Lecture Notes in Computer Science 16406

Founding Editors

Gerhard Goos
Juris Hartmanis

The series Lecture Notes in Computer Science (LNCS), including its subseries Lecture Notes in Artificial Intelligence (LNAI) and Lecture Notes in Bioinformatics (LNBI), has established itself as a medium for the publication of new developments in computer science and information technology research, teaching, and education.

LNCS enjoys close cooperation with the computer science R & D community, the series counts many renowned academics among its volume editors and paper authors, and collaborates with prestigious societies. Its mission is to serve this international community by providing an invaluable service, mainly focused on the publication of conference and workshop proceedings and postproceedings. LNCS commenced publication in 1973.

Chandan Karfa · Navid Asadi ·
Anupam Chattopadhyay

Editors

Security, Privacy, and Applied Cryptography Engineering

15th International Conference, SPACE 2025
Guwahati, India, December 16–19, 2025
Proceedings

 Springer

Editors
Chandan Karfa
Indian Institute of Technology
Guwahati, Assam, India

Anupam Chattopadhyay
Nanyang Technological University
Singapore, Singapore

Navid Asadi
University of Florida
Gainesville, FL, USA

ISSN 0302-9743 ISSN 1611-3349 (electronic)
Lecture Notes in Computer Science
ISBN 978-3-032-16341-7 ISBN 978-3-032-16342-4 (eBook)
https://doi.org/10.1007/978-3-032-16342-4

Preface

This volume contains the papers presented at SPACE 2025: International Conference on Security, Privacy and Applied Cryptographic Engineering, held on December 16–19, 2025 in Guwahati.

The conference received overall 103 submissions, in two submission cycles. This is the first time the conference adopted a multi-cycle review and acceptance format, which resulted in boosting the quality of reviews as well as manuscripts. Every submission received at least 3 reviews, meticulously performed by the technical program committee members, each of whom reviewed more than 10 manuscripts over two review cycles. There were in total 45 technical program committee members, who represented 11 different countries through their current affiliation.

This was the fifteenth edition of the conference, and it also observed the highest number of paper submissions in the history of this conference. Despite the two-cycle submission, it was daunting task for the technical program committee members, who were further helped by 27 external reviewers. Their timely, thorough and detailed review of all the manuscripts undoubtedly contributed to the excellent quality of the conference program.

The committee decided to accept 22 papers, including 1 paper that was resubmitted after it received a major revision in the first cycle of reviews. This puts the overall acceptance rate at 21%. Throughout the review process, strict conflicts of interest and double-blind review processes were followed.

Beyond regular research presentations, the conference program included 3 tutorial sessions, 2 keynote talks and one adjoining workshop on Post-Quantum Security, which was held as a bilateral event between NTU Singapore and IIT Kharagpur, sponsored by ISEA, MeitY. Moreover, the conference program featured a poster session and multiple concurrently running booths by industrial participants and spinoffs.

The conference received generous support from Qualcomm India, TCS Research, Anusandhan National Research Foundation and DRDO, for which we are really thankful.

We used EasyChair for managing the paper submissions, reviews and online discussions, which was very convenient. The conference proceedings are published by LNCS, Springer, whom we would like to thank for their excellent editorial support.

The conference organization was ably led by the general chairs, Sukumar Nandi and Debdeep Mukhopadhyay, whom we sincerely thank for their efforts. The entire organization team at IIT Guwahati showed exemplary dedication to make the conference program memorable. We are grateful for their efforts.

Finally, we are grateful to the vibrant community of researchers in security, privacy and applied cryptography, who submitted excellent research works to this conference.

We sincerely hope that these proceedings will bring valuable knowledge toward a better, more secure world.

November 2025

Anupam Chattopadhyay
Navid Asadi
Chandan Karfa

Michael Pehl	Technical University of Munich, Germany
Rajesh Pillai	Government, India
Rupesh Raj Karn	New York University Abu Dhabi, United Arab Emirates
Prasanna Ravi	Temasek Laboratories, NTU, Singapore
Raghvendra Rohit	IIT Roorkee, India
Kala S.	IIIT Kottayam, India
Rajat Sadhukhan	IIT Kharagpur, India
Sayandeep Saha	Indian Institute of Technology, Kharagpur, India
Somitra Sanadhya	IIT Jodhpur, India
Sourav Sen Gupta	imec, Belgium
Dean Sullivan	University of New Hampshire, USA
Mostafa Taha	Carleton University, Canada
Adithya Vadapalli	IIT Kanpur, India

Additional Reviewers

Ahmed, Shazly
Baddour, Issa
Basu Roy, Prithwish
Boyapally, Harishma
Chaudhuri, Arunava
Das, Sayan
Defranceschi, Marco
Ghosh, Bishakh Chandra
Gupta, Sanchit
Hasan, Md Ajoad
Hassan, Neelofar
Jap, Dirmanto
Kumar, Sanjay
Lin, Da

Manoj, Anjali
Music, Tim
Rajendran, Gokulnath
Ruchti, Jonas
Sayed, Mahmoud Abdelhafeez
Shukla, Shubhi
Sinha, Sayani
Stein, Niklas
Talapatra, Debadrita
Varshney, Aarav
Wang, Zeng
Yadav, Tarun
Yassin, Mahmoud

Contents

A Custom Entropy Harvester for Consistent Entropy Supply to the */dev/random*

Kunal Abhishek[(✉)] and Anuyog Chauhan

Centre for Development of Advanced Computing (C-DAC), Patna, India
`kunalabh@gmail.com`

Abstract. An entropy harvester digitizes analog signals received from hardware sources such as disk input/output (I/O) events, thermal noise, diode resistance, etc. and produces binary values called the digitized analog signals (das) numbers. These das numbers are considered as good entropy bits which are used by */dev/random* to produce true random bits of arbitrary length in Linux-based operating systems. However, due to hardware limitations, regular emittance of digitized analog signals is not possible by the entropy harvesters, and a zero-entropy state is created where */dev/random* suffers significant delay to produce true random bitstreams of reasonably large lengths. Though Linux uses a cryptographically secure pseudo-random number generator (CSPRNG) called */dev/urandom* to immediately overcome the zero-entropy state, it significantly reduces the entropy of the generated bitstreams. We propose a novel entropy refilling architecture to allow */dev/random* to consistently generate true random bitstreams without the need of */dev/urandom* anymore in Linux-based operating systems. Our proposal is backed up with rigorous evaluation of entropy generation and management processes along with experimentation and benchmarking reports which make custom entropy harvester a viable candidate for Linux-based operating systems. Our contributions also help other operating systems to maintain consistent entropy supply using the proposed custom entropy harvester.

Keywords: Entropy · */dev/random* · Linux · zero-entropy state · random number generator · CSPRNG

1 Introduction

Entropy is a measure of uncertainty that represents the unpredictability of a system. In an ideal entropy system, the probability of obtaining either a 0 or 1 bit in each independent and identical trial is equal, each having a 50 percent likelihood. The ideal entropy is quantified on a scale of 1, representing the maximum randomness. The quality of entropy depends on the sources from which it is derived. These sources must be either physical or non-physical noise sources, or a combination of both. Notably, the operating bandwidth of an entropy source

C. Karfa et al. (Eds.): SPACE 2025, LNCS 16406, pp. 1–20, 2026.
https://doi.org/10.1007/978-3-032-16342-4_1

should be maximized to ensure that a random number generator maintains a constant power spectral density across the bandwidth, supporting consistent randomness [4,8].

Entropy harvesting poses a significant challenge, as it relies on obtaining true randomness from genuine noise sources. True random numbers are inherently unpredictable, meaning that even when provided with the same inputs, the generator produces entirely different and uncorrelated bit sequences each time [20]. Although physical noise sources can generate such randomness, they are often slow, resource-intensive, and limited by specific hardware dependencies. Consequently, there is increasing interest in exploring non-physical noise sources that can provide comparable reliability and deliver high quality randomness in a more efficient manner [7,12]. Representative examples of both physical and non-physical entropy sources are summarized in Table 1.

Table 1. Entropy contribution by various noise sources

True physical noise source	True non-physical noise source
Zener diode noise	Operating system interrupt timing
Disk Interrupts	System data such as Application Programing Interface (API) data, RAM data etc.
Thermal noise	Network activity
Electronic circuits	CPU execution timing
Ring oscillator's delays	User input timing
Other physical sources	Other non-physical sources

/dev/random in Linux-based Operating Systems (OSs) is a True Random Number Generator (TRNG) that is designed to collect entropy bits for crucial kernel applications, such as generating Address Space Layout Randomization (ASLR) offsets, cryptographic keys, and salts [1]. However, */dev/random* is inherently restrictive because of the limited entropy supply available in the system. To overcome this limit, Linux uses */dev/urandom*, which provides an uninterrupted supply of randomness through a deterministic process. While */dev/urandom* is effective for ensuring availability, it clearly compromises on the basic notion of entropy, which allows randomness to be derived from true noise sources instead of some deterministic methods.
In general, the following are the key contributions of this paper.

1. An evaluation of entropy harvesters used by Linux-based OSs is presented.
2. A new entropy refilling architecture is proposed for Linux-based OSs that uses the timing difference between successive disk and system interrupts to efficiently eliminate zero-entropy states and ensure a continuous entropy supply.
3. Experiments and benchmarking of entropy harvesters used by Linux-based OSs are presented.

4. The contributions of this paper address the limitations of entropy harvesters that provide inconsistent randomness in Linux-based OSs, while also eliminating the dependency on */dev/urandom*.

1.1   Organization of Paper

The paper is organized as follows. Section 2 presents an in-depth evaluation of entropy harvesters used by Linux-based operating systems. Section 3 proposes a new entropy refilling architecture for Linux-based OSs, while Sect. 4 gives experimentation, benchmarking and comparison of the proposed entropy refilling architecture with that of the current */dev/(u)random* in Linux-based OSs. Section 5 gives recommendations and suggestions based on our empirical results. Finally, Sect. 6 concludes the paper with a future scope of the utility of the proposed entropy refilling scheme.

2   Evaluation of Entropy Harvesters of Linux-Based OSs

Entropy harvesting in Linux systems requires close scrutiny. Since random number generators form the foundation of most cryptographic primitives, any weakness in the entropy collection, estimation, or expansion process directly undermines overall system security. Many persistent challenges such as small pool sizes, blocking behavior, and zero-entropy states, and contrasting them with modern improvements such as ChaCha20-based non-blocking generators in Linux-based operating systems, are still open to be evaluated and counteracted. In this section, we evaluate their entropy generation and management schemes, with particular focus on the zero-entropy state where */dev/random* fails to consistently deliver true random bits.

2.1   Entropy Generation Process

Generation of entropy in its pure form is an intricate task. It involves a systematic process of collecting entropy from true noise sources available with the system, their post-processing, and entropy estimation. The harvested entropy bits are accumulated in the entropy pool created by Linux-based OSs to provide the desired number of entropy bits. The entire process of entropy generation is shown in Fig. 1. Multiple physical noise sources are usually selected to produce good entropy bits. Regular sampling of the signal is performed from the true noise sources available with the system to generate good entropy bits. In a general

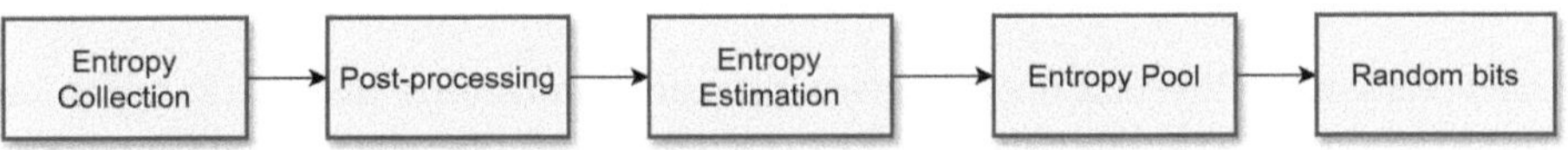

Fig. 1. Entropy generation process

scenario, regular sampling of noise signals is compared with Gaussian white noise (constant power spectral density with Gaussian distributed amplitude) [5], and their comparison forms an entropy source for random number generation [4]. As physical noise resources are limited with the system, accumulating good quantum of entropy is not often possible, and therefore, entropy pools are made limited to a fixed size. In case of Linux-based OSs, the kernel restricts its entropy pool with a fixed size of 256 bits in its current versions i.e., kernel versions 4.8 and above.

Entropy Collection. Entropy collection is the first step of the entropy generation process which requires random noise signals to be collected from multiple physical noise sources. The */dev/random* and */dev/urandom* are the special files (technically a TRNG and a CSPRNG file, respectively) which use entropy sources to generate randomness for various kernel applications. The physical and non-physical entropy sources used by */dev/(u)random* typically include the following events [11]:

- *Interrupt Events:* This event includes the timing intervals between hardware interrupts and OS interrupts.
- *Disk I/O Events:* This event includes the precise timing of operations on storage devices, such as hard drives or Solid State Devices (SSD).
- *User Interaction Events:* This event includes the timing and other input events from the keyboard and mouse.
- *Network Activity Events:* This event includes the precise timing of incoming network packets, network-related events such as changes in the state of the TCP/IP stack, connection attempts, and other protocol-specific operations that can add to the entropy pool.
- *Thermal Noise:* This event includes electronic noise generated by thermal agitation of charge carriers (usually electrons) inside an electrical conductor.
- *CPU Execution Timing:* This event includes variations in CPU processing times caused by different execution paths, interrupts, and other factors.

The operating systems use these entropy sources to retrieve good entropy bits for construction of the seed, which is used to produce random bitstreams of arbitrary size using a deterministic scheme known as a pseudo random number generation algorithm. Physical noise sources produce noise in the form of distorted signals that look quite different from a clean sine wave signal. The noise signals emitted from its source are continuous time-continuous analog signals that are digitized periodically to obtain binary values called the digitized analog signals (das) numbers [13]. Since the das numbers originate from true physical noise sources, they are considered as good entropy bits. One may refer to [10,16,21] for a detailed discussion on the physical noise sources.

Post-processing. Physical noise sources produce bitstreams that are random but often biased and correlated. To remove such residual bias and correlation, post-processing methods such as Hashing [3], Mixing, Von Neumann Debiasing [19], and Fast Fourier Transform are used. Among these, the Linux OS primarily uses hashing to enhance per-bit entropy through compression. Hashing applies a hash function to input bits of arbitrary length to generate a fixed-length output (hash value), which is mathematically expressed as

$$H : \{0,1\}^* \rightarrow \{0,1\}^n \tag{1}$$

where $\{0,1\}^*$ represents the set of all possible bit strings and $\{0,1\}^n$ represents the set of all possible bit strings of length n. */dev/(u)random* does not directly use entropy bits from noise sources, instead, it applies a cryptographic hash function (a hash chain) to process raw entropy. The Linux */dev/urandom* device implements a non-blocking pseudorandom number generator (PRNG) that expands the entropy collected from noise sources into an arbitrarily long output stream. Unlike */dev/random*, which blocks when the entropy estimate is low, */dev/urandom* relies on a forward-secure hash chain construction to continuously derive outputs without depleting the entropy counter. In the legacy design, the internal pool state is periodically re-seeded with system entropy and compressed using SHA-1; subsequent outputs are then generated by iteratively applying the hash function to the previous state, *i.e.*, $s_{i+1} = H(s_i)$. This provides forward secrecy, since knowledge of the current state does not compromise past outputs, while also ensuring a strong mixing of newly injected entropy [6,14]. In modern kernels, SHA-1-based chaining has been replaced by the ChaCha20 stream cipher to improve performance and cryptographic robustness, although the underlying principle of entropy-pool extraction and one-way expansion remains unchanged [2,15].

Entropy Estimation. Entropy estimation is carried out after the sampling and post-processing of the entropy bits to add the random bitstream into the entropy pool. The Linux Random Number Generator (LRNG) estimates the amount of entropy of an event (both physical and non-physical) as a function of its timing only, and not of the event type. The estimate is carried out in the following manner:

Definition. Let t_n denote the timing of the event number n. Define

$$\delta_n = t_n - t_{n-1}$$
$$\delta_n^2 = \delta_n - \delta_{n-1}$$
$$\delta_n^3 = \delta_n^2 - \delta_{n-1}^2$$

where t_n, δ_n, δ_n^2, and δ_n^3 are each 32 bits long.
The estimator then takes the minimum of the absolute values of the differences

$$\Delta_i = \min\left(|\delta_i|, |\delta_i^2|, |\delta_i^3|\right).$$

Finally, it applies the following entropy estimation function [14],

$$H_i = \begin{cases} 0 & \text{if } \Delta_i < 2, \\ 11 & \text{if } \Delta_i \geq 2^{12}, \\ \lfloor \log_2(\Delta_i) \rfloor & \text{otherwise.} \end{cases}$$

where H_i is the entropy estimate of an interrupt event recorded with a timestamp in terms of jiffies (which is a kernel unit of time, defined as the duration of one tick of the computer's system clock, and we usually denote it in nanoseconds (ns) for a finer resolution). For example, Table 2 shows sample jiffy values for an event along with jiffy differences up to three levels.

Table 2. Jiffies Differences Table

Jiffies	1st differences	2nd differences	3rd differences
1004	8	–	–
1012	12	4	–
1024	1	11	7
1030	5	4	7
1041	11	6	2

The entropy contributed by a particular event based on the given entropy estimation method will be shown below:

$$\delta_{1041} = 1041 - 1030 = 11; \delta^2_{1041} = 11 - 5 = 6; \delta^3_{1041} = 6 - 4 = 2;$$
$$\Delta_i = \min(|11|, |6|, |2|) = 2$$

Hence, the entropy estimate for the jiffy value 1041 will be

$$H_{1041} = \lfloor \log_2(2) \rfloor = 1$$

According to the estimation, the event at time 1041 brings 1 bit of entropy.

Entropy Pool. The Linux kernel maintains an entropy pool where collected entropy bits are stored. This pool is often a fixed size buffer that accumulates entropy from various entropy sources. Each bit of collected entropy is added to the pool, which is determined by the entropy estimator. Current entropy harvesters in Linux-based systems (*/dev/(u)random*) use primary and secondary pools for entropy management. The kernel keeps track of an estimate of how much entropy has been collected in the primary pool. This estimation is conservative; each event adds a small, unpredictable portion to the pool, and when the kernel's entropy counter reaches the maximum (256 bits), it indicates that the pool is completely filled with sufficient amount of entropy bits. The key feature of the primary entropy pool is its use to generate random data through */dev/random*, as shown in Fig. 2a. When entropy bits are requested from */dev/random*, the system checks whether there is sufficient entropy in the primary pool. If not, it will block the supply of entropy bits until more entropy is collected, and this leads to the zero-entropy state, as discussed in Sect. 2.1. However, the secondary entropy pool is used in situations where the primary pool does not have sufficient entropy bits to supply. In such situations, */dev/urandom* uses a CSPRNG (which uses the ChaCha20 stream cipher) to supply consistent random bits to the kernel. The secondary pool actually supplements the primary pool in situations where the kernel needs to provide random bits quickly and uninterruptedly, as shown in Fig. 2b.

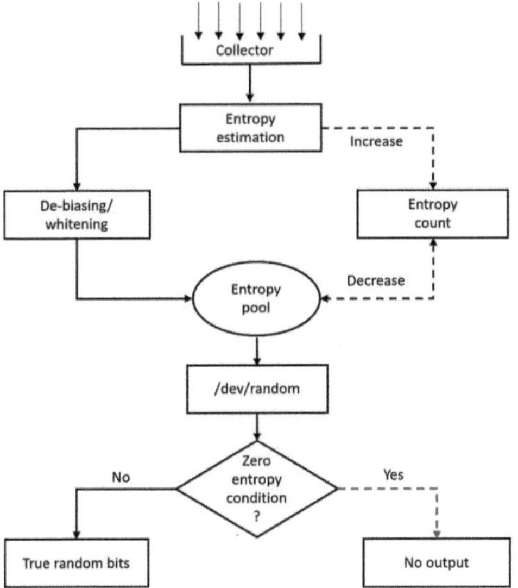

(a) Flow diagram showing working of */dev/random*

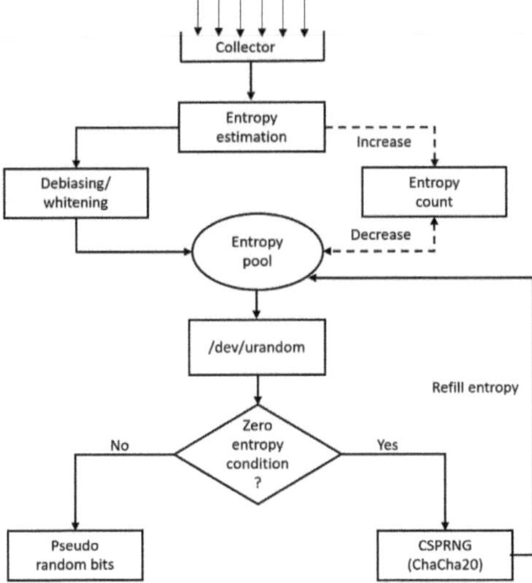

(b) Flow diagram showing working of */dev/urandom*

Fig. 2. Entropy management in Linux OS

Table 3 details the entropy contributions of the physical and non-physical noise sources used in the Linux operating system.

Table 3. Entropy Contribution by physical and non-physical noise sources

Entropy Sources	Category	Entropy Contribution (in bits)	Entropy Quality
Interrupt Timing	Physical	1 bit for every 64 interrupts	*High*, as the exact timing of these events is unpredictable and varies greatly
Disk I/O Timing	Non-physical	0–11 bits based on delta estimation. Refer Sect. 2.1	*High*, depending on the underlying hardware fundamental properties which are extremely unpredictable
Thermal Noise	Physical	*	*High*, as thermal noise is fundamentally random and difficult to predict
System Data Interrupts	Non-physical	0–11 bits based on delta estimation. Refer Sect. 2.1	*Moderate to high*, depending on the nature and frequency of system data interrupts
Keyboard and Mouse Events	Non-physical	*	*Moderate*, as human input tends to be less unpredictable
Network Activity	Non-physical	*	*Variable*, depending on network traffic patterns and external factors influencing packet arrivals
CPU Execution Timing	Non-physical	*	*Moderate*, due to the complexity and variability of modern CPU operations
User Input Timing	Non-physical	*	*Moderate*, as human input tends to be less unpredictable

* *Data not available.*

The Zero-Entropy State. The zero-entropy state refers to a condition in which the entropy pool possesses an insufficient number of entropy bits to meet the actual demands. As illustrated in Fig. 2a, */dev/random* blocks the supply of entropy bits in case sufficient entropy is not available in the system entropy pool.

Definition. Let e be the required number of entropy bits in the entropy pool, a be the available number of entropy bits in the entropy pool, then

$$e > a \geq 0 \tag{2}$$

is the condition for the zero-entropy state of the entropy pool.

The entropy pool of the Linux OS is used by the */dev/(u)random* for the extraction of the desired number of entropy bits to construct the seed to the output random number generation function of the generator. Linux kernel versions 4.8 and above limit the entropy pool to a maximum of 256 bits at a time. Sensitive user applications usually require huge entropy multiple times, which is not possible for the entropy pool to supply every time to the generator. In such a situation, the Linux OS observes a zero-entropy state where the Linux OS waits for further collection of the entropy bits from its true noise sources keeping the */dev/random* suspended for some time. This exact condition is shown in Eq. 2. This was the case with Linux kernel versions earlier than 4.8. The whole process of entropy management in the Linux OS is presented in Fig. 2. The versions of the Linux kernel earlier than 4.8 used the entropy management scheme as depicted in Fig. 2a, whereas the versions after 4.8 used the entropy management scheme as depicted in Fig. 2b.

3　The Proposed Entropy Refilling Architecture

We propose a novel entropy harvester to prevent the Linux entropy pool from reaching a zero-entropy state. The proposed architecture achieves this by fixing the true random noise sources, i.e., both the physical and non-physical ones. A new entropy pool, that is, a custom entropy pool is created in the Linux kernel space to store raw entropy data retrieved from true noise sources, including timing interrupts, system data interrupts, user interactions through keyboard and mouse key press events, and disk interrupts. The size of custom entropy pool is currently fixed at 256 bits or 32 bytes, which can be doubled to a reasonable extent according to the OS's convenient policy. The proposed architecture fetches entropy bits from the disk as well as system interrupts to avoid the zero-entropy state. Figure 3 presents the proposed entropy refilling architecture that relies more on hardware and software interrupts, as they are abundant with the system in pure entropy form, which can be updated every tick of the clock. Each identifier *nvme(k)* as shown in Fig. 3 represents the queue associated with disk interrupts.

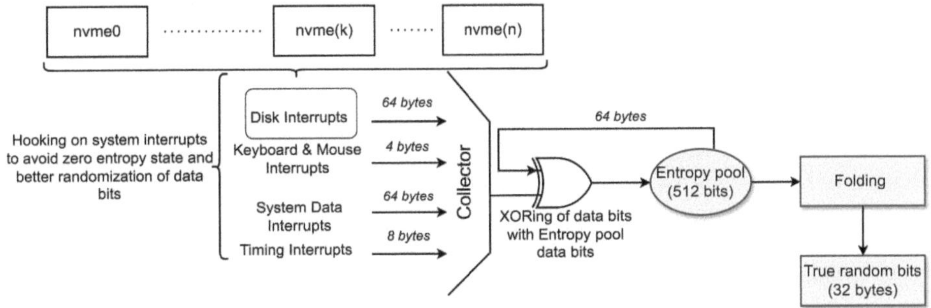

Fig. 3. The proposed entropy refilling architecture

3.1 Time Delta Model Using Interrupts to Overcome Zero-Entropy State

The proposed entropy refilling architecture is based on the concept of obtaining entropy from the timing difference of the occurrence of successive disk and system interrupts. It has been observed in Section II, Part C of [9] that for an L-bit block, the entropy is inherently less than L due to hardware limitations of the physical noise source (in this case, an oscillator). To address this limitation of the physical noise source, a potential solution of building a non-physical true random number generator based on CPU time jitter is discussed in [18]. Building on this notion of deriving entropy from non-physical sources, we extend the idea of leveraging jitter in the form of disk and system interrupts to extract quality entropy.

Interrupts as a Source of Entropy. An interrupt is an event that stops the processor from performing a task. It is classified as a hardware interrupt, a software interrupt, or a trap. Hardware interrupts are triggered by devices, whereas software interrupts are triggered by programs that invoke system calls though traps originate from the CPU to signal errors. We focus on hardware and software interrupts and the CPU response to them. A key point towards understanding how entropy can be extracted from system interrupts is to understand what the CPU does when an interrupt occurs. The CPU performs the following actions in response to an interrupt [17]:

1. The execution of the current instruction is complete.
2. The execution of the currently running program is suspended, pushing eight registers on the stack (R0, R1, R2, R3, R12, LR, PC, and PSR with R0 on top).
3. The LR register is set to a specific value that indicates that an interrupt service routine (ISR) is running.
4. The IPSR is set to the interrupt number that is being processed.
5. The PC is loaded with the address of the ISR vector.

Thus, interrupt handling by CPU involves various complex operations such as storing and fetching CPU register values, use of TLB caches, branch prediction units, moving of the execution of processes from one CPU to another by the scheduler, etc. This implies that the handling of interrupts may have considerable variations in execution time. In addition, modern CPUs have a high-resolution timer or instruction counter that is so precise that they are impacted by these variations. For example, modern x86 CPUs have a TSC clock whose resolution is in the nanosecond range [18]. These variations in the handling of system interrupts by the CPU can be visualized in Fig. 4. Notably, Fig. 4 illustrates the relative frequency of the delta values generated by the system interrupts through a bar diagram. The red line overlays a half-normal distribution, defined by the measured mean and standard deviation. A half-normal distribution is used instead of a normal distribution, as the time delta values (in nanoseconds) cannot be negative. As these variations are based on the aforementioned complexity of the operating system and its use of hardware mechanisms, no observer can deduce the next variation with complete certainty, although the observer can fully monitor the operation of the system. This non-deterministic behavior forms the foundation of the proposed random number harvester.

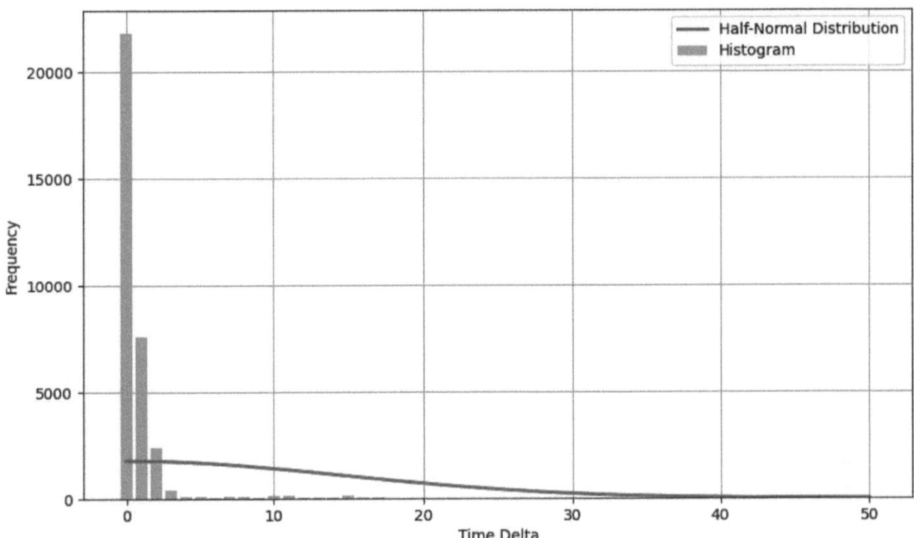

Fig. 4. Half-normal distribution of Time Delta values of system generated interrupts

Obtaining the Time Delta. The time delta is the timing difference for each successive disk or system interrupt. The time delta is obtained by the following operations.

- Storing the current timestamp of the interrupt in terms of jiffies by the interrupt handler. For interrupt handling, the structure 'irq_state' holds various pieces of information related to an interrupt request (IRQ) state. This includes the status of the interrupt, the last servicing time of the interrupt, and other relevant data.
- Subtracting the current timestamp of the interrupt from the last servicing time of the interrupt. This time delta is the time difference between two successive interrupts.

The corresponding values of successive time deltas will vary depending on the arrival time of the interrupts. This variation has been visualized in Fig. 4.

Folding Operation. The folding operation is performed on the extracted entropy bits before true random bits are generated as output. The folding operation is applied before delivering true random bits from the custom entropy pool. This step is introduced to prevent the generation of identical random bits when the entropy pool is accessed simultaneously. During the folding operation, the first half of the entropy pool is XOR-ed with the second half in a specific pattern: the first bit is XOR-ed with the last bit, the second bit with the second-to-last, the third bit with the third-to-last, and so on. The resulting output is then provided to the user as true random bits. Mathematically, the folding operation is defined as follows.

Let the entropy pool be defined as a 64-byte sequence:

$$P = \{p_0, p_1, \ldots, p_{63}\}, \quad \text{where } p_i \in \{0, 1\}^8$$

Split P into two 32-byte halves:

$$A = \{p_0, p_1, \ldots, p_{31}\}, \quad B = \{p_{32}, p_{33}, \ldots, p_{63}\}$$

Define the output sequence $O = \{o_0, o_1, \ldots, o_{31}\}$ using the folding operation:

$$o_i = p_i \oplus p_{63-i}, \quad \text{for } i = 0, 1, \ldots, 31$$

Equivalently, at the bit level

$$o_i^{(j)} = p_i^{(j)} \oplus p_{63-i}^{(j)}, \quad \text{for } j = 0, 1, \ldots, 7$$

The resulting 32-byte output O is provided as true random bits to the user.

Overcoming the Zero-Entropy State. The blocking nature of */dev/random* often results in a zero-entropy state, making it unsuitable for time-sensitive cryptographic applications. Its refresh mechanism updates the entropy pool only when the available entropy count falls below the requested amount. In [18], a CPU time jitter-based approach is suggested to overcome the blocking nature of */dev/random*. This method uses a loop counter to generate timing differences and produce 64 bits of entropy data. However, increasing the entropy size with this approach significantly increases the overhead associated with the loop counter. Consequently, this method may not be suitable for applications that require entropy within nanoseconds. For such cases, a novel solution capable of updating the entropy pool at every clock tick is essential.

To address this limitation, our proposed entropy harvester, which is based on the timing differences of system interrupts, offers an efficient alternative. We estimate that systems connected to peripherals experience approximately one interrupt per clock tick. The average interrupt frequency, i.e., the number of interrupts per clock tick, can be obtained by directly using the actual interrupt counts per time delta bin (bucketed distribution of time differences between interrupt events expressed in nanoseconds) generated during experimentation. In the experiment, the histogram is plotted by recording the number of interrupts occurring within specific time-delta ranges as shown in Fig. 4, omitting the 0 ns spike and assigning "< 1 ns" events to the 1 ns bin. The representative counts for each Δ are: 1 ns $\rightarrow$ 6,738; 2 ns $\rightarrow$ 2,500; 3 ns $\rightarrow$ 900; 4 ns $\rightarrow$ 850; 5 ns $\rightarrow$

820; 7 ns $\rightarrow$ 800; 10 ns $\rightarrow$ 790; 14 ns $\rightarrow$ 780 and so on. The mean time delta is then calculated as a weighted average of these raw counts:

$$\bar{\Delta} = \frac{\sum_i \Delta_i \times C_i}{\sum_i C_i},$$

where Δ_i is the representative delta for bin i and C_i is the corresponding interrupt count. The inverse of this mean delta gives the average interrupt frequency

$$f_{\text{avg}} = \frac{1}{\bar{\Delta}} = \frac{1}{1.075} \approx 0.93$$

interrupts per clock tick.

Furthermore, [18] notes that each timing delta event generates one entropy bit. Based on this, the harvester illustrated in Fig. 3 produces one entropy bit per clock tick. Additionally, the proposed architecture incorporates a folding operation before delivering true random bits. This step prevents the delivery of duplicate bit streams to applications accessing the entropy pool simultaneously. It is noted from Fig. 3 that disk interrupts and system data interrupts constitute 128 bytes together to consistently maintain the proposed entropy pool with true entropy bits and that they are available in abundance with the system. As a result, the proposed harvester continuously supplies non-reproducible entropy bits, effectively eliminating blocking while providing true entropy.

As noted in [18], each timing delta event contributes an entropy bit. Consequently, the harvester shown in Fig. 3 generates one entropy bit per tick of the clock. To further enhance randomness, the proposed architecture applies a folding operation prior to releasing true random bits to ensure that applications accessing the entropy pool concurrently do not receive duplicate bit streams. From Fig. 3, it is evident that disk interrupts and system data interrupts together contribute 128 bytes, thus consistently sustaining the entropy pool with genuine entropy bits and also they remain abundantly available within the system. Consequently, the proposed harvester achieves a continuous supply of non-reproducible entropy bits, eliminating blocking conditions while reliably delivering true entropy.

4 Experimentation and Benchmarking of Entropy Harvesters

We conducted extensive experiments to propose our benchmarks comparing the entropy refilling architecture used by the *dev/random* and *dev/urandom* generators and that of our proposed entropy refilling architecture.

4.1 Hardware Configuration

Table 4 presents the hardware specifications of the standard desktop computer used for the experiments.

Table 4. Hardware configuration

Processor	Intel(R) Core(TM) i7-10700 CPU @ 2.90 GHz
Memory	16 GB DDR4 RAM
Storage	512 GB NVMe SSD
Operating System	Ubuntu 22.04.4 LTS
Linux Kernel Version	6.5.0-44-generic

4.2   The Proposed Kernel Module Implementation

A custom kernel module is proposed and loaded into the Linux kernel version 6.5.0 that includes the following components:

- Entropy Pool Initialization: A fixed-size custom entropy pool of 256 bits.
- Timing Events: At regular intervals (i.e. 10ns), the system time in terms of jiffies is recorded.
- Keyboard and Mouse Interrupts: Captures raw data based on key press events and mouse movements.
- System Interrupts: Captures raw data from interrupts generated on *INTER-RUPT_LINE 0.*
- Disk I/O Events: A function that keeps track of all disk-related interrupts generated in a system by hooking onto disk interrupt queues.
- Entropy Addition: A function that collects raw data from all of the above sources and mixes them into a custom entropy pool.

4.3   Experimental Procedure

The kernel module was compiled using the standard *make* utility and loaded using the $<$ *insmod* $>$ command. The module's initialization function *(entropy_module_init)* as shown in Algorithm 1 allocates memory for the custom entropy pool, collects raw data from various hardware sources, including disk data, populates the custom entropy pool with the entropy bits, and creates a proc file */proc/entropy_pool* to read the custom entropy data.

Algorithm 1. Initialization of Entropy Module

1: Create proc file using *proc_create("entropy_pool", 0666, NULL, &proc_file_ops)*
2: Register keyboard notifier using *init_keyboard_notifier()*
3: Register mouse event handler using *input_register_handler(&mouse_handler)*
4: Capture System generated interrupts using *request_irq(irq_line →irq, (irq_handler_t)add_interrupt_randomness, IRQF_SHARED, "interrupt_randomness", &custom_pool)*
5: Capture Disk I/O interrupts using *request_irq(irq_line →irq, (irq_handler_t)add_disk_randomness, IRQF_SHARED, "disk_randomness", &custom_pool)*

4.4 Entropy Collection and Addition

The randomness of the system in the form of entropy is collected using various physical and non-physical noise sources. The noise sources have been kept limited to timing events, keyboard & mouse interrupts, and all system-generated interrupts including disk interrupts for experimentation purposes. The pseudocode for collecting the entropy from these noise sources is shown below.

– Timing Events: At regular intervals, the current_time in the form of jiffy, i.e. the total number of ticks since the system boot-up time, is recorded and added to the custom entropy pool. The entropy contribution can be calculated as described in Table 2. Algorithm 2 gives a method for estimating the entropy of timing interrupts.

Algorithm 2. Estimation of entropy from timing interrupts

Require: struct timer_rand_state *state
1: Set current time as *now* ←*jiffies*
2: Initialize *time_ data[sizeof(current_ time)]*
3: *delta* ← *now - READ_ONCE(state →last_ time)*
4: *delta2* ← *delta - READ_ONCE(state →last_ delta)*
5: *delta3* ← *delta2 - READ_ONCE(state →last_ delta2)*
6: Estimate entropy bits using *min(abs(delta, delta2, delta3), 11)*

– Keyboard and Mouse Interrupts: Algorithm 3 is used to obtain keyboard interrupts wherein the values of the keys pressed are passed as raw data and the values of the mouse buttons pressed are used together to fill the entropy pool.

Algorithm 3. Fill entropy pool with keyboard and mouse events

---

1: Initialize key data →*key_ data[sizeof(param →value)]*
2: Copy keyboard key press data in param to key data →*memcpy(key_ data, ¶m →value, sizeof(param →value))*
3: Add entropy to pool →*add_ entropy_to_ pool(key_ data, sizeof(key_ data))*
4: Use *input_register_ handle()* function to register mouse events

---

– System Interrupts: To handle system interrupts, an interrupt request handler is created and attached to the INTERRUPT_LINE number 0. As soon as an interrupt is generated on this line, the jiffy value of the interrupt is used as raw data. The entropy contribution can be calculated as described in Table 2. Algorithm 4 gives an overview of interrupt handling.
– Disk I/O Interrupts: The module continuously hooks on the disk interrupt queues, which are used to store the interrupts generated by disk I/O operations. For each successive interrupt, a time delta method is used to estimate the entropy as described in Table 2. Algorithm 5 gives an overview of the collection of entropy from disk I/O interrupts.

Algorithm 4. Get Interrupt Handler

Require: Interrupt Line `irq` **return** IRQ_HANDLED
1: Set current time as *now ←jiffies*
2: *delta ← now - READ_ ONCE(state →last_ time)*
3: *delta2 ← delta - READ_ ONCE(state →last_ delta)*
4: *delta3 ← delta2 - READ_ ONCE(state →last_ delta2)*
5: Estimate entropy bits using *min(abs(delta, delta2, delta3), 11)*
6: Return IRQ_HANDLED

Algorithm 5. Add Disk Entropy

1: Parse output of */proc/interrupts* to get all disk I/O interrupt lines
2: Store all such interrupt lines as a list in *irq_ list*
3: Insert hooks on all such disk interrupt lines to handle disk I/O operations
4: For each such disk interrupt, estimate entropy using delta method describes below
5: *delta ← now - READ_ ONCE(state →last_ time)*
6: *delta2 ← delta - READ_ ONCE(state →last_ delta)*
7: *delta3 ← delta2 - READ_ ONCE(state →last_ delta2)*
8: Estimate entropy bits using *min(abs(delta, delta2, delta3), 11)*

Algorithm 6. Add Entropy data to the Pool

Require: Input data `data` of length `len`
1: Acquire lock using *spin_ lock_ irqsave(&custom_ pool.lock, flags)*
2: **for** `int i = 0; i < CUSTOM_ENTROPY_POOL_SIZE; i++` **do**
3:     `custom_pool.data[i] ^= ((unsigned char *)data)[i]`
4: **end for**
5: Release the lock using *spin_ unlock_ irqrestore(&custom_ pool.lock, flags)*

The collected entropy is added to the custom entropy pool using the XOR operation as shown in Fig. 3. An overview of the addition of raw entropy bits to the custom entropy pool is presented in Algorithm 6. In this experiment, we have created only a single entropy pool which continuously supplies on-demand random data bits. The proposed entropy harvester is benchmarked against the current Linux-based entropy harvesters in Sect. 4.5.

4.5   Benchmarking of the Entropy Harvesters

The generation of entropy bits from various physical noise sources in a system is subject to several factors, including the nature of the noise source, the frequency of events, and the method of collection of entropies. It is evident from Table 5 that the proposed entropy refilling architecture provides excellent entropy quality with minimal serial correlation coefficient using available noise sources. The natural entropy harvested from the noise sources in the proposed entropy refilling architecture is observed to be very close to 1.0, except for the case of keyboard and mouse interrupts, where it is slightly lower due to reduced user interaction. Table 6 shows the entropy values and the serial correlation coef-

Table 5. Benchmark of the entropy harvester using multiple noise sources

Noise sources used	ETR[a]	SCC[b]
Timing Interrupts	0.991598	0.026065
Keyboard Mouse Interrupts	0.733270	0.268542
System Interrupts	0.999994	0.002262
Disk I/O Interrupts	0.999996	−0.008717

[a]Per bit entropy

[b]Negative Serial Correlation Coefficient (SCC) implies that bit patterns 01 and 10 have more probabilities than 00 and 11. Positive Serial Correlation Coefficient implies higher probabilities for 00 and 11 as compared to 01 and 10.

ficient with the Arithmetic Mean Value (AMV) and the throughput observed in the */dev/(u)random* and our proposed entropy refilling architecture during our experimentation. The blue digits are shown as a similar figure, whereas the red digits represent the difference in the values for the reader's comfort.

Table 6. Quality comparison of the proposed and the */dev/(u)random* entropy harvesters

Entropy Harvester	Entropy	Serial Correlation Coefficient	AMV[a]	Throughput in Mbps
/dev/random	0.9999998765691542	0.000249	0.4998	16
/dev/urandom	0.9999998228567102	−0.000355	0.4998	16
Proposed entropy harvester	1.000000	−0.034020	0.5003	19

Note: Red and Blue colors are used for better readability and differentiation among digits.

[a]Arithmetic mean value (average frequency of 0 and 1); ideal with value 0.5.

It is also evident from Table 6 that the proposed entropy refilling architecture provides a better quality entropy with higher throughput compared to the one provided by */dev/random* and */dev/urandom*. Hence, the proposed entropy pool outperforms the existing scheme in two ways: first, with the increased unpredictability by incorporating system interrupts with almost ideal per bit entropy, higher throughput value, and ideal AMV and second, maintaining the unblocked entropy supply to the entropy harvester.

Table 7 presents a comparative analysis of the existing */dev/(u)random* mechanism and the proposed method, demonstrating the superiority of the latter with respect to the use of the noise source, the size of the entropy pool, the concurrent access, uninterrupted supply of entropy, the quality of the entropy and the overall throughput of the entropy harvesters.

Table 7. Comparison between existing */dev/(u)random* method and the proposed method

Contribution	Existing */dev/(u)random* Method	Proposed Method
Noise Sources	Relies more on non-physical noise sources such as timing interrupts, user interactions in terms of keyboard and mouse events, system data interrupts etc.	Relies more on hardware and software interrupts (disk and system interrupts), which are abundant and closer to true entropy. Interrupt frequency observed: approx. 0.93 per clock tick, with one entropy bit per timing delta event
Entropy Pool	Fixed entropy pool of 256-bit size.	Introduced a new dynamic custom entropy pool in the Linux kernel space
Simultaneous Access to the Entropy Pool	Produces identical random bits when accessed simultaneously by multiple applications	Implements a novel "folding operation" to prevent identical outputs under simultaneous access by multiple applications
Entropy Supply	Not consistent (blocking nature of */dev/random*)	Consistent supply of entropy due to unblocking design
Entropy Quality	Not explicitly optimized	Optimized to achieve ideal entropy (1.0 per bit), minimal serial correlation, and ideal Arithmetic Mean Value (AMV) of 0.5
Throughput*	16 Mbps	19 Mbps

tested on same operational platform

5   Recommendations and Suggestions

The zero-entropy state is a critical issue faced by the */dev/(u)random* harvesters in the Linux-based OSs. Also, these entropy harvesters in the Linux-based OSs do not maintain entropy pool with ideal quality entropy bits because of the way they interact with underlying hardware resources acting as the true noise sources. Based on the discussion presented in this paper, the following are recommendations and suggestions to resolve entropy-related issues in Linux-based OSs.

- Physical noise sources such as environmental noise, unusual hardware events, power supply fluctuations, and noise from components such as zener diodes must be considered for entropy generation. These can offer truly random signals which enrich the quality of the entropy pool.
- Efforts must be directed towards designing new hardware for generation of good entropy bits. This could involve integrating specialized circuits or sensors

into the system to provide a dedicated source of good entropy bits for true randomness.

- Linux systems inherently provide various non-deterministic variations, for example, CPU and GPU utilization, RAM usage patterns, system configuration settings, patterns of usage of user applications, user's browsing history, typing patterns, cache hits and misses, fluctuations in Wi-Fi signal strength, and network activity. These sources, though not truly random, can still provide good entropy bits, as they capture the complexity and variability of system operations.
- A combination of simple operations such as folding, permutations, and XOR-ing can be used instead of merely using a hashing technique to enhance the entropy of the bitstream.
- A dynamic entropy pool size is preferable along with an enhanced number of noise sources to efficiently eliminate the zero-entropy state. The proposed entropy refilling architecture is one of such desired options.
- Implement mechanisms for continuous monitoring and auditing of the entropy pool. This helps detect anomalies or potential vulnerabilities and can also help ensure the ongoing reliability and security of the entropy harvesting process.

6   Conclusion and Future Scope

The Linux-based OSs use */dev/(u)random* as the entropy harvesters, which were evaluated on important grounds such as entropy quality, serial correlation coefficients, AMV, noise sources used and, on handling the most critical zero-entropy state. A new entropy refilling architecture based on a new custom entropy pool is proposed to avoid a zero-entropy state in the Linux-based OSs while handling sensitive kernel operations. The customized pool is created in the kernel space whose size can vary according to the user's convenient policy. Empirical validations through extensive experimentation revealed that the proposed entropy-refilling architecture overcomes the limitation of */dev/random* harvester with the same existing hardware resources, and therefore */dev/urandom* is not required anymore. The contribution of this paper will help to improve the design of entropy refilling scheme for other than Linux OSs as well in the future. The proposed methodology may be further extended through additional experiments to analyze the dynamics of the entropy pool among heterogeneous workloads and to examine potential side-channel information sources.

Acknowledgments. The authors gratefully acknowledge the Ministry of Electronics and Information Technology (MeitY), Government of India and the Centre for Development of Advanced Computing (C-DAC) for their support and the opportunity to present this work. They also extend their gratitude to Mr. Aditya Kumar Sinha and Mr. Abhinav Dixit, C-DAC Patna, for their valuable guidance and encouragement.

Disclosure of interests. The authors have no competing interests.

References

1. Abhishek, K., et al.: On random number generation for kernel applications. Fundamenta Informaticae **185** (2022)
2. Bernstein, D.J.: Chacha, a variant of salsa20 (2008). https://cr.yp.to/chacha.html
3. Chi, L., Zhu, X.: Hashing techniques: a survey and taxonomy. ACM Comput. Surv. (Csur) **50**(1), 1–36 (2017)
4. Demir, K., Ergün, S.: An analysis of deterministic chaos as an entropy source for random number generators. Entropy **20**(12), 957 (2018)
5. Diebold, F.X.: Elements of forecasting. Citeseer (1998)
6. Eastlake, D., Crocker, S., Schiller, J.: Randomness requirements for security. Technical Report. RFC 4086, IETF (2001)
7. Ferguson, N., Schneier, B., Kohno, T.: Cryptography Engineering: Design Principles and Practical Applications. John Wiley & Sons, Hoboken (2011)
8. Göv, N.C., Mıhçak, M.K., Ergün, S.: True random number generation via sampling from flat band-limited gaussian processes. IEEE Trans. Circuits Syst. I Regul. Pap. **58**(5), 1044–1051 (2010)
9. Guo, C., Zhou, Y., Liu, H., Zhu, N.: On the jitter and entropy of the oscillator-based random source. In: 2015 6th International Conference on Computing, Communication and Networking Technologies (ICCCNT), pp. 1–5. IEEE (2015)
10. Hennebert, C., Hossayni, H., Lauradoux, C.: Entropy harvesting from physical sensors. In: WiSec '13, pp. 149–154. Association for Computing Machinery, New York (2013). https://doi.org/10.1145/2462096.2462122
11. for Information Security, F.O.: Documentation and analysis of the linux random number generator (2022). https://www.bsi.bund.de
12. Killmann, W., Schindler, W.: A proposal for: Functionality classes for random number generators. ser. BDI, Bonn (2011)
13. Koç, Ç.K.: About Cryptographic Engineering. Springer, Heidelberg (2009)
14. Lacharme, P., Röck, A., Strubel, V., Videau, M.: The linux pseudorandom number generator revisited. In: Proceedings of the 9th International Conference on Security and Cryptography (SECRYPT) (2012)
15. Linux Kernel Community: Linux random number generator documentation (2023). https://www.kernel.org/doc/html/latest/admin-guide/lrng.html
16. Ma, Y., Chen, T., Lin, J., Yang, J., Jing, J.: Entropy estimation for adc sampling-based true random number generators. IEEE Trans. Inf. Forensics Secur. **14**(11), 2887–2900 (2019)
17. Mejia-Alvarez, P., Leyva-del Foyo, L.E., Diaz-Ramirez, A.: Interrupt Handling Schemes in Operating Systems. Springer, Heidelberg (2018)
18. Müller, S.: Cpu time jitter based non-physical true random number generator. In: Ottawa Linux Symposium, pp. 23–48 (2014)
19. Naccache, D.: von Neumann Correction, pp. 1364–1364. Springer US, Boston (2011). https://doi.org/10.1007/978-1-4419-5906-5_520
20. Schneier, B.: Applied Cryptography: Protocols, Algorithms, and Source Code in C. John Wiley & Sons, Hoboken (2007)
21. Sönmez Turan, M., Barker, E., Kelsey, J., McKay, K., Baish, M., Boyle, M.: Recommendation for the entropy sources used for random bit generation. Technical report, National Institute of Standards and Technology (2016)

Efficient Time Share Masking of AES

Subhadeep Banik[1(✉)] and Francesco Regazzoni[1,2]

[1] Universita della Svizzera Italiana, Lugano, Switzerland
`subhadeep.banik@usi.ch`, `f.regazzoni@uva.nl`
[2] University of Amsterdam, Amsterdam, The Netherlands

Abstract. Time sharing was a novel approach to small area and low latency first-order masking in hardware presented by Kumar S.V. et al. at IACR TCHES 2024. The principal underlying idea behind the approach was to separate the processing of shares in the time domain in order to achieve non-completeness. The authors used this approach to construct masked round-based implementations of the `PRINCE` and `AES-128` block ciphers which were considerably smaller than state of the art.

In this paper, we observe that the cost in terms of number of gates and amount of random bits required for the time sharing approach is considerably smaller, if the algebraic degree of the underlying S-box is small. Using the well known decomposition of the inverse power map, (i.e. $f(x) = x^{254}$ over $GF(2^8)$ as $f(x) = x^{26} \circ x^{49}$) we present a more efficient approach to mask the `AES` S-box that requires much lower gate area and randomness to implement and only 2 additional clock cycles. Using this technique we present three implementations of `AES-128`: **(a)** Bit-Serial, **b)** Byte-Serial and **(c)** Round based circuit, all of which require much lower gate area and randomness to construct. We present synthesis results from three different Standard Cell libraries to validate our results.

1 Introduction

Over the years, Side-channel attacks have become an increasingly important tool in the cryptographic community. Power analysis has been particularly effective partly because the equipment required to mount such attacks are not particularly sophisticated or expensive. In differential power analysis [?] (DPA) and its generalizations [?], [MS16], an attacker observes the power consumption traces of a cryptographic implementation and applies statistical analysis to infer the underlying secret. Cryptographic literature has also seen a number of counter-measures proposed to protect circuits against such power attacks. Masking is one such approach which uses secret sharing to randomize input and intermediate values within a circuit. To standardize the designing of secure masked circuits, Threshold Implementations (TI) were introduced which provide provable security with respect to side-channel attacks [?], [DNR19], [?]. When implemented in hardware, a TI is secure even in the presence of glitches, an inherent side effect not considered in earlier schemes [?]. TI comes with enormous overheads in terms of implementation area, particularly when the algebraic degree of the

C. Karfa et al. (Eds.): SPACE 2025, LNCS 16406, pp. 21–40, 2026.
https://doi.org/10.1007/978-3-032-16342-4_2

function to be masked is high. It is known that for a degree d function, a secure TI circuit requires at least $d + 1$ shares, increasing the hardware requirement proportionally with increase in degree. Apart from this several techniques such Consolidating Masking Schemes (CMS) [RBN+15], and Domain Oriented Masking (DOM) [GMK16], Generic low latency masking (GLM) [GIB18] and Generic hardware private circuits (GHPC) [KSM20] have been proposed to securely mask hardware in the presence of glitches.

1.1 Time Share Masking

Time Share Masking (TSM) was a generic technique introduced in [VDB+24] to mask S-boxes by separating out in time, the processing of shares. This method secures any vectorial Boolean function against first-order attacks and uses only a single register stage, thus executes in a single clock cycle. Every function is masked using two additive shares. In the first cycle, the first share is processed and re-masked and carried over using a register stage to the second cycle along with the second share. In the second cycle all cross-product terms involving the two shares are computed and furthermore all such terms are combined to give the final result. The authors also showed that the method is first-order probing secure and that it is, moreover, composable first-order secure in the Probe-Isolating Non-Interference (PINI) framework by Cassiers et al. [CS20]. This security notion is particularly important since it allows for the composition between gadgets without the need to place additional registers between them.

1.2 Contribution and Organization

In this paper, we make a crucial observation that it becomes increasingly diffi-cult to securely mask S-boxes with higher degree functions. This makes S-boxes like the one used in **AES** difficult to mask since its algebraic degree is 7. Start-ing with an observation made in [WMM20] that the inverse power map over $GF(2^8)$ can be decomposed as the composition of lower degree power maps $x \to x^{26}$ and $x \to x^{49}$, we first show that the **AES** S-box can be masked using much lower gate area and random bits as compared to the figures reported in [VDB+24]. Next we try to used this masked S-box to create low area imple-mentations of **AES-128**. We target three design philosophies: **(a) Bit-Serial** We design a bit-serial **AES-128** circuit that takes $131 \times 11 = 1441$ cycles to complete every an encryption operation and occupies around 12 kGE in hardware, **(b) Byte-Serial** We design a byte-serial **AES-128** circuit that takes $20 \times 11 = 220$ cycles to complete every an encryption operation and occupies around 14 kGE in hardware, and **(c) Round based** We design a round based **AES-128** circuit that takes $3 \times 11 = 33$ cycles to complete every an encryption operation and occupies around 177 kGE in hardware.

We benchmark the circuits using three standard cell libraries. The rest of the paper is organized in the following manner. Section 2 introduces the introductory notions of Time Sharing and some related mathematics required to read the paper. In Sect. 3, we describe in detail our construction of the time shared **AES** s-box. Sections 4, 5 and 6 describe the three implementations. Section 7 presents all the simulation results from the synthesis of the circuits so designed. Section 8 concludes the paper.

2 Preliminaries

We give a brief introduction to the theory of time share masking. In order to do so seamlessly, we borrow some of the symbols and terminology that originally appeared in [VDB+24]. Let $x \in \mathbb{F}_2^k$ be a k-bit word, where its two-share Boolean masking is denoted as $(a, b) \in \mathbb{F}_2^{2k}$ with $a \oplus b = x$. We denote the individual bits of a, b, x as $a_0, a_1, \ldots, a_{k-1}, b_0, b_1, \ldots, b_{k-1}, x_0, x_1, \ldots, x_{k-1}$, with $a_i \oplus b_i = x_i$ for all i. Consider the monomial $x_0 x_1 x_2 = (a_0 \oplus b_0)(a_1 \oplus b_1)(a_2 \oplus b_2)$. We have that

$$
\begin{aligned}
x_0 x_1 x_2 &= (a_0 \oplus b_0)(a_1 \oplus b_1)(a_2 \oplus b_2) \\
&= a_0 a_1 a_2 \oplus a_0 a_1 b_2 \oplus a_0 b_1 a_2 \oplus a_0 b_1 b_2 \oplus \\
&\quad b_0 a_1 a_2 \oplus b_0 a_1 b_2 \oplus b_0 b_1 a_2 \oplus b_0 b_1 b_2 \qquad \text{①} \\
&= \sum_{v \in \mathbb{F}_2^k} \prod_{v_i=0} a_i \cdot \prod_{v_i=0} b_i \qquad \text{②}
\end{aligned}
$$

Note that there are 8 terms in the expression marked by ①, each corresponding to one element in the canonical listing of all the 3 bit strings over a binary alphabet. Thus the expression ② immediately follows. The main idea in TSM is to compute all the monomials $\prod_{v_i=0} a_i$ in the first clock cycle and in the second cycle compute the terms $\prod_{v_i=0} b_i$ and combine them to get the final result.

Indeed the above process is to be repeated for all monomials present in the algebraic expression of the S-box. In general for an arbitrary Boolean function $f : \mathbb{F}_2^k \to \mathbb{F}_2 : (x_0, x_1, \ldots, x_{k-1}) \to f(x_0, x_1, \ldots, x_{k-1})$, of algebraic degree d, we can generalize the above to write

$$
f(a \oplus b) = \sum_{I \in \mathcal{P}_{k,d}} g_{\pi(I)}(a_0, a_1, \ldots, a_{k-1}) \cdot h_{\pi(I)}(b_0, b_1, \ldots, b_{k-1})
$$

In the above expression, $\mathcal{P}_{k,d}$ denotes all binary strings of length k with hamming weight less than or equal to d (or equivalently all sets of cardinality at most d in $[0, k-1]$). This is because if the algebraic degree is bounded by d, we do not need to construct higher degree monomials. g_j, h_j are functions over the shares a, b respectively, which are essentially monomials of degree upto d. And the strings in $\mathcal{P}_{k,d}$ are numbered and indicated by the function π.

The above sharing scheme needs further randomness for security, and so the authors of [VDB+24] update the expression as follows

$$
f(a \oplus b) = \sum_{I \in \mathcal{P}_{k,d}} \left(g_{\pi(I)} + r_{\pi(I)} \right) \cdot h_{\pi(I)} \oplus \sum_{I \in \mathcal{P}_{k,d}} r_{\pi(I)} \cdot h_{\pi(I)}
$$

Finally the two output shares are computed as

$$
F_0 = \sum_{I \in \mathcal{P}_{k,d}} \left(g_{\pi(I)} + r_{\pi(I)} \right) \cdot h_{\pi(I)}, \quad F_1 = \sum_{I \in \mathcal{P}_{k,d}} r_{\pi(I)} \cdot h_{\pi(I)}
$$

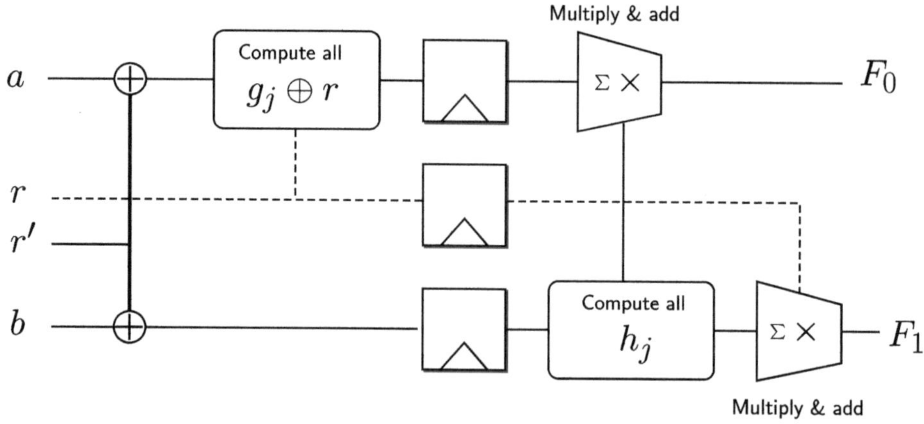

Fig. 1. An overview of Time Share Masking Circuit

2.1   Circuit for TSM

Figure 1 presents a brief overview of the circuit of a TSM S-box. We briefly take the reader through the steps involved.

Step 1: Initial Refreshing: We refresh the input shares with initial randomness to get $a' = a \oplus r'$ and $b' = b \oplus r'$. This requires a total of k bits of randomness.

Step 2: Compute all g_j: We now compute all the functions g_j over a' and mask them with additional randomness to get $g_j \oplus r_j$. Essentially this implies that we have to construct all monomials of degree up to d in a'. Define $\binom{k}{\downarrow d} = \sum_{\ell=1}^{d} \binom{k}{\ell}$. Then this step requires $\binom{k}{\downarrow d}$ bits if randomness.

Step 3: Carry forward to next clock cycle: We use register stages to carry forward the following signals: (a) All the functions $g_j \oplus r_j$ computed so far, (b) All the bits of randomness r_j used so far and (c) the share b' that has been unused at this point of time. This would require a total of $2\binom{k}{\downarrow d} + k$ flip-flops.

Step 4: Compute the functions h_j: In the next clock cycle we compute the functions h_j.

Step 5: Compute F_0: This is done by evaluating $F_0 = \sum_{I \in \mathcal{P}_{k,d}} (g_{\pi(I)} + r_{\pi(I)}) \cdot h_{\pi(I)}$.

Step 5: Compute F_1: This is done by evaluating $F_1 = \sum_{I \in \mathcal{P}_{k,d}} r_{\pi(I)} \cdot h_{\pi(I)}$. Note that we now have $F_0 \oplus F_1 = f(a' \oplus b')$. Since $a' \oplus b' = a \oplus b$, the output shares are mathematically correct.

It can be seen that we need $\mathbf{F} = 2\binom{k}{\downarrow d} + k$ flip-flops and a total of $\mathbf{R} = \binom{k}{\downarrow d} + k$ bits of randomness. For the AES and PRINCE S-boxes $d = k - 1$, and so the above expressions boil down to $\mathbf{F} = 2^{k+1} + k - 4$ and $\mathbf{R} = 2^k + k - 2$. However we can see that for smaller d the cost in terms of randomness and flip-flops is considerably lesser, not to mention the circuit savings for constructing g_j, h_j.

3   Masked S-Box

It is well known that the AES S-box is constructed by composing an affine transformation over the inverse map $x \to x^{254}$ over $GF(2^8)$. It is also well known that the algebraic degree of the power map $x \to x^p$ over any field of characteristic 2, is exactly the hamming weight of p. Since $\mathsf{HW}(254) = 7$, the algebraic degree of the AES S-box is 7. It was shown in [WMM20], that the inverse power map over $GF(2^8)$ can be written as the composition of the power maps $x \to x^{26}$ and $x \to x^{49}$. Indeed since $[x^{26}]^{49} = x^{26 \times 49 \bmod 255} = x^{254}$. Now we have that $\mathsf{HW}(26) = \mathsf{HW}(49) = 3$, and so these smaller power maps are essentially cubic S-boxes over 8-bit inputs. Thus if we were to construct the TSM S-box of AES in 2 stages, i.e.

Stage 1: Construct the TSM S-box for the power map $x \to x^{26}$ and then
Stage 2: Construct the TSM S-box for the power map $x \to x^{49}$ and construct the circuit for the affine map,

then we may hope for some savings in both circuit area and randomness, at the cost of additional time. The cost for constructing a degree 7 S-box for $8 - bit$ inputs is given by $\mathsf{F}_7 = 2^9 + 8 - 4 = 516$ flip-flops and $\mathsf{R}_7 = 2^8 + 8 - 2 = 262$ bits of randomness. Now consider the same costs for a cubic S-box: we have $\mathsf{F}_3 = 2\binom{8}{\downarrow 3} + 8 = 202$ and $\mathsf{R}_3 = \binom{8}{\downarrow 3} + 8 = 100$. Even when we need to double the costs for constructing two successive power maps, we have that $2 \times \mathsf{F}_3 < \mathsf{F}_7$ and $2 \times \mathsf{R}_3 < \mathsf{R}_7$. Even the costs of designing the other parts of the circuit are considerably lower even we have to duplicate them to construct two power maps.

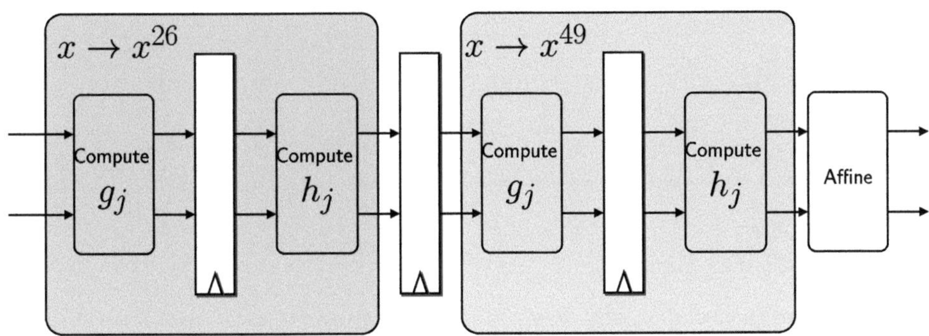

Fig. 2. An overview of Decomposed and Masked AES S-box

3.1   Circuit

Figure 2 shows the construction of the masked AES S-box. We construct the TSM circuits for the individual cubic power maps separately and add the affine transform in the end. The circuit takes 3 cycles to compute the S-box. We synthesized the S-box using three standard cell libraries: (a) Nangate 15 nm OCL, (b)TSMC 65 nm and (c) UMC 40 nm. The results are tabulated in Table 1. We compare the results with the original TSM S-box that appeared in [VDB+24], and whose source code is available online at [tsm]. We used the `compile_ultra` directive with the Synopsys Design Compiler to arrive at the results. A timing analysis is then performed on the synthesized netlist using sufficient number of randomly generated test vectors, which outputs the switching statistic of every node in the circuit. This information is used by the Synopsys Power Compiler software to estimate the average power consumed by the circuit. Energy is computed as the product of the average power and the total physical time taken for the circuit to execute a given operation. The synthesis results confirm, that for all the three libraries the decomposed S-box is around 50% smaller than the original S-box reported in [VDB+24], while the energy consumption is slightly higher but of the same order as the original S-box.

Table 1. Synthesis results for the decomposed and undecomposed **AES** S-boxes. Note that power has been evaluated at 10 MHz.

#	Architecture	Area (μm^2)	'(GE)	#Random Bits	#Cycles	Power (mW)	Energy (pJ)
	Nangate 15 nm						
1	Original [VDB+24]	3110.5	15821	262	1	0.4086	40.86
2	Decomposed (This work)	1608.3	8180	200	3	0.1400	42.00
	TSMC 65 nm						
3	Original [VDB+24]	20852.3	14481	262	1	0.8444	84.44
4	Decomposed (This work)	10488.6	7284	200	3	0.4123	123.69
	UMC 40 nm						
5	Original [VDB+24]	7960.5	14505	262	1	0.5361	53.61
6	Decomposed (This work)	4057.7	7394	200	3	0.1927	57.81

3.2 Can We Do Better?

One question the reader may have is why we stopped after decomposing the AES S-box into two smaller cubic power maps. Is it not possible to decompose the S-box further: may be into three/four quadratic power maps that would have resulted in more savings in area/randomness? The short answer is no. It is impossible to decompose the inverse power map further using quadratic power maps, at least over $GF(2^8)$. To find the reason for this, one has to delve into the cyclotomic coset structure mod 255, and define a particular operation between two cosets. This operation gives the set of cosets a group structure. However the coset arithmetic over $GF(2^8)$ is such that not all the cosets are part of this group. In particular all the cosets that have hamming weight two are outside the group structure, and the hamming weight 3,7 cosets are inside the group. Which is why it is not possible to combine any number of hamming weight 2 cosets to reach the coset in which 254 lies. Since this is of only mathematical interest, we give a more complete detailed analysis in Appendix B.

4   Bit Serial Circuit

One of the main objectives of designing a smaller masked S-box, is to see if one can implement a smaller masked implementation of the AES-128 block cipher, and this was the next objective. The smallest implementations of unmasked AES-128 are those reported in [BCB21, JMPS17]. We chose to pursue the implementation in [BCB21], which only takes 128 cycles per round and $128 \times 11 = 1408$ cycles to compute the entire encryption. This is theoretically the lowest possible for a bit-serial circuit that advances only one bit per clock cycle. Initially our aim was to design the masked circuit also in 128 cycles per round. However unlike [BCB21], in which the S-box is a purely combinatorial circuit, we could not fit all operations in the pipeline if we budgeted for only 128 cycles per round. In stead, since the S-box takes 3 cycles, we found a working solution at 131 cycles per round.

Figure 3 presents an overview of the circuit we use to construct the 131 cycle per round masked circuit (note that we show the datapath for only one of the shares for ease of representation). The circuit closely resembles the 128-cycle per round implementation presented in [BCB21] but with some differences. In the following we present the salient features of the circuit vis-a-vis the [BCB21] circuit.

(A) Three additional flip-flops: We need the extra storage elements in the pipeline to accommodate seamlessly a 131 cycle round. Note that the plaintext and key enter bit by bit through the top left corner of the state and key datapaths as shown in Fig. 4.

(B) S-box Operations: Consider an up-counter t modulo 131 that controls the data movement. At all $t \equiv 7 \bmod 8$, data is fed into the S-box via the register locations 124 to 130 and the signal on the wire leading to FF 130. At $t \equiv 2 \bmod 8$ (with $t > 8$) the S-box output is written back to the flip-flops 120 to 127.

(C) Swaps in the state pipeline: Swapping bits are performed by placing multiplexers in the circuit. We keep the original placement of multiplexers in the circuit (with one exception). Only the intervals in which a swap is activated are moved forward by 3 clock cycles, i.e. we have

$$\textbf{swap}(80, 112) \quad \text{at } t \in [59, 66] \cup [91, 98] \cup [123, 130] \cup [8, 15]$$
$$\textbf{swap}(56, 120) \quad \text{at } t \in [91, 98] \cup [123, 130] \cup [0, 7]$$
$$\textbf{swap}(25, 121) \quad \text{at } t \in \{130\} \cup [0, 7]$$

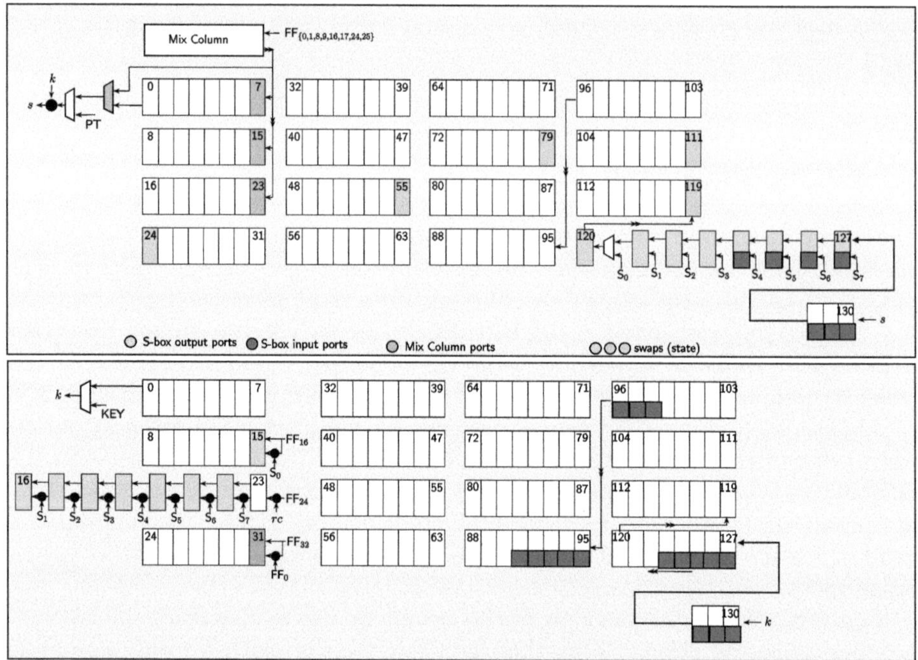

Fig. 3. The bit-serial **AES** circuit. Note that we show circuit for only one share for ease of representation.

(D) Sequential Mixcolumn: The whole reason of scheduling the swaps in this manner is to make sure that the correct state bits are available as input to the Mixcolumns circuit. Note that we use a sequential version of the Mixcolumn circuit, first introduced in [JMPS17]. In order for the circuit to work correctly, the first 2 bits of each byte must be present at FFs 0,1,8,9,16,17,24,25 at the beginning of each Mixcolumn cycle. We will see that this holds for all the 8 clock cycles: bits at position $t, t+1$ must be in place for the circuit to to work correctly at time t.

Mixcolumn operations are carried out at $t \in [0, 7] \cup [32, 39] \cup [64, 71] \cup [96, 103]$. The circuit is explained pictorially in Fig 4. It may appear a little complicated, but one can understand it thus: in the 0th cycle, the MSB of each byte of the column is stored in the column of FFs marked MSB. This is important because the MSB controls multiplication by 2, 3 in $GF(2^8)$. As shown in the figure, let us call the four signals after the first set of NAND gates (from right to left) Fsig, the second set of NAND gates BSig and the first set of XOR gates Xsig. Note that these are 4-bit signals indexed from 3 to 0 from top to bottom as they appear in the figure. notLSB is a signal that is always 1 except in the last cycle i.e. at $t = 7, 39, 71, 103$. Poly is a signal that encodes the irreducible polynomial used to extend $GF(2)$ to $GF(2^8)$: it is 0 at cycles 0,1,2,5 otherwise 1.

	Index	0	1	2	3	4	5	6	7
Fsig	3	1	1	1	$1 + a_0$	$1 + a_0$	1	$1 + a_0$	$1 + a_0$
	2	1	1	1	$1 + b_0$	$1 + b_0$	1	$1 + b_0$	$1 + b_0$
	1	1	1	1	$1 + c_0$	$1 + c_0$	1	$1 + c_0$	$1 + c_0$
	0	1	1	1	$1 + d_0$	$1 + d_0$	1	$1 + d_0$	$1 + d_0$
Bsig	3	$1 + a_1$	$1 + a_2$	$1 + a_3$	$1 + a_4$	$1 + a_5$	$1 + a_6$	$1 + a_7$	1
	2	$1 + b_1$	$1 + b_2$	$1 + b_3$	$1 + b_4$	$1 + b_5$	$1 + b_6$	$1 + b_7$	1
	1	$1 + c_1$	$1 + c_2$	$1 + c_3$	$1 + c_4$	$1 + c_5$	$1 + c_6$	$1 + c_7$	1
	0	$1 + d_1$	$1 + d_2$	$1 + d_3$	$1 + d_4$	$1 + d_5$	$1 + d_6$	$1 + d_7$	1
Xsig	3	$a_1 + b_0$	$a_2 + b_1$	$a_3 + b_2$	$a_0 + a_4 + b_3$	$a_0 + a_5 + b_4$	$a_6 + b_5$	$a_0 + a_7 + b_6$	$a_0 + b_7$
	2	$b_1 + c_0$	$b_2 + b_1$	$b_3 + c_2$	$b_0 + b_4 + c_3$	$b_0 + b_5 + c_4$	$b_6 + c_5$	$b_0 + b_7 + c_6$	$b_0 + c_7$
	1	$c_1 + d_0$	$c_2 + d_1$	$c_3 + d_2$	$c_0 + c_4 + d_3$	$c_0 + c_5 + d_4$	$c_6 + d_5$	$c_0 + c_7 + d_6$	$c_0 + d_7$
	0	$d_1 + a_0$	$d_2 + a_1$	$d_3 + a_2$	$d_0 + d_4 + a_3$	$d_0 + d_5 + a_4$	$d_6 + a_5$	$d_0 + d_7 + a_6$	$d_0 + a_7$

Let a, b, c, d be the bytes incident at the Mixcolumn circuit. The above encoding means that Fsig equals "1111" at cycles 0,1,2,5, and "$1 + a_0, 1 + b_0, 1 + c_0, 1 + d_0$" otherwise. Bsig equals "$1 + a_{t+1}, 1 + b_{t+1}, 1 + c_{t+1}, 1 + d_{t+1}$" at all cycles except for the last cycle when it equals "1111". And then we have Xsig = Fsig + Bsig + Rotleft(a_t, b_t, c_t, d_t). the above table gives the expressions for Xsig, Fsig, Bsig at all the 8 clock cycles. After that it is easy to check that [MC3,MC2,MC1,MC0] = Xsig + Rotleft(Xsig) + Rotright(a_t, b_t, c_t, d_t) correctly computes the bit level expressions of all the four Mixcolumn outputs at all the 8 clock cycles. After this computation, MC3 is added to the next roundkeybit and cycled back to the state pipeline. The remaining outputs MC2,MC1,MC0 are written back to FFs 7,15,23.

(E) Arrangement of Swaps: As we have seen, for the Mixcolumn circuit to function correctly, at all the 8 cycles bits at locations $t, t + 1$ much be at the correct location i.e. FFs 0,1,8,9,16,17,24,25. If we run a simple script (like the one listed in Appendix A) to see if the sequence of swaps given in **(C)** produces the correct sequence of bits at the above FFs at all the Mixcolumn cycles i.e. $t \in [0, 7] \cup [32, 39] \cup [64, 71] \cup [96, 103]$. We find that swaps generally produce the correct sequence of bits with a few exceptions. Only at $t \in [0, 7]$ the bit at the second position is not present in FF 25. The required bit is however stored at FF 121. So at cycle 0 to 7 we need an extra multiplexer to bring this bit into the Mixcolumn circuit.

To give a clearer picture, note that the first **AES** Mixcolumn operation requires as input the bytes indexed 0,5,10,15, i.e. (bits $0 \to 7, 40 \to 47, 80 \to 87, 120 \to 127$). So, we need that the state bits at $t = 0$ at FFs 0,1, 8,9, 16,17, 24,25 be those indexed by 0,1, 40,41, 80,81, 120, 121. While all the other bits are in place the state bit 121 is still at FF 121, if we use the swap sequence in **(C)**. Thus an additional mux is needed.

(F) Key Path: There are two issues in the key path. We need 4 S-box accesses which must be scheduled at cycles in which it is not used by the state pipeline. And we need to consider the effect of rotating the last column of the key state by one byte before applying S-box, adding round constant and adding it back to the first column. We take inputs to the S-box at cycles $112, 120, 128, 5$ to avoid conflict with the state path and the output is written back three cycles later i.e. at cycles $115, 123, 0, 8$. We always add the S-box output to content

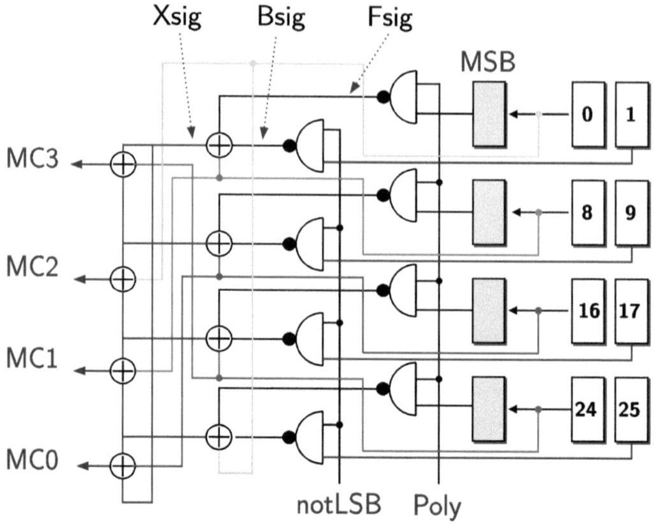

Fig. 4. The sequential Mixcolumn Circuit.

of FFs 16 to 23 and write it back to FFs 15 to 22. In order to accommodate for the Rotword operation on the last key column, we take the S-box inputs from FFs 123 to 130 at $t = 112, 120, 128$, and FFs 91 to 98 at $t = 5$ (it is easy to check that this notionally rotates the last column by a byte before applying the S-box). The only other operations remaining in the key path are addition of the updated first column to the second, second to the third etc. This is done by executing FF [32] =FF [32] +FF [0] at all $t < 96$, which is written to FF 31 in the next cycle.

5   Byte Serial Circuit

The byte serial circuit is probably the most efficient of the three AES circuits when we consider both area and latency parameters. There are numerous byte serial implementations of AES-128 present in literature. The first such circuit was proposed in [MPL+11], which computed one round in 21 cycles. Since the number of S-box accesses in one round of AES-128 is 20, then if the circuit uses a single S-box, this represents close to optimal latency. In [BBR16], the authors combined encryption and decryption into one circuit. [BBR17] improved the above work further by using the fact that the Mixcolumn matrix had multiplicative order 4. This obviated the need for inverse Mixcolumn circuit for decryption, since the same functionality could be achieved by running the Mixcolumn circuit thrice. [BCB21] proposed a 16-cycle per round implementation that however required 2 S-box circuits. In this paper we try to design a 20-cycle per round using a single masked S-box which therefore is theoretically optimal.

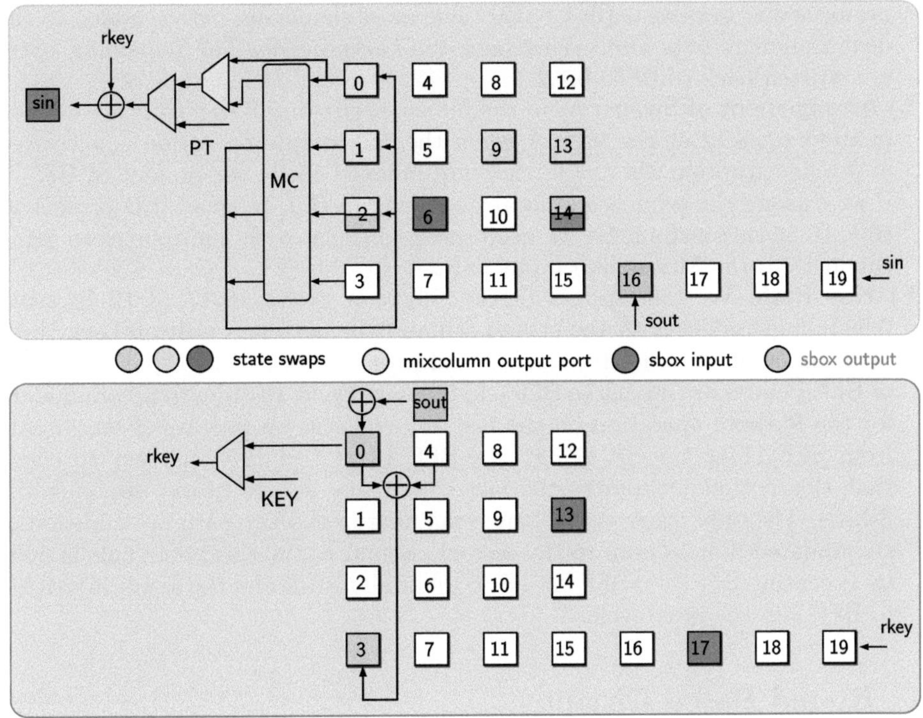

Fig. 5. The byte-serial `AES-128` circuit. Note we only show the datapath of one share.

We represent pictorially the byte-serial circuit (only the datapath of one share) in Fig. 5. The salient features of the circuit are as follows:

(A) Four additional byte flip-flops: Since we aim to design a 20-cycle per round implementation, we add four additional byte flip-flops (BFFs) to accommodate this.

(B) S-box Operations: Consider an up-counter t modulo 20 that controls the data movement. At all $t < 16$, data is fed into the S-box after the roundkey addition operation i.e. via the signal on the wire leading to BFF 19. At $t \in [3, 18]$ the S-box output is written back to BFF 17.

(C) Swaps in the state pipeline: We perform the following swaps in the state pipeline

$$\mathbf{swap}(10, 14) \quad \text{at } t \in \{11, 15, 19, 1\}$$
$$\mathbf{swap}(3, 15) \quad \text{at } t \in \{0\}$$
$$\mathbf{swap}(7, 15) \quad \text{at } t \in \{15, 19, 0\}$$

(D) Combinatorial Mixcolumn: Since all bits of a byte move together in a byte-serial circuit, there is no real advantage in using a sequential Mixcolumn circuit. We use the combinatorial Mixcolumn circuit designed by [Max19] that uses only 92 XOR gates, connected to BFFs 0,4,8,12. The operation is performed at cycles $t \in \{0, 4, 8, 12\}$. The most significant byte is added to the next roundkey byte and cycled back 9in the pipeline. The remaining bytes are written back to BFFs 0,1,2.

(E) Arrangement of Swaps: As in the bit serial circuit, all the bytes are aligned in BFFs 0,4,8,12 at the instant when the Mixcolumn operation is activated with one exception. At $t = 0$, the byte indexed 15, is not present at BFF 3, if we execute the sequence of swaps outlined in **(C)**. In stead it is present at BFF 15 at this instant. So we need one additional byte multiplexer to bring this byte to the Mixcolumn input port.

(F) Key Path: We take inputs to the S-box at cycles $16, 17, 18, 19$ to avoid scheduling conflict with the state path and the output is written back three cycles later i.e. at cycles $19, 0, 1, 2$. We always add the S-box output to content of BFF 1 and write it back to BFF 0 in the next cycle. In order to accommodate for the **Rotword** operation on the last key column, we take the S-box inputs from BFF 17 at $t = 16, 17, 18$, and BFF 13 at $t = 19$ (it is easy to check that this notionally rotates the last column by a byte before applying the S-box). The only other operations remaining in the key path are addition of the updated first column to the second, second to the third etc. This is done by executing BFF $[4]$ =BFF $[4]$ +BFF $[0]$ at all $t < 12$ and the result is written to BFF 3 in the next cycle.

6   Round Based Circuit

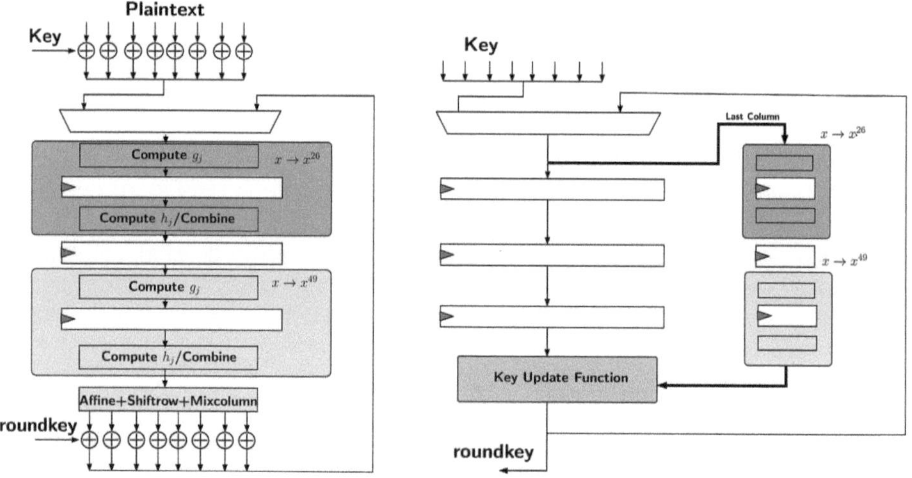

Fig. 6. The round-based AES-128 circuit. Note we only show the datapath of one share.

The round based circuit is simplest to describe since the circuit for processing one round in a single clock cycle is already available, and one just needs to iterate over 10 cycles for the result. In this case however, one encryption operation needs 31 cycles, since each S-box computation needs 3 cycles as shown in Fig. 2. The circuit for one share of the round based circuit is shown in Fig. 6. Although the circuit needs 31 cycles to do one encryption, it can encrypt 3 plaintexts in the first 33 cycles. It can be seen that the register stages used for the S-box operation form a natural pipeline, and so if three plaintext/key pairs are input to the circuit at $t = 0/1/2$ successively, the result can be obtained from the circuit at $t = 31/32/33$ respectively.

7   Implementation Results

We synthesized all the ciphers using the Nangate 15nm, TSMC 65 nm and UMC 40nm standard cell libraries. All the designs were initially implemented in VHDL their functionality has been verified using Mentor Graphics Model-Sim SE. The designs were synthesized using the Synopsys Design Compiler using the `compile_ultra -no_autoungroup -no_boundary_optimization` command. The switching activity was collected while performing a timing simulation on the synthesized netlist using Synopsys VCS. The switching activity was then back annotated to estimate the power consumption using Synopsys Power Compiler. Table 2, reports the result of our implementations. Since the a large part of the design is the masked s-box, it can be seen that the byte serial design offers the most in terms of area-throughput ratio.

Table 2. Synthesis results for the three **AES-128** architectures. Note that power has been evaluated at 10 MHz.

#	Architecture	Area		#Random Bits	#Cycles	Power (mW)	Energy (pJ)
		(μm^2)	'(GE)				
Nangate 15 nm							
1	Bit-Serial	2392.4	12168	40000	1441	0.1413	20.36
	Byte-Serial	2808.7	14286		220	0.2010	4.42
	Round-Based	34926.1	177643		31	1.0071	3.12
TSMC 65 nm							
2	Bit-Serial	14908.0	10353		1441	0.5686	81.93
	Byte-Serial	17401.0	12084		220	0.7138	15.70
	Round-Based	227506.7	157991		31	7.0350	21.81
UMC 40 nm							
3	Bit-Serial	6019.0	10968		1441	0.2107	30.37
	Byte-Serial	7016.1	12784		220	0.3670	8.74
	Round-Based	87793.5	159974		31	1.6400	5.08

8   Conclusion

Starting from the observation that Time Share masking is significantly more efficient in masking smaller degree S-boxes, we put this premise to test by using the power map decomposition of the **AES** S-box. We found that the standalone S-box occupied almost half the area when the internal inverse map is decomposed into lower degree power maps. We then tried to fit this masked S-box into the pipeline of a bit-serial, byte-serial and round-based circuit. As a result we get fairly compact masked implementation of **AES-128** in around 12 kGE, 14kGE and 177 kGE across three standard cell libraries.

Acknowledgment. The authors wish to thank all the reviewers whose feedback helped improve the paper. The research presented in this paper was partially funded by the European Union, by grant No. 101135183 (MYRTUS). Views and opinions expressed are however those of the author(s) only and do not necessarily reflect those of the European Union. Neither the European Union nor the granting authority can be held responsible for them.

A   Appendix A: Python script for keeping track of state

```
def rotate(S, newb):
    for i in range(130):
        S[i] = S[i + 1]
    S[130] = newb

def show(x,r,i):
    print("Round ",r," cycle",i)
    l= [x[num] for num in range(0,8)]+[x[num] for num in range
    (32,40)] + [x[num] for num in range(64,72)] + [x[num] for num
     in range(96,104)]
    print (1)
    l= [x[num] for num in range(8,16)]+[x[num] for num in range
    (40,48)] + [x[num] for num in range(72,80)] + [x[num] for num
     in range(104,112)]
    print (1)
    l= [x[num] for num in range(16,24)]+[x[num] for num in range
    (48,56)] + [x[num] for num in range(80,88)] + [x[num] for num
     in range(112,120)]
    print (1)
    l= [x[num] for num in range(24,32)]+[x[num] for num in range
    (56,64)] + [x[num] for num in range(88,96)] + [x[num] for num
     in range(120,128)]
    print (1)

    l= [x[num] for num in range(128,131)]
    print (1)


State = ['x'] * 131
B = [0]*128
for i in range(128):
```

```python
23        B[i] = 'b%03d' % i
24
25 for round in range(2):
26     for i in range(131):
27
28         if (round==1 and (i==0 or i==32 or i==64 or i==96)):
29             show(State,round,i)
30         if i < 128 and round == 0:
31             newbit = B[i]
32         elif i >= 128 and round == 0:
33             newbit = '0000'
34         else:
35             newbit = State[0]
36
37         if (i >= 59 and i < 67) or (i >= 91 and i < 99) or (i >=
123 ) or (i >= 8 and i < 16):
38             t = State[80]
39             State[80] = State[112]
40             State[112] = t
41
42         if (i >= 91 and i < 99) or (i >= 123 ) or (i >= 0 and i <
8):
43             t = State[56]
44             State[56] = State[120]
45             State[120] = t
46
47         if (i==130 or (i >= 0 and i < 8))  :
48             t = State[25]
49             State[25] = State[121]
50             State[121] = t
51
52         rotate(State , newbit)
```

B   Appendix B: Mathematics of composition of Power maps

It can be seen that if we compose two power maps $x \to x^a$ and $x \to x^b$ over any characteristic 2 field $GF(2^c)$, the resultant power map is given by $x \to x^{a \times b \bmod 2^c - 1}$. This is naturally because the multiplicative group of $GF(2^c)$ has order $2^c - 1$, and so the above follows from Fermat's law. Note that all the integers in the set $[0, 2^c - 2]$ can be naturally partitioned with respect to the relation R defined thus:

$$(a, b) \in R, \text{ if } \exists \, t, \text{ such that } a \equiv b \cdot 2^t \bmod (2^c - 1)$$

This is an equivalence relation, and thus partitions the set $[0, 2^c - 2]$. these partitions are well studied in mathematical literature and are more well known by the name cyclotomic cosets. For example the cyclotomic cosets modulo $2^4 - 1 = 15$ are

$$C_0 = \{0\}, \ C_1 = \{1, 2, 4, 8\}$$
$$C_3 = \{3, 6, 12, 9\}, \ C_5 = \{5, 10\}$$
$$C_7 = \{7, 14, 13, 11\}$$

The smallest entries of the cyclotomic cosets are called coset representatives. Note each coset is sub-scripted by the representative. Moreover the entire coset can be generated by successively multiplying the representative by 2 and reducing modulo $2^c - 1$. The following lemma can be easily proven.

Lemma 1. *All elements of in a single coset have same hamming weight when seen as a binary string. In fact all elements in a single coset are finite rotations of one another.*

Proof. This fact is easily borne out by the example above. For example, C_3 when viewed as a set of binary strings can be written as $\{0011, 0110, 1100, 1001\}$. Let $a \in C_i$, for some i. If $2a < 2^c - 1$, then it is obvious that there is no overflow and so a and $2a$ do have the same weight and are rotations of one another. If $b = 2a \geq 2^c - 1$, note that $2^c \equiv 1 \bmod (2^c - 1)$, and that the msb of a equals 1. Consider $\ll, \lll$ to be the left-shift, left-rotate over c-bit words. In that case $b = 2a = (a \ll 1) + 2^c$, where $(a \ll 1)$, is simply the c-bit representation of a left shifted by 1. The overflowing bit is represented by the addition of 2^c. Reducing modulo $2^c - 1$, we have $b \equiv (a \ll 1) + 1 \bmod (2^c - 1) \equiv (a \lll 1) \bmod (2^c - 1)$ which is what we need to prove. The equality of hamming weight immediately follows.

The following are also easy to see/prove

A: Since $x \to x^{2^t}$ are linear maps over characteristic 2 fields, all elements in a single coset represent affine equivalent power maps. That is if $a, b \in C_i$ for some i, then $x \to x^a$ and $x \to x^b$ are affine equivalent maps.

B: Since we have already proven that all elements of a single coset are bit-rotations of each other, this immediately gives us the number of cosets modulo $2^c - 1$. This is just the number of length c necklaces over the binary alphabet minus 1, since the all one string is equivalent to the all 0 string modulo $2^c - 1$. It is a well known fact in combinatorics that there are $M(c) = \frac{1}{c} \sum_{d|c} \phi(d) 2^{c/d}$ different binary necklaces of length c, where $\phi()$ is the Euler totient function. So the number of cosets is given by $M(c) - 1$, and the number of non-zero cosets is $M(c) - 2$.

Group Operation

We try to define an operation $\odot$ between 2 cosets as follows. Let $a \in C_i$ and $b \in C_j$ for some i, j. Now let $p = a \cdot b \bmod (2^c - 1)$ and $p \in C_k$ for some k. Then we claim that for any arbitrary $a^* \in C_i$ and $b^* \in C_j$, $p^* = a^* \cdot b^* \bmod 2^c - 1 \in C_k$. Indeed this is true since

$$a^* \cdot b^* \equiv a \cdot 2^t \cdot b \cdot 2^s \bmod (2^c - 1) \equiv a \cdot b \cdot 2^{t+s} \bmod (2^c - 1)$$

$$\equiv p \cdot 2^{t+s} \bmod (2^c - 1) \in C_k \text{ as required.}$$

So this naturally gives rise to the operation $\odot$, between two cosets. $C_i \odot C_j = C_k$ if the product modulo $2^c - 1$ of any element of C_i, and any element of C_j, lies in C_k. This sometimes gives rise to a group structure among the set of cosets, especially if $2^c - 1$ is prime, because then it guarantees the existence of an inverse for each element and thus also each coset. Note that since modular multiplication is associative and commutative, the coset operation is also associative and commutative. And the coset in which 1 lies, can serve as the identity element. For example, when $c = 7$, $2^c - 1 = 127$ is a prime number. All the 18 non-zero cosets modulo 127 form a group. For $c = 4$, the cosets that don't have divisors of 15, i.e. C_1, C_7 forms a group of 2 elements. But $2^8 - 1 = 255$ is not a prime. So the group structure of these cosets is slightly tricky.

As can be seen in Table 3, over $GF(2^8)$, not all the 35 cosets are in the Group defined by $\odot$. There are 16 elements in the group (marked in cyan background in the above table), and it has 2 cyclic subgroups generated by the elements C_7 of order 8, and C_{127} of order 2. Hence all cosets can be factored as $C_7^x \odot C_{127}^y$, where $x \in [0, 7]$ and $y \in [0, 1]$. In the paper we use the fact that $C_{13} \odot C_{49} = C_7^6 \odot C_{127} \odot C_7^2 = C_{127}$, which leads to the decomposition of the inverse map $x \to x^{254}$ into the power maps $x \to x^{26}$ and $x \to x^{49}$. However all the Hamming weight 2 cosets contain either divisors of 255, or integers that are not co-prime with 255, hence they don't have inverses. Hence these cosets are not part of the group. This means that no matter how many quadratic power maps we combine we will not reach the inverse map over $GF(2^8)$.

Table 3. All cyclotomic cosets modulo 255

Rep	Coset	HW	Remark
C_0	0	0	Null
C_1	1,2,4,8,16,32,64,128	1	Identity
C_3	3,6,12,24,48,96,129,192	2	*
C_5	5,10,20,40,65,80,130,160	2	*
C_7	7,14,28,56,112,131,193,224	3	C_7
C_9	9,18,33,36,66,72,132,144	2	*
C_{11}	11,22,44,88,97,133,176,194	3	C_7^3
C_{13}	13,26,52,67,104,134,161,208	3	$C_7^6 \odot C_{127}$
C_{15}	15,30,60,120,135,195,225,240	4	*
C_{17}	17,34,68,136	2	*
C_{19}	19,38,49,76,98,137,152,196	3	C_7^2
C_{21}	21,42,69,81,84,138,162,168	3	*
C_{23}	23, 46, 92, 113, 139, 184, 197, 226	4	$C_7^5 \odot C_{127}$
C_{25}	25, 35, 50, 70, 100, 140, 145, 200	4	*
C_{27}	27, 54, 99, 108, 141, 177, 198, 216	4	*
C_{29}	29, 58, 71, 116, 142, 163, 209, 232	4	C_7^5
C_{31}	31, 62, 124, 143, 199, 227, 241, 248	5	$C_7 \odot C_{127}$
C_{37}	37, 41, 73, 74, 82, 146, 148, 164	3	C_7^7
C_{39}	39, 57, 78, 114, 147, 156, 201, 228	4	*
C_{43}	43, 86, 89, 101, 149, 172, 178, 202	4	$C_7^4 \odot C_{127}$
C_{45}	45, 75, 90, 105, 150, 165, 180, 210	4	*
C_{47}	47, 94, 121, 151, 188, 203, 229, 242	5	C_7^6
C_{51}	51, 102, 153, 204	4	*
C_{53}	53, 77, 83, 106, 154, 166, 169, 212	4	C_7^4
C_{55}	55, 110, 115, 155, 185, 205, 220, 230	5	*
C_{59}	59, 103, 118, 157, 179, 206, 217, 236	5	$C_7^2 \odot C_{127}$
C_{61}	61, 79, 122, 158, 167, 211, 233, 244	5	$C_7^3 \odot C_{127}$
C_{63}	63, 126, 159, 207, 231, 243, 249, 252	6	*
C_{85}	85, 170	4	*
C_{87}	87, 93, 117, 171, 174, 186, 213, 234	5	*
C_{91}	91, 107, 109, 173, 181, 182, 214, 218	5	$C_7^7 \odot C_{127}$
C_{95}	95, 125, 175, 190, 215, 235, 245, 250	6	*
C_{111}	111, 123, 183, 189, 219, 222, 237, 246	6	*
C_{119}	119, 187, 221, 238	6	*
C_{127}	127, 191, 223, 239, 247, 251, 253, 254	7	C_{127}

References

[BBR16] Banik, S., Bogdanov, A., Regazzoni, F.: Atomic-AES: a compact implementation of the AES encryption/decryption core. In: Dunkelman, O., Sanadhya, S.K. (eds.) INDOCRYPT 2016. LNCS, vol. 10095, pp. 173–190. Springer, Cham (2016). https://doi.org/10.1007/978-3-319-49890-4_10

[BBR17] Banik, S., Bogdanov, A., Regazzoni, F.: Compact circuits for combined AES encryption/decryption. J. Cryptogr. Eng. 9(1), 69–83 (2019)

[BCB21] Balli, F., Caforio, A., Banik, S.: The area-latency symbiosis: towards improved serial encryption circuits. IACR Trans. Cryptogr. Hardw. Embed. Syst. 2021(1), 239–278 (2021)

[CS20] Cassiers, G., Standaert, F.-X.: Trivially and efficiently composing masked gadgets with probe isolating non-interference. IEEE Trans. Inf. Forensics Secur. 15, 2542–2555 (2020)

[DNR19] Dhooghe, S., Nikova, S., Rijmen, V.: Threshold implementations in the robust probing model. In: Bilgin, B., Petkova-Nikova, S., Rijmen, V. (eds.) Proceedings of ACM Workshop on Theory of Implementation Security, TIS@CCS 2019, London, UK, 11 November 2019, pp. 30–37. ACM (2019)

[GIB18] Groß, H., Iusupov, R., Bloem, R.: Generic low-latency masking in hardware. IACR Trans. Cryptogr. Hardw. Embed. Syst. 2018(2), 1–21 (2018)

[GMK16] Groß, H., Mangard, S., Korak, T.: Domain-oriented masking: compact masked hardware implementations with arbitrary protection order. In: Bilgin, B., Nikova, S., Rijmen, V. (eds.) Proceedings of the ACM Workshop on Theory of Implementation Security, TIS@CCS 2016, Vienna, Austria, October 2016, p. 3. ACM (2016)

[JMPS17] Jean, J., Moradi, A., Peyrin, T., Sasdrich, P.: Bit-Sliding: a generic technique for bit-serial implementations of SPN-based primitives. In: Fischer, W., Homma, N. (eds.) CHES 2017. LNCS, vol. 10529, pp. 687–707. Springer, Cham (2017). https://doi.org/10.1007/978-3-319-66787-4_33

[KSM20] Knichel, D., Sasdrich, P., Moradi, A.: SILVER – statistical independence and leakage verification. In: Moriai, S., Wang, H. (eds.) ASIACRYPT 2020. LNCS, vol. 12491, pp. 787–816. Springer, Cham (2020). https://doi.org/10.1007/978-3-030-64837-4_26

[Max19] Maximov, A.: AES mixcolumn with 92 XOR gates. IACR Cryptol. ePrint Arch. 833 (2019)

[MPL+11] Moradi, A., Poschmann, A., Ling, S., Paar, C., Wang, H.: Pushing the limits: a very compact and a threshold implementation of AES. In: Paterson, K.G. (ed.) EUROCRYPT 2011. LNCS, vol. 6632, pp. 69–88. Springer, Heidelberg (2011). https://doi.org/10.1007/978-3-642-20465-4_6

[MS16] Moradi, A., Standaert, F.X.: Moments-correlating dpa. In: Proceedings of the 2016 ACM Workshop on Theory of Implementation Security, pp. 5–15 (2016)

[RBN+15] Reparaz, O., Bilgin, B., Nikova, S., Gierlichs, B., Verbauwhede, I.: Consolidating masking schemes. In: Gennaro, R., Robshaw, M. (eds.) CRYPTO 2015. LNCS, vol. 9215, pp. 764–783. Springer, Heidelberg (2015). https://doi.org/10.1007/978-3-662-47989-6_37

[tsm] Time share masking. htttps://github.com/KULeuven-COSIC/TSM

[VDB+24] Dilip Kumar, S.V., Dhooghe, S., Balasch, J., Gierlichs, B., Verbauwhede, I.: Time sharing-a novel approach to low-latency masking. IACR Trans. Cryptogr. Hardw. Embed. Syst. **2024**(3), 249–272 (2024)

[WMM20] Wegener, F., De Meyer, L., Moradi, A.: Spin me right round rotational symmetry for fpga-specific AES: extended version. J. Cryptol. **33**(3), 1114–1155 (2020)

Investigation on the Impact of Practical Fault Model for Commercial Edge Machine Learning Devices

Shivam Bhasin[1], Dirmanto Jap[1], Marina Krček[2(✉)], and Stjepan Picek[2,3(✉)]

[1] Temasek Laboratories and National Integrated Centre for Evaluation (NiCE),
Nanyang Technological University, Singapore, Singapore
`{sbhasin,djap}@ntu.edu.sg`
[2] Radboud University, Nijmegen, The Netherlands
`{marina.krcek,stjepan.picek}@ru.nl`
[3] Faculty of Electrical Engineering and Computing, University of Zagreb,
Zagreb, Croatia
`stjepan.picek@fer.hr`

Abstract. Fault Injection Attacks (FIAs) are well-studied in information security and have proven capable of breaking even highly secure cryptographic implementations. However, their application to other targets, such as edge machine learning (ML) systems on commercial devices, has not received much attention. Edge ML, where pretrained models are deployed on resource-constrained embedded devices for Internet-of-Things (IoT) and critical infrastructure applications, presents new security challenges. Recent work demonstrated practical electromagnetic (EM) pulse-based FIA on a commercial edge ML device (Intel Neural Compute Stick 2), achieving misclassification by inducing faults in a small, toy Convolutional Neural Network (CNN) model. To our knowledge, there is no other work that targets explicitly a commercial edge ML product using Laser or EM FIAs.

In this work, we extend this investigation by evaluating the applicability and generalizability of these fault models across a range of publicly available, more complex neural network architectures. By observing and mapping practical fault behaviors, we validate the fault models across different types of layers and analyze their overall impact on neural network accuracy. Our experiments reveal that faults injected at the Fully-Connected layer can cause an average 80.7% reduction in classification accuracy, highlighting the significant security risks FIA poses to real-world edge ML deployments.

Keywords: Edge Machine Learning · Fault Injection Attacks · Model Evasion

1 Introduction

Over the past few decades, the field of machine learning (ML) has experienced tremendous growth, both in academia and industry. One of the reasons is the

© The Author(s), under exclusive license to Springer Nature Switzerland AG 2026
C. Karfa et al. (Eds.): SPACE 2025, LNCS 16406, pp. 41–57, 2026.
https://doi.org/10.1007/978-3-032-16342-4_3

advancement of technology, which enables researchers to study and investigate deep learning algorithms in depth, contributing to their growth. As such, it has now been widely applied for various applications, with mostly great success. Due to their high resource requirements, most deep learning algorithms have been applied on high-performance computing systems for training the model and running inference. On the other hand, another growing paradigm in ML coincides with the growth of the Internet of Things (IoT). Since model inference requires less computational effort than training, it can be deployed on more resource-constrained devices, and as such, there is now a growing demand for ML on smaller embedded or edge devices.

These smaller devices will typically have lower processing capacity and will be expected to perform similarly to higher-performance devices. Various edge ML accelerators have then been developed and optimized to allow ML acceleration on embedded edge devices. Since edge ML can be used for critical applications, ensuring its performance, especially its security, is of utmost importance. This has been demonstrated in the field of hardware security that any physical deployment of the implementation, no matter how theoretically secure, is subject to physical threats [9], for example, a fault injection attack [10], or a side-channel analysis [3].

1.1 Related Works

Most investigations have been conducted on evaluating the side-channel vulnerability of ML implementations on different target platforms, where the attacker can recover the information regarding the ML model. However, the fault injection attacks (FIA) remain interesting threats [5], where they corrupt the inference process, resulting in misclassification, and it could be severe in critical applications. Thus, the aim of the FIA is different from the side-channel analysis, and they are more similar in nature to adversarial examples [12]. In addition to misclassification, FIA can be utilized for other attacks like model stealing, model inversion, and model evasion [11].

To conduct FIA on ML models, different methods to physically inject the fault on the target device have been reported, mainly targeting inference. For example, a practical fault targeting the activation function was reported by Breier *et al.* [5], on an 8-bit microcontroller platform. This work serves as a proof-of-concept, and it is tested on a small ML model to illustrate the potential threat from FIA. Another work, done on a different target, was reported by Yao *et al.* [15]. This work targets a quantized ML model running on cloud servers, and utilizes the Rowhammer [8] method to inject faults by flipping multiple bits to degrade the accuracy from resulting misclassification.

However, to our knowledge, most of the reported works have only been conducted in a simulation setting or on a standard target, such as a development board or a microcontroller. As far as we are aware, only one recent work [4] has reported the results targeting a commercial device, Intel NCS 2.[1] The work

---

[1] Intel NCS 2 has been subjected to side-channel [14] and cold boot attacks [13], which are out of scope for this paper.

demonstrates the feasibility of fault injection resulting in misclassification on a small CNN example; however, the implications of such physical faults on commercial neural network accelerators have never been analyzed.

1.2 Motivations and Contributions

As demand for edge machine learning (ML) in critical infrastructure grows, ensuring the integrity of devices running these models is essential, particularly given the threat of fault injection attacks (FIA) that can cause critical failures. Understanding fault behaviors and their practical impact is, therefore, vital. Unlike ML models deployed on GPUs, edge devices face strict memory constraints, requiring smaller models. By investigating models approaching these memory limits, we can better characterize vulnerabilities and generalize our findings to improve the security of edge ML deployments.

In this work, we advance the findings of [4] by not only replicating the original fault model but also rigorously analyzing its implications for realistic neural network deployments. We extend and test the generalizability of these practical fault-injection models through simulation across a range of widely used public CNN architectures of varying sizes and depths, providing new insights into their vulnerability profiles and informing more robust edge ML security design. We again emphasize that this work extends previous work by focusing on more complex public models and aims to demonstrate the practicality of the observed practical fault models on a commercial target in a black-box setting, not to present novel fault attacks.

2 Background

2.1 Machine Learning

Machine learning (ML) is a subfield of artificial intelligence that empowers computer systems to learn from data and make decisions or predictions without being explicitly programmed. A prominent class of ML models is Artificial Neural Networks (ANNs), and in this work, we focus on a specific type of ANNs, namely Convolutional Neural Networks (CNNs) [7].

The core of a CNN is the convolutional layer. It automatically extracts key visual characteristics (like lines or textures) using small, specialized filters. The filter slides across the image, identifying where each specific feature exists and recording its strength. This process breaks the input down into manageable features. Most often, the network ends with fully connected (FC) layers. These layers take the collected visual features and use them to perform the final task, such as classifying an image (e.g., determining if it is a cat or a dog). In these layers, every single processing unit is connected to every unit in the previous layer. This final step uses the combined knowledge from all previous layers to calculate the probabilities for each possible outcome.

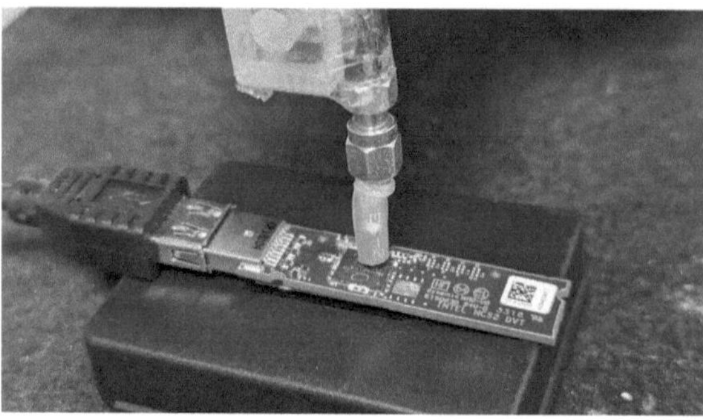

Fig. 1. An example of EMFI setup: the EM probe is positioned on top of Intel NCS 2 running inference process.

2.2   Target Device

The commercial edge ML that was investigated in previous work [4] is Intel NCS 2 [2], which is a compact, plug-and-play development kit designed to accelerate neural network inference. To convert the trained model into a proper format that can be loaded onto the target device, the OpenVINO library is used [1].[2] It supports the models trained in popular frameworks, such as PyTorch, TensorFlow, Keras, *etc.*. The OpenVINO also provides a list of popular pretrained models supported for execution on NCS 2.[3] Note that NCS 2 is a limited-resource device, and, as such, due to its memory constraints (internal memory of 500MB), large models cannot be loaded to NCS 2. Thus, for this work, we have chosen several supported popular models from this library as a basis for our investigations.

2.3   EM Fault Injection (EMFI)

The general idea of conducting EMFI is to inject a very high, but short, voltage pulse directly onto the surface of the chip using a near-field EM probe. Since the EM probe can be placed to target different locations on the chip, EMFI could be used to precisely target different sub-blocks within the target. However, the effect of EMFI is more global, in the sense that the EM field will affect a larger portion of the device where the probe is positioned, as compared to, e.g., laser fault injection spot [6]. Figure 1 illustrates a typical EMFI setup, with the EM probe positioned on top of a target device. In this case, we see NCS 2 without its plastic case, allowing the probe to be placed closer to the main processing unit. Note that this setup is used in [4].

---

[2] https://software.intel.com/content/www/us/en/develop/tools/openvino-toolkit.html.

[3] https://github.com/openvinotoolkit/open_model_zoo/blob/2022.3.1/models/public/device_support.md.

The pulses can also be injected as single or multiple pulses. In some applications, it is more desirable to inject multiple consecutive EM pulses in a burst. For instance, it was shown in [15] that, to achieve successful misclassification in ResNet20 when trained on CIFAR-10, multiple bit flips are required; thus, multiple injections are performed, resulting in bit-flip faults. Similarly, in [4], *burst mode* is used, where multiple EM pulses are injected sequentially onto the target device, in order to introduce multiple faults into the computations. Since the target device is a commercial product, the internal functionality is not revealed, hence, a black-box setting. The multiple fault injections are preferable in this scenario, since the attacker could not precisely target a specific operation, but could operate within a large segment, for example, focusing on a layer in the network.

2.4   Observed Practical Fault Models

The first practical EMFI experiment on a commercial edge device, Intel NCS 2, was reported in [4]. The aim of the study was to induce misclassification by making the model predict an incorrect class in an untargeted manner. Due to a lack of documentation for the target platform, the EMFI is performed in a black-box setup with no injection optimizations and no knowledge of the model implementation.

Overall, from the practical EMFI, there are two main categories for successful faults that could be injected on Intel NCS 2, as found and reported in [4]. The faults are also reported to have high repeatability. There are also other types of faults, but they are not interesting to investigate, since they do not result in any observable misclassification. Note that previous work used a CNN with two convolutional layers, followed by two fully-connected layers in the practical EMFI testing.

- *Fully-Connected Layer Faults*: The faults are observed to be from the first fully-connected (dense) layer.
  Based on the analysis, only a small portion of the values are changed. Indeed, as reported, only 8 values on average are changed, and the absolute differences are reported to be quite large (about 2 000), which, when propagated to the output, will bias towards a certain (random) class, resulting in (untargeted) misclassification.
- *Convolution Layer Faults*: The faults are reported to cause changes in the second convolutional layer, mostly at the output of *ReLU* activation function. The changes caused by this fault are observed to be small, with an average difference of 1.06 and a maximum absolute difference of 6.09. Since these faults resulted in misclassifications, it means that a significant number of the values will change, propagating the difference to the output layer. As expected, it requires around 300–400 faults in this layer's output for the classification to be impacted.

It is also reported that similar faults occur at the very first convolution layer. However, the changes are small, and the neural network is able to correct them during propagation, leading to the correct label. This also indicates that the poor propagation of these faults results in minimal changes in the output. Hence, from the observation, it can be safely assumed that, in order to achieve useful faults, the faults have to be injected at the deeper layers.

In this work, we have replicated the experiments from [4] and validated the previously reported fault behavior by mapping the faults on more complex public models. We first tested on the same CNN model, which we will denote as the Toy CNN model, and then on larger public models. We want to re-emphasize that the fault models used for the experiments were observed and derived in the previous work from the practical settings.

3   Experimental Evaluation

The models supported for NCS 2 can be found in the OpenVINO GitHub library.[4] Following that list of models, we select several models for these simulation experiments, namely 1) *efficientnet-b0-pytorch*, 2) *mobilenet-v2-pytorch*, 3) *resnet-18-pytorch*, 4) *resnet-34-pytorch*, and 5) *resnet-50-pytorch*. The rationale is that these models are larger than the utilized toy CNN model for the MNIST dataset, and are considered among the most popular for image classification tasks. In the rest of the paper, we will remove the *pytorch* notion from the name, so respectively, models will be noted as *efficientnet-b0*, *mobilenet-v2*, *resnet-18*, *resnet-34*, *resnet-50*.

These models are pretrained on the ImageNet-1k dataset; in Table 1, we provide information on the models, their size, and expected accuracy on the ImageNet-1k dataset. Some models have two sets of pretrained weights for the dataset, both of which are reported, but we use the version with better accuracy in our experiments. As the models are pretrained, we avoid any training of the models, and use only the ImageNet-1k validation set of 50 000 images (samples) for testing. This aligns with the following threat model.

Table 1. Model information. The number of total and trainable parameters is equal, as there are 0 non-trainable parameters in all of these models.

	Trainable params	Params size (MB)	Expected acc. (top-1, %)
efficientnet-b0	5,288,548	21.15	77.69
mobilenet-v2	3,504,872	14.02	71.88/72.15
resnet-18	11,689,512	46.76	69.76
resnet-34	21,797,672	87.19	73.31
resnet-50	25,557,032	102.23	76.13/80.86

---

[4] https://github.com/openvinotoolkit/open_model_zoo/blob/2022.3.1/models/ public/device_support.md.

3.1 Threat Model

This work focuses on pretrained neural networks deployed on edge devices for inference only. Since training is resource-intensive, it is assumed to occur separately in a secure cloud environment and remains uncompromised. The adversary instead targets inference on the edge device using fault injection attacks via electromagnetic probes, which require physical access. The deployed models store values (such as weights) in IEEE 754 floating-point format. A standard 32-bit (single-precision) floating-point number consists of 1 sign bit, 8 exponent bits, and 23 fraction (mantissa) bits. The fault model, as previously reported in [4] and validated on our setup, is approximated as random word-level bit flips.

For *Fully-Connected Layer Faults*, we assume changes occur in the upper bits, affecting the exponent and sign bits, while for *Convolution Layer Faults*, they are assumed to target the mantissa bits, leading to smaller value changes. In our experiments, we adopt these assumptions and first validate whether we can reproduce results consistent with those reported in prior practical studies.

3.2 Experimental Setup

We first derive the fault model from the practical experiments and then analyze the chosen neural networks under this fault model. For the first fully-connected layer, we introduce faults into a neural network's parameters (weights and biases) based on a given probability. Secondly, for the convolutional layer, we introduce faults on the output of the second convolutional layer after the activation function. The aim is to test *Fully-Connected Layer Faults* and *Convolutional Layer Faults* respectively. For each individual parameter or output of a targeted layer, there is a certain probability that a "fault" will be introduced. This simulates the stochastic nature of real-world errors or variations. The probability is adjusted to adhere to the observed number of changes in the real EMFI experiments. The probability of fault is noted with each experiment, as we needed to adjust it based on the number of parameters (weights and bias) and outputs in each of the tested models.

Another parameter used in the experiments is *magnitude*. For *Fully-Connected Layer Faults*, a relative change is applied by multiplying the weight parameters by a factor from the range $[-magnitude, magnitude]$ chosen uniformly at random. As we increase the *magnitude*, the weight modification gets more extreme, and sign flipping is possible. We also round the number to an integer, as this was observed with practical EMFI.

We aim to match the *magnitude* to achieve similar changes observed with the EMFI on NCS 2 in practical settings. In the practical experiment, the changes were observed from values in a smaller range, somewhere between $\{-3, 0\}$ to integer values of large numbers, $\sim 2\,000$. We tested several *magnitudes*, and they will be noted in the corresponding experiments. However, the closest results in the weight modification were achieved with *magnitude* of 30 000, so we use this setup to test with the new models. For biases, an absolute change is applied by adding a value to the original bias value, scaled by the standard deviation of the bias array (*change * std_dev*, where *change* is a random value from the [−*magnitude*, *magnitude*] range). This same approach is used for *Convolutional Layer Faults*, where the output of the activation function of a convolutional layer is modified in the same manner as the bias. Note that for *Fully-Connected Layer Faults* we used low fault probabilities since we aim to achieve, on average, around 8 trainable parameters to be modified. Due to the low number of trainable parameters being modified, the bias was never modified (faulted). However, with larger probabilities, as we allow more parameters to get modified, we did observe changes in bias as well.

The *Fully-Connected Layer Faults* occur in the model's trainable parameters. Therefore, once the injection is complete, we evaluate the faulted model's performance on the entire validation set. On the other hand, for *Convolutional Layer Faults*, the fault is done per input sample, during the inference time, because the layer output values are not fixed properties of the model itself but are dynamically generated based on the specific input data. Consequently, injecting faults at this stage inherently introduces more randomness, which helps to understand our experimental results. Presumably, identifying a specific fault pattern per model-input combination would be beneficial in this setting, while changing weights can impact different inputs automatically. We repeat the experiments 10 times, and report the average. Only the baseline accuracy with the original and pretrained models is not repeated, as they stay the same, since this process only involves running the inference operation. For the original toy CNN model, we use the MNIST dataset, while for the larger models, the ImageNet-1k validation set is used.

3.3   Experimental Results

We first verify our fault model on a toy CNN example (original CNN) that matches the practical observations. Upon verification, we adopted the fault models onto the larger public models.

Experiments on Toy CNN Model

Fully-Connected Layer Fault Model. First, we test our approach on the same model that was used in previous work. The model used is a CNN with two convolutional and two fully-connected layers. It was trained and tested on the MNIST dataset. Here, we use the reported weights of the original CNN that were used while running the EMFI experiments. This model has 77 568 parameters for the first fully-connected layer. Therefore, we set the probability of faulting to 0.0001. This should lead to around 8 parameters faulted on average. We tested with *magnitudes* ranging from 2 000, 20 000, 30 000 and 200 000, and with *magnitude* of 30 000, we achieved the closest difference in the weight value change when compared to the physical EMFI results. The results are presented in Table 2.[5]

---

[5] "Acc." means *accuracy* and "params" means *parameters* in all the table headers.

Table 2. Reproducing Toy CNN [4] results with fault simulation on MNIST dataset for *Fully-Connected Layer Faults*. The setup is with a fault probability of 0.0001 and magnitude 30 000. Only weights from one (first) fully-connected layer are faulted. The results are averaged over 10 simulations.

Baseline Acc.	Acc. w/ Faults	Acc. Drop	Params	Faulty Params
96.05%	44.52%	51.53	77 568	6.4

We observe that on average 6.4 out of 77 568 weights of the first fully-connected layer were changed in the model. We observe an accuracy drop of 51.53% from the baseline of 96.05%, confirming successful misclassifications occurring. Next, we look at the difference between the original weight values and the faulted ones. In Table 3, we can see again the number of weights that are changed on average (column named "Count"). Note that the bias values were not changed in any of the simulations, so we exclude them from the table. Over 10 simulations, the mean difference was around 681, with a minimal difference of 171, and a maximum difference of 1 556 on average. Specifically, the maximum value differences ranged from 846 to 3 089, averaging at 1 556 for 10 repetitions.

Table 3. Results on weight value differences from simulated faults. The values are mean, median, min, and max of the difference between the original and the modified (faulted) weight values, averaged over 10 simulations. These different statistics are related to the reproduction of Toy CNN [4] results on the MNIST dataset for the *Fully-Connected Layer Faults*. The setup is with a fault probability of 0.0001 and magnitude 30 000.

Layer Name	Count	Mean	Median	Min	Max
dense_1_2.weight	6.4	681.17	587.36	171.99	1 556.51

Overall, we observe that the resulting pattern is similar in nature to the results for the *Fully-Connected Layer Faults* from practical experiments. Thus, we can use this approach to test larger public networks to investigate if this fault model can also successfully cause misclassifications, and how it could affect the performance accuracy of the utilized models.

Convolutional Layer Fault Models. After verifying the first fault model, we then test the second fault model. In the practical setting, the faults occurred on the output of the second convolutional layer (out of two convolutional layers, followed by two fully-connected layers). Note that this output was input for the first fully-connected layer in this model. Again, we use the reported weights of the toy CNN model. The output of this convolutional layer had 605 output values, and in the practical EMFI, 300 − 400 of them were modified with the EM injection. Thus, we investigate the faults using a fault probability of 0.58 to randomly introduce around 350 output value changes. We tested with *magnitudes* ranging from 1 − 4, and the most similar results to practical EMFI can be seen in Table 4. We use the same range for simulation on other models.

Table 4. Reproducing Toy CNN [4] results with fault simulation on MNIST dataset for the *Convolutional Layer Faults*. The setup is with fault probability set to 0.58, and the magnitude is noted in the rows. Only the output values of the second convolutional layer are faulty. The results are averaged over 10 simulations.

Magnitude	Baseline Acc.	Acc. w/ Faults	Acc. Drop	Params	Faulty Params
1	96.05%	95.19	0.86	605	350.82
2	96.05%	92.06	3.99	605	350.81

For this fault model, in contrast to the previous one, the accuracy drop is lower, $\sim 1\%$ for the magnitude of changes set to 1, and $\sim 4\%$ for the magnitude 2. This confirms the possibility of achieving misclassification; however, it is not very significant, especially compared to results with the first fault model (Table 2). Since the impact of the fault is quite negligible, we conclude that the fault in earlier layers (typically in convolutional layers) does not result in good fault propagation. Nevertheless, based on the changes in value, as summarized in Table 5, we observe that the changes are consistent with the practical results. As such, we can simulate the *Convolutional Layer Fault* for the larger models as well.

Table 5. Results on convolutional layer output value differences from simulated faults. The values are mean, median, min, and max of the difference between the original and the modified (faulted) output values, averaged over 10 simulations. These different statistics are related to the reproduction of Toy CNN [4] results on the MNIST dataset for the *Convolutional Layer Fault*. The setup is using a fault probability of 0.58.

Magnitude	Layer Name	Count	Mean	Median	Min	Max
1	conv2d_1_1/Relu	350.82	1.16	1.15	6.10E-07	3.08
2	conv2d_1_1/Relu	350.81	2.33	2.31	1.92E-06	6.17

Experiments on Larger Public Networks. Similarly to the result for the toy CNN model, we report results on different neural network models. When we compare the achieved baseline accuracy to that reported on the PyTorch website[6] and shown in Table 1, we can observe that the differences are small. For example, the largest difference is in the *resnet-50* model, which is 0.518, where our obtained accuracy was 80.34% compared to the reported 80.858%.

---

[6] https://docs.pytorch.org/vision/main/models.html.

Overall, the average decrease is 0.139 in the obtained baseline accuracy in our experiments. We find these differences negligible, so we will proceed with our experiments using these.

Fully-Connected Layer Fault Model. In Table 6, we report the experimental results on the larger selected public models. The setup used is mentioned in the first column with the model. The probabilities differ between different models as the faulted fully-connected layer has a different number of parameters that could be faulted, and we aim to have, on average, around 8 faulted parameters. We do this to adhere to the practical fault model. Note also that we are introducing faults in the first fully-connected layer, as was the case in the practical EMFI with the toy CNN model. However, the toy CNN model had two fully-connected layers overall, while the public models have a single last layer that is used for the final classification task. This might impact the experiment, but conceptually, we deem this a fair choice as the public models do not have the same structure and are more complex than the toy CNN model.

The *magnitude* parameter is kept at 30 000 as this was found to result in similar weight value difference as observed in the practical results. Our experiment results show significant accuracy drops for all of the tested models with this fault model. The lowest accuracy drop is for the largest model *resnet-50* (the accuracy drop of 35.6). The most significant accuracy drop is observed for the *resnet-34* model, where the accuracy dropped by **73.14**, leading to the performance accuracy of the model to 0.155%. Thus, the performance of this model was greatly compromised. The number of faulted models on average is kept around 8 parameters, so we conclude that this fault model can greatly impact even larger models than those tested with a practical setup. Therefore, the fault model is generalized to different networks for achieving untargeted misclassifications and lowering the performance of the deployed model, compromising its accuracy and reliability.

To observe the achieved modifications, we show the average parameter value differences for each of the tested models in Table 7. We can see that the maximum absolute difference on average for these models was between 1 025 and 2 759, while the minimum changes ranged 8−114 between different models. The number of parameters modified was approximately 8–9 on average for models, as intended and controlled by the fault probability. These results show that the fault model was kept as the one observed in practice. We conclude that the fault model extends and generalizes to even larger models, having a significant impact on the model's performance. We achieve successful and consistent misclassifications, degrading the model's performance and integrity.

We observe that using a smaller *magnitude* also allows us to achieve lower model accuracy, although not as significant as in the previous setting. For the *resnet-18* and *resnet-34* models, with only around 2 − 3 modified parameters on average, the accuracy dropped by 44.78 for the *resnet-18* model. In general, we observe a drop between **17.8 − 49.96%** in the accuracy for all five tested models, which can be quite significant in some critical applications. These are achieved, with usually fewer faulted parameters, and a smaller weight value difference

Table 6. Results of *Fully-Connected Layer Fault Model* simulation on different larger models. The results are averaged over 10 simulations. In the first column p stands for probability of faults. Magnitude is set to 30 000 for all the models.

Model and Setup	Baseline Acc.	Acc. w/ Faults	Acc. drop	Params	Faulty Params
efficientnet-b0; $p = 6.2\text{e-}06$	77.67%	6.24%	71.43	1 281 000	8.5
mobilenet-v2; $p = 6.2\text{e-}06$	72.01%	15.95%	56.06	1 281 000	9.1
resnet-18; $p = 1.6\text{e-}05$	69.76%	7.16%	62.60	513 000	9.3
resnet-34; $p = 1.6\text{e-}05$	73.30%	0.16%	73.14	513 000	8.4
resnet-50; $p = 3.9\text{e-}06$	80.34%	44.73%	35.61	2 049 000	9.9

Table 7. Fault simulation setting for achieved parameter value differences. The results are averaged over 10 simulations. The setup is the same as for the results in Table 6.

Model and Setup	Layer name	Count	Mean	Median	Min	Max
efficientnet-b0; $p = 6.2\text{e-}06$	classifier.1.weight	8.5	784.51	669.03	114.19	1 983.95
mobilenet-v2; $p = 6.2\text{e-}06$	classifier.1.weight	9.1	586.48	340.11	40.99	1 875.59
resnet-18; $p = 1.6\text{e-}05$	fc.weight	9.3	800.16	475.67	81.40	2 759.86
resnet-34; $p = 1.6\text{e-}05$	fc.weight	8.4	548.26	430.32	79.80	1 520.05
resnet-50; $p = 3.9\text{e-}06$	fc.weight	9.9	288.91	164.35	8.39	1 025.81

between original and faulted values. We exclude the tables with results due to the page limit.

Convolutional Layer Fault Model. We then experiment on the fault model where the faults are injected in the output of a convolutional layer. In the Toy CNN model, this was the second convolutional layer's output (specifically after the *ReLU* activation function). Since we are again working with larger and more complex models, we again had to select an alternative, as directly using the second convolutional layer would not be conceptually the same, since these models use convolutional blocks, and sometimes the convolutional layer is not followed by an activation function immediately. So, in this case, we aim to inject faults on the last convolutional layer before the first fully-connected layer, which is followed by an activation function. Some of these models also use different activation functions, such as *SiLU* in the *efficientnet-b0*, *ReLU6* for *mobilenet-v2*, while *resnets* use *ReLU*. In all the tested models, the last convolutional layer was followed by an activation function, however, for the *resnet-18* and *resnet-34* that is not the case, so a convolutional layer before (which is followed by a ReLU function) was the targeted output. From the practical results, there were $300 - 400$ output values that were successfully modified in these successful injections. Thus, per model, we again select a fault probability that will keep the number of faulty output values around 350. We also set the magnitude to keep the absolute difference around 1 on average.

Table 8. Results of *Convolutional Layer Fault Model* simulation on different larger models. The results are averaged over 10 simulations. In the first column, p stands for fault probability. Magnitude is set to 3 for all the models except resnet-50 which had 4 to keep the average absolute difference close to the practical EMFI.

Model and Setup	Baseline Acc.	Acc. w/ Faults	Acc. Drop	Outputs	Faulty Outputs
efficientnet-b0, $p = 0.00558$	77.67%	77.648	0.027	62 720	349.99
mobilenet-v2, $p = 0.00558$	72.01%	72.009	0.003	62 720	349.93
resnet-18, $p = 0.01395$	69.76%	69.675	0.089	25 088	349.99
resnet-34, $p = 0.01395$	73.30%	73.244	0.052	25 088	349.99
resnet-50, $p = 0.01395$	80.34%	80.332	0.008	50 176	699.94
resnet-50, $p = 0.01395$ and $p = 0.003488$	80.34%	80.339	0.005	50 176	349.99

The same number of outputs in the targeted layer is observed for *efficientnet-b0* and *mobilenet-v2* (62 720), as is for the *resnet* models (25 088). However, for the *resnet-50* model, it happens that the output of that targeted layer, while most of the time is 25 088 output values, sometimes ends with 100 352 output values. Thus, in this case, we first report the results using the same fault probability for both, but then we also test by adjusting the probability for those outputs of 100 352 to keep the number of faulty outputs around 350. This is why we report two instances for the *resnet-50* model, with one noting two fault probabilities. The results are shown in Table 8, with the average differences achieved shown in Table 9.

From the results, we can observe, as was seen for the original toy CNN model, that the accuracy drop is significantly less than with the *Fully-Connected*

Layer Fault. The accuracy drop on these larger models is in the range 0.003–0.089, which is even less significant than the accuracy drop of 1–4 for the toy CNN model. We conclude that this fault type is not as successful as the weight modifications in the first fully-connected layer. The reason might come from the smaller absolute differences, despite a larger number of values being changed. The following fully-connected layers for final classification can mitigate these small changes and prevent the fault propagation to the prediction. Moreover, the nature of the fault type is quite different, as the fault injections happen on the output of the layer, while in the other fault model, the model weights are targeted. Due to the added randomness in the output changes, stemming from different inputs obtaining different outputs even for the same layer, and the random faults introduced, the fault type is not very successful in general. So, while it might misclassify some samples, it does not lead to a large decrease in the model's performance.

Table 9. Achieved layer output value differences. The results are averaged over 10 simulations. The setup is the same as for the results in Table 8

Model	Layer name	Count	Mean	Median	Min	Max
efficientnet-b0, $p = 0.00558$	features.8.2	349.99	1.27	1.26	2.37E-07	3.20
mobilenet-v2, $p = 0.00558$	features.18.2	349.93	0.90	0.89	1.86E-07	2.12
resnet-18, $p = 0.01395$	layer4.1.relu	349.99	1.20	0.25	3.03E-08	5.24
resnet-34, $p = 0.01395$	layer4.2.relu	349.99	1.21	0.20	1.87E-08	5.27
resnet-50, $p = 0.01395$	layer4.2.relu	699.94	1.05	0.99	1.09E-07	3.23
resnet-50, $p = 0.01395$ and $p = 0.003488$	layer4.2.relu	349.99	0.96	0.90	1.06E-07	3.23

Discussion. Our experimental results match the practical results on the toy CNN model. We then extend it to larger public models and observe the generalization of the found fault types. We found that the *Fully-Connected Layer Fault Model* works quite well on these larger models, even if a lower absolute difference can be achieved, with even fewer weights modified. Specifically, we observe, on average, **80.7%** reduction in performance accuracy for this fault type on the five public, commonly utilized image classification models. On the other hand, the second *Convolutional Layer Fault Model* does not generalize as well to larger models. This fault model can work, but it might need optimization for each input sample given to the model, while the weight changes affect different inputs without additional consideration or optimization.

As per our knowledge, this is the only work we are aware of that investigated fault injection attacks using EM on a commercial target device in a black-box setting. As this is a black-box scenario, and we don't know the internal structure, the attacker has to resort to a random fault model, which is suboptimal in comparison to other existing works with bit flip faults, etc. Thus, it is hard to come up with a fair comparison between this work and other existing works. Again, we would like to emphasize that we are not aiming for optimal attack, and our goal is to demonstrate the practicality of the observed practical fault models on a commercial target in a black-box setting.

We note that execution time for all models, including all 10 simulations, was at most $1.67\,h$ (some took less than an hour also), using at most $6.4\,GB$, while running on Nvidia RTX A6000 ($48\,GB$) or RTX A5000 ($24\,GB$) GPU. The execution time is related mostly to the repeated inference over $50\,000$ images from the ImageNet-1k validation set.

Limitations and Future Works. The experiments have been solely conducted on a single Intel NCS 2 device. Regarding the portability of the fault model, we expect these fault models to work on a similar family of devices, as the faults are not targeting a specific architecture within the device. However, since this is a black-box design, we do not know many details about the internal component, and as such, we cannot perform an in-depth analysis of what is happening internally. Thus, we cannot claim that these fault models would be fully transferable without adaptation to other families of devices, since each family has its own specific processing units, hardware, and implementation, as well as different model optimization requirements. However, this could be a significant future work. With regards to future works, it would also be an interesting direction to consider the following:

- To investigate and have a theoretical modeling of the fault attacks, along with an analysis regarding the efficacy of the attacks.
- Our current investigation was limited to public CNN models because we focused on establishing a proof-of-concept using architectures found on the NCS 2 supported list. A valuable extension of this work would be to explore other architectures, e.g., for natural language processing tasks.
- Another interesting direction to explore, which also deals with the limitation of edge ML, is for the countermeasure or mitigation. In the edge ML paradigm, there are physical or resource constraints, so standard countermeasures, such as redundancy, might not be applicable.

4   Conclusion

It is known that any physical implementation of an algorithm is prone to hardware attacks. In the case of edge ML, this leads to potential threats of compromising the performance accuracy. In previous works, it is shown that a common edge ML device, Intel NCS 2, can be faulted using EMFI during the inference process, resulting in misclassification. However, one of the limited aspects is that the analysis is performed only on a toy CNN model.

In this study, we aim to extend the work by investigating the scalability of EMFI on different target models, using more complex public models. We first analyze the fault models obtained from the practical experiments, and we construct a suitable fault simulation setting. We first confirmed the validity of the simulation on the same toy model and reported similar performance to that reported in the previous paper. We then use the simulation setting to perform the FIA on several public models. We observe that the practical fault model could indeed compromise and degrade the performance accuracy, even on larger and more complex models.

Acknowledgments. This work was (in part) supported by the Dutch Research Council (NWO) through the Challenges in Cyber Security (CiCS) project of the Gravitation research program under the grant 024.006.037. It is also supported in parts by the National Research Foundation, Singapore, and Cyber Security Agency of Singapore under its National Cybersecurity Research & Development Programme (Development of Secured Components & Systems in Emerging Technologies through Hardware & Software Evaluation NRF-NCR25-DeSNTU-0001). Any opinions, findings and conclusions or recommendations expressed in this material are those of the author(s) and do not reflect the view of National Research Foundation, Singapore and Cyber Security Agency of Singapore.

References

1. Intel OpenVINO Toolkit. https://software.intel.com/content/www/us/en/develop/tools/openvino-toolkit.html
2. Neural Compute Stick 2. https://software.intel.com/content/www/us/en/develop/hardware/neural-compute-stick.html
3. Batina, L., Bhasin, S., Jap, D., Picek, S.: CSI NN: reverse engineering of neural network architectures through electromagnetic side channel. In: Heninger, N., Traynor, P. (eds.) 28th USENIX Security Symposium, USENIX Security 2019, Santa Clara, CA, USA, 14–16 August 2019, pp. 515–532. USENIX Association (2019). https://www.usenix.org/conference/usenixsecurity19/presentation/batina
4. Bhasin, S., Jap, D., Ravi, P., Krček, M., Picek, S.: Late breaking results: practical electromagnetic fault injection on intel neural compute stick 2. In: 2025 Design, Automation & Test in Europe Conference (DATE), pp. 1–2. IEEE (2025)
5. Breier, J., Hou, X., Jap, D., Ma, L., Bhasin, S., Liu, Y.: Practical fault attack on deep neural networks. In: Proceedings of the 2018 ACM SIGSAC Conference on Computer and Communications Security, pp. 2204–2206 (2018)
6. Dumont, M., Lisart, M., Maurine, P.: Electromagnetic fault injection: how faults occur. In: 2019 Workshop on Fault Diagnosis and Tolerance in Cryptography (FDTC), pp. 9–16. IEEE (2019)
7. Goodfellow, I., Bengio, Y., Courville, A.: Deep Learning. MIT Press, Cambridge (2016). http://www.deeplearningbook.org
8. Kim, Y., et al.: Flipping bits in memory without accessing them: An experimental study of DRAM disturbance errors. In: ACM/IEEE 41st International Symposium on Computer Architecture, ISCA 2014, Minneapolis, MN, USA, 14–18 June 2014, pp. 361–372. IEEE Computer Society (2014). https://doi.org/10.1109/ISCA.2014.6853210

9. Kocher, P.C.: Timing attacks on implementations of Diffie-Hellman, RSA, DSS, and other systems. In: Koblitz, N. (ed.) CRYPTO 1996. LNCS, vol. 1109, pp. 104–113. Springer, Heidelberg (1996). https://doi.org/10.1007/3-540-68697-5_9
10. Liu, Y., Wei, L., Luo, B., Xu, Q.: Fault injection attack on deep neural network. In: 2017 IEEE/ACM International Conference on Computer-Aided Design (ICCAD), pp. 131–138. IEEE (2017)
11. Papernot, N., McDaniel, P., Sinha, A., Wellman, M.P.: Sok: security and privacy in machine learning. In: 2018 IEEE European symposium on security and privacy (EuroS&P), pp. 399–414. IEEE (2018)
12. Szegedy, C., et al.: Intriguing properties of neural networks. arXiv e-prints arXiv:1312.6199 (2013)
13. Won, Y.S., Chatterjee, S., Jap, D., Basu, A., Bhasin, S.: Deepfreeze: cold boot attacks and high fidelity model recovery on commercial edgeml device. In: 2021 IEEE/ACM International Conference On Computer Aided Design (ICCAD), pp. 1–9. IEEE (2021)
14. Won, Y.S., Chatterjee, S., Jap, D., Bhasin, S., Basu, A.: Time to leak: cross-device timing attack on edge deep learning accelerator. In: 2021 International Conference on Electronics, Information, and Communication (ICEIC), pp. 1–4. IEEE (2021)
15. Yao, F., Rakin, A.S., Fan, D.: {DeepHammer}: depleting the intelligence of deep neural networks through targeted chain of bit flips. In: 29th USENIX Security Symposium (USENIX Security 20), pp. 1463–1480 (2020)

A New Perspective on the Decomposition in the Jacobian of Small Genus Hyperelliptic Curve

Deepak Bhati[1(✉)] and Shashank Singh[2]

[1] CISPA Helmholtz, Saarbrücken, Germany
deepak2602161@gmail.com
[2] Indian Institute of Science Education and Research Bhopal, Bhopal, India
shashank@iiserb.ac.in

Abstract. The decomposition step is a major bottleneck in the effectiveness of the index-calculus algorithm for solving the discrete logarithm problem on the Jacobian of hyperelliptic curves with low genus, as it requires solving a nonlinear system of multivariate polynomial equations. Sarkar and Singh, in the year 2016, proposed a decomposition method for the curves, defined over quadratic extensions, which avoids solving multivariate polynomial systems. In this paper, building on the Sarkar-Singh work and using the cyclic group of the underlined extension field, we identify a class of weak curves for which the decomposition is easy to handle. In the new decomposition, we completely avoid solving the system of multivariate polynomial equations, and the time complexity remains the same as that of the Sarkar-Singh decomposition. The new decomposition applies to specific curves defined over extension fields. For a given random hyperelliptic curve, it can be efficiently checked whether this decomposition attack applies to it or not, using the discrete logarithms in the cyclic group of the underlying extension field. The discrete logarithm problem (DLP) over finite fields is generally easier than the DLP over the Jacobian of hyperelliptic curves. Therefore, we can reasonably assume that discrete logarithms over the underlying finite field are accessible. This assumption aids in determining whether the given curve is susceptible to this type of attack.

MSC: 11Y16 · 11T71 · 94A60

1 Introduction

The index calculus technique [11] offers some of the most advanced algorithms for solving the discrete logarithm problems in finite fields. However, when it comes to low-genus hyperelliptic curves, this technique is less effective than in finite fields. This reduced effectiveness is primarily attributed to the decomposition step of the algorithm. In the year 2000, Gaudry [3] proposed an index calculus algorithm for solving the hyperelliptic curve discrete logarithm problem

C. Karfa et al. (Eds.): SPACE 2025, LNCS 16406, pp. 58–78, 2026.
https://doi.org/10.1007/978-3-032-16342-4_4

(HCDLP). This algorithm has exponential-time complexity, yet it is more efficient than the generic Pollard's rho algorithm for genus $g \geq 4$. Improvements to this algorithm, particularly the large prime variants, are discussed in the papers by Gaudry et al. [4,17]. Sarkar and Singh proposed a practically faster decomposition algorithm in their paper [14] in 2017. It is important to note that all subsequent variants and improvements to Gaudry's algorithm maintain similar asymptotic complexities, and they are all applicable to curves defined over finite fields $\mathbb{F}_q$.

Nagao [10] introduced a new decomposition method for the hyperelliptic curve defined over the finite field of the form $\mathbb{F}_{q^n}$, where $n \geq 2$. Joux and Vitse later improved this method in their work [6]. Both studies consider a factor base that is defined over the subfield $\mathbb{F}_q$ and involves a relation collection step that requires solving a system of multivariate polynomial equations. On the other hand, Sarkar-Singh [15] examined a similar setup but showed that their decomposition method avoids the necessity of solving multivariate polynomial equations, for a specific class of hyperelliptic curves. However, in the Sarkar-Singh approach, one final Nagao-type decomposition is still needed during the individual discrete logarithm step.

Our Result. In this work, we adapt the Sarkar-Singh approach and utilise the cyclic group structure of $\mathbb{F}_{q^n}^{\star}$. We identify a class of hyperelliptic curves for which the decomposition is significantly simplified, as it avoids the need to solve a system of multivariate polynomial equations. It is important to note that the Sarkar-Singh approach applies specifically to some hyperelliptic curves defined over quadratic extensions, while the new decomposition proposed in this paper is applicable to a class of hyperelliptic curves defined over odd characteristic extension field.

Paper Outline. In Sect. 2, we mention the required notations and preliminaries needed for the understanding of this work. Section 3 gives a brief introduction to the decomposition technique proposed by Nagao [10]. This section motivates our main idea, which is presented in Sect. 4 of the paper. In this section, we give a detailed account of the new decomposition technique. Here, we describe a class of hyperelliptic curves where the decomposition step doesn't require solving non-linear system of multivariate polynomial equations. The Sect. 5 describes how we can efficiently check whether a given random curve is vulnerable to our attack or not. In Sect. 6, we briefly discuss how our technique can be employed in the characteristic 2 case. Finally, we provide our experimental results in Sect. 7, and the appendix contains Magma scripts to test the decompositions provided in the paper.

2 Notations and Prerequisites

Let $K := \mathbb{F}_{q^n}$ be a finite field of characteristic $p > 2$, $n \geq 2$, and $\mathcal{C}/K : y^2 = f(x)$ be a hyperelliptic curve of genus g defined over K, where $\deg f(x) = 2g+1$, and

f is a monic polynomial. For a finite point $P \in \mathcal{C}(K)$ ($\mathcal{C}(K)$ denotes the set of all K-rational points of $\mathcal{C}$), we define by $x(P)$ and $y(P)$ the respective x-coordinate and y-coordinate of the point P. We are interested in the discrete logarithm problem in the cyclic subgroup G of the Jacobian $J_{\mathcal{C}}(K)$ of hyperelliptic curve $\mathcal{C}$. Elements of the $J_{\mathcal{C}}(K)$ are represented by the reduced divisors of a form

$$(P_1) + (P_2) + \ldots + (P_r) - r(\infty),$$

with $P_i = (x_i, y_i) \in \mathcal{C}$, and ∞ is a special point on the curve called point at infinity, $P_i \neq \tilde{P}_j$ for $i \neq j$ where $\tilde{P}_j = (x_j, -y_j)$, and the multiset $\{P_i : 1 \leq i \leq r\}$ is stable under the action of Galois group $\mathrm{Gal}\left(\bar{K}, K\right)$. More conveniently an element of $J_{\mathcal{C}}(K)$ is represented by its Mumford representation i.e. by a pair of polynomial $(u(x), v(x))$, with $u(x), v(x) \in K[x]$ where $\deg(v) < \deg(u) \leq g$, and $u(x) \mid (v^2(x) - f(x))$. For more details on hyperelliptic curves and the above-mentioned notations, we refer to the paper [8].

Let D_1 be an element of $J_{\mathcal{C}}(K)$ of prime order, $D_2 \in \langle D_1 \rangle$, and our aim is to find $\log_{D_1}(D_2)$. We further denote a multiplicative group $K^* = \langle \alpha \rangle$ for some $\alpha \in K^*$.

Let $\tilde{\mathcal{C}}/K : y^2 = \tilde{f}(x)$ be a transformation of curve $\mathcal{C}$ where

$$\tilde{f}(x) := f(\alpha^a x) \tag{1}$$

for some $a \in \{1, 2, \ldots, q^n - 2\}$.

Claim 1. *If $\tilde{f}$ has no repeated root, then $J_{\tilde{\mathcal{C}}}(K)$ is isomorphic to $J_{\mathcal{C}}(K)$.*

Proof. Let $P = (x(P), y(P))$ be a K-rational point of $\mathcal{C}$, then we define $\tilde{P} := (\alpha^{-a} x(P), y(P))$. We can easily verify that $\tilde{P}$ is a K-rational point of $\tilde{\mathcal{C}}$ and this gives an isomorphism of projective varieties. Let's consider the following map,

$$\phi : J_{\mathcal{C}}(K) \to J_{\tilde{\mathcal{C}}}(K)$$
$$D \hookrightarrow \tilde{D},$$

where $D = \sum_{i=1}^{s}(P_i) - s(\infty)$ is a K-rational reduced divisor of $\mathcal{C}$ and $\tilde{D} = \sum_{i=1}^{s}(\tilde{P}_i) - s(\infty)$. We observe that the multiset $\{\tilde{P}_i\}_{i=1}^{s}$ remains stable under the action of $\mathrm{Gal}\left(\bar{K}, K\right)$ and hence $\tilde{D} \in J_{\tilde{\mathcal{C}}}(K)$. Secondly, we will prove that ϕ is a well-defined map.

Let $D_1 = \sum_{i=1}^{r}(Q_i) - r(\infty)$ such that $D_1 \sim D$, so there exists $R(x, y) \in K(\mathcal{C})^*$ such that $\mathrm{div}(R) = D_1 - D$. Let $R(x, y) = \frac{G(x,y)}{H(x,y)}$. We define $\tilde{R} := \frac{\tilde{G}}{\tilde{H}}$, where $\tilde{G}(x, y) := G(\alpha^a x, y)$ and $\tilde{H}(x, y) := H(\alpha^a x, y)$. Note that $\tilde{R}(\tilde{Q}_i) = 0$ for $i \in \{1, 2, \ldots, r\}$, $\tilde{R}(\tilde{P}_i) = \infty$ for $i \in \{1, 2, \ldots, s\}$ and $\tilde{R}$ does not have any other zero or a pole. Thus $\mathrm{div}(\tilde{R}) = \sum_{i=1}^{r}(\tilde{Q}_i) - \sum_{i=1}^{s}(\tilde{P}_i) - (r - s)(\infty)$ which means $\mathrm{div}(\tilde{R}) = \tilde{D}_1 - \tilde{D}$ and hence $\tilde{D}_1 \sim \tilde{D}$.

Now we prove the group isomorphism. Let D_1, and D_2 be two elements of $J_{\mathcal{C}}(K)$ such that $D_1 = \sum_{i=1}^{s}(P_i) - s(\infty)$ and $D_2 = \sum_{i=1}^{r}(Q_i) - r(\infty)$. Let $D \sim \sum_{i=1}^{s}(P_i) + \sum_{j=1}^{r}(Q_j) - (s + r)(\infty)$, then

$$\phi(D) = \phi\left(\sum_{i=1}^{s}(P_i) + \sum_{j=1}^{r}(Q_j) - (s+r)(\infty)\right)$$

$$= \sum_{i=1}^{s}(\tilde{P}_i) + \sum_{j=1}^{r}(\tilde{Q}_j) - (s+r)(\infty)$$

$$= \left(\sum_{i=1}^{s}(\tilde{P}_i) - s(\infty)\right) + \left(\sum_{j=1}^{r}(\tilde{Q}_j) - r(\infty)\right)$$

$$= \phi(D_1) + \phi(D_2).$$

The bijection of ϕ is straightforward.

3 Nagao's Type Decomposition

In this section, we revisit Nagao's Type Decomposition given in the Sarkar-Singh Decomposition [15]. Let $\mathcal{C}/K : y^2 = f(x)$ be a hyperelliptic curve as defined in Sect. 2. Let

$$\mathcal{F} = \{(P) - (\infty) \mid P \in \mathcal{C}(K), \text{ and } x(P) \in \mathbb{F}_q\} \tag{2}$$

be a factor base of $J_\mathcal{C}(K)$. Let $D = (u(x), v(x)) \in J_\mathcal{C}(K)$ and the aim is to decompose D into the elements of the factor base. Consider a bivariate polynomial

$$G(x,y) := u(x)\lambda(x) - (y - v(x))\mu(x), \tag{3}$$

where $\lambda(x), \mu(x) \in K[x]$. It is easy to see that the points in the support of D are the zeros of the $G(x,y)$. In addition, these are all possible curves that pass through all the points in the support of D. The x-coordinates of additional zeros are given by the polynomial

$$H(x) = S(x)/u(x), \tag{4}$$

where $S(x) = (-u(x)\lambda(x) + v(x)\mu(x))^2 - \mu^2(x)f(x)$ is a polynomial obtained by eliminating y between $y^2 = f(x)$ and $G(x,y) = 0$. If $H(x)$ is smooth over $\mathbb{F}_q$ i.e., $H(x) = \prod_i(x - \gamma_i)$, we have $\delta_i = v(\lambda_i) - \dfrac{u(\gamma_i)\lambda(\gamma_i)}{\mu(\gamma_i)}$, and $P_i := (\gamma_i, \delta_i) \in \mathcal{F}$. Thus

$$\mathrm{div}(G(x,y)) = D + \sum_{i=1}^{\deg(H)} ((P_i) - (\infty)), \tag{5}$$

and hence we have a decomposition

$$-D \sim \sum_{i=1}^{\deg(H)} ((P_i) - (\infty)), \tag{6}$$

If we choose $D = (1, 0)$, i.e. the identity of $J_{\mathcal{C}}(K)$, we get a decomposition involving the elements of the factor base only, and in this case the above-mentioned polynomial $H(x)$ simplifies to

$$H(x) = \lambda^2(x) - \mu^2(x) f(x). \tag{7}$$

In the relation collection step, both the Joux-Vitse and Sarkar-Singh methods aim to choose/obtain $\lambda(x)$ and $\mu(x)$ in such a way that the resulting $H(x)$ given by Equation (7) is smooth over $\mathbb{F}_q$. Note that the coefficients of two polynomials $\lambda(x)$ and $\mu(x)$ are the control variables for us. Joux-Vitse by suitably choosing the control variables obtains $H(x) \in F_q[x]$ by solving a system with $ng(n-1) + 2(n-1)$ many multivariate polynomial equations, and $ng(n-1) + 2n$ variables. Solving this results in a triangular system with two free variables, and these two free variables are varied to get enough smooth $H(x)$'s.

4   Decomposition, a New Perspective

In this section, we search for a Joux-Vitse-type decomposition. We follow the setup provided in the Sect. 3. Let

$$f(x) = x^{2g+1} + \sum_{i=0}^{2g} f_i x^i \tag{8}$$

where $f_i = \alpha^{j_i} \ \forall \ i \in \{0, 1, 2, \ldots, 2g\}$, for some $j_i \in \{0, 1, \ldots, q^n - 2\}$. Note that α is a generator of the cyclic group $\mathbb{F}_{q^n}^*$.

Without loss of generality, we can work within an isomorphic group $J_{\widetilde{C}}(K)$. Recall that that curve $\tilde{C}/K$ is given by equation $y^2 = \tilde{f}(x)$, where $\tilde{f}(x) := f(\alpha^a x)$. This represents a transformation of the curve $\mathcal{C}$ as defined in the Sect. 2. We define the following factor base for $J_{\widetilde{C}}(K)$:

$$\widetilde{\mathcal{F}} := \{(\tilde{P}) - (\infty) \mid \tilde{P} \in \tilde{C}(K), \text{ and } x(\tilde{P}) \in \mathbb{F}_q\} \tag{9}$$

We aim to find relations among the elements of the factor base described in Eq. (9). Continuing with the analysis from Sect. 3, we obtain the following polynomial:

$$\tilde{H}(x) = \tilde{\lambda}^2(x) - \tilde{\mu}^2(x) \tilde{f}(x). \tag{10}$$

We intend to find $\tilde{\lambda}(x)$ and $\tilde{\mu}(x)$ such that $\tilde{H}(x) \in \mathbb{F}_q[x]$. If we find $\tilde{\mu}(x)$ such that $\tilde{\mu}^2(x) \tilde{f}(x) \in \mathbb{F}_q[x]$, then we can achieve our goal easily. Therefore, we focus solely on this term. First, we set $\tilde{\mu}(x) := \alpha^l$, a constant polynomial, for some l. We further define

$$\psi(x) := \tilde{\mu}^2(x) \tilde{f}(x) = \sum_{i=0}^{2g+1} \alpha^{2l + j_i + ia} x^i, \tag{11}$$

where $j_{2g+1} := 0$. The reason for defining $\tilde{\mu}(x)$ in this way is based on our assumption that we have access to the discrete logarithms to the base α.

Let $\mathbb{F}_q^\star = \langle \gamma \rangle$ with $\gamma = \alpha^t$, $M = q^n - 1$, and $d = \gcd(t, M)$. We note that $\alpha^i \in \mathbb{F}_q^\star$ if and only if d divides i. Consider a set

$$L := \{\alpha^{d\eta_0}, \alpha^{d\eta_1}, \ldots, \alpha^{d\eta_{2g+1}}\} \subset \mathbb{F}_q^\star, \tag{12}$$

where $\{\eta_i\}_{i=0}^{2g+1}$ are mutually coprimes and $\gcd(d, \eta_i) = 1$ for all $i \in \{0, 1, \ldots, 2g+1\}$. We note that $\psi(x) \in \mathbb{F}_q[x]$ provided the following system of congruence has a solution for l:

$$\left.\begin{aligned}
2l + j_0 &\equiv 0 \quad \mathrm{mod}\ d\eta_0 \\
2l + j_1 + a &\equiv 0 \quad \mathrm{mod}\ d\eta_1 \\
&\vdots \\
2l + j_{2g} + 2ga &\equiv 0 \quad \mathrm{mod}\ d\eta_{2g} \\
2l + (2g+1)a &\equiv 0 \quad \mathrm{mod}\ d\eta_{2g+1}
\end{aligned}\right\}. \tag{13}$$

Solving such a modular system requires working out some mathematical details. Consider the following system,

$$\left.\begin{aligned}
z &\equiv t_0 \quad \mathrm{mod}\ d\eta_0 \\
z &\equiv t_1 \quad \mathrm{mod}\ d\eta_1 \\
&\vdots \\
z &\equiv t_{n-1} \quad \mathrm{mod}\ d\eta_{n-1}
\end{aligned}\right\}, \tag{14}$$

where d, and $\eta_i's$ are defined as above. Let's consider the following modular equation,

$$z \equiv t_i \quad \mathrm{mod}\ d\eta_i$$

The solution of this equation will also satisfy the following equations, and vice versa

$$\begin{aligned}
z &\equiv t_i \quad \mathrm{mod}\ d \\
z &\equiv t_i \quad \mathrm{mod}\ \eta_i
\end{aligned}$$

Hence, the System 14 breaks down to the following system of congruences,

$$\left.\begin{aligned}
z &\equiv t_0 \quad \mathrm{mod}\ \eta_0 \\
z &\equiv t_1 \quad \mathrm{mod}\ \eta_1 \\
&\vdots \\
z &\equiv t_{n-1} \quad \mathrm{mod}\ \eta_{n-1} \\
z &\equiv t_0 \equiv \cdots \equiv t_{n-1} \quad \mathrm{mod}\ d
\end{aligned}\right\}, \tag{15}$$

So the modular system given by Eq. (14) has a solution if and only if the following condition is satisfied

$$t_0 \equiv t_1 \equiv \cdots \equiv t_{n-1} \quad \mathrm{mod}\ d. \tag{16}$$

Assume that this condition is satisfied, then consider $l_2 := t_0 \mod d$. Considering this assumption, we get the following system

$$\left.\begin{array}{l} z \equiv t_0 \mod \eta_0 \\ z \equiv t_1 \mod \eta_1 \\ \quad \vdots \\ z \equiv t_{n-1} \mod \eta_{n-1} \\ z \equiv l_2 \mod d \end{array}\right\}, \tag{17}$$

which can be solved by CRT.

Now we will use this result to solve the system given by the Eq. (13). Consider $z = 2l$, and $t_i = -(j_i + ia) \ \forall i \in \{0, 1, \ldots, 2g+1\}$ where $j_{2g+1} = 0$. Then the system, given by Eq. (14), represents the system given by the Eq. (13). Assuming Eq. (16) is satisfied for this system, we can get a solution for z. The solution of l is given by the following congruence

$$2l \equiv z \mod d\eta_0\eta_1\ldots\eta_{2g+1}. \tag{18}$$

Observe that

$$d = \frac{q^n - 1}{q - 1} = \underbrace{q^{n-1} + q^{n-2} + \ldots + q + 1}_{n \text{ terms}}.$$

Since q is an odd prime power, if n is odd, then d is odd and therefore $2^{-1} \mod d$ exists; otherwise it doesn't.

- n is odd : In this case $2^{-1} \mod d$ exists, and therefore the solution for $l = 2^{-1}z \mod d\eta_0\eta_1\ldots\eta_{2g+1}$;
- n is even : In this case, the inverse doesn't exist. Firstly, we can observe that if the solution of z is odd, then there doesn't exist any solution for l. Secondly, if the solution of z is even, then taking $l = z/2$ will satisfy Eq. (18).

Thus, we have an l for which $\psi(x) = \tilde{\mu}^2(x)\tilde{f}(x) \in \mathbb{F}_q[x]$. If we choose $\tilde{\lambda}(x)$ from $\mathbb{F}_q[x]$ and vary its coefficients over $\mathbb{F}_q$, we can get a smooth $\tilde{H}(x) = \tilde{\lambda}^2(x) - \tilde{\mu}^2(x)\tilde{f}(x)$ and hence a relation among factor basis elements.

The rest of the analysis remains similar to that of Sarkar-Singh [15] analysis. Let $\deg \tilde{\lambda}(x) = m$, then $\deg \tilde{H}(x) = \max\{2m, 2g+1\}$. Since we have m coefficients of $\tilde{\lambda}(x)$ to vary over $\mathbb{F}_q$, we can find approximately $\frac{q^m}{(2g+1)!}$ many smooth $\tilde{H}(x)$'s. Since $\#\tilde{\mathcal{F}} = \mathcal{O}(q)$, we set m to be the smallest positive integer such that $2m < 2g + 1$ (in order to keep the degree of $\tilde{H}$ equal to $2g + 1$ only), and

$$q^{(m-1)} \geq (2g+1)!. \tag{19}$$

The sieving technique of the Sarkar-Singh approach also works well in this case.

4.1 Sieving Technique

In this section, we describe the sieving method used by Sarkar-Singh [15] in our setting Let $\mathcal{B} := \{x(\tilde{P}) | (\tilde{P}) - (\infty) \in \tilde{\mathcal{F}}\}$, and $\lambda(x) = x^m + \sum_{i=1}^{m-1} \lambda_i x^i + \lambda_0$. For a fixed value of $\bar{\lambda}$ $(\in \mathbb{F}_q^{m-1}) =: (\lambda_1, \cdots, \lambda_{m-1})$, the polynomial $\tilde{H}$, given by Eq. (10), can be written as

$$\tilde{H}_{\bar{\lambda}}(x) = \left(\lambda_0 + \sum_{i=1}^{m-1} \lambda_i x^i \right)^2 - \psi(x), \tag{20}$$

Now the aim is to vary λ_0 to get a smooth $\tilde{H}_{\bar{\lambda}}(x)$. We note that $\tilde{H}_{\bar{\lambda}}(\delta)$, for some $\delta \in \mathbb{F}_q$, is smooth and the corresponding two roots are $\lambda_0^{(1)}$ and $\lambda_0^{(2)}$. Let $\mathtt{ctr}$ be an associate array of size q. We vary δ through $\mathcal{B}$ for a fixed $\bar{\lambda}$ and compute the values of $\lambda_0^{(1)}$ and $\lambda_0^{(2)}$. If $\lambda_0^{(1)} \neq \lambda_0^{(2)}$, then increment $\mathtt{ctr}[\lambda_0^{(1)}]$ and $\mathtt{ctr}[\lambda_0^{(2)}]$ by 1, else just increment $\mathtt{ctr}[\lambda_0^{(1)}]$. Since the degree of $\tilde{H}$ is $2g + 1$, there will be approximately $q/(2g + 1)!$ many indices in $\mathtt{ctr}$ with the value $2g + 1$ after traversing through the entire $\mathcal{B}$. The corresponding indices of $\mathtt{ctr}$ will give us the value of λ_0, and hence of $\lambda(x)$, for which $\tilde{H}(x)$ is smooth over $\mathbb{F}_q$.

We then choose different value of $\bar{\lambda} := (\lambda_1, \cdots, \lambda_{m-1})$ and start sieving for λ_0 again, until we get enough relations.

4.2 Individual Logarithm Step

In this step, we decompose a random element of the form $a_1 \tilde{D}_1 + b_1 \tilde{D}_2$, in our factor base $\tilde{\mathcal{F}}$. For this decomposition, we refer to the paper by Nagao [10] for details. After getting such a decomposition, we take the discrete logarithm to the base D_1 on the two sides and thereby compute the final value of the logarithm of $\tilde{D}_2$ to the base $\tilde{D}_1$. And this value will remain the same as the discrete logarithm of D_2 to the base D_1, since $J_{\mathcal{C}}(K) \cong J_{\tilde{\mathcal{C}}}(K)$.

4.3 Complexity Analysis

The asymptotic complexity of this work remains the same as that of Sarkar-Singh work [15]. Both this work and the work of Sarkar-Singh avoid solving multivariate non-linear system for getting a smooth $\tilde{H}(x)$. Sarkar-Singh technique works for curves defined over a quadratic extension field, whereas our technique works for any extension degree, with some constraints as explained above.

5 Attack on a Random Curve

Let $\mathcal{C}/K : y^2 = f(x)$ be a random hyperelliptic curve as defined in Sect. 2 is given to us. We want to find whether this curve is vulnerable to our attack or not. Let $K^\star = \langle \alpha \rangle$ and assume that the discrete logarithms of the coefficients of f to the base α are known to us. The assumption is not unrealistic, and for the recent works on DLP in the finite fields, we refer to the following papers [1, 2, 5, 7, 9, 12, 13, 16]. Recall $f(x) = x^{2g+1} + \sum_{i=0}^{2g} f_i x^i$, where $f_i = \alpha^{j_i}$. We assume that the j_i's are known to us. The condition for our method to work is given by the Eq. (16). But the system of congruences to be solved depends on the degree of extension, i.e. n (Refer to Sect. 4). So we need to find an $a \in \{1, 2, \ldots, q^n - 2\}$ such that the following condition is satisfied:

$$t_0 \equiv t_1 \equiv \ldots \equiv t_{2g} \equiv t_{2g+1} \mod d$$

$t_i's$ are defined as in Sect. 4. Since $t_0 \ (= -j_0)$ is independent of a, the value of a gets fixed by $t_0 \equiv t_1 \mod d$ i.e. $a = (j_0 - j_1) \mod d$. Then we need to check the remaining congruences in the condition (Eq. (16)) for this particular value of a. If this a satisfies all the congruences, then the System 14, for the above defined values of $t_i's$, has a solution. Then, for the solution of l, and the remainder of the attack, refer to Sect. 4.

6 Curves over Characteristic 2 Fields

In this section, we briefly discuss how our technique can be employed in the characteristic 2 case. Hyperelliptic curves defined over characteristic 2 fields have the following equation

$$\mathcal{C}/K : y^2 + h(x)y = f(x),$$

where $h(x), f(x) \in K[x]$, $\deg f(x) = 2g + 1$, $\deg h(x) \leq g$, f is monic, g is the genus of the curve, and $K = \mathbb{F}_{q^n}$, where q is a power of 2, and $n \geq 2$.

Working along the same lines as in Sect. 4 to get the relations among the factor basis elements, we consider the polynomial $G(x, y) = \lambda(x) + y\mu(x)$ where $\lambda(x)$ and $\mu(x)$ are polynomials of degrees m_1 and m_2 respectively in $K[x]$. We are interested in finding the zeroes of G on the above defined hyperelliptic curve $\mathcal{C}/K$. Let $(a, b) \in \mathcal{C}(K)$ be a finite point s.t. $G(a, b) = 0$, then by eliminating b from both the equations, we get the polynomial $H(x)$ of the following form

$$H(x) = \lambda^2(x) + h(x)\lambda(x)\mu(x) + \mu^2(x)f(x). \tag{21}$$

Our aim is to find $\lambda(x)$ and $\mu(x)$ s.t. $H(x) \in \mathbb{F}_q[x]$, and it is smooth over $\mathbb{F}_q$. We can apply our technique to a special form of curves $\mathcal{C}/K$; in the next paragraph, we provide a more detailed explanation.

Consider a hyperelliptic curve defined as above, such that $h(x) = c$, where $c \in K$. Then using Eq. (21), we have

$$H(x) = \lambda^2(x) + c\lambda(x)\mu(x) + \mu^2(x)f(x). \tag{22}$$

Consider the term $\mu^2(x)f(x)$ in Eq. (22), we will use the same approach as we did in Sect. 4 to find a transformation curve $\tilde{\mathcal{C}}/K : y^2 + cy = \tilde{f}(x)$ s.t. $\tilde{\mu}^2(x)\tilde{f}(x) \in \mathbb{F}_q[x]$ where $\tilde{\mu}(x) = \alpha^l$, and $K^\star = \langle \alpha \rangle$. For more details, we refer to the Sect. 4.

So now we have a transformed curve $\tilde{\mathcal{C}}/K$, which is isomorphic to $\mathcal{C}/K$, whose corresponding $H(x)$ polynomial is

$$\tilde{H}(x) = \tilde{\lambda}^2(x) + \underbrace{c\alpha^l}_{=:c^\star \in K}\tilde{\lambda}(x) + \underbrace{\alpha^{2l}\tilde{f}(x)}_{\in F_q[x]}.$$

Now, we define an auxiliary polynomial $H_1(x) := \tilde{\lambda}^2(x) + c^\star\tilde{\lambda}(x)$, and our aim is to find $\tilde{\lambda}(x) \in K[x]$ s.t. $H_1(x) \in \mathbb{F}_q[x]$. There must be some control variables when we define $\tilde{\lambda}(x)$ so that we can find smooth polynomials $\tilde{H}(x)$.

We set $\tilde{\lambda}(x)$ to be a constant degree polynomial. Using this and Weil Descent, we have the following

$$\tilde{\lambda}(x) = \sum_{j=0}^{n-1} s_j w^j,$$

$$c^\star = \sum_{j=0}^{n-1} c_j w^j,$$

where $s_j, c_j \in \mathbb{F}_q$, and w is algebraic over $\mathbb{F}_q$ with degree n. Putting these values of $\tilde{\lambda}(x)$ and $c^\star$ in H_1, we get the following

$$H_1(x) = \sum_{i=0}^{n-1} g_i(s) w^i,$$

for some $g_i(s) \in \mathbb{F}_q[s]$, and $s = (s_0, s_1, \ldots, s_{n-1})$. For $H_1(x) \in \mathbb{F}_q[x]$, $g_i(s)$ should vanish $\forall\ i \geq 1$. Hence, we have an underdetermined system of multivariate quadratic equations with $n - 1$ equations and n variables. We can use Gröbner basis or resultant methods to solve this system. After getting a solution, we have $H_1(x) \in \mathbb{F}_q[x]$ and therefore $\tilde{H}(x) \in \mathbb{F}_q[x]$. Then, we look for the smoothness of $H(x)$. If it is smooth, we get one relation; else, we consider another solution of the above system. Unfortunately, this is not enough to get the desired number of relations to carry out the linear algebra step.

7　Experimental Results

Recall $K^\star = \langle \alpha \rangle$. As mentioned in the Sect. 4, our method works for the curves $\mathcal{C}/K : y^2 = f(x)$, where

$$f(x) = x^{2g+1} + \sum_{i=0}^{2g} \alpha^{j_i} x^i, \tag{23}$$

for which $\exists\, a \in \{1, 2, \ldots, q^n - 2\}$ s.t. the condition given by Eq. (16) is satisfied i.e.,

$$t_0 \equiv t_1 \equiv \ldots \equiv t_{2g} \equiv t_{2g+1} \mod d,$$

where $t_i's$ are defined as in Sect. 4. In order to find such curves, we try to solve the linear system generated by Eq. (16), for the values of a and j_i's. As it turns out, the linear system is under-determined (with nullity being 1) and hence there will be many solutions, and the corresponding curves will be vulnerable to this attack. The following are a few examples of such curves and a decomposition for illustration.

Example 1. Let $q = 1354523531, n = 7, K = \mathbb{F}_q[w]$ with $x^7+x^6+1354523513x^5+1354523496x^4 + 38x^3 + 104x^2 + 7x + 1354523482$ as the minimal polynomial of w. Let $\alpha = (w+1)$ be a generator of $K^\star$ and

$$f(x) = x^5 + \sum_{i=0}^{4} \alpha^{j_i} x^i.$$

The condition 16 translates into a system of linear equations in $a, j_0, j_1, \ldots, j_4$ below:

$$\left. \begin{array}{l} j_0 + 6176171118343794545313934281278559099501295306 2846430632a \\ j_1 + 6176171118343794545313934281278559099501295306 2846430633a \\ j_2 + 6176171118343794545313934281278559099501295306 2846430634a \\ j_3 + 6176171118343794545313934281278559099501295306 2846430635a \\ j_4 - a \end{array} \right\} . \qquad (24)$$

Since there are 6 variables and 5 independent equations $\mod d$, we can get $\mathcal{O}(q^n)$ many solutions of this system by varying the value of a. Hence we are able to find $\mathcal{O}(q^n)$ many hyperelliptic curves which will be vulnerable to the attack. The following is one of the solutions of the above system (Eq. (24)):

$$a = 40786346522457119140033113332608027022325454240019 41544664543424$$
$$j_0 = 44981297145480137586615993876992058523836162107127 93443,$$
$$j_1 = 23632695349508219163014109476022464829043023560009 48627,$$
$$j_2 = 22840935535363007394122250750528711342498850128910 3811,$$
$$j_3 = 42697203591943836847203768801939187389586277094236 89632,$$
$$j_4 = 40786346522457119140033113332608027022325454240019 41544664543424$$

So,

$$\begin{aligned} \tilde{f}(x) =& f(\alpha^a x) \\ =&(780022053w^6 + 760928178w^5 + 170989435w^4 + 662222802w^3 \\ & + 702422979w^2 + 601651399w + 636757065)x^5 \\ & + (780022053w^6 + 760928178w^5 + 170989435w^4 + 662222802w^3 \\ & + 702422979w^2 + 601651399w + 636757065)x^4 \\ & + (789992515w^6 + 271076474w^5 + 641593893w^4 + 60273850w^3 \\ & + 1118544582w^2 + 1168055942w + 523388883)x^3 \\ & + (615249757w^6 + 538160793w^5 + 134609138w^4 + 287039557w^3 \end{aligned}$$

$$+\ 47910319w^2 + 159765934w + 734765645)x^2$$
$$+\ (986949060w^6 + 603254005w^5 + 469173590w^4 + 369803482w^3$$
$$+\ 1083057270w^2 + 1021615666w + 1036052397)x$$
$$+\ 1250291512w^6 + 541668418w^5 + 648336894w^4 + 93981211w^3$$
$$+\ 1209366817w^2 + 123242898w + 285752852$$

The following value of z is obtained by using CRT

$$z = 128859803375396182927468696220301079158464515636913142174087 4$$

and hence the value of l is, using Eq. (18),

$$l = 6442990168769809146373434811015053957923225781845657108704 37$$

and hence $\tilde{\mu}(x)\ (= \alpha^l)$ is

$$\tilde{\mu}(x) = 1096004451w^6 + 72204545w^5 + 1031970086w^4 + 850013668w^3$$
$$+\ 667154540w^2 + 50674261w + 1212050995$$

For these values of a, j_i's, and l the corresponding $\psi(x)\ (= \tilde{\mu}^2 f(\alpha^a x)) \in \mathbb{F}_q[x]$,

$$\psi(x) = 140224146x^5 + 140224146x^4 + 163649504x^3 + 288749419x^2$$
$$+\ 506022088x + 952059020$$

The polynomial $\tilde{\lambda}(x)$ is randomly chosen to ensure a $\mathbb{F}_q$-smooth $\tilde{H}(x)$. In the following, we provide a value for one such $\tilde{\lambda}(x)$ and the corresponding smooth polynomial $\tilde{H}(x)$:

$$\tilde{\lambda}(x) = x + 1133867401$$
$$\tilde{H}(x) = 1214299385x^5 + 1214299385x^4 + 1190874027x^3 + 1065774113x^2$$
$$+\ 407189183x + 936216086$$

For illustrative purposes, we provide the corresponding decomposition below:

$$\sum_{i=1}^{5}((\tilde{P}_i) - (\infty)) \sim 0,$$

where $\tilde{P}_i$ are the points of $\widetilde{\mathcal{F}}$.

$$\tilde{P}_1 = (807542330, 716687265w^6 + 843761534w^5 + 828265313w^4 + 159145829w^3$$
$$+\ 686345735w^2 + 700861992w + 509324809)$$
$$\tilde{P}_2 = (620447586, 813283073w^6 + 318977187w^5 + 267032198w^4 + 35254994w^3$$
$$+\ 844429980w^2 + 369850187w + 214843875)$$
$$\tilde{P}_3 = (582043617, 134707935w^6 + 32178915w^5 + 41003762w^4 + 373212771w^3$$

$$+ 69947485w^2 + 533130081w + 1094103612)$$

$$\tilde{P}_4 = (548956658, 314837163w^6 + 1345447603w^5 + 380080922w^4 + 807574817w^3$$
$$+ 985485077w^2 + 893517804w + 1139064555)$$

$$\tilde{P}_5 = (150056870, 85834289w^6 + 675835336w^5 + 951227639w^4 + 362195701w^3$$
$$+ 972755872w^2 + 328519770w + 389619817)$$

The above decomposition can be easily verified using the MAGMA script given in the Appendix A. In the following, we provide another example that demonstrates the idea.

Example 2. Let $q = 13545235267, n = 4, K = \mathbb{F}_q[w]$ with $x^4 + x^3 + x^2 + x + 1$ as the minimal polynomial of w. Let $\alpha = w + 8$ be a generator of $K^\star$.

$$a = 18873717481056311115904417284347496327892$$
$$j_0 = 20830259616715189032412281460$$
$$j_1 = 16664207693372151225929251888$$
$$j_2 = 12498155770029113419447368916$$
$$j_3 = 83321038466860756129649125944$$
$$j_4 = 18873717481056311115904417284347496327892$$

$$f(x) = x^5 + (10389434500w^3 + 8503457960w^2 + 1804331189w + 7652432451)x^4$$
$$+ (4496414736w^3 + 3012914952w^2 + 4914608386w + 13530656394)x^3$$
$$+ (1563939549w^3 + 2029154388w^2 + 10721694268w + 12640846479)x^2$$
$$+ (9480766090w^3 + 12046505315w^2 + 11847794918w + 1761196756)x$$
$$+ 8555796245w^3 + 3896712384w^2 + 2849733199w + 7361159113;$$

$$\tilde{f}(x) = (8311487827w^3 + 668903640w^2 + 746585135w + 10112627890)x^5$$
$$+ (8311487827w^3 + 668903640w^2 + 746585135w + 10112627890)x^4$$
$$+ (11887251939w^3 + 4448133116w^2 + 3493295058w + 10674514901)x^3$$
$$+ (7967576419w^3 + 7786992992w^2 + 10961177735w + 857524719)x^2$$
$$+ (1613278559w^3 + 12653224429w^2 + 9436869140w + 9250569911)x$$
$$+ 8555796245w^3 + 3896712384w^2 + 2849733199w + 7361159113;$$

$$z = 12558534558337594956102391477136651340$$
$$l = 62792672791687974780511957385682567 0$$
$$\tilde{\mu}(x) = 8480343835w^3 + 10345332833w^2 + 2496233379w + 11776077527$$
$$\psi(x) = 10076073713x^5 + 10076073713x^4 + 533270342x^3 + 12633136871x^2$$
$$+ 163035135x + 9900534212$$
$$\tilde{\lambda}(x) = x + 5631025385$$
$$\tilde{H}(x) = 3469161554x^5 + 3469161554x^4 + 13011964925x^3 + 912098397x^2$$
$$+ 11099015635x + 933023164$$

For illustrative purposes, we provide the corresponding relation among the elements of factor basis $\widetilde{\mathcal{F}}$, given by the Eq. (9).

$$\sum_{i=1}^{5}((\tilde{P}_i) - (\infty)) \sim 0$$

where

$\tilde{P}_1 = (13539352170, 9808490675\,w^3 + 11848496349\,w^2 + 10783891627\,w + 11360816798)$

$\tilde{P}_2 = (7708342780, 8476725686w^3 + 12354179980w^2 + 5399924307w + 10535120119)$

$\tilde{P}_3 = (3683205295, 2470303628w^3 + 6406203858w^2 + 9996767999w + 350144386)$

$\tilde{P}_4 = (1428292391, 12661012320w^3 + 9191091394w^2 + 3111319514w + 771379433)$

$\tilde{P}_5 = (731277897, 1467582925w^3 + 1476361776w^2 + 6522982528w + 1852301214)$

The above decomposition can be easily verified using the MAGMA script given in the Appendix B.

Example 3. This is an example of the characteristic 2 case. Let $q = 2^{40}$, $n = 3$, $\mathbb{F}_q = \mathbb{F}_2[v]$ with $x^{40} + x^{23} + x^{21} + x^{18} + x^{16} + x^{15} + x^{13} + x^{12} + x^8 + x^5 + x^3 + x + 1$ as the minimal polynomial of v, $K = \mathbb{F}_q[w]$ with $x^3 + (v^{39} + v^{38} + v^{35} + v^{32} + v^{31} + v^{30} + v^{28} + v^{27} + v^{26} + v^{23} + v^{22} + v^{20} + v^{17} + v^{12} + v^9 + v^8)x^2 + (v^{38} + v^{35} + v^{34} + v^{30} + v^{29} + v^{26} + v^{24} + v^{23} + v^{19} + v^{18} + v^{17} + v^{16} + v^{15} + v^{13} + v^{12} + v^{10} + v^8 + v^6)x + v$ as the minimal polynomial of w.

$$H(x) = \lambda^2(x) + c\lambda(x)\mu(x) + \mu^2(x)f(x)$$

Firstly, our aim is to employ the same technique, as been used in the above two examples, to find curves (i.e. $f(x)$), the transformation constant (i.e. a), and l s.t. the term $\mu^2(x)\tilde{f}(x) = \alpha^{2l}\tilde{f}(x) \in \mathbb{F}_q[x]$. The following is an example of one such curve

$$\begin{aligned}
f(x) = x^5 &+ ((v^{38} + v^{37} + v^{35} + v^{34} + v^{33} + v^{32} + v^{30} + \\
&v^{28} + v^{27} + v^{25} + v^{23} + v^{21} + v^{18} + v^{16} + v^{15} + v^{12} \\
&+ v^{11} + v^8 + v^6 + v^5 + v^2 + 1) + (v^{38} + v^{36} + v^{32} + v^{27} \\
&+ v^{25} + v^{23} + v^{20} + v^{19} + v^{16} + v^{15} + v^{13} + v^4 + v^3 \\
&+ v^2)w + (v^{36} + v^{34} + v^{32} + v^{31} + v^{30} + v^{25} + v^{24} + v^{23} \\
&+ v^{20} + v^{19} + v^{18} + v^{17} + v^{16} + v^{15} + v^{14} + v^{12} + v^{10} \\
&+ v^9 + v^8 + v^6 + v^5 + v^3 + v^2 + v)w^2)x^4 + ((v^{39} + v^{36} \\
&+ v^{35} + v^{32} + v^{26} + v^{24} + v^{23} + v^{20} + v^{17} + v^{16} + v^{15} \\
&+ v^{14} + v^{12} + v^{11} + v^5 + v^4 + v^2 + v + 1) + (v^{39} + v^{38} \\
&+ v^{37} + v^{36} + v^{34} + v^{33} + v^{32} + v^{30} + v^{28} + v^{27} + v^{26} \\
&+ v^{24} + v^{23} + v^{22} + v^{21} + v^{20} + v^{18} + v^{17} + v^{15} + v^{14} \\
&+ v^{13} + v^{11} + v^5 + v^3 + v)w + (v^{38} + v^{36} + v^{33} + v^{29} + v^{28}
\end{aligned}$$

$$+ v^{26} + v^{25} + v^{24} + v^{23} + v^{20} + v^{17} + v^{16} + v^{14} + v^{12}$$
$$+ v^8 + v^7 + v^4 + v^3 + v^2)w^2)x^3 + ((v^{38} + v^{36} + v^{35}$$
$$+ v^{32} + v^{30} + v^{27} + v^{26} + v^{23} + v^{22} + v^{21} + v^{19} + v^{17}$$
$$+ v^{16} + v^9 + v^7 + v^6 + v^5 + v^4 + v^3 + v^2 + 1) + (v^{38}$$
$$+ v^{35} + v^{31} + v^{30} + v^{29} + v^{27} + v^{25} + v^{24} + v^{21} + v^{20}$$
$$+ v^{18} + v^{14} + v^{13} + v^{11} + v^{10} + v^6 + v^5 + v^4 + 1)w + (v^{38}$$
$$+ v^{37} + v^{34} + v^{29} + v^{27} + v^{23} + v^{22} + v^{21} + v^{20} + v^{19}$$
$$+ v^{18} + v^{16} + v^{11} + v^{10} + v^9 + v^7 + v^5 + v^3 + v)w^2)x^2$$
$$+ ((v^{38} + v^{36} + v^{35} + v^{34} + v^{32} + v^{30} + v^{29} + v^{25} + v^{24}$$
$$+ v^{21} + v^{19} + v^{18} + v^{15} + v^{14} + v^{13} + v^{12} + v^{11} + v^9$$
$$+ v^8 + v^6 + v^4 + v^2) + (v^{37} + v^{36} + v^{35} + v^{34} + v^{32}$$
$$+ v^{30} + v^{29} + v^{27} + v^{25} + v^{23} + v^{20} + v^{19} + v^{18} + v^{15}$$
$$+ v^{14} + v^{12} + v^9 + v^8 + v^7 + v^6 + v^4 + v^3 + v + 1)w$$
$$+ (v^{37} + v^{32} + v^{31} + v^{30} + v^{29} + v^{28} + v^{27} + v^{26} + v^{24}$$
$$+ v^{22} + v^{20} + v^{19} + v^{17} + v^{14} + v^7 + v^6 + v^2 + 1)w^2)x$$
$$+ (v^{35} + v^{33} + v^{29} + v^{27} + v^{24} + v^{22} + v^{21} + v^{20} + v^{19}$$
$$+ v^{17} + v^{11} + v^7 + v^6 + v^2) + (v^{39} + v^{34} + v^{30} + v^{27}$$
$$+ v^{24} + v^{23} + v^{21} + v^{20} + v^{19} + v^{18} + v^{16} + v^{13} + v^{12}$$
$$+ v^{11} + v^9 + v^7 + v^4)w + (v^{39} + v^{37} + v^{36} + v^{30} + v^{29}$$
$$+ v^{28} + v^{26} + v^{24} + v^{23} + v^{22} + v^{19} + v^{15} + v^{13} + v^{10}$$
$$+ v^8 + v^7 + v^6 + v^4 + v^3)w^2$$

$$a = 108997347519202283412386595063382120$$
$$l = 128763563410208436223620 95876480$$

$$\mu(x) = (v^{38} + v^{37} + v^{35} + v^{34} + v^{33} + v^{31} + v^{29} + v^{28} + v^{25}$$
$$+ v^{24} + v^{23} + v^{22} + v^{20} + v^{19} + v^{17} + v^{15} + v^{14} + v^{13}$$
$$+ v^8 + v^4 + v^3 + 1) + (v^{39} + v^{38} + v^{36} + v^{34} + v^{33} + v^{32}$$
$$+ v^{29} + v^{28} + v^{26} + v^{25} + v^{23} + v^{21} + v^{19} + v^{18} + v^{12}$$
$$+ v^8 + v^7 + v^6 + v^4 + v^3 + v^2 + 1)w + (v^{39} + v^{38} + v^{36}$$
$$+ v^{35} + v^{34} + v^{32} + v^{30} + v^{26} + v^{25} + v^{20} + v^{19} + v^{18}$$
$$+ v^{17} + v^{16} + v^{15} + v^{14} + v^{11} + v^{10} + v^9 + v^8 + v^5$$
$$+ v^4 + v^3 + v^2 + 1)w^2$$

$$\psi(x) = (v^{39} + v^{36} + v^{35} + v^{34} + v^{31} + v^{28} + v^{27} + v^{26}$$
$$+ v^{25} + v^{22} + v^{17} + v^{10} + v^9 + v^7 + 1)x^5 + (v^{39} + v^{36}$$
$$+ v^{35} + v^{34} + v^{31} + v^{28} + v^{27} + v^{26} + v^{25} + v^{22} + v^{17}$$
$$+ v^{10} + v^9 + v^7 + 1)x^4 + (v^{39} + v^{38} + v^{36} + v^{35} + v^{34}$$

$$+ v^{29} + v^{26} + v^{25} + v^{23} + v^{22} + v^{21} + v^{17} + v^{16} + v^{15}$$
$$+ v^{14} + v^{12} + v^{10} + v^6 + v^2)x^3 + (v^{39} + v^{38} + v^{37}$$
$$+ v^{34} + v^{32} + v^{31} + v^{29} + v^{28} + v^{27} + v^{26} + v^{21} + v^{20}$$
$$+ v^{19} + v^{18} + v^{17} + v^{16} + v^{11} + v^7 + v^6 + v^4 + v^2)x^2$$
$$+ (v^{39} + v^{38} + v^{37} + v^{36} + v^{35} + v^{34} + v^{32} + v^{30} + v^{29}$$
$$+ v^{27} + v^{26} + v^{21} + v^{19} + v^{18} + v^{17} + v^{13} + v^{11} + v^8$$
$$+ v^7 + v^5 + v^3 + v^2 + 1)x + v^{34} + v^{33} + v^{28} + v^{26} + v^{25}$$
$$+ v^{24} + v^{19} + v^{16} + v^{15} + v^{13} + v^{12} + v^{11} + v^{10} + v^8$$
$$+ v^5 + v^3 + v^2 + 1$$

After achieving this feat, we will consider the following term

$$H_1(x) = \lambda^2(x) + c^\star \lambda(x)$$

where $c^\star = c\alpha^l$. After following the analysis of Sect. 6, we get the following results. The following is one such example of $\lambda(x)$ for which $H_1(x)$, and hence $H(x) \in \mathbb{F}_q[x]$, and $H(x)$ is smooth over $\mathbb{F}_q$.

$$\lambda(x) = (v^{38} + v^{37} + v^{35} + v^{33} + v^{30} + v^{26} + v^{25} + v^{24}$$
$$+ v^{23} + v^{18} + v^{16} + v^{14} + v^{12} + v^9 + v^6 + v^5 + v^3 + 1)$$
$$+ (v^{39} + v^{37} + v^{33} + v^{27} + v^{25} + v^{23} + v^{22} + v^{20}$$
$$+ v^{19} + v^{18} + v^{15} + v^{13} + v^{11} + v^{10} + v^8 + v^5 + v^3$$
$$+ v^2)w + (v^{39} + v^{36} + v^{33} + v^{32} + v^{29} + v^{27} + v^{26}$$
$$+ v^{21} + v^{18} + v^{16} + v^{15} + v^{11} + v^8 + v^5 + v^4 + v^2)w^2$$

$$H_1(x) = v^{38} + v^{36} + v^{33} + v^{31} + v^{30} + v^{29} + v^{28} + v^{26}$$
$$+ v^{25} + v^{23} + v^{19} + v^{18} + v^{17} + v^{15} + v^{14} + v^{13}$$
$$+ v^{11} + v^9 + v^2 + 1$$

$$H(x) = (v^{39} + v^{36} + v^{35} + v^{34} + v^{31} + v^{28} + v^{27} + v^{26}$$
$$+ v^{25} + v^{22} + v^{17} + v^{10} + v^9 + v^7 + 1)x^5 + (v^{39}$$
$$+ v^{36} + v^{35} + v^{34} + v^{31} + v^{28} + v^{27} + v^{26} + v^{25}$$
$$+ v^{22} + v^{17} + v^{10} + v^9 + v^7 + 1)x^4 + (v^{39} + v^{38}$$
$$+ v^{36} + v^{35} + v^{34} + v^{29} + v^{26} + v^{25} + v^{23} + v^{22}$$
$$+ v^{21} + v^{17} + v^{16} + v^{15} + v^{14} + v^{12} + v^{10} + v^6$$
$$+ v^2)x^3 + (v^{39} + v^{38} + v^{37} + v^{34} + v^{32} + v^{31}$$
$$+ v^{29} + v^{28} + v^{27} + v^{26} + v^{21} + v^{20} + v^{19} + v^{18}$$
$$+ v^{17} + v^{16} + v^{11} + v^7 + v^6 + v^4 + v^2)x^2 + (v^{39}$$
$$+ v^{38} + v^{37} + v^{36} + v^{35} + v^{34} + v^{32} + v^{30} + v^{29}$$
$$+ v^{27} + v^{26} + v^{21} + v^{19} + v^{18} + v^{17} + v^{13} + v^{11}$$

$$+ v^8 + v^7 + v^5 + v^3 + v^2 + 1)x + v^{38} + v^{36} + v^{34}$$
$$+ v^{31} + v^{30} + v^{29} + v^{24} + v^{23} + v^{18} + v^{17} + v^{16}$$
$$+ v^{14} + v^{12} + v^{10} + v^9 + v^8 + v^5 + v^3$$

For illustrative purposes we provide the corresponding decomposition below:

$$\sum_{i=1}^{5} ((\tilde{P}_i) - (\infty)) \sim 0,$$

where $\tilde{P}_i$ are the points of $\widetilde{\mathcal{F}}$.

$$\tilde{P}_1 = ((v^{32} + v^{31} + v^{29} + v^{28} + v^{25} + v^{24} + v^{23} + v^{22}$$
$$+ v^{21} + v^{19} + v^{16} + v^{14} + v^{11} + v^{10} + v^8 + v^7$$
$$+ v^5 + v^4 + v^3 + v^2, (v^{39} + v^{33} + v^{32} + v^{30}$$
$$+ v^{29} + v^{27} + v^{26} + v^{24} + v^{23} + v^{22} + v^{21} + v^{18}$$
$$+ v^{15} + v^{13} + v^{11} + v^8 + v^7 + v^6 + v^5 + v^4 + 1)$$
$$+ (v^{39} + v^{35} + v^{33} + v^{32} + v^{31} + v^{29} + v^{28} + v^{25}$$
$$+ v^{23} + v^{22} + v^{20} + v^{18} + v^{16} + v^{14} + v^{12} + v^{11}$$
$$+ v^{10} + v^5 + v^4 + v^3 + v^2 + v + 1)w + (v^{39} + v^{36}$$
$$+ v^{35} + v^{33} + v^{32} + v^{30} + v^{28} + v^{27} + v^{24} + v^{18}$$
$$+ v^{17} + v^{16} + v^{15} + v^{14} + v^7 + v^5 + v^3 + v^2 + v)w^2)$$
$$\tilde{P}_2 = ((v^{36} + v^{35} + v^{33} + v^{31} + v^{29} + v^{28} + v^{24} + v^{23}$$
$$+ v^{19} + v^{18} + v^{17} + v^{16} + v^{15} + v^{14} + v^{13} + v^{12}$$
$$+ v^{11} + v^{10} + v^8 + v^5 + v^4 + v^2, (v^{39} + v^{33} + v^{32}$$
$$+ v^{30} + v^{29} + v^{27} + v^{26} + v^{24} + v^{23} + v^{22} + v^{21}$$
$$+ v^{18} + v^{15} + v^{13} + v^{11} + v^8 + v^7 + v^6 + v^5 + v^4 + 1)$$
$$+ (v^{39} + v^{35} + v^{33} + v^{32} + v^{31} + v^{29} + v^{28} + v^{25} + v^{23}$$
$$+ v^{22} + v^{20} + v^{18} + v^{16} + v^{14} + v^{12} + v^{11} + v^{10} + v^5$$
$$+ v^4 + v^3 + v^2 + v + 1)w + (v^{39} + v^{36} + v^{35} + v^{33} + v^{32}$$
$$+ v^{30} + v^{28} + v^{27} + v^{24} + v^{18} + v^{17} + v^{16} + v^{15} + v^{14}$$
$$+ v^7 + v^5 + v^3 + v^2 + v)w^2)$$
$$\tilde{P}_3 = ((v^{38} + v^{37} + v^{36} + v^{35} + v^{34} + v^{33} + v^{32} + v^{27}$$
$$+ v^{26} + v^{23} + v^{21} + v^{19} + v^{18} + v^{16} + v^{13} + v^{10} + v^6$$
$$+ v^4 + v^3 + v, (v^{39} + v^{33} + v^{32} + v^{30} + v^{29} + v^{27} + v^{26}$$
$$+ v^{24} + v^{23} + v^{22} + v^{21} + v^{18} + v^{15} + v^{13} + v^{11} + v^8$$
$$+ v^7 + v^6 + v^5 + v^4 + 1) + (v^{39} + v^{35} + v^{33} + v^{32} + v^{31}$$
$$+ v^{29} + v^{28} + v^{25} + v^{23} + v^{22} + v^{20} + v^{18} + v^{16} + v^{14}$$
$$+ v^{12} + v^{11} + v^{10} + v^5 + v^4 + v^3 + v^2 + v + 1)w$$

$$+ (v^{39} + v^{36} + v^{35} + v^{33} + v^{32} + v^{30} + v^{28} + v^{27} + v^{24}$$
$$+ v^{18} + v^{17} + v^{16} + v^{15} + v^{14} + v^{7} + v^{5} + v^{3} + v^{2} + v)w^{2})$$
$$\tilde{P}_4 = ((v^{39} + v^{36} + v^{32} + v^{30} + v^{29} + v^{28} + v^{27} + v^{26} + v^{21}$$
$$+ v^{17} + v^{16} + v^{15} + v^{13} + v^{11} + v^{9} + v^{8} + v^{7} + v^{6} + v^{4} + 1,$$
$$(v^{39} + v^{33} + v^{32} + v^{30} + v^{29} + v^{27} + v^{26} + v^{24} + v^{23} + v^{22}$$
$$+ v^{21} + v^{18} + v^{15} + v^{13} + v^{11} + v^{8} + v^{7} + v^{6} + v^{5} + v^{4} + 1)$$
$$+ (v^{39} + v^{35} + v^{33} + v^{32} + v^{31} + v^{29} + v^{28} + v^{25} + v^{23} + v^{22}$$
$$+ v^{20} + v^{18} + v^{16} + v^{14} + v^{12} + v^{11} + v^{10} + v^{5} + v^{4} + v^{3} + v^{2}$$
$$+ v + 1)w + (v^{39} + v^{36} + v^{35} + v^{33} + v^{32} + v^{30} + v^{28} + v^{27} + v^{24}$$
$$+ v^{18} + v^{17} + v^{16} + v^{15} + v^{14} + v^{7} + v^{5} + v^{3} + v^{2} + v)w^{2})$$
$$\tilde{P}_5 = ((v^{39} + v^{38} + v^{37} + v^{36} + v^{34} + v^{32} + v^{30} + v^{29} + v^{28}$$
$$+ v^{25} + v^{23} + v^{22} + v^{21} + v^{19} + v^{13} + v^{12} + v^{11} + v^{10}$$
$$+ v^{9} + v^{8} + v, (v^{39} + v^{33} + v^{32} + v^{30} + v^{29} + v^{27} + v^{26}$$
$$+ v^{24} + v^{23} + v^{22} + v^{21} + v^{18} + v^{15} + v^{13} + v^{11} + v^{8} + v^{7}$$
$$+ v^{6} + v^{5} + v^{4} + 1) + (v^{39} + v^{35} + v^{33} + v^{32} + v^{31} + v^{29}$$
$$+ v^{28} + v^{25} + v^{23} + v^{22} + v^{20} + v^{18} + v^{16} + v^{14} + v^{12} + v^{11}$$
$$+ v^{10} + v^{5} + v^{4} + v^{3} + v^{2} + v + 1)w + (v^{39} + v^{36} + v^{35} + v^{33}$$
$$+ v^{32} + v^{30} + v^{28} + v^{27} + v^{24} + v^{18} + v^{17} + v^{16} + v^{15} + v^{14}$$
$$+ v^{7} + v^{5} + v^{3} + v^{2} + v)w^{2})$$

8 Conclusion and Future Work

In this paper, we have proposed a new way of decomposition for a class of special low genus hyperelliptic curves defined over odd characteristic extension field. For any given finite field $\mathbb{F}_{q^n}$, where $2 \nmid q$, we can find $\mathcal{O}(q^n)$ many distinct hyperelliptic curves that are vulnerable against our attack, and we have given an efficient method to check for a *weak curve*. We note that the new decomposition provides relations consisting of the elements of the factor base, and we get enough such relations to carry out the linear algebra step. We further want to stress that for computing the discrete logarithm of a random element of the Jacobian, we still need to carry out individual discrete logarithm step using a specific method, such as Nagao's decomposition. In the future, we plan to explore the application of our idea to complete the individual discrete logarithm phase as well, thereby completely avoiding solving any system of multivariate polynomial equations. The applications of this idea are far-reaching; one of the avenues we plan to explore is the characteristic 2 case.

A   Magma Script to Verify Example 1

```
q := 1354523531;
assert(IsPrime(q));
n := 7;
Fq := GF(q);
Ry<z> := PolynomialRing(Fq);
gz := z^7 + z^6 + 1354523513*z^5 + 1354523496*z^4 + 38*z^3 +
104*z^2 + 7*z + 1354523482;
assert(IsIrreducible(gz));
Fqn<w> := ext<Fq|gz>;
alpha := w+1;
Rx<x> := PolynomialRing(Fqn);
a := 40786346522457119140033113332608027022325454240019415446664543424;
fx_tilde := (780022053*w^6 + 760928178*w^5
    + 170989435*w^4 + 662222802*w^3
    + 702422979*w^2 + 601651399*w + 636757065)*x^5
    + (780022053*w^6 + 760928178*w^5 + 170989435*w^4 + 662222802*w^3
    + 702422979*w^2 + 601651399*w + 636757065)*x^4
    + (789992515*w^6 + 271076474*w^5 + 641593893*w^4 + 60273850*w^3
    + 1118544582*w^2 + 1168055942*w + 523388883)*x^3
    + (615249757*w^6 + 538160793*w^5 + 134609138*w^4 + 287039557*w^3
    + 47910319*w^2 + 159765934*w + 734765645)*x^2
    + (986949060*w^6 + 603254005*w^5 + 469173590*w^4 + 369803482*w^3
    + 1083057270*w^2 + 1021615666*w + 1036052397)*x
    + 1250291512*w^6 + 541668418*w^5 + 648336894*w^4 + 93981211*w^3
    + 1209366817*w^2 + 123242898*w + 285752852 ;

H_tilde := HyperellipticCurve(fx_tilde);
J_tilde := Jacobian(H_tilde);
inf := PointsAtInfinity(H_tilde)[1];

pts := [
        [(807542330, 716687265*w^6 + 843761534*w^5 + 828265313*w^4
        + 159145829*w^3 + 686345735*w^2 + 700861992*w + 509324809)],
        [(620447586, 813283073*w^6 + 318977187*w^5 + 267032198*w^4
        + 35254994*w^3 + 844429980*w^2 + 369850187*w + 214843875)],
        [(582043617, 134707935*w^6 + 32178915*w^5 + 41003762*w^4
        + 373212771*w^3 + 69947485*w^2 + 533130081*w + 1094103612)],
        [(548956658, 314837163*w^6 + 1345447603*w^5 + 380080922*w^4
        + 807574817*w^3 + 985485077*w^2 + 893517804*w + 1139064555)],
        [(150056870, 85834289*w^6 + 675835336*w^5 + 951227639*w^4
        + 362195701*w^3 + 972755872*w^2 + 328519770*w + 389619817)]
    ];

sum := &+[J_tilde!Divisor([<Place(H_tilde!pt),1>,<Place(inf),-1>])
            : pt in pts];
print sum eq Identity(J_tilde);
```

B   Magma Script to Verify Example 2

```
q := 13545235267;
assert(IsPrime(q));
n := 4;
Fq := GF(q);
Ry<z> := PolynomialRing(Fq);
gz := z^4 + z^3 + z^2 + z + 1;
assert(IsIrreducible(gz));
Fqn<w> := ext<Fq|gz>;
alpha := w+8;
Rx<x> := PolynomialRing(Fqn);
a := 18873717481056311115904417284347496327892;
fx_tilde :=
(8311487827*w^3 + 668903640*w^2 + 746585135*w + 10112627890)*x^5
+ (8311487827*w^3 + 668903640*w^2 + 746585135*w + 10112627890)*x^4
+ (11887251939*w^3 + 4448133116*w^2 + 3493295058*w + 10674514901)*x^3
+ (7967576419*w^3 + 7786992992*w^2 + 10961177735*w + 857524719)*x^2
+ (1613278559*w^3 + 12653224429*w^2 + 9436869140*w + 9250569911)*x
+ 8555796245*w^3 + 3896712384*w^2 + 2849733199*w + 7361159113;

//fx := Evaluate(fx_tilde, x*alpha^(-a));
H_tilde := HyperellipticCurve(fx_tilde);
J_tilde := Jacobian(H_tilde);
inf := PointsAtInfinity(H_tilde)[1];

pts := [
        [(13539352170, 9808490675*w^3 + 11848496349*w^2
        + 10783891627*w + 11360816798)],
        [(7708342780, 8476725686*w^3 + 12354179980*w^2
        + 5399924307*w + 10535120119)],
        [(3683205295, 2470303628*w^3 + 6406203858*w^2
        + 9996767999*w + 350144386)],
        [(1428292391, 12661012320*w^3 + 9191091394*w^2
        + 3111319514*w + 771379433)],
        [(731277897, 1467582925*w^3 + 1476361776*w^2
        + 6522982528*w + 1852301214)]
        ];

sum := &+[J_tilde!Divisor([<Place(H_tilde!pt),1>,<Place(inf),-1>])
            : pt in pts];
print sum eq Identity(J_tilde);
```

References

1. Barbulescu, R., Gaudry, P., Guillevic, A., Morain, F.: Improving NFS for the discrete logarithm problem in non-prime finite fields. In: Oswald, E., Fischlin, M. (eds.) EUROCRYPT 2015. LNCS, vol. 9056, pp. 129–155. Springer, Heidelberg (2015). https://doi.org/10.1007/978-3-662-46800-5_6

2. Barbulescu, R., Gaudry, P., Kleinjung, T.: The tower number field sieve. In: Iwata, T., Cheon, J.H. (eds.) ASIACRYPT 2015. LNCS, vol. 9453, pp. 31–55. Springer, Heidelberg (2015). https://doi.org/10.1007/978-3-662-48800-3_2

3. Gaudry, P.: An algorithm for solving the discrete log problem on hyperelliptic curves. In: Preneel, B. (ed.) EUROCRYPT 2000. LNCS, vol. 1807, pp. 19–34. Springer, Heidelberg (2000). https://doi.org/10.1007/3-540-45539-6_2

4. Gaudry, P., Thomé, E., Thériault, N., Diem, C.: A double large prime variation for small genus hyperelliptic index calculus. Math. Comput. **76**(257), 475–492 (2007)

5. Guillevic, A., Singh, S.: On the alpha value of polynomials in the tower number field sieve algorithm. Math. Cryptol. **1**(1), 1–39 (2021)

6. Joux, A., Vitse, V.: Cover and decomposition index calculus on elliptic curves made practical. In: Pointcheval, D., Johansson, T. (eds.) EUROCRYPT 2012. LNCS, vol. 7237, pp. 9–26. Springer, Heidelberg (2012). https://doi.org/10.1007/978-3-642-29011-4_3

7. Kim, T., Barbulescu, R.: Extended tower number field sieve: a new complexity for the medium prime case. In: Robshaw, M., Katz, J. (eds.) CRYPTO 2016. LNCS, vol. 9814, pp. 543–571. Springer, Heidelberg (2016). https://doi.org/10.1007/978-3-662-53018-4_20

8. Menezes, A., Zuccherato, R., Yi-Hong, W.: An elementary introduction to hyperelliptic curves. Faculty of Mathematics, University of Waterloo (1996)

9. De Micheli, G., Gaudry, P., Pierrot, C.: Asymptotic complexities of discrete logarithm algorithms in pairing-relevant finite fields. In: Micciancio, D., Ristenpart, T. (eds.) CRYPTO 2020. LNCS, vol. 12171, pp. 32–61. Springer, Cham (2020). https://doi.org/10.1007/978-3-030-56880-1_2

10. Nagao, K.: Decomposition attack for the Jacobian of a hyperelliptic curve over an extension field. In: Hanrot, G., Morain, F., Thomé, E. (eds.) ANTS 2010. LNCS, vol. 6197, pp. 285–300. Springer, Heidelberg (2010). https://doi.org/10.1007/978-3-642-14518-6_23

11. Odlyzko, A.M.: Discrete logarithms in finite fields and their cryptographic significance. In: Beth, T., Cot, N., Ingemarsson, I. (eds.) EUROCRYPT 1984. LNCS, vol. 209, pp. 224–314. Springer, Heidelberg (1985). https://doi.org/10.1007/3-540-39757-4_20

12. Sarkar, P., Singh, S.: Fine tuning the function field sieve algorithm for the medium prime case. IEEE Trans. Inf. Theory **62**(4), 2233–2253 (2016)

13. Sarkar, P., Singh, S.: New complexity trade-offs for the (multiple) number field sieve algorithm in non-prime fields. In: Fischlin, M., Coron, J.-S. (eds.) EUROCRYPT 2016. LNCS, vol. 9665, pp. 429–458. Springer, Heidelberg (2016). https://doi.org/10.1007/978-3-662-49890-3_17

14. Sarkar, P., Singh, S.: A new method for decomposition in the Jacobian of small genus hyperelliptic curves. Des. Codes Crypt. **82**(3), 601–616 (2017)

15. Sarkar, P., Singh, S.: A simple method for obtaining relations among factor basis elements for special hyperelliptic curves. Appl. Algebra Eng. Commun. Comput. **28**(2), 109–130 (2017)

16. Sarkar, P., Singh, S.: A unified polynomial selection method for the (tower) number field sieve algorithm. Adv. Math. Commun. **13**(3), 435–455 (2019)

17. Thériault, N.: Index calculus attack for hyperelliptic curves of small genus. In: Laih, C.-S. (ed.) ASIACRYPT 2003. LNCS, vol. 2894, pp. 75–92. Springer, Heidelberg (2003). https://doi.org/10.1007/978-3-540-40061-5_5

A Multi-view Contrastive Graph Neural Network Framework for Malware Detection in IoMT Environments

Bhagyasri Bora[iD], Saunav Barman[iD], Rahul Bardhan[iD], Dharitri Brahma[iD], and Amitava Nag[(✉)][iD]

Central Institute of Technology, Kokrajhar 782442, Assam, India
{ph24cse1002,u22cse1062,u22cse1076,ph24cse1004,amitava.nag}@cit.ac.in
https://www.cit.ac.in/

Abstract. The Internet of Medical Things (IoMT) has emerged as a transformative domain in healthcare, offering unprecedented opportunities for remote monitoring, smart diagnosis, and automated medical services. However, the rapid development and deployment of IoMT applications have inadvertently attracted the attention of attackers, leading to an increased risk of security breaches. Attackers will use malware to exploit IoMT systems to get unauthorized access to them. To address this challenge, the proposed work introduces a Multi-View Contrastive Graph Neural Network (MVC-GNN) for malware detection in IoMT environments. The proposed approach leverages graph-based deep learning and contrastive representation learning to effectively distinguish benign and malicious network traffic to enable timely and accurate detection of malware. This work uses CICIoMT 2024 dataset, a state-of-the-art publicly available dataset, for a comprehensive evaluation of the proposed approach. Experimental results highlight the high efficacy of the approach, with an accuracy of 99.69% and an F1-score of 99.61%, indicate that the proposed work is robust and generalizable for malware detection in IoMT framework.

Keywords: Internet of Medical Things · Deep Learning · Network Security · Traffic Classification

1 Introduction

A transformative era in healthcare is marked by the advent of the Internet of Medical Things (IoMT), which integrates medical devices, software applications, and health systems to enable real-time health monitoring, remote diagnostics, and automated treatment delivery [13,25]. This interconnected ecosystem, which includes everything from wearable health monitors like smartwatches to implanted devices like pacemakers, holds the promise of enhancing patient care and optimizing medical workflows [5]. However, the intrinsic sensitivity of medical data and the life-critical nature of IoMT operations render these systems

C. Karfa et al. (Eds.): SPACE 2025, LNCS 16406, pp. 79–96, 2026.
https://doi.org/10.1007/978-3-032-16342-4_5

highly susceptible to cyberattacks, posing significant risks to patient privacy, safety, and the continuity of essential medical services [7,24,27]. Multifaceted challenges, including an expansive attack surface, diverse device types, and the severe consequences of security breaches, underscore the urgent need for robust security mechanisms in IoMT [4].

Traditional security approaches, such as rule-based Intrusion Detection Systems, often prove insufficient against the dynamic and heterogeneous traffic patterns of IoMT environments [4,15]. These conventional methods frequently struggle with scalability, require manual updates for evolving attack vectors, and may suffer from high false positives due to class imbalances [7,15,16]. Therefore, effective network traffic classification is paramount for identifying and mitigating malicious activities within IoMT systems, safeguarding critical infrastructure, and ensuring patient trust and data integrity [7,14].

In recent years, the integration of machine learning and deep learning into IDS has shown considerable promise in identifying malicious actions and enhancing threat detection accuracy within IoT and IoMT networks [3,11,15,23]. Deep learning models, in particular, are well-suited to process and analyse the extensive and complex datasets generated by IoMT devices, automatically learning intricate patterns that might elude traditional methods [2,3,15]. Their success in general IoT traffic classification highlights their potential for developing advanced, adaptive, and context-aware security frameworks capable of protecting life-critical healthcare systems against evolving cyber threats [14,20]. Despite these advancements, significant research gaps remain in addressing IoMT-specific challenges. Existing datasets often fall short of meeting essential criteria for training robust ML-based IDS, frequently lacking representativeness or balance between benign and malicious traffic [17,22]. Furthermore, many prior studies on deep learning for network traffic classification primarily address generic IoT scenarios, neglecting critical IoMT-specific concerns such as ultra-low latency requirements, the prioritisation of life-critical data, and the unique challenges posed by the diversity of IoMT protocols and devices [13,24]. There is a pronounced need for comprehensive datasets and tailored deep learning models that can effectively handle the dynamic nature and specific threat landscape of IoMT environments [10,22].

This study focuses on using advanced deep learning techniques to address these issues and achieve reliable network traffic classification in IoMT systems. The principal contributions of this study are:

- The development and implementation of a novel Multi-View Contrastive Graph Neural Network (MVC-GNN) architecture that integrates contrastive learning with graph-based modeling for enhanced IoMT malware detection.
- A comprehensive benchmark and performance evaluation of the proposed MVC-GNN compared with Convolutional Neural Network (CNN) and Long Short-Term Memory (LSTM) models on the CIC IoMT Dataset 2024, assessing their effectiveness in handling heterogeneous traffic and imbalanced data.
- The provision of empirical evidence demonstrating the superior performance of the MVC-GNN architecture for enhancing cybersecurity in the critical

domain of healthcare, thereby advancing the development of tailored security solutions.

2 Related Work

Various deep learning architectures have been explored for network traffic classification in IoT and IoMT environments. CNNs (Convolutional Neural Networks) are highly effective at extracting spatial features from data. In the context of network traffic, this involves converting raw traffic data into representations that CNNs can process, similar to image processing. Kharoubi et al. [15] proposed a CNN-based Network Intrusion Detection System designed for real-time threat detection in IoT environments, demonstrating its capability to handle large volumes of data and achieve high performance across diverse datasets, including CICIoT2023, Edge-IIoTset, and CICIoMT2024. Their work highlights the CNN's effectiveness in extracting complex patterns from sequential data with fewer computations compared to other DL models [15]. Abbasi et al. also investigated CNNs for intrusion detection in IoT, emphasising dimensionality reduction for efficient processing [1].

Several studies have explored traditional ensemble learning approaches and neural architectures on these datasets. For instance, Dadkhah et al. [10] introduced the CICIoMT2024 dataset and evaluated Random Forest (RF), AdaBoost, and Deep Neural Network (DNN) models for both binary and fine-grained (19-class) multiclass classification. While these models performed robustly in binary scenarios—achieving a top accuracy of 97.1%—their effectiveness sharply deteriorated in multiclass contexts, with accuracy declining to 73.3% and F1-scores reduced for rare attack types. These findings underscore the challenges posed by class imbalance and the subtlety of complex IoMT-specific threats.

In other comparative evaluations, SVM, LSTM, and RF models were applied to multiclass (six-category) tasks on the CICIoMT2024 dataset. Despite leveraging advanced sequential neural network architectures, maximum reported accuracies plateaued at 77.3%. Limitations such as inter-class confusion and reduced recall for attacks like DDoS and MQTT highlight the persistent difficulties in distinguishing nuanced medical cyber-attacks.

Beyond the specific domain of medical devices, Dong et al. leveraged the CICIoT2023 dataset, using CNNs and SVMs for IoT traffic classification. Their CNN model achieved a binary classification accuracy of 98.61%, but, similar to earlier studies, generalizability to more granular or healthcare-specific threats remained unaddressed due to the dataset's semantic gap with IoMT protocol diversity.

Additional research utilising the Edge-IIoTset and UNSW-NB15 datasets typically focused on multiclass IoT attack detection using CNNs, Stacked Autoencoders, and Bidirectional LSTMs. These models yielded multiclass accuracies ranging between 67.6% and 70%. Notably, these contributions reiterated common limitations: low F1-scores for minority (rare) classes, a generic IoT focus lacking medical device heterogeneity, and limited effectiveness under severe class imbalance.

Contrastive learning has emerged as a powerful paradigm for learning discriminative representations [19]. Chen et al. [9] introduced SimCLR, which uses NT-Xent (Normalized Temperature-scaled Cross Entropy) loss for self-supervised representation learning. The basic idea underlying contrastive learning is to minimize agreement between various data points and maximize agreement between variously augmented perspectives of the same data.

Botnet attacks pose a significant threat to IoMT systems, capable of orchestrating large-scale distributed attacks. Research in this area has explored various ML and DL algorithms for detection. Saif et al. [27] analysed the performance of several ML and DL algorithms, including CNNs, for botnet attack detection in IoMT, using the N-BaIoT dataset. Their work also investigated feature engineering techniques to enhance detection performance. Krishnan & Shrinath [18] proposed a robust IoT botnet detection framework resilient to gradient-based adversarial attacks, employing a weighted multi-layer perceptron model. This highlights the ongoing challenge of making detection systems robust against sophisticated evasion techniques.

GNNs (Graph Neural Networks) are gaining traction in network security due to their ability to model complex relationships and interdependencies within networked environments. IoMT networks, with devices acting as nodes and communication links as edges, naturally lend themselves to graph-based representations. While GNNs have shown promise in general network security applications beyond healthcare, their application to IoMT-specific challenges is still an emerging area [31,32]. Zhang et al. utilised GNNs to model IoT device interactions to detect botnet activity, achieving high precision by capturing relational patterns in device communication [31]. This demonstrates the unique strength of GNNs in understanding the holistic context of IoMT traffic.

3   Graph Neural Networks for Cybersecurity and IoMT

GNNs have emerged as powerful tools in cybersecurity because they can model interdependencies between entities (devices, packets, or events) that traditional ML/DL models often ignore [29]. Unlike CNNs or LSTMs that process samples independently, GNNs leverage the connectivity and structure of data, enabling improved detection of stealthy or multi-stage cyber-attacks. Traditional IDS models treat network flows as isolated samples, which leads to false positives/negatives. GNNs learn from relationships among nodes (devices, flows, or attack stages), making them better suited for detecting correlated and evolving attacks. By combining attack graphs (static vulnerabilities, system configuration) with real-time measurements (traffic, host logs), GNN-based IDS can detect which node is under attack and what attacker action caused it [8]. This dual perspective improves explainability and reduces uncertainty in predictions.

Experiments show GNNs outperform baselines in precision, recall, and F1-score across intrusion detection tasks. GNNs excel at detecting False Data Injection Attacks (FDIAs) in smart grids by capturing spatio-temporal correlations between sensors and meters. Unlike shallow models, GNNs adapt to topological changes in the power grid, making them robust to stealthy, coordinated attacks.

A critical challenge in developing effective IoMT security solutions is the availability of representative datasets. Many prior studies rely on outdated or generic IoT datasets that do not adequately reflect the unique characteristics and attack scenarios prevalent in IoMT. Neto et al. [22] emphasise the need for comprehensive and realistic IoT attack datasets, introducing CICIoT2023 as a benchmark that includes a variety of attacks executed in an extensive IoT topology with real devices. This addresses the limitation of many previous efforts that do not consider an extensive network topology with real IoT devices. The CIC IoMT Dataset 2024 further extends this effort to specifically address the medical domain [10].

Despite the advancements, several research gaps persist. Many existing works often lack time-cost evaluation, which is crucial for real-time IoMT scenarios [15]. In addition, some models are limited in the number and variety of attacks they can detect, focusing on specific threats rather than a broader range [15]. A need for comprehensive datasets that capture real-world medical device traffic and contemporary attack vectors is paramount. This study aims to address these gaps by leveraging the CIC IoMT 2024 dataset and benchmarking GNNs, CNNs, and LSTMs across various classification tasks, including fine-grained (19-class) classification, and by considering computational efficiency and real-time deployment feasibility. Boosting and feature reduction techniques, as explored by Hamdouchi and Idri [12], also play a vital role in optimising model performance for multiclass intrusion detection.

4 Proposed Multi-view Contrastive Graph Neural Network

4.1 GNN for Malware Detection

Graph Neural Networks are well-suited for malware detection in IoMT because they model network traffic as connected flows rather than isolated events. Each network flow is represented as a node in a graph, and edges connect flows that are related in time or context (e.g., flows from the same device or within the same session). This graph structure naturally captures communication patterns between devices, which is essential for identifying malicious behavior in IoMT networks.

The GNN uses message-passing to share information between connected nodes, allowing it to detect suspicious activities that span multiple flows. Such coordinated attacks might appear benign when each flow is examined in isolation. We enhance the model with contrastive learning, which improves its ability to distinguish between similar-looking benign and malicious patterns by learning from multiple augmented views of the data. The final output is a binary classification (benign or malicious) for each network graph, providing clear security alerts for IoMT administrators.

4.2 Problem Formulation

We represent network traffic as a graph $G = (V, E, X)$, where V is the set of nodes (network flows), E is the set of edges (connections between flows), and $X \in \mathbb{R}^{|V| \times d}$ is the feature matrix containing d features for each node. Our goal is to learn a function f_b that classifies network graphs as either benign or malicious:

$$f_b : G \rightarrow \{0, 1\} \tag{1}$$

4.3 Graph Construction from Network Flows

The construction of the graph from network traffic data involves three main steps. First, each network flow becomes a node with features including source IP, destination IP, protocol type, packet count, duration, and statistical properties (total bytes, TCP flags). Second, we connect two nodes with an edge if their flows are related by: (1) originating from the same source device within a 60-second window, (2) sharing the same destination, or (3) belonging to the same communication session. These connections capture how IoMT devices communicate, where multiple related flows from one device may indicate an attack. Third, edge weights reflect the time difference between flows and their similarity in traffic patterns, which helps distinguish normal periodic communication from suspicious coordinated activity.

4.4 MVC-GNN Architecture

The Multi-View Contrastive Graph Neural Network (MVC-GNN) uses the constructed graph structure to model relationships in network traffic. The architecture has three main components: (1) a GNN encoder for learning features, (2) a classification head for predicting malware, and (3) a contrastive learning module with attention for better representation.

The feature encoder transforms raw network traffic features $x \in \mathbb{R}^d$ (where $d = 33$) into a compact embedding space through a series of nonlinear transformations:

$$h^{(1)} = \mathrm{ReLU}(W_1 x + b_1), \tag{2}$$

$$h^{(2)} = \mathrm{Dropout}(\mathrm{ReLU}(W_2 h^{(1)} + b_2)), \tag{3}$$

$$z = W_3 h^{(2)} + b_3, \quad z \in \mathbb{R}^{d_{embed}}, \ d_{embed} = 64, \tag{4}$$

where W_i and b_i denote the learnable parameters. The initial layer projects the 33 input features into a higher-dimensional space before subsequent processing. On top of the encoder, a binary classification head is employed to detect malicious or benign traffic flows. It is modeled as a shallow feedforward network:

$$\hat{y}_{binary} = \sigma\left(W_b^{(out)} \, \mathrm{ReLU}(W_b^{(hidden)} z + b_b^{(hidden)}) + b_b^{(out)} \right), \tag{5}$$

where $\sigma(\cdot)$ denotes the sigmoid activation function. To strengthen representation learning, the framework incorporates a contrastive learning module. For two augmented views z_i and z_j of the same input, the NT-Xent loss is defined as

$$\mathcal{L}_{contrastive} = -\log \frac{\exp(\text{sim}(z_i, z_j)/\tau)}{\sum_{k=1}^{2N} \mathbf{1}_{k \neq i} \exp(\text{sim}(z_i, z_k)/\tau)}, \tag{6}$$

where $\text{sim}(u, v) = \frac{u^T v}{\|u\|\|v\|}$ represents cosine similarity, $\tau = 0.5$ is the temperature parameter, and N is the batch size. A projection head maps embeddings into the contrastive space according to

$$p = W_p^{(2)} \, \text{ReLU}(W_p^{(1)} z + b_p^{(1)}) + b_p^{(2)}. \tag{7}$$

To improve interpretability, an attention mechanism assigns feature importance weights, computed as

$$\alpha = \sigma(W_\alpha z + b_\alpha), \tag{8}$$

where α captures the contribution of individual features to the decision-making process.

The overall training objective combines the binary classification loss with the contrastive objective:

$$\mathcal{L}_{total} = \mathcal{L}_{binary} + \lambda \mathcal{L}_{contrastive}, \tag{9}$$

where $\mathcal{L}_{binary}$ is the binary cross-entropy loss and λ is a weighting parameter that balances the two objectives. In practice, we set λ equal to the mean attention weight to adaptively weight the contrastive loss based on feature importance.

Finally, to further support contrastive learning, data augmentation is applied by injecting Gaussian noise into the input features:

$$x_{aug} = x + \epsilon, \quad \epsilon \sim \mathcal{N}(0, 0.1^2 I), \tag{10}$$

which generates perturbed but semantically consistent views of the same flow, ensuring robust representation learning.

5 Experimental Setup

5.1 Data Collection

This section of the development utilised the CIC IoMT 2024 dataset [10]. Data were collected from a network designed to simulate a realistic IoMT environment. To ensure correct operation, this network comprises various IoMT device types, as well as the necessary support devices, including switches, routers, and access points. Since some devices require an Internet connection to function properly, an iPad is connected to an access point, which is connected to a switch that connects to the router and the public Internet. A collection of Raspberry Pi 4 devices, acting as malicious actors, is linked to the same access point. Finally, the switch is connected to an additional access point that connects all IoMT devices and provides iPad and Internet connectivity.

5.2   Data Preprocessing

In this study, the CICIoMT2024 dataset, a comprehensive, multiprotocol benchmark designed to evaluate the cybersecurity of Internet of Medical Things (IoMT) devices, was used. It includes network traffic recorded from 40 devices, comprising 15 simulated and 25 real systems, and encompasses 18 different attack types categorized into five main groups: Spoofing, MQTT-based threats, reconnaissance, distributed denial of service (DDoS), and denial of service (DoS).

5.3   Data Cleaning

The data cleaning process ensures that the collected data are reliable and ready for analysis by eliminating errors and inconsistencies. To preserve alignment between features and labels, we first identify missing values (NaN) and remove columns containing incomplete data, then delete rows with remaining missing values to retain only complete features. To guarantee numerical stability, infinite values (such as those resulting from arithmetic errors) are replaced with NaN and subsequently removed. Label standardization is also employed to remove numerical identifiers and suffixes (e.g., "train", "test") from attack labels.

5.4   Feature Selection

This approach employs a hybrid feature selection strategy to methodically refine the feature set. We use a correlation-based method with a threshold of 0.90 to identify strongly associated feature pairs using Pearson correlation coefficients. Concurrently, we assess feature importance by determining each feature's absolute correlation with the target variable, giving priority to features with higher predictive relevance. When two features exceed the correlation threshold, we eliminate the feature with the lower absolute correlation to the target, retaining the feature that makes a more significant contribution to the model's predictive power. This intelligent removal strategy eliminates redundancy among correlated features. To maximize the feature subset for downstream modeling tasks, this hybrid technique leverages both inter-feature interactions and target relevance while balancing dimensionality reduction with informative feature preservation.

This feature selection filter approach combines correlation analysis and target-based relevance scores to minimize dimensionality while maintaining the most relevant features. The resulting relationships are visualized in the correlation matrix shown in Fig. 1.

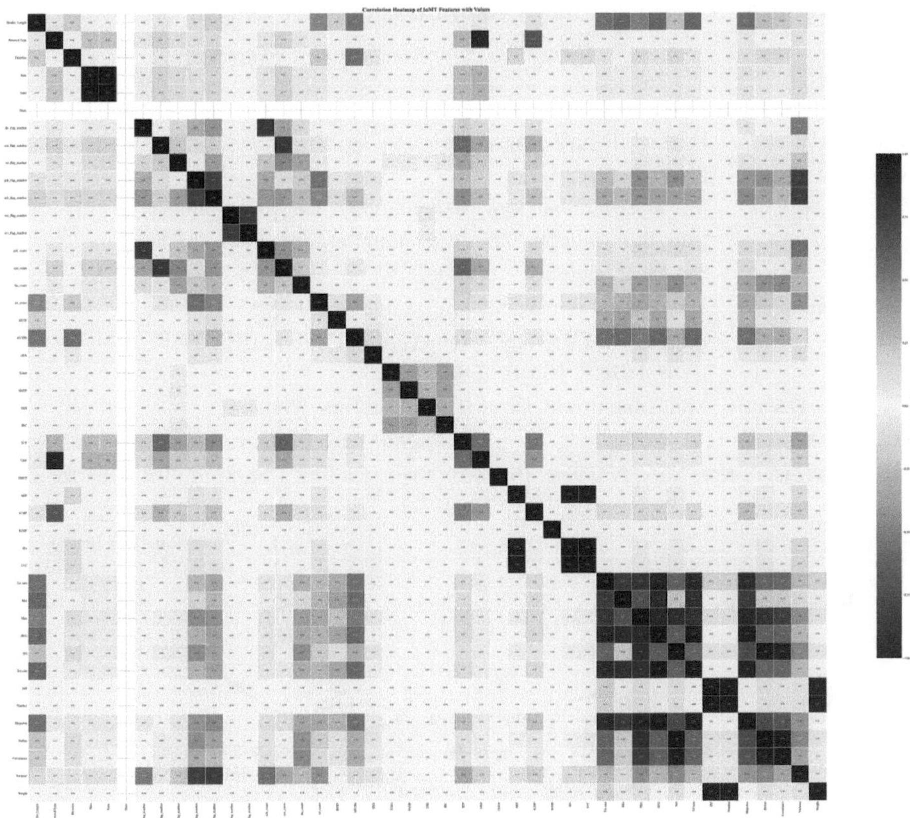

Fig. 1. Correlation Matrix showing Correlation Coefficients.

The goal of the feature selection procedure was to eliminate duplicate or less discriminative features while maintaining statistical and protocol-specific features, as summarized in Table 1. The original dataset contained 45 features, from which 33 were selected and 12 were removed. Due to the dataset's imbalance, it may be difficult to differentiate certain attacks from legitimate traffic, especially when dealing with the most prevalent attack types (DoS and DDoS).

5.5 Data Normalization

This phase normalizes all data to the same scale to improve machine learning model performance and accuracy, preventing scale-sensitive models from creating inaccurate associations. Various scaler types can be employed depending on the data characteristics. This study utilizes the Standard Scaler, a machine learning preprocessing method that transforms features to have a mean of 0 and a standard deviation of 1. To standardize a feature x, the following mathematical formula is used:

Table 1. Selected and Removed Features from the Original Set of 45

Selected Features (33)	
Category	Features
Header-related	Header_Length, Duration
Rate-related	Srate, Drate
TCP Flags	fin_flag_number, syn_flag_number, rst_flag_number, psh_flag_number, ack_flag_number, ece_flag_number, cwr_flag_number
Flag Counts	ack_count, syn_count, fin_count, rst_count
Protocols	HTTP, HTTPS, DNS, Telnet, SMTP, SSH, IRC, TCP, UDP, DHCP, ICMP, IGMP, LLC
Statistical Features	Min, Magnitude, Covariance, Variance, Weight
Removed Features (12)	
ARP, AVG, IAT, IPv, Max, Number, Protocol Type, Radius, Rate, Std, Tot size, Tot sum	

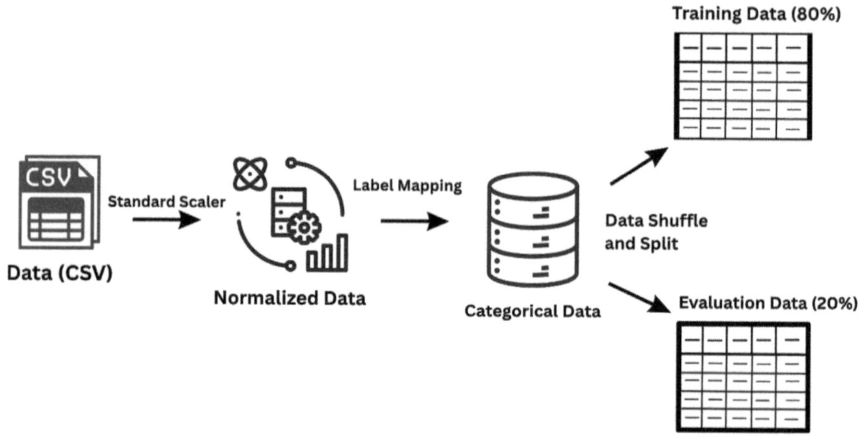

Fig. 2. Data Pipeline for flow analysis.

$$z = \frac{(x - \mu)}{\sigma} \tag{11}$$

where z is the standardised value of the feature, x is the original value of the feature, μ is the mean of the feature column, and σ is the standard deviation of the feature column.

5.6 Label Data Mapping

This stage converts the output classes into numerical values that serve as the model's output. For binary classification, attack traffic is classified as 1 and benign traffic as 0. While the dataset supports multiclass classification structures

(6-class and 19-class), this study focuses exclusively on the binary setting, which is most relevant for real-time intrusion detection in IoMT environments. All of the data are shuffled to have a random distribution to prevent the model from identifying patterns in the training order. After that, these data are divided into datasets for training and evaluation. Following these procedures, as illustrated in Fig. 2, the data are prepared for model evaluation and training. Graph Neural Networks (GNNs) model relational data, such as IoMT networks, where devices are nodes and communications are edges. Formally, a graph is $G = (V, E, F)$, with V the set of nodes, E the set of edges, and $F \in \mathbb{R}^{n \times D}$ the node feature matrix. The core operation is message passing:

$$h_v^{(l)} = f^{(l)} \left(h_v^{(l-1)}, \mathrm{AGG}^{(l)} \left(\{ h_u^{(l-1)} : u \in N_v \} \right) \right) \tag{12}$$

where N_v are neighbors of v, $\mathrm{AGG}^{(l)}$ is an aggregation function, and $f^{(l)}$ is a learnable transformation. For graph convolutional networks, the normalized Laplacian is $L = I_n - D^{-1/2} W D^{-1/2}$, with W the weighted adjacency matrix and D the degree matrix. Spectral filtering uses Chebyshev polynomials:

$$y = g_\theta *_G x = \sum_{k=0}^{K-1} \theta_k T_k(\tilde{L}) x \tag{13}$$

where T_k is the k-th Chebyshev polynomial, $\tilde{L} = 2L/\lambda_{\max} - I_n$, and θ_k are learnable coefficients. This enables GNNs to capture both local and global structures, supporting the detection of complex attacks in IoMT. A proposed system architecture, illustrated in Fig. 3, outlines the workflow from data acquisition to classification.

Figure 3 presents the detailed architectures of the proposed deep learning models used in this study. For feature aggregation, the Graph Neural Network (GNN) utilized a three-layer graph convolutional network with global mean pooling and ReLU activation. A dense layer with softmax activation was used after two stacked LSTM layers (128 units each) in the Long Short-Term Memory (LSTM) network. Three convolutional layers with a kernel size of 3×3 were constructed using the Convolutional Neural Network (CNN), which also included max-pooling and dropout (rate $= 0.3$) to prevent overfitting.

5.7 Evaluation Metrics

Model performance was evaluated using standard classification metrics: accuracy, precision, recall, and F1-score. These metrics are essential for assessing the effectiveness of binary classification in intrusion detection, particularly in IoMT contexts where both missed attacks (false negatives) and false alarms (false positives) carry significant operational and safety implications. Alrefaei and Ilyas [3] emphasize these metrics for real-time intrusion detection in IoT environments.

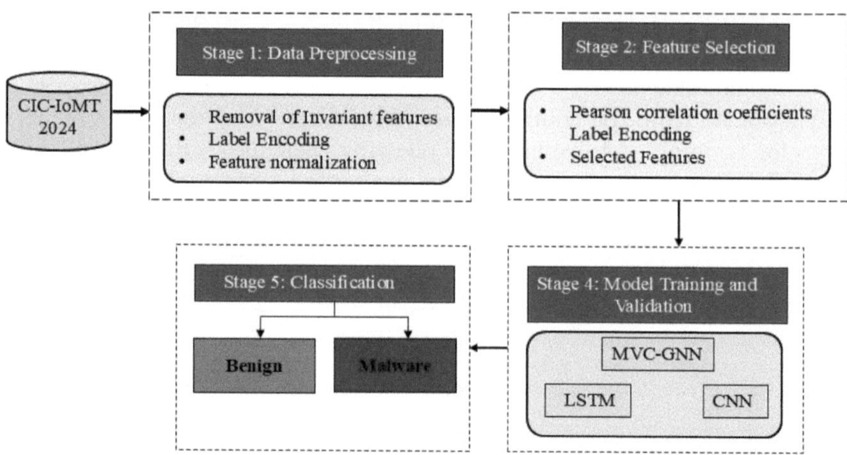

Fig. 3. Three-stage workflow of the proposed deep learning–based malware detection framework.

5.8   Results and Analysis

Models were evaluated on the binary classification task (benign vs. attack). The key results are summarized in Table 2.

Table 2. Performance Comparison of Deep Learning Models for Binary Classification

Classification Task	Metric	MVC-GNN	CNN	LSTM
Binary	Accuracy	**0.9969**	0.9862	0.9767
	Recall	0.9963	0.9831	0.9765
	Precision	0.9959	0.9774	0.9539
	F1-Score	0.9961	0.9802	0.9652

An evaluation of binary classification performance for deep learning models, as shown in Fig. 4, revealed distinct patterns of effectiveness across architectures. The proposed Multi-View Contrastive Graph Neural Network (MVC-GNN) demonstrated the best results, achieving an accuracy of 0.9969, a recall of 0.9963, a precision of 0.9959, and an F1-score of 0.9961, significantly outperforming traditional deep learning approaches. The Convolutional Neural Network (CNN) achieved an accuracy of 0.9862 and an F1-score of 0.9802, showing competitive yet notably lower performance. The Long Short-Term Memory (LSTM) model ranked last, obtaining an accuracy of 0.9767 and an F1-score of 0.9652.

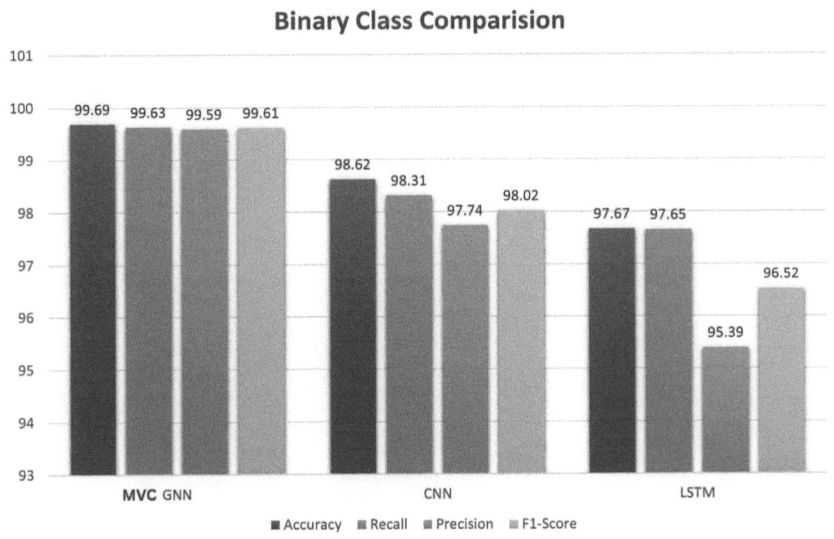

Binary Class Comparision

Fig. 4. Performance Metrics for Binary Classification.

The confusion matrix in Fig. 5 further illustrates the superior classification capability of the MVC-GNN in distinguishing between the two classes.

5.9 Computational Efficiency

The practical deployment of deep learning models in IoMT environments requires evaluation of computational efficiency alongside classification performance. All experiments were conducted on an NVIDIA GeForce RTX 3050 GPU 4GB VRAM with AMD Ryzen 7 5800H processor using PyTorch 2.0.1. Training used batch size 256 for 50 epochs with early stopping. Table 3 presents the computational metrics for all models.

CNN exhibited superior computational efficiency with shortest training time 78.3 min and lowest latency 2.1 ms, though at the cost of significantly reduced accuracy in capturing complex attack patterns. LSTM required the longest training time of 145.8 min due to sequential processing constraints and higher memory consumption of 2.8 GB. The proposed MVC-GNN achieved balanced efficiency with 135.2 min training time and 6.8 ms inference latency, which remains acceptable for near real-time IoMT monitoring scenarios. The MVC-GNN framework achieves optimal balance between detection accuracy (99.69%) and computational feasibility, with its graph-based architecture and contrastive learning components providing superior threat detection capabilities critical for healthcare security.

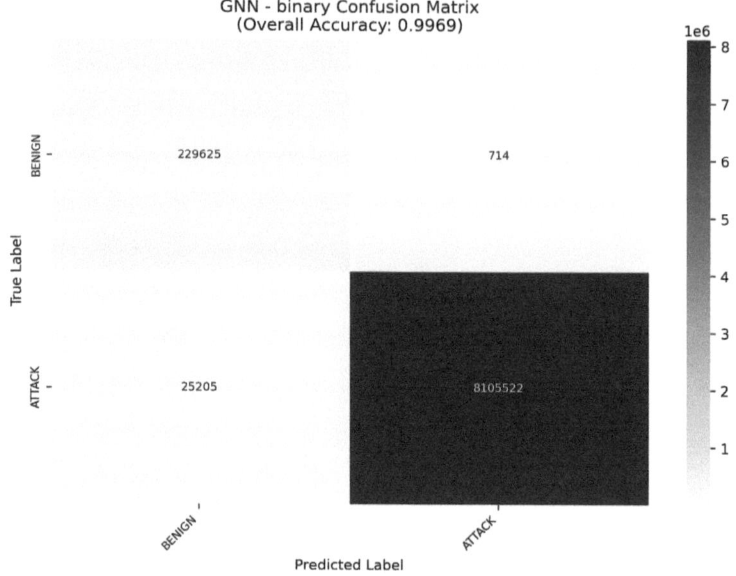

Fig. 5. Confusion Matrix for MVC-GNN Model (Binary Classification).

6   Discussion

Experimental results demonstrate the significant potential of deep learning models for IoMT security, with the proposed Multi-View Contrastive Graph Neural Network (MVC-GNN) consistently outperforming traditional and other deep architectures for binary traffic classification. The MVC-GNN architecture represents a significant advancement in Internet of Medical Things security through its integration of contrastive learning with graph-based modeling, providing enhanced interpretability through attention mechanisms.

The superior performance of the MVC-GNN can be attributed to several key factors. First, the contrastive learning component maximizes agreement between differently augmented views of the same data sample while minimizing agreement between views of different samples, allowing the network to acquire robust, discriminative representations. This approach is particularly effective in IoMT environments where subtle differences between benign and malicious traffic patterns need to be captured. Second, the graph-based structure naturally captures relational patterns and device interactions that are critical for detecting coordinated attacks in IoMT networks. Third, the attention mechanism provides interpretability by highlighting the most important features for each prediction, which is crucial for deployment in critical healthcare environments where explainability is paramount.

Table 3. Computational Efficiency Metrics for Deep Learning Models

Model	Training Time (min)	Inference Latency (ms)	GPU Memory (GB)	Throughput (samples/s)
CNN	78.3	2.1	1.5	476
LSTM	145.8	9.8	2.8	102
MVC-GNN (Proposed)	135.2	6.8	2.4	147

Note: All measurements averaged over 5 runs. Throughput calculated as 1000/latency for single-sample inference.

In this section, the performance of the proposed MVC-GNN model on the CIC IoMT 2024 dataset is compared with the results reported in contemporary literature, particularly studies employing deep learning or machine learning approaches for network intrusion and anomaly detection in IoMT/IoT contexts. A comparison is presented for binary traffic classification tasks, as summarized in Table 4.

Table 4. Comparative analysis of proposed model and existing works for binary classification

Dataset	Ref	Model	Type	Acc	Prec	Rec	Limitation
Custom Malware Dataset	[21]	RUSBoost + Ensemble DNN (Late Fusion)	Binary	95.36	79.9	86.5	Precision lower than recall, fusion complexity
IoT Malware Dataset	[26]	CNN + LSTM Ensemble	Binary	99.5	99.1	99.3	Results limited to IoT malware, lacks medical focus
CICIoMT 2024	[10]	Benchmark Dataset (Profiling + ML)	Binary	97.1	96.1	95.1	Benchmark only, no optimized model, imbalance issues
IoMT-TrafficData	[6]	ML + Deep Models	Binary	99.07	99.2	99.01	Dataset specific, flow-based, no resource efficiency focus
CICIoMT 2024	[28]	MI + Ensemble FS + RF	Binary	93.48	92.46	93.45	Trade-off between accuracy and efficiency, feature selection overhead
CICIoMT 2024	[10]	RF, AdaBoost, DNN	Binary	97.1	95.1	95.1	Class imbalance, rare class issues
CICIoT 2023	[12]	CNN, SVM	Binary	98.6	96.0	91.0	Not medical specific
CICIDS 2017	[30]	CNN	Binary	96.0	95.0	94.0	IoT general
CICIoMT 2024	**This Study**	**MVC-GNN**	**Binary**	**99.69**	**99.59**	**99.63**	**Contrastive learning + graph modeling, robust to imbalance**

Note: Bold values indicate the highest in each metric.

The proposed MVC-GNN demonstrates superior accuracy in binary classification for IoMT security, achieving 99.69% on CIC IoMT 2024, significantly surpassing existing methods like Random Forest (97.1%), AdaBoost [10], and other deep learning approaches. Comparative benchmarks on related IoT datasets, including CICIoT2023 [22] and CICIDS2017 [14], yield 96–98.6% accuracy but often suffer reduced recall and F1-scores due to class imbalance. While Convolutional Neural Networks (CNNs) excel in simpler contexts (e.g., 96.37% on CICIoT2023 [22]), their performance degrades in more complex classification tasks due to challenges with rare classes and an inability to capture relational patterns. This finding underscores the necessity of representative, balanced datasets like CIC IoMT 2024 for advancing robust intrusion detection models.

Overall, the MVC-GNN outperforms all baseline approaches in both accuracy and robustness to real-world IoMT dataset challenges, positioning it as a highly promising solution for future IoMT security deployments.

7   Conclusion

This research introduced and evaluated a novel Multi-View Contrastive Graph Neural Network (MVC-GNN) architecture for binary network traffic classification in IoMT systems using the CIC IoMT Dataset 2024, comparing it against established deep learning models including CNNs and LSTMs. Findings of this proposed work confirm that the MVC-GNN significantly enhances IoMT security, demonstrating superior performance due to its integration of contrastive learning with graph-based modeling, proving particularly effective for binary malware detection. The MVC-GNN architecture addresses critical limitations in existing approaches by: (1) leveraging contrastive learning to learn discriminative representations that are robust to subtle variations in IoMT traffic patterns, (2) utilizing graph structure to capture device interactions and relational patterns essential for detecting coordinated attacks, (3) incorporating attention mechanisms for enhanced interpretability, which is crucial in healthcare environments, and (4) employing data augmentation strategies to improve model robustness. While CNNs and LSTMs are also capable, the MVC-GNN shows distinct advantages in handling binary IoMT malware detection and capturing intricate IoMT network characteristics through its contrastive learning framework. The mathematical foundations provided, including the NT-Xent contrastive loss formulation, establish a solid theoretical basis for the approach. In order to achieve even more reliable detection, future research should concentrate on creating hybrid deep learning models that incorporate the advantages of several architectures. Extending MVC-GNN to multiclass IoMT attack categorization is an important direction for future work. Optimizing models for real-time deployment on resource-constrained IoMT devices, enhancing their resilience against adversarial attacks, and improving interpretability through Explainable AI are crucial next steps. Additionally, exploring federated learning for privacy-preserving model training, investigating the scalability of the MVC-GNN architecture to larger IoMT networks, and continuously updating datasets with novel attack scenarios will ensure the long-term effectiveness of IoMT cybersecurity. The proposed MVC-GNN represents a significant step forward in IoMT security, providing a comprehensive framework that balances accuracy, interpretability, and practical deployment considerations essential for protecting critical healthcare infrastructure.

Data Availibility Statement. The CIC dataset page makes the dataset used in this investigation freely accessible at: https://www.unb.ca/cic/datasets/iomt-dataset-2024.html.

References

1. Abbasi, M., Shahraki, A., Taherkordi, A.: Dimensionality reduction with deep learning for botnet detection in IoT. IEEE Access **12**, 15234–15247 (2024)
2. Almiani, M., AbuGhazleh, A., Al-Rahayfeh, A., Atiewi, S., Razaque, A.: Deep recurrent neural network for IoT intrusion detection system. Simul. Model. Pract. Theory **101**, 102031 (2020)
3. Alrefaei, A.F., Ilyas, M.: Real-time intrusion detection for IoT devices using machine learning. Comput. Netw. **234**, 109912 (2024)
4. Alsaedi, A., Moustafa, N., Tari, Z., Mahmood, A., Anwar, A.: IoT intrusion detection taxonomy, reference architecture, and open challenges. Wireless Netw. **26**(8), 6153–6181 (2020)
5. Alsubaei, F., Abuhussein, A., Shiva, S.: Internet of medical things security: a review. Comput. Netw. **153**, 86–105 (2019)
6. Areia, J., Bispo, I.A., Santos, L., Costa, R.L.D.C.: IoMT-trafficdata: dataset and tools for benchmarking intrusion detection in internet of medical things. IEEE Access **12**, 115370–115385 (2024)
7. Berguiga, A., Haloui, I., Alshomrani, S., Ben Jemaa, Y.: A hybrid deep learning-based intrusion detection system for IoMT networks. Comput. Netw. **234**, 109913 (2025)
8. Boyaci, O., et al.: Graph neural networks based detection of stealth false data injection attacks in smart grids. IEEE Syst. J. **16**(2), 2946–2957 (2021)
9. Chen, T., Kornblith, S., Norouzi, M., Hinton, G.: A simple framework for contrastive learning of visual representations. In: International Conference on Machine Learning, pp. 1597–1607 (2020)
10. Dadkhah, S., Neto, E.C.P., Ferreira, R., Molokwu, R.C., Sadeghi, S., Ghorbani, A.A.: Ciciomt2024: attack vectors in healthcare devices-a multi-protocol dataset for assessing IoMT device security. Internet Things **28**, 101351 (2024). https://doi.org/10.1016/j.iot.2024.101351. https://www.unb.ca/cic/datasets/iomt-dataset-2024.html
11. Ferrag, M.A., Maglaras, L., Moschoyiannis, S., Janicke, H.: Deep learning for cyber security intrusion detection: approaches, datasets, and comparative study. J. Inf. Secur. Appl. **50**, 102419 (2020)
12. Hamdouchi, Y., Idri, A.: Boosting and feature reduction techniques for multiclass intrusion detection. Expert Syst. Appl. **237**, 121486 (2025)
13. Hasan, M.K., Islam, M.M., Hashem, I.A.T., Dawan, M.A., Ahmed, M., et al.: A comprehensive survey on security issues in internet of medical things. Comput. Secur. **117**, 102691 (2022)
14. Hussain, F., Hussain, R., Hassan, S.A., Hossain, E.: Machine learning in IoT security: current solutions and future challenges. IEEE Commun. Surv. Tutor. **22**(3), 1686–1721 (2020)
15. Kharoubi, F., Alshomrani, S., Ben Jemaa, Y.: CNN-based network intrusion detection system for real-time threat detection in IoT environments. Comput. Netw. **235**, 110041 (2025)

16. Khraisat, A., Gondal, I., Vamplew, P., Kamruzzaman, J.: Survey of intrusion detection systems: techniques, datasets and challenges. Cybersecurity **2**(1), 1–22 (2019). https://doi.org/10.1186/s42400-019-0038-7
17. Koroniotis, N., Moustafa, N., Sitnikova, E., Turnbull, B.: Towards the development of realistic botnet dataset in the internet of things for network forensic analytics: Bot-IoT dataset. Futur. Gener. Comput. Syst. **100**, 779–796 (2019)
18. Krishnan, P., Shrinath, N.: A robust IoT botnet detection framework resilient to gradient-based adversarial attacks. Comput. Commun. **198**, 1–12 (2024)
19. Liu, X., et al.: Self-supervised learning: generative or contrastive. IEEE Trans. Knowl. Data Eng. **35**(1), 857–876 (2023)
20. Lopez-Martin, M., Carro, B., Sanchez-Esguevillas, A., Lloret, J.: Network traffic classifier with convolutional and recurrent neural networks for internet of things. IEEE Access **5**, 18042–18050 (2017)
21. Nazim, S., Alam, M.M., Rizvi, S., Mustapha, J.C., Hussain, S.S., Su'ud, M.M.: Multimodal malware classification using proposed ensemble deep neural network framework. Sci. Rep. **15**(1), 18006 (2025)
22. Neto, E.C.P., Dadkhah, S., Ferreira, R., Zolanvari, M., Jain, R., Ghorbani, A.A.: CICIoT2023: a real-time dataset and benchmark for large-scale attacks in IoT environment. Sensors **23**(13), 5941 (2023)
23. Otoum, S., Kantarci, B., Mouftah, H.T.: DL-IDS: a deep learning-based intrusion detection framework for securing IoT. Trans. Emerg. Telecommun. Technol. **32**(6), e3803 (2021)
24. Qureshi, K.N., Tayyab, M., Rehman, S.U., Jeon, G.: An intrusion detection system for the internet of medical things. IEEE Access **9**, 20067–20076 (2021)
25. Ravi, V., Alazab, M., Srinivasan, S.K., Arunachalam, A., Soman, K.: Attention-based multidimensional deep learning approach for cross-architecture IoMT malware detection. Futur. Gener. Comput. Syst. **127**, 389–406 (2022)
26. Riaz, S., et al.: Malware detection in internet of things (IoT) devices using deep learning. Sensors **22**(23), 9305 (2022)
27. Saif, S., Das, P., Biswas, S., Khari, M., Shanmuganathan, V.: Analysis of ml and dl algorithms for botnet attack detection in IoMT. Wireless Pers. Commun. **129**(4), 2681–2705 (2023)
28. Salehpour, A., Balafar, M.A., Souri, A.: An optimized intrusion detection system for resource-constrained IoMT environments: enhancing security through efficient feature selection and classification. J. Supercomput. **81**(6), 783 (2025)
29. Sun, Z., Teixeira, A.M., Toor, S.: GNN-IDS: graph neural network based intrusion detection system. In: Proceedings of the 19th International Conference on Availability, Reliability and Security, pp. 1–12 (2024)
30. Wang, H., Li, Z., Zheng, L., Sun, Y., Liu, J.: Contrastive learning for network anomaly detection. In: 2021 IEEE International Conference on Data Mining (ICDM), pp. 652–661. IEEE (2021)
31. Zhang, Y., Li, X., Zhao, J.: Graph neural networks for botnet detection in IoT networks. IEEE Trans. Netw. Sci. Eng. **8**(2), 1563–1576 (2021)
32. Zhou, L., Wang, X., Zhang, Y.: Graph neural networks for IoT security: a comprehensive survey. In: Proceedings of the IEEE International Conference on Communications, pp. 1–6. IEEE (2020)

PAC-Guided Design Strategies
for Resilient Priority Arbiter PUFs

Durba Chatterjee[1]([✉])(iD), Simranjeet Singh[2](iD), Debdeep Mukhopadhyay[3](iD),
Farhad Merchant[2](iD), and Anupam Chattopadhyay[4](iD)

[1] Radboud University, Nijmegen, The Netherlands
durba.chatterjee94@gmail.com
[2] University of Groningen, Groningen, The Netherlands
[3] IIT Kharagpur, Kharagpur, India
[4] Nanyang Technological University, Singapore, Singapore

Abstract. Silicon Physically Unclonable Functions (PUFs) exploit intrinsic manufacturing variations to generate unique device-specific responses and serve as hardware roots of trust. Despite their promise, PUFs remain vulnerable to modeling attacks. Recent works propose using PAC learnability bounds as a formal measure to assess the modeling robustness of delay-based PUFs. In this work, we assess Priority Arbiter PUF (PA-PUF), a variant of the classical Arbiter PUF that incorporates a three-path chain and a priority-based arbitration mechanism. We provide the first provable learnability results for PA-PUF under the Deterministic Finite Automata (DFA) class. We extend the analysis to Feedforward PA-PUF. We empirically validate the PAC learnability bounds using an implementation of Angluin's L* algorithm, which achieves a modeling accuracy of 80% for a 32-bit PA-PUF with 8000 queries. Based on the formal analysis, we propose a generalization of the PA-PUF construction and analyze how the learnability outcomes change with varying design parameters. Finally, we evaluate the proposed generalized construction using state-of-the-art multi-layer perceptron (MLP)-based modeling attacks. Extensive experiments reveal that approximately 2^{20} challenge-response pairs (CRPs) are sufficient to model a 64-bit PA-PUF with feed-forward with nearly 100% accuracy, while increasing the configuration to a generalized 12-path architecture reduces this accuracy to approximately 65%.

Keywords: Physically Unclonable Functions · PAC Learning · Modeling Attack

1 Introduction

Since the advent of delay-based PUFs, most design efforts have centered on enhancing security against model-building attacks. To this end, various strategies have been proposed, such as ① combining multiple PUF responses using cryptographic Boolean functions [10, 13, 15] or ② composing PUFs hierarchically [11, 19] or ③ incorporating cryptographic constructs such as Sponge function [3] or LWE decryption module [17]. While these approaches significantly bolster resistance to ML-based modeling attacks, they come with substantial hardware overhead. To address this challenge, PUFs with multiple delay chains have been proposed [1,14] that achieve enhanced robustness against such attacks whilst having efficient implementations and good statistical properties. The underlying rationale of these constructions is to enhance the nonlinearity of the challenge-response mapping, such that the responses are not linearly separable by a hyperplane, thereby thwarting the modeling attacks based on the linear additive delay model [8].

The linear additive delay model derived in [7] represents the response as a scalar product of the parity bits (derived from transforming the challenge) and the delay parameters. It is to be noted that this is applicable for constructions comprising two delay paths, as in Arbiter PUF-based constructions. The additive delay model provides the challenge transformations (such as converting it to a parity vector) that segregate the input data into two linearly separate classes. Changing the number of delay paths and their connections alters this mathematical model. Thus, attacks solely based on the model derived in [7] do not perform well.

In this work, we analyze one such construction - priority arbiter PUF (PA-PUF) comprising a 3-input delay chain, followed by a nonlinear combiner function as shown in Fig. 1. This priority arbiter in the construction decides the final response based on the priority assigned to the delay signals [14]. This mechanism results in responses with close to ideal uniformity. We choose this PUF design for analysis for these primary reasons: ① This generalizes the 2-input delay chain to the 3-input delay chain, thereby enhancing the complexity of the linear additive delay model. ② the construction takes relative arrival times of signals into consideration (by means of configurable combiner functions). Thus, the same construction can realize distinct challenge-response mappings solely with the change of the arbitration circuit and the combiner function, without changing the placement of the delay chains. Additionally, PA-PUF has close to ideal performance metrics with minimal additional overhead compared to APUF [14]. While a recent work [5] analyses the cryptographic properties of this construction, such as strict avalanche criteria, its modeling robustness is not explored.

In this work, we perform a rigorous analysis of the modeling robustness of PA-PUF with respect to empirical and provable modeling attacks. We state the core contributions of this work as follows:

- We provide the first provable learning results for PA-PUF and feed-forward. We prove that both constructions are learnable in the Probably Approximately Correct (PAC) model under the DFA representation class.
- We highlight the vulnerability of PA-PUF against LR-based attacks, owing to the existence of an additive delay model.
- We propose a generalization of PA-PUF to a k-input chain construction from the insights obtained from the learnability bounds, and additive model.

- We experimentally validate our DFA-based PAC learning bounds on simulated instances of PA-PUF.
- We empirically validate the modeling robustness of PA-PUF and its generalized variants using state-of-the-art modeling attacks, including Logistic Regression, Least Squares Mean, and Multi-Layer Perceptron-based modeling attacks on simulated as well as real-world FPGA implementations.

The paper is organized as follows. Section 2 provides a brief description of the concepts required for this work. Section 3 presents the PAC learnability results of PA-PUF and feed-forward PA-PUF. Section 4 describes the generalization of PA-PUF construction. Section 5 provides an overview of related multi-chain PUF constructions and their differences with PA-PUF. Section 6 provides the experimental results that validate our theoretical results. Section 7 concludes the paper.

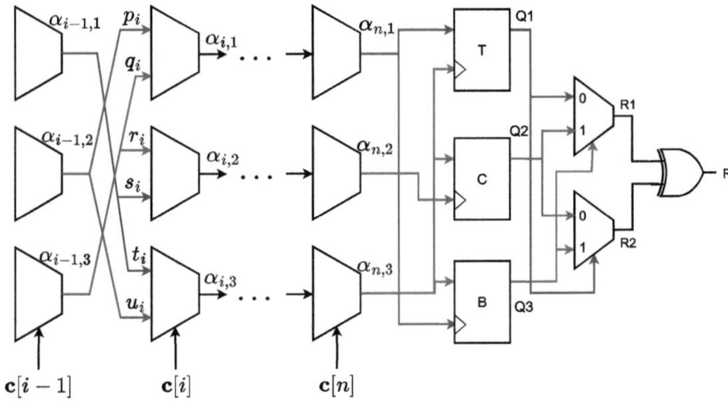

Fig. 1. Schematic Representation of Priority Arbiter-PUF (PA-PUF).

2   Background

This section presents the PA-PUF construction and its feed-forward variant, followed by a brief overview of the Deterministic Finite Automata representation class and the Probably Approximately Correct (PAC) Learning model.

2.1   Priority Arbiter PUF (PA-PUF) and Feed-Forward PA-PUF

Priority Arbiter-PUF (PA-PUF) is a delay-based PUF construction comprising a delay chain and a three-input priority arbiter. Each stage of the delay chain consists of three MUXs [14]. The priority arbiter includes three D flip-flops followed by a combiner function (AND and OR gates) that leverages the order in which the input signals arrive and their priority, thereby creating a complex challenge-response than traditional two-input arbiters. Figure 1 depicts the schematic representation of PA-PUF. FPGA implementations of PA-PUF achieve close to optimal 50% uniformity.

Feed-Forward PA-PUF. PA-PUFs incorporate feed-forward arbiters in the delay chains to further increase the non-linearity [14]. The feed-forward arbiters pass intermediate signals from the primary arbiter through additional logic, thus contributing to the enhanced nonlinearity contributed by the feed-forward output bits. The feed-forward (FF) arbiter generates the challenge bits, which are used to drive the next line of MUXs in the PA-PUF delay chain. Adding the FF increases the number of challenges with the $3\times$ number of FF. The design of the PA-PUF is scalable, allowing for various configurations based on the specific needs of the application, such as different lengths of data paths or the number of feed-forward arbiters.

2.2 Deterministic Finite Automaton Representation for PUFs

Deterministic Finite Automaton (DFA) is a formal representation used to recognize regular languages and is denoted as $= (Q, \Sigma, q_0, f, \delta)$. It consists of a set of finite states (Q), one of which is the start state (q_0), and some are designated as accepting states (F). A DFA processes an input string (challenge $\mathbf{c}$ in case of PUFs) defined over the alphabet set (Σ) one symbol/bit at a time, transitioning between states according to a set of deterministic rules defined by a transition function $\delta : Q \times \Sigma \to Q$. For each state and input symbol, there is exactly one transition to another state. If the transitions end in an accepting state $(q \in F)$ after processing the entire input $(\mathbf{c})$, the string is considered accepted; otherwise, it is rejected.

In the context of PUFs, $\Sigma = \{0, 1\}$. The challenges for which the PUF instance generates a response of 1 are considered part of the language. PUFs were first mapped to regular languages in [4]. This work presents the DFA representation of Arbiter PUF [7], the preliminary delay-chain-based PUF. The DFA resembles a binary tree of depth n (challenge length). Each state captures the cumulative delay values for each of the delay paths. It has outgoing transitions to two distinct states, resulting in 2^i states in i^{th} level, thus resulting in $\mathcal{O}(2^n)$ active states (exponential in challenge length).

2.3 Probably Approximately Correct Learning

The Probably Approximately Correct (PAC) learning model, introduced by Valiant [16], provides a formal framework for analyzing the performance of machine learning algorithms. In this model, a learning algorithm is provided with examples drawn from the input space according to an arbitrary distribution and labeled by the target function. The algorithm aims to deliver an approximately correct hypothesis with high probability. Formally, let $\mathcal{C}_n$ be a class of Boolean functions defined over instance space $\mathcal{X}_n = \{0, 1\}^n$, with target function $f \in \mathcal{C}_n$ to be learned. A concept class $\mathcal{C}_n$ is PAC learnable if there exists an algorithm

$\mathcal{A}$, polynomial $p(n, 1/\epsilon, 1/\delta)$, such that for every $\epsilon, \delta \in (0, 1)^2$, and for any distribution $\mathcal{D}$ over $\mathcal{X}_n$, $\mathcal{A}$ can return a hypothesis $h \in \mathcal{H}n$ with probability at least $(1 - \delta)$, with $error_{\mathcal{D}}(h) \leq \epsilon$ after observing $p(n, 1/\epsilon, 1/\delta)$ examples. The error function is defined as:

$$error_{\mathcal{D}}(h) = Pr_{x \sim \mathcal{D}}[f(x) \neq h(x)]$$

In the context of PUFs, the challenge-response mappings realized for a PUF design represent the concept class that an adversary targets to model. The hypothesis class corresponds to the function representation that an adversary decides, based on the information it has about the challenge response mapping. In this work, we analyse PA-PUF and Feed-forward PA-PUF under the DFA representation class. To this end, we represent these constructions as polynomial-sized DFAs and analyse their learnability bounds.

2.4   PAC Learning of Deterministic Finite Automata

The PAC model supports several function representation classes, with DFA being one such class. It has been proven that DFAs, when polynomial in size, are PAC learnable using Angluin's L* algorithm [2].

Polynomial-Sized DFA Representation. To obtain a polynomial-sized representation, we leverage the following discretization technique proposed in [4]. The core rationale behind this technique is that the difference between the arrival times of two signals is only observable by an arbiter if the difference is greater than the precision of the arbiter (γ). In practice, arbiters are realized by D-flip flop or NAND latch, and they can only set the response of 0 (low signal) or 1 (high signal) if the absolute difference in their arrival times is at least γ.

Discretization of Delay Values. This is based on the observation that the cumulative delay of an excitation signal follows a Gaussian distribution [9]. Consequently, the majority of significant delay values fall within a limited interval, spanning six times the standard deviation of the cumulative distribution. Owing to limited precision, the arbiter can only differentiate between signals with delay differences above (γ). Thus, the real delay values can be mapped to integer values within the range $[-d, d]$, where d denotes the maximum discretized delay value. We refer the reader to Sect. 3.1 in [4] for details. Given the polynomial-sized representation of DFA. We state the fundamental PAC learnability result for DFAs as follows.

Result 1: [4] Let $\mathcal{N}$ represent the number of live states in a DFA. A PAC learning algorithm $\mathcal{A}$ returns a hypothesis h after at most $\mathcal{O}(\mathcal{N} + (1/\epsilon)(\mathcal{N} \log(1/\delta) + \mathcal{N}^2))$ calls to the EX oracle. With probability at least $(1 - \delta/2)$, h is an $\epsilon/2$-approximation of the target DFA.

3   PAC Learning of Priority Arbiter PUF and Its Variants

In this section, we prove the PAC learnability of PA-PUF and feed-forward PA-PUF. First, we establish a polynomial-sized DFA representation of the constructions, leveraging its physical properties. Next, we compute the time and sample complexity of the corresponding learning algorithm.

3.1   PAC Learning PA-PUF

We start with the PA-PUF construction without a feed-forward loop.

Polynomial-Sized Representation of PA-PUF. For this, we extend the DFA representation employed to represent APUF [4] to represent PA-PUF. Figure 2 illustrates the DFA representation of the PA-PUF given by $\mathcal{A} = (Q, \Sigma, \delta, q_0, F)$, where Q is the state space, $\Sigma = \{0, 1\}$ the input alphabet, $\delta : Q \times \Sigma \to Q$ the transition function, $q_0 \in Q$ the start state, and $F \subseteq Q$ the set of accepting states. . The DFA consists of n levels, where each state at the ith level tracks the accumulated delays of the signals $(\alpha_{i,1}, \alpha_{i,2}, \alpha_{i,3})$ over the first i stages. Here, $(\alpha_{i,1}, \alpha_{i,2}, \alpha_{i,3})$ represents the cumulative delay of the top, center, and bottom signals, respectively. Every state has two outgoing transitions to the subsequent layer's states, determined by the next challenge bit, either 0 or 1. The parameter $u[i]$ computes the parity of the challenge bits up to the ith state, thereby encoding the transitions between states in the earlier layers.

Since each stage has two outgoing connections to two distinct states, the total number of states in the last layer amounts to 2^n, as each state corresponds to a unique path taken by the excitation signal. By applying delay discretization, we map the delay values to integers within a finite interval $[0, d]$, limiting the number of distinct states in a given layer (corresponding to a delay stage) to $(d+1)^3$. Consequently, the total number of distinguishable DFA states for an n-stage PA-PUF is bounded by $\mathcal{O}(n(d+1)^3)$, as depicted in Fig. 2. The final states in the DFA are computed as follows

$$F = \{q_{n,l}|q_{n,l} = ((\alpha_{i,1}, \alpha_{i,2}, \alpha_{i,3}), u[n], n), |$$
$$\alpha_{i,1} < \alpha_{i,2} < \alpha_{i,3} \text{ or } \alpha_{i,1} < \alpha_{i,3} < \alpha_{i,2} \text{ or } \alpha_{i,1} < \alpha_{i,1} < \alpha_{i,3}, 1 \leq k \leq 2^n\} \tag{1}$$

From the above equation, we can understand that the response depends on the priority defined by the combiner function. Note that the combiner decides the final states in the last layer of the DFA while the size of the DFA remains unchanged.

Learnability Bounds of PA-PUF. Given the polynomial-sized representation of PA-PUF, we can compute the sample complexity of the PAC learning algorithm using Result 1. Substituting the value of the number of states ($\mathcal{N} = \mathcal{O}(n(d+1)^3)$), we obtain the sample complexity to be $\mathcal{O}(n(d+1)^3 + (1/\epsilon)(n(d+1)^3 log(1/\delta) + n(d+1)^6))$. The sample complexity is polynomial in the PUF design parameters (n) and $\frac{1}{\epsilon}, \frac{1}{\delta}$, thereby implying it is PAC learnable under the DFA representation class.

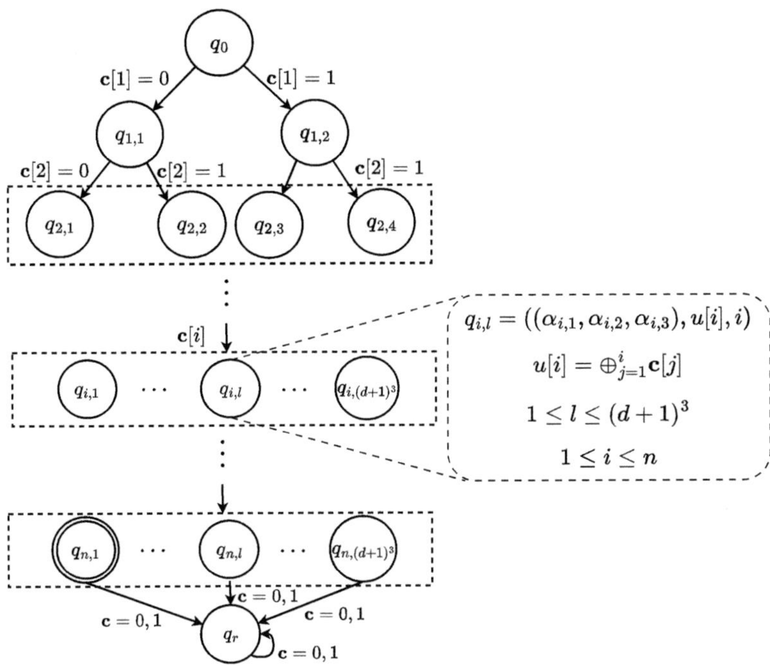

Fig. 2. DFA Representation of PA-PUF (after applying delay discretization).

3.2 PAC Learning PA-PUF with Feed-Forward

In the feed-forward PA-PUF, the feed-forward loop generates three output bits that are fed into three distinct stages in the subsequent part of the delay chain. We start from the DFA representation of the baseline PA-PUF denoted by $\mathcal{A} = (Q, \Sigma, \delta, q_0, F)$.

NFA Representation. To incorporate the feed-forward behavior, we extend $\mathcal{A}$ into an ϵ-NFA $\mathcal{N} = (Q', \Sigma, \delta', q_0, F')$, where $\delta' : Q' \times (\Sigma \cup \{\epsilon\}) \to 2^{Q'}$. The ϵ-transitions encode the dependencies introduced by the feed-forward arbiters. The addition of the feed-forward loop from ff_{in} to $ff_{out1}, ff_{out2}, ff_{out3}$ stages in the original PA-PUF construction translates to the addition of the following ϵ-transitions in the PA-PUF DFA:

1. *Feed-forward outputs:* From all states in layers $ff_{out1}, ff_{out2}, ff_{out3}$ to the start state of the DFA representation. This is added as feed-forward output bit (say O_1) depends on the cumulative delay difference at the end of ff_{in} stage. Thus, feeding the bit O_1 to stage ff_{out1} implies that the switching decision at ff_{out1} depends on the relative delay of signals till stage ff_{in}. Mathematically, $\delta'(q, \epsilon) \ni q_0, \quad \forall q \in Q_{ff_{outj}}$. This reflects that the switching decision at ff_{outj} depends on the cumulative delay up to ff_{in}.

2. *Dummy states for arbiter outputs:* From every state in $Q_{ff_{in}}$, we introduce ϵ-transitions to two auxiliary states q_{acc} and q_{rej}, representing the two possible outcomes of the feed-forward arbiter:

$$\delta'(q, \epsilon) = \{q_{\text{acc}}, q_{\text{rej}}\}, \quad \forall q \in Q_{ff_{in}}.$$

3. *Redefining output transitions:* At the ff_{out} stages, the next transition is determined by the outcome of the feed-forward arbiter rather than the direct challenge bit. The last modification includes adding ϵ transitions from the accept dummy state to states $\{q_{out1,i}, i = 2, 4, \dots\}$, $\{q_{out2,i}, i = 2, 4, \dots\}$, $\{q_{out3,i}, i = 2, 4, \dots\}$ and from the reject dummy state to states $\{q_{out1,i}, i = 1, 3, \dots\}$, $\{q_{out2,i}, i = 1, 3, \dots\}$, $\{q_{out3,i}, i = 1, 3, \dots\}$. Note that the states $\{q_{out1,i}, i = 2, 4, \dots\}$ are reached when the input bit is 1 and $\{q_{out1,i}, i = 1, 3, \dots\}$ are reached when the challenge bit is 0. Sames holds for states in levels *out2* and *out3*. Since the input bit at these levels (out1, out2, out3) is determined by O_1, the transitions from the accept dummy state replace the transitions for input=1, and transitions from the reject dummy state replace the ones for input=0. Concretely, we add

$$\delta'(q_{\text{acc}}, \epsilon) \ni q_{outj,i}, \quad i \in \{2, 4, 6, \dots\}, \quad \delta'(q_{\text{rej}}, \epsilon) \ni q_{outj,i}, \quad i \in \{1, 3, 5, \dots\}.$$

NFA to DFA Conversion. Since every ϵ-NFA has an equivalent DFA, we apply the standard subset construction to obtain $\mathcal{A}' = (Q'', \Sigma, \delta'', q_0, F'')$, $Q'' = 2^{Q'}$. This operation interposes the DFA fragment from the start state up to ff_{in} at each of the feed-forward output levels. The resulting automaton has depth $n + 3ff_{in}$, since the path up to ff_{in} is replicated three times.

Delay Discretization and Learnability Bound Computation. We apply the delay discretization technique, which bounds the number of distinct active states. The size of the resulting DFA is

$$\mathcal{N} = \mathcal{O}\big((n + 3ff_{in})(d + 1)^3\big).$$

Substituting this expression into the PAC sample complexity bound (Result 1), we obtain

$$\mathcal{O}\left((n + 3ff_{in})(d + 1)^3 + \frac{1}{\epsilon}\left((n + 3ff_{in})(d + 1)^3 \log \tfrac{1}{\delta} + (n + 3ff_{in})(d + 1)^6\right)\right),$$

which remains polynomial in the design parameters n, ff_{in} and in $\frac{1}{\epsilon}, \frac{1}{\delta}$. This establishes that both the PA-PUF and its feed-forward variant are PAC learnable under the DFA representation class.

4   Generalization of k-Chain PA-PUF

This section proposes a generalization of the original PA-PUF [14] for a k-chain configuration. The number of parallel lines (T, C, and B in the original design, refer to Fig. 1) is extended to a k-chain construction. Consequently, modifications to the feed-forward arbiter and the final priority arbiter are required to handle the k-chain. The feed-forward arbiter is extended by connecting k D flip-flops according to the connection as shown in Fig. 3, which generates k forward signals. This extends the challenge size from $n \rightarrow n + (k \times F)$, where n is the original challenge size, and F denotes the number of feed-forwards in the design. Similarly, the final arbiter is extended by incorporating k number of D flip-flops, and $(k-1)$ MUX $(2:1)$ are used to generate $k-1$ response signals. These $k-1$ signals are then XORed together to produce a single response bit as depicted in Fig. 4. Note that the final combiner function at the end of the delay chain can be adapted to reconfigure the priority of the signals. In the following section, we compute the learnability bounds for the generalized version of PA-PUF.

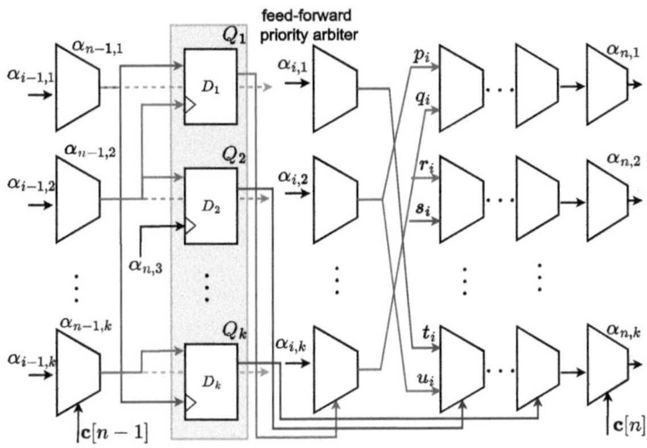

Fig. 3. Generalized PA-PUF with feed-forward arbiter.

4.1   PAC Learning of Generalized k-Chain PA-PUF

The DFA representation for generalized PA-PUF can be constructed similarly to PA-PUF, with the modification in the number of cumulative delays tracked in each stage. In this case, each stage now tracks the cumulative delays of all the k paths, along with the challenge encoding. Leveraging the delay-discretization technique, the number of active states in the representation amounts to $\mathcal{O}(n(d+1)^k)$. Substituting the value in Result 1 provides the sample complexity to be $poly(n, (d+1)^k, \frac{1}{\epsilon}, \frac{1}{\delta})$. Note that although the sample complexity is still polynomial in the design parameters, the number of CRPs increases drastically with k. Notably the value of k can not be increased indefinitely as it degrades the reliability of the construction.

5   Comparison with Related Works

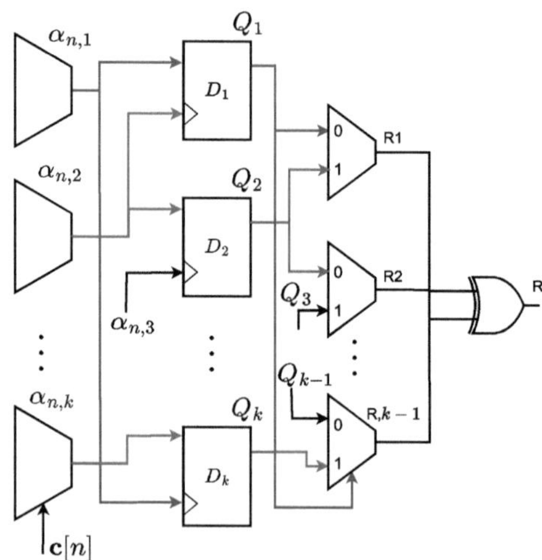

Fig. 4. Combiner function for Generalized k-chain PA-PUF (without arbiter chain).

In this section, we discuss how the DFA representation (and consequently the PAC learning bound) changes for delay-based PUFs with multiple delay paths and that can not be represented by the classic linear additive delay model.

Sensitized-Path PUF [12]. The sensitized path PUF introduces a race condition between two nearly identical paths in conventional or complex circuit blocks. Modeling it with DFA requires capturing all possible delay paths, resulting in a polynomial-sized DFA. Unlike conventional delay-based PUFs comprising one or more delay chains, for sensitive path PUFs, the DFA size depends on the number of parallel paths and challenge lengths in the circuit blocks. Consequently, the sample complexity and learnability bounds of modeling attacks vary based on the underlying circuit architecture.

Beli PUF [1]. The Beli PUF is a Multiple Permuted Delay Line PUF comprising four delay paths traversing through two parallel 2×2 switches and a fixed permutation. The DFA representation for this design captures the cumulative delay across the four delay paths, resulting in $(d+1)^4$ states in each level. Thus, for an n-bit Beli PUF, the number of states is $n(d+1)^4$, which is polynomial in the challenge length, implying that the sample complexity is also polynomial in the PUF design parameters.

6   Experimental Results

In this section, we describe the experimental setup, followed by modeling attack results on the PA-PUF constructions and their generalized variants.

6.1   Experimental Setup

The experiments were conducted by designing the PA-PUF architecture using the PyPuf simulation framework. The original PA-PUF design was adapted and extended to a generalized k-chain PA-PUF, as described in Sect. 4. The PyPuf simulations enabled testing against various attack models, using multi-layer perceptron (MLP), logistic regression (LR), and least squares regression mean (LSM) models implemented in TensorFlow to attack the PA-PUF. We select Logistic Regression (LR), Least Squares Mean (LSM), and Multi-Layer Perceptron (MLP)-based attacks for our experiments because these methods have been empirically demonstrated to effectively model delay-based PUF constructions.

Logistic Regression: The linear additive delay model of delay-based PUFs allows PUF responses to be expressed as the scalar product of a weight vector (representing delay differences) and a parity vector. This structure makes LR a particularly efficient and widely adopted modeling attack for such constructions [8].

Multi-layer Perceptron: Neural networks, particularly MLPs, have been shown to outperform traditional modeling attacks in several delay-based PUF constructions. Their ability to capture complex non-linear challenge-response mappings makes them a powerful tool for breaking PUF designs [18]. While there are numerous other machine-learning methods available, our focus was on these established approaches due to their strong empirical performance and relevance in the context of delay-based PUFs.

Attacks targeted a 32-bit challenge length with different k values to evaluate the effect of the k-chain in PA-PUF. A feed-forward (FF) arbiter was introduced after the 5th challenge line, driving subsequent lines from the 20th position in the delay chain. Since the primary objective is to assess the influence of the k-chain on the response bit, the FF arbiter remains in a fixed location.

Design Characterization on FPGA Data. Alongside the PyPuf simulations, similar attacks were also tested on the PA-PUF hardware implementation (3-bit), deployed on a Nexys Video Artix-7 FPGA board. For a 16-bit challenge length, each PUF chain utilized approximately 47 slices on the Artix-7 FPGA. By integrating these chains, a 128-bit response PA-PUF was developed, yielding performance metrics of 49.63% uniqueness, 49.45% uniformity, 49.66% bit-aliasing, and 94.5% reliability. In the attack analysis, results without the FF arbiter were also considered to isolate the delay chain's effects. Next, we look at the attack models used to break the PA-PUF using the PyPUF simulation.

6.2   DFA Modeling Attack Results on PA-PUF Simulation

We employ the implementation of Angluin's L* learning algorithm [6]. We model simulations of PA-PUF taking a 16-bit and a 32-bit challenge with noise rates of 0 and 0.1. Noise rate refers to the fraction of responses perturbed by Gaussian noise introduced during the simulation. We implement this using the `noisiness` parameter in PyPuf simulation. We observe that the attack accuracy is 80.3%

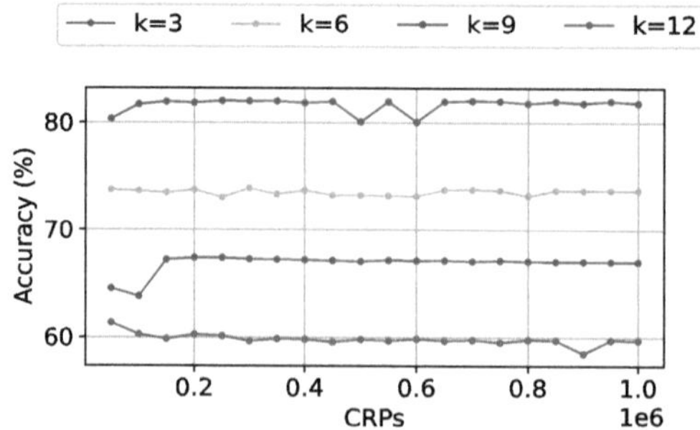

Fig. 5. Improved Logistic Regression Attack results on noiseless simulations of 64-bit PA-PUF with $k = \{3, 6, 9, 12\}$ chains.

with 8000 equivalence queries for noiseless simulation and 80.1% with 11500 equivalence queries for a 0.1 noise rate.

6.3   Modeling Attack Results on PA-PUF Simulation

This section presents the modeling attack performed using different algorithms on the generalized PA-PUF design. The attack model is implemented and performed on an Intel Core i5 processor running at 3.20GHz with 16 GB RAM.

1. Multilayer Perceptron: The Multilayer Perceptron (MLP) attack employs a neural network with three fully connected hidden layers of sizes 2^{k-1}, 2^k, and 2^{k-1} to attack a k-path PA-PUF with a generalized combiner function, following the model proposed in [18]. As the value of k increases, the number of parameters required by the MLP grows exponentially. However, a more dense network can be designed to break the design, but a relation between the number of neurons in a layer and k is maintained. The training is carried out on 1M CRPs data for 300 epochs with a batch size of 1000 and a learning rate of 0.001 per instance. A total of 10 instances are executed, and the highest accuracy among these instances is considered.

Figure 6 presents the results of the MLP attack on the PA-PUF design incorporating an FF arbiter. As the value of k increases from 3 to 12, the learning process becomes progressively more challenging, leading to a decrease in attack accuracy from nearly 100% to approximately 65%. Figure 6a illustrates the attack performance in a noiseless system with a reliability of 100%, highlighting the influence of the k-chain on the PA-PUF. Similarly, Figs. 6b and 6c depict the results under noise levels of 0.1 and 0.15, respectively. With increasing noise in the responses, the accuracy drops by $\approx$ 5–10% for the same k values compared to the noiseless case. Table 1 provides a comprehensive overview of the trade-off between reliability and accuracy for various k-values for 32-bit PA-PUF design with FF. It demonstrates that as k increases from 3 to 12, with noise levels ranging from 0 to 0.15, both accuracy and reliability decrease significantly. Further increasing k would result in a greater drop in accuracy; however, it would also render the PUF increasingly unreliable.

Figure 7 illustrates the results on generalized 64-bit PA-PUF for varying noise rates $\{0, 0.1, 0.15\}$ across different k-values. Noise rates refer to the fraction of CRPs that are impacted by Gaussian noise. The k value was increased in multiples of 3, reflecting the original 3-bit PA-PUF design. However, in the MLP attack, accuracy decreased as k increased. Specifically, as k rose from 3 to 12, the accuracy of the MLP attack dropped from approximately 95% to about $\approx 82\%$ in the case of 0.15 noise level. Table 2 illustrates the trade-off between accuracy and reliability for a 64-bit PA-PUF without FF. It highlights that increasing the k-value and noise level leads to a decline in both accuracy and reliability. For instance, at a noise level of 0.15, the accuracy decreases from 93.74% to 83.27%, with a corresponding drop in reliability by a similar factor. The MLP attack achieved higher accuracy, compared to Logistic Regression (LRA) and Least Square Means (LSM) attacks on the PA-PUF.

2. Logistic Regression: The improved Logistic Regression Attack (LRA) has been employed in the PyPuf simulation, allowing control over the number of parameters and enabling batch processing of training samples. This approach enhances computational performance and provides higher confidence in the gradient direction. In this case, 1M CRPs are processed in 1000 training samples per batch, with an optimization learning rate of 0.001. Training is performed for 300 epochs for 10 instances. In the LRA attack with zero noise, we achieve the $\approx 65\%$ accuracy for $k = 3$, which drops to $\approx 55\%$ for $k=12$ as depicted in Fig. 5.

3. Least Square Means: In this attack, the PA-PUF is framed as a linear regression problem. The responses of PA-PUF can be modeled as a linear function, where the feature vector represents the challenge, and the weights are the parameters to be learned. To improve the accuracy of the attack, multiple measurements are taken for each challenge, and the mean of these responses is used as the target in the linear regression. We have used five response measurements to reduce the noise from the individual response, leading to a more accurate approximation of the underlying linear function that governs the PUF behavior. The LSM attack using noiseless responses achieves an accuracy of $\approx 60\%$, indicating PA-PUF is difficult to model with LSM.

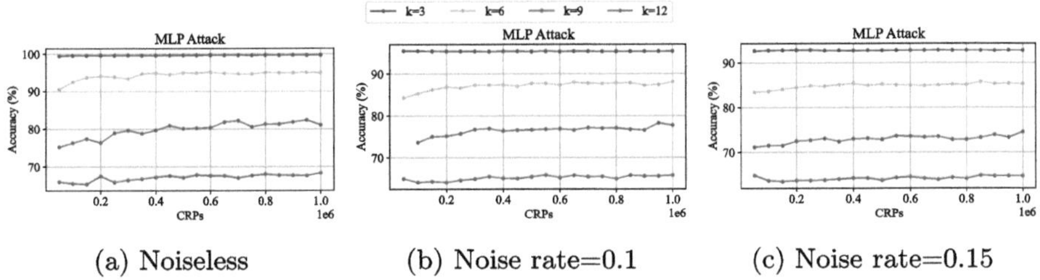

(a) Noiseless   (b) Noise rate=0.1   (c) Noise rate=0.15

Fig. 6. MLP accuracy on generalized 32-bit PA-PUF with feed-forward arbiter for varying noise rates $\{0, 0.1, 0.15\}$, computed over 1M test challenges. Here $k = \{3, 6, 9, 12\}$.

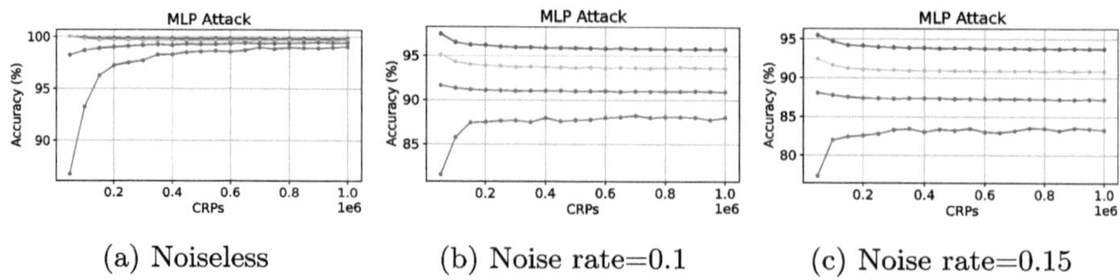

(a) Noiseless   (b) Noise rate=0.1   (c) Noise rate=0.15

Fig. 7. MLP accuracy on generalized 64-bit PA-PUF for varying noise rates $\{0, 0.1, 0.15\}$, computed over 10K test challenges. Here $k = \{3, 6, 9, 12\}$.

6.4 Modeling Attack Results on Real Data

To implement the PA-PUF attack on real data, a single delay chain with a 3-bit priority arbiter, excluding the FF arbiter, is designed on an Artix-7 FPGA, utilizing 47 slices. The delay chain length is set to 32 bits, and 2^{16} CRPs are gathered to carry out the attack. The user input challenge is fed into the MUX lines after passing through a Linear Feedback Shift Register (LFSR). The output response bit corresponding to a specific challenge is captured using the UART protocol.

The ML attack is performed using both an MLP and a linear regression (LR) model. After training for 200 epochs, the MLP model demonstrates higher accuracy than the LR model. Results from the pyPuf simulation are consistent with those obtained from real data. Figure 8 illustrates the MLP and LR attacks on a dataset of 2^{16} CRPs, showing how accuracy varies across epochs.

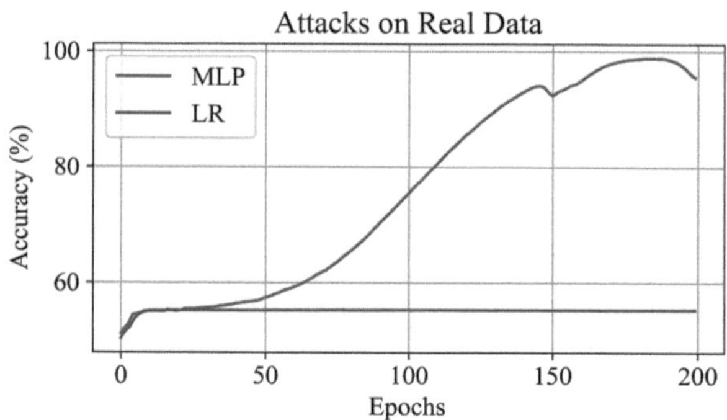

Fig. 8. Attacks on real data using original design with CRPs.

6.5 Impact of k-Chain Generalization

It has been shown that with the increase in the k value in PA-PUF, the accuracy of the ML attack decreases. However, it is also at the cost of reliability. Table 2 illustrates the trade-off between accuracy and reliability in the PA-PUF system

Table 1. Accuracy of MLP-attack and reliability of n-stage k-path PA-PUF *with feed-forward* (simulated using PyPUF). Reliability is computed for 1M randomly chosen challenges and 17 measurements with $\sigma = 15\%$. MLP architecture: $(2^{k-1}, 2^k, 2^{k-1})$

n	k	Noise	Training CRPs	Accuracy (%)	Reliability (%)
32	3	0	1M	99.71	100
32	6	0	1M	94.92	100
32	9	0	1M	81.06	100
32	12	0	1M	68.31	100
32	3	0.1	1M	95.49	86.9
32	6	0.1	1M	88.07	81.33
32	9	0.1	1M	77.71	72.04
32	12	0.1	1M	65.78	65.40
32	3	0.15	1M	92.78	81.07
32	6	0.15	1M	85.3	74.2
32	9	0.15	1M	74.5	62.19
32	12	0.15	1M	64.76	55.11

as the number of k-paths is varied. As the k-path value increases from 3 to 12, accuracy decreases from 99.45% to 65.4%, while reliability declines from 83.4% to 62.8%.

This trend highlights a trade-off between accuracy and reliability: increasing the number of k-paths improves the complexity and security of the PA-PUF but reduces its accuracy and reliability. Conversely, a lower k-path value yields higher accuracy and reliability but may compromise system robustness.

Table 2. Accuracy of MLP-attack and reliability of n-stage k-path PA-PUF (simulated using PyPUF). Reliability is computed for 1M randomly chosen challenges and 17 measurements. MLP architecture: $(2^{k-1}, 2^k, 2^{k-1})$

n	k	Noise	Training CRPs	Accuracy (%)	Reliability (%)
64	3	0	1M	99.81	100
64	6	0	1M	99.66	100
64	9	0	1M	99.40	100
64	12	0	1M	99.03	100
64	3	0.1	1M	95.75	93.81
64	6	0.1	1M	93.5	91.28
64	9	0.1	1M	90.91	87.94
64	12	0.1	1M	88.01	85.08
64	3	0.15	1M	93.74	90.90
64	6	0.15	1M	90.86	87.56
64	9	0.15	1M	87.22	83.08
64	12	0.15	1M	83.27	79.42

7   Conclusion

In this work, we conduct a comprehensive analysis towards modeling robustness of the Priority Arbiter PUF (PA-PUF), a novel delay-based PUF construction. We begin by establishing that the PA-PUF is PAC-learnable using automata-based models, with sample complexity polynomial in the challenge length, the number of delay paths, and the discretized delay value. This is the first work that establishes the provable learnability of a non-APUF based construction in the PAC model and provides formal insights on the impact of design parameters on modeling robustness. Based on this, we generalize the PA-PUF design to a k-chain architecture and propose a combiner function to ensure the resultant mapping remains non-linear. However, the generalization comes at the cost of a reduction in reliability as the number of paths increases. We further analyze the impact of adding a feed-forward chain to the PA-PUF and observe that the feed-forward loop introduces additional non-linearity, further bolstering its resistance to modeling attacks. The findings are substantiated through extensive experimental evaluations, including simulations using PyPUF and real-world FPGA implementations. These results validate the theoretical learnability bounds and establish the role of PAC-guided frameworks to construct provably secure constructions.

References

1. Aghaie, A., Moradi, A., Tobisch, J., Wisiol, N.: Security analysis of delay-based strong PUFs with multiple delay lines. In: 2022 IEEE International Symposium on Hardware Oriented Security and Trust (HOST), pp. 125–128. IEEE (2022)
2. Angluin, D.: Learning regular sets from queries and counterexamples. Inf. Comput. **75**(2), 87–106 (1987)
3. Chen, Z., Sato, T., Shinohara, H.: SpongePUF: a modeling attack resilient strong puf with scalable challenge response pair. In: 2024 IEEE International Symposium on Hardware Oriented Security and Trust (HOST), pp. 244–253. IEEE (2024)
4. Ganji, F., Tajik, S., Seifert, J.P.: Pac learning of arbiter PUFs. J. Cryptogr. Eng. **6**(3), 249–258 (2016)
5. Kansal, M., Roy, A., Roy, D., Bodapati, S., Chattopadhyay, A.: Priority arbiter PUF: analysis. Discret. Appl. Math. **356**, 71–95 (2024)
6. Khmelnitsky, I., et al.: Analyzing robustness of angluin's l* algorithm in presence of noise. arXiv preprint arXiv:2209.10315 (2022)
7. Lim, D.: Extracting Secret Keys from Integrated Circuits. Ph.D. thesis, Massachusetts (2004)
8. Rührmair, U., Sehnke, F., Sölter, J., Dror, G., Devadas, S., Schmidhuber, J.: Modeling attacks on physical unclonable functions. In: Proceedings of the 17th ACM Conference on Computer and Communications Security, pp. 237–249 (2010)
9. Rührmair, U., et al.: PUF modeling attacks on simulated and silicon data. IEEE Trans. Inf. Forensics Secur. **8**(11), 1876–1891 (2013)
10. Sahoo, D.P., Mukhopadhyay, D., Chakraborty, R.S., Nguyen, P.H.: A multiplexer-based arbiter PUF composition with enhanced reliability and security. IEEE Trans. Comput. **67**(3), 403–417 (2018). https://doi.org/10.1109/TC.2017.2749226

11. Sahoo, D.P., Saha, S., Mukhopadhyay, D., Chakraborty, R.S., Kapoor, H.: Composite PUF: a new design paradigm for physically unclonable functions on FPGA. In: 2014 IEEE International Symposium on Hardware-Oriented Security and Trust, HOST 2014, Arlington, VA, USA, 6–7 May 2014, pp. 50–55. IEEE Computer Society (2014). https://doi.org/10.1109/HST.2014.6855567

12. Sauer, M., Raiola, P., Feiten, L., Becker, B., Rührmair, U., Polian, I.: Sensitized path PUF: a lightweight embedded physical unclonable function. In: Design, Automation & Test in Europe Conference & Exhibition (DATE), pp. 680–685. IEEE (2017)

13. Siddhanti, A.A., Bodapati, S., Chattopadhyay, A., Maitra, S., Roy, D., Stănică, P.: Analysis of the strict avalanche criterion in variants of arbiter-based physically unclonable functions. In: Hao, F., Ruj, S., Sen Gupta, S. (eds.) INDOCRYPT 2019. LNCS, vol. 11898, pp. 556–577. Springer, Cham (2019). https://doi.org/10.1007/978-3-030-35423-7_28

14. Singh, S., Bodapati, S., Patkar, S., Leupers, R., Chattopadhyay, A., Merchant, F.: PA-PUF: a novel priority arbiter PUF. In: 2022 IFIP/IEEE 30th International Conference on Very Large Scale Integration (VLSI-SoC), pp. 1–6. IEEE (2022)

15. Suh, G.E., Devadas, S.: Physical unclonable functions for device authentication and secret key generation. In: Proceedings of the 44th Design Automation Conference, DAC 2007, San Diego, CA, USA, 4–8 June 2007, pp. 9–14. IEEE (2007). https://doi.org/10.1145/1278480.1278484

16. Valiant, L.G.: A theory of the learnable. Commun. ACM **27**(11), 1134–1142 (1984)

17. Wang, Y., Xi, X., Orshansky, M.: Lattice PUF: a strong physical unclonable function provably secure against machine learning attacks. In: 2020 IEEE International Symposium on Hardware Oriented Security and Trust (HOST), pp. 273–283. IEEE (2020)

18. Wisiol, N., Thapaliya, B., Mursi, K.T., Seifert, J., Zhuang, Y.: Neural network modeling attacks on arbiter-PUF-based designs. IEEE Trans. Inf. Forensics Secur. **17**, 2719–2731 (2022). https://doi.org/10.1109/TIFS.2022.3189533

19. Wu, Z., Patel, H.D., Sachdev, M., Tripunitara, M.V.: Strengthening PUFs using composition. In: Pan, D.Z. (ed.) Proceedings of the International Conference on Computer-Aided Design, ICCAD 2019, Westminster, CO, USA, 4–7 November 2019, pp. 1–8. ACM (2019). https://doi.org/10.1109/ICCAD45719.2019.8942176

Toward Crypto Agility: Automated Analysis of Quantum-Vulnerable TLS via Packet Inspection

Subeen Cho[1], Yulim Hyoung[1], Hagyeong Kim[1], Minjoo Sim[1], Anupam Chattopadhyay[2], Hwajeong Seo[1], and Hyunji Kim[1(✉)]

[1] Hansung University, Seoul, South Korea
`yu0harrypotter@hansung.ac.kr`, `khj1594012@gmail.com`
[2] Nanyang Technological University, Singapore, Singapore
`anupam@e.ntu.edu.sg`

Abstract. Quantum computing threatens traditional public-key algorithms such as RSA and ECC, both vulnerable to Shor's algorithm, making the transition to NIST-standardized Post-Quantum Cryptography (PQC) urgent for most TLS deployments. We present an open-source framework for automated TLS packet analysis to detect quantum-vulnerable algorithms using hierarchical filtering and hybrid certificate extraction that enables TLS 1.3 analysis without full decryption, achieving over 96% detection accuracy. This hierarchical filtering is expected to be particularly effective for large-scale packet analysis, enabling efficient and selective inspection of relevant TLS sessions. A practical evaluation of our work on real TLS traffic demonstrates its applicability in real-world environments, showing that most major service providers have largely transitioned to TLS 1.3, with a few already experimenting with hybrid handshake mechanisms. These findings illustrate that the framework can be readily applied for practical cryptographic inventory and migration planning, providing visibility into actual deployments rather than relying solely on theoretical compliance.

Keywords: Cryptographic Agility · Transport Layer Security · Post-Quantum Cryptography · Packet Inspection · Automated Analysis

1 Introduction

In the digital era, data transmission security is of paramount importance, and the Transport Layer Security (TLS) protocol serves as the standard for ensuring confidentiality, integrity, and authentication in internet communications. However, advancements in quantum computing pose significant risks to the public-key algorithms currently employed in TLS 1.2 and 1.3, such as RSA, Diffie-Hellman, and Elliptic Curve Cryptography, which are vulnerable to quantum algorithms like Shor's algorithm. Consequently, the adoption of post-quantum cryptography (PQC) and the upgrading of TLS protocols are imperative to safeguard future data protection and internet security. However, while the theoretical vulnerabilities of current cryptographic algorithms to quantum attacks are well-documented, the actual deployment status across heterogeneous enterprise environments remains largely unknown, hampering effective migration planning. To address this challenge, it is necessary to develop systems capable of real-time analysis of TLS traffic to automatically assess the cryptographic algorithms in use and provide visibility into actual deployment configurations. Such systems collect and classify TLS handshake information from network packets generated by diverse applications and operating systems, enabling organizations to understand their current quantum resilience posture and develop data-driven transition strategies.

1.1 Contributions

The main contributions of this study are as follows:

- **Open-source Framework for Automated Packet-Level Detection of Vulnerable TLS Configurations**: The proposed framework, released as an open-source implementation[1]. It automatically identifies TLS configurations containing insecure cipher suites and protocol implementations across various platforms without requiring access to server-side keys.
- **Comprehensive Framework for Cryptographic Agility in the Quantum Era**: This work assess post-quantum readiness and provides theoretical insights and practical guidelines for achieving sustainable cryptographic agility and long-term system resilience in the quantum era. Its effectiveness has been demonstrated through experimental validation across diverse environments.
- **Detection of TLS Hybrid Handshake with Emerging Post-Quantum Algorithms**: This work also incorporates the analysis of hybrid handshake packets. In particular, post-quantum algorithms corresponding to NIST security level 1 are classified as quantum-vulnerable due to the uncertainties of evolving quantum threat models.
- **Efficient and Robust Packet Filtering**: Our approach combines hierarchical filtering with protocol-aware parsing that leverages the structural characteristics of the data to achieve robustness and efficiency. In particular, we introduce a hybrid certificate parsing method that uses OID-based matching and selective OpenSSL parsing to accurately extract certificate fields and support precise analysis without full decryption.

2 Related Works

2.1 Transport Layer Security

Transport Layer Security (TLS) is the standard protocol for protecting communications over the Internet and other open networks, with the primary goals of

---

providing confidentiality, integrity, and authentication between communicating parties. Currently, TLS 1.2 and TLS 1.3 are the most widely deployed versions. Figure 1 illustrates the handshake sequences between client and server for each TLS version, including key negotiation, authentication, and the establishment of encrypted communication [1]. While TLS 1.2 follows a complex handshake procedure, TLS 1.3, standardized in 2018, simplifies it by reducing message exchanges and removing obsolete features. Through the keyshare extension, it further decouples key exchange algorithms from cipher suites, enabling more flexible combinations (see Fig. 1).

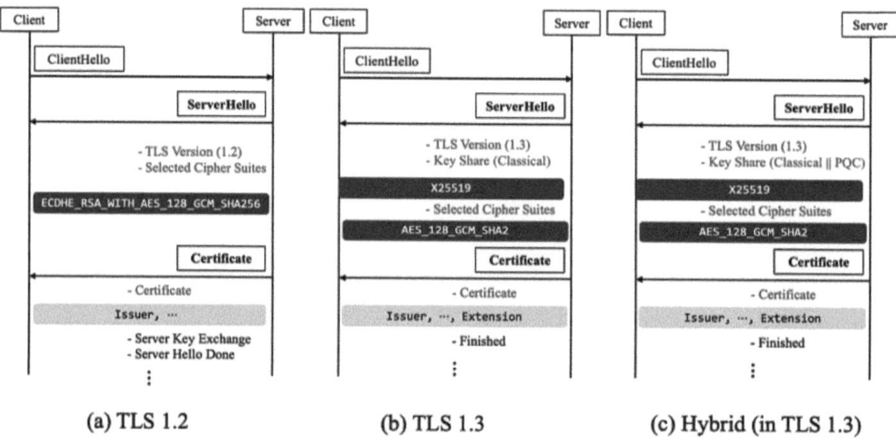

Fig. 1. Comparison of TLS 1.2, TLS 1.3, and hybrid handshake in TLS 1.3.

Hybrid Handshake in TLS 1.3. Hybrid handshake denotes a key exchange and certificatation mechanism wherein a classical algorithm (e.g., X25519) is combined with a post-quantum algorithm (e.g., ML-KEM) to establish a cryptographic session. This strategy is intended to provide robustness against both classical and quantum-capable adversaries. By concurrently executing both key exchange operations and deriving the session key from the aggregation of the resulting shared secrets, hybrid TLS maintains confidentiality even in the event that one of the constituent algorithms is subsequently broken. This also applies to digital signatures used for certificate (see Sect. 2.1).

Cipher Suites. The cipher suite field represents the results of the negotiation (e.g., key exchange, authentication, encryption, and integrity protection) between the client and server of the cryptographic parameters to be used for this connection. In TLS 1.2, the cipher suite includes key exchange and the authenticated encryption with associated data (AEAD) algorithm[2]. In TLS 1.3, a cipher suite specifies only AEAD and the hash function for record protection, while key exchange mechanisms are negotiated separately during the handshake via distinct messages—such as *key_ share* extension in the ServerHello message.

Certificate. TLS employs X.509 certificates [2] to authenticate servers and clients. Certificate includes critical fields such as the issuer, validity period, and a digital signature that ensures the authenticity and integrity of the certificate contents.

Starting from TLS 1.3, however, the certificate message transmitted after the *ServerHello* is encrypted to prevent man-in-the-middle attacks. As a result, it becomes significantly more difficult to directly inspect certificate contents by simply capturing network traffic. This encryption poses a substantial challenge to traditional vulnerability analysis tools, which typically rely on unencrypted certificate data to assess security weaknesses.

Quantum-Safe Certificates. To ensure long-term cryptographic resilience, a migration to post-quantum signature schemes is essential. A representative approach to incorporating post-quantum cryptography into certificates is the hybrid certificate, in which a classical and a post-quantum signature algorithm are used at different levels of the certificate chain. In addition to this strategy, other methods such as composite certificates [3,4], which combine multiple public keys and signatures within a single certificate structure, and parallel certificates [4], where distinct certificates are issued and validated separately for each algorithm, have also been proposed. Recent experimental studies [5,6] have explored the integration of PQC-based certificates into TLS 1.3 handshakes, providing early evidence of the feasibility of post-quantum authentication within the existing TLS infrastructure.

2.2   Security Vulnerabilities in TLS

The security properties and vulnerabilities of TLS primarily stem from its protocol version and supported cipher suites. Accordingly, we categorize them into protocol-level vulnerabilities and quantum vulnerabilities (QV) based on the applicable attack. TLS 1.2 and TLS 1.3 employ RSA- and ECC-based algorithms that are vulnerable to Shor's and Grover's algorithms. TLS 1.2, however, is additionally exposed to downgrade attacks and uses the legacy algorithms such as RC4 and 3DES, whereas TLS 1.3 eliminates these deprecated primitives.

Protocol Vulnerability. TLS 1.2 greatly improved security over previous versions, but remains vulnerable if legacy options are enabled. Notable risks include lack of mandatory forward secrecy, support for deprecated algorithms (e.g., RC4,

---

[2] AEAD algorithms provide both confidentiality and integrity by combining encryption and authentication in a single cryptographic primitive.

3DES), and susceptibility to attacks such as POODLE and Lucky13 [7,8]. TLS 1.3 addresses these issues by enforcing forward secrecy, removing insecure algorithms, encrypting more handshake data, and providing built-in downgrade protection.

Quantum Vulnerability. Even in the case of TLS 1.3, It is uses public-key cryptographic algorithms vulnerable to Shor's algorithm and symmetric-key cryptography that is weakened by Grover's algorithm. In terms of the post quantum cryptography, according to [9], the estimated attack cost of Kyber-512 is roughly 2^{151} gates, while the realistic cost including memory-access overheads is estimated around 2^{160}, within an uncertainty range of 2^{140}-2^{180}. In [10], a refined cost estimation of the Shortest Vector Problem (SVP) indicates that the estimated cost for ML-KEM-512 (Kyber-512) lies close to the lower bound of NIST's intended level 1 security range, suggesting a relatively narrow security margin. Moreover, a recent quantum circuit-based evaluation shows that the security level of ML-KEM and ML-DSA decreases by 15-27 bits compared to the classical sieve [11]. These findings imply that the security margin of level 1 parameters continues to narrow; therefore, under conservative design assumptions, level 1 may not always provide sufficient robustness.

Accordingly, quantum vulnerabilities in PQC must be taken into account. In this work, our analysis includes PQC algorithms that offer a security level comparable to AES-128, as defined by NIST.

2.3   Cryptographic Agility

Cryptographic agility refers to the capability of a system to transition between cryptographic algorithms or configurations with minimal operational disruption. As highlighted in NIST's Cyber Security White Paper (CSWP) [12], crypto agility is not merely the ability to support multiple algorithms, but rather hinges on the ability to accurately identify which algorithms, cipher suites, and protocol parameters are currently in use. This identification enables timely responses to newly discovered vulnerabilities, algorithm deprecation, or evolving compliance requirements.

Accordingly, this work aims to identify protocol configurations and cryptographic algorithms that potentially undermine the security of TLS, thereby establishing the anticipatory response capability required for the implementation of cryptographic agility.

2.4   Overview of TLS Packet Analysis Technologies

In modern network environments, the TLS protocol is extensively utilized across a broad spectrum of applications, including web browsers, messenger services, and cloud platforms. However, each application employs a distinct TLS implementation, resulting in differences in supported cipher suites and security policies, which clearly limits the effectiveness of manual analysis. Consequently, the development and deployment of reliable packet analysis tools and automated frameworks have become essential requirements.

Focus and Gaps in Previous Works. Prior studies mainly examined protocol structures and server vulnerabilities, while automated systems for assessing quantum vulnerabilities in TLS components remain limited. The proposed framework automates packet parsing and cipher extraction, integrating real-time capture with a PQC-based engine to evaluate quantum risks in cryptographic algorithms and key exchanges.

Table 1 presents a comparative analysis of existing studies, focusing on automated systems that systematically evaluate the quantum vulnerability of cryptographic components used in TLS packet communication. A ✓ indicates that the tool supports detection of quantum vulnerabilities in TLS traffic. A ✗ symbol denotes the absence of support for detecting cryptographic algorithms that are vulnerable to quantum attacks.

Table 1. Comparison of related works for automated analysis of TLS packet.

Reference	TLS Type	QV Detection	Target algorithms
IBM Guardium [13]	Classical	✓	Legacy ciphers
TYCHON [14]	Classical	✓	Legacy ciphers
AâĂŚPackets [15]	Classical	✗	Deprecated ciphers
TLS-attacker [16]	Classical	✗	Legacy ciphers
This Work	Classical, Hybrid	✓	Legacy ciphers, PQC

IBM Guardium [13] supports TLS traffic inspection and assessment of cryptographic configurations for quantum vulnerabilities, but does not explicitly provide automated detection of hybrid key exchange in PQC environments. TYCHON [14] is a cybersecurity platform offering endpoint visibility and behavioral analytics, with TLS metadata analysis to identify insecure or non-compliant cryptographic configurations. A-Packets [15] is a TLS traffic analysis framework focused on detecting deprecated cipher suites such as RC4 and 3DES. TLS-Attacker [16] primarily focuses on analyzing TLS implementation flaws and protocol vulnerabilities using legacy algorithms, without supporting quantum threat analysis. Unlike prior works, the proposed framework specifically targets hybrid TLS configurations and provides automated detection of quantum-vulnerable components. Notably, it extends its detection scope to include PQC algorithms corresponding to NIST-defined security level 1, in addition to legacy cryptographic algorithms.

In addition to the TLS-focused tools summarized in Table 1, several broader commercial tools address cryptographic visibility and PQC migration at an enterprise scale (see Table 2). These offerings extend beyond TLS inspection to support multiple protocols—such as SSH, VPN, and application-level encryption—thereby providing end-to-end coverage of cryptographic assets.

Table 2. Overview of enterprise-grade tools supporting PQC migration.

Product	Scope	Supported Protocols
Palo Alto [17]	Firewall & governance	TLS 1.3
PQStation [18]	Cryptographic management	TLS, SSH, VPN
SandboxAQ [19]	Governance	TLS, File systems

A unifying characteristic is their orientation toward post-quantum migration strategies, which combine cryptographic inventory, risk assessment, and phased deployment of quantum-resistant algorithms. By targeting diverse protocols and enterprise-wide infrastructures, these commercial solutions highlight the growing industry focus on comprehensive readiness for the post-quantum era [17–19].

While commercial portfolios excel in delivering enterprise-grade governance and migration capabilities at scale, we propose an open-source framework that aims to provide transparency and accessibility, offering a research-oriented resource for further study and experimentation.

3   Proposed Methods

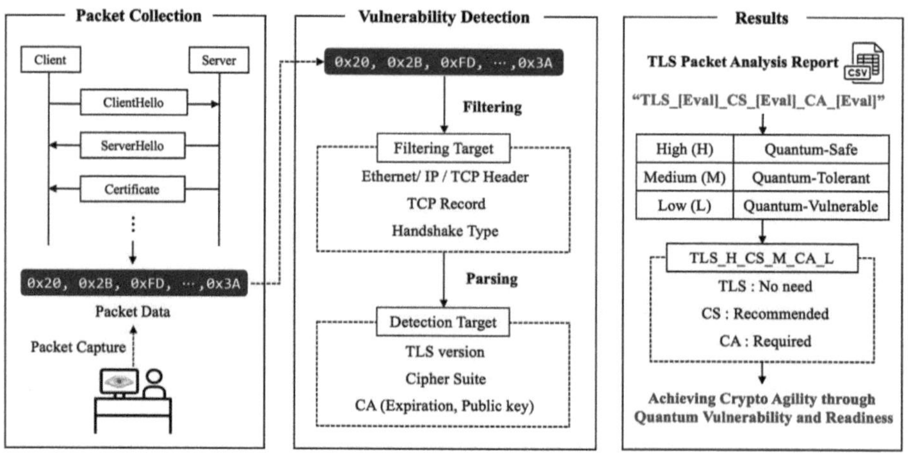

Fig. 2. System Overview.

The proposed method achieves quantum-safe TLS security by automatically detecting and evaluating the vulnerability of TLS cryptographic elements from network packets. It comprises three core components: packet filtering, vulnerability detection, and evaluation with result report (see Fig. 2).

Our system captures network packet from the TLS handshake process during client–server communication and automatically analyzes the packets to identify potential quantum vulnerabilities. The evaluation focuses on three key elements: TLS version, cipher suite, and the certificate. Each element is assessed based on its security level—classified as high, medium, or low. The results are presented in a compact format: TLS_Evaluation result_CS_Evaluation result_CA_Evaluation result. For instance, if TLS 1.3 is used with AES-128 and SHA-256, the result is represented as TLS_H_CS_M. The certificate is also evaluated based on its expiration date: if it is set to expire within 90 days[3], it is considered due for renewal. Therefore, Certificates with an expiry date within 90 days are marked as True, while all others are marked as False.

In our work, TLS records that fail to meet the prescribed length requirements are classified as incomplete and discarded. Parsing proceeds by interpreting length fields and their associated values, but any inconsistency or truncation results in immediate termination to prevent misinterpretation.

3.1   Efficient Packet Filtering

Prior to the detection phase, we capture network traffic to obtain raw packet data. Since the packets vary in type, we apply a two-phase filtering process to extract only the traffic relevant to our analysis.

Network Filtering. To improve analytical efficiency and avoid unnecessary inspection of the entire network, the proposed system employs a hierarchical traffic filtering approach. It supports two types of targeting: selection of the network interface and Server Name Indication (SNI) filtering. Packets are first filtered from a user-specified network interface, after which only traffic associated with selected domains is retained for analysis.

Packet Filtering. Figure 3 illustrates the structure of the Ethernet, IPv4, and TCP headers. Each of these headers contains multiple fields, and they are filtered in sequence to identify and extract TLS handshake packets. The purpose of this procedure is to precisely determine the offset of each protocol layer (i.e., Ethernet, IP, and TCP layers) to reduce parsing error. To achieve this, field-level information is extracted based on standardized header structures.

Ethernet Header Filtering. The Ethernet header has a fixed size of 14 bytes, and packets are passed to the next parsing step only if the ethernet type field indicates IPv4 [20]. Since the vast majority of real-world Internet traffic—particularly in the context of encrypted communication and attack detection—is based on IPv4, non-IPv4 packets are excluded from subsequent processing[4].

---

[3] Certificates are generally renewed within 90 days prior to their expiration. See DigiCert documentation https://docs.digicert.com/en/certcentral/manage-certificates/renew-an-ssl-tls-certificate.html.

[4] See https://www.potaroo.net/ispcol/2025-01/bgp2024.html.

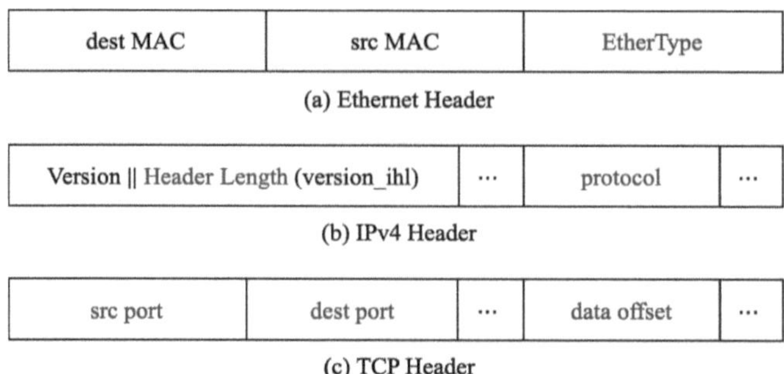

Fig. 3. Header Structure of Ethernet, IPv4 and TCP.

IPv4 Header Filtering. The IPv4 header is typically 20 bytes when no options are present, but its length varies if options are included. Therefore, the *version_ihl* field, which contains the length information of the IPv4 header, is used to extract the actual header length. Most encrypted application-layer traffic (e.g., HTTPS) is based on TCP, so only packets with the *protocol* field set to TCP are extracted during the filtering process to reduce unnecessary overhead in the analysis [21].

TCP Header Filtering. Similar to the IPv4 header, the TCP header parsing step requires extracting the header length. This is accomplished by interpreting the *data_offset* field, which specifies the length of the TCP header.

TLS Record Filtering. A TLS Record is a logical unit for transmitting application data and control messages, consisting of a header and payload [22]. Its location is determined by adding the TCP header length to the TCP layer start, since the TLS record begins immediately thereafter.

TLS Handshake Type Filtering. If the TLS record corresponds to a handshake message, it contains a handshake header, wherein the first field specifies the type of handshake message. As cryptographic vulnerability analysis primarily depends on key exchange and authentication information, only three handshake types are parsed in this work: *ClientHello*, *ServerHello*, and *Certificate* types. They are the parts where cryptographic negotiation information and certificates are first explicitly specified.

Port Filtering. TLS traffic is isolated by filtering on destination port numbers, allowing us to narrow the target traffic scope. Specifically, this work focuses on traffic associated with ports 443, 8443, and 4450. Port 443 is the default for HTTPS and serves as the global standard for TLS-encrypted communications [23], while port 8443 is commonly used as an alternative SSL/TLS service port in major web application servers [24,25]. Port 4450 is additionally included based on user-specific configurations.

3.2   Vulnerability Detection

In this section, we describe the parsing procedure used to detect cryptographic elements relevant to vulnerability analysis. Our work aims to extract essential cryptographic information from TLS packets to support lightweight and efficient vulnerability detection. From the records filtered in the previous stage, the system selectively parses only the fields directly related to the cryptographic configuration and vulnerability assessment.

Detection Targets. Handshake-type records contain several protocol fields (e.g., server version, session ID and extension[5]). Table 3 summarizes the selected TLS handshake fields and their corresponding extracted elements used for cryptographic vulnerability evaluation.

Table 3. Selected fields and information of TLS handshake.

Handshake Type	Field	Extracted Information
ClientHello	Extension	SNI
ServerHello	Cipher Suite Extension	cryptographic algorithm protocol version, key share
Certificate	Certificate	public key algorithm, issuer, validity expiration

SNI. It is used for domain filtering and session identification. Within the SNI field, the type of SNI is distinguished by the name type; however, in practice, only the domain type (i.e., a type value of 0x00) is utilized [27]. This enables selective traffic analysis based on user-configured domain addresses, which is essential for targeting specific TLS sessions during vulnerability evaluation.

Cipher Suite. The cipher suite filed, which specifies the collection of algorithms used for encryption, key exchange, and authentication, serves as a critical indicator for assessing quantum vulnerability and overall security. In this work, to comprehensively analyze the latest standards in network security and recent trends in post-quantum cryptography adoption, the focus is placed on the representative protocols of TLS 1.2 and TLS 1.3 (conventional and hybrid handshake).

Parsing Strategies for Robust and Efficient Detection. To ensure accurate and reliable vulnerability detection, we propose two core parsing strategies. These methods are applied in the certificate detection phase and are designed to

---

[5] In TLS 1.2, extensions are optional; however, in TLS 1.3, certain extensions are mandatory, resulting in a consistently present extension structure [26].

address structural variability and practical limitations associated with real-world TLS packet inspection.

Protocol Version. The *supported_versions*) field is used to indicate the TLS version employed in a given session. For backward compatibility, TLS 1.3 mandates that the protocol version field be set to the same value as TLS 1.2 (i.e., its field value is 0x0303) [28]. Consequently, it is not possible to distinguish between TLS 1.2 and TLS 1.3 solely based on the protocol version field. The presence of the supported_versions extension reveals TLS 1.3, explicitly indicating its use

Key Share. In TLS 1.3, cipher suites are composed solely of AEAD and hash algorithms [28]. Consequently, the *key_share* extension is mandatory in TLS 1.3 to facilitate key exchange. Therefore, key exchange information cannot be determined from the cipher suite alone, necessitating additional parsing. The key share algorithm value is located 4 bytes from the starting offset of the key_share extension.

Public Key Algorithm. The public key algorithm is identified based on the OID value specified in the X.509 certificate [29]. It enables the detection of certificate forgery, such as system errors or man-in-the-middle attacks, by comparing with the cipher suite [30].

As target algorithms, we consider RSA and ECDSA, which are widely recommended for use in TLS 1.2 and TLS 1.3 [31]; Ed25519, standardized in TLS 1.3 [28]; and ML-DSA 44, a post-quantum digital signature algorithm recently standardized by NIST [32].

Issuer. Issuer field is parsed to evaluate the trustworthiness of the certificate issuer. Although the issuer field in a certificate contains various subfields as defined in the standard [33], the Common Name (CN) is considered the most suitable identifier for general users to assess trustworthiness. Therefore, the CN field[6] is chosen for parsing and output as the issuer's name.

Validity Expiration. The certificate's validity expiration date is a key factor in renewal decisions and migration timing. Since the ASN.1 TIME field may be encoded in either UTCTime or GeneralizedTime, simple pattern matching is unreliable [34]. Thus, the certificate is converted into an X.509 structure via OpenSSL, and the notAfter field is directly retrieved.

Effective Certificates Detection. Conventional TLS packet analysis tools primarily evaluate vulnerabilities based on certificate information contained in captured traffic. However, since the certificate message is encrypted in TLS 1.3 and beyond, extraction of certificates by packet capture alone is impossible (see Sect. 2.1). Therefore, additional decryption procedures are required, such as obtaining secret keys or session keys (e.g., session key log file) from the client side to verify certificate information [35,36].

To reduce overhead, the system immediately establishes a separate TLS client connection via a dynamic server connection method using the SNI value based

---

[6] To obtain the issuer's CN, the process involves searching the certificate for the CN OID byte value. The OID value is \x06\x03\x55\x04\x03.

on OpenSSL. This connection automatically negotiates the protocol version with the server and sends the SNI extension during the handshake to retrieve the latest certificate chain in real time, thereby eliminating the overhead of decrypting encrypted certificate messages and significantly enhancing the reliability of vulnerability analysis. The reason for not parsing all packets using the OpenSSL-based approach is processing efficiency. Full parsing with OpenSSL requires significantly more time compared to simple byte matching[7]. As the goal of this work is real-time packet analysis, it is necessary to minimize processing delays. Therefore, to minimize processing delays for real-time analysis, the study prioritizes byte matching when information can be extracted without decryption, resorting to OpenSSL-based matching only when decryption is necessary or when packet errors hinder information retrieval.

Precise OID-based Extraction of Certificate Fields. The public key algorithm and issuer fields are extracted from the certificate by searching for their OID-encoded values within the entire byte sequence. For example, when a certificate is represented as a 32-byte hexadecimal sequence, the public key algorithm and issuer fields appear only in the form of OIDs within this data, making them uniquely identifiable. This structure-agnostic approach was adopted to address the unreliability of offset-based parsing, as the standard X.509 certificate format features variable field lengths and non-fixed ordering (see Sect. 2.1). For instance, when a certificate is represented as a 32-byte hexadecimal sequence, the public key algorithm and issuer fields appear only as OIDs within this data, enabling unique identification.

Experimental validation shows that the hybrid parser produces public-key and issuer field values equivalent to those obtained from the OpenSSL-only baseline. The quantitative analysis of fallback frequency remains as future work, where the number of fallback cases will be explicitly measured and reported.

Table 4. Comparison of certificate parsing strategies.

Component	OpenSSL-Only Parsing	This work
Public key	OpenSSL	OID
Issuer	OpenSSL	CN/ORG OID
X. 509 conversion	Always performed	On-demand
Validity period	OpenSSL	
Execution time (ms/certificate)	182.5720	179.1399

Advantages of the Certificate Parsing Strategy. Table 4 compares the conventional OpenSSL-based certificate parsing method with the proposed hybrid

---

[7] Performance concerns with the OpenSSL d2i_X509 function for ASN.1 DER-encoded certificate parsing have been previously discussed. https://github.com/openssl/openssl/issues/17950.

approach. The traditional model processes all certificate fields—including the public key, issuer, validity period, and X.509 conversion—through the OpenSSL API, ensuring accuracy but incurring computational overhead in real-time analysis environments. The hybrid approach introduces selective OID-based pattern matching for extracting public key and issuer information, invoking OpenSSL only when matching fails. Validity parsing remains OpenSSL-based due to the ASN.1 TIME structure, and X.509 structure conversion is deferred until explicitly required. This selective strategy enhances performance by replacing full OpenSSL operations with lightweight byte-pattern matching when possible. Experiments conducted on 597 certificates over ten runs showed an average parsing time of 179.14 ms per certificate—1.88% faster than the conventional method (182.57 ms)—indicating substantial efficiency gains in large-scale packet analysis scenarios.

3.3   Vulnerability Evaluation

Finally, the vulnerability of TLS packets is evaluated based on the security-relevant information extracted from the filtered packets. Each level reflects both classical and quantum-era considerations, incorporating protocol versions, algorithm strength, and susceptibility to known attacks. To adopt a conservative stance toward security threats, the cryptographic level is determined based on the weakest algorithm among the key exchange, encryption, and hash functions used in the cipher suite.

- **High (H):** This includes TLS 1.3 with enhanced protocol security features and symmetric primitives and post-quantum algorithms (e.g., AES-256, ML-DSA-2/3/5, ML-KEM-1024) that conform to NIST post-quantum security levels 2–5, which can withstand quantum attacks using Grover's algorithm.
- **Medium (M):** This includes TLS 1.2 and symmetric primitives such as AES-128 and SHA-256, which may be exposed to vulnerabilities due to legacy components. In particular, symmetric encryption and hashing components are emphasized in this category, while public-key algorithms used for key exchange or authentication remain purely classical and are not treated as post-quantum secure.
- **Low (L):** This includes TLS versions (≤ 1.1) and quantum-vulnerable public-key systems, which are considered insecure due to both cryptographic and protocol-level flaws, regardless of quantum considerations.
- **True and False (T/F):** To reflect the trend of adopting short renewal cycles within 90 days to maintain cryptographic agility, this criterion applies only to certificates to note the migration timing: certificates set to expire within 90 days are marked as True, while all others are marked as False.

4   Results

In this section, we present the results of our proposed approach. In particular, we provide an in-depth analysis of quantum vulnerability and readiness, along with a case study focusing on domestic (i.e., South Korea) and global enterprises.

4.1   Experimental Setup

Table 5 summarizes the experimental setup including operating systems, packet capture tools, and PQC libraries used in this work. In this work, we collected and analyzed a large volume of real-time TLS packets generated by 20 major enterprises (e.g., Google and YouTube) across both Windows 11 and Kali Linux environments. This dataset enabled a comprehensive evaluation of the proposed framework across heterogeneous platforms and real-world usage scenarios.

Table 5. Experimental environment including operating systems and libraries.

OS	Library		
	Packet capture	PQC	Crypto/Comm.
Windows	WinPcap	OQS	OpenSSL
Linux	libpcap		

4.2   Performance

Confusion Matrix and Recall. We utilize a multi-class confusion matrix (with classes High, Medium, and Low) to visualize the classification results of our system across the three key TLS-related fields. Each matrix compares the predicted labels against manually verified ground truth, enabling observation of the distribution of true positives (TP), true negatives (TN), false positives (FP), and false negatives (FN) for each class. We collected and classified quantum vulnerability and readiness data from a total of 192 TLS sessions (SNI) through real-time packet analysis. This confirms that the three core elements—TLS version, cipher suite, and PQC migration requirements—were successfully classified.

Figure 4 visualizes the confusion matrix for each classification item. For example, in the case of (a) TLS version classification, there were 164 actual TLS 1.3 (High) sessions out of 192 total, and our system correctly classified 158 of these as High. To evaluate the performance of our system, we focus on $recall$[8], which quantifies the proportion of actual positives correctly identified by the system. Recall is formally defined as $TP/(TP + FN)$. A high recall indicates that the system successfully captures the majority of relevant instances, which is particularly critical in security contexts to minimize overlooked vulnerabilities. In our evaluation, recall is computed separately for each key element—TLS version, cipher suite, and certificate—to assess how accurately the system extracts each field from TLS packet data. In cases of errors, our framework may have failed to receive complete TLS packets due to unexpected interruptions. However, such errors constitute only a small fraction of the dataset. Despite these limitations, the proposed framework demonstrates consistently high accuracy overall.

---

[8] Recall and related evaluation metrics are computed by comparing the result of our work against manually verified ground truth.

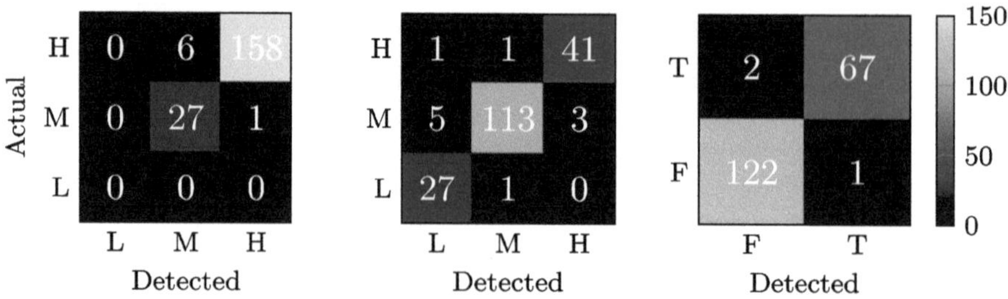

Fig. 4. Visualization of the confusion matrix of (a) TLS version, (b) cipher suite, and (c) migration requirements.

Table 6 shows the recall results of our system. The overall recall for TLS version classification is approximately 96.35% (= 185/192). For cipher suite classification, the overall recall is approximately 94.27% (= 181/192). For PQC migration requirement classification, the overall recall is approximately 98.44% (= 189/192). These results indicate that the proposed system can accurately extract critical security information from real-time TLS packets, ensuring that potential vulnerabilities are not overlooked.

Table 6. Recall for TLS version, cipher suite, and PQC migration requirement.

Evaluation Category	Recall (%)	Correct/Total
TLS Version	96.35	185/192
Cipher Suite	94.27	181/192
PQC Migration Requirement	98.44	189/192

4.3   Application to Real-World Enterprise TLS Traffic

Quantum-readiness is comparatively analyzed for both domestic and global enterprises based on the vulnerability evaluation proposed in this work. Table 7 and Table 8 present the analysis results of the cryptographic algorithms used in TLS communications and the certificate status for domestic and global enterprises, respectively. According to the quantum-vulnerability and quantum-readiness analysis of this work, major domestic service providers in Korea still predominantly utilize TLS 1.2-based communication, and their certificates primarily employ the RSA algorithm, which is known to be vulnerable. In contrast, leading global enterprises have mostly adopted the latest standard, TLS 1.3, by default, and operate with cipher suites that provide a higher level of security.

Table 7. Security level and quantum readiness in domestic enterprises (based on our system; see Sect. 3.3).

Enterprise	TLS ver.	Key Exchange	Cipher Suite	Certificate	Renewal Cycle
Naver	1.3 (H)	ECDHE (L)	AES_128_SHA256 (M)	RSA (L)	90
Coupang					393
Kakao			AES_256_SHA384 (H)		392
SK Telecom					396
Samsung	1.2 (M)	ECDHE_RSA (L)	AES_128_SHA256 (M)		396
Hyundai					322
YES24					396
Kiwoom					335
Toss			AES_256_SHA384 (H)		335
Shinhan Bank					335

Table 8. Security level and quantum readiness in global enterprises (based on our system; see Sect. 3.3).

Enterprise	TLS ver.	Key Exchange	Cipher Suite	Certificate	Renewal Cycle
Google	1.3 (H)	ML-KEM-768_ECDHE (H)	AES_128_SHA256 (M)	ECC (L)	84
Instagram					90
YouTube					84
Netflix		ECDHE (L)		RSA (L)	396
Amazon					359
Microsoft					180
Apple					85
PayPal		ML-KEM-768_ECDHE (H)			364
Tesla		ECDHE (L)	AES_256_SHA384 (H)		90
Mastercard	1.2 (M)	ECDHE_RSA (L)			364

In order to provide a fair, normalized comparison between domestic and global enterprises, the security configuration data from Tables 7 and 8 are transformed into quantitative *quantum readiness* scores for five evaluation indicators. TLS 1.3 adoption was 40% domestically versus 90% globally; post-quantum hybrid key exchange usage was 0% (low-security ECDHE only) domestically, 40% globally. Cipher suite adoption was 100% for medium/high security in both groups; ECC/PQC certificate usage was 0%. Certificate renewal within 90 days was 40% domestically and 50% globally. These metrics collectively indicate the level of post-quantum migration preparedness. In all five indicators, a higher percentage reflects a greater degree of preparedness for post-quantum security migration (see Fig. 5).

This analysis of major domestic and global enterprises reveals a clear contrast in quantum-readiness. While global enterprises have largely adopted the TLS 1.3 and some are even taking proactive steps by experimenting with hybrid PQC key exchange methods like ML-KEM-768_ECDHE, domestic enterprises still predominantly use TLS 1.2 and rely on vulnerable RSA-based certificates. This

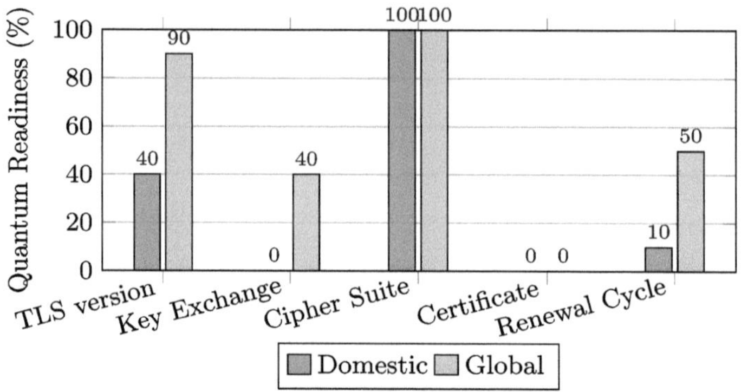

Fig. 5. Comparison of quantum readiness across five indicators: TLS version, key exchange, cipher suite, certificate, and renewal cycle.

disparity highlights a relative lack of cryptographic agility in domestic enterprises compared to their global counterparts.

Certificate Expiry and Migration. Based on the analysis of certificate validity periods and associated vulnerabilities, an appropriate timeline for PQC transition can be established. This study observed a significant number of certificates with impending expiration dates. Despite a global trend towards shorter certificate lifetimes to minimize exposure[9], domestic enterprises predominantly utilize certificates with approximately one-year validity periods[10]. This practice implies potential delays in system-wide updates, as legacy certificates must expire before deploying new quantum-safe certificates.

Toward Quantum-Readiness Infrastructure. The analysis reveals that major domestic enterprises exhibit significantly lower quantum security readiness than global counterparts, primarily due to reliance on TLS 1.2 and vulnerable algorithms. As quantum threats materialize, this imbalance may cause severe long-term risks. Urgent establishment of a comprehensive PQC transition roadmap—beyond mere TLS upgrades to include replacing RSA with PQC-based key exchange and authentication—is imperative. The proposed framework aids enterprises in objectively assessing quantum vulnerabilities and planning effective migration.

---

[9] Internationally, there is a growing mandate to gradually reduce the maximum validity period of certificates to as little as 47 days. See https://www.digicert.com/blog/tls-certificate-lifetimes-will-officially-reduce-to-47-days.

[10] With the exception of Naver, the domestic enterprises survey all had certificate validity periods of approximately one year, whereas about half of the global enterprises had periods of around 90 days.

5   Conclusion

This paper presented a framework for automatically detecting the cryptographic algorithms used in the TLS protocol and identifying those vulnerable in the presence of quantum computers. By analyzing network packets to extract cipher suite information and applying targeted filtering strategies, including a method for examining encrypted TLS 1.3 certificates without decryption, the framework enables systematic evaluation of TLS deployments with respect to quantum-related vulnerabilities.

The necessity of this framework lies in the fact that although NIST has already established concrete standards and identified algorithms vulnerable to quantum attacks, it is essential to provide visibility and awareness of the actual deployment status of these "already known vulnerable algorithms" to realize cryptographic agility. Furthermore, this framework aims to serve as a practical foundation for effectively managing post-quantum cryptographic (PQC) migration based on specific standards in the future.

Our approach achieves over 96% accuracy in packet-based detection. Notably, the proposed hybrid certificate parsing strategy minimizes unnecessary decryption overhead by combining lightweight OID-based pattern matching with selective OpenSSL parsing. This design not only preserves parsing accuracy but also reduces processing time in large-scale analyses, making the framework more practical for real-time TLS traffic evaluation. In addition, our analysis of domestic and international TLS deployments reveals significant quantum-readiness gaps: global enterprises show 90% TLS 1.3 adoption and 40% post-quantum hybrid implementations, while domestic enterprises lag with only 40% TLS 1.3 adoption and zero post-quantum implementations. These findings highlight the urgent need for domestic services to accelerate PQC migration and demonstrate the framework's utility for data-driven transition planning.

Acknowledgment. This work was supported by Institute of Information & communications Technology Planning & Evaluation (IITP) grant funded by the Korea government(MSIT) (No. RS-2025-02306395, Development and Demonstration of PQC-Based Joint Certificate PKI Technology, 50%) and this work was supported by the Institute of Information & Communications Technology Planning & Evaluation(IITP) grant funded by the Korea government(MSIT) (No. RS-2025-25394739, Development of Security Enhancement Technology for Industrial Control Systems Based on S/HBOM Supply Chain Protection, 50%).

References

1. Dierks, T., Rescorla, E.: The Transport Layer Security (TLS) Protocol Version 1.2. Request for Comments RFC 5246, Internet Engineering Task Force (2008)
2. Cooper, D., Santesson, S., Farrell, S., Boeyen, S., Housley, R., Polk, W.: Internet X.509 public key infrastructure certificate and certificate revocation list (CRL) profile. Technical report, Internet Engineering Task Force (IETF) (2008)

3. Ounsworth, M., Gray, J., Pala, M., Klaußner, J.: Composite public and private keys for use in internet PKI (2023)
4. Wang, C., Xue, W., Wang, J.: Integration of quantum-safe algorithms into X.509v3 certificates. In: 2023 IEEE 3rd International Conference on Electronic Technology, Communication and Information (ICETCI), pp. 384–388. IEEE (2023)
5. Paul, S., Kuzovkova, Y., Lahr, N., Niederhagen, R.: Mixed certificate chains for the transition to post-quantum authentication in TLS 1.3. In: Proceedings of the 2022 ACM on Asia Conference on Computer and Communications Security, pp. 727–740 (2022)
6. Chen, A.C.: Post-quantum cryptography X.509 certificate. In: 2024 International Conference on Smart Systems for applications in Electrical Sciences (ICSSES), pp. 1–6. IEEE (2024)
7. AlFardan, N.J., Paterson, K.G.: Lucky thirteen: breaking the TLS and DTLS record protocols. In: Proceedings of the 2013 IEEE Symposium on Security and Privacy. Springer (2013)
8. Möller, B., Duong, T., Kotowicz, K.: This POODLE bites: exploiting the SSL 3.0 fallback. Technical report, Google (2014)
9. National Institute of Standards and Technology: FAQ on Kyber512 (2023). https://csrc.nist.gov/csrc/media/Projects/post-quantum-cryptography/documents/faq/Kyber-512-FAQ.pdf
10. Zhao, Z., Ding, J., Yang, B.-Y.: Sieving with streaming memory access. IACR Trans. Cryptogr. Hardw. Embed. Syst. **2025**(2), 362–384 (2025)
11. Cho, S.-M., Lee, C., Seo, S.-H.: Quantum security analysis of module-LWE PQC based on practical cost estimates. IACR Trans. Cryptogr. Hardw. Embed. Syst. **2025**(4), 437–462 (2025)
12. Scarfone, K., Polk, T., Ouyang, L., Davidson, M.: Considerations for achieving cryptographic agility: strategies and practices. Technical Report CSWP 39 (Initial Public Draft), National Institute of Standards and Technology (NIST). Initial Public Draft (2025)
13. IBM: IBM guardium for quantum-safe data security (2024). https://www.ibm.com/products/guardium-quantum-safe. Accessed 21 July 2025
14. TYCHON: PQC management module (2024). https://tychon.io/products/tychon/pqc-management-module/. Accessed 21 July 2025
15. A-Packets: A-packets: AI-powered network security solutions (2024). https://apackets.com/. Accessed 21 July 2025
16. Somorovsky, J.: TLS-attacker: breaking TLS by exploiting cryptographic vulnerabilities. In: Proceedings of the 2016 ACM SIGSAC Conference on Computer and Communications Security, pp. 2053–2054. ACM (2016)
17. Palo Alto Networks: Post-quantum migration planning and preparation (2024). https://docs.paloaltonetworks.com/network-security/quantum-security/administration/quantum-security-concepts/post-quantum-migration-planning-and-preparation. Accessed 23 Aug 2025
18. PQStation: Qvision: Cryptographic visibility and PQC migration support (2025). https://www.pqstation.com/offerings/qvision. Accessed 23 Aug 2025
19. SandboxAQ: Aqtive guard: unified cryptography management (2025). https://www.sandboxaq.com/solutions/aqtive-guard. Accessed 23 Aug 2025
20. Hedrick, C.L.: A Standard for the Transmission of IP Datagrams over Ethernet Networks. Request for Comments RFC 894, Internet Engineering Task Force. Ethernet (1984)
21. Rescorla, E.: HTTP Over TLS. Request for Comments RFC 2818, Internet Engineering Task Force. Informational (2000)

22. Dierks, T., Allen, C.: The Transport Layer Security (TLS) Protocol Version 1.0. Request for Comments RFC 2246, Internet Engineering Task Force (1999)
23. Reynolds, J., Postel, J.: Assigned Numbers. Request for Comments RFC 1700, Internet Engineering Task Force. Obsoleted by: RFC 3232 (1994)
24. Service name and transport protocol port number registry (2025). Accessed 22 July 2025
25. The Apache Software Foundation: Apache tomcat 9 (9.0.107) - SSL/TLS configuration how-to (2025). Accessed 22 July 2025
26. Eastlake, D.: Transport Layer Security (TLS) Extensions: Extension Definitions. Request for Comments RFC 6066, Internet Engineering Task Force (2011)
27. Ghedini, A., Varga, M.: SNI) Encryption. Request for Comments RFC 8744, Internet Engineering Task Force (2020)
28. Rescorla, E.: The Transport Layer Security (TLS) Protocol Version 1.3. Request for Comments RFC 8446, Internet Engineering Task Force (2018)
29. Cooper, D., Santesson, S., Farrell, S., Boeyen, R., Housley, W., Polk, T.: Internet X.509 Public Key Infrastructure Certificate and Certificate Revocation List (CRL) Profile. Request for Comments RFC 5280, Internet Engineering Task Force (2008)
30. de la Hoz, E., Cochrane, G., Moreira-Lemus, J.M., Paez-Reyes, R., Marsa-Maestre, I., Alarcos, B.: Detecting and defeating advanced man-in-the-middle attacks against TLS. In: 2014 6th International Conference on Cyber Conflict (CyCon), pp. 210–221. NATO CCD COE Publications, Tallinn (2014)
31. Federal Office for Information Security (BSI): Technical Guideline TR-02102-2: Cryptographic Mechanisms - Recommendations and Key Lengths, Part 2 – Use of Transport Layer Security (TLS). Technical report, Federal Office for Information Security (BSI) (2025). Accessed 29 July 2025
32. National Institute of Standards and Technology: Module-lattice-based digital signature standard. Federal Information Processing Standard FIPS 204, U.S. Department of Commerce (2024). Final version
33. Santesson, S., Polk, W., Barzin, P., Nystrom, M.: Internet X.509 Public Key Infrastructure Qualified Certificates Profile. Request for Comments RFC 3039, Internet Engineering Task Force (2001)
34. The OpenSSL Project Authors: ASN1_TIME_set and Related Functions - OpenSSL Manual. OpenSSL Project (2025). Accessed 29 July 2025
35. Wireshark Foundation: Wireshark - Official Website (2025). https://www.wireshark.org/. Accessed 27 July 2025
36. Wireshark Foundation: Transport Layer Security (TLS) - Wireshark Wiki (2020). https://wiki.wireshark.org/TLS. Accessed 27 July 2025

GhostWriter: Exploiting GPU-Cache Contention to Steal and Steer Multi-tenant Large-Language-Model Inference

Satyajit Das[1,2]( ) and Sreenath Vijayakumar[1]

[1] Indian Institute of Technology Palakkad, Palakkad, India
{satyajit,sreenath}@iitpkd.ac.in
[2] Indian Institute of Technology Guwahati, Guwahati, India

Abstract. Cloud providers routinely batch unrelated user prompts on shared Graphics Processing Units (GPUs) to amortize the escalating operational costs of large-language-model (LLM) inference. This paper demonstrates that such efficiency-driven optimizations introduce a potent microarchitectural side channel. We present *GhostWriter*, the first attack framework that *(i)* extracts private prompt tokens from co-located victims and *(ii)* covertly biases their generated text, all without requiring code execution privileges within the victim's process or access to the LLM's internal parameters. The attack exploits a subtle phenomenon: the residency of key–value (KV) cache entries in the GPU's L2 cache persists across batched tenants. This persistence manifests as minute, per-token latency skews—often only a few milliseconds—which, as we show, are statistically amplifiable. We formalize the threat model under realistic cloud deployment conditions and develop a robust statistical detector based on a frequentist z-test, which recovers target tokens with up to 96.2% accuracy on a GPT-Neo-125M model. Furthermore, we introduce an adversarial cache pre-loading strategy capable of increasing victim perplexity by up to 11% and flipping sentiment in 42% of news-style generations. Our end-to-end evaluation spans contemporary NVIDIA T4, A100, and consumer-grade RTX 4090 GPUs, popular inference stacks (including Triton Inference Server, vLLM, and Hugging Face Text Generation Inference), and realistic cloud batch sizes, confirming cross-tenant leakage under default configurations.

1 Introduction

The proliferation of LLMs has catalyzed transformative advancements across diverse natural language processing (NLP) applications, including sophisticated conversational agents, virtual assistants, automated content generation, programming assistance, and scientific discovery [16]. Models such as GPT-3 [2], PaLM, and LLaMA, which encompass hundreds of billions of parameters, exhibit remarkable capabilities in understanding complex queries, engaging in nuanced reasoning, and generating human-like text at an unprecedented scale. However, the substantial computational and memory resources demanded by these

C. Karfa et al. (Eds.): SPACE 2025, LNCS 16406, pp. 134–153, 2026.
https://doi.org/10.1007/978-3-032-16342-4_8

models—primarily driven by dense matrix multiplications within transformer blocks, computationally intensive attention mechanisms, and the maintenance of extensive key–value (KV) caches—present formidable challenges for their efficient and economically viable deployment. To surmount these challenges, cloud service providers increasingly adopt *inference-as-a-service* architectures. These platforms offer LLM capabilities via abstracted APIs, shielding users from the underlying hardware complexities and operational burdens. A cornerstone of these services is the pervasive optimization strategy of batching: the practice of combining prompts from multiple, often unrelated, users into a single inference pass. This maximizes GPU utilization, thereby amortizing the escalating serving costs. Paradoxically, this very optimization introduces a critical vulnerability: cross-tenant side-channel leakage, wherein a malicious tenant can infer sensitive information pertaining to co-located users by observing the side effects of shared hardware resource contention.

Side-channel attacks, which meticulously extract information from secondary physical effects such as timing variations, cache contention patterns, or power consumption fluctuations, have historically targeted CPU-based environments, virtualized infrastructures, and cryptographic workloads [6]. Recent research has extended these concerns to GPU architectures, exposing timing channels in CUDA kernel execution, shared memory contention, and even speculative execution behaviors within warp schedulers [3]. Nevertheless, the unique characteristics of LLM inference—particularly those of transformer-based architectures operating in batched, multi-tenant GPU settings—engender fundamentally new and largely underexplored attack surfaces. Our work diverges significantly from existing LLM attack vectors. Unlike gradient-based extraction attacks (e.g., *MemPrompt*, [15]), which typically require access to model gradients or other internal states, or adversarial suffix optimization techniques [18], which often necessitate fine-grained control over prompt construction and output formatting, *GhostWriter* operates without such privileges. Similarly, while coarse-grained timing attacks like LLM Timing Leaks can infer general model properties or aggregate prompt characteristics through API response times, our approach exploits microarchitectural cache contention at a much finer granularity. This allows us to recover exact token sequences from victim prompts and to actively perturb victim outputs, thereby demonstrating a qualitatively stronger and more direct form of leakage.

Specifically, transformer-based LLMs rely heavily on a key–value (KV) cache, a data structure that stores intermediate attention layer representations (keys and values) to accelerate the autoregressive decoding process. This KV cache typically resides in high-speed GPU memory, such as High Bandwidth Memory (HBM) or, for frequently accessed portions, the L2 cache, and persists across token generation steps to avoid redundant computations. In multi-tenant batching scenarios, the prevalent lack of strict cache isolation between tenant processes can lead to KV cache residues from one tenant persisting in shared memory hierarchies when another tenant's request is processed. This inadvertent persistence exposes exploitable leakage channels. While prior GPU attacks (e.g., *MemHam-*

mer, [5]) have targeted DRAM-level row hammer effects, our research focuses on the transformer-specific KV cache footprints within the L2 cache, which are intrinsically governed by token decoding patterns. This creates a unique, persistent, and statistically discernible side channel that an attacker can systematically probe. In this paper, we introduce *GhostWriter*, the first comprehensive end-to-end side-channel attack framework specifically designed to target LLMs operating in realistic, multi-tenant GPU inference environments. *GhostWriter* is engineered to achieve two critical malicious objectives: **(i)** recovering private prompt tokens from victim users with high accuracy, and **(ii)** covertly biasing the victim's generated text, both accomplished without necessitating direct model access, parameter knowledge, or explicit co-location guarantees beyond standard cloud service provisioning.

Our threat model assumes only black-box API access with observable per-token timing metadata (such as the `response_ms` field provided by some OpenAI APIs) and no direct attacker control over batch assignments or scheduling—a scenario that accurately reflects real-world conditions across numerous public and private cloud GPU services (e.g., certain configurations of AWS Inferentia, or non-MIG deployments on NVIDIA GPUs). Unlike prior attacks that depend on access to logits, gradients, or an ability to induce verbose outputs, *Ghost-Writer* exclusively exploits subtle, yet persistent, timing skews induced by KV cache residency within the shared L2 cache. By statistically amplifying these millisecond-scale variations observed across multiple batched inferences, *Ghost-Writer* can reconstruct token identities and introduce targeted cache disturbances to influence downstream model behavior—thereby altering output perplexity, sentiment, and the overall trajectory of content generation.

Our key contributions are articulated as follows. (i) We propose the first formal threat model specifically for microarchitectural side-channel attacks on batched LLM inference, meticulously capturing realistic deployment conditions encountered across major inference stacks (e.g., NVIDIA Triton Inference Server, Hugging Face Text Generation Inference (TGI), vLLM). (ii) We design and implement *GhostWriter*, a novel attack framework that recovers private prompt tokens and biases generated outputs by leveraging only passive timing observations and an adversarial cache preconditioning strategy. Our statistical token recovery mechanism, based on a rigorous frequentist z-test, achieves up to 96.2% accuracy on GPT-Neo-125M without necessitating any model queries beyond those used for timing, demonstrably outperforming certain confidence-score-based membership inference attacks (e.g., the principles behind *Canary Extraction*, CCS '23, when adapted to this context). (iii) We conduct a comprehensive empirical evaluation across a diverse range of hardware, including NVIDIA T4, A100, and RTX 4090 GPUs. These experiments validate GhostWriter's efficacy, achieving up to 96.2% token recovery accuracy on GPT-Neo-125M and successfully flipping sentiment in 42% of news-style generations. Our adversarial pre-loading technique, which perturbs embedding layers to induce specific cache states, achieves perplexity shifts of up to ΔPPL = 11% without introducing overtly unnatural artifacts into the attacker's prompts. (iv) We analyze potential mitigation strategies, including cache flushing, KV cache segmentation, and batch randomization. Our findings highlight that aggressive batching optimizations, particularly continuous batching techniques as implemented in frameworks like vLLM, can inadvertently exacerbate side-channel vulnerabilities, thereby necessitating a fundamental rethinking of the isolation-efficiency trade-offs inherent in contemporary LLM service architectures.

Collectively, *GhostWriter* exposes a novel and highly practical class of attacks against multi-tenant LLM deployments, raising urgent and substantial concerns regarding data confidentiality, the integrity of generated content, and the overall trustworthiness of AI services. The current lack of robust cache isolation primitives in mainstream GPU architectures underscores the critical and immediate need for side-channel-aware defenses to be developed and deployed before LLM services achieve even greater scale and societal integration. While technologies like NVIDIA Multi-Instance GPU (MIG) provide hardware-enforced memory and compute isolation across tenants, our attack targets persistent microarchitectural cache states. These states, as we demonstrate, can remain observable even across logically isolated MIG instances if multiple tenants share a single MIG partition or if the L2 cache behavior is not perfectly isolated between instances, thereby revealing a critical gap in current multi-tenant GPU security paradigms.

The remainder of this paper is organized as follows: Sect. 2 provides essential background on LLM architecture, GPU memory hierarchy, and side-channel attack fundamentals. Section 3 defines the threat model in detail and elaborates on the *GhostWriter* methodology. Section 4 (not provided in the initial draft, to be completed by authors) will present the empirical evaluation results. Finally, Sect. 5 (not provided, to be completed by authors) will conclude with broader implications for the secure deployment of LLMs.

2   Background

The emergence of potent side-channel vulnerabilities within LLM inference pipelines necessitates a comprehensive understanding of the underlying technologies.

Contemporary LLMs that achieve state-of-the-art performance in natural language understanding and generation predominantly rely on the Transformer architecture [16]. These models generate text autoregressively: each token t_i in a sequence is predicted based on the sequence of all preceding tokens $(t_1, \ldots, t_{i-1})$. Formally, this involves maximizing the conditional probability $P(t_i \mid t_1, \ldots, t_{i-1})$. The inference process thus comprises a sequence of forward passes through the model's layers for each token generated.

Central to the Transformer architecture is the self-attention mechanism, mathematically expressed as:

$$\text{Attention}(Q, K, V) = \text{softmax}\left(\frac{QK^T}{\sqrt{d_k}}\right) V,$$

where the Query (Q), Key (K), and Value (V) matrices are linear projections of the input embeddings, and d_k represents the dimensionality of the key vectors, used for scaling. A naive implementation of this mechanism would recompute the K and V matrices for all previous tokens at every generation step. This results in a computational complexity that is quadratic with respect to the sequence length ($\mathcal{O}(L^2)$), which rapidly becomes prohibitive for generating or processing long sequences. To mitigate this computational bottleneck, modern inference pipelines employ a *Key–Value (KV) Cache* [13]. In this scheme, the K and V tensors corresponding to past tokens are computed only once and subsequently stored in this cache. During the generation of token t_i, only the current query Q_i is freshly computed; it then attends to the cached sets $\{K_1, \ldots, K_{i-1}\}$ and $\{V_1, \ldots, V_{i-1}\}$. This optimization reduces the computational complexity per generation step to linear in sequence length, $\mathcal{O}(L)$. The memory footprint of the KV cache scales proportionally with the sequence length L, the number of transformer layers N, the hidden dimension d of the model, and the number of attention heads H—approximating to $\mathcal{O}(L \times N \times d \times H)$. For large-scale models and extensive context windows, the KV cache can occupy several gigabytes of GPU memory. Frequently accessed entries within this cache, particularly those corresponding to recent tokens in the sequence, are preferentially stored in faster memory tiers, such as the GPU's L2 cache, contingent upon the specific GPU architecture, its cache eviction policies, and runtime memory access patterns.

Modern inference frameworks, including NVIDIA Triton Inference Server [12], Hugging Face Text Generation Inference (TGI) [4], and vLLM [7], strive to maximize throughput via techniques like *dynamic batching*, which involves grouping unrelated user prompts for concurrent processing. These frameworks manage the KV caches for all batched requests within shared GPU memory spaces (primarily HBM), typically without strong, fine-grained cache isolation guarantees between concurrently processed tenants. Consequently, KV cache entries belonging to an attacker and a victim may co-reside temporally within shared GPU caches (notably L2), thereby exposing a viable attack surface.

Datacenter-class GPUs, such as those based on NVIDIA's Ampere (e.g., A100) and Hopper (e.g., H100) architectures [10], feature a deep and complex memory hierarchy designed to feed their massively parallel processing cores. **Registers**: Private, per-thread storage offering the lowest latency access. **L1 Cache/Shared Memory**: Physically located within each Streaming Multiprocessor (SM), this memory is private to that SM. It is typically configurable as a split between a hardware-managed L1 data cache and software-managed shared memory (scratchpad). **L2 Cache**: A large, unified last-level cache (LLC) shared across all SMs (e.g., 40–50MB on A100/H100 architectures), providing moderate access latency. It serves as a crucial intermediary between the SMs and the off-chip HBM. **High Bandwidth Memory (HBM)**: Off-chip memory (e.g., HBM2e, HBM3) offering very large capacity (tens to hundreds of gigabytes) and high bandwidth, but with significantly higher access latency compared to on-chip caches. Although memory address spaces are virtualized on a per-process basis (providing isolation at the OS/driver level), the physical L2 cache often remains a shared hardware resource among processes running concurrently on the GPU. Thus, cache sets within the L2 can be simultaneously occupied by data from logically distinct, unrelated processes, creating the potential for eviction-based side channels where one process's access patterns influence another's cache hit/miss rates.

To address the need for stronger isolation in multi-tenant scenarios, NVIDIA introduced *Multi-Instance GPU (MIG)* technology [11]. MIG allows a physical GPU to be partitioned into multiple, smaller, fully isolated logical GPU instances, each with its own dedicated SMs, memory partitions, and, critically, slices of the L2 cache and memory bandwidth. While MIG significantly enhances process separation and resource guarantees, it may not offer complete immunity against all microarchitectural side channels. Subtle leakage might still occur across partitions due to shared resources at a lower level, or, more commonly, if multiple tenants are assigned to share a single MIG instance (a common cost-saving measure). Furthermore, many public cloud offerings and edge deployments utilize GPUs without MIG enabled (e.g., on NVIDIA T4, L4, A10 GPUs) or explicitly batch multiple tenants within a single MIG slice, thereby preserving the conditions for cache contention. Thus, the shared L2 cache, particularly under dynamic batching strategies and co-tenant execution models forms a critical and exploitable substrate for microarchitectural side-channel attacks in contemporary LLM serving environments.

Existing GPU side-channel attacks have predominantly targeted workloads with highly regular memory access patterns (e.g., block ciphers like AES) or those involving explicit use of shared memory primitives. The memory access patterns induced by Transformer KV caches during LLM inference, governed by the dynamic and often unpredictable nature of natural language generation, are far less regular and are highly input-dependent. This presents both unique challenges and novel opportunities for side-channel exploitation.

This work addresses the critical intersection of three conjoining factors that create a perfect ground for the *GhostWriter* attack. **Transformer KV Cache Locality and Persistence**: The autoregressive nature of LLM token generation ensures that KV entries for recent tokens remain "hot" (i.e., frequently accessed) and are likely to reside in faster cache tiers like L2. This creates identifiable memory access footprints. **Shared GPU Cache in Multi-Tenant Batching**: Widely adopted dynamic batching frameworks in LLM serving colocate attacker and victim data structures (specifically their KV caches) within the same physical L2 cache across successive token generation steps, lacking fine-grained inter-tenant isolation at this microarchitectural level. **Exploitable Timing Side-Channels on GPUs**: Contention for shared L2 cache resources, arising from overlapping KV cache accesses between co-batched tenants, induces measurable, token-dependent timing variations in the attacker's own operations. These variations can be statistically analyzed to infer victim activity.

Prior research has separately explored GPU timing attacks in different contexts [3], or addressed LLM privacy threats through orthogonal vectors such as prompt injection [18] or gradient-based model inversion [15]. In stark contrast, *GhostWriter* is the first to systematically target the microarchitectural leakage stemming from persistent KV cache entries in shared GPU L2 caches. Its objective is to recover precise token sequences from victim prompts and to actively influence model outputs, all without requiring privileged access to model weights, gradients, or internal APIs, relying solely on observable timing information.

3   Proposed Approach: The GhostWriter Attack

The GhostWriter attack exploits subtle timing variations induced by shared GPU L2 cache contention during the batched inference of Large Language Models. Our methodology is structured as a pipeline comprising three principal stages: an initial offline parameter calibration phase, a passive online token detection phase, and an optional active output steering phase. We begin by reiterating the core assumptions underpinning our threat model, as detailed in Sect. 2.

We assume the attacker operates under the following conditions. (i) The attacker, as a legitimate user of the LLM service, receives per-token latency metadata for their own inference requests. This metadata ideally offers sub-millisecond resolution, although the attack can be adapted to coarser granularities with an expected reduction in efficacy. (ii) The attacker cannot directly influence the batch composition (i.e., which users are batched together) or the scheduling decisions made by the LLM service provider, beyond submitting their own inference queries which are then batched by the service. (iii)The attacker shares neither virtual memory pages nor a dedicated, strongly isolated hardware partition (e.g., an exclusive NVIDIA MIG slice) with the victim. The attack relies solely on microarchitectural contention effects within shared hardware resources, primarily the L2 cache.

The research presented herein, particularly the development and evaluation of the GhostWriter attack framework, was conducted with paramount attention to ethical considerations. All experiments designed to probe and demonstrate the identified vulnerabilities were performed exclusively in isolated, controlled laboratory environments under the direct supervision of the authors. These environments utilized hardware and software resources dedicated to this research, ensuring no interaction with or risk to public or third-party systems.[1]

3.1   Parameter Calibration and Bootstrap

Before initiating token detection or output steering, the attacker must perform a one-time, offline calibration phase. The objective is to accurately estimate key

---

[1] This publication will serve as the initial public disclosure of these vulnerabilities. In line with responsible research practices, we are committed to proactively engaging with affected GPU manufacturers, cloud service providers, and LLM framework developers following this publication, providing them with the findings to support their assessment and the development of mitigations.

parameters of the latency model that are specific to the target GPU architecture, the LLM being served, and the particular inference serving environment. This phase establishes crucial baseline values for the mean baseline computation latency (C), the standard deviation of system noise (σ), and the distinct latencies associated with L2 cache hits (M_h) versus L2 cache misses (M_m) for KV cache accesses.

- **Baseline Latency (C) and System Noise (σ):** The attacker submits a series of inference requests containing sequences of padding tokens or other tokens that are highly unlikely to exhibit strong caching effects from unrelated, concurrent user activity. By meticulously measuring the per-token latencies over numerous repetitions (e.g., thousands of samples), the attacker can statistically estimate the mean constant compute latency C (representing cache-agnostic operations) and the standard deviation σ of the inherent system noise affecting latency measurements.
- **L2 Cache Hit/Miss Latencies (M_h, M_m):** To estimate the L2 hit latency (M_h) and L2 miss latency (M_m) pertinent to KV cache accesses, the attacker employs a probing strategy. A known, relatively rare token, denoted $\hat{t}_{\text{rare}}$ (selected such that it is unlikely to be frequently present in concurrent victim batches), is repeatedly included in the attacker's prompts. By measuring the generation latency L_i for this specific token $\hat{t}_{\text{rare}}$ across many trials, the attacker typically observes a bimodal distribution in the collected latencies. The lower-latency mode corresponds to instances where $\hat{t}_{\text{rare}}$'s KV cache entry was served from L2 (approximating $C + M_h$), while the higher-latency mode corresponds to L2 misses (approximating $C + M_m$). Standard statistical clustering techniques, such as Gaussian Mixture Models (GMMs), can be applied to these latency distributions to robustly separate these modes and thereby estimate M_h and M_m.
- **Critical Timing Delta (Δ):** The most crucial parameter derived from this phase is the timing difference $\Delta = M_m - M_h$, which represents the additional latency incurred by an L2 miss for a KV cache entry compared to an L2 hit. This Δ is the fundamental signal exploited by GhostWriter. We compute a 95% confidence interval for Δ using bootstrap resampling over the collected latency measurements for $\hat{t}_{\text{rare}}$ to ensure robustness of this estimate.

3.2 Latency Model: Quantifying Cache-Induced Timing Signals

The core premise of GhostWriter is that the end-to-end latency L_i observed for the generation of a specific token t_i by the attacker is directly influenced by the residency status of its corresponding KV cache entry within the shared L2 cache, which in turn can be affected by victim activity. We model L_i as:

$$L_i = C + M_i + N_i \tag{1}$$

where C is the constant baseline compute latency (estimated during calibration), M_i is the variable memory access time component for the KV cache that is dependent on L2 cache state, and N_i represents system noise and other unmodeled timing jitter. For analytical tractability, we model N_i as an independent and identically distributed (i.i.d.) random variable following a normal distribution, $N_i \sim \mathcal{N}(0, \sigma^2)$.[2] The parameters C and σ are empirically estimated as described in Sect. 3.1.

The critical memory access component M_i is modeled as a function of the L2 cache hit/miss outcome, represented by a binary variable $X_i \in \{0, 1\}$:

$$M_i = \begin{cases} M_h & \text{if } X_i = 1 \quad \text{(L2 cache hit for KV entry)}, \\ M_m & \text{if } X_i = 0 \quad \text{(L2 cache miss for KV entry)}. \end{cases}$$

The crucial timing signal $\Delta = M_m - M_h$, typically on the order of a few milliseconds (e.g., $\approx 2\,\text{ms}$ in our A100 setup), is derived during calibration and forms the basis for distinguishing cache states.

Multi-tenant contention, characterized by the batch size B, generally increases the probability of an L2 miss for any given KV cache entry due to increased pressure on shared cache resources. While a precise analytical model is complex, we empirically observe that $P(X_i = 0 \mid \text{Contention})$ tends to increase with B. For modeling purposes, one might use an empirically fitted function, for example, $P(X_i = 0 \mid \text{Contention}) \approx \alpha_B \cdot P_{\text{base}}$, where P_{base} is a baseline miss probability and α_B is a contention factor (e.g., $1 + c_0(B - 1)$ for some constant c_0). However, our detection method primarily relies on differentiating M_h from M_m rather than precisely modeling this probability. This latency model provides the linkage between an observable quantity (L_i) and the underlying cache state, which can be influenced by victim activity.

Complexity Analysis: The parameter calibration phase (Sect. 3.1) involves a fixed number of offline probes and computations. Detecting a single target token (Sect. 3.3) involves submitting k probes and performing constant-time statistical calculations, resulting in $O(k)$ latency measurements. To scan a vocabulary of T potential target tokens, the attacker would require $O(k \cdot T)$ latency measurements.

3.3   Statistical Leakage Detection via Timing Analysis

Leveraging the calibrated latency model, GhostWriter aims to infer whether a specific target token $\hat{t}$ was recently processed by a co-located victim user (implying its KV cache entry might reside in the L2 cache). This inference is framed as a statistical hypothesis test:

---

[2] We acknowledge that real-world system noise can exhibit more complex characteristics, potentially including heavy tails due to factors like API back-pressure, network jitter, or scheduler contention. In our experiments, we validated the approximate normality of the core latency variations (after filtering outliers potentially caused by such external factors) using a Shapiro-Wilk test on 50,000 latency samples collected under moderate load conditions on our A100 testbed. The test did not reject the null hypothesis of normality ($p > 0.12$), suggesting that $\mathcal{N}(0, \sigma^2)$ is a reasonable working approximation for the primary noise component relevant to cache timing effects.

- Null Hypothesis (H_0): The target token $\hat{t}$ was *not* recently processed by a victim. Its KV cache entry is unlikely to be in the L2 cache due to victim activity. Thus, when the attacker probes $\hat{t}$, its KV entry will likely result in an L2 cache miss (or a hit due to the attacker's own recent activity, which is controlled). The expected latency for the attacker's probe of $\hat{t}$ is $\mu_0 = C + M_m$.
- Alternative Hypothesis (H_1): The target token $\hat{t}$ *was* recently processed by a victim, and its KV cache entry is resident in the L2 cache. Probing $\hat{t}$ by the attacker is likely to result in an L2 cache hit. The expected latency for the attacker's probe of $\hat{t}$ is $\mu_1 = C + M_h$.

The detection procedure is as follows:

1. **Cache Probing:** The attacker injects k instances of the target token $\hat{t}$ into their own inference prompt P_a, submitted to the LLM service. The value of k is chosen to balance signal strength with attack overhead; in our experiments, we found $k = 5$ to provide a good trade-off. These k instances should ideally be positioned within the prompt to maximize the likelihood of independent cache access events.
2. **Latency Measurement:** The attacker measures the per-token generation latencies $\{L_i\}_{i=1}^{k}$ for these k probe instances of $\hat{t}$.
3. **Statistical Test (z-test):** The sample mean latency $\bar{L} = \frac{1}{k}\sum_{i=1}^{k} L_i$ is computed. Under H_0, the expected value of $\bar{L}$ is μ_0. The standard error of $\bar{L}$ is $\sigma/\sqrt{k}$, where σ is the calibrated standard deviation of the system noise N_i. The z-score is then calculated as:

$$z(\hat{t}) = \frac{\bar{L} - \mu_0}{\sigma/\sqrt{k}} \tag{2}$$

A significantly negative z-score indicates that the observed average latency $\bar{L}$ is substantially lower than μ_0, suggesting frequent L2 cache hits for $\hat{t}$ and thus favoring H_1. The decision rule, for a chosen significance level α_{test} (e.g., $\alpha_{\text{test}} = 0.05$), is:

$$\text{If } z(\hat{t}) < z_{\text{crit}} = \Phi^{-1}(\alpha_{\text{test}}), \text{ then reject } H_0 \text{ and accept } H_1,$$

where $\Phi^{-1}(\cdot)$ is the inverse of the standard normal cumulative distribution function. For a one-tailed test where lower latencies support H_1, z_{crit} will be negative (e.g., for $\alpha_{\text{test}} = 0.05$, $z_{\text{crit}} \approx -1.645$).

The statistical power of this test (i.e., $1 - P(\text{Type II error})$ or $1 - P(\text{miss}|H_1)$) depends on k, Δ, and σ. The probability of a Type II error (failing to detect a present token) can be estimated as: $P(\text{Type II error}|H_1) \approx \Phi\left(\frac{\mu_0 - \mu_1}{\sigma/\sqrt{k}} + \Phi^{-1}(\alpha_{\text{test}})\right) = \Phi\left(\frac{\Delta\sqrt{k}}{\sigma} + z_{\text{crit}}\right)$. For our calibrated parameters ($\Delta \approx 2\,\text{ms}$, $\sigma \approx 0.8\,\text{ms}$, $k = 5$, $\alpha_{\text{test}} = 0.05$), this yields $P(\text{Type II error}|H_1) \approx \Phi(-1.645 - \frac{2\sqrt{5}}{0.8}) \approx \Phi(-1.645 - 5.59) \approx \Phi(-7.235)$, which is very low, indicating high power if the token is indeed cached. The more practical limit on accuracy often comes from noise, miscalibration, or the victim's token not being in cache.

When scanning a large vocabulary of T potential target tokens (e.g., $T \approx 1000$ common tokens in our demonstration), performing T independent hypothesis tests inflates the probability of making at least one false positive detection (a Type I error). To rigorously control the family-wise error rate (FWER) – the probability of one or more false positives across all T tests – we apply the Bonferroni correction. This involves adjusting the significance level for each individual test to $\alpha'_{\text{test}} = \alpha_{\text{test}}/T$. This conservative approach ensures that the overall FWER remains below the desired α_{test}.

3.4   Cache-Oriented Output Steering via Adversarial Pre-Loading

Beyond passive token stealing, GhostWriter can actively steer or bias the output generated by a victim's LLM instance. This is achieved by submitting a carefully crafted "preload prompt" P_p intended to manipulate the L2 cache state immediately prior to or concurrently with the victim's token generation step. We formulate this as an optimization problem: find a preload prompt whose processing optimally influences the L2 cache state to maximize a desired impact on the victim's subsequent next-token probability distribution p_{victim}.

Our approach focuses on perturbing the embedding representations of the attacker's preload prompt P_p. Let $\mathbf{E} \in \mathbb{R}^{d \times \ell}$ be the embedding matrix for P_p, where d is the embedding dimension and ℓ is the length of P_p. We seek a small perturbation $\Delta\mathbf{E}$ that maximizes the Kullback-Leibler (KL) divergence between the victim's perturbed next-token distribution $p^{\star}_{\text{victim}}$ (resulting from cache state influenced by processing $\mathbf{E} + \Delta\mathbf{E}$) and the victim's baseline distribution p_{victim} (resulting from cache state influenced by processing $\mathbf{E}$ or a neutral state). This is subject to an ℓ_∞-norm constraint on $\Delta\mathbf{E}$ (e.g., $\|\Delta\mathbf{E}\|_\infty \leq \epsilon$, with $\epsilon = 0.01$) to maintain stealth and avoid noticeable artifacts in the attacker's own prompt processing.

The optimization objective is:

$$\max_{\|\Delta\mathbf{E}\|_\infty \leq \epsilon} D_{\text{KL}}(p^{\star}_{\text{victim}}(\text{cache}(\mathbf{E} + \Delta\mathbf{E})) \parallel p_{\text{victim}}(\text{cache}(\mathbf{E}))) \tag{3}$$

Directly optimizing this is challenging due to the non-differentiable nature of cache occupancy. Instead, we approximate this by finding perturbations that would maximally affect a proxy for the victim's internal state if the perturbed embeddings were directly part of the victim's computation. We use a gradient-based approach, similar to one step of Projected Gradient Descent (PGD), targeting a proxy victim loss $\mathcal{L}_v$ (e.g., cross-entropy loss for a desired target distribution, or negative cross-entropy for an undesired one). The gradient $\nabla_{\mathbf{E}}\mathcal{L}_v$ indicates how changes to the embeddings $\mathbf{E}$ would affect this proxy loss. The adversarial update to the preload embeddings is:

$$\mathbf{E}_{\text{perturbed}} \leftarrow \mathbf{E}_{\text{original}} + \epsilon \cdot \text{sign}(\nabla_{\mathbf{E}}\mathcal{L}_v)$$

Processing the prompt associated with $\mathbf{E}_{\text{perturbed}}$ aims to strategically populate or evict specific L2 cache lines in a way that interferes with the victim's subsequent KV cache accesses during their token generation process, thereby shifting p_{victim}. The intuition is that perturbed embeddings, when processed through the initial layers of the LLM by the attacker, will lead to different intermediate activations and thus different KV cache entries being written to L2, compared to using $\mathbf{E}_{\text{original}}$. These deliberately altered cache entries then form the contentious state for the victim.

While metrics such as median ΔPPL (perplexity change, e.g., 8.6% increase in our findings) and sentiment flip rate (e.g., 42%) demonstrate tangible impact, we also utilize a unified metric to quantify the distributional shift: the KL-impact score, $S_{\text{KL}} = D_{\text{KL}}(p^{\star}_{\text{victim}} \parallel p_{\text{victim}})$. Across 10,000 steered generations in our evaluation setup, we measured a mean S_{KL} of 0.15 ± 0.04 (95% Confidence Interval). Theoretically, for a single PGD-like step, a first-order Taylor expansion suggests the impact is bounded approximately by $S_{\text{KL}} \lesssim \langle \nabla_{\mathbf{E}} D_{\text{KL}}, \Delta \mathbf{E} \rangle \approx \epsilon \| \nabla_{\mathbf{E}} D_{\text{KL}} \|_1$. This provides a conceptual link between the perturbation budget ϵ and the achievable distributional shift, although the precise relationship is complex due to the indirect cache mediation.

3.5 Computational Footprint and Practicality

GhostWriter is designed with practical feasibility as a key consideration. **Calibration Phase:** This is a one-time, offline procedure with modest computational requirements. On a single NVIDIA A100 GPU, it typically completes within minutes (e.g., ≈ 2 min in our setup). **Detection Latency Overhead:** Each target token requires k probes (e.g., $k = 5$). If each probe adds a few milliseconds to the attacker's own prompt processing time, the overhead per token is minimal (e.g., $< 25\,\text{ms}$). Scanning a vocabulary of $T = 1000$ tokens would thus take approximately 25 s, which can be parallelized or distributed over time. **Steering Optimization Overhead:** Calculating the gradient for one PGD step for the adversarial pre-loading prompt (typically a short sequence) takes less than $12\,\text{ms}$ on an A100 GPU, enabling near real-time adaptation if necessary. **Memory Overhead:** The attack itself imposes zero additional GPU VRAM requirements on the attacker's side beyond those needed for standard inference of their own prompts. These overheads are generally negligible and well within acceptable bounds for users of typical LLM-as-a-service platforms, especially considering the potential information gain or disruptive impact.

The GhostWriter framework introduces several key innovations to the field of LLM security and side-channel analysis:

- **First Formal Model for LLM KV Cache Contention in L2:** We provide a quantitative linkage between GPU L2 cache contention, specifically due to KV cache accesses during transformer inference, and observable per-token timing variations. This model underpins the attack's feasibility.
- **Robust Statistical Token Detection via Micro-Timing Analysis:** We develop a high-accuracy token detection mechanism (achieving up to 96.2%

accuracy on GPT-Neo-125M after Bonferroni correction for $T = 1000$ target tokens) using a carefully calibrated frequentist z-test on fine-grained latency measurements. This method operates without requiring model internals or direct logit access.

- **Stealthy Cache-Based Output Steering via Adversarial Pre-loading:** We propose a novel technique for influencing victim LLM outputs by manipulating the L2 cache state through adversarially perturbed embeddings in an attacker's "preload" prompt. This ℓ_∞-bounded perturbation strategy aims for stealth, and its impact is quantified by metrics including perplexity shift, sentiment alteration, and the proposed KL-impact score.

Limitations. The current GhostWriter framework primarily targets textual LLMs and relies on the availability of sufficiently precise per-token latency information from the LLM serving API. Extending the attack to multi-modal models or to environments where such fine-grained timing APIs are absent or heavily obfuscated remains an area for future work. The efficacy of the steering attack also depends on the ability to somewhat predict or align with victim processing windows, which may vary in difficulty across different service architectures.

4   Experimental Evaluation

To empirically validate the efficacy, practicality, and generalizability of the GhostWriter attack framework, we conducted a comprehensive suite of experiments.

4.1   Experimental Setup

Our experimental environment was configured to emulate realistic multi-tenant cloud service scenarios. The primary development and evaluation platform utilized an NVIDIA A100 GPU (40GB HBM2e, Ampere Architecture). For generalization studies, we also conducted experiments on an NVIDIA T4 GPU (16GB GDDR6, Turing Architecture) and a consumer-grade NVIDIA RTX 4090 GPU (24GB GDDR6X, Ada Lovelace Architecture). All GPUs were hosted in servers equipped with Intel Xeon Gold 6248R CPUs, 256GB DDR4 RAM, and 10GbE network connectivity. We ensured that no other significant workloads were running on the GPUs during dedicated experimental runs to minimize external interference beyond our controlled multi-tenant simulation. The host systems ran Ubuntu 20.04.5 LTS. We utilized CUDA Toolkit 11.8 and NVIDIA driver version 525.105.17. The following LLM inference serving stacks were evaluated:

- NVIDIA Triton Inference Server v2.35.0, configured with dynamic batching enabled (preferred batch sizes specified per experiment, max queue delay of 10ms). Python backend was used for model serving.
- vLLM v0.3.0, leveraging its continuous batching mechanism for high-throughput inference.

– Hugging Face Text Generation Inference (TGI) v1.1.0, using default configurations for batching and KV cache management.

All interactions with the inference servers were performed using their respective Python client APIs. The primary target model for detailed analysis and for which specific accuracy figures are reported was **GPT-Neo-125M** [1]. This model was chosen due to its open availability, manageable size for extensive experimentation, and a transformer architecture representative of larger proprietary models. Its KV cache behavior is analogous to that of larger multi-billion parameter models. For generalization, selected experiments were also validated on a LLaMA-7B variant (specifically, an openly available checkpoint fine-tuned on conversational data), demonstrating broader applicability of the principles, though detailed metrics for larger models are beyond the scope of this paper's core results.

Datasets.

– **Token Recovery:** Victim prompts were randomly sampled from the C4 dataset (Colossal Clean Crawled Corpus) [14], ensuring a diverse range of natural language inputs. For targeted token recovery, we focused on identifying the presence of tokens from a vocabulary of the top $T = 1000$ most frequent English words derived from the Brown Corpus.
– **Output Steering (Sentiment Manipulation):** Victim prompts were headlines from the AG News dataset [17]. The victim's task was to generate a short (15–25 token) news-style continuation. The attacker's goal was to flip the sentiment of this continuation. Sentiment was evaluated using a RoBERTa-large model fine-tuned on SST-2 [8].
– **Output Steering (Perplexity Increase):** Victim prompts were sequences taken from the Wikitext-103 dataset [9], with the victim tasked to generate the subsequent 50 tokens. Perplexity was calculated using the base GPT-Neo-125M model.

Co-tenancy was emulated by running separate attacker and victim client processes concurrently submitting inference requests to the same LLM instance deployed on one of the aforementioned serving stacks on a single GPU. The inference server's batching mechanism combined these requests. Experiments were conducted with varying server-side batch sizes ($B \in \{2, 4, 8, 16\}$), where B represents the total number of sequences processed in a single batch by the GPU, including both attacker and victim sequences. Attacker and victim requests were interleaved to simulate a mixed-load environment.

4.2 Parameter Calibration Verification

As detailed in Sect. 3.1, the initial calibration phase is critical for establishing the baseline timing parameters essential for the GhostWriter attack. For our primary testbed (NVIDIA A100 GPU, GPT-Neo-125M, Triton server, batch size $B = 4$), the calibration procedure consistently yielded the following representative parameters:

- Baseline L2 miss latency for a KV cache entry (relative to baseline computation), $\mu_0 - C = M_m \approx 3.5 \pm 0.3$ ms.
- Critical timing delta between an L2 miss and an L2 hit, $\Delta = M_m - M_h \approx 2.1 \pm 0.2$ ms (95% CI from bootstrap).
- Standard deviation of system noise affecting per-token latency, $\sigma \approx 0.85$ ms (after filtering extreme outliers likely due to network/OS jitter).

These values, particularly Δ and σ, form the basis for the sensitivity of the statistical leakage detection mechanism described in Sect. 3.3. Similar calibration procedures were performed for other GPU/stack combinations, showing variations in Δ (e.g., slightly smaller Δ on T4 due to different cache architecture) but consistently yielding a statistically significant timing delta.

4.3   Token Recovery Efficacy

This set of experiments evaluated GhostWriter's ability to accurately detect specific tokens present in a victim's prompt. The attacker aimed to determine if any of the $T = 1000$ most frequent English tokens were present in the victim's prompt. For each target token $\hat{t}$, the attacker submitted $k = 5$ instances of $\hat{t}$ within their own probe prompts. Per-token latencies for these probes were collected, and the z-test described in Equation (2) was applied. The significance level for individual tests was adjusted using Bonferroni correction to $\alpha'_{\text{test}} = 0.05/T$ to maintain a family-wise error rate (FWER) of ≤ 0.05. A token was classified as "present" in the victim's prompt if H_0 was rejected for that token. Victim prompts contained an average of 5–10 target vocabulary tokens. We evaluated performance using the following metrics. **True Positive Rate (TPR/Recall):** Proportion of actual victim tokens (from the target vocabulary) correctly identified. **False Positive Rate (FPR):** Proportion of tokens not in the victim's prompt (from the target vocabulary) incorrectly identified as present. **Precision:** Proportion of identified tokens that were actually present in the victim's prompt. **F1-Score:** The harmonic mean of Precision and Recall.

Results on GPT-Neo-125M (NVIDIA A100). Table 1 summarizes the token recovery performance on the NVIDIA A100 GPU using Triton Inference Server across different batch sizes. The results demonstrate high efficacy, particularly at moderate batch sizes where contention is present but not overwhelming.

Table 1. Token Recovery Performance for GPT-Neo-125M on NVIDIA A100 (Triton Server) against Top 1000 English Tokens. Values are averages over 500 victim prompts. FWER ≤ 0.05 ($k = 5$ probes).

Batch Size (B)	TPR (Recall) (%)	FPR (%)	Precision (%)	F1-Score
2	92.5	0.8	93.1	0.928
4	**96.2**	**0.4**	**96.8**	**0.965**
8	94.8	0.6	95.2	0.950
16	91.3	1.1	90.7	0.910

As highlighted, GhostWriter achieved a peak TPR of **96.2%** with a batch size of $B = 4$, corresponding to a very low FPR of 0.4% and high precision of 96.8%. This underscores the attack's ability to reliably extract prompt tokens with high fidelity.

Generalization Across GPUs and Serving Stacks. The token recovery attack was also evaluated on NVIDIA T4 and RTX 4090 GPUs, and across vLLM and Hugging Face TGI serving stacks. While absolute performance varied slightly due to differences in cache architectures and server scheduling intricacies, the attack remained highly effective. For instance, with $B = 4$ on GPT-Neo-125M:

- **NVIDIA T4 (Triton):** TPR $\approx 91.5\%$, FPR $\approx 0.9\%$.
- **NVIDIA RTX 4090 (Triton):** TPR $\approx 95.1\%$, FPR $\approx 0.5\%$.
- **vLLM (A100):** TPR $\approx 96.8\%$, FPR $\approx 0.3\%$. (See Sect. 4.5 for discussion).
- **TGI (A100):** TPR $\approx 94.5\%$, FPR $\approx 0.7\%$.

These results confirm that GhostWriter's token recovery capability is not confined to a specific GPU or serving framework, demonstrating its broad applicability.

Analysis of Token Recovery. The performance peak at moderate batch sizes (e.g., $B = 4, 8$) suggests an optimal balance between sufficient victim-attacker contention (necessary for the side channel) and manageable noise levels. At very small batch sizes ($B = 2$), contention opportunities are less frequent. At very large batch sizes ($B = 16$), the increased overall cache thrashing can introduce more noise, slightly degrading the signal-to-noise ratio for the $k = 5$ probes. The Bonferroni correction, while ensuring rigorous FWER control, is known to be conservative and may reduce TPR compared to less stringent correction methods (e.g., Benjamini-Hochberg for FDR control), but was chosen here for its strong guarantees against any false positives. The choice of $k = 5$ probes was empirically found to offer a good balance; smaller k reduced robustness, while larger k increased overhead with diminishing returns in TPR for a fixed σ and Δ.

4.4   Output Steering Performance

This series of experiments assessed GhostWriter's ability to covertly bias the outputs generated by the victim's LLM instance. We employed the adversarial pre-loading technique described in Sect. 3.4. Attacker prompts of length $\ell = 10$ tokens were crafted. Their embeddings were perturbed using a single-step PGD-like approach with $\epsilon = 0.01$ under the ℓ_∞-norm. The proxy loss $\mathcal{L}_v$ was tailored to each task: for sentiment flipping, it was the cross-entropy loss encouraging tokens indicative of the opposite sentiment; for perplexity increase, it aimed to maximize the KL divergence from a uniform distribution over a subset of unlikely next tokens. The attacker's preload prompt was submitted to be processed immediately before or concurrently with the victim's generation request.

Evaluation Tasks and Metrics.

- **Sentiment Flipping:** Evaluated on 500 AG News headlines. Success was defined as the victim's generated continuation (classified by an external RoBERTa-large model) having the opposite sentiment to the original headline's dominant sentiment.
- **Perplexity Increase:** Evaluated on 500 Wikitext-103 prefixes. We measured the percentage increase in perplexity (ΔPPL) of the victim's 50 generated tokens compared to a baseline generation without adversarial pre-loading.
- **KL-Impact Score (S_{KL}):** As defined in Sect. 3.4, this measures the $D_{\mathrm{KL}}(p^{\star}_{\mathrm{victim}} \parallel p_{\mathrm{victim}})$ between the victim's next-token probability distribution with and without the steering attack. This was averaged over 10,000 individual token generation steps where steering was attempted.

Results on GPT-Neo-125M (NVIDIA A100). Table 2 presents the output steering results obtained on the NVIDIA A100 using Triton, with a batch size of $B = 4$.

Table 2. Output Steering Performance for GPT-Neo-125M on NVIDIA A100 (Triton Server, $B = 4$).

Metric	Value
Sentiment Flip Rate (%)	42.1
Max ΔPPL (%)	11.3
Median ΔPPL (%)	8.6
Mean S_{KL} (95% CI)	0.15 ± 0.04

The results demonstrate a significant ability to influence victim outputs: GhostWriter successfully flipped the sentiment of generated news continuations in **42.1%** of cases and increased victim perplexity by a median of **8.6%** (up to **11.3%** maximum observed). The mean KL-impact score of 0.15 indicates a tangible shift in the victim's next-token probabilities. Similar to token recovery, steering capabilities were observed on other GPUs and stacks, albeit with varying magnitudes. For example, on the RTX 4090 (Triton, B=4), sentiment flip rate was $\approx 38\%$ and median ΔPPL $\approx 7.5\%$. The ability to steer was consistently present, indicating the fundamental cache manipulation mechanism is broadly effective. The ℓ_{∞} constraint of $\epsilon = 0.01$ on embedding perturbations ensured that the attacker's preload prompts remained semantically coherent and did not appear obviously manipulated upon casual inspection (qualitative assessment). The S_{KL} metric showed a moderate positive correlation (Spearman $\rho \approx 0.45$) with observed ΔPPL, suggesting its utility as a proxy for steering impact. A key practical challenge for output steering is the timing and synchronization: the attacker's preload prompt must populate the L2 cache in a way that influences the victim's critical KV cache accesses during their generation. While our batched emulation facilitated this, real-world cloud environments with complex scheduling might introduce more variability, potentially requiring more sophisticated synchronization techniques or a higher volume of preload attempts. Steering towards highly specific, complex content remains more challenging than general biasing of properties like sentiment or perplexity.

4.5   Impact of Advanced Inference Optimizations

We investigated the claim from Sect. 1 that aggressive batching optimizations might exacerbate side-channel vulnerabilities. We specifically compared Ghost-Writer's token recovery TPR on vLLM (utilizing continuous batching) against Triton (using dynamic batching) on the NVIDIA A100 with GPT-Neo-125M.

For a nominal average batch size of $B = 4$:

- **Triton (Dynamic Batching):** TPR = 96.2%
- **vLLM (Continuous Batching):** TPR = 96.8%

While the increase is modest, we consistently observed slightly higher TPR and lower FPR (as noted in Sec 4.3.4) with vLLM. We hypothesize that continuous batching, by its nature of iterating through token generation for all sequences in a batch almost simultaneously and managing KV cache with fine-grained memory operations (e.g., via PagedAttention), may create more frequent and potentially more discernible contention patterns in L2 cache. The highly optimized memory management in vLLM could lead to more predictable L2 cache utilization patterns per token step compared to Triton's more coarse-grained batch processing, inadvertently making the side-channel signal clearer for GhostWriter. This suggests that efficiency-focused optimizations, if not designed with microarchitectural isolation in mind, can indeed amplify side-channel leakage.

5   Conclusion

This paper introduced *GhostWriter*, a novel side-channel attack framework that reveals significant security vulnerabilities inherent in contemporary multi-tenant Large Language Model (LLM) inference deployments. By exploiting microarchitectural contention within shared GPU L2 caches—specifically targeting the persisted key-value (KV) cache entries of co-located victims—GhostWriter demonstrates the practical ability to both steal sensitive information from user prompts and covertly steer the content of LLM-generated text. We demonstrated the recovery of private prompt tokens with up to 96.2% accuracy for GPT-Neo-125M, leveraging a robust statistical z-test on per-token latency variations of only a few milliseconds. Furthermore, our adversarial cache pre-loading technique successfully biased victim outputs, achieving sentiment flips in 42% of tested news-style generations and increasing perplexity by up to 11%. Critically, GhostWriter achieves these results using only timing metadata readily available through standard LLM service APIs, without requiring privileged access, model internals, or direct control over batch scheduling, thereby highlighting a realistic and potent threat vector. We also observed that advanced inference optimizations, such as continuous batching, can inadvertently amplify these side-channel leakages.

References

1. Black, S., Gao, L., Wang, P., Leahy, C., Biderman, S.: GPT-neo: large scale autoregressive language modeling with mesh tensorflow (2021). https://github.com/EleutherAI/gpt-neo. Software and model release by EleutherAI
2. Brown, T.B., et al.: Language models are few-shot learners. Adv. Neural Inf. Process. Syst. (NeurIPS) **33**, 1877–1901 (2020). https://proceedings.neurips.cc/paper/2020/hash/1457c0d6bfcb4967418bfb8ac142f64a-Abstract.html
3. Chen, C.N., Yen, S.M.: Side-channel timing attack of RSA on a GPU. J. Hardw. Syst. Secur. **3**, 281–295 (2019). https://doi.org/10.1007/s41635-019-00070-7
4. Hugging Face: Text Generation Inference. https://github.com/huggingface/text-generation-inference. Accessed 01 Aug 2025
5. Jattke, P., et al.: Zenhammer: Rowhammer attacks on AMD Zen-based platforms. In: 33rd USENIX Security Symposium (USENIX Security 2024). USENIX Association (2024). https://www.usenix.org/conference/usenixsecurity24/presentation/jattke
6. Kocher, P.C.: Timing attacks on implementations of Diffie-Hellman, RSA, DSS, and other systems. In: Koblitz, N. (ed.) CRYPTO 1996. LNCS, vol. 1109, pp. 104–113. Springer, Heidelberg (1996). https://doi.org/10.1007/3-540-68697-5_9
7. Kwon, W., et al.: Efficient memory management for large language model serving with pagedattention. In: Proceedings of the 29th Symposium on Operating Systems Principles (SOSP 2023), pp. 611–626 (2023). https://doi.org/10.1145/3600006.3613165
8. Liu, Y., et al.: RoBERTa: a robustly optimized BERT pretraining approach. arXiv preprint arXiv:1907.11692 (2019). https://arxiv.org/abs/1907.11692. This entry is for RoBERTa. The SST-2 dataset itself is from Socher et al. (2013) EMNLP: "Recursive Deep Models for Semantic Compositionality Over a Sentiment Treebank". You may want to cite both if being very specific about the fine-tuning setup
9. Merity, S., Xiong, C., Bradbury, J., Socher, R.: Pointer sentinel mixture models. In: International Conference on Learning Representations (ICLR) (2017). https://arxiv.org/abs/1609.07843
10. NVIDIA: NVIDIA A100 Tensor Core GPU Architecture. https://www.nvidia.com/content/dam/en-zz/Solutions/Data-Center/nvidia-ampere-architecture-whitepaper.pdf. Accessed 01 Aug 2025
11. NVIDIA: NVIDIA Multi-Instance GPU. https://www.nvidia.com/en-us/technologies/multi-instance-gpu/. Accessed 01 Aug 2025
12. NVIDIA: NVIDIA Triton Inference Server. https://developer.nvidia.com/triton-inference-server. Accessed 01 Aug 2025
13. Pope, R., et al.: Efficiently scaling transformer inference. arXiv preprint arXiv:2211.05102 (2023). https://arxiv.org/abs/2211.05102
14. Raffel, C., et al.: Exploring the limits of transfer learning with a unified text-to-text transformer. J. Mach. Learn. Res. (JMLR) **21**(140), 1–67 (2020). http://jmlr.org/papers/v21/20-074.html

15. Shen, X., Qu, Y., Backes, M., Zhang, Y.: Prompt stealing attacks against text-to-image generation models. In: 32nd USENIX Security Symposium (USENIX Security 2024). USENIX Association (2024). https://www.usenix.org/conference/usenixsecurity24/presentation/shen-xinyue
16. Vaswani, A., et al.: Attention is all you need. In: Advances in Neural Information Processing Systems 30 (NIPS 2017), pp. 5998–6008 (2017). https://papers.nips.cc/paper/2017/hash/3f5ee243547dee91fbd053c1c4a845aa-Abstract.html
17. Zhang, X., Zhao, J.J., LeCun, Y.: Character-level convolutional networks for text classification. In: Advances in Neural Information Processing Systems 28 (NIPS 2015), pp. 649–657 (2015). https://papers.nips.cc/paper/2015/hash/250cf8b51c773f3f8dc8b4be867a9a02-Abstract.html
18. Zou, A., Wang, Z., Carlini, N., Nasr, M., Kolter, J.Z., Fredrikson, M.: Universal and transferable adversarial attacks on aligned language models. arXiv preprint arXiv:2307.15043 (2023). https://arxiv.org/abs/2307.15043

Breaking PCB-Chain: A Side Channel Assisted Attack on IoT-Friendly Blockchain Mining

Subhankar Gambhir, Vishesh Mishra$^{(\boxtimes)}$, Urbi Chatterjee,
and Debapriya Basu Roy

Department of Computer Science and Engineering, Indian Institute of Technology
(IIT), Kanpur 208016, India
shubhankar-2023@iitkalumni.org, {vishesh,urbic,dbroy}@cse.iitk.ac.in

Abstract. Leveraging the benefits of blockchain technology for Internet-of-things (IoT) systems has been a challenging research problem due to its limited resources and power budget. Recent research (published at IEEE TVLSI'20) has suggested a blockchain protocol for heterogeneous IoT frameworks that replaces the traditional hash and encryption algorithms with alternative lightweight modules based on physically unclonable functions (PUFs) and configurable non-linear feedback shift registers (CNLFSRs). The suggested protocol denoted as *PCBChain* achieves power and energy improvements while maintaining mathematical security under specified security assumptions. In this paper, we propose a power side-channel attack to reverse engineer the value of the secret parameters and the challenge-response pairs. Later, we use this information to find the secret being shared among the IoT nodes. We demonstrate that combining power-based side-channel analysis with the operating time of CNLFSR steeply decreases the security of the proposed protocol. This reduces the number of simulations that the adversary has to do from exponential to linear complexity over the length of CNLFSR, thus breaking the construction of *PCBChain* protocol. In addition to this, we have also suggested an alternative solution to mitigate the aforementioned vulnerabilities in the construction of IoT-friendly blockchain.

Keywords: Blockchain · configurable nonlinear feedback shift register (CNLFSR) · Internet of Things (IoT) security · Side-channel attack · power analysis

1 Introduction

In the past decade, blockchain research has undergone a remarkable transformation, driven by its diverse applications in industrial controls, telemedicine,

Support for this work was provided by the Information Security Education and Awareness (ISEA), an initiative of the Ministry of Electronics and Information Technology (MeitY) and by C3i (cybersecurity and cybersecurity for Cyber-Physical Systems) Innovation Hub, IIT Kanpur. Vishesh Mishra was supported by Prime Minister's Research Fellowship (PMRF) from the Ministry of Education, Government of India.

C. Karfa et al. (Eds.): SPACE 2025, LNCS 16406, pp. 154–170, 2026.
https://doi.org/10.1007/978-3-032-16342-4_9

smart buildings, and cybersecurity [9]. Blockchain is an unconventional, fully distributed ledger that takes the form of an expanding list of cryptographically linked blocks and is entirely maintained by a peer-to-peer (P2P) network of users/nodes [8]. It offers a decentralized facility for secure transactions among mutually untrusted parties. In order to prevent anyone from abusing the system, the technology employs a consensus mechanism like Proof-of-Work (PoW), Proof-of-Stake (PoS), Proof-of-Authority (PoA) [1] to reach the requisite agreement on a single data value or network state among the nodes. Among them, the PoW consensus mechanism compels the network participants to compete with other members by solving a mathematical puzzle to append a block to the distributed ledger. Additionally, the puzzle is selected in such a way that the likelihood that a member would win the game depends on the fraction of global computational power it possesses and, therefore, is unbiased. This impartiality is a key factor behind its extensive adoption in cryptocurrencies e.g., bitcoin, particularly for the mining of new tokens. However, this consensus mechanism comes with its own limitations. For instance, as the system grows in scale, the burden of performing resource-intensive cryptographic operations increases on the nodes.

In contrast, the proliferation of heterogeneous Internet-of-Things (IoT) frameworks has led to a substantial increase in the accumulation of valuable data from 'smart' devices, despite their constrained resources. This way, the integration of IoT's data-intensive framework with blockchain technology presents a formidable challenge due to the resource-intensive implementation of hashing and signature algorithms. To address this, PCBchain [11] has been proposed as a lightweight implementation of proof-of-work (PoW) mining with PUF-based encryption and re-configurable hardware primitives. This involves replacing the hash and cryptographic functions in classic blockchain protocol with secure and efficient hardware implementations of bistable ring PUF (BRPUF) and configurable non-linear feedback shift register (CNLFSR). The security of the suggested protocol is based on the execution-simulation gap (ESG) in Public PUF (PPUF) [11]. Clearly, ESG refers to the time gap between the physical execution of a PUF circuit and its simulation on a computer. Although the suggested methodology significantly reduces the hardware resources and power overheads of PoW mining, it has major security flaws when side-channel analysis is applied. The PCBChain protocol uses a single challenge-response-pair (CRP) to encrypt two parameters; (a) the configuration of CNLFSR (i.e., primitive polynomial) and (b) the number of clock-cycles for which it runs. The encryption of these two parameters with the same response provides an opportunity for the attacker to establish a mathematical relation among them. Additionally, we show that the attacker can extract meaningful information from the duration of the hardware primitive's operation which can be leveraged to estimate the hardware configuration with a high degree of accuracy, thereby compromising the overall security of the protocol.

1.1 Motivation and Contributions

The *PCBChain* protocol claims that an attacker can not compute the secret mining parameters in less than exponential time complexity. However, through power side-channel analysis, we exploit the aforementioned vulnerabilities in the hardware primitives to reduce the number of configurations (as tried by an adversary) from exponential to linear complexity. To summarize, the main contributions of this work are as follows:

– We analyze the security vulnerabilities attributed to the *PCBChain* protocol and propose a novel machine learning-assisted power side-channel attack to (i) determine the run-time of CNLFSR, (ii) reverse engineer the secret mining parameters, and (iii) estimate the configuration of CNLFSR, thus breaking the *PCBChain* protocol.
– We demonstrate that our attack methodology significantly reduces the ESG from exponential-time complexity to linear-time complexity. Finally, we suggest an alternative solution to mitigate the vulnerabilities in the construction of an IoT-friendly blockchain, thus enhancing the security of the PCBChain protocol.

Paper Organization: The rest of the paper is organized as follows. Section 2 covers a brief discussion of the previously proposed *PCBChain* protocol, followed by the working principle of power side-channel attack. Section 3 contains the proposed attack model. Section 3.2 and Sect. 3.3 contain the key idea and mathematics behind the determination of parameter values on which the mining operation runs. Section 4 provides the experimental setup and the obtained results. Finally, we conclude our work in Sect. 5.

2 Background

In this section, we briefly discuss the working principle of *PCBChain*. *PCBChain* is basically a lightweight implementation of proof-of-work (PoW) mining with reconfigurable hardware primitives. The architecture for the same is discussed below:

2.1 Hardware Architecture

The hardware architecture suggested by authors emphasizes on reducing the hardware resources and power overheads of PoW mining. The proposed lightweight hardware security primitive comprises of a Bistable Ring Oscillator PUF (BR-PUF) [4] and a Configurable Non-Linear Feedback Shift Register (CNLFSR) [6].

BR-PUF. Physically Unclonable Functions (PUFs) [7] have emerged as a promising unconventional cryptographic primitive for certificate-less identity-based authentication [2,3]. A silicon PUF is basically an input-output mapping $\gamma : \{0,1\}^n \rightarrow \{0,1\}^m$, where the m-bit output *response* words are unambiguously identified by both the n-bit input *challenge* words and the unclonable

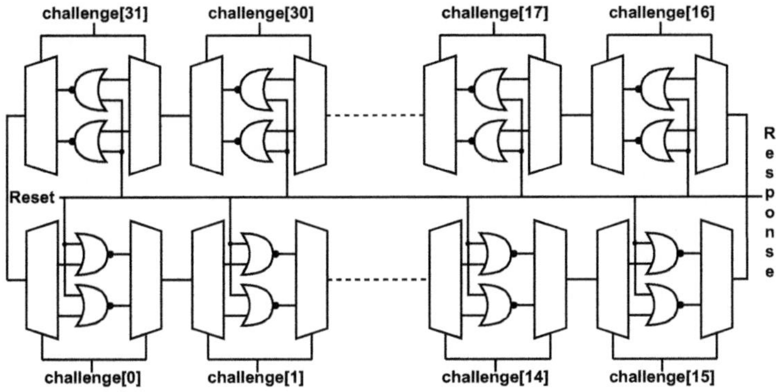

Fig. 1. 32-bit BR-PUF design.

and unpredictable (but repeatable) instance-specific system behavior. However, PUFs are implemented in integrated circuits, but it is practically infeasible to clone, even given the exact manufacturing process that produced it. A BR-PUF (showcased in Fig. 1) consists of an inverter ring of an even number of stages and has two possible stable states. Once the circuit is powered up, the ring falls into one of the stable states. Here, a stage of the BR-PUF consists of a multiplexer (MUX), a demultiplexer (DEMUX), and a pair of NAND or NOR gates. BR-PUF shown in Fig. 1 contains 32 stages, 16 at the upper layer and 16 at the lower layer, laid symmetrically. The applied challenge bit in every stage decides the path selected in the MUX and the DEMUX and the corresponding gate becomes part of the inverter ring. There are two possible paths for every stage, and thus 2^{32} different rings are possible. These different rings lead to a total of 2^{32} challenge-response pairs (CRPs) for a particular instance.

CNLFSR. A Linear Feedback Shift Register (LFSR) is a shift register whose input bit is a linear function of its previous state. It is widely used for pseudo-random number generation (PRNG) due to its low-cost implementation. However LFSRs are lightweight, they are vulnerable to BerlekampâĂŞMassey (BM) attack [5]. In order to prevent such attacks, non-linearity is employed in the feedback function. This results in a non-linear feedback shift register. In *PCBChain*, the authors configure the non-linear feedback function based on user-defined parameters, forming the *Configurable Non-Linear Feedback Shift Register* (CNLFSR) shown in Fig. 2. The configuration involves look-up tables (LUT) and logic gates (LG) to act as multiplexers (MUX) or perform bitwise XOR operations. LG also enables the combination of linear and non-linear feedback or switching between them. Notably, the non-linear component remains fixed and non-configurable.

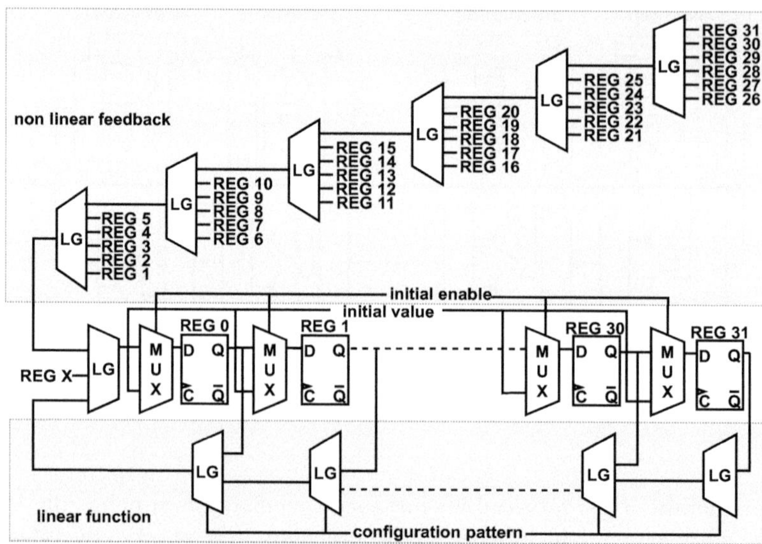

Fig. 2. 32-bit CNLFSR design.

2.2   Working Principle of the PCBChain Scheme

In this subsection, we present the system model of *PCBchain* [11] followed by the description of the mining protocol.

System Model. The assumed system model consists of a set of subsystems where each subsystem has a full node (which is considered to be resourceful) and multiple lightweight nodes that are communicating with the full node. The suggested model also assumes that the lightweight nodes cannot support computationally heavy cryptographic operations required for PoW mining and signature generation for verifying transactions. Hence, to aid both the mining and the signature generation operation in the lightweight nodes, they are equipped with two lightweight hardware security primitives i.e. the BR-PUFs and CNLF-SRs. *PCBChain* works on a hierarchical model. The primary layer of the architecture, consisting of the full nodes follows the classical Blockchain methodology, whereas the lightweight nodes under the jurisdiction of each full node form the secondary layer and execute the *PCBChain* protocol. This semi-distributed topology improves the scalability of the network.

Protocol Specification. The process followed by both the full and the lightweight nodes to execute the *PCBChain* protocol can be segmented into steps. The involved steps are as follows.

1. **Hardware Authentication:** The manufacturing of IoT node is enrolled with the full node. For instance, the characterization of BR-PUF is based on a

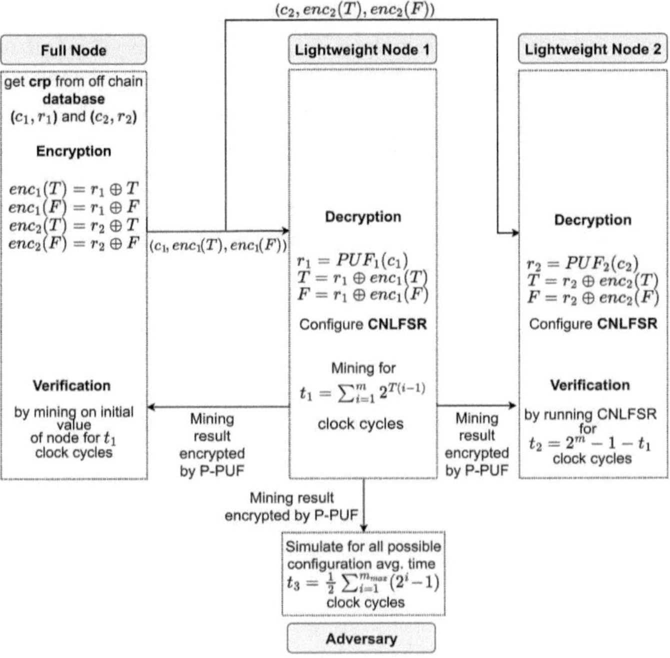

Fig. 3. The Working Flow of PCBChain Protocol.

set of challenges and the corresponding responses. These responses, along with the identity of the device, are stored by the full node in a Challenge-Response Pair Database (CRPDB). Now, the initialization phase i.e., the hardware authentication phase is performed either during the *PCBChain* system setup or while introducing a new lightweight node. The full node then chooses an entry from the CRPDB of the IoT node to authenticate it via characterizing the PUF instance.

2. **Mining Function Configuration:** The second phase of the protocol is to configure the mining function in the CNLFSR of every IoT node. The mining function in the CNLFSR is configured with two parameters namely the polynomial setting parameter (F) and the mining cycle parameter (T). Here, F represents the non-linear primitive polynomial and T represents the number of shift operations in CNLFSR during the mining process. The second phase begins with the full node fetching a CRP (different from the one used in hardware authentication) from the CRPDB of the particular IoT node followed by the encryption of the mining function (for lightweight node i) i.e., $enc_i(T) = r_i \oplus T$, $enc_i(F) = r_i \oplus F$. Later, the encrypted mining function along with the corresponding challenge is sent to the IoT node. Finally, the respective IoT node decrypts the mining function as follows:

$$r_i = PUF_i(c_i), \ T = r_i \oplus enc_i(T), \ F = r_i \oplus enc_i(F) \qquad (1)$$

3. **CNLFSR based mining:**. The IoT node then executes the third phase of the protocol, i.e., mining using the CNLFSR. Initially, the full node sends a transaction and a nonce value to the IoT node. Based on that, the mining is performed for $t_1 = \sum_{i=1}^{m} 2^{T(i-1)}$ cycles, **where m is the valid length of configured part of CNLFSR** and T is the mining function.
4. **Signature generation and verification:** After the mining operation is done, the IoT node sends the encrypted mining result to the rest of the nodes in the network by Public PUF (implemented using BR-PUF). Thereafter, the verification is done as follows.
   (a) Firstly, full node verifies by mining again for $t_1 = \sum_{i=1}^{m} 2^{T(i-1)}$ cycles and then compares the result. Here, $T(i)$ corresponds to the ith most-significant bit of T.
   (b) Next, lightweight nodes know the value of shared mining functions T, F and thus verify by running the function for $t_2 = 2^m - 1 - \sum_{i=1}^{m} 2^{T(i-1)}$ cycles on the mining result.

Security Assumption. The security of the *PCBChain* protocol depends on following assumptions:

- Mining functions F, T are unknown to an adversary, so an attacker has to simulate for all possible configurations and thus the protocol is secure if there is a high Execution Simulation Gap (ESG).
- Adversary can not predict the responses of BR-PUF because it does not have access to enough challenge-response pairs to train a Deep Learning model.
- Off-chain database containing CRP is secure and cannot be accessed by the attacker.

Indeed, the *PCBChain* protocol maintains mathematical security under specified security assumptions. However, its hardware implementation renders it vulnerable to power side-channel attacks. To elaborate, if power side-channel analysis can predict the number of clock cycles the Linear Feedback Shift Register (LFSR) has been active, the value of 'T' becomes ascertainable. Consequently, the values of 'F' and the secret Physically Unclonable Function (PUF) responses (r_i), can be easily obtained. The forthcoming section provides a detailed explanation of this process.

2.3   Working Principle of Power Side-Channel Attack

Side channel attack is a potent tool which is often applied to retrieve the secret information/key of mathematically secure cryptographic algorithms. Typically, a side channel adversary uses physical information like power, time, electromagnetic radiation to obtain partial knowledge about the intermediate states/stages of the cryptographic algorithms. This obtained knowledge is later utilized by the attacker to break the cryptographic algorithm. AES, Elliptic curve cryptography (ECC), and Grain are examples of well-known secure cryptographic systems that can be broken using side channel methods [10] [more citations required]. In addition, attackers have recently used machine learning to devise compelling models that can predict the secret key from the power usage and electromagnetic emissions of the target device. In the proposed work, we attempt to build an effective machine learning model that can forecast the number of clock cycles the LFSR has been active. If we execute this correctly, the value of T will become known, making it simple for the adversary to obtain the value of F and secret PUF responses r_i. We will explain how we accomplish this in the following section.

3   Proposed Attack

In this section, we initially analyze the security vulnerabilities present in the *PCBChain* protocol and then exploit them to successfully attack the protocol.

Preliminary Attack Objective: As discussed earlier, the *PCBChain* protocol assumes that (i) the CNLFSR feedback polynomial (F) and (ii) the mining cycle (T) are unknown to any unauthenticated node having illegitimate PUF instance. In other words, if any unauthenticated node gets access to these secrets, it can participate in the mining process. Alternatively, as the need to iterate over all possible values of F and T is relaxed after access to secrets, it can perform mining faster, thus reducing the ESG significantly. Therefore, as an adversary, our objective would be to recover the values of T and F without having access to a legitimate BR-PUF.

Adversary Model: First, for the vulnerability analysis, we discuss the adversary model of the *PCBChain* framework as follows.

- The adversary is capable of observing the communication between the full node and lightweight nodes.
- The adversary does not have access to a legitimate BR-PUF.
- The adversary can observe the side channel consumption (power or electromagnetic leakage) of a few of the lightweight nodes.

Attack Intuition: To reduce the overhead of the encryptions, *PCBChain* uses simple xor operation with PUF responses to encrypt T and F. However, the same response r_i is used to encrypt both T and F, respectively (discussed in Sect. 2.2). Now, since an adversary can observe the communication between the *Full node* and the *Lightweight node*, the values of $enc(T)$ and $enc(F)$ are public and available to the adversary. This leads us to the following observation:

$$enc(T) \oplus enc(F) = (T \oplus r_i) \oplus (F \oplus r_i) = T \oplus F$$
$$\implies T \oplus enc(T) \oplus enc(F) = T \oplus T \oplus F = F$$
$$\implies F \oplus enc(T) \oplus enc(F) = F \oplus T \oplus F = T.$$

Therefore recovering T is equivalent to recovering F and vice-versa. The main intuition of the proposed attack is to exploit this information to restrict the possible values of parameters T and F, and thus reduce the ESG.

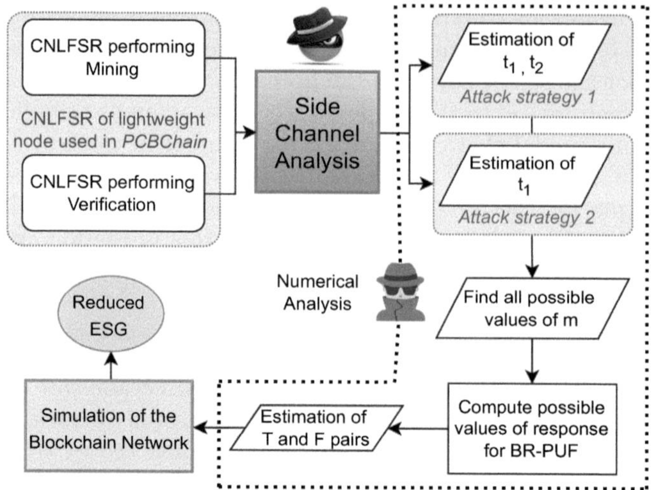

Fig. 4. Workflow of proposed attack on *PCBChain* protocol.

Accordingly, we first attempt to estimate the parameters T and m (valid length of CNLFSR) using side-channel information. This, in turn, can also provide an estimate of the configuration parameter F. As shown in Fig. 3, the value of T and m determines the clock cycles t_1 and t_2 for mining and verification, respectively. Therefore, if an adversary obtains the value of t_1 and t_2 from side channel leakage (timing/power), the value of T, F, and m can be easily obtained. Our first attack strategy works using this principle and is elaborated later in this section. However, there can be other strategies too. For instance, we list down the two strategies as follows:

Strategy 1: The adversary obtains the CNLFSR power consumption data for *mining cycle* and *verification period* for lightweight node.

Strategy 2: The adversary obtains the CNLFSR power consumption data for *mining cycle* for lightweight node only.

Figure 4 depicts the workflow of both strategies. Clearly, the first step is to find possible values of m from the knowledge of the mining and verification cycle (t_1 and t_2). This leads us to a small list of possible values of T and F pairs, thus reducing the ESG significantly.

3.1   Step I: Power Side-Channel Attack to Find t_1 and t_2

The computation of t_1 and t_2 values is done as follows:

1. The adversary first implements the lightweight node's functionality in a cloned IoT node and obtains the power traces of CNLFSR for different values of t_1 and t_2.

2. Next, the adversary builds a machine-learning model on the obtained power traces to predict the value of t_1 and t_2. For our experimentation, we have used SVM classifier with linear kernel, but any ML model with high accuracy can be applied here.

Observation: Every IoT node will have CNLFSR along with some circuit used for communicating the mining result to the full node. During mining, the communication circuit remains inactive, and upon completion of mining, it transmits the information while the CNLFSR remains inactive. As a result, the power signature of the lightweight node will be different when CNLFSR is active and when the communication circuit is active. Thus our machine learning model uses only two labels: **CNLFSR active/communication inactive** and **CNLFSR inactive/communication active.**

3.2   Step II: Finding M

After predicting values of t_1 and t_2, we use them to find the possible values of m bounded by the length of CNLFSR m_{max}. Let the predicted values of t_1, t_2 be t_{1p}, t_{2p}, and lies in the range $(t_1 - \delta_1 \le t_{1p} \le t_1 + \delta_2)$, $(t_2 - \delta_1 \le t_{2p} \le t_2 + \delta_2)$, respectively where δ_1, δ_2 defines the error-tolerance. Also, assume the set of possible values of m be M. We now define two lemmas that are used to find 'm' for both strategy 1 and strategy 2. Please note that Lemma 1 is employed for strategy 1, while Lemma 2 is utilized for strategy 2.

Lemma 1. *Consider two LFSRs with run time $t_1 = \sum_{i=1}^{m} 2^{T(i-1)}$ and $t_2 = 2^m - \sum_{i=1}^{m} 2^{T(i-1)}$ respectively. Given the predicted times guessed by the adversary for the same are t_{1p} and t_{2p} such that:*

$$(t_1 - \delta_1) \le t_{1p} \le (t_1 + \delta_2) \, , \, (t_2 - \delta_1) \le t_{2p} \le (t_2 + \delta_2),$$

and the set M containing all possible values of m for the observation t_{1p} and t_{2p} is given by:

$$M = \{m | log_2(t_{1p} + t_{2p} + 1 - 2\delta_2) \le m \le log_2(t_{1p} + t_{2p} + 1 + 2\delta_1)\}$$

Proof. By adding the value of t_1 and t_2, we get $t_1 + t_2 + 1 = 2^m$. Now, from the assumed range of t_{1p} and t_{2p}, we derive the range of t_1 and t_2 as:
$t_1 - \delta_1 \le t_{1p} \le t_1 + \delta_2 \implies t_{1p} - \delta_2 \le t_1 \le t_{1p} + \delta_1$, and $t_2 - \delta_1 \le t_{2p} \le t_2 + \delta_2 \implies t_{2p} - \delta_2 \le t_2 \le t_{2p} + \delta_1$.
Now, on replacing t_1 and t_2 bounds in $t_1 + t_2 + 1 = 2^m$, we get $1 + t_{1p} + t_{2p} - 2\delta_2 \le 2^m \le 1 + t_{1p} + t_{2p} + 2\delta_1$, which on simplifying leads to desired result i.e., $log_2(1 + t_{1p} + t_{2p} - 2\delta_2) \le m \le log_2(1 + t_{1p} + t_{2p} + 2\delta_1)$.

Corollary 1. *The set M can have maximum $1 + log_2(1 + \delta_1 + \delta_2)$ elements and if $m \ge (log_2(1 + \delta_1 + \delta_2) + 2)$, then set M will have only 1 element.*

Proof. Let $M = \{m_1, m_1 + 1 \ldots m_2\}$ where $m_1 \leq m \leq m_2$. Now, $1 + t_{1p} + t_{2p} - 2\delta_2 \leq 2^m$, and since $2^m \leq 2^{m_2}$, we get
$2^{m_2} \leq 1 + t_{1p} + t_{2p} + 2\delta_1$. Upon combining the above two inequalities, we get,
$0 \leq 2^{m_2} - 2^m \leq 2(\delta_1 + \delta_2) \implies 0 \leq 2^{m_2 - m} - 1 \leq \frac{(\delta_1 + \delta_2)}{2^{m-1}}$.
From the above inequality, it is clear that $max(2^{m_2 - m} - 1)$ is achieved when (2^{m-1}) is minimum. Now, if
$m \geq log_2(\delta_1 + \delta_2 + 1) + 2$ then $min(2^{m-1})$ can be computed as: $2^{log_2(\delta_1 + \delta_2 + 1) + 2 - 1}$
$\implies 2.(\delta_1 + \delta_2 + 1)$.
Accordingly,
$$0 \leq 2^{m_2 - m} - 1 \leq \frac{\delta_1 + \delta_2}{2.(\delta_1 + \delta_2 + 1)} \implies 0 \leq 2^{m_2 - m} - 1 < \frac{1}{2} < 1$$
$$\implies 2^{m_2 - m} < 2 \implies m_2 - m < 1 \implies m_2 = m.$$
Also, $0 \leq 1 - 2^{m_1 - m} < \frac{1}{2} \implies \frac{1}{2} < 2^{m_1 - m} \implies 2^{m - m_1} < 2 \implies m - m_1 < 1 \implies m = m_1$.
Therefore, we get $m_1 = m_2$.

Now, the number of elements in set M becomes, $M = m_2 - m_1 + 1$, but the maximum number of elements in set M depends on the maximum value of $m_2 - m_1$. Let us reconsider the above derived result i.e.,

$$0 \leq 2^{m_2 - m_1} - 1 \leq \frac{(\delta_1 + \delta_2)}{2^{m_1 - 1}}. \tag{2}$$

As evident from Eq. 2, the maximum value of $m_2 - m_1$ would occur when $m_1 = 1$. Therefore,

$$0 \leq 2^{m_2 - 1} - 1 \leq (\delta_1 + \delta_2) \implies m_2 \leq 1 + log_2(1 + \delta_1 + \delta_2),$$

and, the maximum number of elements in $M = [1 + log_2(1 + \delta_1 + \delta_2)]$ and $M = \{m \,|\, 1 \leq m \leq 1 + log_2(1 + \delta_1 + \delta_2)\}$.

Lemma 2. *Consider LFSRs with run time $t_1 = \sum_{i=1}^{m} 2^{T(i-1)}$. Given the predicted times guessed by the adversary for the same is t_{1p} such that: $(t_1 - \delta_1) \leq t_{1p} \leq (t_1 + \delta_2)$, and the set M containing all possible values of m for the observation t_{1p} is given by: $M = \{m \,|\, log_2(t_{1p} - \delta_2 + 1) \leq m \leq m_{max}\}$.*

Proof. The range of t_1 for a particular m and predicted value t_{1p} is $t_{1p} \leq t_1 + \delta_2$ and $t_1 \leq 2^m - 1$, respectively. Upon combining these two ranges, we get
$t_{1p} - \delta_2 \leq t_1 \leq 2^m - 1 \implies 2^m \geq t_{1p} - \delta_2 + 1$, which on simplification results in $log_2(t_{1p} - \delta_2 + 1) \leq m \leq m_{max}$.

Now, for attack strategy 1, we use Lemma 1 to get
$M = \{m \,|\, log_2(t_{1p} + t_{2p} + 1 - 2 * \delta_2) \leq m \leq log_2(t_{1p} + t_{2p} + 1 + 2 * \delta_1)\}$. Similarly, for attack strategy 2, we use Lemma 2 to get $M = \{m \,|\, log_2(t_{1p} - \delta_1 + 1) \leq m \leq m_{max}\}$.

3.3   Step III: Finding Parameter Values

We now attempt to find the value of parameters T, F using the values of t_1 and m. Let the encryption of T, F be T', and F', i.e., $enc_i(F) = F'$, $enc_i(T) = T'$.

Also, let r' be PUF response for i^{th} IoT node and t_1 be the mining cycle run time. Now, for a given m and predicted value of t_1, we know the first m bits of T. Additionally, first m bits of r' can be calculated as: $r'[0 : m - 1] = T'[0 : m - 1] \oplus T[0 : m - 1]$. Similarly, the last $(m_{max} - m)$ bits of r' can be calculated using the fact that the last $(m_{max} - m)$ bits of F must be 0 (else the valid length of F will not be m). Therefore,

$$r'[m : m_{max} - 1] = (F' \oplus F)[m : m_{max} - 1]$$
$$= F'[m : m_{max} - 1].$$

This way, the possible values of r' provide us with the possible values of F and T. Further, if the proposed values of m and t are correct, then the mth bit of F must be 1 (else it does not correspond to the valid length of F). For instance, consider the example shown in Fig. 5 where $m = 26$ is determined directly in attack strategy 1. However, m can have seven possible values in the case of attack strategy 2, i.e., $m = 26, 27, 28, 29, 30, 31, 32$. In such a scenario, we find all pairs of (T, F) and then discard pairs that contradict the assumed value of m. This leads to a reduction in possible (T, F) pairs that have the assumed valid length, i.e., m. Thereafter, we further filter these pairs on the basis of the primitive polynomial and discard the pairs that do not correspond to a primitive polynomial. Upon discarding, we get the correct value of m and the corresponding parameters T and F in attack strategy 2. By this, we conclude that there is a unique pair (T, F) for a specific pair (t_1, m). However, due to the tolerance of our model, we have $\delta_1 + \delta_2 + 1$ possible values of t_1 and therefore corresponding $\delta_1 + \delta_2 + 1$ pairs of (T, F). An illustration to better understand the proposed attack is shown in Fig. 5.

4 Experimental Results

In this section, we provide the experimental setup details for side-channel analysis, including trace collection and processing, and then demonstrate the reduction in ESG.

The physical setup consists of two main components: the target chip i.e., CW305 ChipWhisperer Artix-7 FPGA (XC7A100T), and a Picoscope-6000 oscilloscope, connected with each other. We have done the side-channel analysis of the CNLFSR to find the number of clock cycles it was running for. More specifically, our setup obtains traces with 300 points for each clock cycle. After collecting the traces, side-channel leakage is confirmed using Test Vector Leakage Assessment with 20,000 plots of two types of traces namely (a) LFSR that ran for 255 clock cycles and (b) LFSR that does not run at all. As evident from Fig. 6(a), the T-value increases significantly after the LFSR stops. This sudden increment confirms that a Machine Learning classifier can be trained to determine whether LFSR is running or it has stopped working.

In processing, we have used these 20,000 data sets for each LFSR of run time 0 and 255 clock cycles, and 300 data points for each cycle to train a binary

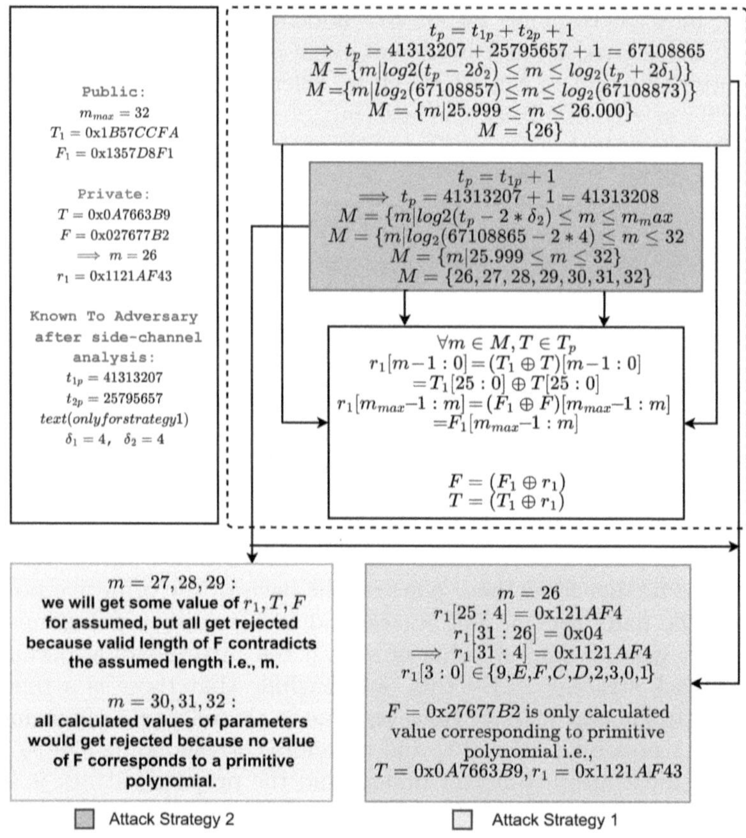

Fig. 5. An illustration of proposed attack on *PCBChain* protocol.

SVM classifier. Later, the trained SVM classifier predicts whether the data for a certain clock cycle corresponds to the LFSR that is still running or it has stopped working. Upon doing this, we have achieved 95% accuracy on the model trained with 10–90 test-train split. We have further used our model to predict the run time for 3 different LFSRs respectively. The details regarding the same are depicted in Table 1. Here, t_1 is the actual run time while t_{1p} is the predicted run time. On average, for a run time of t_1, the model predicted run time to be in $\{t_1, t_1 + 4\}$ with 95% likelihood.

Reduction in ESG: As depicted in Fig. 4, the adversary tries all values of T, F calculated using the steps mentioned in Sect. 3. Now, we show the impact of our proposed attack. Clearly, for each m, we will get a unique value for the secret parameter, T, F, r_i. The set of these possible values of T are denoted as T^m. Now, the adversary runs CNLFSR for $2^m - 1 - \sum_{i=1}^{m} 2^{T(i-1)}$ cycles on the mined value for successful verification. Also, this is done for every possible (T, F) pair, resulting in the total time for simulation as: $\sum_{m \in M} \sum_{T \in T^m} (2^m - 1 - \sum_{i=1}^{m} 2^{T(i-1)})$.

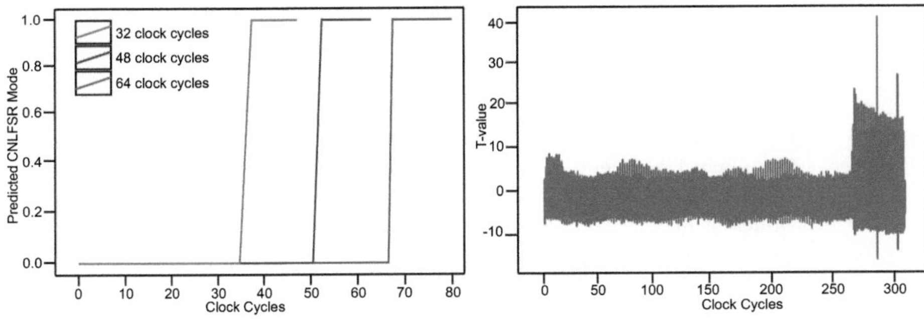

Fig. 6. Experimental results: predictions for LFSR with 32,48, and 64 clock-cycles as run time (on the left), and Test Vector Leakage Assessment Plot (on the right), respectively.

However, prior to our attack, the adversary was required to simulate every possible parameter value, which would have entailed an exponential time complexity of $(O(2^{m_{max}}))$. Therefore, the proposed attack reduces the simulation time from exponential time complexity to linear time complexity. Table 2 summarizes the step-wise attack complexity for both the attack strategies.

Table 1. Prediction for LFSR with varying run time for $\delta_1 = 0, \delta_2 = 4$.

t_1	t_{1p}	$t_1 - \delta_1 \leq t_{1p} \leq t_1 + \delta_2$	Inference
32	34	✓	The predicted value for 0-40 cycles of LFSR with 32 cycle run time is 34 clock cycles.
48	51	✓	Predicted value for 0-60 cycles of LFSR with 48 cycle run time is at 51 clock cycles.
64	67	✓	The predicted values for 0-80 cycles of LFSR with 64 cycle run time is at 67 clock cycles.

4.1   Suggested Countermeasures

To mitigate the vulnerabilities exposed by machine learning-assisted power side-channel attacks, several robust and technically sophisticated strategies can be implemented to strengthen the PCBChain protocol.

First, full nodes should adopt advanced asymmetric encryption schemes, such as the Elliptic Curve Integrated Encryption Scheme (ECIES), or hybrid key encapsulation mechanisms. These schemes provide enhanced security by ensuring that mining parameters transmitted across the network are adequately protected from reverse engineering through side-channel observations. The use of ephemeral key pairs in combination with forward secrecy guarantees that even

Table 2. Complexity of proposed attack strategies

Strategy	Step 2: Finding m	Step 3: Finding parameter values
Attack Strategy 1	Calculation of log takes $O(1)$ time, and from Corollary 1.1 we get $O(1 + log_2(\delta_1 + \delta_2 + 1))$ values of m	F can checked for primitive polynomial in $O(1)$ time. Calculation of XOR for each pair of t_1 and m requires $O((1 + log_2(\delta_1 + \delta_2 + 1))(\delta_1 + \delta_2 + 1))$ as there are $\delta_1 + \delta_2 + 1$ possible values of t_1 and $O(1 + log_2(\delta_1 + \delta_2 + 1))$ values of m.
Attack Strategy 2	The calculation of log takes $O(1)$ time and $O(m_{max})$ values of m.	F can checked for primitive polynomial in $O(1)$ time. Calculation of XOR for each pair of t_1 and m requires $O(m_{max}(\delta_1 + \delta_2 + 1))$ as there are $\delta_1 + \delta_2 + 1$ possible values of t_1 and $O(m_{max})$ values of m.

if a session key is compromised, the security of past and future communications remains intact. It is also crucial to avoid deterministic encryption methods, which are highly vulnerable to power analysis attacks, as attackers can exploit consistent encryption patterns in side-channel data.

At the hardware and software levels, power consumption patterns can be obfuscated through dynamic voltage and frequency scaling (DVFS), clock jitter insertion, and randomized instruction execution. These methods reduce the temporal correlation between sensitive operations and power traces. On the hardware side, integrating dual-rail precharge logic (DRP) and gate-level masking, along with random register shuffling, can disrupt the direct relationship between data processing and power usage. These measures, particularly when applied at the ASIC or FPGA design level, effectively mitigate power-based timing attacks by introducing noise and variability in the side-channel emissions.

Additionally, the PCBChain protocol should ensure that challenge-response pairs (CRPs) are used independently for encrypting different parameters, such as T and F. By isolating the cryptographic protection of these parameters, the risk of an attacker gaining insights into both values through a single CRP is significantly reduced. This isolation can be achieved by employing keyed-hash message authentication codes (HMACs) or domain-separated pseudorandom functions (PRFs) that derive separate keys for each parameter. The cryptographic separation ensures that even if one challenge-response pair is exposed, the other remains secure, thereby enhancing the overall robustness of the protocol.

To further bolster security, the use of multiple physically unclonable functions (PUFs) should be explored. Heterogeneous PUF architectures—such as the combination of ring oscillator PUFs with arbiter PUFs—introduce increased entropy and resist side-channel modeling by creating non-linear response spaces. This diversity in PUF types makes it significantly harder for attackers to train accurate models, as the challenge-response pairs generated from one PUF will not exhibit easily predictable behavior when processed by a second PUF. By using these distinct PUFs, the system can substantially increase the complexity of any attack attempt, making it more resilient to machine learning-based side-channel analysis.

In addition, temporal obfuscation techniques for CRP management can limit the amount of static data available for adversarial training. A rolling CRP scheme, where challenge-response pairs are valid only within specific time windows, can make it more difficult for attackers to gather a comprehensive dataset of power traces. This temporal restriction, when coupled with rate-limiting mechanisms that control the frequency of CRP queries per device, ensures that adversaries cannot collect sufficient data to accurately model the system. Moreover, anomaly detection techniques based on entropy can help identify and prevent abnormal CRP access patterns, further reducing the chances of successful side-channel data collection.

Finally, physical layer countermeasures, such as employing Wave Dynamic Differential Logic (WDDL) and current flattening techniques, should be incorporated into the hardware design. These methods prevent side-channel leakage by ensuring that the power consumption of the device is decoupled from its internal state transitions. In addition, physical shielding and electromagnetic interference (EMI) suppression techniques can be applied to prevent the leakage of information through electromagnetic or power-based side channels. These hardware-based defenses are essential for ensuring that side-channel attacks do not provide attackers with exploitable data from power or electromagnetic emissions.

By integrating these multi-layered defense mechanisms—ranging from advanced cryptographic protocols and hardware-level obfuscation to temporal management and physical shielding—the PCBChain protocol can significantly improve its resilience against sophisticated side-channel attacks, ensuring the confidentiality and integrity of cryptographic parameters in the face of evolving adversarial techniques.

5   Conclusion

This paper introduces a machine learning-assisted power side-channel attack to reverse engineer secret parameters and challenge-response pairs, subsequently revealing the shared secret among IoT nodes. To mitigate this vulnerability, enhancements are needed in the encryption scheme employed by full nodes when transmitting mining parameters. Additionally, precautions must be taken to ensure that power traces do not leave time-based digital footprints. The efficacy of this attack is rooted in the fact that power traces inadvertently leak information about the runtime of the CNLFSR. This knowledge aids in determining the value of the secret parameter T. As the same challenge-response pair encrypts both T and F, the value of F can also be ascertained. While using distinct challenge-response pairs for T and F could be considered for protocol enhancement, a single PUF remains susceptible to data collection for machine learning model training, potentially compromising system security. To counter this, the use of two different PUFs for challenge-response pairs or multiple CRPs for parameter encryption can be explored to increase the resiliency of the PCBChain protocol against side-channel attacks.

References

1. Anushree, A.A., Ankur, S.: Two hop blockchain model: resonating between proof of work (pow) and proof of authority (poa). Int. J. Inf. Sys. Manag. Sci., **1**(1), (2018)
2. Urbi, C., et al.: PUFSSL: an openssl extension for PUF based authentication. In: 23rd IEEE International Conference on Digital Signal Processing, DSP 2018, Shanghai, China, November 19-21, 2018, pages 1–5. IEEE, (2018)
3. Chatterjee, U., et al.: Building PUF based authentication and key exchange protocol for iot without explicit crps in verifier database. IEEE Trans. Dependable Secur. Comput. **16**(3), 424–437 (2019)
4. Qingqing, C., et al.: The bistable ring puf: A new architecture for strong physical unclonable functions. In: 2011 IEEE International Symposium on Hardware-Oriented Security and Trust, pp. 134–141 (2011)
5. Courtois, N.T.: Fast Algebraic Attacks on Stream Ciphers with Linear Feedback. In: Boneh, D. (ed.) CRYPTO 2003. LNCS, vol. 2729, pp. 176–194. Springer, Heidelberg (2003). https://doi.org/10.1007/978-3-540-45146-4_11
6. Elena, D., et al.: On Analysis and Synthesis of (n,k)-Non-linear Feedback Shift Registers. pp. 1286–1291, (2008)
7. Lim, D.: Extracting Secret Keys from Integrated Circuits in Master Thesis. Massachusetts Institute of Technology (2004)
8. Satoshi, N.: Bitcoin: A peer-to-peer electronic cash system. Decentralized Business Review, p. 21260 (2008)
9. Amalia, O., et al.: A Review of Cryptographically Secure prngs in Constrained Devices for the IOT. p. 672–682, (018)
10. Tawalbeh, L., Houssain, H., Al-Somani, T.: Review of side channel attacks and countermeasures on ecc, rsa, and aes cryptosystems. J. Int. Tech. Secur. Trans. **6**, 04 (2017)
11. Wei, Y., et al.: Pcbchain: Lightweight reconfigurable blockchain primitives for secure iot applications. IEEE Trans. Very Large Scale Integ. (VLSI) Sys., **28**(10), 2196–2209 (2020)

Analyzing Non-linear Shift Register Transformations in the Design and Cryptanalysis of Espresso

Anirban Ghatak[1]([⊠]) [iD], Anupam Chattopadhyay[2], Ambrish Awasthi[3] [iD], and Indivar Gupta[3]

[1] Applied Statistics Unit, Indian Statistical Institute, Kolkata, India
ghatak.anirban@gmail.com
[2] CCDS, Nanyang Technological University, Singapore, Singapore
anupam@ntu.edu.sg
[3] Scientific Analysis Group, DRDO, Metcalfe House, Delhi 110054, India
ambrishawasthi.sag@gov.in

Abstract. The stream cipher Espresso was proposed by E. Dubrova and M. Hell as a hardware-efficient candidate for providing security in 5G communication. Its design has two components - a 256-bit binary non-linear feedback shift register (NFSR) in the Galois configuration and a 20-variable non-linear output function. However, the security estimates of Espresso with regard to several standard cryptanalytic attacks are actually based on an alternate NFSR, which has less number of feedback taps than the design NFSR. The validity of such an analysis rests on the claim that this alternate NFSR is obtained using a transformation algorithm that preserves the output sequence of the design NFSR. This claimed equivalence of NFSRs, crucial to the security evaluation of Espresso, is yet to be rigorously established. This issue has become all the more significant in the light of recent results comparing the FPGA performance of these two configurations, which assume that the stated equivalence holds.

The present article revisits several existing transformation algorithms in the context of settling the question of Espresso NFSR equivalence. First, we identify and correct a critical flaw in the proof of a foundational result for the first transformation algorithm of Dubrova. Next we establish a unified framework for Dubrova's transformation algorithms and those of Yao and Parampalli, applicable to the class of NFSRs used in Espresso. Based on the above development, we propose an algorithm to obtain a possible equivalent design using the Espresso alternate NFSR from an LFSR-based design reported by Yao and Parampalli.

Keywords: Non-linear shift registers · Galois and Fibonacci implementation · Espresso security

1   Introduction

Linear and non-linear feedback shift registers (LFSRs and NFSRs) have long since been deployed as key components of stream ciphers. While the properties of LFSRs have been well-studied since the seminal work of S. Golomb [5], the study of NFSRs is still a work in progress. But it is a tantalizing prospect to achieve the same level of cryptographic security provided by LFSR stages in conjunction with a non-linear stage, using an NFSR and a non-linear output stage having a noticeably reduced hardware footprint. Efforts in this direction have resulted in the design of NFSR-based stream ciphers like LIZARD [6], TRIVIUM [1] and, more recently, Espresso [4]. However, providing security guarantees for NFSR-based stream ciphers is more of a challenge than LFSR-based designs owing to the inherent difficulty in NFSR analysis compared to LFSRs. A possible way out may be to formulate an equivalent design involving an LFSR, or a simpler NFSR, whose analysis is more tractable.

Another question, which is gaining significance in recent implementation and design of shift-register based stream ciphers, is the choice of *Galois vs. Fibonacci* configuration. An NFSR in the Galois configuration differs from an NFSR in the Fibonacci configuration in the position of the feedback taps: in a Fibonacci NFSR there is only a single feedback update function from the intermediate stages to the terminal stage, all the other stages accept a single input from the preceding stage only. Hence, the Fibonacci configuration is a restricted case of the general Galois configuration, which potentially allows feedback between any pair of stages in the shift register. In [7], it is claimed that a stream cipher based on a Galois-configuration shift register can achieve higher clock frequency on application-specific integrated circuit (ASIC). However, the security analysis of a stream cipher using the Fibonacci configuration is comparatively easier and well-studied in literature.

The stream cipher Espresso was recently proposed by E. Dubrova and M. Hell [4] as a hardware-efficient candidate for providing security in 5G communication. This cipher also offers an excellent case study for the aforementioned competing design choices - Galois vs Fibonacci and LFSR vs NFSR. As a contender for 5G security, Espresso claims better performance than Grain-128 and Trivium in the under 1500 Gate Equivalence (GE) chip-size regime with the stated parameters: 1497 GE area, 2.22 Gbits/sec throughput and 232 nanosecond latency.

When security claims are considered, Espresso is based on a 256-bit Galois NFSR, having 14 non-linear feedback update functions at different stages, and a non-linear output function, involving the outputs of 20 different stages. However, the security of Espresso against standard cryptanalysis strategies like linear approximation attacks and TMDTO attacks is actually discussed with respect to an "equivalent" NFSR (cf. p. 277 of [4]), having only two non-linear update functions. Thus Espresso is clearly an instantiation of the "analysis-on-equivalent-design" strategy mentioned earlier.

The motivation for the present work arose from an examination of the claimed equivalence of the two NFSRs presented in the Espresso proposal paper in the context of cryptanalysis of Espresso. An immediate issue had already been reported in [12]: no "equivalent" non-linear output function is provided in [4] corresponding to the alternative Galois NFSR. This precludes any comparison between the actual keystreams generated by Espresso and an "equivalent" cipher based on the alternative NFSR. Our preliminary analysis yielded the following additional discrepancies:

1. In [4], as also referred to in subsequent works (cf. for instance, [9,10,12]), the transformation method from *a Fibonacci to a uniform Galois NFSR* presented in [2] is invoked as the theoretical basis for the equivalence of the two NFSR designs in [4]. But, as both the NFSRs obviously have the general Galois configuration, it is not clear how the aforesaid transformation can be applied to validate the equivalence.
2. It is claimed in [4] that the sets of sequences generated by the stages 231 and 193 of the Espresso NFSR are equivalent to the sets of sequences generated by the stages 255 and 217, respectively, of the alternative NFSR. Our preliminary experiments failed to verify this claim.

A series of papers by Yao and Parampalli [11–13] culminated in defining the so-termed 'compensation method' for transformations of several types of Fibonacci and Galois NFSRs. Their method applied to Espresso is claimed to yield (cf. [12], Sect. 6.1):

"... a Fibonacci LFSR with a nonlinear output function. Specifically, the output function consists of 2289 monomials. There are 104 variables in the output function and the algebraic degree is 12."

But the question of whether or not the two NFSRs presented in [4] are actually equivalent is still not resolved. The issue has become urgent of late given the recent works attempting improved implementation of Espresso configurations, for instance [9], which assume the validity of the equivalence as claimed in [4]. In other words, while the security claims of Espresso are based on one design, the implementation is based on another - with several gaps between the equivalence of these two designs. This could potentially manifest in a major design flaw.

In this article, we examine and unify a sequence of transformation techniques, as outlined in E. Dubrova's works, which provide the key ingredients of Yao and Parampalli's analysis of Espresso [12,13]. The main objective of our article is to use our unified framework of the Dubrova and Yao-Parampalli algorithms to gain new insights as to the claimed equivalence of the Espresso designs. Specifically, our contributions are as follows.

1. We identify and correct a critical mis-step in the proof of the foundational theorem of Dubrova's first algorithm (cf. Theorem 1, Section IV, [2]).
2. We establish that Dubrova's first algorithm [2], with a small modification, is subsumed into the framework of the second algorithm [3].
3. We show that the Yao-Parampalli algorithm [12,13] is equivalent to Dubrova's second algorithm in the case of Fibonacci-to-uniform Galois NFSR transformation. It is noted that both the NFSRs in the Espresso paper [4] belong to the latter category.

4. As a final step we formulate, using the Yao-Parampalli framework, a possible
method to resolve the Espresso equivalence problem.

2   Preliminaries and Prior Work

A foundational analysis of non-linear feedback shift registers, in particular, the
cycle structure of the *state transition graph*, is given, like all matters "shift
register", in Golomb's text ([5], Part Three, Chapter VI onwards). We proceed
to outline two major algorithms in the works of E. Dubrova, followed by a brief
account of the Yao-Parampalli transformation framework.

2.1   The Algorithms of E. Dubrova

The first algorithm of E. Dubrova in [2] considers the transformation of a
Fibonacci NFSR to a *uniform* Galois NFSR, which guarantees the following
notion of equivalence between the NFSRs (cf. *Definition 1*, p.5265, [2]):
   "Two NLFSRs are equivalent if their sets of output sequences are equal."
   In [2], the *output bit* of an NFSR is specified to be the 0-th bit (cf. Section
II), and so, the transformation attempts to match the output sequence at the
0-th stage of the original Fibonacci NFSR with that at the 0-th stage of the
transformed Galois NFSR.
   The validity of this transformation is based on the uniform property of a
Galois NFSR, which is defined as follows(cf. *Definition 7*, [2]).

Definition 1. *The* terminal bit *of an n-bit NFSR is the bit with the minimal
index which satisfies the following condition: For all bits i such that $i < \tau$, the
feedback function f_i is of type $f_i = x_{(i+1)_n}$, where $(i+1)_n := (i+1) \mod n$.*

Definition 2. *An n-bit NFSR is* uniform *if*

(a) all its feedback functions are singular functions of the following form:

$$f_i(x_0, x_1, \cdots, x_{n-1}) = x_{(i+1)_n} \oplus g_i(x_0, x_1, \cdots, x_{n-1}) \tag{1}$$

$g_i : \{0,1\}^{n-1} \to \{0,1\}$ be such that $(i+1)_n \notin dep(g_i)$.
(b) for all its bits i such that $i > \tau$, the following condition holds:

$$max\_index(g_i) \leq \tau \tag{2}$$

where τ is the terminal bit of the NFSR.

   In the above context, the *dependence set* of a Boolean function f is denoted
by:

$$dep(f) := \{i \mid f|_{x_i=0} \neq f|_{x_i=1}\}$$

where $f|_{x_i=j} = f(x_0, x_1, \cdots, x_{i-1}, j, x_{i+1}, \cdots, x_{n-1})$, for $j \in \{0,1\}$.
   The main algorithm presented in [2] (cf. Section V) is a transformation algorithm from a Fibonacci to a *fully shifted*, uniform Galois NFSR, which is claimed

to preserve the output sequence at the 0-th stage. The term "fully shifted" refers to the fact that this construction guarantees the maximum possible shift from the Fibonacci configuration while maintaining the uniform property.

In [3], a more general algorithm was presented which handles transformations between two NFSRs in the Galois configuration via the operation of *valid shifting* described as follows.

Definition 3. *Given an n-variate mapping defined by functions of the form in Eq. 1, a shifting $f_i \xrightarrow{m} f_j$, $i, j \in \{0, 1, \ldots, n-1\}$, $i \neq j$, shifts the monomial m in the algebraic normal form (ANF) of f_i to the ANF of f_j, such that every index $a \in dep(m)$ is changed to $b = (a - i + j) \mod n$.*

Definition 4. *Consider an n-variate mapping with functions of the form in Eq. 1, such that the values computed by f_z, $z \in \{0, 1, \ldots, n-1\}$ form the* output *sequence. Then a shifting $g_i \xrightarrow{m} g_j$ is valid if, for every index $a \in dep(m)$ and b as in Definition 3, the following conditions hold.*

1. *For each $c \in [a, b] \setminus i$, $g_c = 0$; if $i \in [a, b]$, then $g_i^* = 0$ ($g_i^* = g_i \oplus m$);*
2. *For each $k \in [i, j]$, $k \notin dep(g_i^*)$.*
   Further, $k \notin dep(g_p)$ for all $p \in \{0, 1, \ldots, n-1\} \setminus i$;
3. *Neither $[a, b]$ nor $[i, j]$ contain both z and $z - 1$.*

In the above definition, $[i, j]$ stands for the set $\{i, i-1, \ldots, j\}$ if $i > j$, and the set $\{i, i+1, \ldots, j\}$ if $i < j$, with similar definitions for $[a, b]$. Further, if multiple indices z constitute the output sequence, the third condition must be fulfilled for all pairs $(z, z - 1)$.

The following result from [3] establishes that when a Galois NFSR is transformed to another through valid shiftings, the output sequences of the two NFSRs may differ only in a specific subset of the stages of the internal state.

Theorem 1 (E. Dubrova [3]). *Let F be a mapping as defined by Eq. 1 and F' be a mapping obtained from F by applying a valid shifting $g_i \xrightarrow{m} g_j$, where $i, j \in \{0, \ldots, n-1\}$ and $i \neq j$. Denote $\mathcal{J} = \{i+1, i+2, \ldots, j\}$ and $\mathcal{I} = \{i, i-1, \ldots, j+1\}$. Let F be initialized to the state $(s_0, s_1, \ldots, s_{n-1})$ and F' to the state $(r_0, r_1, \ldots, r_{n-1})$ such that:*

1. *For $k \in \mathcal{I}$, $r_k = s_k \oplus m|_{k-i-1}$*
2. *For $k \in \mathcal{J}$, $r_k = s_k \oplus m|_{k-j-1}$*
3. *$r_k = s_k$ for all $k \in \{0, 1, \ldots, n-1\}$ not in either $\mathcal{I}$ or $\mathcal{J}$.*

Then the sequences of states generated by F and F' may differ only in the bit positions in $\mathcal{I}$ or $\mathcal{J}$, respectively.

2.2   The Yao-Parampalli Framework

In [13], a classification of Galois NFSRs based on the forms of the feedback functions is discussed, where four types of NFSRs are described and four sets of transformation algorithms are presented. Of interest in this article is the

Type-II Galois NFSR, which corresponds to Dubrova's uniform Galois NFSR. Henceforth, we will refer to this configuration as uniform Galois.

The so-called *compensation method* was defined to satisfy the notion of output equivalence where the output is a function of several stages of the shift register. In this context, we state the following definitions from [13].

Definition 5. *A compensation list is a list with n elements denoted as $C = [c_0, c_1, \ldots, c_{n-1}]$, where each element $c_i(x_0, \ldots, x_{n-1})$, $i \in \{0, \ldots, n-1\}$ is a combination of variants of shifted monomials.*

The combination of two compensation lists C_{m1} and C_{m2}, for two monomials $m1$ and $m2$, is defined as the bitwise XOR $C = C_{m1} \oplus C_{m2}$.

Given an n-bit NFSR, the compensation list for shifting a monomial m from f_a to f_b with $a, b \in [0, n-1]$ and $a > b$, is constructed as

$$C = [c_0, c_1, \ldots, c_{n-1}] = [0, \ldots, 0, m|_{-(a-b)}, \ldots, m|_{-1}, 0, \ldots, 0]$$

where $c_i = 0$ for $i \in [0, b]$ or $[a+1, n-1]$ and $c_i = m|_{-(a-i+1)}$ for $i \in [b+1, a]$.

Given an n-bit Fibonacci NFSR with output function z and initial state X^0, the following steps outline the process of transformation into a uniform Galois NFSR [13].

1. For each monomial m_j, $j \in [1, r]$, compute the lowest permissible shifting index p_j using Dubrova's algorithm in [2] and choose a position τ_j, such that $p_j \le \tau_j \le n - 1$.
2. Shift the r monomials from the feedback functions f_{n-1} to $f_{\tau_1}, f_{\tau_2}, \ldots, f_{\tau_r}$, where $0 \le \tau_1 \le \tau_2 \le \ldots \le \tau_r \le n - 1$.
3. For each monomial m_j, $j \in [1, r]$, construct compensation list

$$C_{m_j} = [0, \ldots, 0, m_j|_{-(n-1-\tau_j)}, \ldots, m_j|_{-1}]$$

   XOR all such lists to compute a combined compensation list:
   $C = C_{m_1} \oplus C_{m_2} \oplus \ldots \oplus C_{m_r}$.
4. Compensate the output function f_z by C iteratively in the descending order to obtain the output function $\overline{f_z}$ for the transformed NFSR.
5. The initial state computed as: $\hat{x}_i^0 = x_i^0 \oplus c_i(X^0)$, $i \in [0, n-1]$.

A similar sequence of steps is presented for the transformation of an n-bit uniform Galois NFSR, with output function f_z and an initial state X^0, to an equivalent Fibonacci NFSR:

1. Shift every monomial $g_i \ne 0$, from f_i, $i \in [\tau, n-2]$ to f_{n-1}.
2. For each $g_i \ne 0$ in the first step, compute the compensation list

$$C_{g_i} = [0, \ldots, 0, g_i, g_i|_{+1}, \ldots, g_i|_{+(n-2-i)}]$$

   XOR all such lists to compute a combined compensation list:

$$C = C_{g_0} \oplus C_{g_1} \oplus \ldots \oplus C_{g_{n-2}}.$$

3. Compensate the output function f_z by C *without iteration* to obtain the output function $\overline{f_z}$ for the transformed Fibonacci NFSR as

$$\overline{f_z} = f_z(x_0 \oplus c_0, \ldots, x_{n-1} \oplus c_{n-1})$$

4. The initial state $\hat{X}^0 = [\hat{x}_0^0, \hat{x}_1^0, \ldots, \hat{x}_{n-1}^0]$ is given by: $\hat{x}_i^0 = x_i^0 \oplus \overline{c_i}(X^0)$, $i \in [0, n-1]$, where $\overline{c_i}$ is obtained from c_i compensated iteratively by C in descending order.

One readily notes the following obvious similarities between the Yao-Parampalli algorithm stated above and Dubrova's generalized algorithm in [3]:

- Both methods use Dubrova's formula in [2] to compute the indices of shifted monomials.
- Both methods attempt to achieve post-transformation equivalence in the sense of identical output sequences, by 'aligning' the initial states.

In the following Sect. 3 we establish the relation between Dubrova's algorithms in [2] and [3]. The connection between the Yao-Parampalli algorithms and the generalized Dubrova formulation is analyzed in Sect. 4.

3 Unifying Dubrova's Transformation Algorithms

In this section, we analyze Dubrova's Fibonacci-to-uniform Galois transformation algorithm, henceforth referred to as D1, and Galois-to-Galois transformation algorithm, henceforth referred to as D2. We begin by correcting the proof of a key result in [2], which forms the basis of the algorithm D1.

3.1 "Fixing" Dubrova's First Algorithm

All transformation algorithms analyzed in the subsequent sections of this article build on the work of E. Dubrova in defining the Fibonacci-to-uniform Galois NFSR transformation in [2]. However, we first show that there is a non-trivial flaw in the proof of the key result - termed the "main theorem" in [2] - that validates the algorithm D1. We then show how this discrepancy can be rectified with a simple modification so that Dubrova's theorem holds intact.

We begin by stating the result in question from [2]:

Theorem 2. *Given a uniform NLFSR with terminal bit a, a shifting $g_a \xrightarrow{P} g_b$, $P \subseteq A_{g_a}$, $b < a$, results in an equivalent NLFSR if the transformed NLFSR is uniform as well.*

The proof uses the *feedback graph* description of an NFSR as defined below [2].

Definition 6. *The* feedback graph *of an n-bit NFSR is a directed graph with n vertices $v_0, \ldots, v_{n-1}$ which represents bits $0, \ldots, n-1$ of the NFSR, respectively. There is an edge from v_i to v_j if $i \in dep(f_j)$.*

We will show that the discrepancies in the proof of this theorem stem from an incorrect application of the 'substitution' operation (Definition 3 of Section III in [2]), stated below.

Definition 7. *The operation* substitution, *denoted by* $sub(v_i, v_j)$, *is defined for any vertex* v_i, *which has a unique predecessor* v_j. *The substitution* $sub(v_i, v_j)$ *removes* v_i *from the feedback graph and, for each successor* v_k *of* v_i, *replaces the edge* (v_i, v_k) *by an edge* (v_j, v_k).

Clearly the operation is defined as $\mathbf{sub}(v(\mathbf{successor}), v(\mathbf{predecessor}))$.

We first outline the steps of the proof provided in [2] which use a flawed definition of the substitution operation. While we adhere to the original notation in [2] as much as possible, we label the first uniform NFSR as N_a and the second as N_b, according to the respective terminal bits. The strategy of Dubrova's proof may be stated as follows:

If the NFSR N_b, with terminal bit b, is uniform, its feedback graph is reducible to a single vertex v_b. Then there exists a non-linear recurrence describing the sequence at v_b. The equivalence between N_a, N_b is established if this recurrence is shown to be identical with that describing the sequence at v_a for N_a.

Relevant Steps in Dubrova's Proof: Let $\tau = a$ and $\tau = b$ represent the respective terminal bits for N_a and N_b. As outlined in the steps of the proof to Theorem 1 of [2], the substitution operation is invoked twice in arriving at the non-linear recurrence for each terminal bit $\tau, \tau \in \{a, b\}$. For instance, for $\tau = a$, the vertices $i < a$ are first removed via the substitution sequence:

$$\text{sub}(v_0, v_1), \text{sub}(v_1, v_2), \ldots, \text{sub}(v_{a-1}, v_a)$$

Then the vertices $v_i, i > \tau = a$ are removed as follows in Section IV of [2], page 5268 (we quote in italics):

"After a sequence of $n-a-1$ substitutions $\text{sub}(v_{n-1}, v_{n-2}), \ldots, \text{sub}(v_{a+1}, v_a)$, *we get a non-linear recurrence describing the sequence of values of bit a*

$$s_a(t) = s_a(t - n) \oplus g_{n-1}(\tilde{s}_a(-n + a + 1)) \oplus g_{n-2}(\tilde{s}_a(-n + a))$$
$$\oplus \cdots \oplus g_a^*(\tilde{s}_a) \oplus s_a(t - 1 - a + k)s_a(t - 1)."$$

The notation $\tilde{s}_a(i)$ has been defined (cf. pages 5267, 5268) to mean that each element $s_a(x)$ of $\tilde{s}_a$ has been replaced by $s_a(x + i)$, where $\tilde{s}_a$ stands for

$$\tilde{s}_a := (s_a(t - a - 1), s_a(t - a), \ldots, s_a(t - 1 - (a - b)))$$

A similar step is described in arriving at the non-linear recurrence for the values of the bit b.

The Discrepancy
We observe that:

- The vertices $i > \tau$, for $\tau = a$ or b, are removed via the sequence:

$$\mathrm{sub}(v_{n-1}, v_{n-2}), \ldots, \mathrm{sub}(v_{\tau+1}, v_\tau) \tag{3}$$

  It is noted that the arguments of the terms in Eq. (3) are not consistent with the definition of the substitution operation (cf. Definition 7) as they have the form

$$(v(\text{predecessor}), v(\text{successor})).$$

- Even if the order of the arguments is reversed in each operation, the second substitution sequence fails to achieve the presumed objective of reducing all the remaining vertices to v_τ.

However, a simple modification to the strategy of applying the substitution operation suffices to remove this discrepancy in the proof, as discussed below.

The Correction
We aver that the correct strategy to evaluate the non-linear recurrence for the sequence of values of the terminal bit is to apply the following sequence of substitutions, *after* all the vertices labelled $i < \tau$ have been removed:

$$\mathrm{sub}(v_{n-1}, v_\tau), \mathrm{sub}(v_{n-2}, v_\tau), \ldots, \mathrm{sub}(v_{\tau+1}, v_\tau)$$

Justification: Our correction stems from the observation that

at the beginning of the second substitution sequence, the vertex v_τ becomes the unique predecessor of v_{n-1} and the reduction proceeds by collapsing the vertices $v_{n-2}, \ldots, v_{\tau+1}$ to the vertex v_τ in this order.

The above is clearly a consequence of the uniform property, with τ as the terminal bit. The first substitution in the second sequence, $\mathrm{sub}(v_{n-1}, v_\tau)$, results in v_τ emerging as the unique predecessor of v_{n-2}, and the process continues.

Changing the time-shifts of $s_\tau(t)$ appropriately at each stage will result in identical non-linear recurrences for both $\tau = a$ and $\tau = b$, thus proving the theorem.

An Illustration of the Correct Reduction. We illustrate the correct procedure for graph reduction using Dubrova's substitution operation with the following toy example.

Consider the 4-bit Galois NFSR given by the feedback update functions:

$$f_3 = x_0; \quad f_2 = x_3 \oplus x_0 x_2; \quad f_1 = x_2; \quad f_0 = x_1.$$

Following Dubrova's graphical representation in Section III of [2], the graph of the NFSR is given in Fig. 1(a). Note that every vertex except the vertex 2 has a unique predecessor. Hence, we can proceed to apply the substitution sequences in two stages as follows:

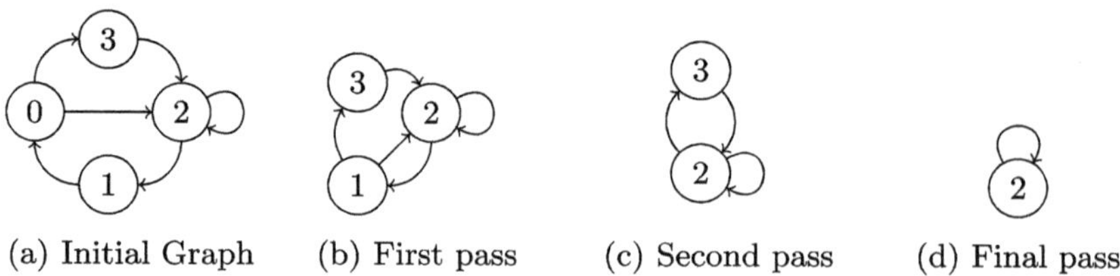

(a) Initial Graph   (b) First pass   (c) Second pass   (d) Final pass

Fig. 1. NFSR Graph Reduction via Substitution

1. The vertices $i < 2$ can be removed by the sequence:

$$\{\mathrm{sub}(0,1),\ \mathrm{sub}(1,2)\}$$

2. Now the vertex 3 can be removed by the substitution: $\mathrm{sub}(3,2)$.

The first sequence exactly matches Dubrova's formulation for vertices v_i with $i < \tau$. Where the proof fails in [2] is in formulating the second sequence for the vertices v_i with $i > \tau$.

The initial sequence of states for the above NFSR is given by the following set of equations.

$$s_3(t) = s_0(t-1)$$
$$s_2(t) = s_3(t-1) \oplus s_0(t-1)s_2(t-1)$$
$$s_1(t) = s_2(t-1)$$
$$s_0(t) = s_1(t-1)$$

After the first substitution pass, which results in the removal of the vertex 0 as shown in Fig. 1(b), the sequence of states are described as:

$$s_3(t) = s_1(t-2)$$
$$s_2(t) = s_3(t-1) \oplus s_1(t-2)s_2(t-1)$$
$$s_1(t) = s_2(t-1)$$

After the final pass, which removes the vertex 3, the equation for the sequence at vertex 2 is obtained as:

$$s_2(t) = s_2(t-2) \oplus s_2(t-3)s_2(t-1).$$

3.2   Unifying Dubrova's Algorithms

In this section we establish the connection between the transformation algorithms discussed in [2] and [3]. We explore this connection in the context of the type of NFSRs featured in the Espresso proposal, and hence, begin with the following definition.

Definition 8. *A uniform NFSR is termed a strict-terminal uniform NFSR, denoted st-uniform NFSR, if it satisfies the following condition for all stages indexed by $i > \tau$:*

$$max\_index(g_i) < \tau$$

where τ is the terminal bit.

For instance, the Espresso NFSR G has terminal bit $\tau = 193$ with the largest $max\_index(g_i) = 189$, while the Espresso alternate NFSR F has terminal bit $\tau = 217$, with $max\_index(g_i) \leq 183$. Hence they are both st-uniform NFSRs.

In what follows we show that:

Dubrova's Fibonacci-to-uniform Galois transformation algorithm [2] D1, restricted to st-uniform Galois NFSRs, is subsumed into the framework of the Galois-to-Galois algorithm D2 [3].

The algorithm D1 effects a transformation between a uniform Fibonacci to a uniform, fully shifted Galois NFSR, which shifts all the monomials from the stage $n-1$ to a stage with index greater than or equal to the terminal bit τ. The rules of this shifting are given in [2] as follows.

Let $max\_index(m)$ denote the largest index of variables in $dep(m)$; likewise $min\_index(m)$ denotes the smallest index. For all $m \in S_{g_{n-1}}$, where $S_{g_{n-1}}$ is the set of monomials of g_{n-1},

1. If $min\_index(m) \leq (n-1) - \tau$, then the monomial m is shifted as

$$g_{n-1} \xrightarrow{m} g_{n-1-\min\_index(m)}$$

2. If $min\_index(m) > (n-1) - \tau$, then the monomial is shifted to g_τ.

We now prove that the above method in the D1 algorithm for generating a fully shifted st-uniform Galois NFSR from a (uniform) Fibonacci NFSR, which preserves the output sequence at the 0-th stage, is consistent with a valid shifting in the D2 algorithm.

Theorem 3. *Let F be a Fibonacci NFSR with feedback functions of the form given in Eq. 1, with the set of feedback monomials at the $(n-1)$-th stage denoted by $\{x_0\} \cup S_{g_{n-1}}$. Then the shift of any monomial $m \in S_{g_{n-1}}$ under the algorithm D1 for st-uniform NFSRs is a valid shifting in the sense of the algorithm D2.*

Proof. We establish that the conditions for a valid shifting are indeed satisfied by the shift operations of the D1 algorithm for st-uniform NFSRs. Consider the setting of Definition 4 for the shift of a monomial m from g_i to g_j.

- **Condition 1:** *For each $c \in [a,b] \setminus i$, $g_c = 0$; if $i \in [a,b]$, then $g_i^* = 0$.*
  In the D1 algorithm, by the st-uniform property of the transformed Galois NFSR, $a, b \in \{\tau - 1, \ldots, 0\}$, where the terminal bit satisfies $n - 1 > \tau \geq 0$. Moreover, for the transformed Galois NFSR, for all $c \in \{\tau - 1, \ldots, 0\}$ the feedback function is $f_c = x_{c+1}$, i.e. $g_c = 0$.
  Further, the condition $i = n - 1 > j \geq \tau$ implies $i \notin [a,b]$, so the second case does not arise.

- **Condition 2:** *For each $k \in [i, j]$, $k \notin \mathrm{dep}(g_i^*)$. Further, $k \notin \mathrm{dep}(g_p)$ for all $p \in \{0, 1, \ldots, n-1\} \setminus i$.*
  In the D1 algorithm, $i = n - 1$ and $j \geq \tau$, with $n - 1 > \tau \geq 0$. By the st-uniform property, any stage $k \in [i, j] = \{n - 1, n - 2, \ldots, j\}$ has possible feedback only from stages $l < \tau$. Hence, no index $k \in [i, j]$ is included in either $\mathrm{dep}(g_i^*)$ or $\mathrm{dep}(g_p)$ for any stage p.
- **Condition 3:** *Neither $[a, b]$ nor $[i, j]$ contain both z and $z - 1$.*
  The set $[a, b]$ (labelled as 'sources' in [3]) is a subset of $\{\tau - 1, \ldots, 0\}$ and the set $[i, j]$ (labelled as 'sinks' in [3]) is a subset of $\{n - 1, n - 2, \ldots, j\}$ with $j \geq \tau$. As the D1 algorithm designates the 0-th stage as the output stage z, it is evident that the admissible sets $[a, b]$ and $[i, j]$ cannot contain both 0 and $n - 1$.

Hence the proof. $\qquad\qquad\square$

The implications of the above result in the context of the Espresso equivalence problem are discussed in the next subsection.

Remark 1. Theorem 3 shows that for Fibonacci to st-uniform Galois transformation, D1 in [2] is subsumed in the framework of D2 in [3]. Hence the post-transformation equivalence conditions (cf. Theorem 1) that are satisfied for D2 will hold for D1 as well.

3.3   Applicability of Dubrova's Algorithms in the Espresso Equivalence Problem

As discussed in the introductory section, an alternate Galois NFSR F is defined in [4] to discuss the security of Espresso, which is claimed to be "equivalent" to the cipher design. However, we point out that there are two aspects to any meaningful equivalence, in the context of security analysis, of the two NFSR configurations so defined.

1. Establishing the equivalence of the generated keystreams at designated stages of the 2-tap Galois NFSR F and the Espresso NFSR G.
2. Defining a corresponding non-linear output function for F, so that both systems generate *identical keystreams*. No such function is provided in [4].

Both of these issues are as yet unresolved and constitute what we term the *Espresso Equivalence Problem*, graphically depicted in Fig. 2.

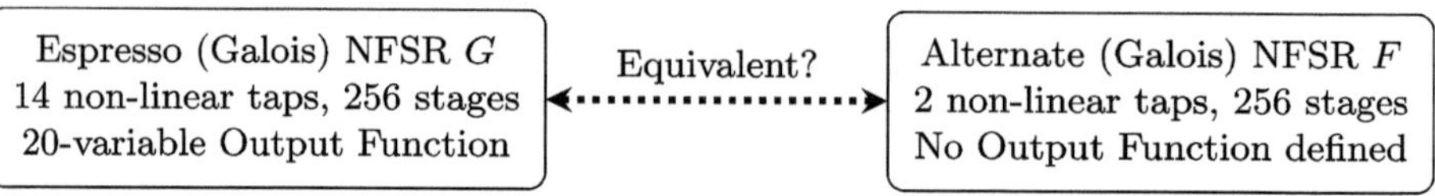

Fig. 2. The Espresso Equivalence Problem

In [4], the only pointer to establishing the claimed equivalence is a reference, on p. 278, to Dubrova's algorithm D1 in [2] which we quote below:

"The equivalence of G and F can be shown by applying the Fibonacci-to-Galois transformation [6]."

In the light of our preceding analysis, we now discuss the applicability of Dubrova's algorithms to the Espresso equivalence problem. We make our case with the following comparison of the relevant features of algorithms D1 and D2.

Table 1. Comparison of Dubrova's NFSR Transformation Algorithms

Algorithm	NFSR Types	Multi-stage Equivalence	Matching Initial States
D1 [2]	Fibonacci to Uniform Galois	No	No
D2 [3]	Galois to Galois	Yes	Yes

The corresponding aspects of the Espresso equivalence problem are enumerated as follows.

1. The Espresso NFSR G has Galois configuration with 14 non-linear taps, and the alternate NFSR F is Galois as well, with 2 non-linear taps.
   Hence any technique to establish their equivalence should be defined to handle Galois-to-Galois transformation.
2. The non-linear output function of Espresso is composed of 20 variables, representing the values at 20 different stages of the NFSR G. Even though the corresponding output function has not been defined for NFSR F, it is likely to involve multiple stages as well.
   Hence the proposed technique should guarantee the equivalence of the sequences at multiple corresponding stages.
3. Finally, matching initial states should be defined for both systems in order to generate identical keystreams.

It now follows from Table 1 that, contrary to the claim in [4], the algorithm D1 cannot be used to resolve the Espresso equivalence problem, while it may be possible to use the algorithm D2 to gain further insights into the problem.

4 Relating Yao-Parampalli and Dubrova's Algorithms

As discussed in Subsect. 2.2, the Yao-Parampalli transformation framework, henceforth denoted as the Y-P framework, analyzes four configurations of Galois NFSRs and back-and-forth transformations with "equivalent" Fibonacci NFSRs, when possible. However, the only proven technical results in [13] deal with the transformation of a Fibonacci NFSR to a uniform Galois NFSR, which is the case treated in [2] by E. Dubrova. Accordingly, we compare the Y-P Fibonacci-to-uniform Galois algorithm with Dubrova's generalized transformation D2 restricted to this particular case.

4.1   Comparing Y-P and Dubrova's Generalized Algorithms

There are exactly three results which are furnished with proofs in [13] as follows:

- In Sect. 2 of [13], Lemma 1 and Lemma 2 relate the internal states of an "original Fibonacci NLFSR" with that of the "transformed Type-II Galois NLFSR".
- The third result is Theorem 1 in Sect. 3 of [13], which establishes that for "an n-bit Fibonacci NLFSR transformed to a Type-II Galois NLFSR according to the Fibonacci-to-Type-II algorithm", the internal states are related by the relations in Lemma 1 and Lemma 2, and, further, the NFSRs are "equivalent".

We first show that the proposed modification to match the initial states before and after the transformation in the Y-P framework yields the same result as that outlined in Dubrova's algorithm D2.

Modification of Initial States. We begin by stating the two lemmas, proved in [13], and compare them with Dubrova's Theorem 1. For facilitating this comparison, we use the following

Notation: Denote the k-th stage at time t of the transformed uniform Galois NFSR as r_k^t, and let s_k^t denote the corresponding entity for the Fibonacci NFSR. The complete states of the said NFSRs at time t are denoted with the boldface $\mathbf{r}^t$ and $\mathbf{s}^t$, respectively.

The lemmas, as stated below, establish that for the shift of a single monomial, using Dubrova's shift formula in [2], a relation between the initial states of the Fibonacci and the transformed uniform Galois NFSRs is preserved for all subsequent states.

Lemma 1 (Lemma 1, [13]). *Given an n-bit Fibonacci NFSR, a monomial m is shifted from f_{n-1} to f_b according to the shift operation in Definition 3 and the resulted feedback functions satisfy the conditions for uniform Galois NFSRs. If the initial state of the uniform Galois NFSR is computed according to (4), then the internal state of the uniform Galois NFSR $r_t^k, k \in \{0, \ldots, n-1\}$ and the internal state of the Fibonacci NLFSR $s_t^k, k \in \{0, \ldots, n-1\}$ also satisfy this relation for $t > 0$.*

$$r_k = s_k \oplus m|_{-(n-k)}(\mathbf{s}^t), \ for \ k \in [b+1, n-1]$$
$$r_k = s_k, \ for \ k \in [0, b] \tag{4}$$

In the following result we establish the equivalence of the procedure of matching the initial states in the Y-P and Dubrova's formulations by proving the equivalence of Lemma 1 of [13] with Dubrova's theorem in [3].

Lemma 2. *For a Fibonacci-to-uniform Galois transformation, the formulation in [13] for the Galois NFSR stages r_k^t in terms of the Fibonacci stages s_k^t, $k \in \{0, \ldots, n-1\}$, is simply obtained by a restriction of the formulation in Dubrova's Theorem in [3] to this particular case.*

Proof. The condition on the initial state stated in Lemma 1 is exactly identical to that stated in Dubrova's Theorem 1 for the case $i = n - 1 > j = b$, which corresponds to $\mathcal{I} = [n - 1, n - 2, \ldots, b + 1]$.

Substituting $i = n - 1$ in the expression $r_k = s_k \oplus m|_{k-i-1}$ yields precisely the formula in Lemma 1 for the indices which are modified in the transformation. Dubrova's theorem further states that all indices outside the set $\mathcal{I}$ are unaffected by the transformation, which translates exactly to the condition $r_k^t = s_k^t$, for $k \in [0, b]$, for all $t > 0$.

Finally, the proof of Dubrova's theorem establishes that if the stages of the two NFSRs indexed by $\mathcal{I}$ are related by Eq. 4 at some time t, the relation holds for $t + 1$ as well. $\qquad\square$

Compensation vs. Iterative Compensation. The second lemma (Lemma 2) in [13] simply re-states the correspondence between the states of the Fibonacci and Galois NFSRs in the converse direction of Lemma 1. However, in the statement and proof of this lemma in [13], the compensation procedure discussed in Sect. 2.2 is employed *iteratively*. Following [13], we briefly outline this in the case where the indices x_i, x_j, $j = i - 1$, are compensated by the entries c_i, c_j of the compensation list, respectively.

Simple compensation results in $x_i \to x_i \oplus c_i$ and $x_j \to x_j \oplus c_j$.

In iterative compensation *in the descending order*, x_i is first transformed to $x_i \oplus c_i$. If $c_i = c_i(\ldots, x_j, \ldots)$, then in the next step, $x_i \to x_i \oplus c_i(\ldots, x_j \oplus c_j, \ldots)$, i.e. the effect of compensation at the next lower index $j = i - 1$ is applied iteratively on the compensated x_i.

The second lemma of the Y-P framework, which features iterative compensation, is stated as follows.

Lemma 3. *[Lemma 2, [13]] In the setting of Lemma 1,*

$$
\begin{aligned}
s_k &= r_k \oplus \overline{m|_{-(n-k)}}(\mathbf{r}^t), \; \text{for } k \in [b+1, n-1] \\
s_k &= r_k, \; \text{for } k \in [0, b]
\end{aligned}
\tag{5}
$$

where $\overline{m|_{-(n-k)}}$ *is m compensated by* $C = [0, \ldots, 0, m|_{-(a-b)}, \ldots, m|_{-1}, 0, \ldots, 0]$ *iteratively in descending order.*

We next build on Lemma 2, and the aforementioned results, to compare the results of Dubrova's and Y-P frameworks on the modification of the initial states through the following series of observations.

Observations:

1. An inspection of the conditions in Theorem 1 and Eq. 4 shows that the proposed modifications on the initial states are identical in both. In other words, the simple compensation formula of Yao-Parampalli is identical with Dubrova's relevant formula in this case (cf. Lemma 2).
2. The only difference in the conditions of Theorem 1 and those in Eq. 5 is the possible difference between the effects of compensation and iterative compensation.

3. If both the Eqs. 4 and 5 hold, as proved separately in [13], we have

$$m|_{-(n-k)}(\mathbf{s}^t) = \overline{m|_{-(n-k)}}(\mathbf{r}^t), \text{ for } k \in [b+1, n-1]$$

Therefore, for the purpose of designing an equivalent Galois NFSR from a Fibonacci NFSR, the correspondence between the states is captured by simple compensation, i.e. Dubrova's formula itself.

5 Applying the Y-P/Dubrova Techniques to the Espresso Equivalence Problem

In this section we bring to bear our analysis of the Y-P transformation techniques on the Espresso Equivalence Problem (cf. Subsection 3.3). As mentioned earlier, it is claimed in [12] that the application of the Yao-Parampalli *uniform Galois-to-Fibonacci* NFSR transformation on the Espresso NFSR G results in a Fibonacci LFSR with feedback function

$$f_L(\mathbf{x}) := f_{255}(x) = x_0 \oplus x_{12} \oplus x_{48} \oplus x_{115} \oplus x_{133} \oplus x_{213} \tag{6}$$

The Y-P algorithm claims to generate an output function, which we denote as $z_{\mathrm{YP}}(\mathbf{x})$, consisting of 2289 monomials and having algebraic degree 12. It is further claimed that the ensemble comprising the LFSR $f_L(\mathbf{x})$ and the output function $z_{\mathrm{YP}}(\mathbf{x})$, with the initial state matched with that of Espresso NFSR G, produces the same keystream as Espresso.

Thus far in this section, we have shown that the NFSR transformation effected by the Y-P Fibonacci-to-uniform Galois method is essentially the same as Dubrova's algorithm D2. We can, therefore, use the Fibonacci-to-uniform Galois algorithm on the Y-P LFSR ($f_L(\mathbf{x})$) to attempt a transformation to the Espresso alternate NFSR F. If the NFSR F is recovered, then, given the equivalence claimed in [12], *the output function obtained using the Y-P algorithm on the LFSR ensemble would complete the gap in the Espresso NFSR F design.* A concept schematic of this strategy is depicted in Fig. 3. We next demonstrate the recovery of the alternate NFSR F from the Y-P LFSR.

5.1 Recovery of Espresso NFSR F from Y-P LFSR

We note that the Espresso alternate NFSR F, which is the basis of several security claims regarding Espresso, is a Galois NFSR with exactly two feedback taps given by:

$$\begin{aligned}
f_{255}(\mathbf{x}) =& x_0 \oplus x_{12} \oplus x_{48} \oplus x_{115} \oplus x_{133} \oplus x_{213} \oplus x_{41}x_{70} \oplus x_{46}x_{87} \\
& \oplus x_{52}x_{110} \oplus x_{55}x_{130} \oplus x_{62}x_{157} \oplus x_{74}x_{183} \oplus x_{87}x_{110}x_{130}x_{157} \\
f_{217}(\mathbf{x}) =& x_{218} \oplus x_3x_{32} \oplus x_8x_{49} \oplus x_{14}x_{72} \oplus x_{17}x_{92} \oplus x_{24}x_{119} \oplus x_{36}x_{145} \\
& \oplus x_{49}x_{72}x_{92}x_{119}
\end{aligned} \tag{7}$$

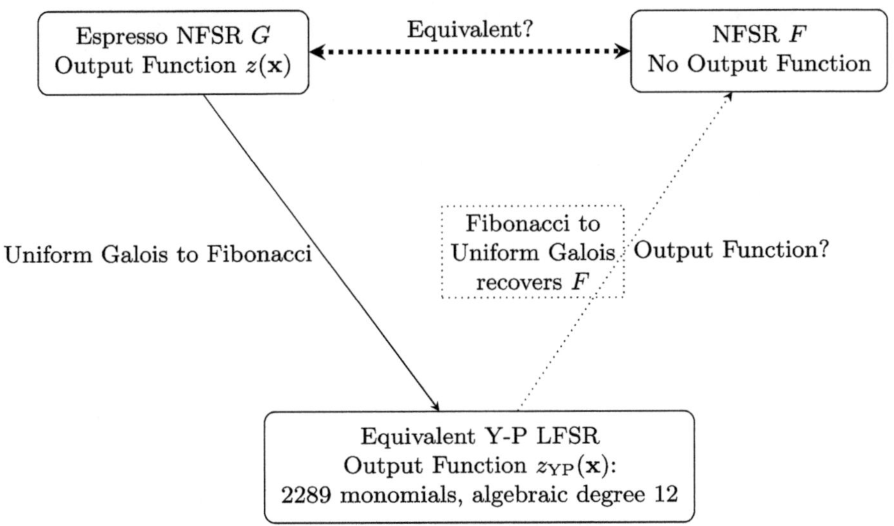

Fig. 3. Using Y-P/Dubrova Algorithms to Resolve Espresso Equivalence

It is remarked in [4] that the feedback functions of the NFSR F are related in the following manner. First it is evident that

$$f_{255}(\mathbf{x}) = f_{\mathrm{Lin}}(\mathbf{x}) \oplus f_{\mathrm{NL}}(\mathbf{x}) \tag{8}$$

where $f_{\mathrm{Lin}}(\mathbf{x})$ is a linear polynomial component and $f_{\mathrm{NL}}(\mathbf{x})$ is a non-linear component. Further the feedback function at stage 217 is given precisely by

$$f_{217}(\mathbf{x}) = x_{218} \oplus f_{\mathrm{NL}}(\mathbf{x})_{(i-38)}$$

where the second term is given by the non-linear component $f_{\mathrm{NL}}(\mathbf{x})$ of f_{255}, with every variable x_i changed to x_{i-38}.

Crucial Observation: From Eq. 6 and Eq. 8 it immediately follows that the Y-P transformed LFSR feedback function $f_L(\mathbf{x})$ is identical with the linear component of the feedback function at stage 255 of the Espresso alternate NFSR, $f_{\mathrm{Lin}}(\mathbf{x})$.

We re-write the feedback function at stage 255 in the Y-P Fibonacci LFSR as

$$f_L(\mathbf{x}) = (f_L(\mathbf{x}) \oplus f_{\mathrm{NL}}(\mathbf{x})) \oplus f_{\mathrm{NL}}(\mathbf{x})$$

Next we use Dubrova's shift formula to transfer all the monomials in $f_{\mathrm{NL}}(\mathbf{x})$ from stage 255 to stage 217. The transformed feedback function at stage 217 then becomes:

$$f_{217} = x_{218} \oplus f_{\mathrm{NL}}(\mathbf{x})_{(i-255+217)} = x_{218} \oplus f_{\mathrm{NL}}(\mathbf{x})_{(i-38)}$$

For instance, the term $x_{41}x_{70}$, on being shifted to the stage 217, becomes x_3x_{32}.

After the shift, the modified feedback function at stage 255 is

$$f_{255}(\mathbf{x}) = f_L(\mathbf{x}) \oplus f_{\mathrm{NL}}(\mathbf{x})$$

Hence, we have recovered the Galois NFSR F with exactly two non-linear feedback taps at stages 255 and 217. Further, all the feedback inputs at the stages 255 and 217 are from the stages x_i with $i \leq 183 < 217$. Clearly this is a uniform Galois NFSR, with terminal bit chosen as 217. Therefore we can use the Y-P Fibonacci-to-uniform Galois algorithm to generate a non-linear filter generator cipher based on the Espresso alternate NFSR F as follows.

Algorithm 1. GENERATION OF ESPRESSO ALTERNATE NFSR CIPHER

1: **Input:** Y-P n-bit Fibonacci LFSR L and Non-linear function $z_{\mathrm{YP}}(\mathbf{x})$; Initial state $\mathbf{s}$ of Fibonacci LFSR.
   Output: Espresso alternate NFSR F and Non-linear function $z_F(\mathbf{x})$; Matching initial state $\mathbf{r}$ of NFSR F.
2: Use Dubrova's shift formula to generate NFSR F:

$$f_{255} \xrightarrow{f_{\mathrm{NL}}(\mathbf{x})} f_{217}$$

3: Generate combined compensation list C for the shift.
4: Obtain matching initial state for F by simple compensation using C (Dubrova's theorem/Y-P lemma).
5: Obtain output function $z_F(\mathbf{x})$ from $z_{\mathrm{YP}}(\mathbf{x})$ by iterative compensation in the descending order using C.

To conclude, we summarize our progress in the resolution of the Espresso equivalence problem and the gap that still remains. As depicted in Fig. 3, we have successfully deployed the published algorithm in [13] on their Fibonacci ensemble to retrieve the Espresso alternate Galois NFSR F. This was done by appropriately applying Dubrova's shift formula to the Yao-Parampalli LFSR, which corresponds to Step 2 of our Algorithm 1. Then, assuming that the algorithms in [13] are correct, iterative compensation of the LFSR ensemble non-linear function, *should* retrieve a valid non-linear function for the NFSR F. This is what is described in the final steps of our proposed algorithm. However, apart from the obvious challenge posed by the iterative compensation of the 2289-monomial non-linear function in the Y-P LFSR ensemble, our preliminary analyses indicate additional issues. Specifically, the equivalence guarantees of the Y-P Fibonacci-to-uniform Galois transformation need careful verification when applied to Espresso. This is a work in progress.

Conclusion and Future Work

The stream cipher Espresso is of practical interest as a candidate for 5G security and its design methodology is significant as it attempts to harness the benefits of a Galois NFSR-based implementation while providing a means of simpler analysis through an equivalent design. But the validity of its security claims against several standard cryptanalytic techniques rests on the equivalence of two designs discussed in [4], which is as yet unsubstantiated. We have termed this the Espresso equivalence problem and have demonstrated the first steps in a proposed road-map for its resolution. Our results are partly based on an analysis of Yao and Parampalli's LFSR-based design [12].

We have achieved a partial unification of E. Dubrova and Yao-Parampalli's transformation techniques, and used this insight to recover the Espresso alternate NFSR F from the Y-P LFSR. However, a complete resolution of Espresso equivalence would require a correct evaluation of a matching non-linear function for F. This is part of an ongoing analysis.

In this context, we mention that there is a growing body of research on NFSR equivalence, for instance, [14,15] and [8][1]. In [15], the authors claim to establish that the 288-stage Galois NFSR of Trivium cannot be shown to be equivalent to a 288-stage Fibonacci NFSR. However, it is somewhat surprising that the case of the Espresso NFSRs is still unresolved. We hope that this investigation would lead to the creation of a general template for equivalence-preserving shift register transformations. Such a template, if rigorously formulated, would open up the exciting possibility of obtaining equivalent circuits for existing designs of proven security like Grain and Trivium, and possibly identify variants with optimized implementation.

Acknowledgement. The authors would like to thank the anonymous reviewers for their detailed comments that improved both the content and presentation. The inputs from Subhamoy Maitra, Mridul Nandi and Sabyasachi Karati are also gratefully acknowledged. The work of Anirban Ghatak is supported by SAG, DRDO, Delhi.

References

1. Cannière, C.: TRIVIUM: a stream cipher construction inspired by block cipher design principles. In: Katsikas, S.K., López, J., Backes, M., Gritzalis, S., Preneel, B. (eds.) ISC 2006. LNCS, vol. 4176, pp. 171–186. Springer, Heidelberg (2006). https://doi.org/10.1007/11836810_13
2. Dubrova, E.: A Transformation From the Fibonacci to the Galois NLFSRs. IEEE Trans. Inf. Theory **55**(11), 5263–5271 (2009). https://doi.org/10.1109/TIT.2009.2030467
3. Dubrova, E.: An equivalence-preserving transformation of shift registers. In: Schmidt, K.-U., Winterhof, A. (eds.) SETA 2014. LNCS, vol. 8865, pp. 187–199. Springer, Cham (2014). https://doi.org/10.1007/978-3-319-12325-7_16
4. Dubrova, E., Hell, M.: Espresso: a stream cipher for 5G wireless communication systems. Cryptogr. Commun. **9**(2), 273–289 (2015). https://doi.org/10.1007/s12095-015-0173-2

---

[1] The authors are grateful to the anonymous reviewer for suggesting this work.

5. Golomb, S.W.: Shift register sequences: secure and limited-access code generators, efficiency code generators, prescribed property generators, mathematical models. World Scientific (2017). https://doi.org/10.1142/9361
6. Hamann, M., Krause, M., Meier, W.: LIZARD - a lightweight stream cipher for power-constrained devices. IACR Trans. Symmetric Cryptol. **2017**(1), 45–79 (2017). https://doi.org/10.13154/tosc.v2017.i1.45-79
7. Mansouri, S.S., Dubrova, E.: An improved hardware implementation of the grain stream cipher. In: 13th Euromicro Conference on Digital System Design: Architectures, Methods and Tools, pp. 433–440 (2010). https://doi.org/10.1109/DSD.2010.49
8. Pan, Y., Zhong, J., Lin, D.: The equivalence between Galois and Fibonacci NFSRs. Theor. Comput. Sci. **1003** (2024). https://doi.org/10.1016/j.tcs.2024.114620
9. Shi, Z., et al.: Design space exploration of galois and fibonacci configuration based on espresso stream cipher. ACM Trans. Reconfigurable Technol. Syst. **16**(3) (2023). https://doi.org/10.1145/3567428
10. Wang, M.X., Lin, D.D.: Related key chosen IV attack on stream cipher espresso variant. In: IEEE International Conference on Computational Science and Engineering (CSE) and IEEE International Conference on Embedded and Ubiquitous Computing (EUC), vol. 1, pp. 580–587 (2017). https://doi.org/10.1109/CSE-EUC.2017.107
11. Yao, G., Parampalli, U.: Improved transformation algorithms for generalized galois NLFSRs. In: Sequences and Their Applications SETA 2020 (2020)
12. Yao, G., Parampalli, U.: Cryptanalysis of the class of maximum period galois NLFSR-based stream ciphers. Cryptogr. Commun. **13**(5), 847–864 (2021). https://doi.org/10.1007/s12095-021-00511-0
13. Yao, G., Parampalli, U.: Improved transformation algorithms for generalized Galois NLFSRs. Cryptogr. Commun. **14**(2), 229–258 (2021). https://doi.org/10.1007/s12095-021-00500-3
14. Zhao, X.-X., Qi, W.-F., Zhang, J.-M.: Further results on the equivalence between Galois NFSRs and Fibonacci NFSRs. Des. Codes Crypt. **88**(1), 153–171 (2019). https://doi.org/10.1007/s10623-019-00677-y
15. Zhong, J., Pan, Y., Kong, W., Lin, D.: Necessary and Sufficient Conditions for Galois NFSRs Equivalent to Fibonacci Ones and Their Application to the Stream Cipher Trivium. Cryptology ePrint Archive (2021). https://eprint.iacr.org/2021/928

Sample Similarity Based Incremental Clustering: An Effective Methodology for Anomaly Detection in Networks

K. Arun$^{(\boxtimes)}$, V. S. Ardra, and S Aji

Centre for Data Science and Information Processing, Department of Computer Science, University of Kerala, Thiruvananthapuram, India
{arunk,aji}@keralauniversity.ac.in

Abstract. The day to day increase of devices connected to the internet has led to an increase in cybersecurity threats, making it essential to develop advanced intrusion detection systems (IDS) that can recognize new and evolving attacks. Traditional methods for clustering in IDS, like K-means and DBSCAN, have their drawbacks, including rigid cluster formation, and difficulties in processing real-time data streams. To address this gap, this paper proposes an unsupervised learning based approach called Incremental Cosine Similarity-based Clustering (ICS) to detecting anomalies in network environments. ICS uses cosine similarity to allow clusters to grow adaptively, update centroids efficiently, and score anomalies dynamically. When evaluated on the BCAST IDS and NSL-KDD datasets, ICS showed impressive results, outperforming incremental K-Means variants in terms of cluster quality (Silhouette Score: 0.504 vs 0.201), runtime efficiency (17.45 s vs 20.66 s), and adaptability (3 clusters vs 2 clusters). The findings show that ICS is effective for detecting intrusion, providing enhanced accuracy, precision, and specificity while effectively identifying outliers and adapting to new attack patterns.

Keywords: Anomaly Detection · Clustering · Similarity · Machine Learning · Incremental clustering · Unsupervised Learning

1 Introduction

Nowadays, the number of devices connected to the network is increasing rapidly, resulting in a larger volume of digital information with complex characteristics. As the volume of data transfer grows, there are higher chances of an increase in cyberthreats, attacks, and exploitation of vulnerabilities in networks [12]. To address these challenges, security mechanisms such as firewalls and intrusion detection systems (IDS) have been implemented to protect devices and sensitive data [3]. IDS are generally classified into three categories: signature-based, anomaly-based and hybrid-based. In signature-based models, the intrusions are

C. Karfa et al. (Eds.): SPACE 2025, LNCS 16406, pp. 191–205, 2026.
https://doi.org/10.1007/978-3-032-16342-4_11

detected based on patterns which are known, whereas in anomaly-based models, they are used to detect network abnormalities to detect threats. The hybrid approach combines both the systems to detect attacks [7]. Research is carried out to develop a security mechanism to protect the devices and their sensitive data against evolving cyber threats using machine learning techniques. It is necessary to create an effective IDS that can detect zero-day attacks using machine learning [8].

Most models struggle to detect novel or evolving attack patterns; their limitation motivates the development of unsupervised learning technique using clustering-based techniques for anomaly detection to identify the cyber threats in the network [5]. Existing clustering methods, like k-means and DBSCAN, require complete dataset availability and reprocessing when new data arrives – a significant limitation in real-world scenarios where the data streams continuously . Incremental clustering helps in updating clusters with incoming data, making it suitable for real-time IDS applications [1]. However the existing models have limitations, like rigid cluster formation, poor handling of outliers, and scalability.

To overcome these limitations, we propose Incremental Cosine Similarity-based Clustering (ICS), a novel unsupervised method tailored for anomaly detection in dynamic environments. ICS leverages cosine similarity to measure data-point affinity incrementally, resulting in three core capabilities: adaptive cluster growth, efficient centroid updates, and dynamic anomaly scoring.

The major contributions of this work are

- An incremental clustering framework that combines samples cosine similarity with density-based centroid initialization.
- Comprehensive evaluation on two IDS benchmarks demonstrating superior performance over incremental K-Means variants in:
  - Cluster quality (Silhouette Score)
  - Runtime efficiency (Execution time)
  - Adaptability (Cluster count flexibility)

Clustering has demonstrated potential for unsupervised intrusion detection; however, current methodologies often face challenges with real-time data streams and concept drift. The next section examines related work and highlights the research gap and the contribution.

2   Related Works

Intrusion Detection Systems (IDS) that use clustering techniques have become increasingly popular because they can detect unknown threats without needing pre-labeled data. Recent studies have explored hybrid models, density-based clustering, and fuzzy logic to improve detection accuracy, lower false positives, and tackle computational challenges.

Leung and Leckie (2005) [9] proposed fpMAFIA, a density- and grid-based clustering method that uses FP-trees for high-dimensional data. Although efficient for large datasets, their experiments only identified a single cluster, which limited its real-world usability.

Zhong et al. (2007) [15] performed an in-depth comparison of centroid-based clustering methods, including K-means, MOSG, SOM, and Neural-Gas, using the DARPA 1998 dataset. While they achieved an impressive 93.6% overall accuracy, their study revealed that computational complexity grows exponentially with higher dimensions, raising scalability concerns for large datasets.

Bharti et al. (2010) [2] developed a hybrid model that combines K-Means clustering with J48 and Random Forest classifiers to overcome limitations like class dominance and forced assignments in K-Means. Their method achieved a detection rate of around 72 – 73% with a false positive rate of 3.6% when tested on the KDD Cup 1999 dataset, effectively identifying attacks.

Wang et al. (2010) [14] integrated Fuzzy C-means with Artificial Neural Networks (FC-ANN), achieving 96.71% average accuracy. While excelling in low-frequency attack detection, the model suffered from higher training complexity, especially for R2L and U2R attacks

Ranjan and Sahoo (2014) [10] enhanced K-medoids by refining initial centroid selection, achieving a 91.2% detection rate while resolving degeneracy problems. While their method showed computational improvements over K-means, it offered only moderate advancements in the broader context of intrusion detection.

Fernando et al. (2024) [4] tested unsupervised methods like K-means++, DBSCAN, LOF, and Isolation Forest (I-Forest) on the BoT-IoT dataset. Among these, I-Forest stood out with 95% purity and only 10% CPU usage, proving to be highly efficient for detecting DDoS, DoS, and Reconnaissance attacks.

Table 1 summarizes key clustering-based IDS techniques, their methodologies, strengths, and limitations.

Table 1. Comparison of existing clustering methods

Method	Clustering Method	Strengths	Limitations
Leung and Leckie (2005)	fpMAFIA (density and grid-based)	Efficient for large datasets,	Only one cluster found in experiments
Zhong et al. (2007)	K-means, MOSG, SOM	Handles new attack types well	Exponential complexity with dimensions
Bharti et al. (2010)	K-Means and J48/Random Forest	Overcomes K-means limitations	Limited to known clustering approaches
Wang et al. (2010)	Fuzzy C-means and ANN	Superior performance on low-frequency attacks	Higher training time complexity
Ranjan and Sahoo (2014)	Modified K-medoids	Eliminates degeneracy, better initial selection	Limited to small improvements over K-means
Fernando et al. (2024)	K-means++, DBSCAN, LOF, I-Forest	Excellent computational efficiency (I-Forest)	Class imbalance still affects some methods

When applied to changing attack patterns, however, current methods have limitations: (1) clustering methodologies struggles with real-time data streams and varying dimensionality, (2) computational complexity escalates for high-dimensional datasets, and (3) slow convergence limits practicality in time-sensitive environments.

To address this gap, we propose an incremental clustering approach that utilizes cosine similarity, which enables continuous adaptation to emerging threats without requiring full retraining. This method shows better clustering performance for changing attack patterns while still being efficient in terms of computation. By combining these capabilities, our solution provides an adaptive and scalable framework to effectively detect and respond to evolving threats in modern network environments.

3   Proposed Methodology

The proposed methodology incremental cosine similarity based clustering (ICS) consist of four stages i) data preprocessing ii) incremental cosine similarity – based clustering iii)Anomaly Detection, iv)Evaluation Metrics. The overall architecture is shown is in Fig. 1.

Step 1: Data Preprocessing During the preprocessing phase the Categorical features were transformed using label encoding, while all numeric features were normalized using min – max scaling as shown in Eq. 1 where x is the normalized value and X is the input.

$$x = \frac{(X - X_{min})}{(X_{max} - X_{min})} \tag{1}$$

This ensures that all numeric features contribute equally to the clustering process.

Step 2: Incremental Cosine Similarity – Based Clustering. The clustering algorithm processes the dataset incrementally in batches of size B, starting with an initial batch size B_0.

Cosine Similarity Given a data point x and a cluster centroid c, cosine similarity is defined as Eq. 2.

$$\text{sim}(x, c) = \frac{x \cdot c}{\|x\| \, \|c\|} \tag{2}$$

Initial Centroid Selection. The initial centroid selection is based on maximum similarity detection. The local similarity score of a point x_i is computed as 3.

$$\rho(x_i) = \frac{1}{k} \sum_{j \in \mathcal{N}_k(x_i)} \text{sim}(x_i, x_j) \tag{3}$$

where $\mathcal{N}_k(x_i)$ denotes the k nearest neighbors of x_i. Local maxima of $\rho(x_i)$ are chosen as initial centroids.

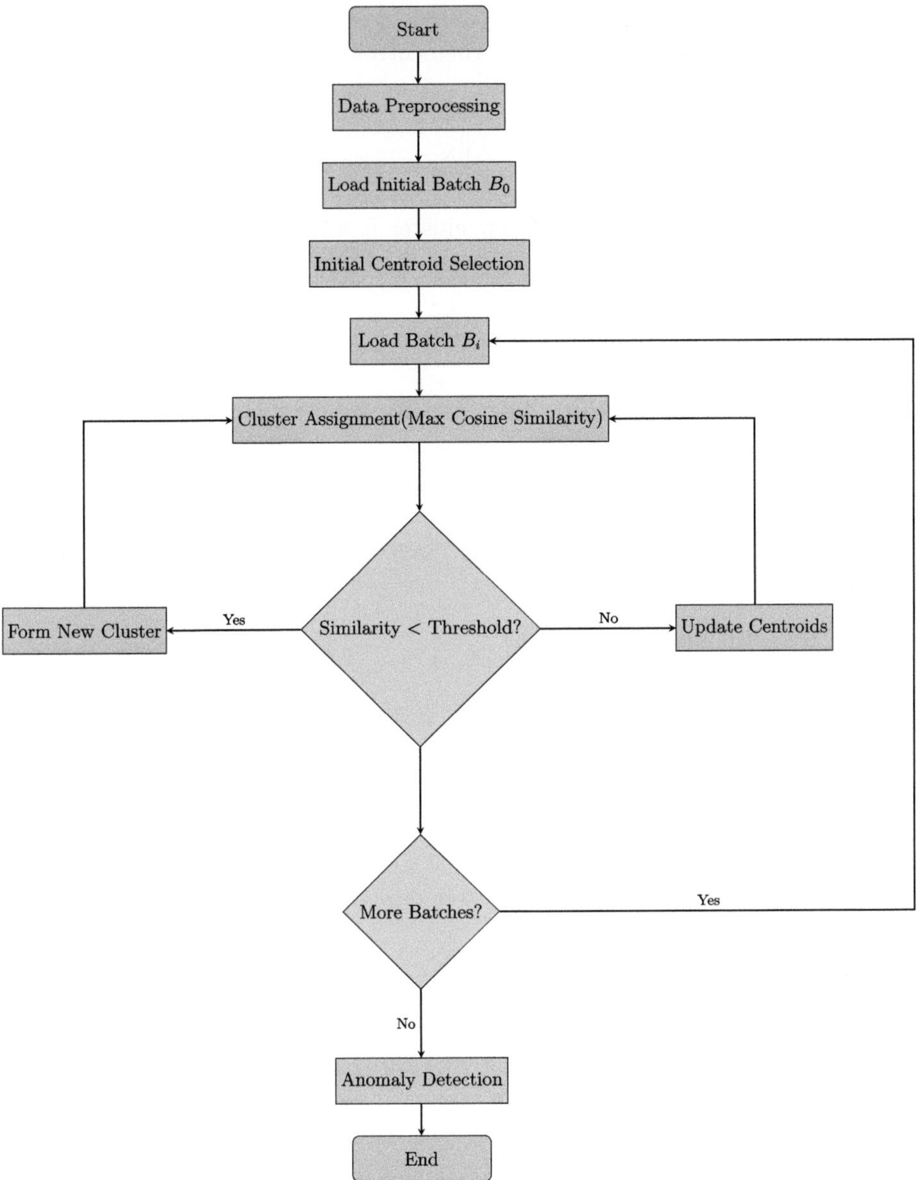

Fig. 1. Incremental Cosine Similarity Based Clustering Methodology.

Cluster Assignment The cluster for each point x is assigned whose centroid has the maximum cosine similarity(Equation 4).If the similarity is less than a threshold then it is marked as outlier.

$$\hat{y}(x) = \arg\max_{c_j \in C} \text{sim}(x, c_j) \tag{4}$$

Centroid Update. Centroids are updated incrementally after each batch. For cluster j with assigned members X_j, the centroid is recalculated as Eq. 5

$$c_j^{(t+1)} = \frac{\sum_{x \in X_j} x}{\left\| \sum_{x \in X_j} x \right\|} \tag{5}$$

New Cluster Formation. The new cluster is formed when a group of unassigned points are found. The new centroid is computed by Eq. 6.

$$c_{\text{new}} = \frac{\sum_{x \in U} x}{\left\| \sum_{x \in U} x \right\|} \tag{6}$$

Step 3: Anomaly Detection. The anomaly score for point x is computed by Eq. 7

$$s(x) = 1 - \max_{c_j \in C} \text{sim}(x, c_j) \tag{7}$$

The anomaly score $s(x)$ measures how dissimilar a sample is from its nearest cluster.

Step 4: Evaluation Metrics
Performance is evaluated through:

- **Silhouette Score:** To measure intra-cluster cohesion and inter-cluster separation over time (Eq. 8) [11].

$$S = \frac{b(x) - a(x)}{\max(a(x), b(x))} \tag{8}$$

  where $a(x)$ is the average intra-cluster dissimilarity and $b(x)$ is the nearest-cluster dissimilarity.
- **Centroid Stability:** measured via Δc_j.
- **Cluster Growth:** number of clusters across batches.
- **Convergence time:** time required for each batch to converge

Algorithm 1 summarizes the entire ICS algorithm by incorporating all of the previously defined steps and equations.

Algorithm 1. Incremental Cosine Similarity Clustering (ICS)

Require: Data stream X, batch size B, similarity threshold τ, number of neighbors k
Ensure: Clusters C, anomaly scores S
 1: Initialize clusters $C \leftarrow \emptyset$
 2: **Data Preprocessing**
 3: **while** data batches available **do**
 4:     Load data batch X_b of size B
 5:     **if** $C = \emptyset$ **then**
 6:         **Initial Centroid Selection** (Eq. 3)
 7:         $C \leftarrow \{c_1, c_2, \dots\}$
 8:     **else**
 9:         **for** each $x_i \in X_b$ **do**
10:             **Cluster Assignment** (Eq. 2, 4)
11:             **if** $\hat{y}(x_i) \geq \tau$ **then**
12:                 Assign x_i to cluster
13:             **else**
14:                 Mark x_i as potential outlier
15:             **end if**
16:         **end for**
17:         **New Cluster Formation** (Eq. 6)
18:         $C \leftarrow C \cup \{c_{new}\}$
19:         **for** each $c \in C$ **do**
20:             **Centroid Update** (Eq. 5)
21:         **end for**
22:     **end if**
23: **end while**
24: **Anomaly Detection** (Eq. 7)

3.1   Computational Complexity

The time complexity per batch of ICS is $O(B \cdot k \cdot d)$, where B represents the batch size, k denotes the number of clusters, and d indicates the data dimensionality. This linear scaling concerning batch size and cluster count guarantees efficient data stream processing, rendering ICS appropriate for real-time intrusion detection applications.

4   Experiments and Results

4.1   Plan of Action

This study evaluated the performance of incremental cosine similarity (ICS)-based clustering against two centroid-based approaches, K-Means (IKM) and K-Means with Cosine Similarity (IKMCS), for incremental clustering on the BCAST IDS and NSL-KDD datasets. For comparison, all the methods were configured with a batch size of 10,000, an initial cluster count of two and a similarity threshold of 0.8. The analysis focuses on assessing cluster quality (Silhouette Score), adaptability (cluster count), runtime efficiency, and outlier detection.

For the labeled dataset, the classification metrics, like accuracy, precision, recall, F1 score, and specificity were computed based on ground truth labels.

The experiments were carried out on a workstation with 24GB of RAM and a 12th generation i5 processor that ran at 1.30GHz. Python, NumPy, scikit-learn, pandas, Matplotlib, and skfuzzy are some of the software that was used.

4.2   Dataset

The experiments where conducted in different scenarios in-order to evaluate the clustering performance. The details of dataset used are shown in Table 2.

Table 2. Summary of Dataset

Dataset	Features	Total Samples
BCAST IDS	15	21806
NSL-KDD	42	148517

The BCAST IDS dataset offers unlabelled network traffic traces targeted for intrusion detection research in broadcast and multicast contexts [6]. It records high-frequency snapshots of network activity at 10-second intervals utilising intrusion detection systems (IDS) sensors across various organisations. The dataset encompasses authentic broadcast patterns, typical behaviour, and anomalies such as scanning, denial-of-service attempts, and ARP disruptions.

The NSL-KDD dataset, derived from the KDD99 dataset, addresses the issue of duplicate instances in KDD99, which hindered the efficiency of detection models. By removing duplicates while preserving all 42 features, NSL-KDD enables the development of more accurate IDS [13].

4.3   Analysis Using BCAST IDS

Table 3 shows the summary of comparative analysis of BCAST IDS using three clustering approaches ICS, IKM and IKMCS.

Table 3. Performance Comparison of ICS, IKM and IKMCS

Metric	ICS	IKM	IKMCS
Avg. Silhouette Score	0.504	0.201	0.454
Total Running Time (s)	17.45	20.66	23.37
Final Cluster Count	3	2	2
Total Outliers	1,037	324	489

The ICS method got a silhouette score of 0.504, while the IKM and IKMCS methods got scores of 0.201 and 0.454, respectively. This indicates that ICS is better at grouping similar data points, which makes clustering work better. The ICS method is better than the IKM and IKMCS methods because it takes 17.45 s to finish clustering instead of 20.66 s and 23.37 s, respectively.

The number of clusters that each method formed is also different: ICS formed 3 clusters, while IKM and IKMCS only formed 2 clusters. This means that ICS is better at finding intrusions because it can find more subtle groupings in the data. The ICS method found 1037 more outliers than IKM (324) and IKMCS (489). The comparative analysis demonstrates that the ICS approach excels across all evaluated metrics.

Batch-wise Convergence Analysis Figure 2 shows the batch-wise development of the clustering metrics over five successive batches, highlighting three significant performance behaviors for ICS, IKM, and IKMCS.

Cluster quality analysis (Fig. 2(a)) indicates that ICS consistently attained high Silhouette Scores ranging from 0.502 to 0.516 across all batches, thereby affirming its stable incremental learning capability. In contrast, IKM consistently fell below 0.23, while IKMCS achieved moderate but stable scores between 0.452 and 0.456.

The execution time analysis (Fig. 2(b)) illustrates ICS's computational efficiency, scaling approximately linearly from 0.51 s to 6.24 s. However, IKM and IKMCS exhibited super-linear growth timelines - IKM escalated from 1.31 s to 7.50 s, whereas IKMCS exhibited the most significant scaling, increasing from 1.25 s to 9.35 s. The divergence became particularly apparent following Batch 3, where IKMCS suffered significant overhead.

The increase in cluster count (Fig. 2(c)) indicates that ICS dynamically expanded from 2 to 3 clusters following Batch 1, autonomously identifying emerging data structures. Simultaneously, both IKM and IKMCS remained limited to their original 2-cluster configuration, despite evident indications of suboptimal partitioning in subsequent batches. This adaptability makes ICS particularly valuable for security applications with evolving attack patterns.

In summary, the comparative analysis demonstrates using BCAST IDS dataset shows that the ICS method outperforms both IKM and IKMCS across all evaluated metrics, showcasing its superior clustering capabilities and efficiency.

4.4 Analysis Using NSL KDD

Table 4 presents a summary of the comparative analysis of three clustering approaches—ICS, IKM, and IKMCS—using the NSL KDD dataset. The evaluation is based on three key metrics: average silhouette score, total running time, and final cluster count.

The clustering quality, as measured by the average silhouette score, indicates that ICS (0.462) outperforms the other methods, followed by IKMCS, while IKM has the lowest score. This suggests that ICS produces more distinct and well-separated clusters compared to IKMCS and IKM. Regarding total running

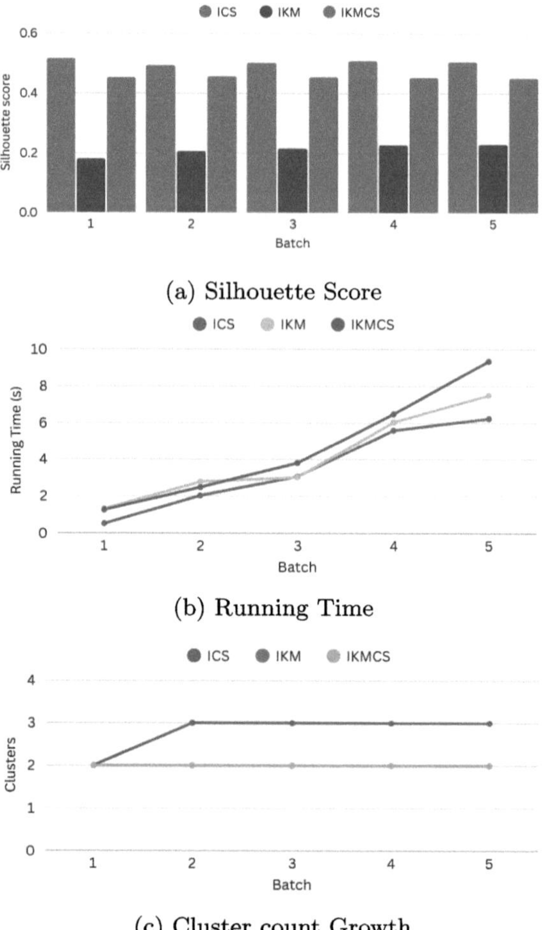

(a) Silhouette Score

(b) Running Time

(c) Cluster count Growth

Fig. 2. Batch Wise Analysis.

Table 4. Performance Comparison of ICS, IKM and IKMCS

Metric	ICS	IKM	IKMCS
Avg. Silhouette Score	0.462	0.365	0.446
Total Running Time (s)	1056.32	1066.80	1646.04
Final Cluster Count	3	12	2

time, ICS and IKM exhibit comparable performance, whereas IKMCS requires significantly more time. In terms of final cluster count, IKM formed 12 clusters, IKMCS converges to 2 clusters due to its initialization, and ICS results in 3 clusters.

Batch-Wise Convergence Analysis. Figure 3 shows the batch-wise development of the clustering metrics over fifteen successive batches, highlighting three significant performance behaviors for ICS, IKM, and IKMCS.

The analysis of cluster quality, as depicted in Fig. 3(a), shows the ICS method consistently achieved high Silhouette Scores, ranging from 0.355 to 0.519 across the 15 batches. This indicates a strong ability to form well-defined clusters. In contrast, the IKM method displayed lower Silhouette Scores, fluctuating between 0.329 and 0.469, which suggests that it struggled to maintain effective clustering performance. The IKMCS method, while better than IKM, produced moderate and stable scores between 0.413 and 0.485, indicating some level of effectiveness but lacking the robustness of the ICS method.

The execution time analysis (Fig. 3(b)) demonstrates the efficiency of the ICS method, exhibiting a linear rise in processing time from 1.07 s in Batch 1 to 191.62 s in Batch 15. The IKM method demonstrated a comparable trend, with durations varying from 1.09 s to 192.52 s. Both IKM and IKMCS exhibited super-linear growth in execution time, with IKMCS demonstrating the most pronounced escalation, increasing from 1.07 s to 285.73 s. The disparity in execution time became particularly apparent following Batch 3, during which IKMCS experienced significant overhead.

The analysis of cluster counts (Fig. 3(c)) reveals that the ICS method effectively adapted to the data, expanding from 2 to 3 clusters after Batch 1. This flexibility allowed it to better capture emerging data structures. Conversely, both IKM and IKMCS remained constrained to their initial 2-cluster configuration, despite clear signs of suboptimal partitioning in later batches.

Comparative Performance Analysis. Table 5 summarizes the key metrics that were adopted to assess the performance of three distinct methods in this study: ICS, IKMCS, and IKM. These metrics included accuracy, precision, recall, F1 score, specificity and false positivity rate are computed based on ground truth labels.

Table 5. Performance metrics comparison of ICS, IKMCS, and IKM models

Method	Accuracy(%)	Precision(%)	Recall(%)	F1-Score (%)	Specificity(%)	False Positivity Rate(%)
ICS	55.70	98.90	54.00	69.60	88.20	11.77
IKM	51.70	80.60	52.20	63.30	49.60	50.43
IKMCS	55.20	98.70	53.70	69.50	85.50	14.52

The findings show that the IKM method trailed behind at 51.7%, while the ICS methods had the highest accuracy at 55.7%, closely followed by IKMCS at 55.2%.

With ICS achieving 98.9%, IKMCS attaining 98.7%, and IKM obtaining 80.6%, precision was significantly high across all methods. This ensures the methods are successful in reducing false positives. Recall values, however, were rather low, with IKM at 52.2%, IKMCS at 53.7%, and ICS at 54.0%.

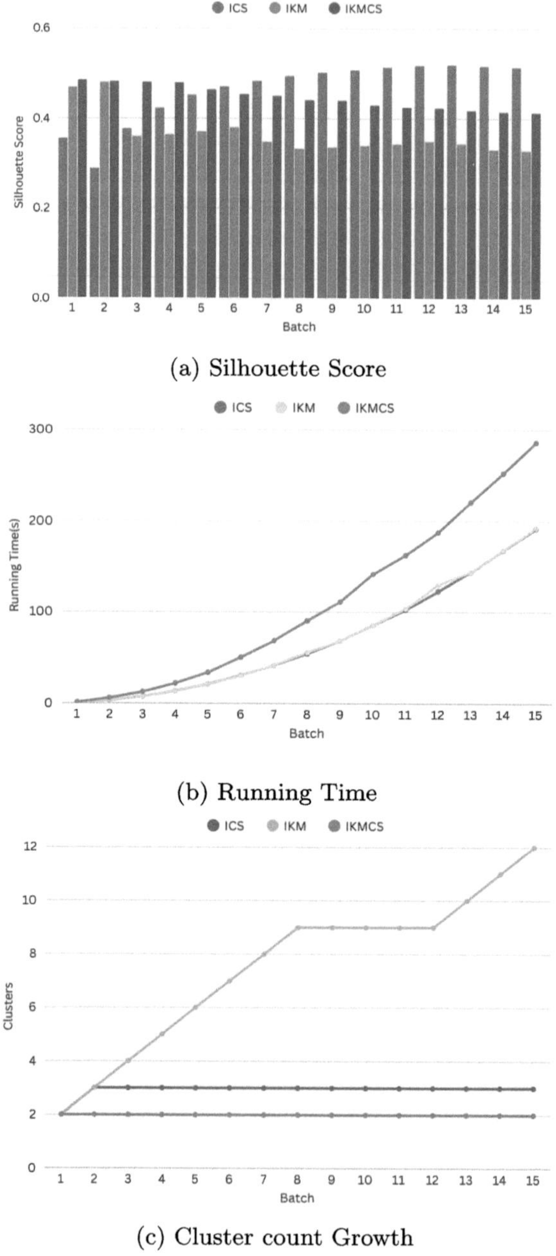

(a) Silhouette Score

(b) Running Time

(c) Cluster count Growth

Fig. 3. Batch Wise Analysis.

Further demonstrating the superior performance of the ICS and IKMCS methods were the F1-scores, which balance precision and recall, which were 69.6% for ICS, 69.5% for IKMCS, and 63.3% for IKM. With a true negative rate of 88.2%, ICS had the highest specificity, followed by IKMCS at 85.5%, while IKM had a much lower specificity of 49.6%. ICS had the lowest False Positive Rate at 11.77%, outperforming IKM (50.43%) and IKMCS (14.52%). This is important for reducing false alarms in operational security environments. Thus ICS method performs the best overall across all assessed metrics, indicating that it may find use in real-world scenarios.

The comparative analysis shows that the ICS method outperforms both IKM and IKMCS in all evaluated metrics, exhibiting enhanced clustering capabilities and computational efficiency. The results point out that ICS is the optimal choice for applications that emphasise superior clustering quality and efficient resource utilization.

5   Discussion

The ICS method is an advancement in the field of unsupervised anomaly detection, especially for dynamic network environments. By applying cosine similarity to initialize centroids, ICS effectively overcomes the common issues that traditional clustering methods face like cluster formation and challenges with scalability. The experiment results on BCAST IDS dataset, shows ICS attained a better clustering measured using Silhouette Score, which is a significant improvement of approximately 150% over IKM and 11% over IKMCS. In terms of computational time ICS completed its clustering process much faster, showing a 15% improvement over IKM and 25% improvement over IKMCS. In the case of dynamic cluster formation ICS was better at fitting data with more clusters discovered whereas other methods remained static. This shows ICS method detected more outliers when compared with IKM and IKMCS methodologies. Similar improvements were observed when experimented with NSL KDD dataset where the clustering quality and computation time using ICS is better compared to IKM and IKMCS methodologies. This shows that ICS as a most effective solution for detection anomalies in rapid changing network environments and effective in detecting cyber threats.

6   Conclusion

This paper proposed Incremental Cosine Similarity-based Clustering (ICS), a novel unsupervised learning framework designed specifically for anomaly detection in network traffic. ICS effectively addresses the key limitations of existing methods by using cosine similarity for adaptive cluster assignments and centroid updates, along with a density-based initialisation method. It enables dynamic cluster formation, efficient processing of data batches, and robust outlier identification without requiring complete dataset retraining. The extensive experimental evaluation on the BCAST IDS and NSL-KDD datasets demonstrates the superior performance of ICS against incremental variants of IKM and IKMCS. The results consistently showed that ICS achieves higher cluster quality, converges faster, and has an improved detection rate. It is also a highly adaptive solution for unsupervised anomaly detection in modern network environments. Its ability to learn incrementally and identify emerging threats efficiently makes it a highly suitable candidate for deployment in real-time IDS.

Author contributions. Conceptualization: A.K., A.V.S, A.S. ; Methodology A.K., A.V.S, A.S.; Formal Analysis: A.K., A.V.S; Validation and Review: A.K., A.S.; Writing (original draft): A.K., A.V.S ;Writing(review and editing): A.S.

Funding Information. This work is not funded.

Data Availibility Statement. The datasets used in this work are available in public.

Conflict of Interest. The authors declare that they have no conflict of interest.

References

1. Amini, A., Wah, T., Saboohi, H.: On density-based data streams clustering algorithms: a survey. J. Comput. Sci. Technol. **29**, 116–141 (2014). 10.1007/s11390-013-1416-3
2. Bharti, K.K., Shukla, S., Jain, S.: Intrusion detection using clustering. Int. J. Comput. Commun. Technol. **1**(4), Article 5 (2010). 10.47893/IJCCT.2010.1052
3. Borky, J.M., Bradley, T.H.: Protecting Information with Cybersecurity, pp. 345–404. Springer International Publishing, Cham (2019). 10.1007/978-3-319-95669-5_10
4. Fernando, G.P., Florina, A., Liliana, C.B.: Evaluation of the performance of unsupervised learning algorithms for intrusion detection in unbalanced data environments. IEEE Access **PP**, 1–1 (2024). 10.1109/ACCESS.2024.3516615
5. Ghesmoune, M., Lebbah, M., Azzag, H.: State-of-the-art on clustering data streams. Big Data Anal. **1**(13) (2016). 10.1186/s41044-016-0011-3
6. Gombao, J.: Bcast ids dataset. IEEE Dataport (2024). 10.21227/kdnn-yp02
7. Jaber, A.N., Rehman, S.U.: FCM–SVM based intrusion detection system for cloud computing environment. Clust. Comput. **23**(4), 3221–3231 (2020). https://doi.org/10.1007/s10586-020-03082-6
8. Krishnaveni, S., Sivamohan, S., Sridhar, S.S., Prabakaran, S.: Efficient feature selection and classification through ensemble method for network intrusion detection on cloud computing. Clust. Comput. **24**(3), 1761–1779 (2021). https://doi.org/10.1007/s10586-020-03222-y
9. Leung, K., Leckie, C.: Unsupervised anomaly detection in network intrusion detection using clusters. In: Proceedings of the Twenty-Eighth Australasian Conference on Computer Science - Volume 38, pp. 333–342. ACSC '05, Australian Computer Society, Inc. (2005)
10. Ranjan, R., Sahoo, G.: A new clutering approach for anomaly intrusion detection. Int. J. Data Min. Knowl. Manage. Process **4** (2014). 10.5121/ijdkp.2014.4203
11. Shahapure, K.R., Nicholas, C.: Cluster quality analysis using silhouette score. In: 2020 IEEE 7th International Conference on Data Science and Advanced Analytics (DSAA), pp. 747–748 (2020). 10.1109/DSAA49011.2020.00096
12. Shiravani, A., Sadreddini, M.H., Nahook, H.N.: Network intrusion detection using data dimensions reduction techniques. J. Big Data **10**(27) (2023). 10.1186/s40537-023-00697-5

13. Tavallaee, M., Bagheri, E., Lu, W., Ghorbani, A.A.: A detailed analysis of the KDD cup 99 data set. In: Proceedings of the Second IEEE International Conference on Computational Intelligence for Security and Defense Applications, pp. 53–58. CISDA'09, IEEE Press (2009)
14. Wang, G., Hao, J., Ma, J., Huang, L.: A new approach to intrusion detection using artificial neural networks and fuzzy clustering. Expert Syst. Appl. **37**(9), 6225–6232 (2010). https://doi.org/10.1016/j.eswa.2010.02.102
15. Zhong, S., Khoshgoftaar, T.M., Seliya, N.: Clustering-based network intrusion detection. Int. J. Reliab. Qual. Saf. Eng. **14**(02), 169–187 (2007). https://doi.org/10.1142/S0218539307002568

Addressing Cache Side-Channel Attacks Using Taint-Guided Fine-Grained Computation Offloading in Near-Memory Processing

Simran Preet Kaur[✉], Asutosh Kumar Sarma, Satanu Maity,
and Manojit Ghose

Department of CSE, IIIT Guwahati, Guwahati, India
{simran.kaur,asutosh.sarma,satanu.maity,manojit}@iiitg.ac.in

Abstract. With the growing demand for resource-intensive applications and the rising popularity of cloud computing, resource sharing has become a standard practice, primarily aimed at enhancing system performance. However, this sharing introduces multiple vulnerabilities, including cache side-channel attacks. Such attacks exploit shared cache states to infer sensitive information, posing a significant threat to the confidentiality of security-critical applications. Although a number of mitigation techniques have been proposed, each has its own limitations. This paper presents a novel strategy, **TaintOff**, a compiler-assisted defense mechanism that employs taint analysis to automatically track the propagation of secret data and utilizes the near-memory processing (NMP) paradigm to mitigate cache-side-channel attacks by restricting the use of shared cache memory. The strategy begins by annotating secret inputs as tainted and propagating these taints through whole program analysis to identify the secure regions of an application at a finer granularity. The proposed strategy offloads fine-grained secure code regions to the NMP cores, while non-secure application regions are executed on the multicore processor. Experimental evaluations, conducted using a set of standard simulators for a wide range of applications from different domains, demonstrate the effectiveness of our proposed strategy *TaintOff*, achieving a significant speedup of 1.86x (maximum) and 3.45x reduction in energy consumption (maximum), along with security guarantees. *TaintOff* outperforms the state-of-the-art strategy (SOAS) both in performance and energy consumption as it offloads 20% (overall) fewer instructions than SOAS to the low-end NMP cores.

Keywords: Near memory processing · security-aware computation offloading · cache side-channel attack · sensitive application in NMP · secret dependency · taint analysis · program analysis using LLVM

1 Introduction

With the rapid evolution of computing technologies, modern applications have grown increasingly resource-intensive, requiring significant computational,

C. Karfa et al. (Eds.): SPACE 2025, LNCS 16406, pp. 206–226, 2026.
https://doi.org/10.1007/978-3-032-16342-4_12

memory, and storage capacities for efficient execution. To address these demands, modern computing systems leverage shared resources to enhance performance and overall throughput [25]. The emergence of cloud computing has further accelerated this trend, positioning computation itself as a utility-based service [6,18]. Resource sharing here is generally accomplished via virtualization methods that provide dedicated execution environments for each user, facilitated by virtual machines [10,15]. Nevertheless, the security provided by this isolation technique is confined to the software level, leaving the underlying hardware still vulnerable [21]. This vulnerability arises because these applications depend on the underlying hardware, which is shared among all the concurrent processes executing on the system. In such scenarios, the hardware environment used by other users' processes becomes observable to a malicious user [26]. The low-level details such as resource utilization (e.g., memory allocation, read/write operations, etc.) can be inferred. These details can potentially expose sensitive information about other processes while they are running. Therefore, the shared hardware becomes prone to significant risks or threats [35]. Furthermore, since many applications are sensitive and critical, addressing these security threats becomes a matter of utmost importance.

In recent years, a wide range of hardware security vulnerabilities have been identified, yet cache-side-channel attacks have emerged as particularly critical due to their practicality and impact [2,27,29,42]. These attacks have not been effectively mitigated and remain a promising area for further research [4,13,26,32]. Two primary factors make the cache memory susceptible to side-channel attacks. First, it is a shared resource, meaning the last-level cache (LLC) is seamlessly accessed by all cores in a multicore system [5]. Consequently, a processor core executing a malicious program can potentially exploit access to cache lines containing secret data. The second reason is the considerable variation in access time between cache hits and misses [20]. As a consequence, an adversary may distinguish between a cache hit and a cache miss and rapidly extract the secret. This threat is particularly critical for security-sensitive applications, such as those implementing the AES encryption algorithm, where operations are performed on data that is either secret or dependent on secret values [35]. Thus, if the adversary successfully executes a side-channel attack on the shared cache, the entire secret information can be inferred [26].

Consequently, a number of strategies have been developed to protect against cache-side-channel attacks. Cache partitioning [5,28] is one such popular defense mechanism that divides the entire cache memory and assigns a particular partition to a particular core. Another strategy is the execution of secure portions of the application code on some special hardware [12,43]. A different category of mitigation strategies focuses on flushing the cache entirely [44]. While such existing defense mechanisms against side-channel attacks have shown effectiveness, they also incur certain costs in other aspects. In addition, the approach in [5] provides security in the L1 private cache by preloading the secret data. However, it fails to handle the cases where the size of the secret data region gets larger than the cache size. In another work, Ojha *et al.* [28] propose a mechanism that maintains a bit for each hardware context, and the first cache access by a process is always treated as a miss irrespective of its residency status. This mitigates the data-reuse-based cache-side-channel attack. However, it adversely affects the system's performance. The work [12] executes the secure regions of a program in the special secure execution environment. However, the entire secure region and data formation must be performed manually by the developer, which is a tedious, error-prone task.

Very recently, Casey *et al.* [26] have proposed a Near-Memory Processing (NMP) computing paradigm-based solution where the secure regions of an application are offloaded to the memory side for execution. As secret data does not use shared cache memory, the authors claim to mitigate the side-channel attack completely. However, the approach adopts a completely manual mechanism to annotate all the functions that work on secure data and offloads them to the NMP side. Further, suppose an entire function region is offloaded to the NMP side. In that case, a significant performance degradation is observed, since NMP cores are inherently less powerful than the host processor cores [7,22,24]. Furthermore, a function typically contains a large code segment comprising many basic blocks, and not all the basic blocks work on secret data. Therefore, a fine-grained automatic identification mechanism of secure regions of an application is crucial to judiciously decide which regions are to be offloaded, balancing both security and performance. In this paper, we propose a taint-based strategy that automatically identifies the secure code regions within the entire application. By propagating the taint from taint sources through data and control flow dependencies, our strategy systematically detects program regions that operate on or are influenced by secret data. Thereafter, the strategy offloads these secure code regions to main memory for execution, ensuring the overall system's security remains intact. To the best of our knowledge, this is the first work that leverages taint-based analysis to find fine-grained offloading regions of applications that operate on secret data, and their execution on the NMP side, thereby addressing cache side-channel attacks. We list the paper's contributions below.

1.1 Our Contribution

1. We design and develop an LLVM compiler-assisted taint analysis strategy that performs taint propagation over the whole program and identifies the secure regions of an application program.
2. We devise a seamless execution framework that performs offloading at a fine-grained basic block level, striking a balance between security and performance.
3. We present a detailed security assessment, including both analysis and empirical validation, of our proposed strategy to demonstrate its resilience against cache side-channel attacks.
4. We perform experiments on applications from diverse technological domains by extending a set of standard simulators to validate the effectiveness of our proposed strategy.

A brief overview of related work is presented in Sect. 2. Section 3 explains the methodology adopted in this work and describes the overall system design. The simulation environment and experimental setup are detailed in Sect. 4, while Sect. 5 presents and analyzes the experimental results. Section 6 provides an extensive security evaluation of the proposed strategy, and Sect. 7 concludes the paper with key findings and directions for future research.

2   Related Work

Cache Partitioning: Cache partitioning mitigates side-channel attacks by assigning exclusive cache regions to processes, either statically or dynamically. Static techniques such as [30] propose dividing the last-level cache (LLC) into sections, each dedicated to a specific process, to enhance security, while [28] presents an approach that triggers cache misses whenever a cache line is loaded by another process. Similarly, several researchers have proposed dynamic cache partitioning methods [14,34,38,39]. The work cited in [39] dynamically allocates cache to public applications to protect secure applications, while [14] prevents timing-based side-channel attacks by enforcing a secure cache allocation policy.

Constant Time: Another method of minimizing cache side-channel attacks is the constant-time technique, which eliminates timing variations in the algorithm. This approach incorporates techniques such as employing compact S-box tables with frequent permutations [3] and masking secret-dependent data before memory writes [41].

Cache Flushing: Additionally, cache side-channel attacks can be mitigated through Cache Flushing, which involves clearing cached data during program execution. For instance, the work cited in [44] addresses timing-based cache exploitation by repeatedly clearing the first-level (L1) cache, while [11] introduced flushing the cache during context switching.

Cache Randomization: Another promising approach to reduce cache side-channel attacks is the use of randomized cache architectures. Remapping-based schemes such as Ceaser [33] and Scatter-Cache [40] strengthen cache security by leveraging cipher-based hash functions with periodically updated secret keys to randomize address-to-set mappings and hinder adversarial analysis. In contrast, Maya-Cache [1] utilizes a pointer-based randomization mechanism that separates tag and data arrays through bidirectional pointers, effectively masking their correlation.

Although all the above-mentioned works have been shown to mitigate cache side-channel attacks and protect our system, the security of the system came at the cost of some other parameters, like efficiency, performance, etc. For instance, in the case of cache partitioning, the cache is divided into several divisions, and each core of the system gets a particular division. However, this lowers resource utilization and hampers the system's performance. Similarly, the cache-flushing mechanism would flush all the content of the cache, thereby significantly increasing the cache miss ratio. Hence, resulting in a decrease in the system performance. Again, for the constant time technique, it is seen that the methods used are costly and require high computation.

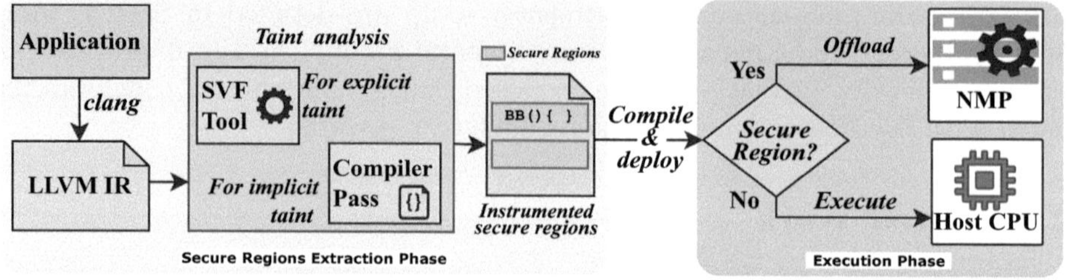

Fig. 1. Overall workflow of TaintOff

To overcome these issues, Casey *et al.* [26] propose a mitigation strategy leveraging an emerging NMP computing paradigm, where the vulnerable computations are performed directly within memory, thus avoiding cache hierarchy walks and reducing the risk of cache-side attacks. The isolated NMP vaults are utilized to store all secret data, and the execution of secure functions is delegated from the overall application to these vaults. This approach effectively minimizes the likelihood of accessing data within the cache hierarchy, thereby providing a promising solution for mitigating cache side-channel attacks. However, this method requires the developer to manually annotate all the secret variables and entire code regions that are secret. This is both tedious and prone to errors. Further, this approach relies on coarse-grained function-level offloading to the NMP side, disregarding the poor computational capabilities of the NMP cores. Since the NMP cores are relatively simple and lack advanced mechanisms like the host multicore systems [7], offloading the entire function results in degraded overall system performance. Furthermore, the entire code segment within a function does not work on secret data. In contrast, our proposed strategy leverages a taint-based program analysis and employs a fine-grained offloading mechanism, striking a balance between security and performance.

3   TaintOff: The Proposed Strategy

This section presents the overall working of our strategy, and it is depicted in Fig. 1. Our proposed strategy works in two steps. The first step is to identify the fine-grained secure regions of an application program using compiler-assisted taint analysis, and the next step is to execute the secure regions on the NMP side. To achieve this, we first convert our application program into LLVM IR representation and employ taint analysis accompanied by a compiler multi-pass approach [17]. In this process, the taint sources are propagated through the whole IR program, and the results of taint propagation precisely determine the code regions directly or indirectly dependent on the taint sources, forming the basis for secure region construction. Thereafter, the secure regions are offloaded to the trusted near-memory processors, while the remaining simple regions are deployed on the host-side core for subsequent execution. We have considered basic blocks as the offloading granularity in our strategy.

3.1 Taint Analysis

We employ taint tracking as a taint analysis technique to determine how secret data propagates across a program. The secret data can be a program variable or any confidential input that is referred to as a taint source. In our work, program variables containing the secret information are identified as a taint source. Any variable that exhibits dependence on a tainted source is treated as a secret-tainted variable. In particular, taint tracking captures the explicit and implicit flow propagation of the variables designated as the taint source. Explicit flows occur through direct data dependencies, where the data values are propagated through program operations (assignment, arithmetic, or string), as well as through function parameters, arguments, or return values. In contrast, implicit flows occur when sensitive information is propagated through control flow (e.g., conditional statements or loops), where the outcome of a conditional branch is dependent on a secret-tainted variable and influences the subsequent execution paths without any direct data assignment. Hence, tracking explicit flows enables the identification of data dependencies, and tracking implicit flows captures the control dependencies of an application program. We divide our taint tracking analysis into two parts: Data-flow taint tracking and Control-flow taint tracking.

1. **Data-flow taint tracking:** We need to track the explicit data flow in order to find the secret-tainted data dependencies. To achieve it, we adapt the state-of-the-art SVF tool [36], which performs value-flow analysis over the generated LLVM IR entities to propagate taint from identified sources throughout the program. SVF uses the LLVM IR and the results of its points-to analysis to construct a graph-based representation of the program. Subsequently, the focus should be on identifying all the secret-tainted variables that express direct or indirect dependence on the taint sources. For this step, we traverse the SVF graph in a breadth-first manner from the taint source along the edges to identify explicit data-dependent variables denoted as $\xrightarrow{dd}$. We employ a taint-aware data dependency as follows:

   Data dependency: Let n_1 and n_2 be nodes in the SVF graph, where each node corresponds to an LLVM IR `instruction` (e.g., `alloc`, `load`, `store`, etc.). Then $n_1 \xrightarrow{dd} n_2$ if and only if:

   (a) n_1 represents a variable or memory object that is directly or transitively dependent on the taint source variable, and

   (b) there exists a value-flow edge in the SVF graph from n_1 to n_2, such that n_2 either allocates, loads, stores, or copies the variable represented by n_1.

   These conditions cover **Def-Use**, and **Memory-Use** type of data dependencies, which account for the direct secret variable dependencies and transitive memory interactions through multiple instructions. Thereafter, we construct a list of secret-tainted variables, along with their taint sources, derived from the above data dependency analysis. The next step involves discovering secret instructions that incorporate the secret-tainted variables. Once the secret instructions have been discovered, we locate the set S_{DD} of appropriate basic blocks that contain them. The designation for this set of code blocks is *secret tainted blocks*. We represent it as:

$$S_{DD} = \{B_i \mid \exists x \in T,\ x \text{ is used in } B_i\}, \forall i \in \{1, .., n\}, \tag{1}$$

where x represents a variable in the set of secret-tainted variables T, B_i is the data-dependent secret code block, and n is the total number of basic blocks in the program. While this establishes the data dependency between secret-tainted variables throughout the program, static value-flow analysis alone is insufficient, as it does not account for implicit flows that arise from control dependencies [8,37]. To overcome this limitation, we extend our analysis with control-flow taint tracking.

2. **Control-flow taint tracking:** While data flow taint tracking captures how values are explicitly propagated between instructions, control flow taint tracking is necessary to reason about information flows that occur from the structure of program execution. We design a set of compiler passes to track the implicit control-flow of the IR application. In LLVM IR, predicates are produced by ordinary instructions (e.g., icmp) and resolved through branching instructions and jumps (e.g., `br`, `switch`, or `loop` instructions). These branching instructions and jumps are basic block terminators. We construct and traverse a control-flow graph (CFG) [9] using compiler passes to analyze the control dependencies of the program at the LLVM IR level. Each IR `instruction` is grouped into a basic block, and edges in the CFG represent the flow of control in the program, denoted as $\xrightarrow{cd}$. We follow conventions for control and transitive control dependency [43] as follows:

   Control dependency Let n_1 and n_2 be nodes of the CFG, where each node represents a basic block B. Then block $n_1 \xrightarrow{cd} n_2$ if and only if:

   (a) there exists at least one path from n_1 to an exit block that does not pass through n_2, and

   (b) there exists a path p from n_1 to n_2 such that, for every intermediate block M on p (excluding n_1 and n_2), all paths from M to any exit block must pass through n_2.

   Transitive control dependency: If block B_1 is control-dependent on block B_2 and B_2 is control-dependent on block B_3, then B_1 is control-dependent on B_3.

   Based on these definitions, our taint-aware control dependency analysis identifies the *secret tainted blocks*. A basic block is classified as tainted if it is either directly or transitively control-dependent on a branch whose predicate involves a secret-tainted variable. In other words, whenever the evaluation of a control predicate depends on a secret-tainted variable, all blocks within its control dependence set are marked as tainted. Hence, we derive a set S_{CD} of all secret code blocks B_i that are implicitly dependent on the secret-tainted variable, which is represented as:

$$S_{CD} = \{B_i \mid \exists B_{ic} \text{ such that } B_i \in CD^*(B_{ic})\}, \tag{2}$$

where,

$$\exists x \in T, \ x \text{ is used in } B_{ic}, \ \forall i \in \{1, \ldots, n\}. \tag{3}$$

Here, B_i denotes the set of control-dependent basic blocks selected from the total of n blocks in the program. T is the set of secret tainted variables, B_{ic} denotes a conditional branch block, x represents the variables used in its predicate and, $CD^*(B_{ic})$ corresponds to the transitive closure of the control dependencies.

3.2   Sensitive Region Formation and Instrumentation

We combine the secret tainted blocks obtained from data and control flow taint analysis in order to obtain a final set of secret blocks, which is represented as:

$$S_{secret} = S_{DD} \cup S_{CD} \tag{4}$$

This collection of these secret blocks (both direct and dependent) is referred to as the secure regions of an application. Once all secret code blocks have been located, the subsequent task is to identify the starting point and termination points of the secret code block, to facilitate their execution on the NMP side at runtime. We have used an LLVM-based compiler pass to annotate the sensitive regions with the machine-readable offloadable tags (we use *NMP-Begin* and *NMP-End* in our case). These offloadable tags indicate that the current region is an offloading region within the application. Finally, our instrumentation approach compiles the instrumented application into an NMP-compatible object file.

3.3   A Running Example

To clearly describe how our approach works, we use a sample C program shown on the left side of Fig. 2 that performs the encryption of a plaintext to its corresponding ciphertext using a secret variable `sVar`. The secret variable `sVar` is identified as a taint source, which can be easily done by using the *attribute method, annotations, decorators,* or *custom comment tags,* available in different programming languages (similar to an approach adopted in [31,43]). As `sVar` is used for the encryption, it is necessary to protect it. Here we can see that if the value of `sVar` is less than zero, we would terminate the code (lines 8 to 11). Otherwise, we would continue with the execution. This means that the execution of the code is determined by the value of the variable `sVar`. Now, the variable `hash` is derived from the variable `sVar` by decrementing it by 2 in line number 14. Therefore, the variable `hash` becomes a secret-tainted variable, as using `hash`, the attacker can retrieve the information related to `sVar`. The variable `cipher text` is further derived by multiplying `plain text` with `hash`, which is related to the secret-tainted variable. Hence, `ciphertext` is also a secret-tainted variable as it is derived from `hash`, which is again derived from the source `sVar` variable. Therefore, the instructions that use the variable `sVar`, `hash`, and `ciphertext`

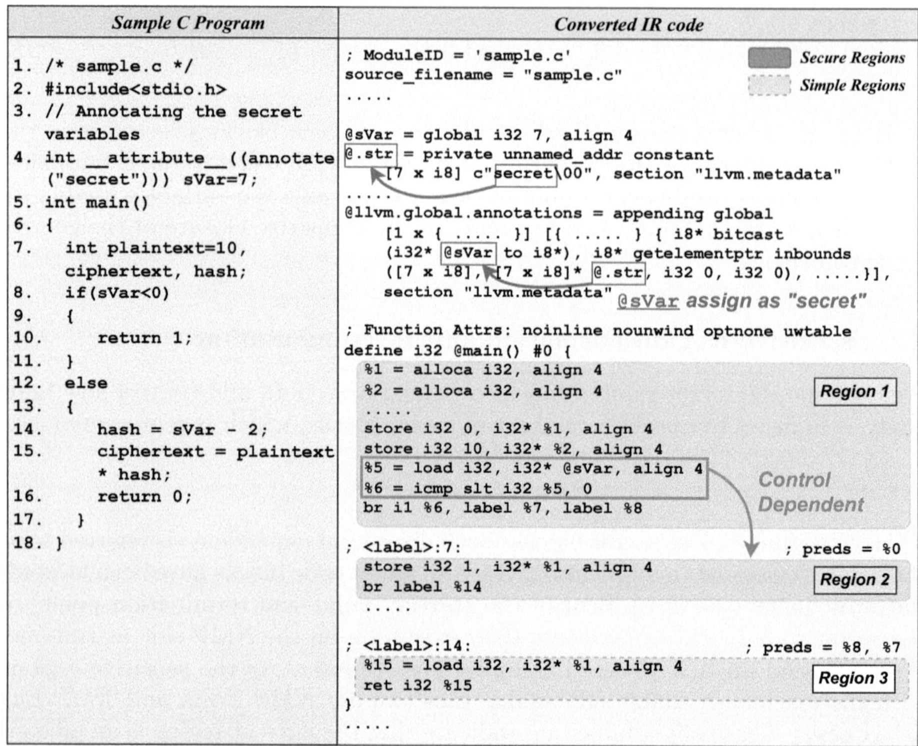

Fig. 2. An intermediate code snippet showing a type of secret control dependency

need to be denoted as secret by the compiler. Next, the program is converted into some low-level intermediate form for the compiler-assisted taint analysis. We use the LLVM compiler framework [17] for the same.

An intermediate code snippet (LLVM IR) of the program is depicted on the right side of Fig. 2. At the beginning of the code, the secret keyword is assigned to the `@.str` register, and then the `@sVar` is annotated as a `secret` variable using the assignment of `@.str` register. Now it is necessary to find all the secret dependent and indirect dependent variables. As discussed previously, we have used the SVF tool for finding the explicit data flows and leverage a set of compiler passes to capture the implicit flows from the IR program. Figure 3 shows a part of the SVF graph in simplified form. SVF recognizes memory allocation sites using *address-of* nodes (green color). The loads and stores from the IR `instructions` are represented in red and blue colors, respectively. The graph illustrates how the source variable taints the other variables. Initially, the integer value of 7 is stored in `sVar`. The value is then loaded into `%5` and `%9` register variables which are further used for comparison and binary operations; thus tainting `%6` and `%10` register variables. The value of `%10` register variable is stored at the memory location pointed to by `%4` and later

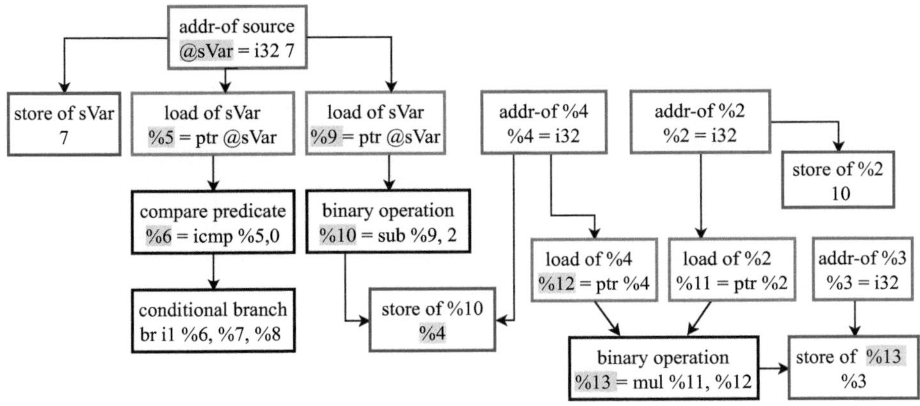

Fig. 3. A part of the SVF graph for the example in Fig. 2

loaded in %12 register variable. It implies that these register variables are secret data dependent on @sVar variable, thereby being classified as secret-tainted variables. Similarly, the %13 register stored the result of the product of a simple register variable (%2) and a secret dependent variable (%12). Thus, it is also dependent on the source variable (@sVar) indirectly. All tainted variables are highlighted and added to the list of secret-tainted variables. Next, a secret control dependency is also shown between the *Region 1* and *Region 2* in Fig. 2, as the execution of code block *Region 2* is dependent on the secret @sVar register variable. Finally, the *secret tainted blocks* are denoted as red boxes, which have at least one operation with the source variables or secret-tainted variables, and simple regions are denoted by the green box where no secure operation will be performed.

3.4   Execution Environment

The execution environment is divided into two primary portions: the *host* side and the *NMP* side, as shown in Fig. 4. As stated earlier, the host side is responsible for executing simple program regions, while the NMP side provides a secure execution environment for executing secure regions through near-memory processing technology. The host side comprises multiple computing cores with multilevel caches, where L1 and L2 caches are private to each core, and L3 (LLC) is shared among all the cores. The memory side comprises a 3D-stacked DRAM memory unit with a near-memory processing capability. The 3D-stacked DRAM comprises numerous vertical memory segments referred to as vaults. Each vault is constructed with multiple layers of DRAM, which are stacked on top of a logical layer. The DRAM layers consist of multiple memory banks, and inter-layer communication is facilitated by the Through-Silicon Via (TSV) technology. In each logic layer, a basic core is put in place to exclusively operate on the corresponding vault. This core establishes a secure computational environment for the

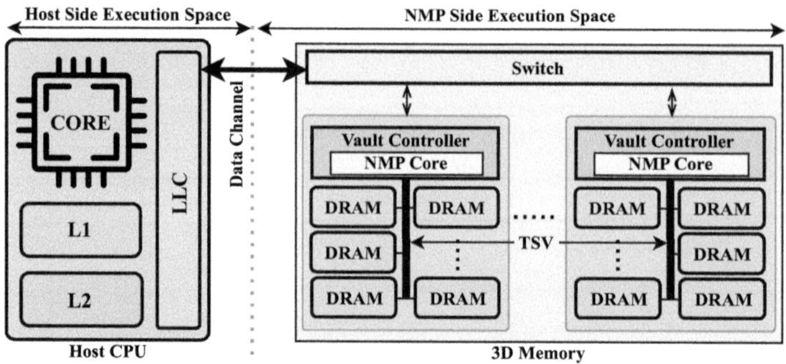

Fig. 4. NMP-enabled system

application. During program execution, the host CPU initiates the execution of the program from its beginning. The execution will persist within the host CPU until the NMP tags (inserted by the compiler analysis mechanism) are detected. Once the NMP tags are identified, the secure code regions located between the *NMP-Begin* and *NMP-End* tags are offloaded to the secure side for further execution. Secret and secret-dependent data are initially allocated in main memory. The decoded instructions and the translated physical memory addresses are then bypassed to the task queue of the corresponding NMP cores based on the vault address location of the data. Then, the NMP cores will execute the queued task accordingly. Therefore, secret and secret-dependent data are processed by the NMP core and used exclusively on the main memory side. As a result, these data will never reach the shared LLC during the course of the application execution, effectively eliminating the risk of cache side-channel attacks.

4   Experimental Details

4.1   Simulation Framework

In the initial phase of our experiment, we utilize several LLVM-based compiler passes (including the SVF tool) to extract taint analysis and instrument the NMP offloading secure regions. In the second phase, we extend two widely used simulation tools to evaluate our proposed work. First, we utilize the PIN tool [19] to extract the execution trace from the instrumented application. The traces contain annotations with special begin and end tags to indicate that the in-between trace lines belong to the offloading secure region. Second, we implement the NMP architecture along with the 3D memory in the Ramulator simulator [16]. This simulator accepts the annotated trace file produced by the PIN tool and runs the simulation. All sets of experiments are carried out on a workstation with an Intel Xeon Silver CPU having 32 cores, running at 2.10 GHz, and equipped with 128 GB of RAM.

Table 1. System configuration parameters

Host Side	Processor	16 Cores, Out-of-Order, 2.4 GHz, 10 W/cycle
	Private L1 Cache	32 KB Cache per core, 8-ways, 4-cycle hit latency, 64 B line size, 0.494 nj/access
	Private L2 Cache	256 KB/core, 8-ways, 12-cycle hit latency, 64B line size, 3.307 nj/access
	Shared L3 Cache	Shared 32 MB, 32-ways, 31-cycle hit latency, 64 B line size, 6.995 nj/access
NMP Side	NMP Logic	32 NCs, In-Order pipeline, 1 NC/vault, 500MHz, 8 mW/cycle
	Private Cache	32 KB/NC, 4-ways, 64 B line size, 0.494 nj/access
	3D Memory	HMC v2.1, 32 vaults, FRFCFS Scheduling, 13.7 pJ/bit (switching link), 3.7 pJ/bit (DRAM) and 6.78pj/bit (logic layer)

4.2   Benchmark Applications

For the evaluation of our work, we have used various well-known algorithms from diverse application domains, namely cryptographic, machine learning (ML), and graph processing algorithms, and these are specified at the bottom of the application name in each resulting figure (see Sect. 5). The cryptographic algorithms used are AES, DES, RSA, RC4, Blowfish, and SHA-2. The keys used in the encryption and decryption are considered as taint sources. Within the ML domain, we have employed K-Means (KM) clustering, k-Nearest Neighbor (NN) classification, and Backpropagation(BP) algorithms. The *attributes* array in KM clustering, the *neighbors* variable in NN, and the *weights* in BP are secret sources, as each parameter directly represents sensitive raw feature values, computed records with distances, or learned mappings, respectively. Next, we have used PageRank (PR) and Breadth-First Search (BFS) algorithms from the domain of graph processing, where the secure information is encoded in the *node rank* array and *graph topology*, respectively. Hence, we consider them as secret in our experiment.

5   Result Evaluation

This section presents the percentage of instruction offloaded to the NMP side, as well as the performance and energy consumption of our proposed strategy, along with other strategies, as described in the following subsections. To ensure a fair comparison, we maintain identical system parameter values across all the policies (mentioned in Table 1). All results have been normalized to the highest outcomes, and the geometric mean of all the workloads (represented by *GM*) has been shown in all resulting figures.

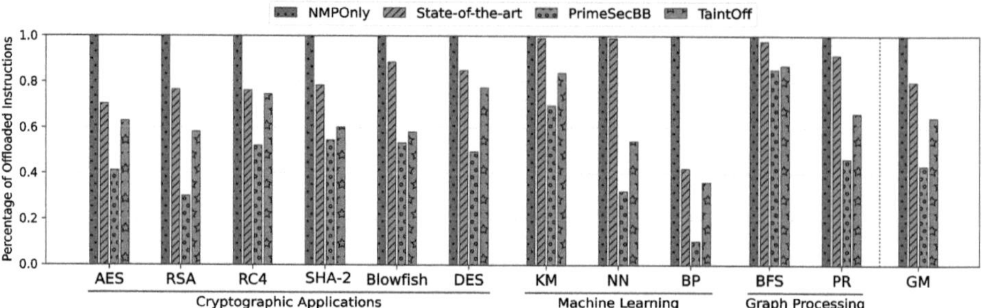

Fig. 5. Instruction offloading percentage for different applications

5.1   Comparable Strategies

To assess the proposed strategy's relative performance, we compare its outcomes with four other strategies, including a state-of-the-art strategy. We briefly explain below.

1. **HostOnly**: This is the conventional approach that follows the standard Von-Neumann architecture, with all computations performed on the multicore host processor, and the NMP capability is turned off at the memory side.
2. **NMPOnly** [23]: This strategy utilizes a straightforward NMP architecture where the entire application executes on the NMP side regardless of its security level.
3. **State-of-the-art strategy** [26]: In this existing strategy, the programmer manually annotates all function bodies that involve operations with secret variables and offloads them to the NMP side.
4. **PrimeSecBB**: This is the basic version of our proposed strategy, where only the basic blocks containing the instructions involving only the primary secret variables are offloaded to NMP cores for execution. All other application regions are executed on the multicore host processor.

5.2   Amount of Offloaded Instructions

Figure 5 shows the percentage of instructions executed and offloaded to the NMP side for different applications. To understand how our proposed strategy influences the system performance, we first assess the percentage of instructions offloaded to the NMP side throughout the application's execution. The NMPOnly strategy offloads 100% of the applications to the NMP side, whereas the state-of-the-art (SOA) strategy offloads 20% fewer instructions to the NMP side. This is because the SOA strategy offloads only a few functions to the NMP side that are manually declared as secure. Further, PrimeSecBB strategy offloads 56% of instructions on the NMP side as only the primary secret basic blocks are offloaded here. However, our proposed strategy (TaintOff) offloads all basic block regions that are directly or indirectly dependent on secure regions, resulting in

21% more instructions offloaded (overall) than the trivial case. The remaining portions of the applications are not offloaded to the NMP side, and they are executed on the host CPU. Compared to the state-of-the-art approach, our strategy results in 15% fewer instructions being offloaded to the NMP side. After reviewing, it is observed that certain ML and graph workloads (KM, NN, and BFS) exhibit an offloading ratio of approximately 99% of instructions to the NMP side for the state-of-the-art strategy. This occurs because secret data is used in every function, thereby necessitating its complete offloading and resulting in the execution of the entire application on the NMP side.

5.3   Performance Evaluation

Figure 6 shows the overall speedup comparison of each strategy with respect to the baseline strategy (HostOnly). Here, the IPC of the overall system is considered as the performance metric. For the *cryptographic applications*, TaintOff improves performance by 41% over the state-of-the-art strategy and by 3.5X over the NMPOnly strategy. However, when contrasting with our naive approach (PrimeSecBB), TaintOff yields a performance reduction of 16%. The PrimeSecBB does not adequately address security concerns, as only the basic blocks with the primary secret variables are offloaded to the NMP side. On the contrary, TaintOff considers basic blocks with both primary and dependent secret variables. For the *ML applications*, TaintOff improves performance by 22% compared to the NMPOnly strategy. However, our approach shows a 15% and 13% performance decline compared to the state-of-the-art and the trivial strategy. This is because ML kernels such as matrix multiplications, convolutions, and activation functions can be localized to NMP, reducing data movement and leading to better performance. For *graph processing applications*, TaintOff achieves an 8% performance improvement over the less secure PrimeSecBB strategy. However, compared to NMPOnly and state-of-the-art strategies, our strategy shows declines of 38% and 49%, respectively. This is because offloading the entire function is beneficial, given the data locality exhibited by irregular graph workloads. Finally, compared to the vulnerable strategy (HostOnly), the TaintOff strategy results in an overall performance decrease of 46% while ensuring that the security of the program is effectively addressed.

The overall results clearly indicate that offloading workloads to the NMP side offers limited performance due to its less capable cores requiring more execution cycles. However, the proposed strategy improves security by avoiding sensitive data transfers to the cache hierarchy and enhances performance compared to the state-of-the-art approach. During the inspection of each cluster, we observe that TaintOff demonstrates the highest effectiveness in cryptographic applications, achieving a speedup of up to 89% in RSA. In contrast, ML applications show the least improvement, with KM clustering with just a 1% increase compared to the state-of-the-art strategy. This variance in performance can be attributed to the variable volume of instructions offloaded in each case.

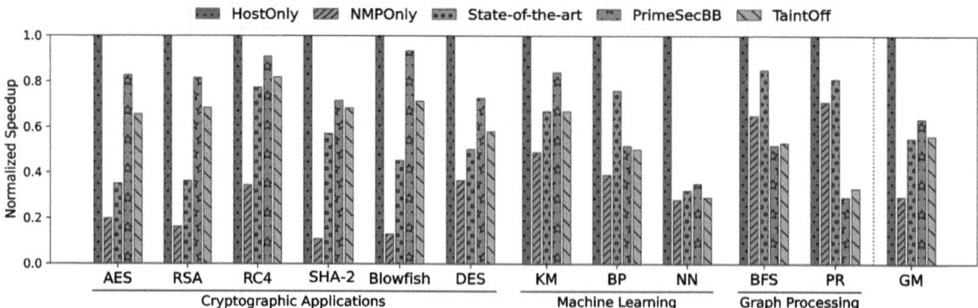

Fig. 6. Speedup comparison

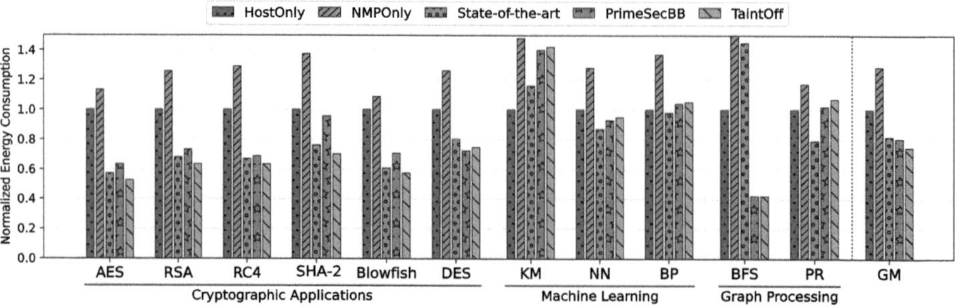

Fig. 7. Energy consumption

5.4   Energy Evaluation

The comparison of overall energy consumption for each strategy is shown in Fig. 7. To assess the system's energy consumption, we have considered the energy consumed by all processing cores, cache memory, and main memory, including DRAM layers and the logic layer. All values for the energy perspective metrics are shown in Table 1. The results indicate that the TaintOff strategy performs better compared to all other strategies. It results in a 42% reduction in overall energy consumption compared to the NMPOnly strategy. Compared to the HostOnly strategy, our approach achieves a reduction in energy consumption of 25%. Further, the TaintOff strategy leads to an overall decrease in energy consumption of 9% when compared with the state-of-the-art strategy. When evaluated against the PrimeSecBB strategy, TaintOff reduces energy consumption by 7% (overall). The energy consumption behavior is different for each application cluster, with cryptographic applications showing a significant reduction of 48% compared to the NMPOnly strategy. For the ML and graph applications, the energy consumption of TaintOff is reduced by 18% and 49%, respectively. This variance of energy among clusters can be attributed to the diversity of workloads executed by different applications. The cryptographic workloads are coupled with regular, data-parallel operations such as substitution or permutation, whereas ML and graph applications show irregular and pointer-chasing patterns leading to higher energy consumption. However, it is essential to note that if an entire application is executed solely on the NMP side, it burdens the NMP cores, leading to higher energy consumption across the system.

6   Security Assessment

6.1   Security Analysis

We reassess the security guarantees of our proposed policy by examining each of its core security objectives. Our analysis follows a structured format: we present relevant arguments from the proposed framework for a set of security objectives, emphasizing how each contributes directly toward fulfilling the corresponding security goal.

Objective 1: Secure data is accessible only to the NMP core and protected from external exposure.

Argument: Cache-based side-channel attacks include the residual data that is present in the LLC. Our proposed policy enables the logic layer to fetch the secure data from the corresponding vault via the vault controller in the memory and establishes a secure computational environment for the secure application. The sensitive code executed by the logic layer on the NMP side completely bypasses the LLC, eliminating the risk of cache-based side-channel vulnerabilities.

Objective 2: Memory accesses initiated from the host CPU reveal no information about secure data or access patterns.

Argument: Attackers frequently use memory access patterns to deduce sensitive information, such as cache-timing or cache-pattern analysis. It is the memory accesses from the application's secure code section that request access to secure data memory regions. The host core does not perform any operation on the secret data; the NMP cores perform operations on secret data at the memory side, keeping no option for any adversary to discover any secure memory access patterns. Sensitive memory regions processed by the NMP side are specifically mapped as uncached, isolated, and inaccessible to regular host CPU caches.

Objective 3: Communication between NMP core and host CPU does not leak information about secret data.

Argument: Our execution framework ensures that operations on all secret data are confined entirely within the memory. After the secure code region is offloaded to the NMP side, all subsequent computation results are stored directly back in memory without transmitting intermediate or secure data to the host CPU. Even if the host CPU requires the results for further computation, the next relevant code region itself will be offloaded to the NMP side due to data and control dependency, rather than transferring sensitive computation results back.

Objective 4: Data transfer occurs only internally between memory banks and the NMP computation unit.

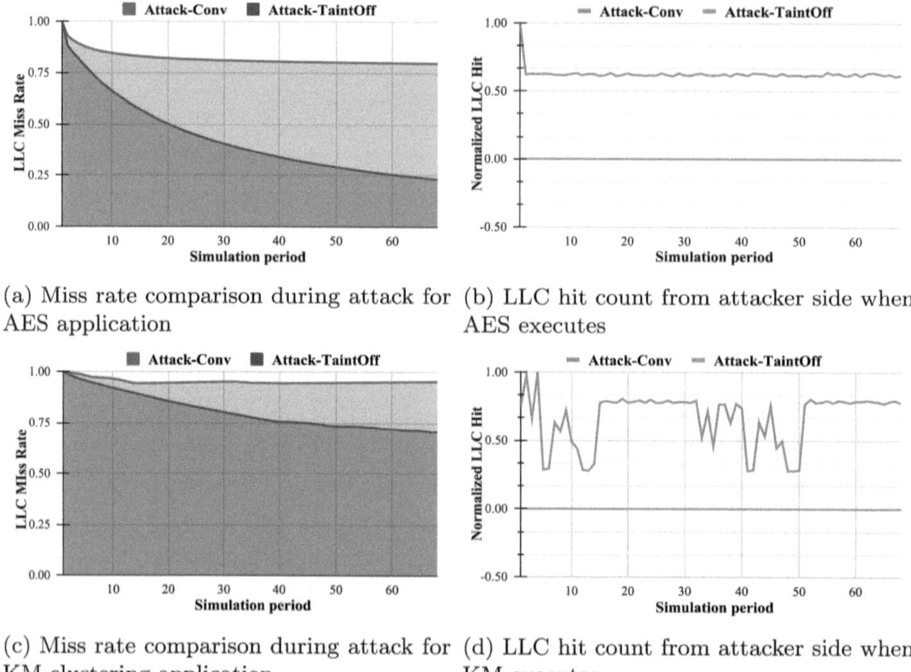

(a) Miss rate comparison during attack for AES application

(b) LLC hit count from attacker side when AES executes

(c) Miss rate comparison during attack for KM clustering application

(d) LLC hit count from attacker side when KM executes

Fig. 8. Attack demonstration under conventional and TaintOff strategy

Argument: External memory buses are a key vulnerability location for side-channel leakage through physical probing or traffic analysis attacks. In our proposed framework, all transfers involving private data take place within the secure memory subsystem itself in our proposed framework, exclusively between the local memory banks and the integrated logic cores, without traversing the external memory buses. The adversary observing the main bus cannot obtain any information regarding the secure data and computation.

6.2 Experimental Validation of Security

To validate the security in our proposed TaintOff, we simulate a cache side-channel attack scenario for two different applications (AES and KM). In our experimental setup, an attacker process runs on a dedicated CPU core, co-located with the victim application, which executes on a separate core. The attacker is assumed to know the memory addresses of the secret data. It periodically probes the LLC for these addresses; upon a successful hit, it records the event (LLC hit) and invalidates the corresponding cache line. This invalidation forces the victim application to fetch the data from main memory on its next access, thereby artificially inflating its cache miss rate. Figure 8 presents the results of this simulation. For a conventional execution strategy, the attacker consistently finds and invalidates secret data in the LLC, as shown by the high number of attacker's LLC hits in Fig. 8(b) and 8(d). This action prevents the legitimate application's LLC miss rate from improving over time, causing it to remain high and constant (Fig. 8(a) and 8(c)). In contrast, when the attack is performed on our NMP-enabled TaintOff strategy, the attacker is unable to locate any secret data in the LLC, resulting in zero hits (Fig. 8(b) and 8(d)). This is because TaintOff offloads sensitive computation regions to the NMP unit, ensuring secret data never populates the shared LLC. Consequently, the application's LLC miss rate decreases naturally as non-sensitive data warms up the cache. These findings demonstrate that TaintOff effectively mitigates this side-channel attack by isolating secure regions having secret data from the shared cache hierarchy.

7   Conclusion

This paper presents a performance-aware taint-based fine-grained computation offloading strategy under the NMP paradigm to address the cache side-channel attacks. The strategy first identifies the taint sources and performs a whole program taint analysis on the basic blocks of the code to form the secure regions. Further, these secure regions are offloaded to the NMP side for execution. We measure the effectiveness of the proposed strategy by performing simulations on a set of standard simulators for a set of benchmark applications from diverse technological domains. The experimental results demonstrate that the proposed strategy *TaintOff* achieves a speedup of 41% over the state-of-the-art strategy. *TaintOff* offloads 20% fewer instructions and achieves a 9% reduction in energy consumption compared to the state-of-the-art approach. The security of our proposed approach is assessed through extensive security analysis and further verified by experimental validation.

Acknowledgment. The research is supported by R&D grant of **ASTEC**, Science, Technology and Climate Change Department, Govt. of Assam (Project Code: R&DP23-98).

References

1. Bhatla, A., Navneet, Panda, B.: The maya cache: a storage-efficient and secure fully-associative last-level cache. In: ISCA 2024, pp. 32–44. IEEE Press (2025)
2. Blömer, J., Krummel, V.: Analysis of countermeasures against access driven cache attacks on AES. In: Selected Areas in Cryptography: 14th International Workshop, SAC 2007, Ottawa, Canada, 16–17 August 2007, pp. 96–109 (2007)
3. Brickell, E., Graunke, G., Neve, M., Seifert, J.P.: Software mitigations to hedge AES against cache-based software side channel vulnerabilities. Cryptology ePrint Archive, Paper 2006/052 (2006)
4. Chakraborty, A., Bhattacharya, S., et al.: Are randomized caches truly random? Formal analysis of randomized-partitioned caches. In: IEEE International Symposium on High-Performance Computer Architecture, pp. 233–246 (2023)

5. Cho, H., Park, J., et al.: SmokeBomb: effective mitigation against cache side-channel attacks on the ARM architecture. In: Proceedings of the 18th International Conference on Mobile Systems, Applications, and Services, pp. 107–120 (2020)
6. Choudhury, A., Nath, K.K., Ghose, M., Thakran, Y.: Memory and CPU utilization-aware energy-efficient VM placement and consolidation in cloud data centers. In: IEEE Guwahati Subsection Conference (GCON), pp. 1–6 (2023)
7. Devic, A., Rai, S.B., Sivasubramaniam, A., Akel, A., Eilert, S., Eno, J.: To PIM or not for emerging general purpose processing in DDR memory systems. In: Proceedings of the 49th Annual International Symposium on Computer Architecture, pp. 231–244 (2022)
8. ElAtali, H., Duan, X., Liljestrand, H., Xu, M., Asokan, N.: BliMe linter. In: 2024 IEEE Secure Development Conference, pp. 46–53 (2024)
9. Ferrante, J., Ottenstein, K.J., Warren, J.D.: The program dependence graph and its use in optimization. ACM Trans. Program. Lang. Syst. 319–349 (1987)
10. Ghose, M., Kaur, S., Sahu, A.: Scheduling real time tasks in an energy-efficient way using VMs with discrete compute capacities. **102**(1), 263–294 (2020)
11. Godfrey, M., Zulkernine, M.: Preventing cache-based side-channel attacks in a cloud environment. IEEE Trans. Cloud Comput. **2**, 395–408 (2014)
12. Gruss, D., Lettner, J., Schuster, F., Ohrimenko, O., Haller, I., Costa, M.: Strong and efficient cache Side-Channel protection using hardware transactional memory. In: 26th USENIX Security Symposium, pp. 217–233 (2017)
13. Gullasch, D., Bangerter, E., Krenn, S.: Cache games – bringing access-based cache attacks on AES to practice. In: 2011 IEEE Symposium on Security and Privacy, pp. 490–505 (2011)
14. Holtryd, N.R., Manivannan, M., Stenström, P.: SCALE: secure and scalable cache partitioning. In: IEEE International Symposium on Hardware Oriented Security and Trust, pp. 68–79 (2023)
15. Kaur, S., Ghose, M., Sahu, A.: Energy efficient scheduling of real-time tasks in cloud environment. In: IEEE 19th International Conference on High Performance Computing and Communications, pp. 178–185 (2017)
16. Kim, Y., Yang, W., Mutlu, O.: Ramulator: a fast and extensible DRAM simulator. IEEE Comput. Archit. Lett. **15**(1), 45–49 (2016)
17. Lattner, C., Adve, V.: LLVM: a compilation framework for lifelong program analysis & transformation. In: International Symposium on Code Generation and Optimization, pp. 75–86 (2004)
18. Lu, Z., Wen, X., Sun, Y.: A game theory based resource sharing scheme in cloud computing environment. In: World Congress on Information and Communication Technologies, pp. 1097–1102 (2012)
19. Luk, C.K., Cohn, R., Muth, R., et al.: Pin: building customized program analysis tools with dynamic instrumentation. In: Proceedings of ACM SIGPLAN Conference on Programming Language Design and Implementation, pp. 190–200 (2005)
20. Lyu, Y., Mishra, P.: A survey of side-channel attacks on caches and countermeasures. J. Hardw. Syst. Secur. **2**(1), 33–50 (2017). https://doi.org/10.1007/s41635-017-0025-y
21. Mahipal, S., Sharmila, V.C.: Virtual machine security problems and countermeasures for improving quality of service in cloud computing. In: International Conference on Artificial Intelligence and Smart Systems (ICAIS), pp. 1319–1324 (2021)
22. Maity, S., Ghose, M., Pasricha, S.: A framework for near memory processing with computation offloading and load balancing. IEEE Trans. Comput.-Aided Des. Integr. Circuits Syst. **44**(9), 1–14 (2025)

23. Maity, S., Ghose, M., et al.: Unguided machine learning-based computation offloading for near-memory processing. In: 38th VLSID, pp. 540–545 (2025)
24. Maity, S., Goel, M., Ghose, M.: Data locality aware computation offloading in near memory processing architecture for big data applications. In: 2023 IEEE 30th International Conference on HiPC, pp. 288–297 (2023)
25. Moses, J., Iyer, R., Illikkal, R., Srinivasan, S., Aisopos, K.: Shared resource monitoring and throughput optimization in cloud-computing datacenters. In: IEEE International Parallel & Distributed Processing Symposium, pp. 1024–1033 (2011)
26. Nelson, C., Izraelevitz, J., et al.: Eliminating micro-architectural side-channel attacks using near memory processing. In: IEEE International Symposium on Secure and Private Execution Environment Design, pp. 179–189 (2022)
27. Neve, M., Seifert, J.P.: Advances on access-driven cache attacks on AES. In: International Workshop on Selected Areas in Cryptography, pp. 147–162 (2006)
28. Ojha, D., Dwarkadas, S.: Timecache: using time to eliminate cache side channels when sharing software. In: ACM/IEEE 48th Annual International Symposium on Computer Architecture, pp. 375–387 (2021)
29. Osvik, D.A., Shamir, A., Tromer, E.: Cache attacks and countermeasures: the case of AES. In: Cryptographers' Track at the RSA Conference, pp. 1–20 (2006)
30. Page, D.: Partitioned cache architecture as a side-channel defence mechanism. Cryptology ePrint Archive, Paper 2005/280 (2005)
31. Qiang, W., Luo, H.: AutoSlicer: automatic program partitioning for securing sensitive data based-on data dependency analysis and code refactoring. In: 2022 IEEE International Conference on Trust, Security and Privacy in Computing and Communications (TrustCom), pp. 239–247 (2022)
32. Qiu, P., et al.: PMU-leaker: performance monitor unit-based realization of cache side-channel attacks. In: Proceedings of the 28th Asia and South Pacific Design Automation Conference (2023)
33. Qureshi, M.K.: Ceaser: mitigating conflict-based cache attacks via encrypted-address and remapping. In: 2018 51st Annual IEEE/ACM International Symposium on MICRO, pp. 775–787 (2018)
34. Sari, S., Demir, O., Kucuk, G.: FairSDP: fair and secure dynamic cache partitioning. In: 4th International Conference on CSE, pp. 469–474 (2019)
35. Shrivastava, N., Sarangi, S.R.: Toward an optimal countermeasure for cache side-channel attacks. IEEE Embed. Syst. Lett. **15**(3), 141–144 (2023)
36. Sui, Y., Xue, J.: SVF: interprocedural static value-flow analysis in LLVM. In: Proceedings of the 25th International Conference on Compiler Construction, pp. 265–266 (2016)
37. Wang, T., He, H., et al.: Conftainter: static taint analysis for configuration options. In: 38th ACM International Conference on Automated Software Engineering, pp. 1640–1651 (2023)
38. Wang, X., Wen, X., et al.: A dynamic cache partitioning mechanism under virtualization environment. In: IEEE 11th International Conference on Trust, Security and Privacy in Computing and Communications, pp. 1907–1911 (2012)
39. Wang, Y., Ferraiuolo, A., Zhang, D., Myers, A.C., Suh, G.E.: SecDCP: secure dynamic cache partitioning for efficient timing channel protection. In: 53nd ACM/EDAC/IEEE Design Automation Conference (DAC), pp. 1–6 (2016)
40. Werner, M., Unterluggauer, T., Giner, L., Schwarz, M., Gruss, D., et al.: Scattercache: thwarting cache attacks via cache set randomization. In: Proceedings of the 28th USENIX Confernce on Security Symposium, pp. 675–692. USENIX Association (2019)

41. Wichelmann, J., Pätschke, A., Wilke, L., Eisenbarth, T.: Cipherfix: mitigating ciphertext side-channel attacks in software. In: 32nd USENIX Security Symposium, pp. 6789–6806 (2023)
42. Yarom, Y., Falkner, K.: FLUSH+RELOAD: a high resolution, low noise, L3 cache side-channel attack. In: 23rd USENIX Security Symposium, pp. 719–732 (2014)
43. Zhang, R., Bond, M.D., Zhang, Y.: Cape: compiler-aided program transformation for HTM-based cache side-channel defense. In: Proceedings of the 31st ACM SIGPLAN International Conference on Compiler Construction, pp. 181–193 (2022)
44. Zhang, X., Xiao, Y., Zhang, Y.: Return-Oriented Flush-Reload Side Channels on ARM and Their Implications for Android Devices, pp. 858–870 (2016)

Gradient-Guided Adversarial Patch Attack for Deep Neural Networks

Rishav Kumar, Umesh Kashyap, and Sk. Subidh Ali$^{(\boxtimes)}$

Indian Institute of Technology, Bhilai, Bhilai, India
{rishavkuma,umeshk,subidh}@iitbhilai.ac.in

Abstract. Deep neural networks (DNNs) have achieved remarkable success across vision tasks, yet they remain highly vulnerable to adversarial perturbations. While patch-based attacks have been explored as a localized and efficient adversarial attack strategy on DNNs, existing methods often require large perturbation areas or lack precise placement, making them either perceptually noticeable or less effective. To address these limitations, this paper proposes a gradient-guided adversarial patch attack that targets model-specific vulnerable regions. Using gradient-based sensitivity analysis, we are able to pinpoint the most important pixels in the input image that influence the decision of target DNNs. The backgrounds of these sensitive pixels are initially considered as patches. Subsequently, these patches are converted into imperceptible and highly lethal patches through an iterative alpha-controlled blending method. Extensive experiments on multiple benchmark datasets demonstrate that our patches achieve high attack success rates while covering only a small fraction of the original image. These findings underscore the vulnerability of DNNs to compact, well-placed adversarial patches and provide valuable insights for designing stronger defenses against such localized attacks. The source code of our work is available at the given link: https://github.com/ RishavKumarIIT/Gradient-Guided-Adversarial-Patch-Attack.

Keywords: Multiple Adversarial Patches · DNN models · Sensitive Pixels · Gradient-Based Attack

1 Introduction

Deep Neural Networks ($DNNs$) have revolutionized computer vision, delivering state-of-the-art ($SOTA$) results in tasks such as image classification, object detection, and semantic segmentation. Despite these achievements, $DNNs$ remain highly vulnerable to adversarial manipulation. In practice, even small, carefully crafted changes to an input image, which are imperceptible to human eyes, can cause a DNN model to misclassify [8,28]. This vulnerability of the DNN models raises serious concerns in highly sensitive domains such as autonomous driving [23], healthcare [15], and security [17], where a single incorrect prediction may result in accidents, compromised patient safety, or system breaches.

C. Karfa et al. (Eds.): SPACE 2025, LNCS 16406, pp. 227–245, 2026.
https://doi.org/10.1007/978-3-032-16342-4_13

Adversarial attacks on images generally fall into two categories: perturbation-based and patch-based. Perturbation attacks spread subtle noise across the entire image, remaining nearly invisible to human eyes [24]. In contrast, patch attacks modify only a small, localized region of the image to fail the model prediction [35]. Unlike perturbations, adversarial patches can be physically printed and attached to real-world objects, where they remain effective under different lighting conditions, viewing angles, and backgrounds [18]. This paper focuses on patch-based attacks.

However, designing adversarial patches involves trade-offs between visibility, robustness, and generalization across multiple models. Some patch-based attack methods rely on large and visible patterns [3], which are effective but easy to detect. Others prioritize stealth by blending into the scene, such as mimicking natural textures, background patterns, or object colors [12]. While such stealth-oriented designs improve imperceptibility to human eyes, they often struggle to maintain robustness and transferability across different datasets and different DNN models [26,29]. Moreover, stealth-focused methods sometimes overfit to specific local textures, making them less adaptive under transformations such as scaling, rotation, or viewpoint changes [6]. In addition, overlapping patch placements in similar sensitive regions further reduce effectiveness and increase detectability [30], as well as a single large, high-contrast patch is visible to human eyes [1]. Consequently, achieving both high stealth and strong cross-model generalization remains an open challenge in adversarial patch design [19]. Recent research has attempted to bridge this gap with camouflaged or naturalistic designs [31] and adaptive patch optimization guided by model interpretability [14]. While these methods improve realism and adaptability, they are still limited. In particular, Fig. 1, patch placement is often guided by attribution tools such as Grad-CAM, which typically highlight concentrated semantic regions. This results in overlapping patch locations and visible artifacts, reducing stealthness of the patch [33,34,36].

In this work, we introduce a new adversarial patch framework that is initialized with a local image region and refined using alpha-blending, which makes placement more adaptive and less perceptible by leveraging model sensitivity maps. Our approach identifies the pixels that have a strong influence on the classifier's prediction using gradient-based measures. This yields sensitivity maps that reveal a spatially distributed set of high-impact pixels. This allows patches to be blended into different parts of the object surface, increasing stealth while maintaining attack success rate. Our contributions are as follows:

- We develop a gradient-based adversarial patch placement method that automatically identifies model-sensitive regions in each input image. This makes the attack adaptive, image-specific, and more effective than random or fixed placement strategies.
- We propose a progressive patch-growing mechanism, where both the size and opacity of the patch are gradually adjusted during the attack process. This reduces unnecessary visual distortion while ensuring misclassification.

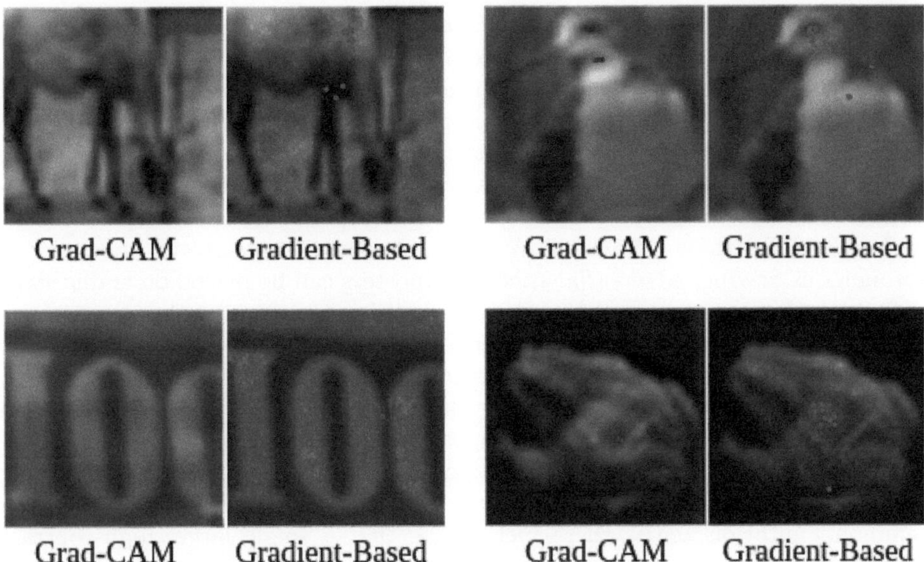

Fig. 1. Comparison between Grad-CAM heatmaps and our gradient-based sensitivity maps for two sample inputs. gradient-based identifies a more spatially distributed set of highly sensitive points.

- Our proposed framework is easy to apply in practice. This generates a stealthy patch and performs a high attack success rate.

2   Related Work

Adversarial examples (AEs) are carefully crafted perturbations that, once added to the input image, will fail the target deep neural network(DNNs) based tasks such as classification, object recognition, etc. The Fast Gradient Sign Method ($FGSM$) [8] is the first adversarial attack that generates a perturbation by taking the gradient of the loss with respect to the input and adding a small step in the direction that increases the loss. This produces a one-shot perturbation that is fast but sometimes less powerful. Projected Gradient Descent (PGD) [21] extends this idea by applying $FGSM$ multiple times in small steps, while projecting the perturbed input back into a fixed bound after each step. This iterative process makes PGD one of the strongest first-order attacks, as it searches more thoroughly for adversarial inputs. Later, studies confirmed that these adversarial attacks can also fool DNN models in real-world settings [17].

2.1   Visible Patch-Based Attacks

Visible patch-based attacks focus on perturbing a small region of an image instead of modifying the whole input. The universal adversarial patch [3] demonstrates that a single patch can reliably drive a model's prediction toward a chosen target label, regardless of where it is placed within an image. The Expectation over Transformation (EOT) framework [2] improved attack success rate by optimizing patches under random transformations such as scaling, rotation, and viewpoint changes, ensuring their effectiveness under diverse conditions. The transferable patch approach [20] further extended this idea by jointly training patches on an ensemble of models, enabling them to generalize across architectures and datasets without the need for retraining.

In practice, these attacks have raised serious concerns. In the case of autonomous driving, adversarial stickers or posters can be placed on traffic signs to fool the classification models and sign recognition systems of the autonomous vehicle [7,35]. Subsequently, more advanced patch attacks were developed [11,23] that can even work in diverse environmental conditions such as varied lighting, occlusion, and viewing angles, making them more effective in many real-world scenarios. In healthcare, the attack proposed in [15] showed that adversarial patterns can fool dermoscopy classifiers, exposing vulnerabilities in medical imaging workflows and raising concerns for patient safety. Despite their effectiveness, a common limitation across these methods is that a single large, high-contrast patch is noticeable, making it easier to detect by both human eyes and automated deep learning based defense systems [16].

2.2 Imperceptible Patch-Based Attacks

While visible patch-based attacks are powerful, their biggest challenge is visibility. A patch that is too large or has high contrast becomes easy to notice, which limits its usefulness in real-world scenarios. To address this, several methods have been developed that focus on stealthiness, making patches less detectable to both humans and automated defenses while keeping their adversarial strength. The *CamoPatch* method [31] uses evolutionary optimization to search for patch textures that visually blend with their surroundings. Instead of producing random noise, the optimization process evolves patterns that look like natural elements, such as drawings or wall stains, while still forcing the model into misclassification. This balance makes the patch less suspicious to human eyes. However, its reliance on natural-looking textures may not always generalize across diverse backgrounds, limiting its robustness in unseen environments. The style-transfer patch method [5] embeds perturbations into textures by borrowing patterns from the image's own background. Using style transfer, the patch is generated in such a way that its colors and textures should look like natural surfaces (*e.g.*, wood, grass, or concrete). This helps hide the adversarial patch inside realistic patterns of the image. But if the background is plain or uniform, the patch has nothing to blend with and becomes easier to notice.

The deformal-shape patch method [4] generates irregular shapes instead of simple squares or circles. By following object boundaries or scene geometry, these patches look more like natural markings and less like foreign elements pasted onto the image. This reduces visual patterns and improves usability in physical settings. However, designing and applying such irregular shapes can be harder in practice, and their adversarial strength may drop compared to larger square patches. The camouflage-aware masking technique [33] guides patches into semantically meaningful regions, such as natural edges, textures, or object parts, where humans are less likely to notice changes. This makes the patch appear integrated into the scene while still preserving adversarial strength. However, its dependency on accurate masks can be a weakness, if the mask misaligns with the scene, the patch becomes more visible and less effective. Diffusion-based generative attacks have also emerged to enhance patch realism. *AdvLogo* [22] leverages diffusion models to create adversarial patches resembling natural brand logos, maintaining strong attack performance against object detectors while remaining visually inconspicuous. However, its generative optimization is computationally intensive and may limit patch diversity.

Recent explainability-guided approaches aim to improve patch stealth by leveraging model interpretation maps. *VIPA* [36] selects contributing feature regions (*CFRs*) from activation maps and applies perturbations only to these high-impact pixels. This targeted approach reduces visual artifacts while maintaining adversarial effectiveness. Its limitation is that *CFRs* can shift under adversarial training or model variations, producing residual artifacts and reducing attack reliability. Similarly, Focus-Shifting Attack (*FS Attack*) [14] redirects the original saliency maps away from true features of the original image, while still causing misclassification. This strategy compromises both predictions and model explanations, making the attack less detectable. However, with low perturbation budgets, patches often become irregular or patchy, increasing their visibility and reducing reliability. *POSES* [18] combines gradient sensitivity and attribution maps to identify optimal patch locations, allowing smaller patches with higher stealth compared to earlier methods. However, it still struggles to balance the trade-off between imperceptibility and robust performance across different models [18]. This limitation motivates the need for methods that reliably achieve both stealth and effectiveness in diverse, real-world conditions.

3   Methodology

We propose a gradient-guided adversarial patch generation framework designed to craft perturbations that are simultaneously effective against *DNNs* and visually imperceptible to human eyes. Unlike traditional patch attacks, which often rely on random placement or heuristic-driven regions, our method leverages gradient-based sensitivity analysis of *DNN* models to systematically identify prediction-critical areas of an input image. This allows for adding patches where they matter most for the model's decision-making, resulting in spatially efficient patches and perceptually stealthy patches.

Our method operates natively in white-box settings, where gradients of the target model are directly accessible to construct sensitivity maps. Because the framework only requires gradients and confidence scores of any classifier. Importantly, although our current experiments optimize patches per model in a white-box manner, the reliance on score-based sensitivity rather than model specific features makes the method naturally extensible to black-box scenarios, where

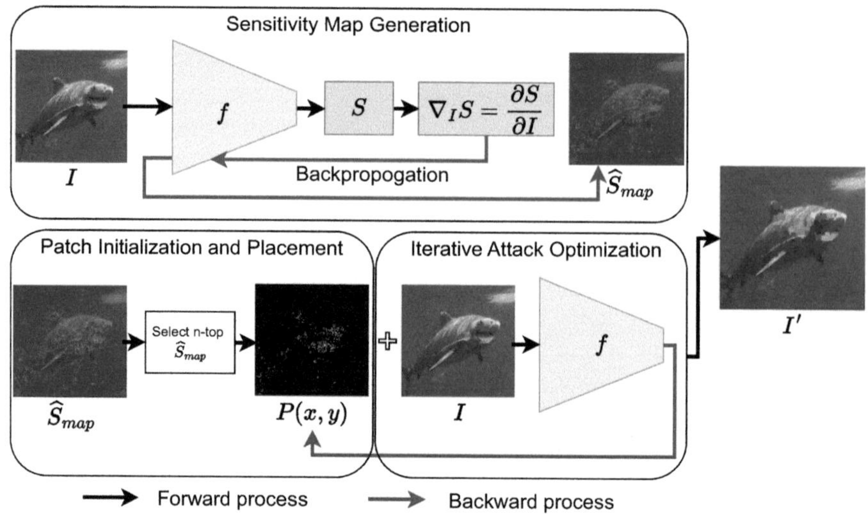

Fig. 2. Overview of proposed method.

gradients can be approximated via confidence score queries on surrogate models. This design ensures the broad applicability of our attack pipeline across diverse threat models.

As shown in the Fig. 2 and Algorithm 3, our proposed pipeline is composed of three integrated components: first *sensitivity map generation*, which localizes the most influential regions of an image with respect to the model's decision boundaries. The second is *Patch Initialization and Placement*, which initializes visually consistent patches and manages their transparency to minimize detectability. The Third component is *iterative attack optimization*, which progressively adjusts patch strength and scale until the attack succeeds, thereby balancing adversarial success with minimal perturbation. Together, these stages establish a unified methodology for generating adversarial patches that maximize both attack efficiency and stealthiness of the patch.

3.1   Sensitivity Map Generation

The first step of our framework is to identify which pixels of the image have the greatest influence on the model's prediction. Intuitively, these are the pixels where even a tiny change can cause a large shift in the classifier's confidence. By localizing such regions, we can place adversarial patches in identified pixel positions while keeping the rest of the image visually unchanged. Let the normalised input image be $I \in \mathbb{R}^{H \times W \times C}$, where H, W, and C represent the input image's height, width and channel, respectively. When I is passed through a pre-trained classifier $f(\cdot)$, we obtain the output logits $O = f(I) \in \mathbb{R}^{1 \times c}$, where c is the number of classes. The logit corresponding to the predicted class y_{pred} is

---

Algorithm 1. Sensitivity Map Generation

Require: Input image I, pretrained classifier $f(\cdot)$
Ensure: Normalized sensitivity map $\hat{S}_{\mathrm{map}}$
1: $O \leftarrow f(I)$
2: $y_{\mathrm{pred}} \leftarrow \arg\max(O)$
3: $S \leftarrow O[0, y_{\mathrm{pred}}]$
4: Compute gradient: $\nabla_I S = \dfrac{\partial S}{\partial I}$
5: $S_{\mathrm{map}}(x, y) \leftarrow \dfrac{1}{C} \sum_{c=1}^{C} |\nabla_I S(x, y, c)|$
6: $\hat{S}_{\mathrm{map}}(x, y) \leftarrow \dfrac{S_{\mathrm{map}}(x, y) - \min(S_{\mathrm{map}})}{\max(S_{\mathrm{map}}) - \min(S_{\mathrm{map}}) + \epsilon}$
7: **return** $\hat{S}_{\mathrm{map}}$

Algorithm 2. Patch Initialization and Placement

Require: Input image I, sensitivity map $\hat{S}_{\mathrm{map}}$, number of candidate locations n, patch size k, initial transparency α_{init}
Ensure: Initial patched image I', patch set $\mathcal{P}$, ROIs, transparency α
1: Select top-n pixels $\{(x_i, y_i)\}$ with highest $\hat{S}_{\mathrm{map}}$
2: Initialize empty lists: $\mathcal{P}$, ROIs
3: Set $\alpha \leftarrow \alpha_{\mathrm{init}}$
4: **for** each pixel (x, y) in I **do**
5:     **if** (x, y) lies inside some ROI centered at (x_0, y_0) **then**
6:         $P(x, y) \leftarrow \frac{1}{k^2} \sum_{i=x_0-\frac{k}{2}}^{x_0+\frac{k}{2}} \sum_{j=y_0-\frac{k}{2}}^{y_0+\frac{k}{2}} I(i, j)$ ▷ Initialize patch for that ROI
7:         $\mathcal{P}.append(P)$
8:         $\mathrm{ROIs}.append(ROI)$
9:         $I'(x, y) \leftarrow \alpha \cdot P(x, y) + (1 - \alpha) \cdot I(x, y)$ ▷ Blend pixel with patch
10:    **else**
11:        $I'(x, y) \leftarrow I(x, y)$
12:    **end if**
13: **end for**
14: **return** $(I', \mathcal{P}, \mathrm{ROIs}, \alpha)$

---

written as $S = O[0, y_{\mathrm{pred}}]$. To measure how sensitive this score is to each pixel, we compute the gradient of S with respect to I:

$$\nabla_I S = \frac{\partial S}{\partial I}. \tag{1}$$

This gradient shows how much a small change at each pixel would increase or decrease the model's confidence in the predicted class. To make the patches easier to interpret, we average the gradient values across color channels, producing a single saliency value for each pixel, denoted as $S_{\mathrm{map}}(x, y)$. We then normalize the saliency map to the range $[0, 1]$ so that it can be visualized as a heatmap:

Algorithm 3. Gradient-Guided Adversarial Patch Generation

Require: Input image I, pretrained classifier $f(\cdot)$, ground-truth label y_{true}, number of candidate locations n, patch size k, initial transparency α_{init}, transparency step α_{step}, patch growth h_{step}, step size η, maximum iterations max_iter

Ensure: Adversarial image I'

    Stage 1: Sensitivity Map Generation

1: $\hat{S}_{\text{map}} \leftarrow$ Algorithm $1(I, f)$

    Stage 2: Patch Initialization and Placement

2: $(I', \mathcal{P}, \text{ROIs}, \alpha) \leftarrow$ Algorithm $2(I, \hat{S}_{\text{map}}, n, k, \alpha_{\text{init}})$

    Stage 3: Iterative attack Optimization

3: $I'_{\text{best}} \leftarrow I'$

4: best_conf $\leftarrow f(I')[0, y_{\text{true}}]$

5: **for** $t \leftarrow 1$ **to** max_iter **do**

6:     $O' \leftarrow f(T(I'))$

7:     $y'_{\text{pred}} \leftarrow \arg\max(O')$

8:     $S \leftarrow O'[0, y'_{\text{pred}}]$

9:     **if** $y'_{\text{pred}} \neq y_{\text{true}}$ **then**

10:         **return** I'_{best}

11:     **end if**

12:     **for** each (P, ROI) in $(\mathcal{P}, \text{ROIs})$ **do**

13:         **for** each pixel (x, y) in I **do**

14:             **if** $(x, y) \in ROI$ **then**

15:                 $P(x, y) \leftarrow P(x, y) + \eta \cdot \text{sign}\left(\dfrac{\partial S}{\partial P(x, y)}\right)$

16:                 $I'(x, y) \leftarrow \alpha \cdot P(x, y) + (1 - \alpha) \cdot I(x, y)$ ▷ Blend pixel with patch

17:             **else**

18:                 $I'(x, y) \leftarrow I(x, y)$

19:             **end if**

20:         **end for**

21:         $\alpha \leftarrow \min(\alpha + \alpha_{\text{step}}, 1.0)$

22:         $\text{size}(ROI) \leftarrow \text{size}(ROI) + h_{\text{step}}$

23:     **end for**

24:     current_conf $\leftarrow f(I')[0, y_{\text{true}}]$

25:     **if** current_conf $<$ best_conf **then**

26:         $I'_{\text{best}} \leftarrow I'$

27:         best_conf $\leftarrow$ current_conf

28:     **end if**

29: **end for**

30: **return** I'_{best}

$$\hat{S}\text{map}(x, y) = \frac{S_{\text{map}}(x, y) - \min(S_{\text{map}}(x, y))}{\max(S_{\text{map}}(x, y)) - \min(S_{\text{map}}(x, y)) + \epsilon}. \tag{2}$$

Here, ϵ is a small constant included to ensure numerical stability during normalization, preventing division by zero when the saliency map has uniform values. The resulting sensitivity map $\hat{S}_{\text{map}}$ highlights the image regions that contribute most strongly to the classifier's decision. Unlike Grad-CAM [25], which typically produces a single coarse region around the most important part of the object, our gradient-based map often reveals multiple smaller but critical points across the object. This richer distribution allows us to place adversarial patches more flexibly and stealthily, making them harder for human eyes to notice and more difficult for defense systems to detect.

3.2   Patch Initialization and Placement

After computing the sensitivity map $\hat{S}_{\mathrm{map}}$, the next step is to select candidate locations for adversarial patch placement. We pick the top pixels with the highest saliency values, as these regions influence the prediction of the classifiers. Around each selected pixel, we define a square region of interest (ROI) of size $k \times k$ to host the patch. The patch is initially set to the average RGB values of its local neighborhood to blend naturally with the surrounding texture:

$$P(x,y) = \frac{1}{k^2} \sum_{i=x_0-\frac{k}{2}}^{x_0+\frac{k}{2}} \sum_{j=y_0-\frac{k}{2}}^{y_0+\frac{k}{2}} I(i,j), \quad (x,y) \in \mathrm{ROI}, \tag{3}$$

where (x_0, y_0) is the center of the ROI. We further apply an *alpha-blending* strategy, placing the patch with partial transparency to reduce visual detectability:

$$I'(x,y) = \begin{cases} \alpha \cdot P(x,y) + (1 - \alpha) \cdot I(x,y), & (x,y) \in \mathrm{ROI}, \\ I(x,y), & \text{otherwise}, \end{cases} \tag{4}$$

where α is the transparency factor. Initially, α is small, making the patch nearly imperceptible.

3.3   Iterative Attack Optimization

Once the patch is initialized and placed in sensitive regions, the attack proceeds in an iterative manner. At each step, the current patched image I' is passed through the classifier, and the output distribution is monitored. If the predicted label differs from the ground-truth y_{true}, the attack is considered successful and the process stops. If the model still predicts the correct class, the patch is adaptively updated using gradient information. Specifically, the gradient of the predicted class score S with respect to the patch pixels is computed:

$$\nabla_P S = \frac{\partial S}{\partial P}. \tag{5}$$

The patch is then updated in the direction that reduces the classifier's confidence in the true class (or increases confidence in the target class for targeted attacks):

$$P(x,y) = P(x,y) + \eta \cdot \mathrm{sign}(\nabla_P S), \quad (x,y) \in \mathrm{ROI}, \tag{6}$$

where η is the step size controlling the magnitude of each update. At the same time, the transparency factor α can be gradually increased, and the patch area can expand from a small seed region to a larger one if required. This progressive patch-growing mechanism ensures that both the strength and size of the patch increase only as needed, maintaining stealth while improving attack effectiveness. Throughout the iterations, the framework keeps track of intermediate patched images that cause the greatest drop in the model's confidence for the true class. Among these, the most effective adversarial image is selected as the final output. After optimization, the adversarial image is converted back to the RGB domain by reversing preprocessing steps, to use for visualization and evaluation.

4   Experiments and Setup

4.1   Datasets

We evaluated our method on five widely-used image classification datasets spanning a range of visual complexities. $ImageNet$ consists of over 1.2 million high-resolution natural images across $1,000$ object categories, representing a large-scale and challenging classification task. $SVHN$ (Street View House Numbers) contains more than $600,000$ real-world digit images extracted from street view scenes, introducing variability in lighting, background, and digit orientation. $CIFAR$-10 includes $60,000$ RGB images across 10 classes, while $CIFAR$-100 contains $60,000$ RGB images across 100 classes, providing inter-class complexity. $Fashion$-$MNIST$ is a benchmark dataset of $70,000$ grayscale images of fashion products across 10 categories, offering a controlled, low-dimensional classification task. This diverse selection ensures that our experiments evaluate the robustness and effectiveness of our method across both simple and complex classification scenarios, covering a broad spectrum from controlled to real-world visual domains.

4.2   Target Models

Experiments were conducted on a variety of deep neural network architectures representative of different design paradigms. These included the VGG family (VGG13, VGG16, VGG19) [27], the ResNet family ($ResNet$18, $ResNet$34, $ResNet$50) [10], and the DenseNet family ($DenseNet$121, $DenseNet$169, $DenseNet$201) [13]. All networks were used in their pre-trained forms, aligned with the standard training protocols of the respective datasets.

4.3   Baseline Methods for Comparision

To ensure a fair and comprehensive evaluation, our approach was compared against several representative adversarial patch methods from prior literature. Specifically, the Universal Patch [3] was evaluated on $InceptionV3$, $ResNet$50, $Xception$, VGG16, and VGG19 models using the $ImageNet$ dataset, while the $FS\ Patch$ [14] employed VGG19, VGG19-BN, Wide ResNet, and $ResNeXt$ architectures trained on the same dataset. The $CamoPatch$ [31] was implemented on VGG16, $ResNet$50, and $DenseNet$121 models, also trained with

ImageNet, whereas the *VIPA* (Visually Imperceptible Adversarial Patch Attacks) method [36] conducted experiments on *ResNet*50 and *DenseNet*201 models using *ImageNet*. In contrast, the *POSES* (Patch Optimization Strategies for Efficiency and Stealthiness Using *XAI*) approach [18] utilized *VGG*16, *ResNet*50, *InceptionV*3, and *MobileNetV*2 architectures, evaluated on the *COCO* and *PASCAL-VOC* datasets. For all these baselines, we adhered to the original evaluation protocols, employing the same pretrained model checkpoints and dataset configurations to ensure consistency and reproducibility across comparisons.

4.4 Patch Initialization and Placement

Adversarial patches were initialized based on gradient-derived sensitivity maps. For each input image, we selected the top $1,000$ pixels with the highest normalized saliency scores as candidate locations for patch placement. Each patch was initially defined as a small square region of size 1×1 pixel, with its color set to the average RGB value of the surrounding pixels to ensure smooth blending with the local texture and reduce visible artifacts.

To maintain stealth, we applied an alpha-blending strategy, starting with a low transparency value ($\alpha = 0.01$), making the patches almost imperceptible in the early stages. During the iterative optimisation, the patch size was gradually increased using a geometric growth factor, while the transparency α was incremented linearly in each step as shown in Algorithm 3 lines 20 and 21. The patch expansion continued until reaching a predefined maximum size, and transparency was increased up to full opacity ($\alpha = 1.0$) only as needed to achieve successful misclassification. This progressive growth strategy ensures that both the patch's strength and size increase gradually, preserving visual subtlety while effectively influencing the classifier's decision.

4.5 Iterative Optimization Attack

Each adversarial attack was run for a maximum of 1000 iterations. At every iteration, the patched image was passed through the target classifier, and the predicted label was compared against the original ground-truth label. The optimization terminated early upon successful misclassification, otherwise continuing with adaptive updates to patch parameters (size and opacity). Among all generated candidates, the instance producing the highest misclassification score was designated as the final adversarial example.

4.6 Evaluation Metrics

We employed multiple quantitative metrics to evaluate the performance of our adversarial patches, considering both their effectiveness in deceiving the classifier and their visual stealthiness. Attack Success Rate (ASR) [32] measures the proportion of images for which the adversarial patch successfully changes the classifier's prediction from the true class to a different class. It is calculated as the number of successfully attacked images divided by the total number of test images. A higher ASR indicates a more effective attack, reflecting the overall capability of the adversarial patches to cause misclassification. Average Patch Visibility (APV) [37] quantifies the mean opacity of all patches applied during successful attacks. Since our method uses an alpha-blending strategy, patches start nearly transparent and increase in opacity only when necessary. Lower APV values indicate that the patches remain largely transparent and are less noticeable to human observers, reflecting the perceptual stealth of the perturbations.

Formally, let $\alpha_{i,j}$ denote the opacity value of the j-th patch in the i-th successfully attacked image. If P_i is the total number of patches applied to image i, then the patch visibility for that image is:

$$\text{APV} = \frac{1}{N_s} \sum_{i=1}^{N_s} \left(\frac{1}{P_i} \sum_{j=1}^{P_i} \alpha_{i,j} \right) \tag{7}$$

Average Perturbation Coverage (APC) [9] measures the fraction of image pixels that are modified by the adversarial patch. It is computed as the pixel difference between the original and adversarial patch image, and then that is divided by the total number of pixels. A lower APC indicates that only a small region of the image was modified, ensuring minimal visual disturbance while maintaining attack effectiveness. Together, ASR, APV, and APC provide a comprehensive evaluation of adversarial patches, capturing their effectiveness, visibility, and spatial efficiency, which are crucial for designing attacks that are both strong and stealthy.

5   Results and Discussion

The proposed gradient-guided adversarial patch framework was evaluated on five benchmark classification datasets ($Fashion\text{-}MNIST$, $SVHN$, $CIFAR\text{-}10$, $CIFAR\text{-}100$, and $ImageNet$) across three families of deep neural networks (VGG, ResNet, DenseNet). The evaluation included both qualitative and quantitative analyses to assess the attack's effectiveness, stealthiness, and efficiency.

5.1   Attack Performance

The evaluation of our proposed method was carried out under predefined stealth constraints: APV, which quantifies the perceptual conspicuity of the patch, and APC, which denotes the fraction of the image area occupied by the patch. For each dataset and architecture, we enforce fixed (APV, APC) pairs and report the ASR measured under those settings. The framework achieved consistently high attack success rates across all datasets and architectures, as summarized in Table 1. For instance, $VGG13$ achieved a success rate of 34% on $CIFAR\text{-}10$ under strict stealth constraints ($APV < 30\%$, $APC < 2\%$), which increased to

Table 1. Attack Success Rate for Different Models and Datasets (in %)

Model	Dataset	$APV < 30\%$		$APV < 50\%$		$APV < 70\%$	
		APC < 2	APC < 6	APC < 2	APC < 6	APC < 2	APC < 6
VGG13	SVHN	58.90	58.90	79.45	79.45	94.52	97.26
	CIFAR-10	34.00	34.00	54.00	60.00	62.00	90.00
	CIFAR-100	42.00	42.00	70.00	72.00	78.00	88.00
	Fashion-MNIST	26.67	26.67	60.00	76.67	65.00	85.00
	ImageNet	26.00	26.00	33.50	53.50	34.00	69.50
VGG16	SVHN	43.84	43.84	69.86	69.86	89.04	94.52
	CIFAR-10	40.00	40.00	62.00	68.00	66.00	86.00
	CIFAR-100	40.00	40.00	60.00	68.00	66.00	86.00
	Fashion-MNIST	31.67	31.67	55.00	68.33	58.33	85.00
	ImageNet	34.00	34.00	44.00	57.00	44.00	73.00
VGG19	SVHN	60.27	60.27	87.67	87.67	98.63	100.00
	CIFAR-10	38.00	38.00	54.00	70.00	56.00	92.00
	CIFAR-100	42.00	42.00	78.00	86.00	80.00	94.00
	Fashion-MNIST	53.33	53.33	73.33	76.67	78.33	93.33
	ImageNet	21.00	21.00	30.00	50.00	32.00	65.00
ResNet18	SVHN	30.14	30.14	71.23	71.23	86.30	89.04
	CIFAR-10	26.00	26.00	54.00	68.00	56.00	90.00
	CIFAR-100	14.00	14.00	40.00	50.00	48.00	74.00
	Fashion-MNIST	40.00	40.00	60.00	68.33	63.33	88.33
	ImageNet	24.00	24.00	28.00	45.00	28.00	59.00
ResNet34	SVHN	34.25	34.25	57.53	57.53	84.93	89.04
	CIFAR-10	12.00	12.00	30.00	32.00	32.00	68.00
	CIFAR-100	18.00	18.00	36.00	40.00	44.00	70.00
	Fashion-MNIST	25.00	25.00	40.00	50.00	51.67	78.33
	ImageNet	16.50	17.00	27.00	40.00	27.50	52.00
ResNet50	SVHN	56.16	56.16	64.38	64.38	78.08	79.45
	CIFAR-10	26.00	26.00	38.00	42.00	48.00	66.00
	CIFAR-100	28.00	28.00	50.00	52.00	54.00	62.00
	Fashion-MNIST	13.33	13.33	30.00	30.00	36.67	45.00
	ImageNet	14.00	14.00	22.00	26.00	24.00	39.00
DenseNet121	SVHN	54.79	54.79	73.97	73.97	86.30	89.04
	CIFAR-10	22.00	22.00	40.00	46.00	48.00	60.00
	CIFAR-100	20.00	20.00	44.00	44.00	60.00	70.00
	Fashion-MNIST	23.33	23.33	41.67	45.00	56.67	70.00
	ImageNet	10.00	10.00	15.00	27.00	16.00	42.00
DenseNet169	SVHN	41.10	41.10	65.75	65.75	83.56	87.67
	CIFAR-10	06.00	06.00	36.00	38.00	52.00	78.00
	CIFAR-100	14.00	14.00	54.00	62.00	58.00	82.00
	Fashion-MNIST	21.67	21.67	46.67	48.33	56.67	61.67
	ImageNet	14.00	14.00	28.00	30.00	31.00	45.00
DenseNet201	SVHN	46.58	46.58	71.23	71.23	87.67	89.04
	CIFAR-10	26.00	26.00	46.00	46.00	52.00	64.00
	CIFAR-100	18.00	18.00	44.00	48.00	48.00	62.00
	Fashion-MNIST	21.67	21.67	53.33	53.33	66.67	76.67
	ImageNet	13.00	13.00	17.26	26.00	21.00	40.00

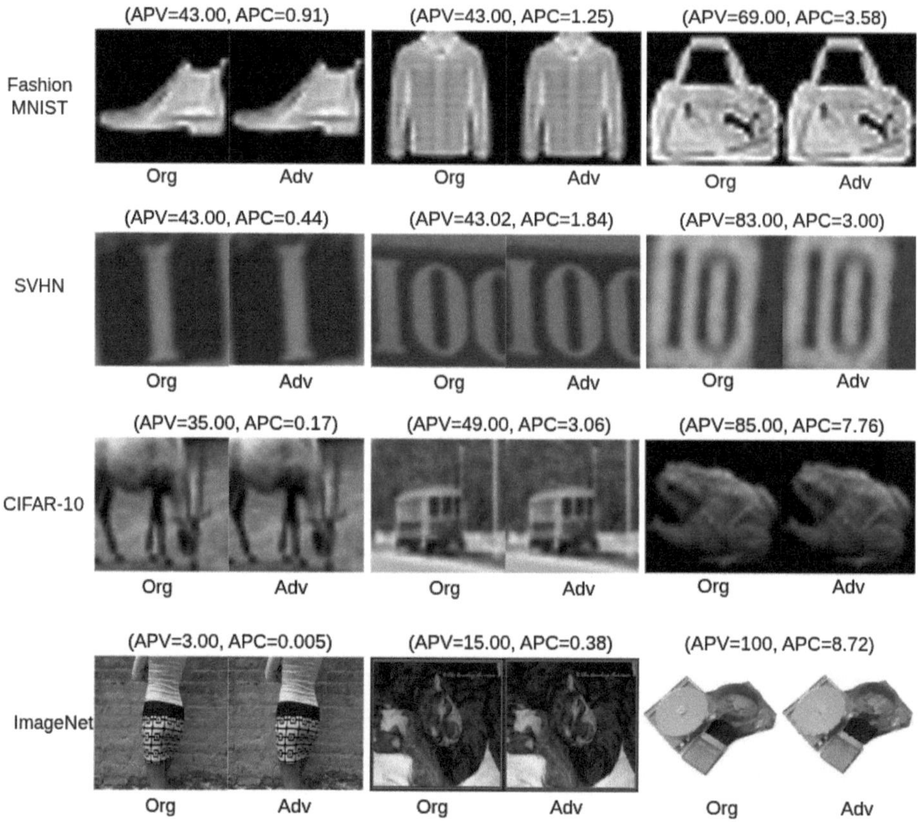

Fig. 3. Visual comparison between clean images (Org) and adversarially patched images (Adv), with patch quality measured using APV and APC.

90% when relaxed to $APV < 70\%$ and $APC < 6\%$. On $SVHN$, the same model reached 58.9% success under tight constraints and 97.3% under relaxed limits. Deeper networks such as $ResNet34$ and $ResNet50$ required higher opacity and coverage values for comparable success. $ResNet34$ on $CIFAR$-10 achieved 12% success at $APV < 30\%$ and $APC < 2\%$, which rose to 68% under $APV < 70\%$ and $APC < 6\%$. Similarly, $DenseNet201$ on $CIFAR$-100 achieved 18% success under strict constraints and 62% under relaxed limits. These results indicate that deeper networks distribute critical features more widely, requiring slightly stronger or larger patches to induce misclassification. Across all datasets, the framework adaptively updates patch parameters during iterative optimization, ensuring maximum reduction of classifier confidence in the true label with minimal updates.

Table 2. Average Patch Visibility and Average Perturbation Coverage analysis across different classifiers and datasets.

Model	SVHN		CIFAR10		CIFAR100		Fashion-MNIST		ImageNet	
	APV	APC	APV	APC	APV	APC	APV	APC	APV	APC
vgg13	27.00	0.34	34.48	1.22	47.80	2.57	44.23	2.74	50.70	5.03
vgg16	28.29	0.47	42.36	2.09	42.90	2.17	50.63	3.55	45.89	4.24
vgg19	29.05	0.47	37.52	1.45	41.22	1.88	43.37	3.18	53.90	6.00
resnet18	34.99	0.49	42.82	2.01	55.02	3.47	66.85	5.74	57.54	7.32
resnet34	43.84	1.28	53.82	3.64	49.96	2.49	51.12	3.56	61.02	8.37
resnet50	37.26	2.52	56.46	7.46	57.46	9.29	52.70	5.29	70.84	16.24
densenet121	35.00	0.61	50.08	2.92	58.56	3.52	55.80	3.50	71.85	9.77
densenet169	38.03	0.78	57.58	3.38	51.46	2.82	62.12	2.41	67.07	8.23
densenet201	36.29	0.53	56.74	3.85	57.82	6.20	65.70	3.74	69.36	9.32

5.2   Patch Visibility and Stealth

The adversarial patches were both stealthy and highly effective, as reflected in Table 2 and Table 1. Despite low Average Patch Visibility (APV) and Average Perturbation Coverage (APC) values, the Attack Success Rate (ASR) remained substantial across datasets and models. For example, on $CIFAR$-10, VGG13 achieved an ASR of 34% under stringent constraints ($APV < 30\%$, $APC < 2\%$), which rose to 90% ASR when thresholds were relaxed ($APV < 70\%$, $APC < 6\%$). Similarly, $ResNet$34 required slightly higher $APV = 53.82\%$ and $APC = 3.64\%$ to achieve comparable ASR on $CIFAR$-10. On simpler datasets such as $SVHN$ and $Fashion$-$MNIST$, APV often remained below 30% with APC under 2%, yet ASR exceeded 7595%. For more complex datasets like $CIFAR$-100 and $ImageNet$, achieving high success rates required larger perturbations, with $DenseNet$201 reaching APV = 69.36% and $APC = 9.32\%$ on $ImageNet$, corresponding to ASR above 60%. Representative examples in Fig. 3 illustrate that patches remain visually imperceptible while being placed in sensitivity-critical regions via gradient-based saliency maps. The progressive patch-growing mechanism ensures that perturbations expand only as necessary, balancing minimal visual artifacts with high attack effectiveness.

5.3   Comparison

Compared to existing adversarial patch approaches (as shown in Table 3), our method is more spatially efficient and visually stealthy. Prior methods such as $Universal\ Patch$ [3] and $FS\ Patch$ [14] required perturbation coverage between 1520%, and camouflage-driven designs such as $CamoPatch$ [31] averaged 9.5% APC. In contrast, the gradient-guided framework consistently maintains APC around 4%, nearly halving the required coverage. Despite the smaller patch size, the method achieves higher success rates across models and datasets. For

Table 3. Comparative analysis of perturbation coverage (APC) and computation time across different adversarial patch methods stealthiness.

Method	APC (%)	Computation Time (sec/img)
Universal Patch [3]	20 ± 5	9.068
FS Patch [14]	15 ± 5	14.351
CamoPatch [31]	9.5 ± 2.5	1262.781
VIPA [36]	9 ± 1	657.784
POSES [18]	8 ± 2	176.163
gradient-guided Patch (Our Method)	4 ± 2	210.972

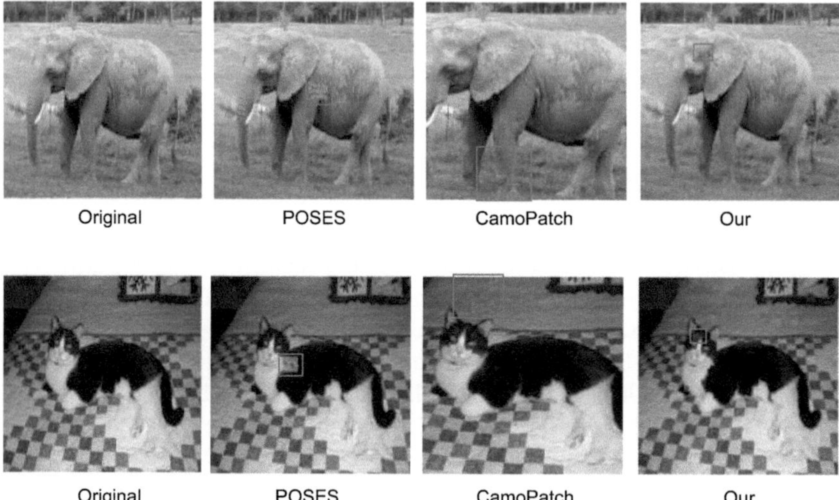

Fig. 4. Qualitative comparison of adversarially patched images of the Proposed method and different existing patch attack methods

instance, $VIPA$ [36] reported $APC = 9\%$, $POSES$ [18] achieved $APC = 8\%$, while our method required only $APC = 4\%$ to achieve high ASR. The computation time of our method is 210.972 sec/img, which is significantly lower compared to $CamoPatch$ (1262.781 sec/img) and $VIPA$ (657.784 sec/img). These results confirm that our method attains a strong balance between stealthiness, attack success, and computational efficiency.

Existing patch attack methods like XAI based approaches such as Grad-CAM or POSES, which depend on intermediate feature maps and produce coarse, visually clustered activation regions, our sensitivity guided framework operates directly on pixel level gradients of the model output. This enables finer localization of truly influential pixels rather than semantically dominant ones, allowing the generated patches to be smaller, more distributed, and visually stealthier. Furthermore, since our method requires only output gradients and no internal feature access, it remains architecture-agnostic and applicable in both white-box and limited black-box settings.

To further illustrate the advantage, Fig. 4 presents a qualitative comparison between our method and existing patch attack methods. As seen, adversarial patches from prior works are larger and more noticeable, often disrupting natural image content. In contrast, the proposed gradient-guided patches remain visually subtle while still causing strong misclassification. This highlights that our approach not only minimizes perturbation size but also enhances stealth, making it less perceptible to human eyes.

6   Conclusion

This work presented a gradient-guided adversarial patch generation framework that exploits model-specific vulnerability regions to craft stealthy yet highly effective perturbations. By employing gradient-based saliency maps to localize the most influential pixels and introducing an iterative alpha-controlled blending method, the proposed method achieves a balance between attack strength and visual imperceptibility. Comprehensive experiments conducted on five benchmark datasets ($SVHN$, $CIFAR$-10, $CIFAR$-100, $Fashion$-$MNIST$, and $ImageNet$) and multiple DNN architectures families (VGG, $ResNet$, and $DenseNet$) yield-ed three key observations. First, deeper and feature-rich models demonstrate greater resilience against low-opacity, small scattered patches. Second, datasets with higher semantic complexity demand a larger patch size to reliably induce misclassification. Third, across all settings, the generated patches remained compact ($APC < 6\%$) and visually imperceptible (low APV), thereby satisfying the dual objective of maximizing classifier degradation while minimizing perceptual distortion. Our results confirm that identifying and exploiting model-specific weak spots is more effective than random placement, giving a clear path toward stronger and stealthier patch attacks.

References

1. Adhikari, A., et al.: Adversarial patch camouflage against aerial detection. In: Proceedings of SPIE—Artificial Intelligence and Machine Learning in Defense Applications II, vol. 11543, p. 115430F. SPIE (2020). https://doi.org/10.1117/12.2575907
2. Athalye, A., Engstrom, L., Ilyas, A., Kwok, K.: Synthesizing robust adversarial examples. In: Proceedings of the 35th International Conference on Machine Learning (ICML) (2018)
3. Brown, T.B., Mané, D., Roy, A., Abadi, M., Gilmer, J.: Adversarial patch. arXiv preprint arXiv:1712.09665 (2017)
4. Chen, Z., Li, B., Wu, S., Xu, J., Ding, S., Zhang, W.: Shape matters: deformable patch attack. In: European Conference on Computer Vision, pp. 529–548. Springer, Cham (2022)
5. Duan, R., Ma, X., Wang, Y., Bailey, J., Qin, A.K., Yang, Y.: Adversarial camouflage: hiding physical-world attacks with natural styles. In: Proceedings of the IEEE/CVF Conference on Computer Vision and Pattern Recognition, pp. 1000–1008 (2020)

6. Duan, Y., Chen, J., et al.: Learning coated adversarial camouflages for object detectors. In: IJCAI (2022)
7. Eykholt, K., et al.: Robust physical-world attacks on deep learning models. In: Proceedings of the IEEE Conference on Computer Vision and Pattern Recognition (CVPR), pp. 1625–1634 (2018)
8. Goodfellow, I.J., Shlens, J., Szegedy, C.: Explaining and harnessing adversarial examples. arXiv preprint arXiv:1412.6572 (2014)
9. He, C., et al.: Dorpatch: distributed and occlusion-robust adversarial patch to evade certifiable defenses. In: NDSS (2024)
10. He, K., Zhang, X., Ren, S., Sun, J.: Deep residual learning for image recognition. In: Proceedings of the IEEE Conference on Computer Vision and Pattern Recognition, pp. 770–778 (2016)
11. Hingun, N., Sitawarin, C., Li, J., Wagner, D.: Reap: a large-scale realistic adversarial patch benchmark. In: Proceedings of the IEEE/CVF International Conference on Computer Vision, pp. 4640–4651 (2023)
12. Hu, Y.C.T., Chen, J.C., Kung, B.H., Hua, K.L., Tan, D.S.: Naturalistic physical adversarial patch for object detectors. In: ICCV (2021)
13. Huang, G., Liu, Z., Van Der Maaten, L., Weinberger, K.Q.: Densely connected convolutional networks. In: Proceedings of the IEEE Conference on Computer Vision and Pattern Recognition, pp. 4700–4708 (2017)
14. Kang, H., Kim, H., et al.: Robust adversarial attack against explainable deep classification models based on adversarial images with different patch sizes and perturbation ratios. IEEE Access **9**, 133049–133061 (2021)
15. Kügler, D., et al.: Physical attacks in dermoscopy: an evaluation of robustness for clinical deep-learning (2021)
16. Kumar, V., Agarwal, A.: A unified, resilient, and explainable adversarial patch detector. In: Proceedings of the Computer Vision and Pattern Recognition Conference, pp. 30387–30397 (2025)
17. Kurakin, A., Goodfellow, I.J., Bengio, S.: Adversarial examples in the physical world. In: Artificial Intelligence Safety and Security, pp. 99–112. Chapman and Hall/CRC (2018)
18. Lee, H.J., Kim, J.S., Lee, H.J., Choi, S.H.: Poses: patch optimization strategies for efficiency and stealthiness using explainable AI. IEEE Access (2025)
19. Li, C., Liu, Z., et al.: Capgen: an environment-adaptive generator of adversarial patches (2024)
20. Liu, X., Yang, X., Chen, C., Song, D.: Universal adversarial patch attack against object detectors. In: Proceedings of the IEEE/CVF Conference on Computer Vision and Pattern Recognition (CVPR), pp. 652–661 (2019)
21. Madry, A., Makelov, A., Schmidt, L., Tsipras, D., Vladu, A.: Towards deep learning models resistant to adversarial attacks. arXiv preprint arXiv:1706.06083 (2017)
22. Miao, B., et al.: Advlogo: adversarial patch attack against object detectors based on diffusion models. arXiv preprint arXiv:2409.07002 (2024)
23. Nesti, F., Rossolini, G., Nair, S., Biondi, A., Buttazzo, G.: Evaluating the robustness of semantic segmentation for autonomous driving against real-world adversarial patch attacks. In: Proceedings of the IEEE/CVF Winter Conference on Applications of Computer Vision, pp. 2280–2289 (2022)
24. Rafferty, A., Ramaesh, R., Rajan, A.: Corpa: adversarial image generation for chest x-rays using concept vector perturbations and generative models. arXiv preprint arXiv:2502.05214 (2025)

25. Selvaraju, R.R., Cogswell, M., Das, A., Vedantam, R., Parikh, D., Batra, D.: Grad-cam: visual explanations from deep networks via gradient-based localization. In: Proceedings of the IEEE International Conference on Computer Vision, pp. 618–626 (2017)
26. Shekhar, P., Devkota, B., Samaraweera, D., Kandel, L.N., Babu, M.: Cross-model transferability of adversarial patches in real-time segmentation for autonomous driving. arXiv preprint arXiv:2502.16012 (2025)
27. Simonyan, K., Zisserman, A.: Very deep convolutional networks for large-scale image recognition. arXiv preprint arXiv:1409.1556 (2014), published in ICLR 2015
28. Szegedy, C., et al.: Intriguing properties of neural networks. arXiv preprint arXiv:1312.6199 (2013)
29. Wang, C., Duan, J., Xiao, C., et al.: Semantic adversarial attacks via diffusion models. In: BMVC (2023)
30. Wang, J., Li, F., He, L.: A unified framework for adversarial patch attacks against visual 3D object detection in autonomous driving. IEEE Trans. Circuits Syst. Video Technol. (2025)
31. Williams, P., Li, K.: Camopatch: an evolutionary strategy for generating camoflauged adversarial patches. Adv. Neural. Inf. Process. Syst. **36**, 67269–67283 (2023)
32. Wu, J., Zhou, M., Zhu, C., Liu, Y., Harandi, M., Li, L.: Performance evaluation of adversarial attacks: Discrepancies and solutions. arXiv preprint arXiv:2104.11103 (2021)
33. Wu, T., Guo, Y., Li, M., Zhang, H., Xu, C.: Extended spatially localized perturbation: Robust adversarial perturbation with camouflage patch. Sensors **21**(16), 5323 (2021)
34. Xu, W., Jia, X., Zhang, Y., Song, D.: A survey on physical adversarial attacks in computer vision. arXiv preprint arXiv:2209.14262 (2022)
35. Ye, B., Yin, H., Yan, J., Ge, W.: Patch-based attack on traffic sign recognition. In: 2021 IEEE International Intelligent Transportation Systems Conference (ITSC), pp. 164–171. IEEE (2021)
36. Zhang, H., Hu, W., Fu, H., Zhu, F., Zhang, Z.: Visually imperceptible adversarial patch attacks. Comput. Secur. **125**, 102984 (2023)
37. Zolfi, A., Kravchik, M., Elovici, Y., Shabtai, A.: The translucent patch: a physical and universal attack on object detectors. In: Proceedings of the IEEE/CVF Conference on Computer Vision and Pattern Recognition, pp. 15232–15241 (2021)

High Throughput 64-Bit Implementation of SNOW-V Stream Cipher

Kakumani Kushalram, Majji Harsha Vardhan, and Raghvendra Rohit$^{(\boxtimes)}$ ⓘ

Department of Computer Science and Engineering, Indian Institute of Technology Roorkee, Roorkee 247667, Uttarakhand, India
{kakumani_k,majji_hv,raghvendra.rohit}@cs.iitr.ac.in

Abstract. SNOW-V is a stream cipher designed by Ekdahl et al. (ToSC 2019(3)) and mainly used for protecting 5G network communications. Existing works on SNOW-V focused on optimizing its performance with respect to 16-bit registers which are part of ciphers' linear feedback shift registers. In this paper, we present a 64-bit implementation of SNOW-V by extending all core round components and state update functions of the cipher to operate on 32 bits. We verify the correctness of our implementation with SNOW-V test vectors and provide benchmarking results on two different software platforms – Intel Core i7 and AMD Ryzen 5. Our results demonstrate a throughput gain of 90% and 107% on Intel Core i7 and AMD Ryzen 5 compared to SNOW-V implementations using 16-bit registers, respectively.

Keywords: SNOW-V · AES · Linear Feedback Shift Register · Finite State Machine

1 Introduction

Stream ciphers are symmetric encryption algorithms that secure data by combining message with pseudo random keystream bits. They provide efficient and high throughput performance for real-time applications such as mobile communications and embedded systems. Their deployment in mobile networks, from A5 in GSM to SNOW 3G and ZUC in UMTS and LTE highlights how important they are in maintaining data privacy. With increase in usage of the 5G and 6G networks, a requirement of higher throughput, software-driven solutions and optimized stream cipher implementations has emerged to meet the industrial demands.

SNOW-V is a stream cipher designed for 5G networks, provides reliable security and high speed software performance [4]. The ciphers' design consists of two linear feedback shift registers operating on 16-bit words and a finite state machine consisting of three 128-bit registers. From the implementation perspective, the prior software implementations of SNOW-V either target the 16-bit words or 32-bit architectures [5,7,8,10]. While the focus of this work is on software implementation, there exist works that target the hardware area, energy and throughput efficiency [2,6,9].

C. Karfa et al. (Eds.): SPACE 2025, LNCS 16406, pp. 246–261, 2026.
https://doi.org/10.1007/978-3-032-16342-4_14

The 32-bit C++ implementations of SNOW-V provided in [4,5,10] have many unoptimized components for 64-bit architectures, leading to suboptimal throughput. This paper addresses these limitations by developing a 64-bit implementation of SNOW-V.

Our Contributions. We propose a 64-bit implementation of SNOW-V using 32-bit registers instead of 16-bit registers for LFSR and FSM, and consequently exploit 64-bit instructions. We give the detailed and step-by-step procedures of converting each of the underlying functions (e.g., multiplication in Galois Field, modular addition, etc.) based on 32-bit registers. We then provide implementation and benchmarking results on two different software platforms – Intel Core i7 and AMD Ryzen 5. Our results demonstrate a throughput gain of 90% and 107% on Intel Core i7 and AMD Ryzen 5 compared to SNOW-V implementations using 16-bit registers, respectively.

The implementation codes are publicly available at https://github.com/harsha-050/High-throughput-64-bit-implementation-of-SNOW-V-stream-cipher.

Organization of the Paper. The rest of the paper is organized as follows. In Sect. 2, we provide the description of SNOW-V algorithm and the tool we use to analyze the performance. Section 3 presents the 64-bit implementation of SNOW-V while in Sect. 4 we provide the performance results. We conclude the paper in Sect. 5.

2   Preliminaries

In this section, we give a description of SNOW-V algorithm and discuss the profiling tool utilized for analyzing our implementations.

2.1   SNOW-V Algorithm

SNOW-V is a stream cipher designed by Ekdahl et al. [4] and mainly used for protecting 5G network communications. It retains the architectural features of prior SNOW versions with two main components: a Linear Feedback Shift Register (LFSR) and a Finite State Machine (FSM). The LFSR is composed of a circular structure interconnected by two shift registers which alternately feed one another, as shown in Fig. 1. The FSM contains three 128-bit registers and implements two copies of a single-round AES [3].

In the following, we explain the core components of cipher in detail.

Linear Feedback Shift Registers. The cipher has two shift registers, labeled as LFSR-A and LFSR-B. Each shift registers has 16 stages, and each stage contains 16 bits. The 32 cells are denoted by $(a_{15}, \ldots, a_0)$ and $(b_{15}, \ldots, b_0)$, respectively.

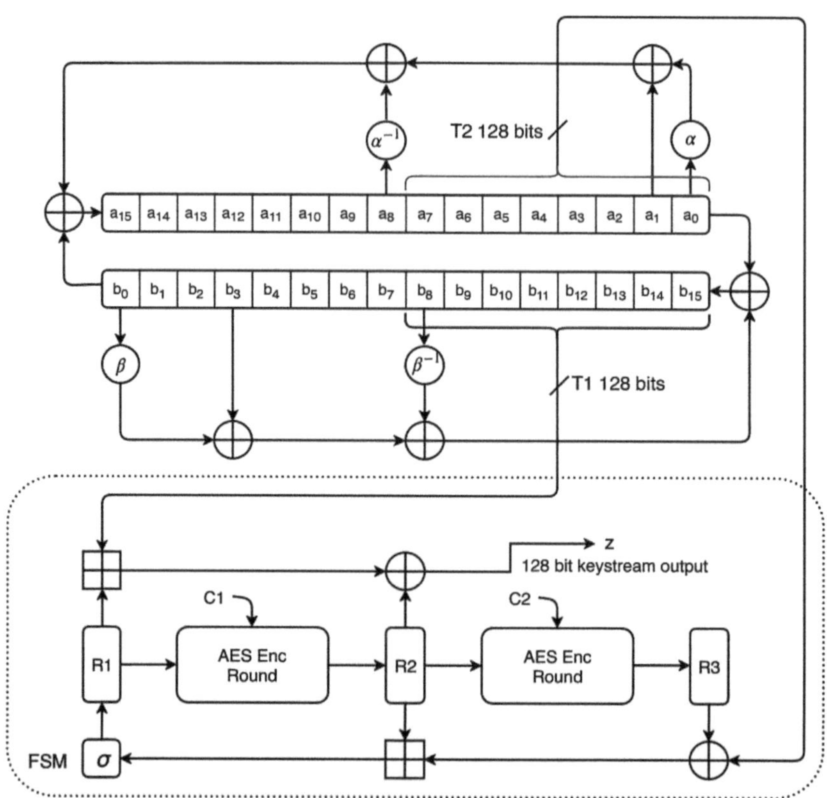

Fig. 1. Schematic of SNOW-V algorithm [4]

At time $t \geq 0$, we denote the LFSR states as $(a_{15}^{(t)}, \ldots, a_0^{(t)})$ and $(b_{15}^{(t)}, \ldots, b_0^{(t)})$ for LFSR-A and LFSR-B, respectively. The LFSRs produce sequences a^t and b^t, $t \geq 0$ which are given by the following expressions:

$$a^{(t+16)} = b^{(t)} \oplus \texttt{mul\_x}(\alpha, a^{(t)}) \oplus a^{(t+1)} \oplus \texttt{mul\_x\_inv}(\alpha^{-1}, a^{(t+8)}) \tag{1}$$

$$b^{(t+16)} = a^{(t)} \oplus \texttt{mul\_x}(\beta, b^{(t)}) \oplus b^{(t+3)} \oplus \texttt{mul\_x\_inv}(\beta^{-1}, b^{(t+8)}). \tag{2}$$

Here $\texttt{mul\_x}$ and $\texttt{mul\_x\_inv}$ denotes the multiplication over Galois Field $GF(2^{16})$. For the underlying polynomials defining the field, we refer the reader to [4][Section 2]. The implementations of $\texttt{mul\_x}$ and $\texttt{mul\_x\_inv}$ are provided in at our publicly repository.

In Figs. 1 and 2, the tap T1 is formed by considering $(b_{15}^{(t)}, \ldots, b_8^{(t)})$ as a 128-bit word where $b_8^{(t)}$ is the least significant part. Similarly, T2 is formed by considering $(a_7^{(t)}, \ldots, a_0^{(t)})$ as a 128-bit word where a_0 is the least significant part.

At time $t \geq 0$, these two taps are given as follows.

$$T1^{(t)} = \left(b_{15}^{(t)}, \ldots, b_{8}^{(t)} \right) \tag{3}$$

$$T2^{(t)} = \left(a_{7}^{(t)}, \ldots, a_{0}^{(t)} \right) \tag{4}$$

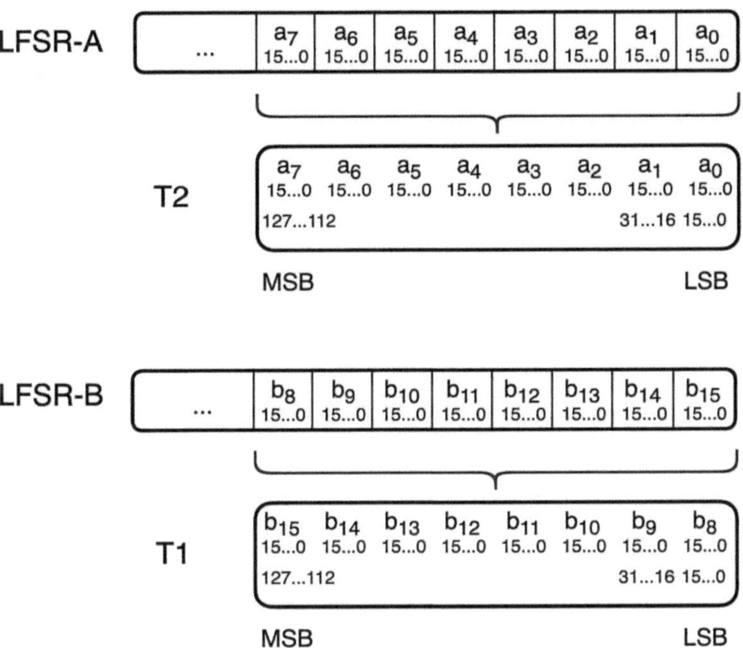

Fig. 2. Mapping the 16-bit words of LFSRs into 128-bit words T1 and T2

The entire LFSR update function is given in Algorithm 1.

Finite State Machine. In FSM, we have R_1, R_2, and R_3 which are 128-bit registers. Let $\boxplus_{32}$ denotes a parallel application of four additions modulo 2^{32} over each sub-word. The four 32-bit segments of the 128-bit words are added up with carry, though the carry is restricted to each 32-bit segment and does not propagate to the next higher segment. The three register R_1, R_2, and R_3 are updated according to the functions described in Algorithm 2.

The `permute_sigma` function applies a fixed byte-level permutation to a 128-bit state using a predefined permutation. The full implementation of the above functions is provided at our public repository.

Algorithm 1. The LFSR update function

1: **procedure** LFSR_UPDATE
2:     **for** $i = 0$ to 7 **do**
3:         $u \leftarrow \mathtt{mul\_x}(a_0, \mathtt{0x990f}) \oplus a_1 \oplus \mathtt{mul\_x\_inv}(a_8, \mathtt{0xcc87}) \oplus b_0$
4:         $v \leftarrow \mathtt{mul\_x}(b_0, \mathtt{0xc963}) \oplus b_3 \oplus \mathtt{mul\_x\_inv}(b_8, \mathtt{0xe4b1}) \oplus a_0$
5:         **for** $j = 0$ to 14 **do**
6:             $a_j \leftarrow a_{j+1}$
7:             $b_j \leftarrow b_{j+1}$
8:         **end for**
9:         $a_{15} \leftarrow u$
10:        $b_{15} \leftarrow v$
11:     **end for**
12: **end procedure**

Algorithm 2. The FSM update function

1: **procedure** FSM_UPDATE
2:     **Initialize:** $R_1' \leftarrow R_1$
3:     **for** $i = 0$ to 3 **do**
4:         $T2 \leftarrow \mathtt{MAKEU32}(a_{2i+1}, a_{2i})$ ▷ Converts two 16-bit words into a 32-bit word
5:         $R_1[i] \leftarrow (T2 \oplus R_3[i]) \boxplus_{32} R_2[i]$
6:     **end for**
7:     $\mathtt{permute\_sigma}(R_1)$
8:     $\mathtt{aes\_enc\_round}(R_3, R_2, 0)$ ▷ AES round key $= 0$
9:     $\mathtt{aes\_enc\_round}(R_2, R_1', 0)$ ▷ AES round key $= 0$
10: **end procedure**

Initialization and Keystream Generation. SNOW-V takes 256-bit key K and a 128-bit initialization vector (IV) as inputs. The key and IV are denoted by $K = (k_{15}, \ldots, k_0)$ and $IV = (iv_7, \ldots, iv_0)$, where each k_i, iv_i is a 16-bit word. The state is first loaded with key and IV into the LFSRs as follows:

$$(a_{15}, \ldots, a_0) = (k_7, \ldots, k_0, iv_7, \ldots, iv_0) \tag{5}$$

$$(b_{15}, \ldots, b_0) = (k_{15}, \ldots, k_8, 0, 0, \ldots, 0). \tag{6}$$

The initialization phase has 16 steps, and in each step, the LFSRs and FSM run similar to the keystream generation mode. However, instead of using the 128-bit z as actual output, we XOR it back into the LFSR, specifically into positions $(a_{15}, \ldots, a_8)$. Moreover, during the last two steps of initialization, we XOR the key into R_1. The key and IV setup phase is shown in Algorithm 3.

Algorithm 4 describes the keystream generating function. When the KEYSTREAM function is called with a specified number of blocks, it generates a 128-bit keystream output from the FSM in each iteration. This is done by taking two blocks, $T1$ and $T2$, as inputs from LFSR. After generating the keystream, the registers in both LFSR and FSM are updated by calling the LFSR_UPDATE and FSM_UPDATE functions, respectively. This process is repeated for the given number of blocks. Combining Algorithms 3 and 4, the complete SNOW-V algorithm is given in Algorithm 5.

Algorithm 3. The key and IV setup phase

```
 1: procedure KEYIV_SETUP(K, IV, is_aead_mode)
 2:     (a₁₅, a₁₄, ..., a₈) ← (k₇, k₆, ..., k₀)
 3:     (a₇, a₆, ..., a₀) ← (iv₇, iv₆, ..., iv₀)
 4:     (b₁₅, b₁₄, ..., b₈) ← (k₁₅, k₁₄, ..., k₈)
 5:     (b₇, b₆, ..., b₀) ← (0, 0, ..., 0)
 6:     R₁, R₂, R₃ ← 0, 0, 0
 7:     for t = 1 ... 16 do
 8:         T1 ← (b₁₅, b₁₄, ..., b₈)
 9:         z ← (R₁ ⊞₃₂ T1) ⊕ R₂
10:         FSM_UPDATE()
11:         LFSR_UPDATE()
12:         (a₁₅, a₁₄, ..., a₈) ← (a₁₅, a₁₄, ..., a₈) ⊕ z
13:         if t = 15 then
14:             R₁ ← R₁ ⊕ (k₇, k₆, ..., k₀)
15:         end if
16:         if t = 16 then
17:             R₁ ← R₁ ⊕ (k₁₅, k₁₄, ..., k₈)
18:         end if
19:     end for
20: end procedure
```

Algorithm 4. The keystream generation function

```
 1: procedure KEYSTREAM(z)
 2:     for i = 0 ... 3 do
 3:         T1 ← MAKEU32(b₂ᵢ₊₉, b₂ᵢ₊₈)    ▷ Converts two 16-bit words into a 32-bit word
 4:         v ← (T1 + R₁[i]) ⊕ R₂[i]
 5:         Store the 32-bit word v into 4 consecutive bytes of z starting at index 4i
 6:     end for
 7:     FSM_UPDATE()
 8:     LFSR_UPDATE()
 9: end procedure
```

Algorithm 5. SNOW-V algorithm

```
 1: procedure SNOW-V(K, IV)
 2:     KEYIV_SETUP(K, IV, is_aead_mode)
 3:     while keystream blocks needed do
 4:         KEYSTREAM(z)
 5:     end while
 6: end procedure
```

Remark 1. Algorithm 5 is referred as 32-bit implementation of SNOW-V.

2.2   Tools for Analysis

We use `perf` [1], a powerful Linux profiling tool, to benchmark and analyze the performance of our implementations. We use `perf record` command to collect execution data, while `perf report` command is used to identify the time spent for each function. The codes are compiled with the `-g` flag to enable symbol resolution, and execution was isolated to a single CPU core with a fixed frequency to ensure consistent measurements.

We use perf as it provides better support for modern multi-core systems. It also eliminates the need for special instrumentation (`-pg`) and provides detailed and accurate profiling, making it a suitable choice for fine-grained performance analysis.

Self Time Calculation from Perf Report. An example of perf report is shown in Fig. 3. To determine the actual self time of each function, we use the self percentage reported by perf alongside the total execution time measured using C++'s chrono library. In perf report, the self percentage represents the proportion of the program's total execution time that a function spent executing its own instructions, excluding the time spent in any called sub-functions. This percentage reflects the direct CPU usage of that function. By multiplying the self percentage with the total runtime, we obtain the self time in seconds as follows.

$$\text{Self time} = \left(\frac{\text{Self percentage from perf}}{100} \right) \times \text{total execution time}$$

```
Samples: 2M of event 'cycles:P', Event count (approx.): 1778990845410
  Children      Self  Command       Shared Object    Symbol
+   95.69%     0.00%  snowv32_30b   snowv32_30b      [.] _start
+   95.69%     0.00%  snowv32_30b   libc.so.6        [.] __libc_start_main_impl (inlined)
+   95.69%     0.00%  snowv32_30b   libc.so.6        [.] __libc_start_call_main
+   94.86%     0.19%  snowv32_30b   snowv32_30b      [.] main
+   92.00%     4.21%  snowv32_30b   snowv32_30b      [.] SnowV32::keystream(unsigned char*)
+   72.76%    63.87%  snowv32_30b   snowv32_30b      [.] SnowV32::lfsr_update()
+   10.95%     3.01%  snowv32_30b   snowv32_30b      [.] SnowV32::fsm_update()
+    9.64%     9.57%  snowv32_30b   snowv32_30b      [.] SnowV32::mul_x_inv(unsigned short, unsigned short)
+    9.51%     9.44%  snowv32_30b   snowv32_30b      [.] SnowV32::mul_x(unsigned short, unsigned short)
+    7.88%     7.85%  snowv32_30b   snowv32_30b      [.] SnowV32::permute_sigma(unsigned int*)
+    2.30%     0.00%  snowv32_30b   [unknown]        [.] 0xffffffffffffffff
+    1.36%     1.34%  snowv32_30b   snowv32_30b      [.] SnowV32::aes_enc_round(unsigned int*, unsigned int*, unsigned int*)
```

Fig. 3. Example output of perf report command for 32-bit implementation of SNOW-V

This method provides an accurate way to quantify the exact amount of time each function consumes independently, helping to identify performance-critical code segments. We refer the reader to [1] for more information on perf tool.

3   The 64-Bit Implementation of SNOW-V

In this section, we present the 64-bit implementation of SNOW-V stream cipher. We first explain our core idea and then discuss in detail the methods to optimize individual components: FSM, LFSRs, and keystream generation of SNOW-V.

3.1   The Core Idea

While the overall algorithmic structure remains consistent with the previously explained 32-bit version (Algorithms 1 to 5), we propose key changes in two main components – the FSM and LFSR, in order to better leverage the capabilities of 64-bit architectures. These changes are carefully implemented to ensure that the output keystream bits remain identical to the one produced by original 32-bit version, thereby preserving the functional correctness of the cipher, even though the performance characteristics differ.

In FSM, instead of using four 32-bit registers $(R_j[0], R_j[1], R_j[2], R_j[3])$ to represent the 128-bit state, we now use two 64-bit registers $(R_j^{64}[0], R_j^{64}[1])$ for $j = 1, 2, 3$, thereby reducing the number of operations and improving registers usage efficiency.

In LFSRs, the original implementation used sixteen 16-bit registers. In the 64-bit version, we implement them as eight 32-bit registers. This reduces the number of right shifts from 8 to 4 while recalculating the new register values in a more compact manner, resulting in performance gain. The new representations of LFSR-A and LFSR-B are given by :

$$(a_7^{32}, a_6^{32}, a_5^{32}, a_4^{32}, a_3^{32}, a_2^{32}, a_1^{32}, a_0^{32}) \tag{7}$$

$$(b_7^{32}, b_6^{32}, b_5^{32}, b_4^{32}, b_3^{32}, b_2^{32}, b_1^{32}, b_0^{32}) \tag{8}$$

The `mul_x` and `mul_x_inv` functions are modified accordingly based on 32-bit registers.

3.2   Optimizing the FSM

The original 32-bit version relied on 2^{32} modular addition, which inherently discards the carry to maintain integrity within 32-bit arithmetic. However, in 64-bit implementation, to replicate the same behavior and preserve correctness, we apply bit masking to extract and operate on the upper and lower 32-bit segments of $R_3^{64}[i], R_2^{64}[i]$.

The above approach allows to explicitly eliminate the carry, ensuring the mathematical behavior aligns with the 32-bit version. Algorithm 6 explains our implementation of the `fsm_update` function.

3.3   Optimizing LFSRs

In the 32-bit implementation, both LFSR-A and LFSR-B were represented using 16 elements of 16-bit each. An update cycle involved shifting these registers to right by one position, repeated 8 times. After each shift, the updated value of last register a_{15} was computed using a linear feedback function on the previous state.

Algorithm 6. The FSM update function

1: **procedure** FSM_UPDATE
2:     Initialize $R_1' \leftarrow R_1^{64}$
3:     **for** $i = 0$ to 1 **do**
4:         $T21 \leftarrow a_{2i+1}^{32} \lll 32, \ T22 \leftarrow a_{2i}^{32}$
5:         $lower R_3 \leftarrow R_3^{64}[i] \ \& \ \texttt{0xffffffff}$
6:         $lower R_2 \leftarrow R_2^{64}[i] \ \& \ \texttt{0xffffffff}$
7:         $upper R_3 \leftarrow R_3^{64}[i] \ \& \ \texttt{0xffffffff00000000}$
8:         $upper R_2 \leftarrow R_2^{64}[i] \ \& \ \texttt{0xffffffff00000000}$
9:         $v22 \leftarrow ((T22 \oplus lower R_3) + lower R_2) \ \& \ \texttt{0xffffffff}$
10:         $R_1^{64}[i] \leftarrow v22 \boxplus_{64} (T21 \oplus upper R_3) + upper R_2$
11:     **end for**
12:     permute_sigma(R_1^{64})
13:     aes_enc_round$(R_3^{64}, R_2^{64}, 0)$ ▷ AES round key $= 0$
14:     aes_enc_round$(R_2^{64}, R1', 0)$ ▷ AES round key $= 0$
15: **end procedure**

In 64-bit implementation, the new representations of LFSR-A and LFSR-B are given by

$$(a_7^{32}, a_6^{32}, a_5^{32}, a_4^{32}, a_3^{32}, a_2^{32}, a_1^{32}, a_0^{32}) \tag{9}$$

$$(b_7^{32}, b_6^{32}, b_5^{32}, b_4^{32}, b_3^{32}, b_2^{32}, b_1^{32}, b_0^{32}) \tag{10}$$

This change reduces the number of shifts from 8 to 4, while maintaining the same functionality. The feedback function is modified accordingly to work with wider registers and fewer iterations.

The entire 64-bit implementation of **LFSR_UPDATE** is given in Algorithm 7. In Algorithm 7, we use a temporary 32-bit register s_1 to process the data for a_0, a_1; since these are present in two different 32 bit LFSR-A elements a_1^{32} and a_0^{32}, we use bit-shifting to extract partial a_0, a_1 from them. Similarly, we use another 32-bit register s_2 for LFSR-B.

Notice that `mul_x` and `mul_x_inv` have also been adapted to process 32-bit words instead 16-bit words. Accordingly, b_0^{32} consists of b_0, b_1 which means that the essentially we are merging

$$u \leftarrow \texttt{mul\_x}(a_0, \texttt{0x990f}) \oplus a_1 \oplus \texttt{mul\_x\_inv}(a_8, \texttt{0xcc87}) \oplus b_0 \ , \tag{11}$$

$$u \leftarrow \texttt{mul\_x}(a_1, \texttt{0x990f}) \oplus a_2 \oplus \texttt{mul\_x\_inv}(a_9, \texttt{xcc87}) \oplus b_1 \tag{12}$$

into one operation, i.e., Line 5 in Algorithm 7. A similar thing is done for LFSR-B in Line 6. The updated `mul_x` and `mul_x_inv` operating on 32-bit words are given in Algorithms 8 and 9.

Algorithm 7. The LFSR update function

```
1: procedure LFSR_UPDATE
2:     for i = 0 to 3 do
3:         s_1 ← (a_1^32 ≪ 16) | (a_0^32 ≫ 16)
4:         s_2 ← (b_2^32 ≪ 16) | (b_1^32 ≫ 16)
5:         u ← mul_x(a_0^32, 0x990f990f) ⊕ s_1 ⊕ mul_x_inv(a_4^32, 0xcc87cc87) ⊕ b_0^32
6:         v ← mul_x(b_0^32, 0xc963c963) ⊕ s_2 ⊕ mul_x_inv(b_4^32, 0xe4b1e4b1) ⊕ a_0^32
7:         for j = 0 to 6 do
8:             a_j^32 ← a_{j+1}^32
9:             b_j^32 ← b_{j+1}^32
10:        end for
11:        a_7^32 ← u
12:        b_7^32 ← v
13:    end for
14: end procedure
```

Algorithm 8. The `mul_x` function operating on 32-bit words

```
1: procedure MUL_X(v, c)
2:     v_1 ← v ≪ 1
3:     v_1 ← v_1 & ∼(1 ≪ 16)                      ▷ Clear bit 16 of v_1
4:     if v & 0x80000000 then
5:         mask_upper ← c & 0xffff0000
6:     else
7:         mask_upper ← 0
8:     end if
9:     if v & 0x8000 then
10:        mask_lower ← (c & 0x0000ffff)
11:    else
12:        mask_lower ← 0
13:    end if
14:    mask ← mask_upper | mask_lower
15:    return v_1 ⊕ mask
16: end procedure
```

Algorithm 9. The `mul_x_inv` function operating on 32-bit words

1: **procedure** MUL_X_INV(v, d)
2:      $v_1 \leftarrow v \gg 1$
3:      $v_1 \leftarrow v_1 \,\&\, \sim (1 \ll 15)$ ▷ Clear bit 15 of v_1
4:      **if** $v \,\&\, \texttt{0x0001}$ **then**
5:          $mask\_lower \leftarrow d \,\&\, \texttt{0x0000ffff}$
6:      **else**
7:          $mask\_lower \leftarrow 0$
8:      **end if**
9:      **if** $v \,\&\, \texttt{0x00010000}$ **then**
10:          $mask\_upper \leftarrow d \,\&\, \texttt{0xffff0000}$
11:      **else**
12:          $mask\_upper \leftarrow 0$
13:      **end if**
14:      $mask \leftarrow mask\_upper \mid mask\_lower$
15:      **return** $v_1 \oplus mask$
16: **end procedure**

3.4 Optimizing the Keystream Generation

The change in the KEYSTREAM function is a direct consequence of updated FSM logic as discussed earlier. Since the FSM now uses 64-bit registers (R_1^{64} and R_2^{64}), the keystream function is modified accordingly.

In 64-bit implementation, the 64-bit temporary value T is formed by combining two 32-bit values from LFSR-B. To preserve correctness and prevent unintended carry propagation across 32-bit boundaries during addition with R_1^{64}, the addition is split into two independent 32-bit operations. Algorithm 10 outlines the implementation of the KEYSTREAM generation function.

Algorithm 10. The keystream generation function

1: **procedure** KEYSTREAM(z)
2:      **for** $i = 0$ to 1 **do**
3:          $T \leftarrow (b_{2i+5}^{32} \ll 32) \mid b_{2i+4}^{32}$
4:          $lower32 \leftarrow (T \,\&\, \texttt{0xffffffff}) \boxplus_{64} (R_1^{64}[i] \,\&\, \texttt{0xffffffff})$
5:          $lower32 \leftarrow lower32 \,\&\, \texttt{0xffffffff}$
6:          $upper32 \leftarrow (T \gg 32) \boxplus_{64} (R_1^{64}[i] \gg 32)$
7:          $upper32 \leftarrow upper32 \,\&\, \texttt{0xffffffff}$
8:          $v \leftarrow ((upper32 \ll 32) \mid lower32) \oplus R_2^{64}[i]$
9:          Store v as bytes in $z[i \times 8]$ to $z[i \times 8 + 7]$
10:      **end for**
11:      FSM_UPDATE()
12:      LFSR_UPDATE()
13: **end procedure**

The entire 64-bit implementation of SNOW-V cipher is provided at our public repository.

4 Experimental Results

In this section, we present our experimental results. First, we give a brief overview of our experimental setup. We then provide the performance comparison and analysis for 32-bit and 64-bit implementations of SNOW-V.

4.1 Experimental Setup

To evaluate the performance, we conducted experiments on two different software platforms – an Intel Core i7-12700H with the frequency fixed at 3.48 GHz, and an AMD Ryzen 5 5600H with the frequency fixed at 4.16 GHz. To ensure consistent and controlled measurements, we disabled frequency scaling and executed all tests using an isolated single core on Linux OS.

The evaluation consists of running both the 32-bit and 64-bit versions of SNOW-V on different input sizes, with the number of blocks set to 2^{21}, 2^{24}, 2^{27}, and 2^{30}, where the size of each block is 128 bits.

4.2 Benchmarking with Perf

We use the perf tool (see Sect. 2.2) to analyze the performance of SNOW-V 32- and 64-bit implementations. Table 1 gives the performance comparison on Intel Core i7 and AMD Ryzen 5 processors.

Performance Analysis. From Table 1, we notice throughput improvements of 90.58% and 107.09%, for Intel Core i7 and AMD Ryzen 5, respectively. This notable gain is primarily due to the optimization of LFSR_UPDATE function.

While the KEYSTREAM function also shows a performance gain mainly due to the use of the memcpy() function in the 64-bit version; its contribution to the overall throughput improvement is minimal. The actual time improvement is around 9 s for Intel Core i7 and 10 s for AMD Ryzen 5, which is small compared to the total execution time. Hence, KEYSTREAM should not be considered a major factor in the throughput gain.

On the other hand, functions such as permute_sigma, and aes_enc_round exhibit noticeable percentage changes; their absolute time improvements are relatively small. For example, the improvement in permute_sigma is only 1.61 s (for Intel Core i7) and 8.66 s (for AMD Ryzen 5), which is negligible compared to the total runtime. A similar trend is seen for aes_enc_round function.

In the case of FSM_UPDATE, although we replaced 32-bit segments with 64-bit segments, the change does not reflect any meaningful performance improvement. As seen from the table, the time difference is around -1.2 s (for Intel Core i7) and +1.4 s (for AMD Ryzen 5). The difference in sign arises due to variations in processor architecture and frequency between the two testing environment.

Other percentage changes are below 10% and have a negligible effect on total execution time. The variations in the percentage change for each function for both architectures can be attributed to differences in the underlying hardware platforms and operating frequency.

Table 1. Performance comparison for 2^{30} blocks on Intel Core i7 and AMD Ryzen 5 processors (throughput is measured in Mbps). The definition of self time is given in Sect. 2.2. The significant improvement is due to LFSR update and is shown in blue in the table.

Function	SNOW-V 32-bit implementation		SNOW-V 64-bit implementation		% change
	Self %	Self time (s)	Self %	Self time (s)	
Intel Core i7-12700H					
main	0.59	3.7684	1.03	3.4518	−8.40
KEYSTREAM	4.28	27.3366	5.25	17.5942	−35.64
LFSR_UPDATE	56.92	363.5512	13.57	45.4679	−87.49
mul_x_inv	13.69	87.4388	27.98	93.7689	7.23
mul_x	12.22	78.0498	23.13	77.5152	−0.68
FSM_UPDATE	2.47	15.7760	4.32	14.4775	−8.23
permute_sigma	7.85	50.1384	15.44	51.7438	3.20
aes_enc_round	1.84	11.7522	3.98	13.3381	13.49
Throughput		215.183		410.108	90.58
AMD Ryzen 5 5600H					
main	0.19	1.0701	0.61	1.6590	55.03
KEYSTREAM	4.21	23.7117	4.75	12.9187	−45.52
LFSR_UPDATE	63.87	359.7311	14.42	39.2184	−89.10
mul_x_inv	9.57	53.9005	21.00	57.1142	5.96
mul_x	9.44	53.1683	20.94	56.9510	7.11
FSM_UPDATE	3.01	16.9530	6.74	18.3309	8.13
permute_sigma	7.85	44.2131	19.44	52.8715	19.58
aes_enc_round	1.34	7.5472	3.39	9.2199	22.16
Throughput		244.022		505.341	107.09

Trend in Throughput with Number of Blocks. Table 2 depicts how the throughput change with varying number of keystream blocks.

Table 2. Throughput (in Mbps) for different number of blocks

Encryption Only	Processor	Number of blocks			
		2^{21}	2^{24}	2^{27}	2^{30}
		Throughput (in Mbps)			
SNOW-V (32-bit)	Intel Core i7	213.358	213.944	213.784	215.183
	AMD Ryzen 5	242.493	243.488	244.131	244.022
SNOW-V (64-bit)	Intel Core i7	442.548	415.076	418.567	410.108
	AMD Ryzen 5	496.928	500.408	504.068	505.341

From Table 2, we observe a seemingly increasing trend in throughput for AMD Ryzen 5 across both 32-bit and 64-bit implementations. However, for the Intel Core-i7, no consistent pattern is apparent. This variation is due to how throughput is calculated as the ratio of the number of bytes generated to the time taken by the code. For large block sizes, i.e., 2^{30}, the numerator in the throughput calculation becomes significantly large (i.e., $(1 \ll 30) \times 16$ bytes).

Furthermore, though the CPU frequency is fixed during execution and core is isolated while running the code, there is always some inherent variability in execution time due to system-level factors such as interrupts or background tasks. This timing variability affects smaller block sizes (e.g., 2^{21}, 2^{24}, 2^{27}) more significantly, resulting in fluctuations in the computed throughput. In contrast, for 2^{30} blocks, the large data size dampens the impact of such timing noise, leading to more stable throughput values.

5 Conclusion

This paper presented an improved implementation of SNOW-V stream cipher by changing the structures of its internal components from 16-bit registers to 32-bit registers resulting an implementation that utilizes the 64-bit system architectures. We verified the correctness of our implementations with test vectors and provide benchmarking results on two different software platforms – Intel Core i7 and AMD Ryzen 5. We boosted the throughput by up to 107%, while our LFSR optimizations slashed execution time by an impressive 8789% compared to the 32-bit implementation of the same cipher.

As a future work, we plan to investigate the constant-time version of our proposed 64-bit implementation. Moreover, exploring SIMD instructions, large register sizes for LFSRs, optimizing the AES round encryption and permute sigma routines, and exploiting data-level parallelism could significantly enhance performance.

A   Test Vectors

```
== SNOW-V test vectors :
key = 00 00 00 00 00 00 00 00 00 00 00 00 00 00 00 00
      00 00 00 00 00 00 00 00 00 00 00 00 00 00 00 00
iv  = 00 00 00 00 00 00 00 00 00 00 00 00 00 00 00 00

Initialization phase, z =
      00 00 00 00 00 00 00 00 00 00 00 00 00 00 00 00
      63 63 63 63 63 63 63 63 63 63 63 63 63 63 63 63
      a5 a5 a5 a5 a5 a5 a5 a5 a5 a5 a5 a5 a5 a5 a5 a5
      ea ea ea ea eb eb eb eb eb eb eb eb eb eb eb eb
      55 f7 f7 c2 e8 e8 d4 d4 ae 8d d4 4a e8 d4 4a e8
      c7 2a 23 bf e8 93 73 30 23 bc b6 ce b6 3c b6 b2
      a7 dd ca f3 13 87 61 02 de ad f4 2b 54 e3 ef cf
      6a 67 62 3e 6f 8a f9 79 1c ed 81 63 c5 86 8e 3a
      45 10 be 13 a2 c6 dd eb 40 96 38 2d cf fb 3b 6f
```

```
3c c4 df 56 cf bf c1 06 82 05 f0 2c 83 2e 39 3a
0c cb e1 de 2e 41 af da 70 98 05 e5 29 10 06 98
53 cd 98 69 c7 78 ca de d7 db 45 96 bf 45 b8 1b
8d 94 0b e5 9f bd b1 c1 61 21 f6 29 7a 3d 0a 15
12 23 14 9e af 12 cc d3 2f 35 76 f6 68 b6 8c 94
0e 75 be 09 54 18 1e f5 8a 60 a9 a9 54 3a 05 ff
dc 77 a4 97 23 eb 65 6a e1 8f 28 2c f1 de 1d 00
```

Keystream phase, z =
```
69 ca 6d af 9a a3 b7 2d b1 34 a8 5a 83 7e 41 9d
ec 08 aa d3 9d 7b 0f 00 9b 60 b2 8c 53 43 00 ed
84 ab f5 94 fb 08 a7 f1 f3 a2 df 18 e6 17 86 3b
48 1f a3 78 07 9d cf 04 db 53 b5 d5 99 5e 6c 2f
03 1c 15 9d cc d0 a5 0c 5d b4 bf 51 15 e6 a6 35
c0 d0 3c a1 37 0c 49 03 47 a0 b4 0b d2 e9 db 05
cb ca 60 14 a2 25 6c df 68 09 8b 14 a3 5c 1d 03
95 4f df 30 84 af 02 f6 a8 e2 48 1d e6 bf 82 79
```

References

1. Perf Tool. https://perfwiki.github.io/main/
2. Caforio, A., Balli, F., Banik, S.: Melting SNOW-V: improved lightweight architectures. J. Cryptogr. Eng. **12**(1), 53–73 (2022). https://doi.org/10.1007/s13389-020-00251-6
3. Daemen, J., Rijmen, V.: Rijndael for AES. In: The Third Advanced Encryption Standard Candidate Conference, 13–14 April 2000, pp. 343–348. National Institute of Standards and Technology, New York (2000)
4. Ekdahl, P., Johansson, T., Maximov, A., Yang, J.: A new SNOW stream cipher called SNOW-V. IACR Trans. Symmetric Cryptol. **2019**(3), 1–42 (2019). https://doi.org/10.13154/TOSC.V2019.I3.1-42
5. Ekdahl, P., Maximov, A., Johansson, T., Yang, J.: SNOW-Vi: an extreme performance variant of SNOW-V for lower grade CPUs. In: Pöpper, C., Vanhoef, M., Batina, L., Mayrhofer, R. (eds.) WiSec 2021: 14th ACM Conference on Security and Privacy in Wireless and Mobile Networks, Abu Dhabi, United Arab Emirates, 28 June–2 July 2021, pp. 261–272. ACM (2021). https://doi.org/10.1145/3448300.3467829
6. Konstantopoulou, E., Athanasiou, G., Sklavos, N.: Towards secure and efficient multi-generation cellular communications: multi-mode SNOW-3G/V ASIC and FPGA implementations. In: Palumbo, F., Keramidas, G., Voros, N.S., Diniz, P.C. (eds.) Applied Reconfigurable Computing. Architectures, Tools, and Applications - 19th International Symposium, ARC 2023, Cottbus, Germany, 27–29 September 2023, Proceedings. LNCS, vol. 14251, pp. 159–172. Springer, Cham (2023). https://doi.org/10.1007/978-3-031-42921-7_11
7. Molina-Gil, J., Álvarez, Ó.C., González, Y.G., Corbella, I.M.: Improving the lightweight implementation of SNOW-V. Wirel. Netw. **30**(6), 5823–5835 (2024). https://doi.org/10.1007/S11276-023-03348-Y

8. Molina-Gil, J., Álvarez, Ó.C., González, Y.G., Márquez-Corbella, I.: Analysis of SNOW-V software implementation. In: Bravo, J., Ochoa, S.F., Favela, J. (eds.) Proceedings of the International Conference on Ubiquitous Computing & Ambient Intelligence, UCAmI 2022, Córdoba, Spain, 29 November - 2 December 2022. LNNS, vol. 594, pp. 957–964. Springer, Cham (2022). https://doi.org/10.1007/978-3-031-21333-5_95

9. Pyrgas, L., Kitsos, P.: 5G Security: FPGA implementation of SNOW-V stream cipher. In: Leporati, F., Vitabile, S., Skavhaug, A. (eds.) 24th Euromicro Conference on Digital System Design, DSD 2021, Virtual Event/Palermo, Sicily, Italy, 1–3 September 2021, pp. 381–384. IEEE (2021). https://doi.org/10.1109/DSD53832.2021.00064

10. Wei, M., Yang, G., Kong, F.: Software implementation and comparison of ZUC-256, SNOW-V, and AES-256 on RISC-V platform. In: 2021 IEEE International Conference on Information Communication and Software Engineering (ICICSE), pp. 56–60. IEEE (2021)

A Security Analysis of CNN Partitioning Strategies for Distributed Inference at the Edge

Fatemeh Mehrafrooz[1]([✉]), Roozbeh Siyadatzadeh[1], Nele Mentens[1,2], and Todor Stefanov[1]

[1] Leiden Institute of Advanced Computer Science (LIACS), Leiden University, Leiden, The Netherlands
`f.mehrafrooz.mayvan@liacs.leidenuniv.nl`
[2] Department Electrical Engineering Department (ESAT), KU Leuven, Leuven, Belgium

Abstract. The inference of Convolutional Neural Networks (CNNs) at the Edge poses significant challenges due to resource limitations of edge devices. One approach to addressing these challenges is to distribute a CNN model across multiple edge devices. While much attention has been paid to improving the performance, memory utilization, energy efficiency, and robustness of distributed CNN inference at the Edge, security implications of such inference remain largely unexplored. Therefore, in this paper, we investigate the security vulnerabilities of the three main partitioning strategies for distributing CNN models across multiple edge devices, namely vertical partitioning, horizontal partitioning, and data partitioning. More specifically, we assess how accurately an attacker can reconstruct the input image given to a CNN model and predict the image class by eavesdropping on the communication link between two edge devices. We devise a simple, yet realistic attack scenario in which the attacker attempts to reconstruct the input image from intermediate data obtained from the communication link. In order to evaluate the vulnerability of the system, the reconstructed image is fed back into the model to see if its class can be determined. We conduct extensive experiments using different CNN models and datasets. Our results show that data partitioning is less vulnerable to this attack scenario compared to the other partitioning strategies, while vertical partitioning is the most vulnerable.

Keywords: Distributed Edge Computing · Neural Networks · Security

1 Introduction

Deep Neural Networks (DNNs) play a crucial role in our daily lives and are used in various applications like healthcare, smart home, and autonomous vehicles. One of the most popular type of DNN models are Convolutional Neural Networks

(CNNs), thanks to their effectiveness in image recognition and classification tasks. Typically, large CNN models are computationally intensive and require a significant amount of memory for storing weights and biases to perform inference. Cloud servers usually have the computational power and sufficient memory to handle the inference of such CNN models. However, for some modern machine learning-based applications like autonomous vehicles, face recognition, and voice assistance, large CNN models need to be deployed on resource-constrained edge devices. This is because edge devices, unlike cloud servers, bring computing power closer to data sources, thereby significantly reducing data communication delays and making such devices suitable for running time-sensitive tasks in the aforementioned applications.

The deployment of CNNs on edge devices poses a significant challenge due to the inherent limitations in computational resources and memory capacity of these devices [1]. One approach to overcome this challenge is to use lightweight CNN models, i.e., a compressed version of larger CNN models, obtained by pruning [2], quantization [3], and knowledge distillation [4] techniques. Although lightweight models are more resource-efficient, they often suffer from reduced accuracy [5]. Another approach is to distribute a CNN model by running a part of it on an edge device and the rest on a cloud server [6]. Such edge-cloud distribution approach, although effective in overcoming resource limitations of edge devices, introduces increased latency and potential security vulnerabilities, as some data has to be transmitted over a communication network to cloud servers for processing [7].

An alternative approach to tackling the aforementioned challenge involves distributing entirely a CNN model across multiple edge devices [8]. Such an approach uses the collective processing power and resources of several edge devices while it maintains the original CNN model accuracy instead of using a lightweight version of the CNN model. Additionally, this approach mitigates the delay issue associated with the edge-cloud distribution approach.

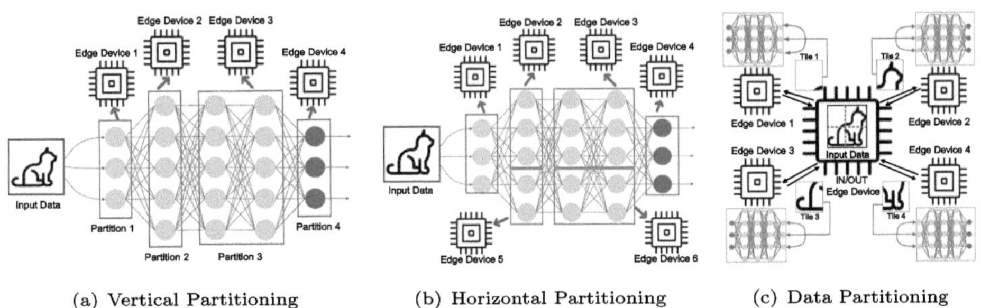

(a) Vertical Partitioning   (b) Horizontal Partitioning   (c) Data Partitioning

Fig. 1. Partitioning strategies for distributing a CNN model across multiple edge devices.

Entirely distributing a CNN model for inference on multiple edge devices requires to split the model into several partitions and map each model partition onto an edge device. There exist three main strategies for splitting a CNN model into partitions: *vertical partitioning* [9], *horizontal partitioning* [10], and *data partitioning* [7]. In vertical partitioning, a layer or a group of CNN layers comprises a partition as illustrated in Fig. 1(a). Horizontal partitioning involves splitting every CNN layer into segments, where a segment or a group of segments from different CNN layers comprises a partition (Fig. 1(b)). In data partitioning, the input data to a CNN model is split into tiles, and every tile together with a copy of the whole CNN model comprises a partition (Fig. 1(c)).

Several studies have been conducted to examine the overall system performance [7–14], memory requirements [7–9,11,13,15], energy consumption [8,11, 16], and robustness [17] when distributing CNN models at the edge using vertical, horizontal and data partitioning strategies. However, to the best of our knowledge, there are no research studies addressing security implications when these different partitioning strategies are used to distribute CNNs. Studying such implications is important because CNN partitions run on different edge devices and these devices need to communicate data in order to collaboratively execute the CNN model. Typically, the communication links between resource-constrained edge devices, running the CNN partitions, are not protected by data encryption. This is because the very large time and energy overhead due to running cryptographic algorithms on such devices is unacceptable. The unprotected communication links increase the vulnerability of the system. For example, an attacker might eavesdrop on the communication link between two edge devices and obtain intermediate data in transit. One action the attacker might take with this intermediate data is to attempt reconstructing the input data provided to the CNN model for processing. In certain scenarios, such as sensitive healthcare or virtual assistants applications, reconstructing the input data can compromise users' privacy.

Therefore, in this paper, we investigate and examine how each strategy for partitioning a CNN model across edge devices affects the vulnerability of the system to attacks attempting to reconstruct the CNN input data from intermediate data communicated between two edge devices. To assess the vulnerability, we devise and utilize a machine learning method to reconstruct, as much as possible, the CNN input data from intermediate data exchanged between layers in the CNN model. Then, to examine the vulnerability, we classify this reconstructed input data with the same CNN model to determine whether the inferred class is the same as the class inferred by utilizing the original input data. Our main novel contributions can be summarized as follows:

- To the best of our knowledge, this is the first paper to examine the security aspect of distributed CNN inference across multiple edge devices. We analyze the three main existing strategies for distributing a CNN model, namely the vertical, horizontal and data partitioning strategies. Our analysis provides important insights from a security point of view and offers guidance for selecting the most appropriate partitioning strategy based on specific application requirements with security in mind.

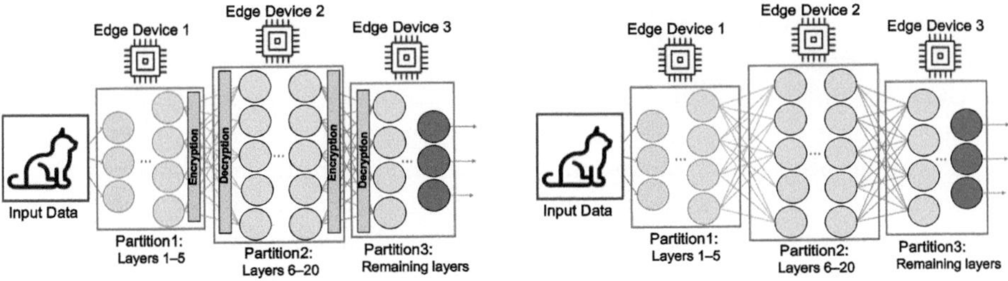

Fig. 2. Illustration of two scenarios for distributing a CNN model vertically across three edge devices with and without encryption–decryption.

- We propose a machine learning based attack scenario in which an attacker can obtain intermediate data exchanged between layers in the CNN model by eavesdropping on the communication between two edge devices. Using machine learning, the attacker attempts to reconstruct the input image from this intermediate data and then classify the reconstructed input. Through this approach, we aim to examine the vulnerability of the three partitioning strategies.
- We evaluate the three partitioning strategies using different CNN models and datasets in terms of the aforementioned vulnerability. Our findings indicate that the data partitioning strategy is significantly less vulnerable compared to the vertical and horizontal partitioning strategies.

The remainder of this paper is organized as follows. In Sect. 2, we motivate, in more detail, why unsecured communication links between resource-constrained edge devices are typically utilized. Section 3 provides a brief overview of related studies on distributed CNN inference across edge devices. In Sect. 4, we provide a detailed description of our method for analysis and evaluation of the vulnerability of the existing CNN partitioning strategies. Section 5 presents and discusses the evaluation results. Finally, the paper is concluded in Sect. 6.

2   Motivation

In this section, we give a quantitative example of the overhead in terms of delay and performance of a distributed CNN system in which the communicated data are encrypted and authenticated. This serves as a motivation why a network with secured communication links is often not practical and why unsecured communication links between resource-constrained edge devices are typically utilized when a trained CNN model is distributed across multiple edge devices for inference. As mentioned earlier, in such case, an attacker with non-authorized access to a communication link between two edge devices can eavesdrop on transmitted data. This allows the attacker to obtain intermediate data, which is closely related to the private and potentially sensitive input data being processed by the CNN model.

Although authentication encryption can protect the transmitted intermediate data against potential attacks, deploying even the most lightweight existing cryptographic algorithms on resource-constrained edge devices presents significant challenges. These devices often have limited computational resources and energy budgets, and they are commonly employed in time-sensitive applications where rapid and efficient processing is crucial. Therefore, in some cases, the large time and energy overhead caused by authentication encryption and decryption is not practically acceptable for applications involving distributed CNN inference on resource-constrained edge devices. To support this statement, we present and compare two scenarios that reveal the large time and energy overhead caused by deploying a lightweight cryptographic algorithm to protect data communication links between such devices.

Figure 2 illustrates these two scenarios where in one of the scenarios authenticated encryption-decryption algorithm is applied to protect the data transmitted between edge devices. In both scenarios, we consider the MobileNet CNN model which is distributed by vertical partitioning across three edge devices. In Fig. 2(a), Edge Device 1 receives the input data and processes it up to Layer 5. The output of Layer 5 is encrypted using the ASCON authenticated encryption algorithm, which is currently regarded as the most lightweight cryptographic algorithm, offering state-of-the-art efficiency and security for resource-constrained devices [18]. After encryption, the authenticated and encrypted data is transmitted to Edge Device 2. This device decrypts the data and verifies the authenticity using ASCON, processes it up to Layer 20, authenticates and encrypts the results, and sends the result to Edge Device 3. This device decrypts and verifies the received data and completes the remaining layers to produce the final classification result. For comparison, Fig. 2(b) shows the same CNN model and vertical partitioning across three edge devices without applying any encryption-decryption on the data transmitted between the devices.

Figure 3 shows the processing time (Fig. 3(b)) [19] and energy consumption (Fig. 3(a)) per edge device for the two scenarios mentioned above. The processing time and energy consumption are evaluated for edge devices utilizing three different ARM microprocessors: Cortex-A7 [20], Cortex-A9 [21], and Cortex-A17 [22]. The x-axis indicates the three edge devices (ED1, ED2, and ED3) together with the microprocessor within each device. The bars represent the corresponding metric, i.e., the processing time (in seconds) in Fig. 3(b) and the energy consumption (in joules) in Fig. 3(a). Each bar is divided into two sections where the dark-colored section corresponds to the scenario without data encryption-decryption and the bright-colored section corresponds to the scenario with data encryption-decryption.

For example, in Fig. 3(b), the dark-blue and bright-blue bar sections denote the processing time for Edge Device 1 without and with data encryption, respectively. Similarly, in Fig. 3(a), the dark-green and bright-green sections indicate

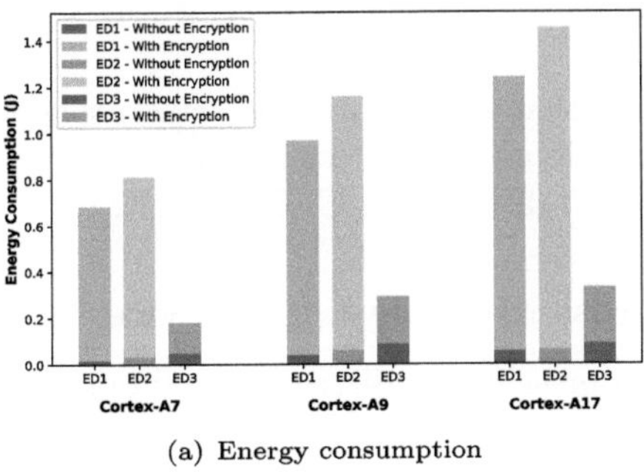

(a) Energy consumption

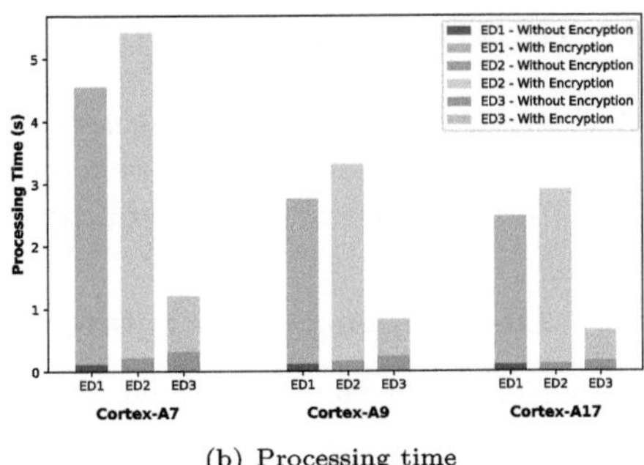

(b) Processing time

Fig. 3. Comparison of processing time and energy consumption for edge devices with and without encryption–decryption.

the energy consumption for Edge Device 1 without and with data encryption, respectively.

The results, shown in Fig. 3, clearly demonstrate that applying even the most lightweight cryptographic algorithm (ASCON) on resource-constrained edge devices, when running a partitioned CNN model, imposes significant time and energy overheads. As can be seen in Fig. 3, these overheads range from at least 3 times up to as much as 36 times, significantly affecting both the processing time and energy consumption. For example, looking at the results for device ED1 with Cortex-A7 in Fig. 3(b), the processing time without data encryption (the dark-blue bar) is approximately 0.122 s, whereas applying data encryption raises this value to 4.432 s (the bright-blue bar), which is an increase of nearly 36.3 times. Similar excessive overhead but in terms of energy consumption can be seen for device ED2 with Cortex-A17 in Fig. 3(a). Such significant/excessive overheads are generally not acceptable for low-power, time-sensitive applications, where rapid inference and efficient energy usage are crucial. Consequently, to maintain acceptable performance levels, many system implementations rely on unsecured communication links between resource-constrained edge devices, thereby leaving data transmissions vulnerable to potential adversaries.

Based on these findings, the following sections present a specific attack scenario aimed at reconstructing input data from unprotected intermediate data transmitted between edge devices running a partitioned CNN model for inference. Our objective is to use this attack scenario in order to analyze how different CNN partitioning strategies for distributed CNN inference are vulnerable to such a scenario as well as to offer guidance for selecting the most appropriate partitioning strategy that inherently enhances the security of distributed CNN inference against the aforementioned attack scenario.

3   Related Work

In this section, we focus on related studies that cover three relevant aspects, namely distributed CNN inference on multiple edge devices, machine learning for data reconstruction and security attacks in distributed CNN models.

3.1   Distributing CNN Inference Across Multiple Edge Devices

Numerous research studies have proposed approaches to distribute and optimize CNN model inference across multiple edge devices to improve the overall system performance [7–14], to reduce memory requirements [7–9,11,13,15] and energy consumption [8,11,16], and to increase the system robustness [17]. For example, MoDNN [14] and DeepThings [7] improve CNN inference on mobile and IoT devices by leveraging parallel execution and efficient task distribution methods. MoDNN uses partitioning schemes to balance the workload and optimize data delivery, while DeepThings employs a novel partitioning and layer fusion method, called Fused Tile Partitioning (FTP), and a distributed work-stealing runtime to reduce the CNN memory footprint and communication overhead between CNN partitions. CoEdge [13] focuses on optimizing memory, computation, and communication. It dynamically partitions workloads based on device capabilities and network conditions, thereby optimizing workload allocation without altering DNN structures. AutoDiCE [8,11] and RobustDiCE [17] introduce frameworks for automated multi-objective exploration and implementation of distributed CNN inference at the edge by focusing on system performance, memory, energy, and robustness optimizations.

The main focus of the aforementioned studies has been on optimizing objectives such as performance, memory, energy, and robustness when distributing CNN models across multiple edge devices. However, security implications have not been addressed in these studies. In contrast, our work focuses on examining a specific security aspect, namely eavesdropping attacks on the communication between edge devices. By analyzing the three main existing strategies for distributing a CNN model, namely the vertical, horizontal, and data partitioning strategies, we provide important insights from a security point of view for selecting the most resilient partitioning strategy against such attacks. Thus, our work significantly complements the aforementioned studies.

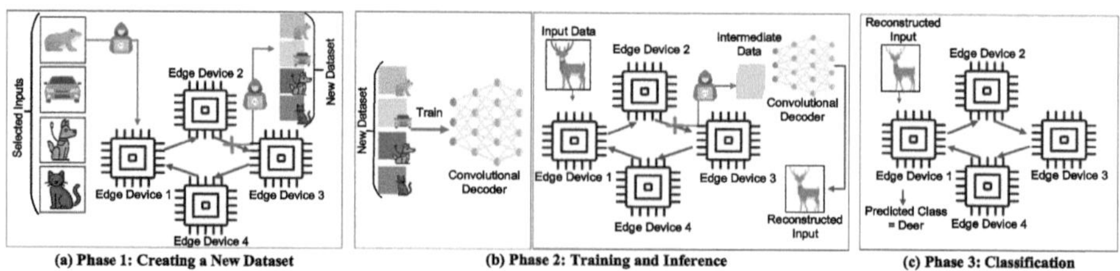

Fig. 4. Overall workflow of our simple attack to evaluate CNN partitioning strategies in terms of security.

3.2 Data Reconstruction Using Machine Learning

Several studies introduce deep learning approaches for reconstructing images from noisy or incomplete data using CNNs. One approach [23] leverages a CNN within an iterative framework to reduce artifacts and improve image quality, outperforming traditional methods. Another method [24], called RPGD, iteratively refines intermediate data through gradient descent and CNN projections to achieve high-quality image reconstruction. In [25], an approach utilizing deep CNNs performs missing data reconstruction tasks in remote sensing, such as dead lines and cloud removal, by integrating spatial, temporal, and spectral information.

In the domain of medical imaging, iCT-Net [26] employs CNNs to refine initial CT reconstructions from specific kernels, enhancing accuracy across various conditions. Another approach [27] uses DNNs to processes limited view projection data to produce high-quality CT images, addressing challenges in applications such as CT scans. A cascaded architecture of multiple CNNs is utilized in [28] to reconstruct ultrasound images, correcting artifacts and enhancing resolution. In [29], an autoencoder processes noisy Monte Carlo rendered images to produce high-quality, stable image sequences.

Beyond image reconstruction, deep learning techniques have also been applied to audio restoration. For example, [30] demonstrates the use of deep learning to restore audio files affected by background noise and signal loss. Another paper [31] proposes a novel method for reconstructing lost audio signals by combining steganography, halftoning, and deep learning models like LSTM and Random Forest.

As described above, many studies utilize machine learning techniques to reconstruct data from noisy or incomplete sources. Inspired by the strong performance of the aforementioned approaches, we devise and apply a specific approach targeting a CNN input data reconstruction from intermediate data processed within a CNN model and obtained in an attack scenario. Our approach involves training and using a convolutional decoder network to reconstruct the input given to the CNN model. The model is distributed across multiple edge devices and its input is reconstructed from intermediate data, exchanged between CNN layers mapped on different devices, in order to evaluate the vulnerability of different partitioning strategies used to distribute the CNN model.

3.3 Security Attacks in Distributed CNN Models

Recent studies have highlighted vulnerabilities in split learning frameworks, where neural networks are partitioned between clients and servers to preserve data privacy. These works demonstrate that intermediate representations exchanged during training or inference can leak sensitive information. Pasquini et al. [32] introduce the Feature-Space Hijacking Attack (FSHA), showing that a malicious server can reconstruct clients' private training data by manipulating the learning process. Erdoğan et al. [33] present UnSplit, a suite of attacks including model inversion, model stealing, and label inference, demonstrating that even with limited knowledge, a server can recover input data and model parameters. Liu et al. [34] propose similarity-based label inference attacks that exploit gradients and intermediate representations to infer private labels during both training and inference phases. Yu et al. [35] develop SIA, a sustainable inference attack framework that reconstructs client data while evading detection mechanisms.

While the aforementioned studies focus on split learning scenarios, our work examines the security implications of distributing CNN inference across multiple edge devices. Specifically, we analyze the vulnerability of different partitioning strategies (vertical, horizontal, and data partitioning) to eavesdropping attacks by reconstructing input data from intermediate representations exchanged between devices. Our approach provides insights into selecting partitioning strategies that enhance resilience against such attacks, thereby complementing the findings of the aforementioned studies.

4 Our Method for Vulnerability Analysis

In this section, we sketch a realistic machine learning based attack scenario which we use as a method for evaluating the three main CNN partitioning strategies, introduced in Sect. 1 and illustrated in Fig. 1, with respect to security. First, we assume that a trained CNN model is distributed across multiple edge devices for inference and the model inference is provided as a service to users. By booking a time slot, any user can exclusively reserve the service to classify own private input data. Thus, an attacker, acting as a legitimate user, can input data into the distributed CNN model for classification. Second, we assume that the attacker has access to a communication link between two edge devices and can eavesdrop on the communicated data. By accessing the communication link, the attacker can obtain intermediate data related to private input data provided by any user and currently processed by the CNN model.

The aforementioned assumptions are realistic in many practical edge computing setups. For example, edge devices might communicate over a shared but physically segmented (wireless) network. Suppose some devices use local 5G connectivity while others use Wi-Fi or a dedicated Ethernet channel. An attacker physically close to a Wi-Fi router (or using a compromised intermediate network device) may be able to eavesdrop on one link, such as the communication between Device 1 and Device 2, without having access to links involving other devices that are routed through separate, isolated network paths or encrypted channels. This partial access could result from exploiting a vulnerability in a specific router or switch, from being in range of an unencrypted wireless transmission, or from compromising a device connected to a specific network segment. Importantly, we assume that it is not possible for the attacker to access all communication links due to network segmentation, physical isolation of devices, and the possible use of secure protocols on some links.

A third assumption is that the attacker does not have access to the internals of any edge device, and does not know the structure of the CNN model, its architecture, parameters, or layer mappings. Their only access point is the intercepted intermediate data flowing through a single link between two edge devices. This reflects a black-box, passive attacker model in which the attacker's objective is to reconstruct private input data from intermediate data and infer the corresponding label.

Considering the above realistic assumptions, we can setup and perform an attack, which utilizes and trains a convolutional decoder network [36]. The purpose of this convolutional decoder is to reconstruct input data provided to the distributed CNN model from intermediate data communicated between two edge devices. Figure 4 shows the overall workflow of our simple attack, which consists of three phases. Phase 1 involves the creation of a dataset that is used to train the convolutional decoder. Phase 2 focuses on the training of the convolutional decoder with the dataset created in Phase 1 and uses the trained decoder to reconstruct the input from intermediate data. Phase 3 determines the class of the reconstructed input obtained in Phase 2. In the rest of this section, we explain the three phases of our attack approach and how we use it to evaluate the vulnerability of distributed CNN inference in more detail.

4.1   Phase 1: Creating a New Dataset

As mentioned above, the goal of this phase is to generate a dataset D used for training the convolutional decoder. This dataset is based on intermediate data that the attacker can obtain from the communication link between two edge devices. Since the attacker has access to the distributed CNN model by acting as a legitimate user, the attacker can input any data into the model for inference. Therefore, the process of generating the training dataset D begins by giving the CNN model a set of selected input data samples $I = \{x_1, x_2, ..., x_n\}$ illustrated by the Frog, Car, Dog, and Cat images in Fig. 4a. For each selected input sample $x_i \in I$, the attacker collects the corresponding intermediate data z_i exchanged between two edge devices via the eavesdropped communication link, e.g., the link between Edge Device 2 and 3 in Fig. 4a.

Since the attacker does not know the internal structure or the mapping of layers of the distributed CNN model, the z_i is collected as a bitstream and stored into a vector shape. Then, the attacker creates a pair (z_i, x_i) and stores it as a new labeled data sample in dataset D where z_i is the new training data sample and x_i is its label. By repeating the above steps for every $x_i \in I$, the new training dataset $D = \{(z_1, x_1), (z_2, x_2), \ldots, (z_n, x_n)\}$ is created.

4.2   Phase 2: Training and Inference

The goal of this phase is to prepare and perform the attack using dataset D created in Phase 1. Phase 2 consists of two steps: training and inference. In the training step, illustrated in the left part of Fig. 4b, any available training algorithm [37] can be used to train a convolutional decoder with dataset D. Based on the length and complexity of the intermediate data samples, the attacker designs a decoder to reconstruct the original input. The attacker can iteratively evaluate the output of the decoder and modify its structure if necessary to improve reconstruction quality.

Once the convolutional decoder is trained, it is ready to reconstruct original input data samples from intermediate data obtained by eavesdropping on the communication link between two edge devices. The inference step, illustrated in the right part of Fig. 4b, is the actual attack where the user provides an input data sample to the distributed CNN model and the attacker collects the corresponding intermediate data. Then, this intermediate data is given as input to the convolutional decoder which outputs the reconstructed input data sample.

4.3   Phase 3: Classification

In the third phase, illustrated in Fig. 4c, the goal is to determine the class of the data reconstructed in Phase 2. The attacker can use the distributed CNN model as a legitimate user for this purpose. Therefore, the reconstructed data is given to the distributed model as input, and the model predicts the class of the reconstructed data.

We evaluate the vulnerability of the distributed CNN inference by performing the attack, described above and illustrated in Fig. 4, with the following modifications. In Phase 2, we play the role of the user and the attacker, i.e., we provide user input data to the distributed CNN model instead of the user, and we collect the corresponding intermediate data and obtain reconstructed input data as the attacker does. In addition, we use Phase 3 to assess whether the attack is successful or not by classifying the reconstructed input data using the distributed CNN model for inference. If the inferred class is the same as the class inferred by utilizing the user input data, then the attack is successful, indicating a vulnerability.

Table 1. Characteristics of the Datasets

Dataset	Number of Images	Image Size	Categories
MNIST	70,000	$28 \times 28 \times 1$	10
CIFAR-10	60,000	$32 \times 32 \times 3$	10
Oxford Flowers	8,189	Variable	102

5   Experimental Evaluation

In this section, we examine the vulnerability of the three main partitioning strategies (Fig. 1) used to distribute a CNN model across multiple edge devices. The goal of this examination is to demonstrate and compare the vulnerabilities of these partitioning strategies to the attack scenario described in Sect. 4. First, we explain the experimental setup in Sect. 5.1. Then, in Sect. 5.2, we present the experimental results and discuss their implications with respect to the vulnerability of the different partitioning strategies.

5.1   Experimental Setup

In this study, we investigate the vulnerability by distributing three distinct CNN models across multiple edge devices, namely LeNet-5 [38], MobileNet [39], and ResNet-50 [40]. These models are selected because of their varied complexity and characteristics, making them ideal for representative evaluation of vulnerabilities when distributing CNN models. LeNet-5 represents CNNs with a small and simple architecture. MobileNet is well known for its efficiency on mobile devices. ResNet-50 is a representative of deep and more complex CNN models.

To train the above CNN models, three datasets are used: MNIST for LeNet-5; CIFAR-10 for LeNet-5, MobileNet and ResNet-50; and Oxford Flowers- for MobileNet and ResNet-50. Table 1 characterizes these datasets by three attributes. For every dataset, the attribute `Number of Images` shows the total image count in the dataset, `Image Size` indicates the dimensions of the images in the dataset, and `Categories` shows the number of classes within the dataset. MNIST consists of grayscale images of handwritten digits, CIFAR-10 includes color images, and the Oxford Flowers dataset contains high-resolution color images. The described datasets vary in the input image size, type, and number of classes, thereby ensuring a robust and trustworthy evaluation. Each dataset is split as follows: 80% of the images are used for training, 10% for validation, and 10% for testing. The CNN models are trained for 10 epochs on each dataset.

To evaluate and compare the vulnerability of the three partitioning strategies, introduced in Sect. 1 and illustrated in Fig. 1, we partition each trained CNN model, using the three strategies, and then deploy the model on a distributed system with multiple edge devices for inference, using Python and the TensorFlow Keras library. After the distributed deployment of a CNN model, we collect intermediate data from the output of specific layers. This data is used to create dataset D as described in Sect. 4.1. Any compatible input data can be used for creating dataset D. Therefore, we use a part of the ImageNet dataset [41], consisting of 40,000 image samples, as the set of input data samples I. These samples are unseen during the training process of the distributed CNN models. Each sample $x_i \in I$ is processed by a distributed CNN model, and the corresponding intermediate data z_i is collected during this processing.

Then, we build a convolutional decoder network to reconstruct the original input of the distributed CNN model using the intermediate data, as described in Sect. 4.2. Table 2 provides a detailed overview of the decoder architectures used for reconstructing the original input from different intermediate representations. Each row in the table corresponds to a specific combination of a model and a layer index, characterized by the input feature map size at that point in the network. Layer 1 in each model is used specifically for our data partitioning strategy. In this approach, we divide the original input image into four equal parts and assign each part to the decoder. As a result, the input size shown in the table for Layer 1 reflects the size of each partition.

In this table, the `Vector Size` column shows the length of the intermediate data received by the attacker. This vector is reshaped into a set of 2D matrices to enable the application of convolutional operations for reconstruction. As

Table 2. Decoder structures used to reconstruct the original input from intermediate data of different models and layers

Model	Layer	Vector Size	Input Size	Output Size	Decoder Structure
MobileNet	Layer 1	37632	(112,112,3)	(224,224,3)	Up(224)$\to$Conv(3, 16, 3)$\to$ReLU$\to$Conv(16, 3, 3)
	Layer 2	401408	(112,112,32)	(224,224,3)	Up(224)$\to$Conv(32, 64, 3)$\to$ReLU$\to$Conv(64, 32, 3)$\to$ReLU$\to$Conv(32, 3, 3)
	Layer 33	200704	(28,28,256)	(224,224,3)	ConvT(256, 128, 3, 2)$\to$ReLU$\to$ConvT(128, 64, 3, 2)$\to$ReLU$\to$ConvT(64, 32, 3, 2)$\to$ReLU$\to$Conv(32, 3, 3)
	Layer 72	100352	(14,14,512)	(224,224,3)	ConvT(512, 256, 3, 2)$\to$ReLU$\to$ConvT(256, 128, 3, 2)$\to$ReLU$\to$ConvT(128, 64, 3, 2)$\to$ReLU$\to$ConvT(64, 32, 3, 2)$\to$ReLU$\to$Conv(32, 3, 3)
ResNet-50	Layer 1	37632	(112,112,3)	(224,224,3)	same as MobileNet Layer 1
	Layer 2	802816	(112,112,64)	(224,224,3)	Up(224)$\to$Conv(64, 32, 3)$\to$ReLU$\to$Conv(32, 3, 3)
	Layer 33	200704	(56,56,64)	(224,224,3)	ConvT(64, 32, 3, 2)$\to$ReLU$\to$ConvT(32, 16, 3, 2)$\to$ReLU$\to$Conv(16, 3, 3)
	Layer 42	100352	(28,28,128)	(224,224,3)	ConvT(128, 64, 3, 2)$\to$ReLU$\to$ConvT(64, 32, 3, 2)$\to$ReLU$\to$ConvT(32, 16, 3, 2)$\to$ReLU$\to$Conv(16, 3, 3)
LeNet-5 (CIFAR-10)	Layer 1	768	(16,16,3)	(32,32,3)	Up(32)$\to$Conv(3, 16, 3)$\to$ReLU$\to$Conv(16, 3, 3)
	Layer 2	2304	(12,12,16)	(32,32,3)	Up(32)$\to$Conv(16, 8, 3)$\to$ReLU$\to$Conv(8, 3, 3)
	Layer 3	576	(6,6,16)	(32,32,3)	ConvT(16, 16, 3, 2)$\to$ReLU$\to$Up(32)$\to$Conv(16, 8, 3)$\to$ReLU$\to$Conv(8, 3, 3)
	Layer 5	480	(2,2,120)	(32,32,3)	ConvT(120, 60, 3, 2)$\to$ReLU$\to$ConvT(60, 30, 3, 2)$\to$ReLU$\to$ConvT(30, 15, 3, 2)$\to$ReLU$\to$Conv(8, 3, 3)
LeNet-5 (MNIST)	Layer 1	196	(14,14,1)	(28,28,1)	Up(28)$\to$Conv(1, 8, 3)$\to$ReLU$\to$Conv(8, 1, 3)
	Layer 2	1600	(10,10,16)	(28,28,1)	Up(28)$\to$Conv(16, 8, 3)$\to$ReLU$\to$Conv(8, 1, 3)
	Layer 3	400	(5,5,16)	(28,28,1)	ConvT(16, 16, 3, 2)$\to$ReLU$\to$Up(28)$\to$Conv(16, 8, 3)$\to$ReLU$\to$Conv(8, 1, 3)
	Layer 5	120	(1,1,120)	(28,28,1)	ConvT(120, 64, 4, 2, 1)$\to$ReLU$\to$ConvT(64, 32, 3, 2)$\to$ReLU$\to$ConvT(32, 16, 3, 2)$\to$ReLU$\to$ConvT(16, 8, 3, 2)$\to$ReLU$\to$Up(28)$\to$Conv(8, 1, 3)

explained in Sect. 4.2, the attacker may adjust both the decoder architecture and the input shape based on the vector length and complexity in order to improve the reconstruction quality. The `Input Size` column shows the size of the feature map that is fed into the decoder while the `Output Size` column displays the size of the output produced by the decoder. The `Decoder Structure` column describes the sequence of operations used by the decoder, which typically include upsampling (Up(n)), transposed convolutions (ConvT), standard convolutions (Conv), and ReLU activation functions. For example, in Layer 33 of MobileNet, the decoder receives a feature map of shape (28, 28, 256) and transforms it to an output of shape (224, 224, 3). This transformation is performed through a series of ConvT, each followed by a ReLU activation. The first ConvT layer reduces the number of channels from 256 to 128 and increases the spatial dimensions using a 3×3 kernel and a stride of 2. This is followed by a ReLU and a second ConvT layer that reduces the channels to 64 using the same kernel and stride. A third ConvT layer further reduces the channels to 32. Finally, a standard 3×3 convolution maps the 32-channel output to 3 channels, yielding the final image-shaped output. The decoder is trained for 10 epochs on the dataset D using the Adam optimizer [42] for gradient descent optimization.

Finally, for every distributed CNN model, partitioned using the data, vertical, and horizontal partitioning strategies, the vulnerability of every strategy

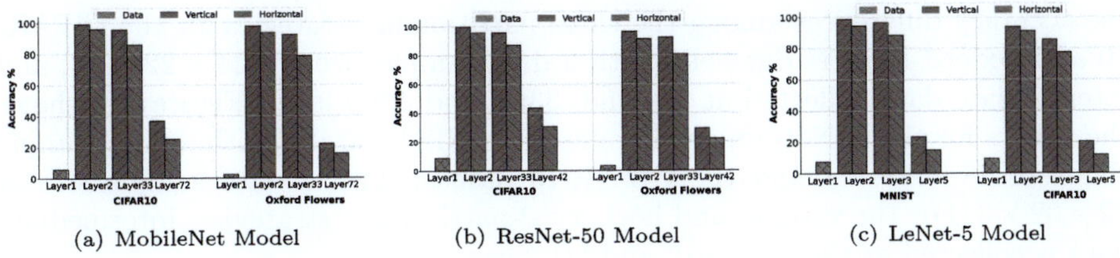

(a) MobileNet Model   (b) ResNet-50 Model   (c) LeNet-5 Model

Fig. 5. Comparison of the Data, Vertical, and Horizontal strategies across different CNN models, datasets, and layers.

is assessed by calculating the accuracy of the reconstructed input images generated by the convolutional decoder. To calculate this accuracy, every image in the aforementioned 10% test data from a dataset in Table 1 is fed into the CNN model for processing, and the predicted class of this original input image is recorded. During the processing, intermediate data produced by a specific layer in the CNN model is collected and given as input to the trained convolutional decoder for reconstruction. The output of the decoder, i.e., the reconstructed image, is then fed back into the CNN model, as explained in Sect. 4.3, and the predicted class is recorded as well. By comparing the predicted class of every reconstructed image with the predicted class of the corresponding original input images, we determine the number of correctly predicted classes of the reconstructed images. The accuracy is calculated by dividing this number by the total number of reconstructed images.

5.2 Experimental Results and Vulnerability Analysis

Figure 5 depicts the results of our experimental evaluation of the three partitioning strategies when they are used to distribute MobileNet, ResNet-50 and LeNet-5 across 4 edge devices, and the attack scenario/method, described in Sect. 4, is applied.

In each bar chart of Fig. 5, the Y-axis shows the accuracy, while the X-axis shows the dataset used to calculate the accuracy as well as the specific layers of the CNN model used to collect the intermediate data. The blue and green bars correspond to the vertical and horizontal partitioning strategies, respectively. The red bars correspond to the data partitioning strategy. For this strategy, we consider only Layer 1 because an attacker, with access to the communication link between two edge devices, can only collect a part of the input image transferred from the IN/OUT edge device to the other device as shown in Fig. 1(c). Therefore, the attacker is limited to the partial input data given to Layer 1 and does not have access to data processed by other layers.

Figure 5(a) plots the results for the MobileNet model, showing the accuracy of the three partitioning strategies for the CIFAR-10 and Oxford Flowers datasets, where each data sample has a size of $224 \times 224 \times 3$. For the vertical and horizontal partitioning, intermediate data is collected at the 2nd, 33rd, and 72nd layers. Similarly, Fig. 5(b) showcases the results for the ResNet-50 model, highlighting the accuracy differences among the three partitioning strategies for the CIFAR-10 and Oxford Flowers datasets, with a data sample size of $224 \times 224 \times 3$, and intermediate data collected at the 2nd, 33rd, and 42nd layer. Figure 5(c) shows the results for the LeNet-5 model, using the MNIST dataset with a data sample shape of $28 \times 28 \times 1$ and the CIFAR-10 dataset with a data sample size of $32 \times 32 \times 3$. For the vertical and horizontal partitioning strategies, intermediate data is collected at the 2nd, 3rd, and 5th layer.

5.2.1 Partitioning Strategies

First, we analyze how the different CNN partitioning strategies, used for distributed CNN inference across edge devices, affect the input data reconstruction accuracy under our attack scenario. The choice of a partitioning strategy directly influences the amount and nature of the intermediate data available to the attacker, which in turn impacts how effectively the attacker's convolutional decoder can reconstruct the input data. For example, it can be seen in Fig. 5 that if the attacker can collect the output of the second layer (Layer 2), the accuracy is higher in vertical partitioning compared to horizontal and data partitioning. This is because vertical partitioning involves more (intermediate) data exchanged between layers mapped on different devices than the other partitioning strategies. In contrast, horizontal partitioning limits the attacker to only a subset of the data, and data partitioning further restricts the attacker to only a small fraction of the original input. As a result, the information available to the attacker in horizontal and data partitioning scenarios is insufficient to achieve the same level of reconstruction accuracy as in vertical partitioning.

Furthermore, the results in Fig. 5 show that the accuracy in data partitioning is significantly lower compared to the other strategies. This is because, in data partitioning, the input data is divided into smaller parts that are processed separately as illustrated in Fig. 1(c). Consequently, the attacker only gains access to a small part of the input data, making it more difficult for the convolutional decoder to accurately reconstruct the full input data from that small part.

5.2.2 Layer Access

As shown in Fig. 5, the positioning of the accessed layer within the CNN's topology greatly influences the attacker's reconstruction capabilities. In general, when an attacker has access to the output of a higher layer, i.e., a layer that is far away from the input layer in the CNN model topology, the accuracy of the reconstructed input decreases. This trend means that the accuracy is higher when the attacker accesses earlier layers, i.e., layers closer to the input layer in the CNN model topology. This is because earlier layers capture more generalized, low-level features, such as edges and textures, that are more directly linked to the original input data. In contrast, higher layers contain more refined, abstract representations that are crucial for the model's decision-making process but are less directly tied to the original input data. These abstract representations are more challenging to reverse-engineer into the original input data. Consequently, the convolutional decoder requires more detailed features to accurately reconstruct

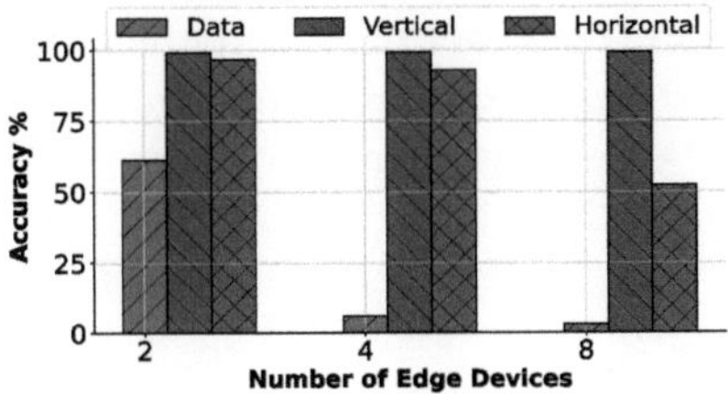

Fig. 6. Comparison of partitioning strategies with respect to the number of devices used to distribute the MobileNet model, based on the CIFAR-10 dataset.

the input data from the intermediate data, that are more readily available in earlier layers.

5.2.3   Dataset Characteristics

The characteristics of the datasets, processed by a partitioned CNN model during inference, play a role in the accuracy of reconstructing input data from intermediate data. One of the important factors that impacts the accuracy is the number of classes in a dataset. For example, in Fig. 5(a) and 5(b), the accuracy for the Oxford Flowers dataset and a given layer is lower compared to the same layer and the CIFAR-10 dataset. This is because reconstructing the input data from intermediate data can introduce errors, and with a larger number of classes, i.e., 102 in the Oxford Flowers dataset, these errors are more likely to occur and cause a wrong class prediction, resulting in lower accuracy. Additionally, the image size plays a role in reconstructing the input image and achieving better accuracy. If the attacker has access to less (intermediate) data due to a small input image size, it becomes more difficult to reconstruct the original input image and correctly predict the class. This can be seen in Fig. 5(c), where the accuracy for Layer 2 in the CIFAR-10 dataset is lower compared to the accuracy for Layer 2 in Fig. 5(a) and 5(b). This difference is due to the smaller image size ($32 \times 32 \times 3$) in CIFAR-10 with LeNet-5, compared to the larger image sizes ($224 \times 224 \times 3$) in CIFAR-10 and Oxford Flowers used with MobileNet and ResNet-50. Furthermore, it is easier to reconstruct MNIST images than CIFAR-10 images, as shown in Fig. 5(c), because MNIST images are simpler and lack the fine details present in CIFAR-10 images.

5.2.4   Number of Edge Devices

Another important factor for the accuracy is the number of edge devices used to distribute a CNN model. A higher number of edge devices means more partitions. Figure 6 compares the accuracy of the three partitioning strategies when the MobileNet model is distributed across 2, 4, and 8 edge devices, with intermediate data collected from Layer 2 for the vertical and horizontal partitioning, and from Layer 1 for the data partitioning. The model is tested with colour images of size $224 \times 224 \times 3$ from the CIFAR-10 dataset. In Fig. 6, the X-axis shows the number of edge devices, while the red, blue, and green bars show the accuracy for the data partitioning, vertical partitioning, and horizontal partitioning, respectively. The results indicate that the number of edge devices directly impacts the accuracy, respectively the vulnerability of the data and horizontal partitioning strategies, whereas the vulnerability of the vertical partitioning strategy remains unaffected by the number of edge devices. This is because, with an increasing number of edge devices and partitions, the volume and content of the intermediate data, collected at Layer 2 and Layer 1, are changing in the horizontal and data partitioning strategies. In vertical partitioning, the collected intermediate data at Layer 2 remains unchanged. Moreover, the accuracy for the data and horizontal partitioning strategies tends to be higher when fewer edge devices are used. This is because, by using fewer edge devices, the (intermediate) data is partitioned into larger, more complete segments, thereby allowing the convolutional decoder to reconstruct the original input data more effectively. In contrast, when the number of edge devices increases, each device handles a smaller part of the (intermediate) data. This fragmentation makes it more challenging for the convolutional decoder to accurately reconstruct the input, leading to a decrease in accuracy.

6   Conclusions

In this paper, we examine and compare the vulnerability of the three main strategies for partitioning a CNN model across multiple edge devices, i.e., vertical partitioning, horizontal partitioning, and data partitioning. To assess their vulnerability, we devise a realistic attack scenario in which an attacker eavesdrops on the communication link between two edge devices, obtains intermediate data, and attempts to determine the class of the input data. In this scenario, the attacker tries to reconstruct the original CNN input data using a convolutional decoder and then feeds the reconstructed data back into the model to obtain the class. We evaluate the vulnerability of each partitioning strategy by calculating the data reconstruction accuracy, i.e., comparing the predicted class of the reconstructed data with the original class.

The experimental results show that data partitioning is significantly less vulnerable to the aforementioned attack scenario compared to vertical and horizontal partitioning, with vertical partitioning being the most vulnerable strategy. Moreover, the size of the CNN input data affects vulnerability, as larger input data leads to higher reconstruction accuracy. The number of CNN partitions/edge devices also impacts vulnerability, i.e., when the number of partitions/devices increases, the reconstruction accuracy decreases, thereby reducing the vulnerability.

Based on our experiments, results, and analysis, we can conclude that by employing the data partitioning strategy for distributed CNN inference and increasing the number of edge devices (partitions) as much as possible, or combining it with horizontal partitioning, we can inherently enhance the security of distributed CNN inference against the aforementioned attack scenario. Furthermore, as demonstrated in the experimental section, earlier CNN layers generate more valuable intermediate data for successful reconstruction of the original input data. Therefore, communicating intermediate data between edge devices, generated by these early CNN layers, must be avoided by running these layers on the same device in order to significantly reduce the overall risk of successful input data reconstruction utilizing the aforementioned attack scenario.

Acknowledgments. This work was supported by European Union (NeuroSoC project - Horizon Europe Grant Agreement n°101070634).

References

1. Yang, L., Zheng, C., Shen, X., Xie, G.: OfpCNN: on-demand fine-grained partitioning for CNN inference acceleration in heterogeneous devices. IEEE Trans. Parallel Distrib. Syst. **34**(12), 3090–3103 (2023)
2. Han, S., Pool, J., Tran, J., Dally, W.J.: Learning both weights and connections for efficient neural networks. In: Proceedings of the 29th International Conference on Neural Information Processing Systems, NIPS 2015, vol. 1, pp. 1135–1143. MIT Press, Cambridge (2015)
3. Nagel, M., Fournarakis, M., Amjad, R.A., Bondarenko, Y., Van Baalen, M., Blankevoort, T.: A white paper on neural network quantization. arXiv preprint arXiv:2106.08295 (2021)
4. Hinton, G., Vinyals, O., Dean, J.: Distilling the knowledge in a neural network. arXiv preprint arXiv:1503.02531 (2015)
5. Prakash, I., Bansal, A., Verma, R., Shorey, R.: Smartsplit: latency-energy-memory optimisation for CNN splitting on smartphone environment. In: 2022 14th International Conference on COMmunication Systems & NETworkS (COMSNETS), pp. 549–557 (2022)
6. Hu, C., Bao, W., Wang, D., Liu, F.: Dynamic adaptive DNN surgery for inference acceleration on the edge. In: IEEE INFOCOM 2019 - IEEE Conference on Computer Communications, pp. 1423–1431 (2019)
7. Zhao, Z., Barijough, K.M., Gerstlauer, A.: Deepthings: distributed adaptive deep learning inference on resource-constrained IoT edge clusters. IEEE Trans. Comput. Aided Des. Integr. Circuits Syst. **37**(11), 2348–2359 (2018)
8. Guo, X., Pimentel, A.D., Stefanov, T.: Automated exploration and implementation of distributed CNN inference at the edge. IEEE Internet Things J. **10**(7), 5843–5858 (2023)
9. Tang, E., Stefanov, T.: Low-memory and high-performance CNN inference on distributed systems at the edge. In: Proceedings of the 14th IEEE/ACM International Conference on Utility and Cloud Computing Companion, UCC 2021. Association for Computing Machinery, New York (2022)
10. Stahl, R., Zhao, Z., Mueller-Gritschneder, D., Gerstlauer, A., Schlichtmann, U.: Fully distributed deep learning inference on resource-constrained edge devices. In: Pnevmatikatos, D.N., Pelcat, M., Jung, M. (eds.) SAMOS 2019. LNCS, vol. 11733, pp. 77–90. Springer, Cham (2019). https://doi.org/10.1007/978-3-030-27562-4_6
11. Guo, X., Pimentel, A.D., Stefanov, T.: Hierarchical design space exploration for distributed CNN inference at the edge. In: Machine Learning and Principles and Practice of Knowledge Discovery in Databases, pp. 545–556. Springer, Cham (2023)

280   F. Mehrafrooz et al.

12. Hou, X., Guan, Y., Han, T., Zhang, N.: Distredge: speeding up convolutional neural network inference on distributed edge devices. In: 2022 IEEE International Parallel and Distributed Processing Symposium (IPDPS), pp. 1097–1107. IEEE Computer Society, Los Alamitos (2022)

13. Zeng, L., Chen, X., Zhou, Z., Yang, L., Zhang, J.: Coedge: cooperative DNN inference with adaptive workload partitioning over heterogeneous edge devices. IEEE/ACM Trans. Netw. **29**(2), 595–608 (2021)

14. Mao, J., Chen, X., Nixon, K.W., Krieger, C., Chen, Y.: MoDNN: local distributed mobile computing system for deep neural network. In: Design, Automation & Test in Europe Conference & Exhibition (DATE), pp. 1396–1401 (2017)

15. Zhang, S., Zhang, S., Qian, Z., Wu, J., Jin, Y., Lu, S.: Deepslicing: collaborative and adaptive CNN inference with low latency. IEEE Trans. Parallel Distrib. Syst. **32**(9), 2175–2187 (2021)

16. Tang, E., Guo, X., Stefanov, T.: The effects of partitioning strategies on energy consumption in distributed CNN inference at the edge. arXiv preprint arXiv:2210.08392 (2022)

17. Guo, X., Jiang, Q., Pimentel, A.D., Stefanov, T.: RobustDiCE: robust and distributed CNN inference at the edge. In: Proceedings of the 29th Asia and South Pacific Design Automation Conference, pp. 26–31 (2024)

18. Dobraunig, C., Eichlseder, M., Mendel, F., Schläffer, M.: Ascon v1.2: lightweight authenticated encryption and hashing. In: International Conference on Selected Areas in Cryptography, pp. 84–115. Springer, Cham (2016)

19. Dobraunig, C., Eichlseder, M., Mendel, F., Schläffer, M.: Implementation comparison: crypto_aead/ascon128v1. https://bench.cr.yp.to/impl-aead/ascon128v1.html. Accessed 11 Dec 2024

20. Arm Limited: ARM Cortex-A7 Processor Datasheet. (2025). Accessed 11 Dec 2024. https://developer.arm.com/documentation/ddi0464/latest/ Accessed 11 Feb 2025

21. Arm Limited: ARM Cortex-A9 Processor Datasheet (2025). Accessed 11 Dec 2024. https://developer.arm.com/documentation/ddi0388/latest/. Accessed 11 Feb 2025

22. Arm Limited: ARM Cortex-A17 MPCore Processor Technical Reference Manual (2025). Accessed 11 Dec 2024. https://developer.arm.com/documentation/ddi0535/latest. Accessed 11 Feb 2025

23. Kelly, B., Matthews, T.P., Anastasio, M.A.: Deep learning-guided image reconstruction from incomplete data. arXiv preprint arXiv:1709.00584 (2017)

24. Gupta, H., Jin, K.H., Nguyen, H.Q., McCann, M.T., Unser, M.: CNN-based projected gradient descent for consistent CT image reconstruction. IEEE Trans. Med. Imaging **37**(6), 1440–1453 (2018)

25. Zhang, Q., Yuan, Q., Zeng, C., Li, X., Wei, Y.: Missing data reconstruction in remote sensing image with a unified spatial–temporal–spectral deep convolutional neural network. IEEE Trans. Geosci. Remote Sens. **56**(8), 4274–4288 (2018)

26. Li, Y., Li, K., Zhang, C., Montoya, J., Chen, G.-H.: Learning to reconstruct computed tomography images directly from sinogram data under a variety of data acquisition conditions. IEEE Trans. Med. Imaging **38**(10), 2469–2481 (2019)

27. Kalare, K.W., Bajpai, M.K.: RecDNN: deep neural network for image reconstruction from limited view projection data. Soft. Comput. **24**(22), 17205–17220 (2020). https://doi.org/10.1007/s00500-020-05013-4

28. Wasih, M., Ahmad, S., Almekkawy, M.: A robust cascaded deep neural network for image reconstruction of single plane wave ultrasound RF data. Ultrasonics **132**, 106981 (2023)

29. Chaitanya, C.R.A., et al.: Interactive reconstruction of Monte Carlo image sequences using a recurrent denoising autoencoder. ACM Trans. Graph. (TOG) **36**(4), 1–12 (2017)
30. Nogales, A., Donaher, S., García-Tejedor, A.: A deep learning framework for audio restoration using convolutional/deconvolutional deep autoencoders. Expert Syst. Appl. **230**, 120586 (2023)
31. Cheddad, Z.A., Cheddad, A.: Active restoration of lost audio signals using machine learning and latent information. In: Arai, K. (ed.) Intelligent Systems and Applications, pp. 1–16. Springer, Cham (2024)
32. Pasquini, D., Ateniese, G., Bernaschi, M.: Unleashing the tiger: inference attacks on split learning. In: Proceedings of the 2021 ACM SIGSAC Conference on Computer and Communications Security, CCS 2021, pp. 2113–2129. Association for Computing Machinery, New York (2021)
33. Erdoğan, E., Küpçü, A., Çiçek, A.E.: Unsplit: data-oblivious model inversion, model stealing, and label inference attacks against split learning. In: Proceedings of the 21st Workshop on Privacy in the Electronic Society, WPES 2022, pp. 115–124. Association for Computing Machinery, New York (2022)
34. Liu, J., Lyu, X., Cui, Q., Tao, X.: Similarity-based label inference attack against training and inference of split learning. IEEE Trans. Inf. Forensics Secur. **19**, 2881–2895 (2024)
35. Yu, F., Wang, L., Zeng, B., Zhao, K., Wu, T., Pang, Z.: SIA: a sustainable inference attack framework in split learning. Neural Netw. **171**(C), 396–409 (2024)
36. Ji, Y., Zhang, H., Zhang, Z., Liu, M.: CNN-based encoder-decoder networks for salient object detection: a comprehensive review and recent advances. Inf. Sci. **546**, 835–857 (2021)
37. Sun, S., Cao, Z., Zhu, H., Zhao, J.: A survey of optimization methods from a machine learning perspective. IEEE Trans. Cybern. **50**(8), 3668–3681 (2019)
38. Lecun, Y., Bottou, L., Bengio, Y., Haffner, P.: Gradient-based learning applied to document recognition. Proc. IEEE **86**(11), 2278–2324 (1998)
39. Howard, A.G., et al.: Mobilenets: efficient convolutional neural networks for mobile vision applications. In: Proceedings of the IEEE Conference on Computer Vision and Pattern Recognition (CVPR) (2017)
40. He, K., Zhang, X., Ren, S., Sun, J.: Deep residual learning for image recognition. In: Proceedings of the IEEE Conference on Computer Vision and Pattern Recognition (CVPR), pp. 770–778 (2016)
41. Deng, J., Dong, W., Socher, R., Li, L.-J., Li, K., Fei-Fei, L.: Imagenet: a large-scale hierarchical image database. In: 2009 IEEE Conference on Computer Vision and Pattern Recognition, pp. 248–255 (2009)
42. Kingma, D.P.: Adam: a method for stochastic optimization. arXiv preprint arXiv:1412.6980 (2014)

MLP is Better than ResNet on ANSSI's Protected AES Implementation on ARM

Akash Gupta[(⊠)], S. P. Mishra, and Atul Prakash

MOD, DRDO, Delhi 110054, India
`akash.23march@gmail.com, sp-mishra.sag@gov.in`

Abstract. This paper target's the ANSSI's protected AES implementation on STM32 platform with ARM cortex-M architecture. The dataset generated using this implementation is available publicly as ASCADv2 [11]. By using this available dataset, we targeted ANSSI's protected AES implementation using multi-task learning (MTL) approach, introduced by Magrehbi in 2020 [17]. Our deep learning based approach is different in terms of model selection, selection of point of interest and targeted operation for attacking as compared to the released paper by Loïc Masure and Rémi Strullu in year 2023 [12]. We proposed two separate MTL Multilayer Perceptron (MLP) neural networks that are used for recovering the complete key byte of the given implementation in *40 traces*.

Keywords: Advanced encryption standard · Deep Learning · Side channel Analysis · Multilayer Perceptron · ANSSI's implementation · Multi-Task Learning

1   Introduction

In the evolving cryptographic security, Side-Channel Attacks (SCAs) have emerged as formidable attacks that exploit unintentional information leakage from cryptographic implementations rather than weaknesses in the algorithms emissions or execution time of the hardware devices performing cryptographic operations [1]. SCAs are classified into several types based on the nature of the leakage they exploit. Power analysis attack utilizes variations in power consumption to recover secret data [2]. Timing attacks exploit variations in computational execution time [3], while Electromagnetic (EM) analysis exploits the electromagnetic radiation to retrieve information [4].

1.1   Side - Channel Attack on AES

AES (Advanced encryption standard) standardized by NIST [5], is one of the most widely adopted symmetric-key encryption algorithms, utilized in applications ranging from embedded devices to large-scale data centres. Although AES is mathematically robust and considered secure against classical cryptanalysis, it is still vulnerable to side-channel attacks. The extensive use of low-cost hardware and the widespread deployment of embedded systems have expanded the attack surface for SCAs. Moreover, recent advancements in Artificial Intelligence (AI) and Machine Learning (ML) have significantly enhanced the potency and efficiency of these attacks. Traditional statistical techniques are increasingly being replaced with deep learning models that can autonomously learn complex leakage patterns from raw trace data, improving key recovery success rates even in noisy environments [6,7].

The SubBytes step-implemented using a nonlinear substitution box (S-box) has been identified as a primary source of side-channel leakage [6]. During encryption, intermediate values such as S-box outputs and round key bytes often exhibit data-dependent variations in power consumption or electromagnetic radiation. Adversaries can exploit this correlation to recover key bytes through techniques like Differential Power Analysis (DPA) [1] and Correlation Power Analysis (CPA) [7]. In recent years, machine learning techniques particularly deep learning models such as Multilayer Perceptron [8] and Convolutional Neural Networks (CNNs) [9,10] have been applied in side-channel analysis, significantly boosting attack performance.

1.2   The ANSSI Implementation

As side-channel attacks (SCAs) have become increasingly practical and effective especially with the integration of AI and deep learning techniques, cryptographic implementations must go beyond algorithmic security and include robust countermeasures at implementation-level. In response to this growing threat, the French national cyber-security agency ANSSI (*Agence Nationale de la Sécurité des Systèmes d'Information*) proposed a hardened version of AES designed specifically for side-channel resistance [11]. The ANSSI-protected AES is an enhanced implementation of AES-128 that incorporates multiple side-channel countermeasures at the software level to disrupt any exploitable correlation between sensitive intermediate values and observable physical leakages.

1.3   Side-Channel Attacks on ANSSI-Protected AES

While the ANSSI's protected AES implementation represents a significant advancement in the defence against side-channel attacks, recent research has shown that even these hardened versions remain vulnerable to sophisticated adversaries. ANSSI's AES is designed with multiple countermeasures to mitigate leakages and complicate trace alignment, making classical attacks significantly more difficult. However, deep learning-based side-channel analysis (DL-SCA) has demonstrated the ability to bypass these protections by learning features across misaligned, noisy, and masked traces. Models such as Convolutional Neural Networks (CNNs) and Residual Networks (ResNets) [12] have been successfully trained to recover secret key bytes from ANSSI's protected AES traces, even when traditional attacks fail to do so. These models excel in identifying non-linear relationships and leveraging subtle patterns spread across large time windows, allowing them to effectively mount attacks without prior knowledge of the masking scheme or shuffling order.

1.4 Our Major Contribution

- We are highlighting a new more vulnerable operation in the ANSSI's protected AES algorithm as not targeted in paper [12]. We are targeting random mask rin & input of maskedSbox instead of rout & output of maskedSbox.
- We are proposing a novel approach using two multi-task MLP frameworks for attacking ASCADv2 dataset. So that the less learnable parameters may not affect the learning of other parameters.
- We are using SNR based approach for selecting Point of Interest (PoIs) in ASCADv2 dataset, which is well studied mechanism for dimensionality reduction and choosing the most information leakage point.
- Based on these changes we are able to successfully mount an attack using 40 EM traces, which is significant reduction (33.3% approx.) in trace count as mentioned in research paper [12].

1.5 Paper Organization

The paper is organised as follows: Sect. 2 provides a brief background about the AES-128 symmetric cipher and about the ANSSI's protected AES. It also provides the idea of countermeasures used in ANSSI's AES encryption. Section 3 describes the details about the ASCADv2 database, its analysis and the pre-processing technique to exploit out the point of interests (POIs) from power traces. Section 4 highlights experiments and analysis that emphasize our two MTL-MLP Model architecture, its hyper-parameter optimization, training and validation. Section 5 summarizes the experimental results. Section 6 concludes the paper and discusses the future work.

2   Background and Literature Review

This section gives background information on standard AES algorithm, ANSSI's countermeasure protected AES algorithm and previous work on SCA over ANSSI's protected AES.

2.1 Standard AES

AES is a symmetric block cipher, operates on 128-bit blocks with key sizes of 128, 192, or 256 bits and consists of multiple rounds 10, 12, or 14 respectively. Each round is having the following steps - *SubBytes*: A non-linear substitution using an S-box; *ShiftRows*: A transposition step where rows of the state are cyclically shifted; *MixColumns*: A mixing operation combining the four bytes in each column. It involves matrix multiplication over the finite field GF 2^8; *AddRound-Key*: A bitwise XOR of the current state with a portion of the expanded key. The last round does not have MixColumn.

2.2   ANSSI's Countermeasure Protected AES

While standard AES processes data in a fixed order without masking, makes it vulnerable to SCA. ANSSI's implementation introduces randomness in both data values and processing order. This implementation introduces countermeasures such as affine masking and shuffling to obfuscate intermediate computations. Interested readers can refer the paper [12] for complete understanding and implementations of ANSSI's countermeasure Protected AES.

Affine Masking. This technique combines both additive and multiplicative masking to obscure intermediate values during encryption. All the bytes of AES at each stage are masked as follows:

$$c[i] = \alpha \cdot s[i] \oplus \beta \quad ; \quad 0 \leq i \leq 15 \tag{1}$$

where $c[i]$ is the state of the ith byte after masking, α is the multiplicative mask, β is the additive mask, and $s[i]$ is the state of the ith byte.

Shuffling. It introduces randomness [13] in the execution sequence of operation, which enhances the effort of attacker. In the ANSSI's implementation, two types of permutations are used:

Byte-Level Shuffling: A permutation (permIndices) is applied to randomize the order of byte processing in operations like SubBytes, Shiftrows and AddRoundKey.

Column-Level Shuffling: During the MixColumns operation, columns are processed in a randomized order, which are controlled by a separate permutation indices.

The inclusion of affine masking randomizes sensitive intermediate values by using randomly generated masks during each encryption [14]. The key difference between a standard AES implementation and ANSSI's protected version lies in data randomization and execution variability. During the SubBytes operation, the use of masked S-boxes ensures that the actual value processed is always hidden behind a randomly generated mask, which significantly reduces the statistical leakages [15]. Similarly, shuffling operations reorder the processing of AES bytes to make trace alignment and pattern recognition more challenging for the attacker [16].

2.3   Related Works

In the paper "Side Channel Analysis against ANSSI's Protected AES Implementation on ARM [12]" the researchers employed a deep learning approach by using a ResNet model to recover the ANSSI's protected AES key from side-channel traces. Despite the countermeasures, it is demonstrated that these protections are vulnerable against the advanced deep learning technique; particularly Multi-Task Learning (MTL) frameworks could effectively recover the full key of AES with countermeasures.

The deployed ResNet architecture is a type of deep neural network known for its ability to model complex functions through residual connections efficiently. The ResNet-based model is explored to process power traces to predict intermediate values. The architecture is having 9 stage deep RESNET and input size is 15,000 sample points per trace. Building upon Maghrebi's 2020 proposal [17], the study introduces enhanced MTL architectures, namely MultiResNetSCA-1 and MultiResNetSCA-2. These models predict multiple intermediate variables, such as the multiplicative mask r_m, additive mask r_{out}, permutation of bytes (permIndices i.e. p) and masked S-box outputs c[i]. The models are trained on extensive datasets where 400,000 traces are used for training. Training labels correspond to intermediate cryptographic computations, such as:

$$c[i] = r_m \times \mathrm{Sbox}[\mathrm{pt}[p[i]] \oplus k[p[i]]] \oplus r_{out} \tag{2}$$

where, pt is the plaintext, k is the key, and p[i] denotes the permutation applied to the ith byte.

For full key recovery, the MultiResNetSCA models perform as follows:

- MultiResNetSCA-1 predicts 34 variables, including r_m, r_{out}, c[i], and p[i], and achieves key recovery with approximately *60 traces*.
- MultiResNetSCA-2, which predicts only 18 variables (excluding the permutation of bytes p[i]), requires around *220 traces* for successful key recovery.

The deep learning model was capable of recovering the complete AES key, even with the presence of strong countermeasures. The success of the ResNet model in this attack emphasizes the importance of considering machine learning techniques when evaluating the security of cryptographic implementations.

3   Database Description and Attack Approach

The ASCADv2 is a public available dataset curated and published by the *Agence Nationale de la Sécurité des Systèmes d'Information* (ANSSI) to support academic and industrial research in side channel analysis and cryptographic implementations. The database can be accessed at https://www.data.gouv.fr/fr/datasets/ascadv2/. The traces of ASCADv2, were captured from an ARM Cortex-M4 microcontroller executing AES-128 encryption algorithm with countermeasure including affine masking and shuffling of bytes. Each trace in the dataset corresponds to a complete execution of one AES encryption with a unique random plaintext and a random secret key, while maintaining variation in the internal masking shares. The traces were captured at a clock frequency of 4MHz and the sampling rate was set to 100 MS/sec (mega samples per second). The database contains 800,000 power traces of complete AES-128; each is having 1 million sample points. The complete dataset of 800 GB was divided into 8 HDF5 file of 100 GB each. Figure 1 depicts the complete trace after averaging over 1000 acquisitions.

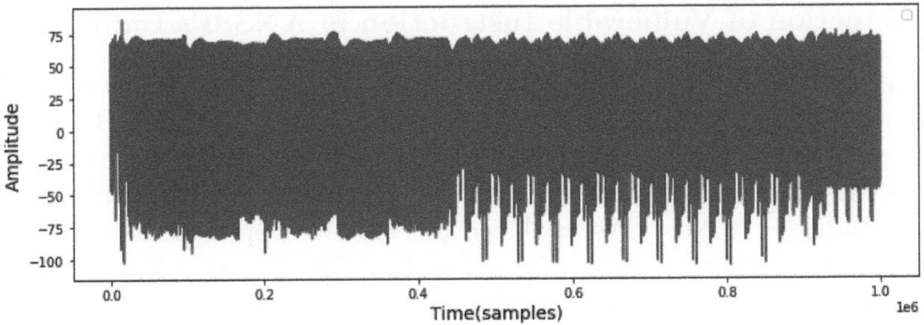

Fig. 1. Complete trace after averaging over 1000 acquisitions

3.1   SNR Computation for the Selection of Point of Interest (POIs)

Considering 1 million sample points is a challenging task with respect to data handling and side channel attack perspective. It increases the computational complexity of the attack, as it demands more resources, time and can also obscure relevant leakage due to the presence of noise and redundant information across samples. To address this, we apply the Signal to Noise ratio (SNR) method, a statistical approach for identifying the Point of Interests (POIs) in side channel traces. SNR effectively highlights the time samples where the variance caused by the data dependent leakage is significantly greater than variance due to noise [18]. For a given sample point 't', the SNR is defined as

$$\mathrm{SNR}(t) = \frac{\mathrm{Var}_k\left[\mathbb{E}[T(t)] \mid K\right]}{\mathbb{E}_k\left[\mathrm{Var}[T(t) \mid K]\right]} \tag{3}$$

where:

- $T(t)$ is the electromagnetic (Power/EM) trace at time sample t.
- K is the sensitive intermediate value (e.g., key-dependent state).
- $\mathbb{E}[T(t) \mid K]$ is the mean of the trace at time t given that the intermediate value is K.
- $\mathrm{Var}[T(t) \mid K]$ is the variance of the trace at time t given that the intermediate value is K.
- $\mathrm{Var}_K[\cdot]$ denotes the variance computed across all classes of K.
- $\mathbb{E}_K[\cdot]$ denotes the expectation (mean) computed over all classes of K.

The SNR computation for each sample point gives most likely meaningful leakage location in the complete trace related to the cryptographic operation under observation. This dimensionality reduction technique allows us to extract a compact informative subset of the original trace. It significantly reduces the computational burden of the analysis. However by isolating high SNR regions, we can enhance the performance of machine learning classifiers and key recovery attacks, as the input features now carry more concentrated leakage information.

3.2   Detection of Vulnerable Instruction in ANSSI's Implementation

We computed SNR's for 39 locations r_m, r_{in}, r_{out}, input of maskedSbox(16 Nos), output of maskedSbox(16 Nos) and permIndices (16 Nos). Based on SNR values we changed the targeted instruction and parameter for attack. In the reference [12] targeted parameters are r_m, r_{out} output of maskedSbox(16 Nos) and permIndices (16 Nos). We analyzed two different operations in the ANSSI's implementation. Those two locations are: (a) combination of r_{in} and input of maskedSbox,

$$c[p[i]] = r_m \times [\text{pt}[p[i]] \oplus k[p[i]]] \oplus r_{in} \tag{4}$$

and (b) combination of r_{out} and output of maskedSbox,

$$c[p[i]] = r_m \times \text{Sbox}[r_m^{-1} \times [\text{pt}[p[i]] \oplus k[p[i]]] \oplus r_{out} \tag{5}$$

We choose the operations performed in equation (4) for our attack, which is the combination of r_{in} (Fig. 5) and input of maskedSbox (Fig. 7) because of their high SNR values as compared to the r_{out} (Fig. 4) and output of maskedSbox (Fig. 6).

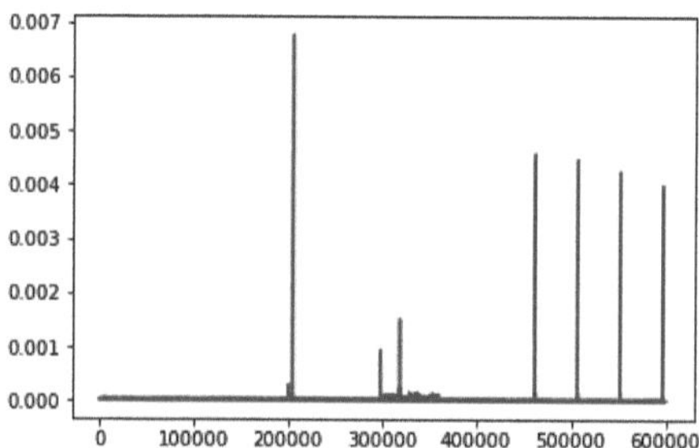

Fig. 2. SNR values of r_m

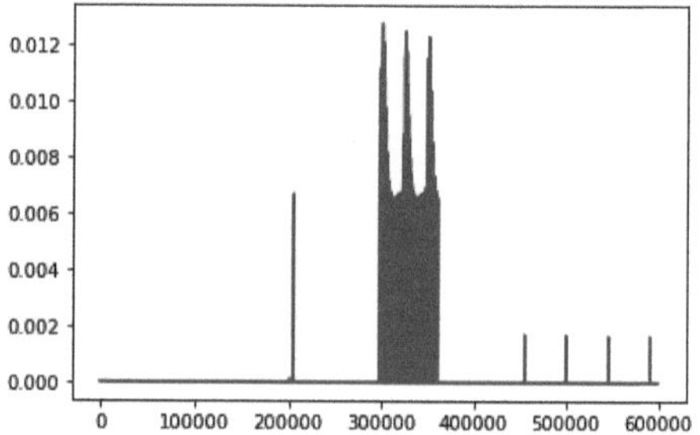

Fig. 3. SNR values of permIndices[0]

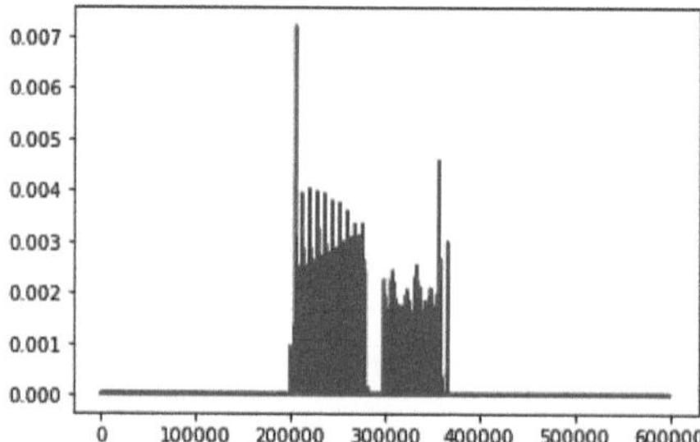

Fig. 4. SNR values of r_{out}

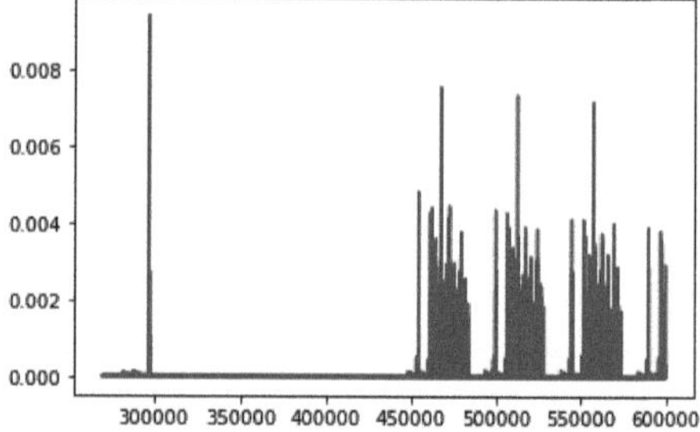

Fig. 5. SNR values of r_{in}

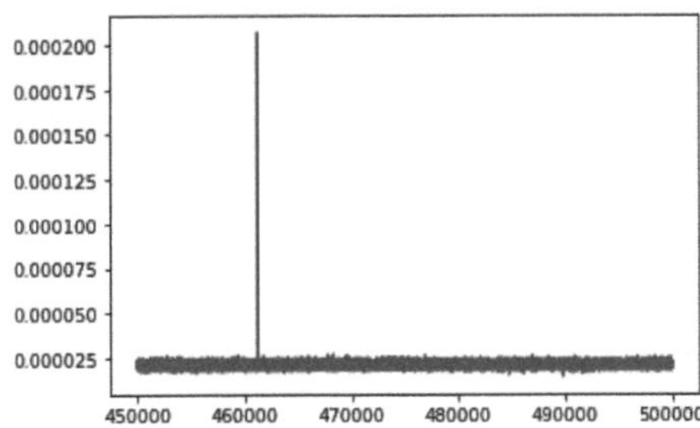

Fig. 6. SNR values of output of maskedSbox[0]

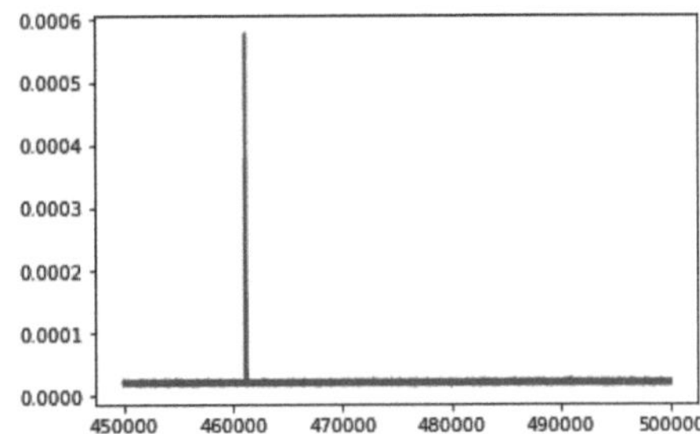

Fig. 7. SNR values of input of maskedSbox[0]

The chosen attack location was taken at the input of maskedSbox, so to recover the secret key at this attack location, demands the information of mask variables r_m, r_{in} and 16 permutations of bytes (permIndices).

- The leakage of r_m ranges from 205,682 to 365,662, where we have considered 1024 POIs having highest SNR values, shown in (Fig. 2).
- The leakage of r_{in} ranges from 205,189 to 590,726, as shown in the (Fig. 5), here we had chosen 3072 POIs.
- The leakage 16 permIndices ranges from 282,009 to 599,976 as shown in (Fig. 3). We considered 384 POIs from each byte leading to 6144 POIs of permIndices for 16 bytes.
- Similarly, the range for the leakage of input of maskedSbox ranges from 450,001 to 499,431, as shown in the (Fig. 7).

The POIs of r_m, r_{in} and 16 permIndices had been combined to merge multiple common POIs into single one, lead to a total of 10,239 POI's, whereas, for input of maskedSbox, 160 POI's with highest SNR values had been selected from each byte which were susceptible to leak the information input of maskedSbox, which after being merged to a total of 2501 points. Our final extracted dataset consists of 700,000 traces with training and validation split of 90:10.

4   Experimental Results and Analysis

We started with the single MTL-MLP Model consisting of 34 parallel networks, but during the training phase it was observed that the 16 parallel networks of input of maskedSbox creating issues in the training of 18 networks. Therefore, we proposed two distinct MTL-MLP (Multilayer Perceptron) parallel architectural network: Model-1 for 18 targets and Model-2 for input of maskedSbox. All experiments were conducted on a local workstation equipped with Intel Xeon Gold 6248R Processor having operating frequency of 3GHz and 48 cores with RAM size of 256 GB and an NVIDIA RTX A6000 graphics card featuring 48 GB GDDR6 of RAM and 10,752 CUDA cores. Both the models were implemented using TensorFlow framework, and trained with GPU acceleration enabled. Model-1 required $\sim$4.5 h to converge, whereas Model-2 took $\sim$3 h depending on the complexity of the architecture and number of training epochs.

4.1 Our MLP Model Architecture

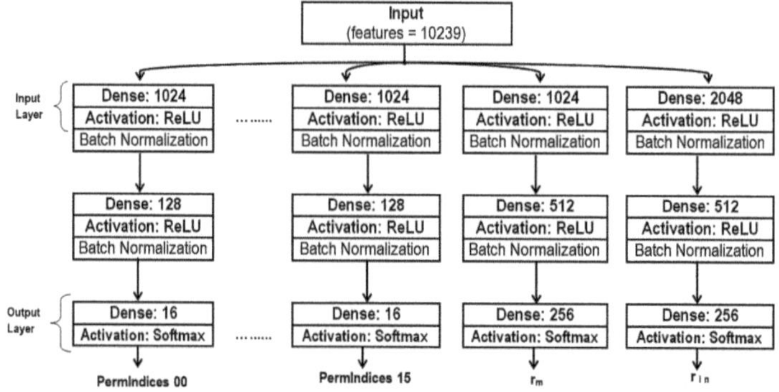

Fig. 8. Model-1 for 16 permutation, r_m and r_{in}

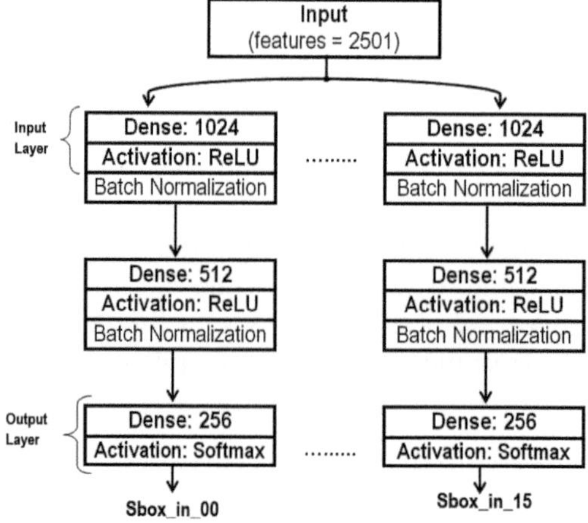

Fig. 9. Model-2 for 16 combinations of input of maskedSbox.

In Model-1, shown in Fig. 8, the first 16 parallel networks, targets the 16 permIndices. It consist fully connected neural networks and the next two parallel network target mask variables r_m and r_{in}. It consists of input layer, fully connected hidden layer and the output layer with Softmax activation. In Model-2, as shown in Fig. 9, there are 16 parallel networks targeting the 256 combination of input of maskedSbox. It consists of three layers of neural networks, where the input layer consists of 1024 neurons followed by a single hidden layer containing 512 neurons and the output layer consists of 256 neurons with Softmax activation, Here also, each input layer and hidden layer has been followed by Batch Normalization, wherein the activation function used is 'ReLU'.

4.2   Training and Validation

Table 1. Final Train - Validation loss and accuracy of Model-1 over r_m, r_{in} and permIndices.

Parameter	Final training loss	Final validation loss	Final training accuracy	Final validation accuracy
r_m	0.0000002	2.33672	1.0	1.0
r_{in}	0.02585	0.31152	0.99133	0.95067
Perm0	0.00030	0.00272	0.99991	0.99908
Perm1	0.00626	0.08180	0.99788	0.97784
Perm2	0.00329	0.05004	0.99898	0.98698
Perm3	0.00114	0.01213	0.99962	0.99642
Perm4	0.00439	0.05843	0.99860	0.98357
Perm5	0.00519	0.06354	0.99833	0.98271
Perm6	0.00321	0.04650	0.99899	0.98744
Perm7	0.00069	0.00580	0.0.999	0.99821
Perm8	0.00329	0.03941	0.99892	0.98862
Perm9	0.00338	0.05059	0.99892	0.98677
Perm10	0.00184	0.03695	0.99942	0.98992
Perm11	0.00052	0.00355	0.99984	0.99900
Perm12	0.00316	0.04430	0.99898	0.98762
Perm13	0.00491	0.07363	0.99849	0.98034
Perm14	0.00268	0.03271	0.99918	0.99078
Perm15	0.00051	0.00319	0.999856	0.99897

Table 2. Final training and validation loss and accuracy of Model-2 over input of maskedSbox

Parameter	Final Training Loss	Final Validation Loss	Final Training Accuracy	Final Validation Accuracy
sbox_in_00	4.53776	4.73742	0.04733	0.03095
sbox_in_01	4.56014	4.74433	0.04563	0.03181
sbox_in_02	4.59444	4.79633	0.04369	0.03007
sbox_in_03	4.59499	4.78019	0.04391	0.03018
sbox_in_04	4.56795	4.76976	0.04625	0.03100
sbox_in_05	4.56827	4.73902	0.04493	0.03098
sbox_in_06	4.56033	4.75321	0.04579	0.03122
sbox_in_07	4.58376	4.81133	0.04429	0.02902
sbox_in_08	4.58945	4.77352	0.04400	0.02950
sbox_in_09	4.60146	4.78180	0.04310	0.02928
sbox_in_10	4.61711	4.79518	0.04230	0.02925
sbox_in_11	4.59104	4.76062	0.04339	0.03001
sbox_in_12	4.57599	4.73933	0.04392	0.03067
sbox_in_13	4.54623	4.74130	0.04633	0.03095
sbox_in_14	4.62433	4.78872	0.04088	0.02885
sbox_in_15	4.56415	4.73349	0.04486	0.03091

The Model - 1 is trained to predict 18 targets comprising of r_m, r_{in} and 16 permIndices. Figure 10 shows the accuracy curve, where r_m shows training and validation accuracy reaches to 100%, reflecting classification performance, For r_{in}, training and validation accuracy also reaches to a 100%, shown in Fig. 11. The training and validation accuracy shown in Fig. 12 and Fig. 13 respectively of permIndices are almost 100%. Table 1 is clearly showing that the validation accuracy of permIndices almost reaches to 100%. Hence, The Model-1 demonstrated stable training dynamics with training accuracies steadily increasing over the epochs for all the 18 targets (r_m, r_{in}, 16 permutation). Validation accuracies are also closely following training accuracy which indicates effectiveness of the architecture of the model used. Training is carried out for 42 epochs.

For Model-2, the training accuracy steadily increased over the epochs for all the 16 targets (i.e., 16 input of maskedSbox), as shown in Fig. 14, Fig. 15. These curves indicate that the model is learning effectively from the training data while also generalizing well to unseen validation data. Validation accuracies are also following training accuracy and the model is trained in 29 epochs. The final training accuracies of Model-2 reaches to about 4.5% and validation accuracies of reaches to about 3%, as mentioned in Table 2. This relatively close alignment between training and validation curves suggests no over-fitting.

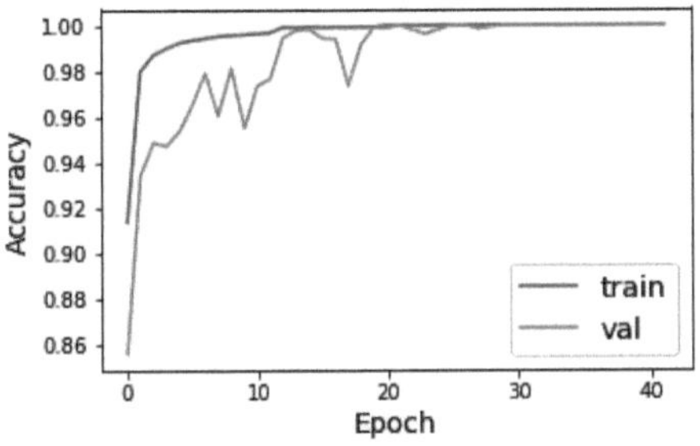

Fig. 10. r_m train and validation accuracy plot

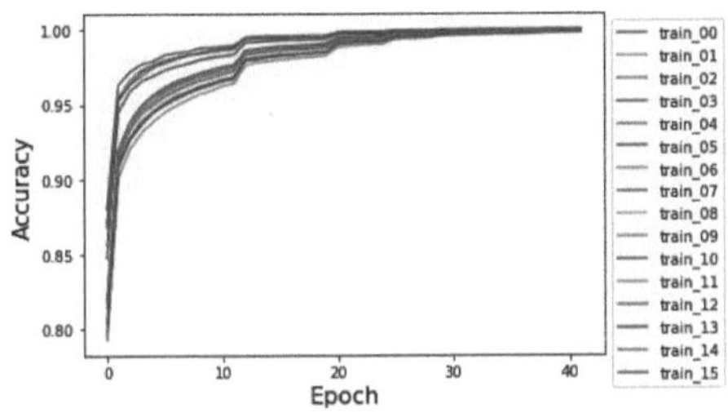

Fig. 12. permIndices- train accuracy plot

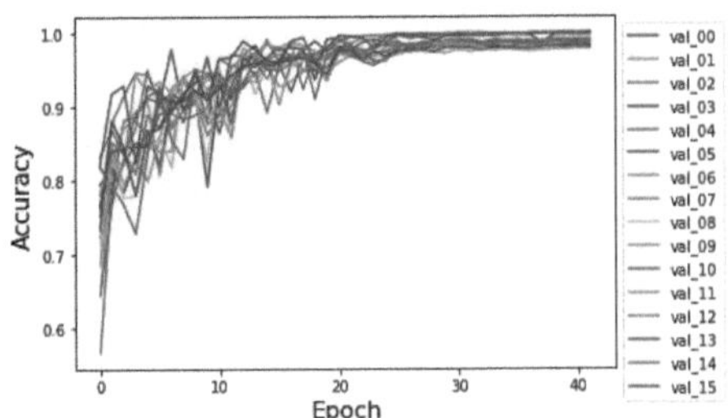

Fig. 13. permIndices- val accuracy plot

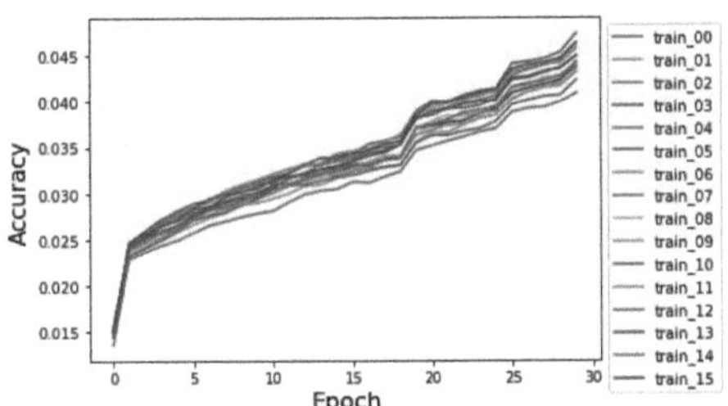

Fig. 14. Input of maskedSbox- train accuracy plot

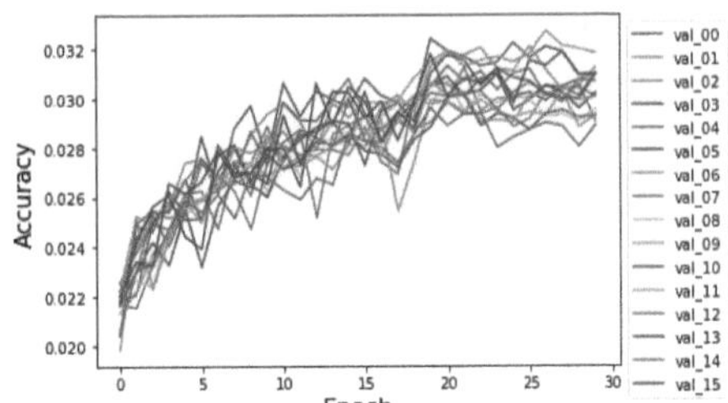

Fig. 15. Input of maskedSbox- val accuracy plot

4.3 Hyper-Parameter Optimization

Table 3. Hyperparameters for Model-1 and Model-2.

Hyperparameters	Model-1 (for r_m, r_{in}, PermIndices)	Model-2 (for maskedSbox)
earlyStopping	Monitor 'val_loss', patience = 11, mode = 'min'	=Monitor = 'val_loss', patience = 11, mode = 'min'
Epochs	42	29
Batchsize	64	64
loss_function	categorical crossentropy	categorical crossentropy
ReduceLROnPlateau	monitor = 'val_loss', factor = 0.3, min_lr = 0.001, min_delta = 0.01, mode = 'min' patience = 3)	monitor = 'val_loss', factor = 0.3, min_lr = 0.001, min_delta = 0.01, mode = 'min' patience = 3)
Activation	ReLU, Softmax	ReLU, Softmax
optimizer	Adam(1e-3)	Adam(1e-3)

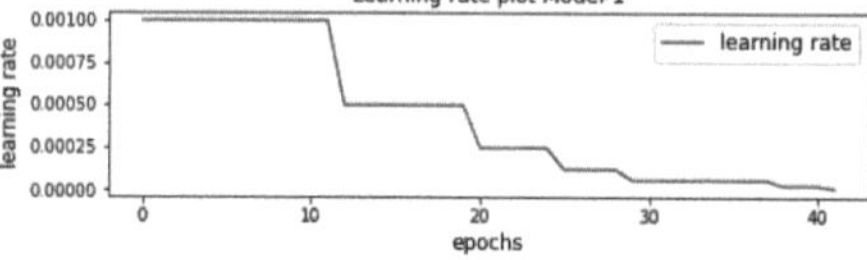

Fig. 16. learning rate curve of Model-1

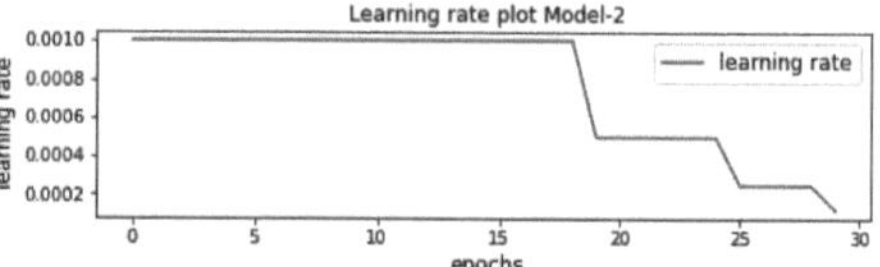

Fig. 17. learning rate curve of Model-2

To ensure optimal training of the model, several hyper parameters and strategies were carefully selected as shown in Table 3. A batch size of 64 was chosen as a balance between computational efficiency and stable gradient updates. The varying learning rate plays a crucial role in the training process across the epochs and can significantly impact model performance. At the very beginning of training of both the Model-1 and Model-2, a higher learning rate of 0.001 is used to enable the model make significant progress toward the optimal solution by taking larger steps in the direction of the gradient. As training advances, the learning rate of Model-1 is typically reduced to 6.25e-05, whereas for Model-2, the learning rate is gradually decreased to 0.00025. The reduction in the learning rate with respect to change in epoch for both Model-1 and Model-2 is depicted in Fig. 16 and Fig. 17 respectively. This reduction in learning rate allows fine-tuning the model parameters, helping the model converge more precisely toward a global minimum. This gradual adjustment in training prevents the model from overshooting optimal values. It also helps to create balance between the speed of learning and the stability of convergence.

To prevent over fitting, an early stopping mechanism was incorporated based on validation loss. Additionally, ReduceLROnPlateau was applied, which was reducing the learning rate by a factor of 0.3 when validation loss plateaued for three epochs to boot up the model fine. A checkpoint mechanism is used to save the best-performing model at each epoch, preventing loss of progress in case of interruptions. The training process also shuffles to maintain randomness in mini-batch selection and a CSV logger to track training history for analysis. By selecting a proper choice of these hyper-parameter and training strategies, the model was in multiple epochs.

5   Result

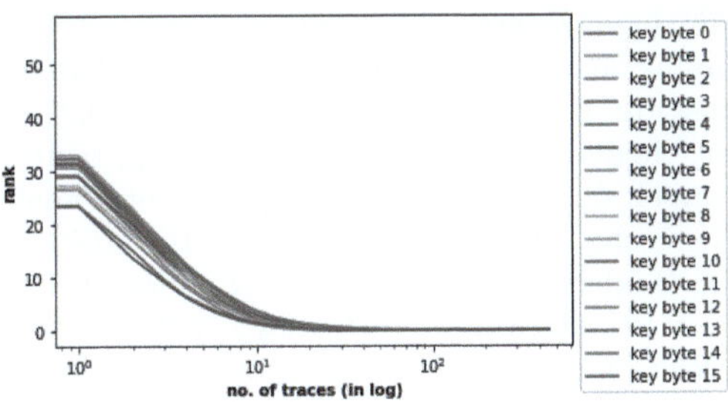

Fig. 18. Full key recovery scenario

To assess the effectiveness of the trained model in terms of recovering the secret key by using the remaining traces of ASCADv2 dataset, a mean rank versus number of traces curve was plotted in Fig. 18. This curve presents the average rank of the correct key bytes across all 16 positions as a function of the number of traces used in the attack. It provides an aggregated metric that reflects the model's ability to consistently identify the correct key bytes with increasing data. The mean rank analysis reveals a rapid convergence toward successful key recovery, with the correct key bytes consistently reaching rank 1 within approximately 40 traces. This indicates that the Model is highly effective in extracting relevant features from the masked and shuffled traces present in the dataset.

6   Conclusions and Future Work

In this paper, we have proposed a new approach of two efficient MLP architecture to target ANSSI's countermeasure implementation. In this paper we have also emphasized the newer parameter (input of maskedSbox and r_{in}) which are more prone to side channel attack. We improved the attack performance approximately 33.3% as claimed earlier [12]. In future work, we intend to extend same approach on the dataset captured on our own hardware, which does not have tap points to capture the clean power traces as available in Chipwhisperer. We will target to mount attack on IoT device using electromagnetic (EM) traces and we will try to reduce the number of trace requirement for the attack.

Acknowledgement. The authors would like to thank the paper reviewing committee and Ms. Rajani Kumari (SAG - DRDO) for their comments and suggestions.

References

1. Kocher, P., Jaffe, J., Jun, B.: Differential power analysis. In: Advances in Cryptology-CRYPTO 1999. Springer (1999)
2. JMangard, S., Oswald, E., Popp, T.: Power Analysis Attacks: Revealing the Secrets of Smart Cards. Springer (2007)
3. Kocher, P.C.: Timing attacks on implementations of Diffie-Hellman, RSA, DSS, and other systems. In: Koblitz, N. (ed.) CRYPTO 1996. LNCS, vol. 1109, pp. 104–113. Springer, Heidelberg (1996). https://doi.org/10.1007/3-540-68697-5_9
4. Gandolfi, K., Mourtel, C., Olivier, F.: Electromagnetic analysis: concrete results. In: Koç, Ç.K., Naccache, D., Paar, C. (eds.) CHES 2001. LNCS, vol. 2162, pp. 251–261. Springer, Heidelberg (2001). https://doi.org/10.1007/3-540-44709-1_21
5. National Institute of Standards and Technology (NIST). FIPS PUB 197: Advanced Encryption Standard (AES) (2001)
6. Mangard, S., Oswald, E., Popp, T.: Power Analysis Attacks: Revealing the Secrets of Smart Cards. Springer (2007)
7. Brier, E., Clavier, C., Olivier, F.: Correlation power analysis with a leakage model. In: Joye, M., Quisquater, J.-J. (eds.) CHES 2004. LNCS, vol. 3156, pp. 16–29. Springer, Heidelberg (2004). https://doi.org/10.1007/978-3-540-28632-5_2
8. Weissbart, L.: On the performance of multilayer perceptron in profiling side-channel analysis. Cryptology ePrint Archive (2019)
9. Cagli, E., Dumas, C., Prouff, E.: Convolutional neural networks with data augmentation against jitter-based countermeasures. In: Fischer, W., Homma, N. (eds.) CHES 2017. LNCS, vol. 10529, pp. 45–68. Springer, Cham (2017). https://doi.org/10.1007/978-3-319-66787-4_3
10. Zaid, A., Bossuet, L., Habrard, A., Prouff, E.: Methodology for efficient CNN architectures in profiling attacks. IACR Transactions on Cryptographic Hardware and Embedded Systems (2020)
11. Benadjila, R., Khati, L., Prouff, E., Thillard, A.: Hardened library for AES-128 encryption/decryption on ARM cortex M4 architecture (2019). https://github.com/ANSSI-FR/SecAESSTM32
12. Masure, L., Strullu, R.: Side-channel analysis against ANSSI's protected AES implementation on ARM: end-to-end attacks with multi-task learning. J. Cryptogr. Eng. **13**(2), 129–147 (2023)
13. Gross, H., Kutzner, D.: Shuffling against side-channel attacks: a comprehensive study with cautionary results. In: FDTC 2016. IEEE (2016)

14. Rivain, M., Prouff, E.: Provably secure higher-order masking of AES. In: CHES 2010. Springer (2010)
15. Coron, J.-S., et al.: Leakage resilient cryptography in practice. J. Cryptogr. Eng. (2013)
16. Gierlichs, B., Batina, L., Tuyls, P., Preneel, B.: Mutual information analysis. In: Oswald, E., Rohatgi, P. (eds.) CHES 2008. LNCS, vol. 5154, pp. 426–442. Springer, Heidelberg (2008). https://doi.org/10.1007/978-3-540-85053-3_27
17. Maghrebi, H.: Deep learning based side-channel attack: a new profiling methodology based on multi-label classification. IACR Cryptol. ePrint Arch. **2020**, 436 (2020)
18. Des Noes, M.: Distribution of signal to noise ratio and application to leakage detection. IACR Trans. Cryptogr. Hardw. Embed. Syst. **2024**(2), 384–402 (2024)

VulScan-LT: A Lightweight Transformer-Based Software Vulnerability Scanning Tool for Resource-Constrained Edge Devices

Dev Saini[1]([✉])(iD), Vivek Chaturvedi[1](iD), and Muhammad Shafique[2](iD)

[1] Indian Institute of Technology (IIT) Palakkad, Palakkad, India
`112113002@smail.iitpkd.ac.in`, `vivek@iitpkd.ac.in`
[2] eBRAIN Lab, Division of Engineering, New York University Abu Dhabi (NYUAD),
Abu Dhabi, UAE
`ms12713@nyu.edu`

Abstract. Software vulnerabilities are security loopholes in software development phases that may turn into a backdoor for potential malicious actors to exploit and pose potent threats such as overflows, DDoS, and data breaches. Traditional vulnerability detection methods are largely computationally intensive and fail to detect these backdoors exploited during runtime. Moreover, edge devices are susceptible to such loopholes due to stringent resource constraints, which makes it difficult to deploy sophisticated security measures. In this work, we propose a novel transformer-based vulnerability scanning tool, VulScan-LT, that envelopes a redesigned state-of-the-art DistilBERT transformer model, customized to be lightweight by reducing the number of encoder layers and attention heads. The model is trained on four publicly available IoT Operating Systems and the SAR-Dataset, making it comprehensive in detecting vulnerabilities with a best-case accuracy of 93.57%, an F1-score of 91.96%, a recall of 93.45%, and a precision of 92.39%. Our tool performs better when compared to the state-of-the-art, with improvements in accuracy for both binary and multi-class classification by an average of 4%.

Furthermore, the tool has also been deployed on the Jetson Orin Nano board, showcasing its compatibility with resource-constrained edge devices. We performed hardware-specific optimizations such as floating-point and layer fusions on the redesigned transformer that reduced its memory footprint by approximately 30%. The optimized model performed with an accuracy of 93.75%, an F1-score of 91.69%, a recall of 93.31%, and a precision of 92.74% on the hardware. VulScan-LT is an end-to-end, platform-independent tool that accepts any C/C++-based source code file as input and generates a comprehensive vulnerability analysis report.

Keywords: IoT · OS Security · Software Vulnerability · Vulnerability Detection · Transformers · DistilBERT

C. Karfa et al. (Eds.): SPACE 2025, LNCS 16406, pp. 298–317, 2026.
https://doi.org/10.1007/978-3-032-16342-4_17

1   Introduction

In recent years, there has been a rapid increase in the usage of edge devices and Internet-of-Things (IoT) platforms across several domains such as power grids [30], healthcare [8], autonomous driving [15] and security surveillance [24]. The number of edge devices is expected to reach around 24 billion by 2030 amounting to almost 3 devices per person [12]. Due to this increased traffic over edge devices, 30% of the total cyberattacks are aimed at edge devices, making them a hotspot for potential hackers and adversaries who impact the confidentiality and integrity of these systems for personal/commercial benefits [34].

These attacks target the inherent software vulnerabilities present in the source code for IoT devices and leverage them as a backdoor to carry out attacks at different abstraction layers, such as network, data, software, and physical, as shown in Fig. 1. For instance, the Mirai botnet attack [2], a massive distributed denial-of-service (DDoS) attack carried out on online consumer devices such as IP cameras and home routers. In [14], colluding injected attacks (CIA) via the network physical layer on mobile ad-hoc networks are presented, causing the failure of other legitimate nodes in the network.

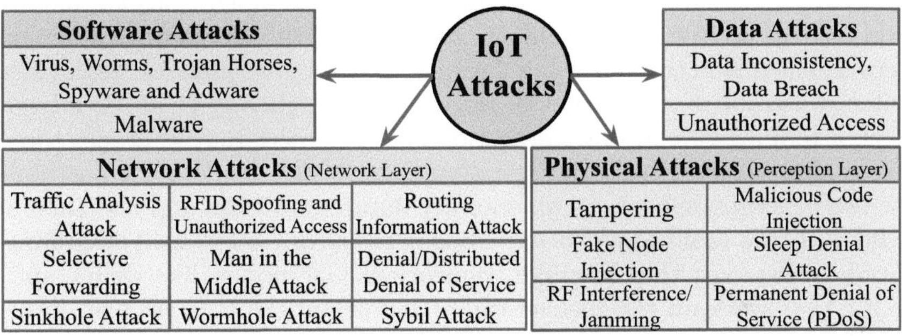

Fig. 1. Attacks on IoT devices/networks due to system vulnerabilities [29].

Several works in the literature have proposed solutions to mitigate the exploitation of software vulnerabilities by various attack methods shown in Fig. 1. Static analysis tools like LCLint [11] and Cppcheck [7] are based on manual code auditing and facilitate the identification of security vulnerabilities in source code during the early phases of software development. LCLint is deficient in identifying several code snippets as problematic, even when they do not constitute genuine issues. Cppcheck also struggles with a conservative approach to minimize false positives making it vulnerable to more false negatives. Smith et al. [31] demonstrated the use of static analysis methods as ineffective, as the interfaces of these tools are often complicated and the software may remain vulnerable to runtime vulnerabilities. Another drawback of these tools is their scalability to large codebases, leading to slower analysis timings for large software projects and deferring feedback in continuous integration environments.

Murshed et al. [21] provide a survey of various machine-learning-based methods for edge devices. In [6], an efficient malicious code detection technique is discussed using N-gram analysis and the SVM. The Random Forest model [35] is used by combining it with misuse detection and anomaly detection to enhance network intrusion and introduce a hybrid intrusion detection system. However, these models also suffer from shortcomings such as feature engineering and scalability to edge devices. Moreover, since edge devices suffer from stringent resource constraints, the machine learning models deployed over these devices should be small with a lower memory footprint and energy consumption.

Multiple studies propose convolutional neural network (CNN) architectures targeting edge devices. VulDeePecker [18] introduces an automated technique for identifying software vulnerabilities via a BLSTM network, a variant of recurrent neural networks that captures the contextual information before and after any given line of code. The model is unsuitable for resource-constrained environments since training and inference in BLSTM networks require considerable computational resources. DP-CNN [17] is another work that uses the CNN model for software vulnerability prediction to produce discriminative features from an Abstract Syntax Tree (AST) that encapsulates the program's semantic and structural information by converting tokens into numerical vectors via word embedding techniques. The drawbacks of this work include the dependence on parameter sensitivity like the filter size, the number of filters, and the number of hidden nodes. Moreover, since it is trained using Java codes, it is infeasible for deployment in resource-constrained environments. Recently, Al-Boghdady et al. [1] introduced iDetect, a tool for vulnerability detection in IoT devices that leverages three different models, CNN, RNN, and Random Forest (RF) to detect vulnerabilities. They also generate dedicated vulnerability datasets to train and test these models. However, the tool has not been tested in resource-constrained environments.

Studies also exist that leverage transformer [33] models like BERT and DistilBERT that work on the mechanism of self-attention. Huang et al. introduce BBVD [13], a BERT-based methodology for vulnerability detection. The study is a comparison of various types of BERT models such as RoBERTa [19], DistilBERT [25], and MobileBERT [32] in vulnerability detection and provides a feasibility study showing that transformers can be deployed for vulnerability detection. Ahmed Bahaa et al. introduce DB-CBIL [4] which is a DistilBERT-based hybrid transformer that uses CNN and BiLSTM to detect vulnerabilities. The study uses Abstract Syntax Tree (AST) code representations and a hybrid DL model that integrates CNN and BiLSTM to detect software vulnerabilities. However, both studies are intended for detecting only application-level vulnerabilities and do not discuss vulnerability detection on resource-constrained devices.

All the works discussed above use pretrained models and fine-tune them for vulnerability classification. They are neither directly intended for the hardware nor showcase any experimental analysis of vulnerability detection in resource-constrained environments. In this work, we propose **VulScan-LT**, a software vulnerability scanning tool designed specifically for operating system softwares and other lightweight applications targeted towards edge devices. VulScan-LT is based on a redesigned DistilBERT transformer model trained on the public

Table 1. Comparison of state-of-the-art solutions with VulScan-LT.

Work	Model(s) Used	Custom Architecture	Vulnerability Detection	Device Implementation
VulDeePecker [18]	CNN	✗	✓	✗
DP-CNN [17]	DNN	✗	✓	✗
iDetect [1]	CNN, RNN, RF	✗	✓	✗
BBVD [13]	DistilBERT	✗	✓	✗
DB-CBIL [4]	DistilBERT	✗	✓	✗
VulScan-LT	**DistilBERT**	✓	✓	✓

releases of four IoT operating systems and the SAR-Dataset [5]. Furthermore, to ensure that the tool has a smaller memory footprint and faster training and inference time, we customize the DistilBERT transformer by reducing the number of encoder layers and the number of attention heads in each encoder layer. In Fig. 2, we present an overall flow of VulScan-LT.

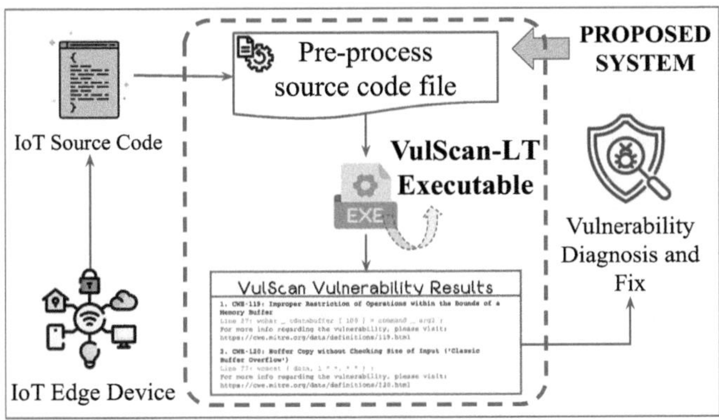

Fig. 2. The overall working methodology of VulScan-LT where the red border highlights the proposed system. (Color figure online)

Next, we perform an end-to-end deployment of VulScan-LT on the Jetson Orin Nano board and conduct experiments on the hardware to evaluate its performance and generate vulnerability reports. We also used the Jetson RT library for memory optimizations to reduce the model size and improve its latency. A detailed hardware implementation is elaborated in Sect. 5. We compare some selected state-of-the-art solutions with VulScan-LT in Table 1 to validate its efficiency for vulnerability detection on edge devices.

Our tool performs vulnerability analysis on the source code of the software as compared to some methodologies that perform this analysis on the Portable Executables (PE)/binaries of the software, as discussed in [27]. VulScan-LT is well-trained and equipped to report any sleeping trojans or untraced loopholes that may get skipped via static analysis, thereby mitigating the possibility of any runtime or zero-day attacks.

The contributions of this paper are summarized below and the novel contributions are highlighted in Fig. 3:

- Similar to [1], we first **develop comprehensive labeled datasets** for both binary and multiclass classifications by combining samples from popular lightweight OSs such as RIOT [3], FreeRTOS [20], Contiki-NG [23], and TinyOS [16]. We also include the Software Assurance Reference Dataset (SARD) [22].
- Next, we propose a novel source code scanning tool, namely, **VulScan-LT**, which is based on a customized DistillBERT transformer model and trained on our comprehensive datasets.
- We achieved accuracy values of **98.73%** in binary classification and **93.57%** in multi-class classification for single encoder layer DistilBERT architecture. The precision and recall values for the same architecture are **92.39%** and **93.45%**, respectively.
- Furthermore, we apply **hardware-specific optimizations** on the custom model to ensure a small memory footprint and carry out an end-to-end deployment of the tool on NVIDIA's Jetson Orin to showcase its compatibility with real-world edge devices.
- We reduce the model size by **30%** post the hardware optimizations and obtain an accuracy of **93.75%**, a precision of **92.74%**, and a recall of **93.31%** when inferencing on the board in multi-class classification.

We have comprehensively compared our work with state-of-the-art solutions and demonstrated the efficiency of VulScan-LT on edge devices. The advantage of this tool over other state-of-the-art solutions like iDetect [1] is its ability to run on edge devices, hence it can provide support for run-time scanning of any suspicious source codes.

The remaining paper is organized as follows: Sect. 2 covers our working methodology, Sect. 3 specifies our experimental setup, Sect. 4 mentions all our results and Sect. 5 elaborates the hardware implementation of the proposed solution. We conclude the paper in Sect. 6.

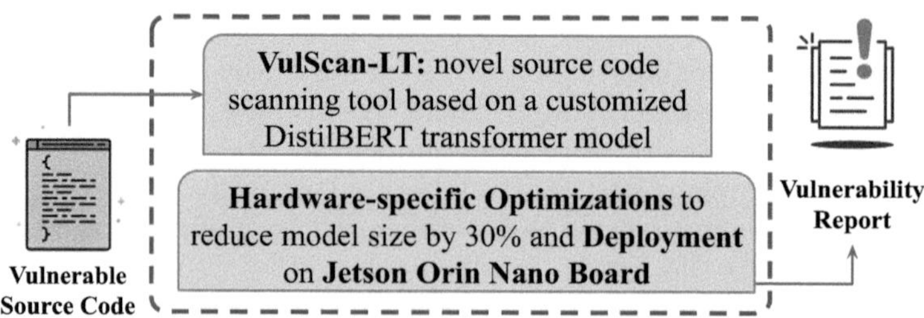

Fig. 3. Blue outline highlights our novel contributions. (Color figure online)

2   Methodology

In this section, we present an in-depth discussion on the design and workflow of VulScan-LT.

2.1   Customized DistilBERT Transformer

The BERT [10] model improves the classification of NLP tasks by enhancing the model's text awareness learning from left to right and right to left. BERT employs an encoder-only architecture unlike the traditional transformer model employing both an encoder and decoder. This ensures more attention towards input sequences rather than generating output sequences. The DistilBERT model [25] is a distilled version of the BERT model, where knowledge distillation from BERT reduces its size by almost 40%. It retains 97% of the language understanding capabilities of the traditional BERT in addition to being almost 60% faster than it [10]. This makes DistilBERT an apt model that can be leveraged to make predictions on resource-constrained devices.

We customize the DistilBERT architecture as shown in Fig. 4. The six-encoder layer architecture of DistilBERT (in purple) is changed and a custom DistilBERT configuration is created which reduces the architecture to a single encoder layer (in green). We explore multiple such configurations where we reduce the encoder layers to 1, 2, and 4. Each encoder layer has a dedicated multi-head attention layer (in blue) containing multiple attention heads. We customize the number of attention heads by changing the number to 4, 8, or 12. We conducted several experiments on these configurations where the number of encoder layers are 1, 2, and 4, and each layer has the number of attention heads as 4, 8, or 12. These experiments with multiple DistilBERT architectures helped us select the best architecture that can be further optimized for hardware deployment and the results are discussed in Sect. 4.

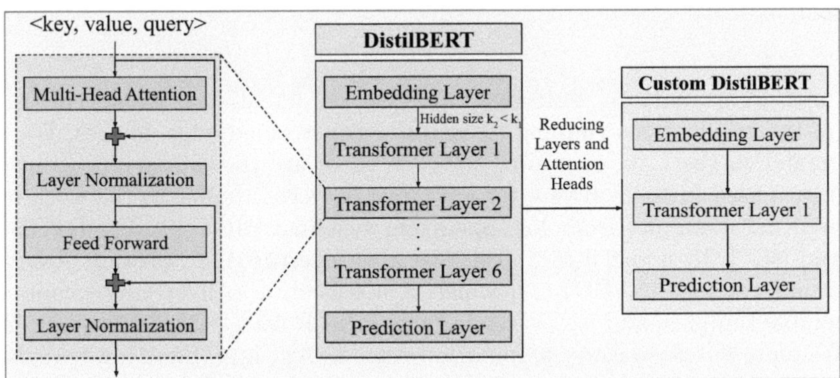

Fig. 4. Reducing encoder layers to create a customized DistilBERT model.

2.2 VulScan-LT Workflow

In this section, we discuss the overall workflow of VulScan-LT in four major stages as highlighted in Fig. 5 (numbered in red):

1. Dataset Preparation
2. Data Pre-Processing
3. Training and Testing
4. Vulnerability Reporting

We perform both binary and multi-class classification using VulScan-LT. Binary classification is carried out to demonstrate the feasibility of vulnerability classification using transformers and is leveraged as a motivational study. Multi-class classification makes the tool comprehensive in vulnerability analysis and reporting.

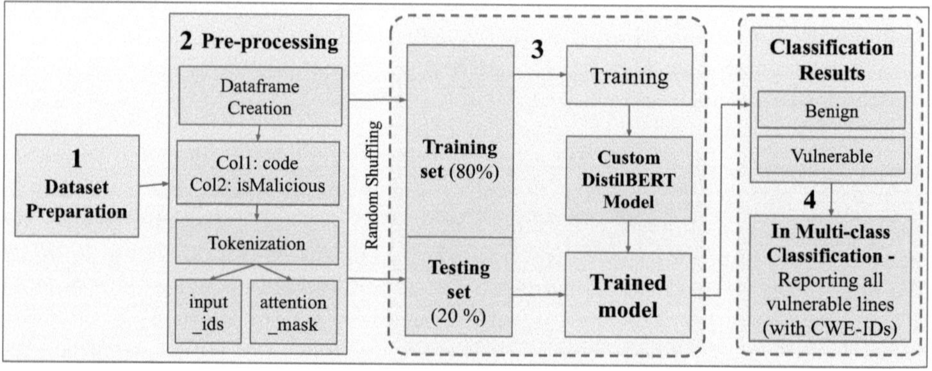

Fig. 5. The overall workflow of VulScan-LT highlighted in four stages. (Color figure online)

Dataset Preparation. VulScan-LT focuses on detecting software vulnerabilities in the applications running on resource-constrained edge devices. We train our model on the C/C++ source codes as these are the primary programming languages used in the software for IoT/edge devices. Similar to the work in [1], we used data samples from IoT operating systems: RIOT [3], FreeRTOS [20], Contiki-NG [23], and TinyOS [16]. We also leverage the Software Assurance Reference Dataset (SARD) [22] which is a collection of test suites containing vulnerable samples, and we particularly use the Juliet C/C++ test suite [26].

We represent the dataset preparation stage using Fig. 6. Firstly, we preprocess the source code files by removing all comments and white spaces. These files are then input to two different Security Analysis Tools (SAT), namely Flawfinder [9] and Rough Auditing Tool for Security (RATS) [28] which scan them to identify the vulnerable lines of code. We create a binary classification dataset by extracting these vulnerable lines and a multi-class classification dataset by extracting the vulnerable line along with its Common Weakness Enumeration ID (CWE-ID). The vulnerable lines extracted from each SAT are combined to create a repository of only vulnerable samples. In this work, benign samples are indistinguishable in the case of binary and multi-class classification. We use only the SAR-Dataset to fetch all benign lines of code (lines not listed as vulnerable by any SAT) and create a repository of only benign samples. These vulnerable and benign samples are combined to form a complete labeled dataset, a snippet of which is shown in Table 2. The vulnerable samples in the binary dataset are labeled as "Vulnerable", and the vulnerable samples in the multi-class dataset are labeled as per their "CWE-ID". The benign samples are labeled as "Benign".

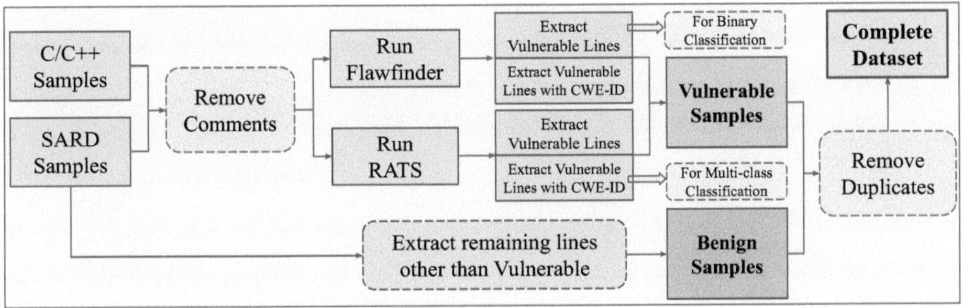

Fig. 6. Outline of the steps involved in the dataset preparation stage.

Table 2. Vulnerability Dataset snippet before preprocessing.

code	malicious (Binary)	malicious (Multi-class)
memcpy(newptr, ptr, chunk.size);	Vulnerable	CWE-120
char pcTaskName[MAX_ TASK_ LEN];	Vulnerable	CWE-119
char buf[10];	Benign	Benign

Data Pre-processing. After preparing the labeled dataset, VulScan-LT further preprocesses it to make it compatible with the customized DistilBERT model's input format. Since the model only operates on numeric labels, the datasets generated in the previous step are incompatible with the model as they contain alphanumeric labels. We encode each such label as a unique numeric integer value. For the binary dataset, the label **"Vulnerable"** is encoded to a numerical value of **1**. For multi-class dataset, the vulnerable labels are encoded using a series of steps outlined in Fig. 7. Multiple vulnerable samples may have the same CWE-ID, indicating that these samples belong to the same type of vulnerability. To encode such labels, which are essentially the same CWE-ID, it is important to identify the number of unique CWE-IDs, otherwise, two same CWE-ID labels may get encoded as two different numeric labels. **36** unique CWE-IDs are identified, implying that all the vulnerable samples in the dataset belong to any one of these 36 types of vulnerabilities. Each of these 36 CWE-ID labels is assigned a unique numeric integer ID, and the vulnerable samples in the multi-class dataset are then assigned these numeric IDs (which are their new encoded labels) according to the vulnerability they belong to. Also, all the **"Benign"** labels are encoded using the numeric integer **0** in both datasets. Table 3 shows a snippet of the pre-processed dataset wherein the previous labels in Table 2 are now encoded as integers.

Table 3. Vulnerability Dataset snippet after preprocessing.

code	malicious (Binary)	malicious (Multi-class)
memcpy(newptr, ptr, chunk.size);	1	5
char pcTaskName[MAX_TASK_LEN];	1	4
char buf[10];	0	0

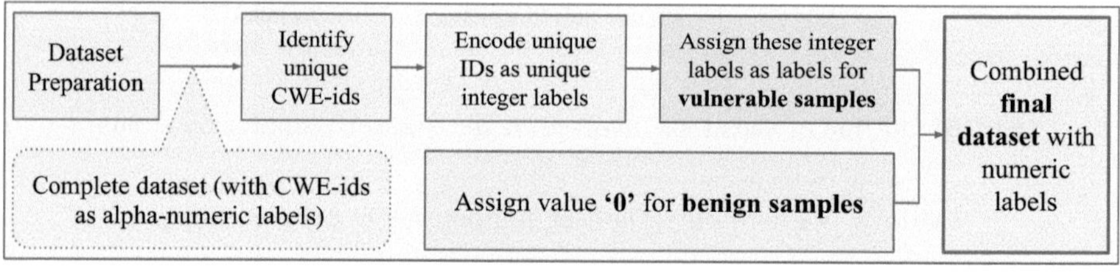

Fig. 7. Data (labels) preprocessing in case of multi-class dataset.

The pre-processed dataset in Table 3 is then tokenized using the DistilBERT 'uncased' tokenizer which converts it into two tensors, the **"input_ids"** which contain the token indices, and the **"attention_masks"**, which give context to the model as to which token to attend to first.

Training and Testing. We have trained the DistilBERT model from scratch on our vulnerability dataset instead of using a pretrained model. The tokenized dataset prepared in the previous stage is divided into the training and testing sets, and the training set is then fed to the model, which initializes its weights, making it learn the relevant features. The trained model is then saved and further validated using the tokenized tensor testing dataset by making predictions on the unseen data. Section 3 highlights the experimental setup and the configuration details of the training and testing phases.

Vulnerability Reporting. We represent the steps involved in reporting software vulnerabilities in both classification types in Fig. 8. The output of the trained model is tensors that envelope the predictions for each line of code the model scans. In the case of binary classification, the predictions are represented in tensor values 'B' and 'V', and in multi-class, these predictions are represented as the values for the 37 classes (one benign (B) class and 36 vulnerable (V) classes). The maximum predicted tensor value is then stored as "P_MAX", which represents the confidence with which the model has made the prediction, hence this P_MAX can be inferred as the class to which the model made the prediction. The actual label index of the maximum predicted value for each tensor is appended to a list "$PREDs$", representing all the predicted targets.

Since the input to the model is tensors, to fetch the actual line of code, the tokenized dataset is decoded. In the decode phase, the *input_ids* and the *attention_masks* in the encoded dataset are used to align the tokens and fetch the original source code line. After decoding, the *PREDs* list is used, where the predictions with index '0' (Benign) are excluded, and the index of vulnerable predictions is used to index into the decoded dataset to fetch the vulnerable line. In binary classification, this fetched line is reported to the user without any additional information. In multi-class, the corresponding CWE-ID for this line (its label) is also decoded and reported, which gives the user more information about the vulnerability. These software vulnerabilities are reported via a dedicated vulnerability report generated by VulScan-LT.

3   Experimental Setup

This section mentions all the configurations, architectures, and values used to create datasets and conduct training, testing, and validations. Our experiments are conducted in Google Colab using the GPU runtime and on the Jetson Orin Nano board, which has an NVIDIA Ampere architecture with 1024 CUDA cores with 8 GB of 128-bit LPDDR5 RAM.

3.1   Dataset Specifications

The four IoT OS and their corresponding release versions used to create vulnerable samples are mentioned in Table 4. The table also mentions the SARD Juliet C/C++ test suite version [26].

The number of vulnerable samples identified by each of the SATs is shown in Table 5. The model is trained on 6,224 vulnerable and 10,000 benign samples, where benign samples are extracted from the SARD test suite [26] only.

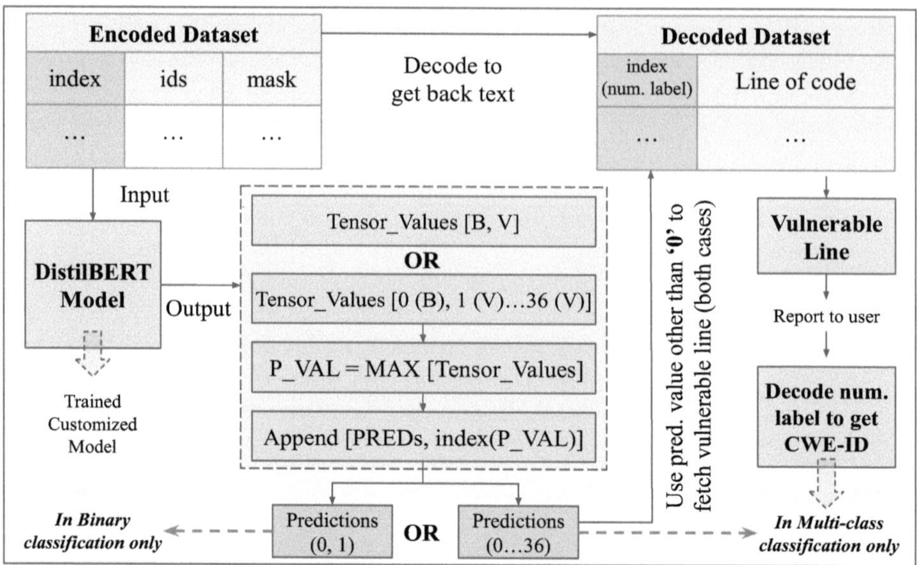

Fig. 8. Steps involved in the vulnerability reporting phase of VulScan-LT.

Table 4. IoT source code and SARD versions used to prepare datasets.

Code Sample	Release
RIOT	2024.04
Contiki-NG	v4.9
Free-RTOS	202212.01
TinyOS	2.1.2.1
Juliet C/C++ Test Suite	1.3

3.2   Training and Testing Specifications

The complete dataset has been divided in the ratio of 80:20, where 80% of the data has been used for training and the rest 20% for testing. All important specifications required in its particular phase are mentioned in Table 6. The *"random_state"* value mentioned in the table is used to sample data randomly while preparing the training and testing sets.

4   Experiments and Results

The custom transformer model architectures used for experiments are shown in Fig. 9 (y-axis labels). We also show the number of total internal layers in each architecture (in red) and the number of trainable parameters (using bars). The number of parameters vary for both binary and multi-class datasets. We

Table 5. Number of vulnerable and benign samples identified by SATs.

SAT Name	Source	Vulnerable
Flawfinder	IoT source code	4828
RATS	IoT source code	741
Flawfinder	SARD	424
RATS	SARD	231

Table 6. Training and Testing specifications.

random_state	200
batch_size	32
Loss Function	Cross-Entropy Loss
Epochs	10

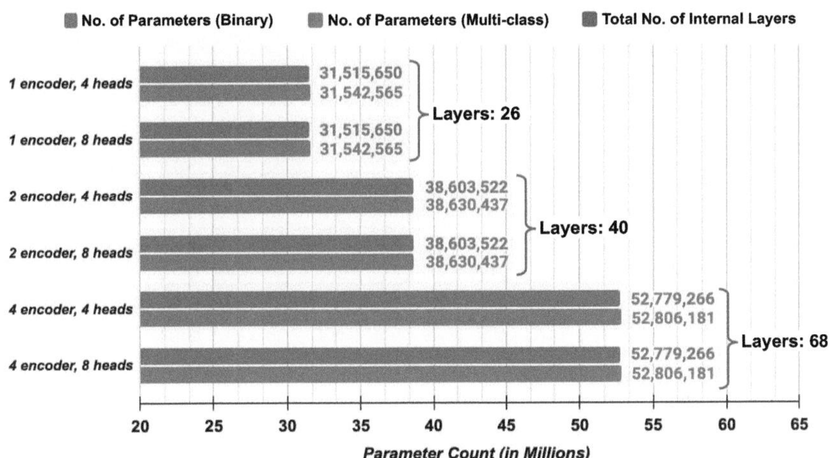

Fig. 9. Varying transformer architectures used for experiments with their corresponding layer and parameter counts.

observe that reducing the number of attention heads in each encoder layer does not impact the total number of internal layers and the number of parameters since the overall output dimension is the same. We validate the performance of these model architectures on various metrics such as Accuracy, Precision, Recall, F1-Score, Model Size, Training, and Inference timings, as discussed further.

4.1 Accuracy Results for Varied Architectures

The accuracy values obtained for multi-class classification on the test dataset are shown in Fig. 10. All the models result in an accuracy of more than 92%, and the model with a **single encoder layer and 12 attention heads** gives a high comparable accuracy of **93.57%** (marked with a green star). The accuracy values in binary classification are shown in Fig. 11. All models result in an accuracy of more than **98%**, and the same model architecture discussed in multi-class (marked with a green star) gives a high comparable accuracy of **98.73%**. In both classifications, these accuracy values are almost equivalent to the accuracy of the models with more encoder layers (like 4 or 6), and we infer that reducing the number of encoder layers does not compromise the performance and is an approach to designing a lightweight transformer. We achieve high accuracy values for vulnerability classification since we train the transformer from scratch, making the model weights and parameters customized for vulnerability classification. Moreover, the heterogeneous nature of our dataset helps the DistilBERT architecture to capture and learn complex vulnerability relationships better than traditional NLP models.

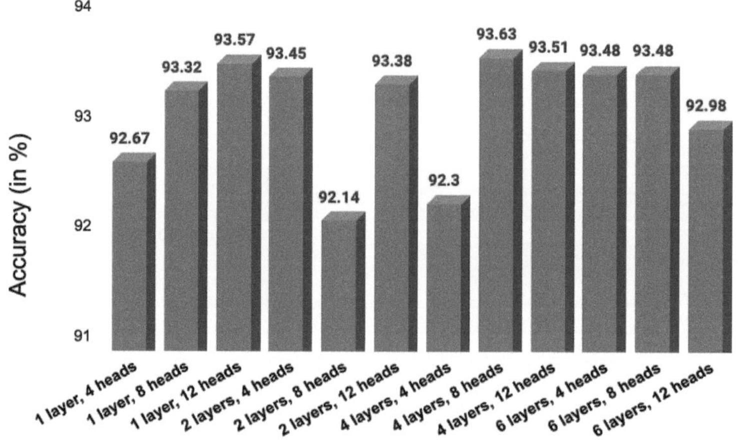

Fig. 10. Accuracy for each model architecture in multi-class classification.

4.2   Precision, Recall, F1-Score and FNR

The results for multi-class classification are highlighted in Fig. 12 and we observe that the same model with **1 encoder layer and 12 attention heads** returns comparable values for **precision** as **92.39%** and **recall** as **93.45%** (marked with a green star). The **F1-Score**, which measures a trade-off between the precision and recall values, stands at **91.96%**. This fares well against the models with 2 or 4 layers having a greater F1-Score but lags either in precision or the recall value. Figure 13 shows the results in binary classification and the same model returns comparable values of **precision** as **98.38%**, **recall** as **98.13%**, and the **F1-Score** as **98.25%**. High precision and recall in both binary and multi-class show that the customized model correctly predicts all the relevant vulnerability

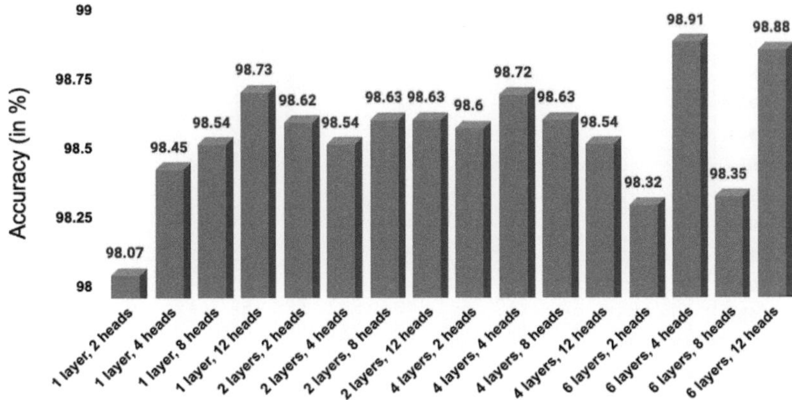

Fig. 11. Accuracy for each model architecture in binary classification.

cases and flags fewer false positives, giving it a significant advantage over the works discussed previously in the literature.

The total number of False Negatives (left) and False Positives (right) that have been classified by each model configuration in binary classification are shown in Fig. 14. A lower False Negative value implies that the number of vulnerabilities the model failed to detect is less. We observe that the number of False Negatives in single encoder layer architecture with 4 attention heads is comparable to the default architecture of six encoder layers. The False Negative Ratio (FNR) measures the proportion of actual vulnerabilities the model fails to detect and is calculated as: $FN/(FN + FP)$. The model with the best comparable accuracy discussed in Sect. 4.1 performs with a **FNR** of **1.86%**. We can also observe that the number of False Positives for the single encoder layer architecture is the least in all configurations compared to the default six-layer architecture. This shows that the number of non-vulnerable instances flagged as vulnerable is the least, hence ensuring reliable performance.

4.3 Memory Footprint Results

The memory footprints of each trained DistilBERT model architecture before hardware optimizations are mentioned in Table 7. We observe that reducing the number of encoder layers significantly reduces the model size, with the model having a single encoder layer only taking **120.3 MB** compared to the default DistilBERT architecture (6 encoder layers), which takes 255.5 MB. It still ensures an optimal benchmark performance, as discussed in Sect. 4.1.

4.4 Training and Inference Timings

The training time and inference time required by each architecture in multi-class classification are shown Fig. 15. The training and inference timings follow an

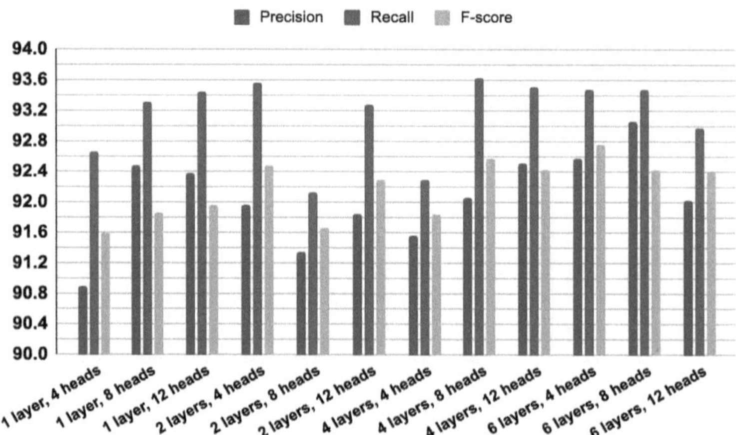

Fig. 12. Precision, Recall, F1-Score for each model in multi-class classification, model with 1 encoder layer fares well against the models with 2 or 4 layers.

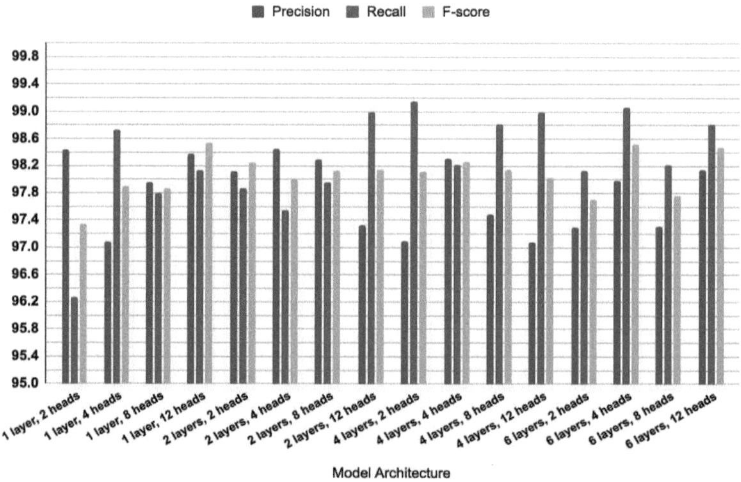

Fig. 13. Precision, Recall, F1-Score for each model in binary classification, model with 1 encoder layer fares well against the models with 2 or 4 layers.

identical trend for binary classification as well. We observe that more the encoder layers, more is the time required to train the model and make vulnerability predictions. This is due to the increased number of parameters that need to be trained with each increased encoder layer, as shown previously in Fig. 9. **1 encoder layer architecture** can make predictions in less than **6 s** in multi-class and in less than **5 s** in binary classification (test dataset).

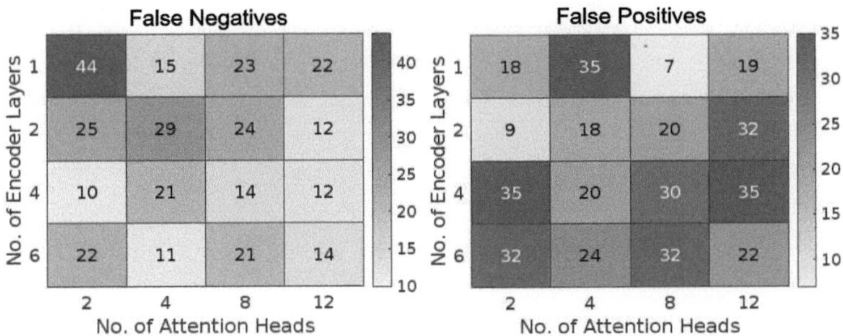

Fig. 14. No. of FN (left) and FP (right) obtained in binary classification.

Table 7. Memory taken by each architecture (before optimization).

DistilBERT Architecture	Model Size (in MB)
1 Encoder Layer	120.3
2 Encoder Layers	147.4
4 Encoder Layers	201.5
6 Encoder Layers (default)	255.5

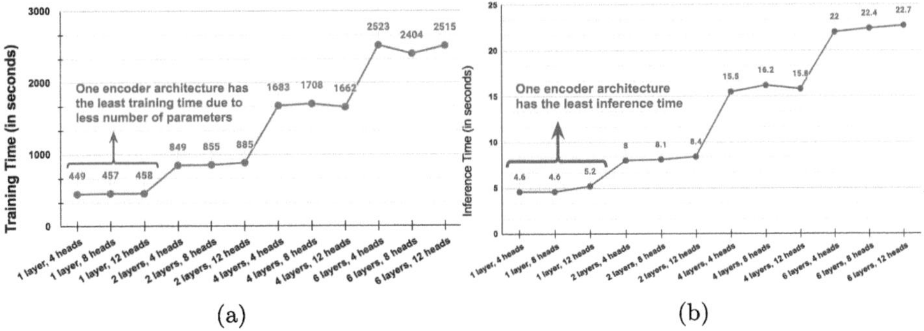

Fig. 15. (a) Training time for each model architecture in multi-class classification. (b) Inference time for each model architecture in multi-class classification.

4.5 Comparison with Other Models

VulScan-LT's custom DistilBERT model performs better than the software vulnerability classification models discussed in iDetect [1] for both binary and multiclass classification. We conduct experiments using iDetect's publicly available code on GitHub for binary and multi-class classification and our labeled dataset. The accuracy, training time, and inference time of our model are compared with the models discussed in [1] and are highlighted in Fig. 16. VulScan-LT performs with a higher accuracy value than the CNN and RNN models in both types of classifications. It also trains faster than the other models. The inference time cited in the figure is for multi-class classification. VulScan-LT's inference performance includes the time required for comprehensive vulnerability reporting, an add-on feature provided by our tool compared to other solutions in [1]. Other works discussed in Table 1 are not used for comparison with VulScan-LT since the working methodology and the dataset used are totally different. Moreover, these works are not focused on C/C++-based vulnerabilities, hence only iDetect [1] is used for comparison.

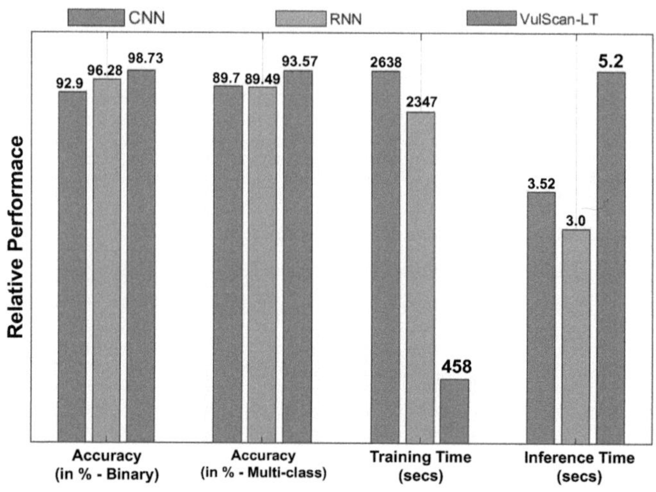

Fig. 16. Accuracy (in %), Training and Inference Time (in secs) comparison with other deep-learning-based models discussed in [1].

5 Hardware Implementation

We demonstrate the real-world compatibility of VulScan-LT with edge devices by performing experiments and inferences on the Jetson Orin Nano board. We achieved a maximum **accuracy** of **93.75%**, an **F1-score** of **91.69%**, a **recall** of **93.31%**, and a **precision** of **92.74%** in multi-class classification when inferencing on the board. The major optimizations on the model are primarily intended to reduce its **memory footprint**. Figure 17 represents the workflow of how we optimize the model and carry out inference on it. We first convert our trained PyTorch model to an intermediate ONNX representation and then optimize it using the TensorRT library, where the following optimizations are carried out:

Floating Point Conversion. Here, all the parameters and activations are dropped from the floating point 32 precision down to floating point 16 precision to reduce the model size.

Layer Fusions. Here, TensorRT fusions fuse the layers that perform similar computations on a routine basis and improve the internal computations of the model, such as reading and writing tensor data more efficiently.

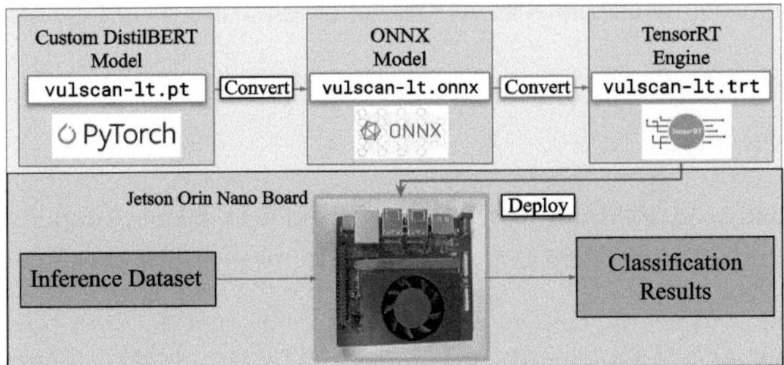

Fig. 17. Deployment of the custom model on Jetson Orin Nano board.

The model sizes obtained after performing the optimizations are represented in Table 8, and the model with the best results in Sect. 4 has a memory footprint of only **63.2 MB**, making it lightweight for edge devices.

Table 8. Memory footprint of each model after optimization

Model Architecture	Model Size (in MB)
1 Encoder Layer	**63.2**
2 Encoder Layers	90.3
4 Encoder Layers	144.4
6 Encoder Layers (default)	198.5

6   Conclusions

We propose a novel solution, VulScan-LT, which is a comprehensive vulnerability scanning tool to detect vulnerable lines of code in the software for resource-constrained edge devices. We performed empirical analysis with multiple Distil-BERT model architectures by changing the number of layers and the number of attention heads to achieve a best-case accuracy of 93.57% in multi-class classification and 98.73% in binary classification by the model with 1 encoder layer and 12 attention heads. Moreover, we have optimized and implemented the model on the Jetson Orin Nano board to show its compatibility with resource-constrained edge devices and have reduced its memory footprint by almost 30%.

Acknowledgments. This work was supported by research grant-in-aid Ministry of Information & Technology (MEITY) India for the project titled Design & Development of Advanced Forensics Data Analytics Tool (Sanction order No. AAA-22/14/2022-CSD).

This work was supported in part by the NYUAD Center for CyberSecurity (CCS), funded by Tamkeen under the NYUAD Research Institute Award G1104.

References

1. Al-Boghdady, A., El-Ramly, M., Wassif, K.: idetect for vulnerability detection in internet of things operating systems using machine learning. Sci. Rep. **12**(1), 17086 (2022)
2. Antonakakis, M., et al.: Understanding the mirai botnet. In: 26th USENIX Security Symposium (USENIX Security 2017), pp. 1093–1110 (2017)
3. Baccelli, E., Hahm, O., Günes, M., Wählisch, M., Schmidt, T.C.: RIOT OS: towards an OS for the internet of things. In: 2013 IEEE Conference on Computer Communications Workshops (INFOCOM WKSHPS), pp. 79–80. IEEE (2013)
4. Bahaa, A., Kamal, A.E.R., Fahmy, H., Ghoneim, A.S.: DB-CBIL: a DistilBert-based transformer hybrid model using CNN and BiLSTM for software vulnerability detection. IEEE Access (2024)
5. Black, P.: SARD: a software assurance reference dataset (1970)
6. Choi, J., Kim, H., Choi, C., Kim, P.: Efficient malicious code detection using n-gram analysis and SVM. In: 2011 14th International Conference on Network-Based Information Systems, pp. 618–621 (2011). https://doi.org/10.1109/NBiS.2011.104
7. Marjamäki, D.: Cppcheck (2007). https://cppcheck.sourceforge.io/
8. Darshan, K., Anandakumar, K.: A comprehensive review on usage of internet of things (IoT) in healthcare system. In: 2015 International Conference on Emerging Research in Electronics, Computer Science and Technology (ICERECT), pp. 132–136. IEEE (2015)
9. Wheeler, D.A.: Flawfinder (2015). https://dwheeler.com/flawfinder/
10. Devlin, J., Chang, M.W., Lee, K., Toutanova, K.: Bert: pre-training of deep bidirectional transformers for language understanding. arXiv preprint arXiv:1810.04805 (2018)
11. Evans, D., Guttag, J., Horning, J., Tan, Y.M.: LCLint: a tool for using specifications to check code. ACM SIGSOFT Softw. Eng. Notes **19**(5), 87–96 (1994)
12. Hatton, M.: The IoT in 2030: which applications account for the biggest chunk of the $1.5 trillion opportunity? (2020)
13. Huang, W., Lin, S., Chen, L.: BBVD: a BERT-based method for vulnerability detection. Int. J. Adv. Comput. Sci. Appl. **13**(12) (2022)
14. Kandah, F., Singh, Y., Zhang, W., Wang, C.: Mitigating colluding injected attack using monitoring verification in mobile ad-hoc networks. Secur. Commun. Netw. **6**(4), 539–547 (2013)
15. Krasniqi, X., Hajrizi, E.: Use of IoT technology to drive the automotive industry from connected to full autonomous vehicles. IFAC-PapersOnLine **49**(29), 269–274 (2016)
16. Levis, P., et al.: Tinyos: an operating system for sensor networks. Ambient Intell. 115–148 (2005)

17. Li, J., He, P., Zhu, J., Lyu, M.R.: Software defect prediction via convolutional neural network. In: 2017 IEEE International Conference on Software Quality, Reliability and Security (QRS), pp. 318–328. IEEE (2017)
18. Li, Z., et al.: Vuldeepecker: a deep learning-based system for vulnerability detection. arXiv preprint arXiv:1801.01681 (2018)
19. Liu, Y., et al.: Roberta: a robustly optimized BERT pretraining approach (2019). https://arxiv.org/abs/1907.11692
20. Melot, N.: Study of an operating system: Freertos. CAPÍTULO XVIII **115** (2009)
21. Murshed, M.G.S., Murphy, C., Hou, D., Khan, N., Ananthanarayanan, G., Hussain, F.: Machine learning at the network edge: a survey. ACM Comput. Surv. **54**(8) (2021). https://doi.org/10.1145/3469029
22. National Institute of Standards and Technology: NIST (2024). https://samate.nist.gov/SARD
23. Oikonomou, G., Duquennoy, S., Elsts, A., Eriksson, J., Tanaka, Y., Tsiftes, N.: The Contiki-NG open source operating system for next generation IoT devices. SoftwareX **18**, 101089 (2022)
24. Quadri, S.A.I., Sathish, P.: IoT based home automation and surveillance system. In: 2017 International Conference on Intelligent Computing and Control Systems (ICICCS), pp. 861–866. IEEE (2017)
25. Sanh, V., Debut, L., Chaumond, J., Wolf, T.: Distilbert, a distilled version of bert: smaller, faster, cheaper and lighter. arXiv preprint arXiv:1910.01108 (2019)
26. SARD: Juliet C/C++ Test Suite (2017). https://samate.nist.gov/SARD/test-suites/112
27. Schaad, A., Binder, D.: Deep-learning-based vulnerability detection in binary executables. In: International Symposium on Foundations and Practice of Security, pp. 453–460. Springer (2022)
28. Secure Software Inc.: Rough Auditing Tool for Security (RATS) (2009). https://code.google.com/archive/p/rough-auditing-tool-for-security/
29. Sengupta, J., Ruj, S., Das Bit, S.: A comprehensive survey on attacks, security issues and blockchain solutions for IoT and IIoT. J. Netw. Comput. Appl. **149**, 102481 (2020). https://doi.org/10.1016/j.jnca.2019.102481. https://www.sciencedirect.com/science/article/pii/S1084804519303418
30. Shahinzadeh, H., Moradi, J., Gharehpetian, G.B., Nafisi, H., Abedi, M.: IoT architecture for smart grids. In: 2019 International Conference on Protection and Automation of Power System (IPAPS), pp. 22–30. IEEE (2019)
31. Smith, J., Do, L.N.Q., Murphy-Hill, E.: Why can't johnny fix vulnerabilities: a usability evaluation of static analysis tools for security. In: Sixteenth Symposium on Usable Privacy and Security (SOUPS 2020), pp. 221–238. USENIX Association (2020). https://www.usenix.org/conference/soups2020/presentation/smith
32. Sun, Z., Yu, H., Song, X., Liu, R., Yang, Y., Zhou, D.: Mobilebert: a compact task-agnostic BERT for resource-limited devices. arXiv preprint arXiv:2004.02984 (2020)
33. Vaswani, A., et al.: Attention is all you need. Adv. Neural Inf. Process. Syst. **30** (2017)
34. Vilandrie, A.: Company. 2017. are your company's iot devices secure. IoT Security White Paper, pp. 1–11 (2017)
35. Zhang, J., Zulkernine, M.: A hybrid network intrusion detection technique using random forests. In: First International Conference on Availability, Reliability and Security (ARES 2006), pp. 8–pp. IEEE (2006)

Enhanced Hardware Trojan Detection with XGBoost Graph Learning: A Glass Box Approach

C. Sneha[✉] and M. Nirmala Devi

Hardware Security Research Lab, Department of Electronics and Communication Engineering, PES University, Bangalore 560085, Karnataka, India
PES1PD24EC009@pesuonline.onmicrosoft.com, nirmaladevim@pes.edu

Abstract. The integrity of modern electronic systems is increasingly being endangered by malignant mutations which are commonly referred to as Hardware Trojans (HTs). Detection of such threats is a complex challenge due to the stealthy nature of Trojans, the diversity of circuit topologies and the opacity of Machine Learning (ML) classifiers. This paper presents an explainable Machine Learning-based framework that incorporates three complementary categories of features such as structural features, Graph Centrality Measures (GCMs) extracted from directed graph transformations and Functional features from gate-level netlist to detect Trojans. The proposed methodology evaluates the combined influence of each feature category on detection accuracy and interpretability, unlike existing approaches that analyze them in isolation or consider only a subset of these feature groups. The eXtreme Gradient Boosting (XGBoost) model is employed as the classifier, and three feature ranking strategies such as SHapley Additive explanations (SHAP), Local Interpretable Model-agnostic Explanations (LIME), and XGBoost's intrinsic importance are utilized for their ability to rank features there by indicating the most influential ones and provide transparent insights into the ML model's behaviour as they are black-box in nature. Filter-based ranking-driven feature selection technique is used to further eliminate redundancy. Beyond conventional evaluation metrics, the study also evaluates feature ranking effectiveness using fidelity, simplicity, stability and coverage, collectively known as eXplainable AI (XAI) metrics marking the first application of such metrics in Trojan detection. Experimental validation on sequential Trust-HUB benchmark circuits demonstrates the efficacy of the proposed approach that establishes a principled path towards explainable and reliable HT detection.

Keywords: Hardware Trojans · XAI metrics · Heterogeneous features · Machine Learning · Feature ranking and selection

1 Introduction

The foundation of digital trust is built not only on the software reliability but also on the robustness of the underlying hardware. Over the decades, circuits

C. Karfa et al. (Eds.): SPACE 2025, LNCS 16406, pp. 318–335, 2026.
https://doi.org/10.1007/978-3-032-16342-4_18

have become the invisible backbone of the critical infrastructures and preserving their integrating has now become an essential factor in ensuring hardware security. The globalization of semiconductor design has increased the dependency on third-party intellectual property (3PIP) vendors, offshore fabrication units and external verification services which has further complicated this challenge. Such a distributed supply chain in order to enable rapid innovation and cost efficiency, created opportunities for the insertion of stealthy alterations into the hardware known as Hardware Trojans [1].

HTs consists of a small trigger and a payload that blends with the original design. The trigger remains dormant for a long period and only gets activated under certain rare conditions, while payload produces the consequences of Trojan activation which can range from sensitive information leakage to system disruption. Hardware Trojans are concealed, tiny, have very small footprint when compared to the overall design, thereby making them extremely difficult to detect using traditional verification methods.

Detecting HTs at the gate-level netlist using Machine learning (ML) classifiers, particularly ensemble-based models [2,3] have seen a tremendous runway of success owing to their ability to learn subtle patterns in circuit features that distinguish infected designs from clean ones. However, even after achieving high detection accuracy, the ML-based approaches for Hardware Trojan Detection (HTD) still face persistent challenges. A crucial technical factor in ML models is the selection of feature representation as they are used to train the model. Structural features, functional attributes and GCMs each with their own significance have been investigated in prior studies either individually or in pairs, a systematic integration of all three categories has not yet been extensively examined. Such integration has the potential to capture complementary information of the circuit characteristics relevant to Trojan behaviour. Another issue lies in interpretability. Machine Learning models are opaque in nature thereby limiting their trustworthiness in security-sensitive applications. Furthermore, quantitative evaluation of explanation quality of many techniques used for interpretability has not been incorporated into existing frameworks. They offer an objective method of evaluating reliability and completeness of explanations which means that the interpretability techniques that are employed are not merely illustrative but verifiable. Finally, feature selection strategies often rely on domain-expert based knowledge, whereas there is a need for systematic approaches for more rigorous mechanisms for identifying the most informative feature subsets.

This paper addresses the above-mentioned challenges by proposing a novel supervised explainable ML framework for HTD at gate-level netlist that integrates heterogeneous feature sets, advanced feature ranking with selection and principled evaluation of explanation quality. The key contributions of this paper can be summarized as follows,

- **Unified feature space**: A combination of structural features and GCMs extracted from Data Flow Graph (DFG) after the conversion from the gate-level netlist and functional features derived directly from the netlist is considered to capture diverse aspects of circuit behaviour. Such graph-based approaches enable node-level HT localization and also help to capture the signal flow so that feature generality and robustness across different Trojan types are enhanced.

- **Explainable ranking strategies**: SHAP, LIME and XGBoost inbuilt importance are comparatively analyzed to guide both feature reduction and provide interpretable insights into model decisions making it a glass-box approach.
- **Systematic feature elimination**: A hybrid filter-based ranking driven Feature Selection Method (FSM) is designed while ensuring deterministic and interpretable feature reduction supported by statistical confirmation.
- **Quantitative explainability evaluation**: XAI metrics such as fidelity, simplicity, stability, and coverage are introduced to evaluate the quality of feature ranking and enhance trust in ML-driven HT detection.
- The proposed framework is validated on Trust-HUB benchmark circuits using XGBoost classifier to demonstrates its generality and effectiveness.

2   Backround and Related Work

Hardware Trojan Detection has been approached through wide spectrum of methodologies where each technique reflects the technological context and design complexity of its time. The evolution of the HTD approaches shows the increasing complexity of the integrated circuits and also reflects the growing globalization of semiconductor manufacturing.

Earlier approaches to detect Trojans were rule-based where they relied on deterministic checks and activation of rare events. MERO [4] attempted to identify malicious entities by generating test patterns that excites rarely activated signals but the scalability of this approach was limited due to exhaustive test generation for larger, real-world circuits. Ref. [5] presented a formal-verification based framework where HTs are identified and removed by checking the functional equivalence between an untrusted implementation and a trusted reference circuit indicating the framework's dependency on golden reference. Since Trojans are stealthy in nature, they exploit rare functional triggers which may remain undetected under limited test or equivalence conditions. Further, Structural reasoning was explored in FANCI [6] where Boolean influence is utilized and signals with negligible influence were labelled as potentially malicious. The technique overcomes the scalability issue but it struggled to separate benign low-activity logic from malicious triggers. Side-channel analysis (SCA) based methods such as [7] leveraged deviation in the physical signatures such as power, delay or electromagnetic emission to detect Trojans but SCA techniques suffered from process variations and measurement noise.

As circuits become more intricate, machine learning emerged as a powerful alternative which framed HTD as a classification task and emerged to automate detection by learning discriminative patterns from circuit features based on connectivity, topology or switching statistics. Many ML-based research works focused on Structural features which describes the design-level characteristics of the circuits. Hasegawa et al. [1] extracted 51 structural features from gate-level netlists out of which 11 features were filtered using importance analysis through

Randon Forest classifier. Functional features which define the behaviour of the circuit during operation is considered in the form of SCOAP measures (Controllability and Observability) in [8] where k-means clustering is used to distinguish Trojan gates from normal gates. However, [9] emphasised that structural features alone cannot detect all Trojans and fails to identify always on-Trojans but can detect nets with low SCOAP measures, on the other hand SCOAP Measures succeeds in pointing out always-on trojans but fail to detect low SCOAP HT nets. Therefore [9] projects the combination of structural and functional features-based HT detection using Light Gradient Boosting model for classification. Ref. [10] considers both structural features and graph-based features known as Graph Centrality Measures, where the features are ranked using SHAP. The result of the research shows that most of the top ranked influential features are Graph Centrality Measures indicating its significance in detecting Trojans. Building upon SHAP-based interpretability, [11] introduced a Shapley Ensemble Boosting framework that combines multiple weak learners to improve detection accuracy and robustness while simultaneously providing feature-level explanations through Shapley value analysis. This ensemble-based approach enhances both performance and interpretability thereby addressing the overfitting limitations of single-model classifiers. In conclusion, all three different categories of features have their own importance in HT detection. Many ML-based frameworks either adopt heuristic approaches for selection of features relying on domain-based expert knowledge [12] which are not reliable and may introduce bias or methodical techniques such as SHAP but neither of those approaches attempt to address the interpretability of the black-box ML model. Recently, [13] proposed SALTY, an explainable AI-guided structural analysis framework for hardware Trojan detection, where model interpretability is leveraged not just for feature ranking but also to guide structural reasoning. This represents an important step towards integrating XAI principles directly into HTD pipelines.

In light of these limitations, we propose a novel unified HTD framework that integrates structural, functional and graph-based features with further employing three feature ranking strategies (SHAP, LIME, XGBoost in-built ranking) which also provide explainability for the ML model's predictions and a principled automated approach for feature selection. Most notably, we introduce the use of eXplainable AI (XAI) metrics to quantitatively assess the quality of model explanations thereby bridging the gap between performance and trustworthiness in ML-based hardware Trojan detection.

3   Proposed Methodology

The proposed framework for Hardware Trojan detection integrates a unified feature space, multiple feature ranking techniques for comparison, systematic feature selection approach and explainable AI (XAI) metrics into a pipeline. The proposed methodology is organized into four integrated phases namely circuit abstraction, feature space construction, feature ranking, selection and classifier (XGBoost) training with explanation validation. All the mentioned phases are elaborated in the following sub-sections.

3.1   Circuit Abstraction

To begin with, for every considered gate-level netlist $N = (S, W)$ where S denotes signals/wires and W denotes physical interconnections (drivers $\rightarrow$ loads). We construct a Directed Flow Graph (DFG) which is a directed graph $D = (V, E_d)$, where each node $v \in V$ represents a signal/wire $s \in S$ and each directed edge $(u \rightarrow v) \in E_d$ represents signal flow from the driver of u to a load that induces v. This signal-centric graph captures propagation and reconvergence patterns independent of gate primitives and enables node-level HT localization which means that the classifier predicts for each signal node, whether it is Trojan-affected thereby identifying the exact nets flagged as infected or clean.

3.2   Feature Engineering

Three categories of features known as Structural features, Graph Centrality Measures and Functional features each with their own significance as described in Sect. 2 are extracted. As mentioned earlier structural and graph-based features are extracted from the DFG representation of each benchmark circuit generated in the previous step and functional attributes are obtained directly from the netlist.

Graph Centrality Measures (GCM) F_g. Trojan infected nets frequently exploit critical communication points within a circuit to maximize their impact while minimizing detectability at the same time. Centrality measures quantifies each signal node importance under different graph-theoretic principles. These metrics allow identification of structurally influential signals that may serve as Trojan triggers or propagation points. 11 different GCMs namely Betweenness Centrality, Hub Centrality, Eigen Vector Centrality, Load Centrality, Clustering Centrality, Degree Centrality, Closeness Centrality, PageRank, Authority Centrality, Harmonic Centrality, Katz Centrality as defined in [14] are considered.

Structural Features F_s. Hardware Trojans often manifest through alterations in the circuit structure therefore structural features are considered to be critical as they capture the topology and connectivity profile of the design. These features highlight deviations in circuit organization that may arise from malicious modifications by identifying how signals are being organized and propagated. Features such as levels which is the hierarchical depth of a node in the circuit measured as the distance from primary inputs and Connectivity – The degree of interconnection of a node quantified through in-degree and out-degree are considered. Additional features such as minimum distance from the Primary Input (PI) and Primary Output (PO), Logical Gate Fan-ins_4 (LGFi_4), Logical Gate Fan-ins_5 (LGFi_5), In_FlipFlop_4, Out_FlipFlop_3, Out_FlipFlop_4, In_ Loop_4, Out_Loop_5, Out_Nearest_Multiplexer, Out_Nearest_FlipFlop wh- ich are mentioned in [1] are also considered.

Functional Features F_f. Controllability (CC/SC) and Observability (CO/SO) which are collectively known as SCOAP Measures of each signal in the netlist is computed as described in [15] under this category. Beyond structural modifications Trojans can alter the dynamic behaviour of circuits and these measures characterize how easily signals can be controlled or observed at the output. Trojan nets are often integrated in the regions of low controllability or observability as a result of which functional features serve as an essential layer to capture behavioural anomalies not directly evident from structure alone.

The combined feature matrix is defined as,

$$F = F_s \cup F_g \cup F_f \tag{1}$$

Altogether, 30 features are extracted across the three categories—structural, graph centrality, and functional—capturing the circuit's topology, key signal interactions and functional behaviour in a comprehensive way.

3.3   Dataset Creation and Balancing

All extracted features from each considered netlists are stored in tabular form. A concatenated dataset, where features (structural, graph centrality measures, functional features) extracted from all circuits are combined for global training and testing. For the concatenated dataset, a 70–30 train–test split is applied with the training set further divided into 90% training and 10% validation. The validation set supports early stopping to prevent overfitting and the entire training dataset is used to train the Machine-learning model. The test dataset is used to only validate the trained model and is kept isolated throughout training. Since Trojan-infected nets are much fewer than Trojan-free nets the data is highly imbalanced. Such imbalance makes the learning process to be skewed towards the majority class which may cause the classifier to misidentify rare Trojan instances. To address this, SMOTE-Tomek Links [16] technique is applied on the training data. where SMOTE generates synthetic Trojan samples to balance the classes while Tomek Links remove borderline samples to refine class separation as a result of which cleaner and balanced dataset is generated for training.

3.4   Classifier

Once the dataset is ready, the next step is to train a Machine-Learning model on them. This work employs the eXtreme Gradient Boosting (XGBoost) model as a classifier due to its ability to handle high-dimensional tabular features, capture complex non-linear relationships, and provide inherent feature importance measures that support interpretability. The model builds an ensemble of boosted decision trees trained sequentially where each tree is built to rectify the errors caused by the previous ones. It also consists of hyperparameters, tuning of which governs the trade-off between model complexity, generalization and training efficiency. The key parameters considered are n_estimators, max_depth, learning_rate, colsample_bytree, subsample, gamma, reg_alpha, reg_lamda, scale_pos_weight and min_child_weight where RandomizedSearchCV strategy is employed to tune those parameters, thereby generating the best-fit model. After constructing the datasets, balancing and training the XGBoost classifier with tuned hyperparameters to obtain the best-fit model which is subsequently employed to perform feature ranking and selection.

3.5   Feature Ranking and Selection

Feature Ranking Techniques. High dimensional feature sets often contain redundant or weakly informative attributes which increases the computational complexity and conceal the discriminative patterns which are required to detect Trojan accurately. Feature ranking techniques are used to address such issues where they systematically arrange the features based on their contribution towards the classification result. Beyond efficiency and predictive generalization, the feature ranking also aids explainability by explicitly revealing which features the model relies upon for Trojan detection, thereby providing concrete insights into the behavioural cues the model associates with HT presence. The following ranking strategies are considered,

XGBoost Feature Importance - In this approach, the most influential features are quantified directly from the ensemble of decision trees generated during the training process. The evaluation metric adopted in this work is called gain, which reflects the improvement in accuracy or reduction in loss brought by a feature when it is used to split the data in a decision tree. The overall importance of feature f_j is computed by summing the gain across all splits where f_j is used,

$$I(f_j) = \sum_{\text{splits } s \text{ using } f_j} \text{Gain}_s \tag{2}$$

Since the ranking is extracted from the classifier itself, it provides a global and model-specific ranking which is consistent with the classifier's training dynamics.

SHapley Additive exPlanations (SHAP) - SHAP interprets feature importance through cooperative game theory [17] where each feature is viewed as a player who is contributing to the model's prediction. The features contribution is evaluated by a metric called Shapley value which is computed as the marginal change in prediction when the feature is added to different subsets of the feature space. SHAP gives both global and local rankings. It identifies the most influential features across the dataset with the former and it defines the contribution of each feature to individual predictions with the latter.

Local Interpretable Model-agnostic Explanations (LIME) - This method which targets local behaviour of the underlying model, builds a locally explainable surrogate model around a particular instance [18]. For a sample i, the method generates perturbed neighbours weighted by a locality kernel π_i and fits a linear model l to approximate the black-box classifier m. The optimization is defined as,

$$\xi(i) = \arg\min_{l \in G} \mathcal{L}(m, l, \pi_i) + \Omega(l), \tag{3}$$

where L is the measure of fidelity of the surrogate of the original model and $\Omega(g)$ is the measure of complexity to maintain the balance of interpretability. Once the features are ranked independently using three different feature ranking strategies generating an ordered list from most influential to weak informative features,

$$R^{(m)} = \{f_1, f_2, \ldots, f_n\}, \quad m \in \{\text{SHAP}, \text{LIME}, \text{XGB}\} \tag{4}$$

Filter-Based Ranking-Driven Feature Selection Method. A filter-based feature selection method is designed which integrates feature importance rankings $R^{(m)}$ where it prunes the features using thresholds derived from ranking distributions. For each of the three different ranking strategies (XGBoost, SHAP, LIME), the procedure followed is as given below:

1. **Normalization of Importance scores:** Raw importance scores (gain for XGBoost, mean absolute SHAP values and average absolute LIME weights) are normalized into (0,1) percentiles.
2. **Filter Rules (Rank-Driven):** Three feature rank-driven filters are applied,
   - **Percentile Cutoff:** Retain features with normalized importance $\geq p_{thresh}$.
   - **Cumulative Contribution:** Retain features until cumulative importance $\geq c_{thresh}$.
   - **Elbow Detection:** Identify the knee point in the sorted importance curve and then retain the features above it
3. **Correlation Pruning:** Highly correlated features ($r \geq r_{thresh}$) are pruned by retaining the higher-ranked features only in the obtained feature importance list from the previous step.
4. **Confirmation Statistics:** Mutual Information, ANOVA F-value and Spearman correlation with the target are computed for both retained and pruned features, not to drive selection but to validate the pruning decision.

This ensures that pruning decisions are deterministic, ranking-based and interpretable, while statistical metrics are used for confirmation and reporting. This process is repeated across the three considered feature ranking techniques to obtained their respective refined subsets.

$$F^* \subseteq F \tag{5}$$

Then each refined subset of features F^* is used to train the XGBoost classifier $C : F^* \rightarrow \{0, 1\}$ independently where labels corresponds to Trojan-free or Trojan-infected nets respectively. The trained classifiers are evaluated with the test dataset which remained isolated during the entire training process using standard performance measures (see Sect. 4) along with the comparison study across different ranking strategies.

3.6 eXplanation AI (XAI) Metrics

The integration of feature ranking methods into HTD will improve classification performance but at the same time it also raises the question of how reliable and interpretable these explanations are. In order to tackle this the eXplainable Artificial Intelligence (XAI) metrics are utilized where they provide a way to define the quality of explanations produced by different ranking strategies. They are meant to evaluate the consistency, comprehensibility and reliability of an explanation. In this study, four complementary XAI metrics are considered such as Fidelity, Simplicity, Stability and Coverage as defined in the Table 1 following the conceptual framework proposed by [19], with the definitions adapted to the specific context of hardware Trojan detection. Together, these metrics ensure that the selected features enhance the Trojan detection and also provide transparent and consistent interpretability addressing the growing demand for explainable machine learning in hardware security. To the best of our knowledge, such quantitative evaluation of explanation quality has not been incorporated into HTD so far marking a novel contribution of this study.

Table 1. Definitions and equations of the selected XAI metrics.

Metric	Definition and Equation	Variables
Stability (Cosine Similarity)	Measures robustness of explanations by comparing original and perturbed importance vectors. $$\text{Stability}_{cos} = \frac{\sum_i gx_i \cdot gx_i'}{\sqrt{\sum_i gx_i^2} \cdot \sqrt{\sum_i (gx_i')^2} + 10^{-8}}$$	gx_i: importance of feature i in original explanation gx_i': importance of feature i in perturbed explanation
Simplicity (Entropy)	Quantifies how concentrated the feature importance distribution is. Lower entropy means reliance on fewer features. $$p_i = \frac{w_i}{\sum_j w_j}, \quad H = -\sum_i p_i \log(p_i + 10^{-12})$$ $$\text{Simplicity}_{entropy} = 1 - \frac{e^H}{d}$$	w_i: importance of feature i d: total number of features H: Shannon entropy of distribution
Coverage (Cumulative Top-k)	Fraction of total feature importance captured by top-k features. $$\text{Coverage}_k = \frac{\sum_{i=1}^{k} w_{(i)}}{\sum_{j=1}^{d} w_j + 10^{-12}}$$	$w_{(i)}$: i-th most important feature (sorted) d: total number of features k: number of top features
Fidelity (Surrogate Accuracy)	Measures how well a surrogate model trained on the top-k features replicates predictions of the original model. $$\text{Fidelity} = \frac{1}{n} \sum_{i=1}^{n} \mathbf{1}(\hat{y}_i^{sur} = \hat{y}_i^{model})$$	n: number of samples $\hat{y}_i^{sur}$: surrogate model prediction $\hat{y}_i^{model}$: original model prediction

4 Experimental Results

4.1 Experimental Setup

This section demonstrates the evaluation of the framework in the proposed methodology. The 17 benchmark circuits (RS232, s15850, s35932, s38417, s38584) with Trojan-inserted netlists obtained from the Trust-HUB repository [20] form the primary dataset. These benchmarks are widely adopted in existing literature for hardware Trojan detection and analysis. To ensure a fair and consistent comparison with previously published works, the same set of benchmark circuits was utilized in this study. Implementation is carried out in Python using Scikit-learn, NetworkX, XGBoost and supporting libraries for analyzing feature ranking (SHAP, LIME) and XAI evaluation.

Feature extraction is performed as described earlier producing structural, GCM and functional features. Training and evaluation configurations include dataset partitioning, balancing with SMOTE-Tomek links, and hyperparameter tuning via RandomizedSearchCV. Performance evaluation is carried out using multiple standard classification metrics such as Accuracy $\frac{TP+TN}{TP+TN+FP+FN}$, Precision $\frac{TP}{TP+FP}$, Recall or TPR $\frac{TP}{TP+FN}$ and F1-score, which balances both as $2 \cdot \frac{\text{Precision} \cdot \text{Recall}}{\text{Precision} + \text{Recall}}$. Specificity or TNR $\frac{TN}{TN+FP}$ captures correct negative detection, whereas FPR $\frac{FP}{FP+TN}$ and FNR $\frac{FN}{FN+TP}$ quantify misclassification rates. Finally, ROC-AUC summarizes overall separability by measuring the area under the ROC curve. Beyond the classification accuracy, explainability metrics as described in the previous section to quantify the interpretability of different feature ranking strategies are evaluated.

4.2 Results and Discussion

Once the training of the machine learning model is carried out, features are ranked using three feature ranking techniques such as XGBoost in-built feature ranking list, Local Interpretable Model-agnostic Explanations and SHapley Additive exPlanations.

Figure 1 presents the XGBoost feature ranking based on gain which is generated as a side-effect of training the ML model. The bar chart places the most influential features at the top, thereby showing how much each feature contributes to improving the model's splits on the leaf nodes across the ensemble model. Larger bars correspond to higher predictive power. According to this approach, Harmonic Centrality ranks as the feature with highest influence on the final model's outcome along with SC0 and Betweenness Centrality features being the dominant ones.

Figure 2 depicts the LIME ranking based on mean absolute weight across explanations as it is mainly designed to generate local explanations using surrogate models. In contrast to global ranking approaches LIME emphasizes on instance-level explanations thereby identifying the specific features that drive individual classification outcomes. Here, Clustering Coefficient, CO and SC1 emerge as the most important features providing a different perspective when compared to XGBoost and SHAP.

Figure 3 shows the SHAP summary plot which explains both ranking and directional impact of the features. Each dot is representing that particular feature's contribution for a single instance. The x-axis shows the range of Shapley values where features are ranked by their overall importance from top to bottom, indicating how strong is their impact on the predictions. SHAP also ranks Harmonic Centrality at the top followed by CO confirming their critical roles while the colour gradient highlights how feature values affect prediction outcomes.

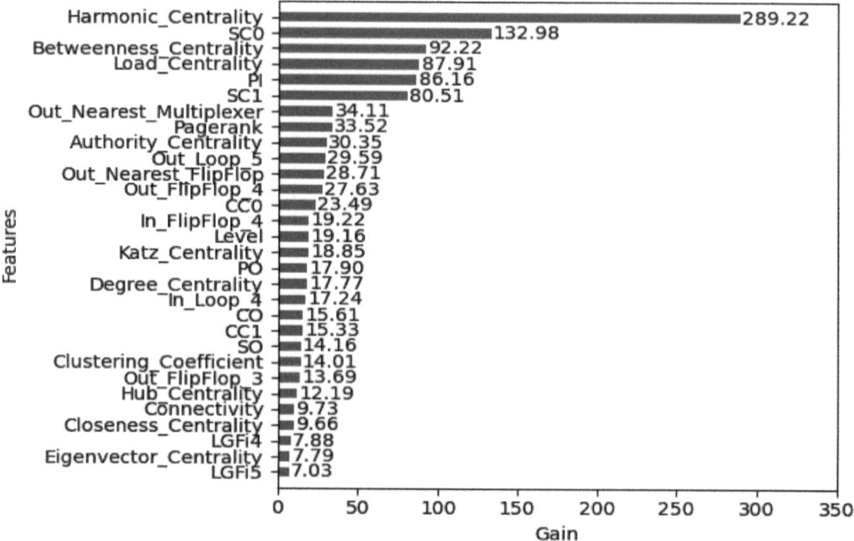

Fig. 1. Intrinsic Feature importance distribution generated by the XGBoost algorithm.

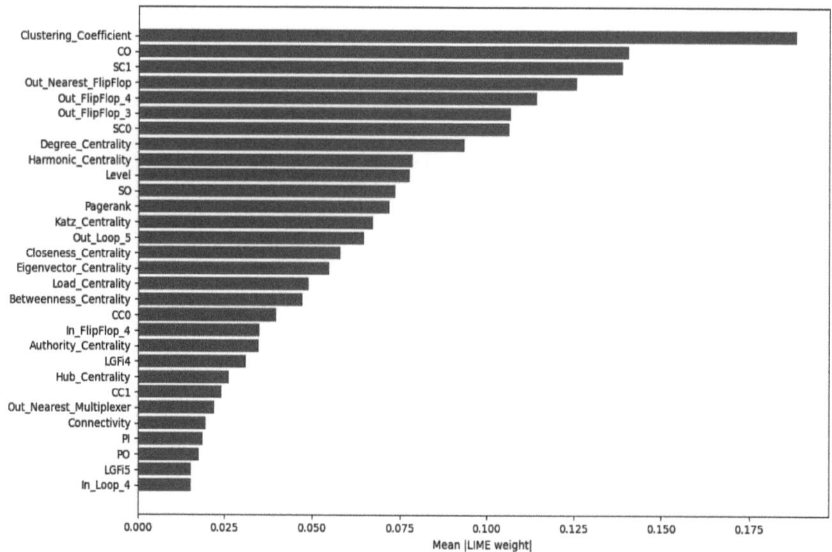

Fig. 2. Global feature importance ranking derived from LIME analysis.

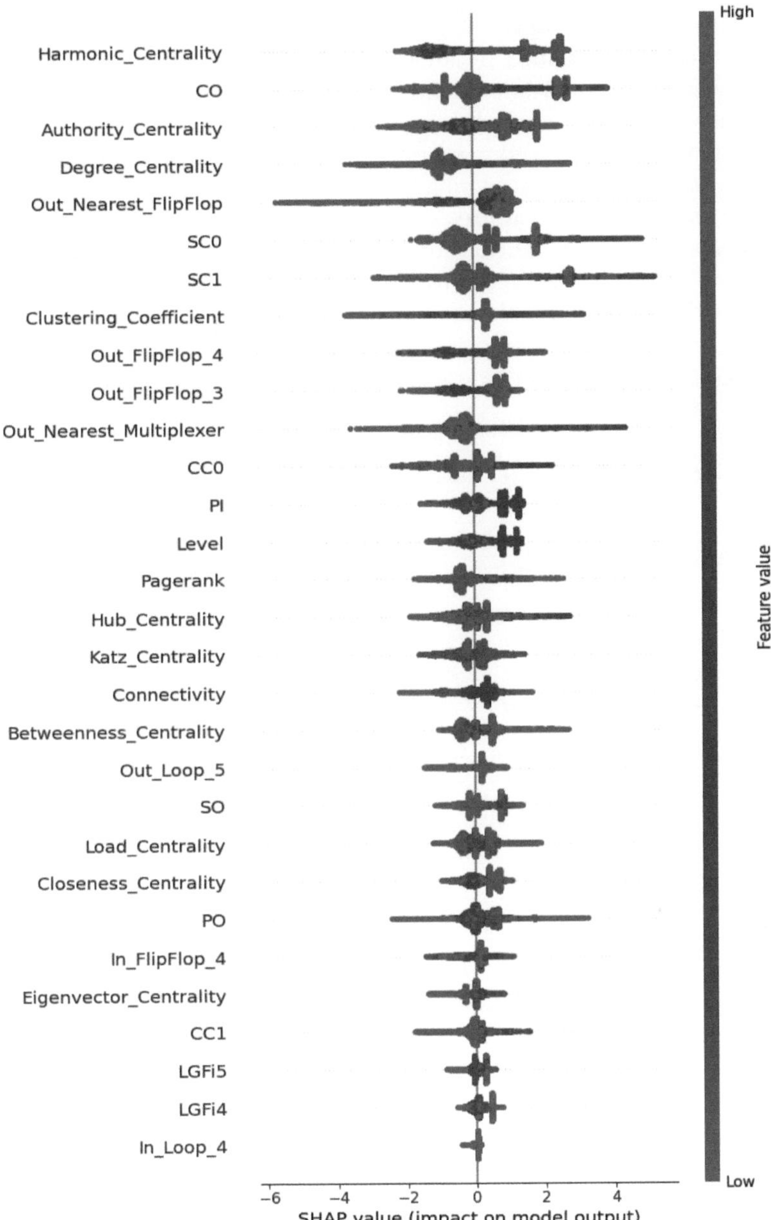

Fig. 3. Distribution of SHAP values on summary plot, indicating the impact of features on model predictions.

After obtaining the rank list across the three feature ranking techniques, the proposed hybrid filter-based ranking driven feature selection strategy to obtain the optimal subset of features for each ranking method is applied.

Table 2 presents the optimal set of features retained across the proposed techniques. Features retained by all three methods (Retained in = 3) indicate strong consensus and high importance, while those retained by only one or two methods show moderate to weak agreement. Features which are not selected by any method (Retained in = 0) can be considered least important and are potential candidates for elimination. Using the proposed FSM applied for three feature ranking list the original 30 features set reduced to 18, 20, 19 for XGBoost, SHAP and LIME respectively. Confirmation statistics (MI, spearman_correlation and ANOVA F-values) validated that dropped features had negligible predictive association with the target variable.

Table 2. Feature retention comparison across XGB, SHAP, and LIME.

Feature	XGB_Kept	SHAP_Kept	LIME_Kept	Retained in
Authority_Centrality	✓	✓	✓	3
CC0	✓	✓	✓	3
CO	✓	✓	✓	3
Degree_Centrality	✓	✓	✓	3
Harmonic_Centrality	✓	✓	✓	3
Katz_Centrality	✓	✓	✓	3
Out_FlipFlop_4	✓	✓	✓	3
Out_Loop_5	✓	✓	✓	3
Out_Nearest_FlipFlop	✓	✓	✓	3
Pagerank	✓	✓	✓	3
SC0	✓	✓	✓	3
SC1	✓	✓	✓	3
Betweenness_Centrality	✓	✓	X	2
Closeness_Centrality	X	✓	✓	2
Clustering_Coefficient	X	✓	✓	2
In_FlipFlop_4	✓	X	✓	2
Out_Nearest_Multiplexer	✓	X	✓	2
PI	✓	✓	X	2
SO	X	✓	✓	2
Connectivity	X	X	✓	1
Eigenvector_Centrality	X	X	✓	1
Hub_Centrality	X	X	✓	1
In_Loop_4	✓	X	X	1
Level	✓	X	X	1
Load_Centrality	✓	X	X	1
PO	X	✓	X	1
CC1	X	X	✓	1
LGFi4	X	X	X	0
LGFi5	X	X	X	0
Out_FlipFlop_3	X	X	X	0

The refined subsets of features obtained were used to train independent XGBoost classifiers again accompanied by balancing using SMOTE-Tomek links, hyperparameter tuning and optimization to obtain the best-fit model whose performance is evaluated on the isolated test dataset.

Table 3 shows a comparative evaluation of the proposed feature selection techniques against the original model without optimizations. Results show that XGBoost, SHAP and LIME achieve competitive performance with fewer features while maintaining high accuracy, precision, and recall. XGBoost achieves strong recall (97.84%) and ROC-AUC (99.78%) but its precision (95.27%) lags behind failing to achieve balance across metrics. LIME with 19 features provides stable results (Accuracy: 99.67%, F1-score: 96.99%). On the other hand SHAP with 20 features, delivers the best balance across metrics, attaining the highest precision (98.60%), F1-score(97.90%) and competitive accuracy (99.76%). Overall, SHAP emerges as the most effective technique offering superior predictive reliability with fewer features.

From Table 2 it is clear that each method (XGBoost, SHAP, LIME) provides a different perspective on each feature's influence on the outcome, which is validated when the performance evaluation on the optimal features set across the techniques are obtained. Performance metrics do not capture how reliable or interpretable the feature selection strategy is. To address this, XAI metrics such as Fidelity, Simplicity, Stability, and Coverage are employed to evaluate the explanatory robustness of each ranking method.

Figure 4 presents the evaluation of XAI metrics highlighting distinct strengths across the three ranking techniques. XGBoost achieves the highest coverage (0.7388) and simplicity (0.4323) which indicates that its global explanations are broad and relatively interpretable but its low stability (0.5610) shows inconsistency under perturbations thereby limiting reliability in dynamic scenarios. This indicates limited robustness to feature-space variability, making XGBoost suitable for global feature exploration but less reliable for process- or design-dependent HTD generalization. LIME provides balanced performance with strong fidelity and stability, moderate coverage suitable for instance-specific insights. This makes it particularly effective for debugging or validating individual design instances, where localized interpretability is more critical than generalization. SHAP in contrast, demonstrates superior fidelity (0.9843) and highest stability (0.9488) with comparable coverage, validating its reliability across varying feature subsets. Although its simplicity (0.1349) is lower, which reflects complex behaviour, SHAP generates explanations which are both faithful to the model and consistent across perturbations, making it a reliable approach. Its high fidelity–stability coupling indicates strong correlation consistency and reproducible attribution across feature subspaces, making SHAP the most technically robust metric for explainable HTD, enabling reproducible feature attribution and enhancing the trustworthiness and auditability of ML-based detection frameworks.

Table 3. Performance comparison of proposed techniques across different feature sets.

Proposed Techniques	Features set	Accuracy (%)	Precision (%)	Recall (%)	F1-score (%)	ROC-AUC (%)	TNR (%)	FPR (%)	FNR (%)
Original Model without Optimizations	30 (All)	99.68	96.40	97.94	97.17	99.75	99.79	0.12	3.85
LIME	19	99.67	96.83	97.16	96.99	99.68	99.82	0.18	5.49
XGBoost	18	99.60	95.27	97.84	96.52	99.78	99.71	0.29	4.03
SHAP	20	99.76	98.60	97.22	97.90	99.73	99.93	0.07	5.49

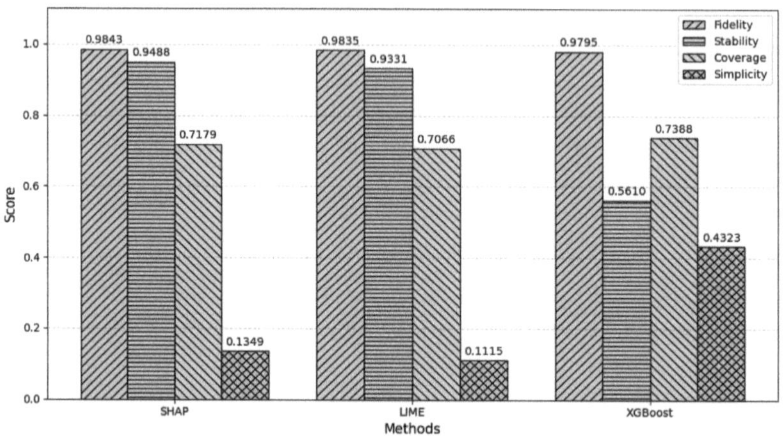

Fig. 4. XAI metrics evaluation results of three feature ranking techniques.

Table 4 shows that structural feature-only approaches [1] are limited in accuracy and recall, while structural+functional features [12] and structural features + GCM [10] improve precision but remain imbalanced. The proposed heterogeneous feature set achieves 99.76% accuracy, 98.60% precision and 97.22% recall offering the best trade-off across all metrics. This highlights the complementarity of structural, GCM and SCOAP features for robust Trojan detection.

Table 4. Evaluation of the best proposed framework versus average results of different existing approaches.

Methods	Features	Accuracy (%)	Precision (%)	Recall (%)	F1-score (%)
[1]	Structural features only	90.0	89.0	88.4	88.4
[12]	Structural + Functional features	99.8	97.8	89.0	92.1
[10]	Structural features + GCM	–	100.0	79.0	88.0
Proposed Technique	Structural, GCM and SCOAP features	99.76	98.60	97.22	97.90

5   Conclusion

The proposed work presents a novel unified feature-based supervised framework for hardware Trojan detection at gate-level netlist that integrates structural features, graph centrality measures, and SCOAP-based functional features. Three distinct feature ranking strategies which also aids for explainability of the black-box model, such as XGBoost intrinsic feature ranking, SHapley Additive exPlanations (SHAP) and Local Interpretable Model-agnostic Explanations (LIME) with XGBoost as the classifier are employed. A hybrid filter-based feature-ranking driven feature selection method is designed to provide systematic automated approach and the proposed method achieved high accuracy (99.76%) with balanced precision (98.60%) and recall (97.22%). Furthermore, a key contribution is the first incorporation of evaluation metrics called XAI metric (fidelity, simplicity, stability, coverage) into hardware Trojan detection application which provided a novel lens to access the quality of explanations, ensuring interpretability alongside performance. The dual focus of the proposed glass-box framework on accuracy and interpretability establishes a new direction for explainable and trustworthy Hardware Trojan Detection (HTD), offering both practical detection capability and valuable insight into model decision-making.

Future extensions will explore Graph Neural Networks (GNNs) to leverage richer circuit graph representations, validate the approach across broader benchmark suites and optimize runtime efficiency to move closer towards deployment in practical design and verification workflows.

Acknowledgments. The authors gratefully acknowledge the Department of Electronics and Communication Engineering, PES University, Bengaluru, and Defense Research and Development Organization (DRDO), Government of India, for the infrastructure and research support.

Disclosure of Interests. The authors have no relevant financial or non-financial interests to disclose.

References

1. Hasegawa, K., Yanagisawa, M., Togawa, N.: Trojan-feature extraction at gate-level netlists and its application to hardware-Trojan detection using random forest classifier. In: IEEE International Symposium on Circuits and Systems (ISCAS), Baltimore, MD, USA, pp. 1–4. IEEE (2017). https://doi.org/10.1109/ISCAS.2017.8050827
2. Helmy, M.M., Abdalla, M.A.Y., Khattab, A.: Detecting hardware trojans using structural features for hardware security and reliability. In: International Telecommunications Conference (ITC-Egypt), Cairo, Egypt, pp. 2345–2358. IEEE (2023). https://doi.org/10.1109/ITC-Egypt58155.2023.10206171
3. Negishi, R., Kurihara, T., Togawa, N.: Hardware-trojan detection at gate-level netlists using gradient boosting decision tree models. In: IEEE 12th International Conference on Consumer Electronics, Las Vegas, NV, USA (2022)

4. Chakraborty, R.S., Wolff, F., Paul, S., Papachristou, C., Bhunia, S.: *MERO*: a statistical approach for hardware trojan detection. In: Clavier, C., Gaj, K. (eds.) CHES 2009. LNCS, vol. 5747, pp. 396–410. Springer, Heidelberg (2009). https://doi.org/10.1007/978-3-642-04138-9_28

5. Hicks, M., Finnicum, M., King, S.T., Martin, M.M.K., Smith, J.M.: Overcoming an untrusted computing base: detecting and removing malicious hardware automatically. In: IEEE Symposium on Security and Privacy (SP), Oakland, CA, USA, pp. 159–172. IEEE (2010). https://doi.org/10.1109/SP.2010.18

6. Waksman, A., Suozzo, M., Sethumadhavan, S.: FANCI: identification of stealthy malicious logic using boolean functional analysis. In: ACM SIGSAC Conference on Computer and Communications Security (CCS), New York, NY, USA, pp. 697–708. ACM (2013). https://doi.org/10.1145/2508859.2516654

7. Faezi, S., Yasaei, R., Al Faruque, M.A.: HTnet: transfer learning for golden chip-free hardware trojan detection. In: Design, Automation and Test in Europe Conference and Exhibition (DATE), Grenoble, France, pp. 1484–1489. IEEE (2021). https://doi.org/10.23919/DATE51398.2021.9474076

8. Salmani, H.: COTD: reference-free hardware trojan detection and recovery based on controllability and observability in gate-level netlist. IEEE Trans. Inf. Forensics Secur. **12**(2), 338–350 (2017). https://doi.org/10.1109/TIFS.2016.2613842

9. Sharma, R., Sharma, G.K., Pattanaik, M., Prashant, V.S.S.: Structural and SCOAP features based approach for hardware trojan detection using SHAP and light gradient boosting model. J. Electron. Test. **39**, 465–485 (2023)

10. Hashemi, M., Momeni, A., Pashrashid, A., Mohammadi, S.: Graph centrality algorithms for hardware Trojan detection at gate-level netlists. Int. J. Eng. (IJE) Trans. A Basics **35**(7), 1375–1387 (2022)

11. Pan, Z., Mishra, P.: Hardware Trojan detection using Shapley ensemble boosting. In: Proceedings of the 28th Asia and South Pacific Design Automation Conference (ASP-DAC 2023), pp. 496–503 (2023)

12. Hasegawa, K., Yamashita, K., Hidano, S., Fukushima, K., Hashimoto, K., Togawa, N.: Node-wise hardware trojan detection based on graph learning. IEEE Trans. Comput. **74**(3), 629–642 (2025). https://doi.org/10.1109/TC.2023.3280134

13. Mahfuz, T., Gaikwad, P., Suha, T., Bhunia, S., Chakraborty, P.: SALTY: explainable artificial intelligence guided structural analysis for hardware Trojan detection. In: Proceedings of the 2025 IEEE 43rd VLSI Test Symposium (VTS), pp. 1–7. IEEE (2025)

14. Alharbi, A., Alsubhi, K.: Botnet detection approach using graph-based machine learning. IEEE Access **9**, 99166–99180 (2021). https://doi.org/10.1109/ACCESS.2021.3094183

15. Goldstein, L.H., Thigpen, E.L.: SCOAP: sandia controllability/observability analysis program. In: 17th Design Automation Conference (DAC), pp. 190–196. IEEE (1980). https://doi.org/10.1145/800139.804528

16. Batista, G.E.A.P.A., Bazzan, A.L.C., Monard, M.C.: Balancing training data for automated annotation of keywords: a case study. In: 2nd Brazilian Workshop on Bioinformatics (WOB 2003), Rio de Janeiro, Brazil, pp. 10–18. IEEE (2003)

17. Lundberg, S.M., Lee, S.-I.: A unified approach to interpreting model predictions. In: Advances in Neural Information Processing Systems (NeurIPS), vol. 30, pp. 4768–4777. Long Beach, CA, USA (2017). https://doi.org/10.48550/arXiv.1705.07874

18. Ribeiro, M.T., Singh, S., Guestrin, C.: "Why should i trust you?": explaining the predictions of any classifier. In: Proceedings of the 22nd ACM SIGKDD International Conference on Knowledge Discovery and Data Mining (KDD), pp. 1135–1144. ACM, San Francisco, CA, USA (2016). https://doi.org/10.1145/2939672.2939778
19. Makridis, G., et al.: Towards a unified multidimensional explainability metric: evaluating trustworthiness in AI models. In: Proceedings of the 2023 19th International Conference on Distributed Computing in Smart Systems and the Internet of Things (DCOSS-IoT). IEEE (2023)
20. Trust-HUB. http://www.trust-hub.org. Accessed 30 Aug 2025

Hard-to-Find Bugs in Public-Key Cryptographic Software: Classification and Test Methodologies

Matteo Steinbach[(✉)], Johann Großschädl, and Peter B. Rønne

DCS and SnT, University of Luxembourg, 6, Avenue de la Fonte,
4364 Esch-sur-Alzette, Luxembourg
`matteo.steinbach.pro@gmail.com`, `{johann.groszschaedl,peter.roenne}@uni.lu`

Abstract. Programming bugs and flaws can have fatal consequences for the security of cryptographic software and may allow an attacker to bypass authentication, forge signatures, decrypt sensitive data, or even completely reveal secret keys. Certain categories of bugs, such as subtle carry-propagation flaws in large-integer or prime-field arithmetic carried out by many public-key cryptosystems, manifest only under very specific and, therefore, extremely rare input conditions, which makes them hard to detect with conventional software testing methodologies. While there exist a few papers that describe such Hard-to-Find Bugs (HFBs) and study their security implications, a more comprehensive treatment and systematization are still lacking. The present paper aims to fill this gap and analyzes the challenges posed by HFBs in software implementations of public-key cryptosystems. More concretely, we define and categorize HFBs, provide a survey of HFBs that have been found in widely-used open-source cryptography libraries (some of which remained undetected for up to 10 years), and discuss the benefits and limitations of common testing and prevention techniques, including differential testing, static analysis, fuzzing, formal verification, and Known Answer Tests (KATs) tailored to HFBs. Raising awareness of HFBs is important for software developers and security auditors who implement and test cryptographic algorithms for mission-critical systems where correctness and robustness are paramount. By shedding light on subtle implementation flaws and how to reduce their occurrence, this paper contributes to improving the real-world security of public-key cryptosystems.

1   Introduction

Cryptographic algorithms are foundational to secure communication over the Internet, safeguarding the confidentiality, authenticity, and integrity of sensitive data. While many of the widely-used cryptosystems stand on a solid theoretical foundation and have been scrutinized for many years, their security in practice is intrinsically related to the correctness of the implementation [22]. Programming errors and resultant defects (i.e., "bugs") can be found in any non-trivial software, and cryptographic software is certainly no exception [7]. According to

C. Karfa et al. (Eds.): SPACE 2025, LNCS 16406, pp. 336–357, 2026.
https://doi.org/10.1007/978-3-032-16342-4_19

McConnell [24, Sect. 22], the "industry average experience is about 1–25 errors per 1000 lines of code for delivered software." Since a software implementation of a single cryptosystem, such as ECDSA, can consist of several hundred Lines of Code (LoC), it is not surprising that a substantial number of bugs have been found in cryptographic libraries [7]. The impact of a bug or flaw in software, in general, and cryptographic software, in particular, can vary significantly. While some bugs are benign and do not cause serious harm, others have catastrophic effects and can even be responsible for a loss of life [34]. More specifically, when it comes to cryptographic software, the immediate consequences of bugs/flaws that slip through quality assurance (e.g., code auditing, testing) and end up in production usually include the incorrect execution of a cryptosystem for certain (potentially very rare) inputs and the leakage of sensitive information via side channels. Indirect (i.e., further) consequences of the former can range from the bypassing of authentication in TLS (e.g., Apple's "goto fail" bug [22]) to the forging of signatures (e.g., by exploiting a padding bug that breaks the collision resistance of the signature's hash function [25]) to the decryption of sensitive data (e.g., by taking advantage of a modular reduction bug to leak the private ECDH key of a TLS server [10]). In the worst case, a single bug can enable an attacker to fully recover a secret key with little effort [14]. However, even if an implementation of a cryptosystem is 100% functionally correct (i.e., produces always a correct result if the input is valid and an error code otherwise), it can still leak sensitive information, e.g., through small input-dependent variations in execution time that could be exploited by a timing attack.

Two commonly-used techniques to discover programming errors and defects are source-code reviewing (including auditing by external experts) and software testing (resp., fuzzing). However, both are particularly challenging for cryptographic software. To maximize efficiency, the performance-critical components of cryptographic algorithms are usually written in Assembly language, which is error-prone not only for the developers but also for reviewers and auditors. In addition, the need for resistance against timing-based side-channel attacks adds an extra layer of complexity, as it prohibits secret-dependent memory accesses and conditional branches, respectively [21]. Furthermore, when a cryptographic library aims to support different processor architectures, a number of separate Assembly implementations have to be reviewed/audited, requiring intricate and rare expertise. Cryptographic software also has a number of unique properties with respect to testing or fuzzing that distinguish it from software in other domains. Namely, certain classes of cryptographic software defects, such as subtle carry-handling flaws [7], emerge only under highly specific and extremely rare input conditions. A good example is the carry-propagation bug in OpenSSL's Karatsuba-based long-integer squaring studied by Weinmann [32]. This bug is triggered with a probability of 2^{-64} on affected 32-bit platforms and 2^{-128} on 64-bit processors, respectively. While conventional testing techniques are vital for basic correctness and regression checks, their odds of finding such an elusive bug are practically zero. Thus, it is not surprising that this carry-propagation bug was present in the OpenSSL code-base for 10 years [32], making it a prime example of a *Hard-to-Find Bug* (abbreviated in the following as HFB).

The main goal of this paper is to raise awareness of the existence of HFBs and their implications among cryptographers on the one hand and software developers on the other, whereby we focus on public-key cryptographic algorithms like RSA and Elliptic Curve Cryptography (ECC). These cryptosystems, due to their reliance on costly mathematical operations (e.g., long-integer arithmetic in RSA and finite-field computations in ECC), are especially susceptible to subtle functional bugs and side-channel flaws. Such defects are a natural consequence of inherent algorithmic complexity, sophisticated optimization, platform-related constraints, and (micro-)architectural nuances of the target processor. Software developers are often unaware of the specifics of cryptosystems and the aspects that make cryptographic software unique. For example, even when a software implementation of a public-key cryptosystem is fully functionally correct, it can still contain an HFB and leak secret data, e.g., via some side channel or due to bad randomness [22]. On the other hand, cryptographers often lack knowledge of the complete spectrum of software testing and formal verification techniques that can be used to tackle HFBs. While each of them has its own benefits and shortcomings, the combination of testing (fuzzing) and formal verification can reduce the number of HFBs that slip through and end up in production.

This paper provides a definition of HFBs, describes different characteristics they share, and exemplifies these characteristics with a famous HFB that made headlines world-wide, namely the Sony PlayStation 3 (PS3) bug [14]. We also discuss the benefits and limitations of state-of-the-art software testing methods (both generally and specifically in the context of HFBs), including differential testing, static analysis, Monte Carlo testing, fuzzing, and Known Answer Tests (KATs) tailored to the rare corner cases where HFBs commonly hide. Beyond "detection and elimination," an alternative way to mitigate HFBs is prevention through formal verification of correctness [2,8]. We survey tools and techniques for the formal verification of cryptographic implementations and highlight the advantages of modern programming languages for building high-assurance software. Another contribution of this paper is a collection of HFBs that have been discovered in various open-source projects and their analysis and categorization into six main classes of bugs: carry propagation flaws, mismanagement of state or context, other implementation issues, incomplete input validation, erroneous parameterization, and vulnerability to timing attacks. A more detailed version of this bug collection, which covers 53 HFBs in total and also includes a small source-code excerpt where each bug manifests, is available on GitHub [30]. The GitHub repository also contains an extended 35-page version of this paper.

2   Hard-to-Find Bugs (HFBs)

In the context of software quality assurance, the term *error* generally refers to a human mistake that produces an unintended or incorrect result. Errors can occur in any phase of the development process, e.g., specification, design, implementation, testing, and maintenance. A *defect* is a deficiency or imperfection in a software artifact that prevents it from satisfying the (intended) requirements or specification [24]. Hence, a defect is the consequence of an error, e.g., a false specification due to a misinterpretation of a requirement or a flaw in the design of the software. A *bug* is the manifestation of a defect and typically discovered during the testing or operation of software artifacts. Bugs can affect any phase of the software development process, from specification to maintenance, but we focus primarily on implementation bugs in this paper. Having established the basic terminology, we define a Hard-to-Find Bug (HFB) as follows.

> An HFB is any kind of imperfection of a delivered cryptographic software implementation that can potentially lead to a security vulnerability and remains undetected by state-of-the-art testing techniques.

The word *delivered* emphasizes that HFBs are bugs in official software versions or releases that made it to production systems, i.e., we explicitly exclude bugs in alpha or beta software. Alpha/beta versions often come with critical bugs and are intended for testers and early adopters to identify these issues.

An important category of HFBs consists of those that cause cryptographic software to produce an incorrect result for at least one input combination. Such input combinations are typically extremely rare, making these bugs difficult to uncover through conventional testing or fuzzing. Even worse, incorrect outputs of a cryptosystem can leak sensitive data (e.g., a secret key) to an attacker, as was shown in [10]. However, not all HFBs manifest as incorrect outputs. Some arise from low-level memory management issues, such as dynamically allocated memory (using, e.g., `malloc` in C) that is never freed. Although these bugs do not affect functional correctness, they can still pose a security risk if sensitive data, e.g., a secret key or a temporary value related to a secret key, remains in memory and becomes accessible to an attacker[1]. Other HFBs stem from flaws in (pseudo-)randomness generation, often referred to as "bad randomness." The security of many cryptosystems depends crucially on random numbers that are unpredictable and uniformly distributed within a specified range; defects in the generation process can have fatal consequences yet are notoriously difficult to detect through standard testing. Timing vulnerabilities represent another class of HFBs: even when outputs are fully correct, variations in execution time can leak information about the secret key via side-channel attacks. These examples illustrate that HFBs encompass a broad range of imperfections, including some that do not affect functional correctness but still can undermine security.

Characteristics of HFBs. Most of the HFBs described in the literature and in bug reports, change logs, mailing lists, and discussion forums of open-source projects share one or more of the following properties.

1. Low Probability of Occurrence: An HFB manifests only under extremely rare and highly specific conditions, such as unique input combinations, special sequences of operations, or particular hardware or timing factors.

---

[1] Note that our HFB definition does not imply the existence of an exploit; it suffices when the bug has the potential to compromise security.

2. High Complexity and Subtlety: An HFB often results from complex system interactions, subtle hardware behavior, or some intricate algorithmic detail (e.g., improper handling of edge cases).
3. Difficulty in Detection and Reproduction: Conventional testing techniques struggle to identify HFBs, and without knowing "the trick" they are hard to reproduce.
4. Cross-Disciplinary Nature: Addressing HFBs often requires expertise across multiple areas, including software, hardware, and cryptographic theory, due to their involvement in various layers of the system stack.

Subtle bugs that are hard to find do not only plague cryptographic software but represent a massive challenge across essentially all segments of the software industry. For example, Bressana et al. [9] discuss the difficulty of finding subtle data plane bugs in networking hardware using their Portable Test Architecture (PTA), which revealed hidden issues like throughput degradation under specific traffic conditions. Although their research is on network devices, the discussed challenges closely mirror those in cryptography: both fields are plagued by bugs that only manifest under rare conditions, evading traditional testing methods.

2.1 HFBs in Public-Key Cryptography

Public-key cryptography involves costly low-level arithmetic operations, such as exponentiation in a multiplicative group with an order of a few thousand bits (e.g., RSA, Diffie-Hellman) or scalar multiplication in an additive group of an order of a few hundred bits (ECC schemes, e.g., ECDH, ECDSA). The latter, in turn, requires operations in a finite field, typically a prime field $\mathbb{F}_p$, where p is chosen to enable fast modular reduction. When implemented in software, these operations are performed on multi-precision integers, which are arrays of words or limbs whose length is determined by the wordsize of the target platform. As discussed in the last section, public-key cryptosystems are prone to many kinds of HFBs, including arithmetic defects (e.g., carry propagation issues, overflows of words/limbs, sign handling lapses), flaws in the generation of pseudo-random numbers, and vulnerabilities to side-channel attacks. The public nature of these cryptosystems, allowing adversaries to craft malicious inputs and probe for bugs without having privileged access, increases the risk that HFBs can be exploited to compromise security. For example, in (EC)DH key exchange, a private key is combined with a public key that may be maliciously crafted by an attacker to trigger leakage of (parts of) the private key via an HFB [10].

Example: Sony PS3 Hack. A well-known example for an HFB is the bug in ECDSA signature generation that affected the Sony PlayStation 3 (PS3) game console and opened doors to widespread software piracy [14]. This bug allowed an attacker to compute Sony's private code-signing key from publicly available signatures, thereby completely breaking the chain of trust of the PS3. With the private key exposed, it was possible to sign arbitrary code as if it were official firmware, which made it relatively easy to create custom firmware and execute unauthorized software, such as illegal copies of PS3 games.

Before explaining the bug and its implications in more detail, we first recap on how ECDSA generates and verifies a signature for a given message m. From a mathematical point of view, ECDSA operates in an elliptic curve (sub-)group of prime order n with generator G. The signer has a key-pair (d, Q) where d is an integer in the range of $[1, n-1]$ and $Q = d \cdot G$ is a point on the curve. To obtain a signature for m, the signer computes the hash $h = H(m)$ and chooses a random nonce $k \in [1, n-1]$. Then, the signer performs a scalar multiplication to get a public nonce $R = k \cdot G$, extracts the x-coordinate r_x of R, and derives $s = k^{-1}(h + d\,r_x) \bmod n$. The signature of m is the pair (r_x, s). To verify this signature, one has to hash m and use the public key Q to check if r_x matches the x-coordinate of the point $T = u_1 \cdot G + u_2 \cdot Q$, where $u_1 = h\,s^{-1} \bmod n$ and $u_2 = r\,s^{-1} \bmod n$. When several or many messages are signed using the same private key d, the security of the ECDSA signature scheme critically hinges on the nonces being unique, unpredictable, and uniformly distributed in the range $[1, n-1]$. Accidental nonce re-use can leak the secret key d.

Suppose two signatures are generated using the same nonce k, one for message m_1 with hash h_1, and the other for m_2 with hash h_2. In this case, the two signatures have the same r_x coordinate, but different s values: s_1 and s_2. The difference $s_1 - s_2 = k^{-1}(h_1 + d\,r_x) - k^{-1}(h_2 + d\,r_x) = k^{-1}(h_1 - h_2) \bmod n$ is sufficient to get $k = (h_1 - h_2)(s_1 - s_2)^{-1} \bmod n$ and, then, recover the private key from either signature by computing, e.g., $d = (s_1\,k - h_1)\,r_x^{-1} \bmod n$. Sony's flawed ECDSA implementation used a fixed nonce k (or insufficiently random nonces), producing signatures with the same r_x for different messages. Hackers collected these signatures and recovered the private key d, which enabled them to sign unauthorized firmware and bypass all security controls.

Cryptanalytic attacks enabled by "bad randomness" (including a complete lack of randomness) have a long history in public-key cryptography and broke the security of many real-world systems. Possible causes for randomness errors range from a lack of implementer awareness to defects in an operating-system or hardware component that is involved in the generation of (pseudo-)random numbers. Modern cryptographic libraries come with their own Pseudo-Random Number Generator (PRNG), which is initially seeded, and then occasionally re-seeded, with "true" (in terms of non-deterministic) randomness collected by the operating system from hardware events, interrupts, or special CPU instructions like `rdseed`. Most standalone ECDSA implementations, on the other hand, use randomness provided by the operating system's PRNG (e.g., `/dev/urandom` in Linux) to avoid the hassle of maintaining a PRNG state. Both approaches can succumb to implementation errors. For example, a bug in the OpenSSL crypto library of Debian Linux distributions from 2008 (CVE-2008-0166) crippled the seeding of OpenSSL's PRNG, making it predictable and causing many of the generated cryptographic keys to be weak. Commenting out two lines of source code reduced the entropy of the seed to the process-ID, i.e., only 15 bits. More recently, it became known that AMD Zen5 CPUs are affected by a flaw in the `rdseed` instruction, which is used by many operating systems as one of several sources of entropy. Under certain conditions, `rdseed` returns the value 0 more often than true randomness would allow and still signals success by setting the carry flag to 1 (CVE-2025-62626). A different kind of mistake, often committed by inexperienced developers, is to use a PRNG that is not suitable for cryptographic purposes. A typical example in the context of the Java language is the generation of ECDSA nonces with the `java.util.Random` class instead of the `java.security.SecureRandom` class. The former employs a non-cryptographic PRNG based on a linear congruential formula with a period of 2^{48}.

Overall, the ECDSA bug in Sony's PS3, and similar bugs due to "bad randomness," aligns well with the characterization of HFBs outlined earlier:

1. Low Probability of Occurrence: Depending on the defect in the generation of (pseudo-)random numbers, a nonce re-use may happen only after a large amount of signing operations (e.g., 2^{48} when `java.util.Random` is used as PRNG to obtain nonces).
2. High Complexity and Subtlety: The nonces for ECDSA signatures have to be unique, unpredictable, and uniformly distributed. Even small deviations may be exploitable and facilitate key recovery [3], making nonce generation a challenging task. In addition, from a purely algorithmic point of view, an ECDSA signature generated with a re-used nonce is still a correct signature (in the sense that the verification yields the correct result).
3. Difficulty in Detection and Reproduction: Conventional testing frameworks for ECDSA check for functional correctness, but are (normally) not able to detect accidental nonce misuse caused by PRNG flaws. While an extension of testing frameworks to catch duplicated nonces is certainly possible, the probability of finding a duplicate can be extremely low and depends on the properties of the defect in (pseudo-)random number generation.
4. Cross-Disciplinary Nature: The generation of (pseudo-)random nonces is an intricate problem as it requires expertise not only in cryptography, but also in operating systems (e.g., entropy collection, reseeding strategies) and even hardware (e.g., failure modes of entropy sources). This task is further complicated by the fact that many relevant implementation details, such as the post-processing/whitening of entropy, are often poorly documented or even completely opaque, especially in closed-source operating systems.

2.2   Exploitability and Impact

The exploitability of an HFB depends less on how often (or rarely) it manifests under benign conditions and more on whether an adversary is able to drive the execution into the HFB's "triggering region" and observe a usable output. In public-key cryptography, attackers often have direct control over certain inputs (e.g., chosen messages, public keys, input encoding), which enables systematic exploration of edge cases that are practically unreachable by arbitrary/random inputs. Equally important is observability: many HFBs become exploitable in practice only when their outputs/effects are externally visible (e.g., in the form of signatures, accept/reject decisions, detailed success/error codes, measurable timing differences, protocol abortions, system crashes). Finally, exploitability is amplified by repeatability; if a bug can be triggered in a deterministic fashion or with a certain probability under repeated trials, an attacker can accumulate evidence and/or reduce uncertainty through statistics. We propose to assess the exploitability of an HFB by considering the following aspects.

1. Adversarial control: Can an attacker directly choose or otherwise influence inputs and/or parameters? Is the execution environment remote or local?
2. Signal strength: Does the HFB produce a clean, low-noise "signal" (e.g., an incorrect result that is public) or only a weak side channel requiring a large number of samples (e.g., a minimal timing bias)?
3. Trigger reliability: Is the HFB's triggering condition deterministic, stateful (i.e., requiring a sequence), or purely probabilistic?
4. Trial or query effort and post-processing complexity: What is the expected number of trials/queries to get the desired "signal" (online complexity) and how costly is the post-processing, e.g., to extract a secret key from a given set of noisy timing measurements (offline complexity)?

As outlined before, an HFB can be simultaneously rare in normal operation yet highly exploitable in adversarial settings. The impact of an exploit can be classified according to the severity of the resulting vulnerability, which enables developers to prioritize fixes based on potential damage. Such a classification is beneficial for a better understanding of the importance and urgency of actions for remedy. Aspects to consider for impact classification include:

1. Security implications, roughly ordered by severity: (a) full key compromise (log-term key vs. short-term key, authentication key vs. encryption key), (b) forgeability or authentication failure, (c) loss of confidentiality without full key compromise (e.g., plaintext recovery), (d) other security/integrity issue (e.g., denial of service, protocol downgrade, policy bypass).
2. Exposure duration: Time between the release of the software containing the HFB and the public disclosure of the bug.
3. Remediation effort: Difficulty of bug-fixing (i.e., patch deployment) and the revocation and/or update of compromised keys.
4. Scale: Number of affected systems before/after the release of a patch.

3   Cryptography Testing Techniques

This section provides a structured analysis of existing software testing methods and evaluates their suitability to uncover HFBs. In contrast to formally verified implementations, which can guarantee the absence of certain HFBs (as will be discussed in the next section), no single testing approach is universally effective across cryptosystems. We assess different testing methods, including differential testing, static analysis, Monte Carlo tests, fuzzing, and known answer tests, on their efficacy for the detection of HFBs. Based on this assessment, we describe a unified framework for robust cryptographic testing.

3.1 Differential Testing

Differential testing applies identical inputs to multiple independent implementations of a procedure or function to find inconsistencies. Discrepancies in the outputs indicate potential bugs caused by errors in arithmetic operations, the handling of parameters, or edge-case logic. This approach is primarily suitable to identify hard-to-find bugs in complex systems, e.g., advanced cryptographic schemes or protocols, where exhaustive specification-based testing may not be practical due to the vastness of input spaces. In the context of public-key cryptography, differential testing is applicable for deterministic operations, such as RSA decryption, RSA/ECDSA signature verification, static (EC)DH, and the validation of TLS certificates [11]. For example, the testing of RSA decryption consists of feeding identical ciphertexts and keys into different implementations and checking for consistency in the obtained plaintexts.

Limitations. Differential testing is able to detect bugs by comparing multiple implementations (without requiring a formal specification), assuming that two or more independent implementations are unlikely to share the same flaw. While it can spot basic flaws, it is less suited to detect elusive bugs that occur only in very rare edge cases, such as HFBs. Instead, differential testing is more useful for confirming bugs once discrepancies arise and to identify buggy code sections by comparing intermediate results. Furthermore, differential testing can not be (straightforwardly) applied to probabilistic operations, such as RSA encryption or signing, as it would require controlling or recording randomness.

3.2 Static Analysis

Static analysis refers to a range of techniques that analyze source code, bytecode, or binaries without execution to spot potential errors, vulnerabilities, and inefficiencies. These methods range from simple approaches, such as linting and type checking, to advanced techniques, e.g., abstract interpretation, translation of source code to mathematical models, proof-oriented equivalence checking.

In cryptographic software, static analysis plays a key role in the verification of security properties. Expressive specification languages like CRYPTOL can be used to describe cryptographic algorithms in a rigorous way and translate them to Satisfiability Modulo Theories (SMT) formulas, often reducing subproblems to SAT/bit-vector queries, which enables automated correctness proofs. Special tools like CT-VERIF focus on the verification of constant-time execution, while BINSEC can detect vulnerabilities in compiled cryptographic binaries.

For example, Amazon Web Services (AWS) uses CRYPTOL as a specification and verification platform to translate cryptographic functions to SMT formulas for analysis by solvers. An important application of this approach is the formal verification of AWS s2n, an open-source TLS implementation that emphasizes simplicity and speed. Thanks to CRYPTOL and associated tools, it was possible to identify and mitigate potential vulnerabilities, such as timing side-channel attacks in the s2n HMAC implementation, prior to deployment [12].

Example: Cryptol for RSA-PSS Signature Generation. Given a message m or its hash $h = \text{Hash}(m)$, an RSA-PSS signature is, in essence, computed as $s = (\text{EMSA}(h, salt))^d \bmod N$, where EMSA is a probabilistic encoding method for h using a random salt. A static analysis of RSA-PSS can ensure that the encoding (including sub-operations like padding and mask generation) and the modular exponentiation are implemented correctly. With help of an appropriate tool, both a high-level specification and low-level implementation of RSA-PSS are translated into SMT formulas. The static analysis verifies the equivalence between the specification and the practical implementation for all inputs in the modeled domain. A discrepancy indicates a potential bug in, for example, the modular arithmetic, bit-manipulation (i.e., padding or encoding), or edge-case handling. The following CRYPTOL specification represents RSA-PSS signing:

```
rsaSign: {n} (fin n) => [n] -> [HLen] -> [SLen] -> [n] -> [n]
rsaSign d h salt N = modExp (EMSA ( h, salt )) d N
```

Here, `d`, `h`, `salt`, and `N` are a private exponent, a hash, a random value, and an RSA modulus, respectively, while `modExp` stands for a modular exponentiation and `EMSA` is the PSS encoding from RFC 8017. The Galois Software Analysis Workbench (SAW) is able to translate both the CRYPTOL code and a low-level implementation in, e.g., C or Java into SMT formulas. An SMT solver, such as Z3 or CVC5, then attempts to prove that this implementation adheres to the mathematical definition. The solver does this by: (a) encoding exponentiation and arithmetic constraints as bit-vector logic; (b) checking that the computed signature is always valid under all possible inputs; (c) finding counterexamples if an invalid transformation exists. The counterexamples, provided only in case the SMT solver detects a discrepancy, help to identify potential bugs related to incorrectly implemented arithmetic or incorrect padding/encoding.

Limitations. Static analysis can provide strong functional assurance (and, in some tools, constant-time execution guarantee), but its conclusions are only as reliable as the specification and the abstraction model used for verification. In particular, properties like randomness quality (entropy, bias, conditioning) and other statistical behaviors are difficult or impossible to capture in SMT-based equivalence proofs and typically require a complementary empirical validation with the help of dedicated statistical test suites, such as the tests described in the NIST special report 800-22 [27]. Finally, solver-based proofs may not scale smoothly to large, highly-optimized code bases without careful modularization and well-chosen invariants.

3.3   Monte Carlo Testing

Monte Carlo testing is a randomized testing technique that evaluates software by sampling inputs from a chosen probability distribution and checking if the executions satisfy expected properties. Unlike deterministic tests that execute a fixed (i.e., limited) set of hand-chosen cases, Monte Carlo testing can explore large input spaces (e.g., millions of cases) relatively quickly and may, thus, be able to reveal failures occurring only under particular input combinations.

When applied to cryptographic software, Monte Carlo testing usually draws random, but valid, inputs (e.g., keys, plaintexts, messages, nonces) and checks algorithm-specific invariants, such as consistency of RSA or ECDSA signature generation/verification (i.e., $\text{verify}(\text{sign}(m)) = m$), symmetry of ECDH shared secret keys (i.e., $a \cdot B = b \cdot A$, where $A = a \cdot G$ and $B = b \cdot G$), and correctness of RSA encryption/decryption round-trips (i.e., $\text{decrypt}(\text{encrypt}(x)) = x$). The distribution of input values can be uniform for wide coverage or biased toward boundary conditions (e.g., values near 0 or $p - 1$ in ECDSA and ECDH, carry-propagation boundaries, or exceptional operand encodings) in order to increase the likelihood of triggering subtle arithmetic and parsing defects.

Limitations. While Monte Carlo testing is self-contained (i.e., does not need any other implementation for reference) and may allow one to execute millions of test cases in a reasonably short time, it can still not provide a completeness guarantee. Extremely rare bugs, e.g., an HFB with a probability of 2^{-32} or even less, may remain undetected without highly targeted test-case generation.

3.4 Fuzzing

A fuzzer is an automated tool for "stress-testing" a program by executing it on a large number of randomized test cases drawn from an extended input space that covers also invalid, malformed, or out-of-specification inputs. Fuzzing can detect many kinds of defect, such as input-buffer overflows and other memory-access errors (if the fuzzer is equipped with static analysis tools, e.g., address sanitizers), incorrect input parsers, missing/insufficient input validation, and so on. These defects manifest not only via an incorrect result or output, but also through crashes, assertion violations, memory-safety errors, or other abnormal behavior. The strategy modern fuzzers adopt to produce pseudo-random inputs can be mutation-based (i.e., existing inputs are perturbed, e.g., by flipping bits or via heuristics), generation-based (i.e., inputs are constructed from grammars or models [19]), coverage-guided (i.e., inputs that explore not-yet-covered code paths are prioritized, e.g., AFL [33]), and differential (i.e., identical inputs are compared across different implementations to detect inconsistencies [31]).

In cryptographic realms, fuzzing is highly valuable for assessing robustness and error handling under incorrect or mis-formatted inputs. Public-key libraries expose many attacker-controllable parsing/decoding surfaces, e.g., ASN.1 and DER objects, X.509 certificates, PEM encodings, representations of points on an elliptic curve, signature/ciphertext formats, protocol messages. Fuzzing can probe how implementations react to NULL pointers, invalid length fields, non-canonical encodings, illegal points/scalars in ECC, malformed public keys, and unspecified parameter sets, and whether such inputs trigger unexpected results or undefined behaviour. Unlike Monte Carlo tests, fuzzing deliberately expands the input-space to inputs that violate syntactic or semantic constraints.

Example: OSS-Fuzz. A well-known example of industrial-strength fuzzing is OSS-Fuzz [15], an open-source framework developed by Google (in cooperation with the Core Infrastructure Initiative and the OpenSSF) to continuously fuzz-test open-source software. Launched in 2016, OSS-Fuzz has helped identify and fix over 10000 vulnerabilities and 36000 bugs across 1000 open-source projects (as of August 2023). Among those were hundreds of cryptography-related bugs found in major libraries like OpenSSL, LibreSSL, GnuTLS, libgcrypt, NSS, and Crypto++. For example, in 2017, OSS-Fuzz discovered multiple vulnerabilities of critical severity in GnuTLS, including CVE-2017-5334, a memory corruption caused by a double-free bug in the X.509 certificate parsing routine. This bug is exploitable from remote via a specifically crafted X.509 certificate that contains a Proxy Certificate Information extension and could, in the worst case, allow an attacker to crash an application using GnuTLS.

Limitations. Many functional HFBs are semantic (e.g., subtle arithmetic defects) and do not manifest as a crash, hang, memory leak, or other unexpected behaviour; without strong oracles (reference models, invariants, or differential checks), fuzzing may miss such flaws even if it executes the relevant code. An other limitation is that detecting common side-channel vulnerabilities, such as key-dependent execution times or memory access patterns, requires specialized measurement and analysis beyond normal fuzzing, and often calls for dedicated tools. Finally, most modern security protocols are stateful (e.g., handshakes in TLS, especially in the case of a renegotiation), whereby "interesting" states can only be reached with sequences of well-formed messages, which requires special fuzzers that are protocol/state-aware rather than purely input-centric [13].

3.5   Known Answer Tests (KATs)

KATs are an essential tool for validating the correctness of a software function (or a full program or system) by checking whether it reproduces a set of known input-output pairs ("test vectors") generated with a reference implementation or specification. Such test-vectors, along with meta-data, are normally stored in hex-format in special KAT files. Unlike differential testing, KATs neither need an "on-the-fly" generation of (pseudo-)random numbers for input data nor the execution of other implementations for output-checking. KAT-based testing is very easy to automate and provides strong regression protection: once a bug is fixed, the corresponding vector is kept to prevent a re-introduction. KATs also support portability (they can find architecture/compiler-dependent deviations in an effective way) and continuous integration (fast pass/fail oracles).

KATs for cryptographic software can serve different purposes, one of which is to determine the correctness of an implementation and its compliance with standards. For example, the NIST provides KAT collections for this purpose as part of their Cryptographic Algorithm Validation Program (CAVP). A second purpose of KATs is to detect HFBs via special test vectors targeting defects in parsing, arithmetic, and boundary handling that may hide in rare edge cases.

Example: Wycheproof. Wycheproof [16], originally developed by Google, is an open-source cryptographic test suite providing KATs to trigger subtle, real-world implementation pitfalls, with emphasis on rare edge cases and historical bug patterns. Whenever a new critical bug or vulnerability in a cryptographic library is reported, corresponding test cases are added to Wycheproof to catch this specific bug and prevent it from appearing in other libraries. Wycheproof's test functions were initially written in Java and later ported to Go, though the test-vectors themselves are language-agnostic [16]. We provide a C-port of the public-key test functions in Wycheproof along with this paper to facilitate the testing of C-based libraries. This port is available on GitHub [30] and enhances the accessibility of Wycheproof without altering its core methodology.

Limitations. Despite their value, KATs are inherently incomplete as they can not cover the full input space: passing a finite set of vectors does not imply the correctness for all inputs. KATs can miss defects that require a specific internal state, long execution history, or extremely rare operand patterns. Even KATs specifically tailored to HFBs, such as Wycheproof, can only find already known bugs, i.e., bugs that have been publicly disclosed.

3.6   Framework for Cryptographic Testing

Given the rarity and subtlety of HFBs, an effective testing environment has to deliberately target the very specific execution conditions where such bugs often hide. We propose a 3-layered approach combining deterministic, statistical, and dynamic techniques, each optimized for HFB discovery.

- *Layer 1: HFB-tailored KATs.* KATs represent the most precise layer of the framework and check an implementation using curated input-output pairs aimed at triggering historical or structurally plausible HFBs. Unlike generic KATs, HFB-specific test-vector suites like Wycheproof deliberately include malformed or non-canonical inputs, and boundary values to cause overflows or carry-mispropagations in multi-precision arithmetic.
- *Layer 2: Monte-Carlo testing with biased distributions.* While KATs are an effective tool to detect known HFBs, they fail to uncover previously unseen flaws. Monte-Carlo testing can address this gap using (valid) inputs drawn from deliberately biased distributions that concentrate probability mass on carry-propagation boundaries, near-0/near-p values in finite-field and group operations, edge-case encodings and borderline valid points or scalars, and atypical but still standards-compliant domain parameters. Such systematic testing of functions around arithmetic or structural "danger zones," where HFBs naturally arise, increases the chance of triggering unknown defects.
- *Layer 3: Continuous coverage-based fuzzing.* This layer ensures robustness and covers not only the core cryptographic operations but also "peripheral functions," which are often complex and can contain many execution paths (e.g., X.509 parsing). Fuzz-testing is especially effective at catching HFBs related to input validation, encoding/decoding, and error-handling.

4   Verified Cryptographic Implementations

Even the most advanced testing regime can not guarantee that a cryptographic software implementation is bug-free. Formal verification can come to the rescue and further improve correctness and security by providing strong (in the sense of mathematically grounded) assurances. In this section, we delve into formal verification methods and the utilization of modern programming languages like Rust and Jasmin to achieve high-assurance cryptographic software.

4.1   Formal Verification of Cryptographic Software

Formal verification applies mathematical logic to rigorously prove that a given implementation adheres to formally specified correctness and security features across all possible executions. Unlike conventional testing, which only inspects a finite subset of possible inputs, formal verification provides global guarantees by exhaustively analyzing every possible execution path. This process ensures the absence of flaws, such as arithmetic errors, incorrect memory handling, and logic inconsistencies, that could compromise security [8].

The verification procedure begins with the formal specification of a cryptographic function $f : \mathcal{X} \rightarrow \mathcal{Y}$ and its desired properties. Taking RSA encryption as a simple example, correctness is typically expressed as

$$\forall(pk, sk), \forall m \in \mathcal{M}, \quad \mathrm{Dec}(sk, \mathrm{Enc}(pk, m)) = m. \tag{1}$$

This property, a global invariant, has to hold under all conditions. Verification tools like COQ, EASYCRYPT, and TAMARIN PROVER translate both the formal specification and an actual software implementation into logical representations (based on first or higher-order logic) and attempt to establish their equivalence through automated theorem proving or model checking [2,4,6].

In addition to cryptographic algorithms, formal verification techniques have also been extensively applied to various security protocols, ensuring properties such as confidentiality, integrity, and authenticity. One common approach uses the symbolic Dolev-Yao model, which abstracts the cryptographic primitives as perfect black boxes while modeling adversarial interactions. Tools such as PRO-VERIF and TAMARIN PROVER automate the verification by analyzing protocol logic to detect vulnerabilities. For example, PROVERIF has been instrumental in verifying the security of some TLS 1.3 draft variants, identifying weaknesses and validating subsequent security enhancements [5].

Challenges and Limitations. Despite its strengths, formal verification faces some challenges. The high complexity of cryptographic schemes and protocols may lead to state-space explosion, making an exhaustive analysis computationally expensive. In addition, ensuring that a formal model accurately represents a real-world implementation is critical, as discrepancies can enable undetected vulnerabilities. Furthermore, formal methods struggle to capture side-channel attacks and compiler-introduced optimizations (e.g., vectorization), which calls for complementary empirical validation techniques, such as differential analysis and fuzz-testing [8]. In summary, while formal verification is a powerful tool to prove the correctness of an implementation, it is most effective in combination with empirical testing to achieve comprehensive security validation.

4.2 Memory Safety and Type Safety

Memory safety is paramount in software since vulnerabilities can lead to severe security breaches. A recent information sheet published by the NSA mentions that a significant portion of software vulnerabilities, namely around 70%, stem from memory safety issues in languages like C, C++, and Assembly [26]. The NSA recommends adoption of memory-safe programming languages to mitigate these risks, particularly in security-critical domains.

Rust is considered as candidate due to its robust memory safety guarantees and performance capabilities. Rust's ownership and borrowing system prevents common memory errors such as null pointer dereferences, buffer overflows, and data races. This is crucial for cryptographic operations, where any unintended memory access can impair security. Formally, the Rust borrow checker ensures that, for any memory state $\mathcal{M}$, a Rust function f will execute safely:

$$\forall \mathcal{M}, \quad \text{BorrowCheck}(f, \mathcal{M}) = \text{safe}. \tag{2}$$

This guarantee is crucial for cryptographic implementations, where unintended memory access can lead to security breaches. Furthermore, Rust's type system enforces that operations are performed on compatible types, which reduces the likelihood of logical errors within cryptographic algorithms. Low-level libraries like `subtle` facilitate the development of constant-time code, essential for preventing timing attacks by ensuring that its operations (e.g., conditional moves and selections, comparisons) have no data-dependent timing variations. Several cryptographic crates, such as `ring` [29], `rustls`, and `RustCrypto`, leverage the memory-safety and type-safety features of Rust. Alternatives like Go sacrifice performance for garbage collection, making them less suitable for applications with low-latency or real-time requirements.

Rust typically exhibits a slight performance penalty compared to C code in cryptographic primitives, but nonetheless remains competitive with aggressive optimization. Benchmarks, such as those for implementations of AES, indicate that Rust approaches C's performance, with any overhead largely coming from higher-level abstractions rather than intrinsic limitations [28]. In contrast, C's minimalism usually provides an advantage in resource-constrained settings like embedded systems [20]. While C excels at low-level efficiency and binary code-size, Rust's richer abstractions, simplified memory management, and extensive libraries can inflate size and complexity if unoptimized, though its optimization potential occasionally surpasses that of C by leveraging advanced integration across function and library boundaries. In addition, Rust supports formal verification through tools like Libcrux (a cryptographic library integrating verified artifacts via hacspec for correctness and security proofs) and HAX (a toolchain to translate Rust into formal languages, e.g., Coq and F*, for security-critical applications) [17,23]. These capabilities are absent in C since the C ecosystem lacks direct verification support. Thus, selecting between Rust's safety and C's raw performance requires a careful trade-off analysis.

4.3 Low-Level Optimization and Verification

Jasmin [1] aims to bridge (high-level) cryptographic specifications and verified Assembly implementations through a certified compiler (`jasminc`) and formal verification in EASYCRYPT. Its core syntax mirrors low-level control flow while enabling mathematical reasoning about correctness and side-channel resistance of an implementation. The methodology to verify code is as follows.

1. Modeling: Translate the Assembly code to Jasmin (this preserves low-level optimizations).
2. Annotation: Add pre-conditions, post-conditions, and loop invariants in the form of EASYCRYPT predicates.
3. Equivalence checking: Use the CRYPTOLINE toolchain to prove equivalence between the Jasmin code and the reference models via algebraic predicates (e.g., $\mathtt{mont\_asm}(x) \equiv \mathtt{mont\_ref}(x) \bmod p$).
4. Compiler certification: Rely on the correctness of the `jasminc` compiler to ensure that the generated Assembly code matches Jasmin semantics.

This approach combines automated SMT solving (for range checks) and interactive theorem proving (for modular equivalences), which allows for verification of both arithmetic correctness and side-channel security. Using single-precision modular reduction for lattice-based cryptography as example, we demonstrate how to employ Jasmin for two critical tasks: ensuring constant-time arithmetic and proving equivalence between optimized code and reference models.

Verified Modular Reduction. Consider Montgomery's reduction technique for a prime modulus p, where $R = 2^{64} > p$ and $p' = -p^{-1} \bmod R$. The Jasmin implementation computes $\mathrm{Mont}(x) = (x + (x \cdot p' \bmod R) \cdot p)/R$, which always has to satisfy $\mathrm{Mont}(x) \equiv x \cdot R^{-1} \bmod p$ and $0 \leq \mathrm{Mont}(x) < 2p$. Below is the Jasmin code in assembly-optimized form with annotations for verification.

```
1  fn montgomery (uint64 x0, x1) -> (uint64 r) {
2      %rax = x0
3      mulx %rax, %rdx, %rax        # x * p' (low)
4      mulx p, %rdx, %rax           # (x * p') * p
5      addc %rax, x0, %rax          # x + (x * p' mod R) * p
6      adc %rdx, x1, %rdx
7      shr $64, %rax, %rdx          # >> 64 (division by R)
8      assert @rpre (x0 + x1*2^64 < 2^128);
9      assert @rpost (result == (x0 + x1*2^64)*R^{-1} mod p);
10     return %rdx
11 }
```

The **assert** clauses specify a pre- and post-condition. EASYCRYPT proves the equivalence between this code and the mathematical specification via symbolic execution and modular arithmetic lemmas. The `jasminc` compiler guarantees "constant-timeness" by rejecting branching on secrets.

Jasmin remains very relevant today, playing a crucial role in post-quantum cryptography (especially lattice-based schemes) and growing its impact beyond integer arithmetic. For example, it turned out to be useful in uncovering issues in an implementation of the Falcon signature algorithm with emulated floating-point arithmetic. Namely, Jasmin helped verify a problem in the multiplication function where intermediate products are zeroized prematurely, which violates IEEE 754 rounding rules [18]. The verification process revealed that, while 692 out of 2048 FFT constants could trigger incorrect zeroization, the impact was mitigated in practice due to lower bounds on intermediate values.

In summary, the combination of formal verification techniques with modern programming languages designed for safety and performance, such as Rust and Jasmin, offers a robust foundation for the development of secure cryptographic implementations. Rust's guarantees of memory and type safety, and Jasmin's support for low-level optimization and formal verification, enable developers to write cryptographic software that is efficient and provably secure. Using these methods—optionally complemented by the testing framework described in the previous section—represents the current "best practice" for the implementation of cryptographic software.

5   HFBs Collection

As mentioned at the end of Sect. 1, this paper is supplemented by some online resources, in particular a collection of HFBs that have been discovered in real-world cryptographic software, including established libraries like OpenSSL. The HFB collection is publicly available on GitHub [30]. At the time of writing this paper, the GitHub repository contained data on more than 50 HFBs, which we collected from numerous open-source projects by studying bug reports, revision histories, discussion forums, mailing lists, research articles, results from large-scale testing/fuzzing initiatives (e.g., Wycheproof, CryptoFuzz), databases like CVE, and various other online resources. Most of the bugs slipped through the testing regime applied by the corresponding projects, and many actually ended up in production. However, not all of these HFBs led to serious vulnerabilities because their impact is often mitigated by system redundancies or the absence of single-point-of-failure dependencies.

This section provides a brief overview of the information about each HFB contained in the repository. The HFBs are summarized in six main Markdown files, roughly corresponding to six main categories of bugs as follows.

- `CARRY_PROPAGATION.md`: Mishandling of carry or borrow bits (resp., chains of carries or borrows) in multi-precision integer arithmetic.
- `CRYPTO_STATE.md`: Incorrect updates to a (secret-dependent) program state or context of a cryptosystem or protocol.

- `IMPLEMENTATIONS.md`: Deviations from formal mathematical or algorithmic specification (other than carry-propagation flaws).
- `INPUT_VALIDATION.md`: Incorrect (incomplete) validation of inputs that are invalid, malformed, or otherwise manipulated.
- `PARAM_HANDLING.md`: Incorrect validation or handling of domain parameters (including encoding/decoding errors).
- `CONSTANT_TIME.md`: Secret-dependent branches or memory access patterns that thwart constant-time execution.

Each bug contained in the repository is documented via the following basic format: *(1) Specification:* description of the bug's context and affected software component(s); *(2) Defect:* the exact defect caused by the bug; *(3) Impact:* the consequences of the defect, especially in terms of cryptographic correctness and potential security risks; *(4) Code Snippet:* an excerpt of the source code where the bug manifests. This structured documentation helps to better understand the nature of HFBs, trace their origins, and identify patterns that can improve future testing and verification efforts. Some examples of HFBs are described in the full version of this paper, which is publicly available on GitHub in the same repository [30] as the collection of HFBs.

5.1   Categorization of HFBs

We group the HFBs into six major categories that recurred across many of the affected cryptographic software projects. Each class captures a distinct failure mode, i.e., a different way the underlying cryptographic guarantees fail. There exist, however, some overlap cases where a bug fits in two categories, e.g., when a bug causes an erroneous computation and also enables a timing attack.

Carry-Propagation Flaws. These bugs arise when carry-bits or borrow-bits are not propagated properly across the words/limbs of multi-precision integers and hide in functions for arithmetic in a prime field or multiplicative group, such as addition, subtraction, multiplication, and squaring, usually including reduction modulo a prime p. Moreover, auxiliary operations like the conversion between full and reduced-radix representation and the final conversion of field-elements into canonical form can be affected. Because triggering inputs often sit at word (resp., limb) boundaries or have highly-specific values (e.g., near 0 or p), these bugs can easily escape conventional software tests.

State or Context Mismanagement. Here, the implementation maintains a state or a context that governs the basic properties and behavior of a cryptographic algorithm (e.g., context of nonce-generation for ECDSA, configuration flag in ECDH indicating whether or not a key can be re-used) or protocol (e.g., state of a TLS session renegotiation), but the state is not initialized and/or updated properly. The resulting failure can be sporadic, manifesting only under specific input sequences or renegotiation patterns, and present in a wrong output, the execution of an exception handler, or abnormal program termination.

Incorrect Implementation. These bugs cause an implementation to deviate from the mathematical or algorithmic specification. A common root-cause are flaws in arithmetic operations, such as exponentiation, scalar multiplication, addition and doubling of elliptic-curve points, and their "low-level" modular operations (other than carry-propagation issues). They can yield wrong results for a small subset of inputs, e.g., acceptance of a carefully-crafted adversarial signature.

Missing or Insufficient Input Validation. Input parsers and API front-ends fail to thoroughly check sizes, lengths, encodings, required parameters, or specific bounds (e.g., ASN.1/DER fields, maximum message sizes). Other examples are non-canonical (or otherwise invalid) exponents or scalars, and group elements (points) of low order. The consequences can range from an overread/overwrite of input buffers to acceptance of ill-formed inputs that should be rejected.

Insecure Domain Parameters. An implementation erroneously accepts insecure or invalid domain parameters (e.g., subgroup generators of wrong order, "prime fields" whose cardinality is actually not a prime) or interprets the parameters inconsistently across different configurations or code paths. Such inconsistencies are always problematic in heterogeneous environments where different libraries interoperate, and can enable attacks through subtle parameter misuse.

Timing-Attack Vulnerabilities. They are caused by secret-dependent branches (e.g., if-then clauses in exponentiation, scalar multiplication, or modular arithmetic) or secret-dependent memory-access patterns (e.g., table lookups).

5.2   Data Collection and Statistics

Collecting, categorizing, and analyzing HFBs discovered in real-world cryptographic software provides insights on subtle implementation pitfalls and traps that even experienced developers may fall into. Apart from the documentation of each HFB, we also generated some statistics, which we hope turn out to be useful when tackling the question of why and how HFBs arise.

For each bug, a statistical record containing the following information was assembled (see file `HFB.csv` in the GitHub repository [30]): *(1) ID:* The unique identifier for the bug, which can be a CVE number or a specific project-related identifier like a Git commit-ID; *(2) Category:* A high-level categorization of the bug, such as "Carry", "State", or "Timing", based on the six HFB categories outlined in the previous subsection; *(3) Language:* The programming language of the affected implementation, e.g., "Assembly" or "C"; *(4) SubType:* A more granular classification of the bug, such as "Montgomery Squaring" for an issue in a function for Montgomery squaring; *(5) Impact:* A description of the bug's immediate effect(s), such as "Incorrect result", "Memory corruption", or "Side-channel"; *(6) Severity:* A numerical value indicating the severity of the bug on a scale from 1 to 10, based on, e.g., CVE severity scores.

A (preliminary) analysis of the statistics we collected about the 50+ HFBs contained in our GitHub repository yields the following observations:

1. Complexity of Assembly: A disproportionately large share of bugs occurred in hand-written or tool-generated Assembly code, whereby readability and maintainability were often sacrificed for performance.
2. Prevalence of carry-propagation flaws: Bugs caused by the mis-propagation of carry/borrow bits are among the most common, highlighting that multi-precision arithmetic operations are error-prone, in particular when they are aggressively optimized for speed.
3. Cross-platform inconsistencies: Slight differences in compiler behavior, the supported instruction set(s) of the CPU (e.g., BMI2, ADX), or endianness caused bugs that remained undetected in single-target test environments.

6   Conclusions

In this survey paper, we delivered a thorough examination of HFBs in cryptographic software, with a specific emphasis on public-key cryptosystems. These subtle bugs pose a number of unique challenges to the security and robustness of cryptographic software due to their low probability of occurrence, high complexity, and resistance to detection by standard testing methods. Our analysis underlines the urgent need to tackle these elusive bugs and further investigate the vulnerabilities and attacks they enable.

We systematically evaluated a spectrum of software testing methodologies tailored to uncover HFBs, including differential testing, static analysis, Monte Carlo testing, fuzzing, formal verification, and KATs. Each methodology offers distinct advantages: differential testing excels at spotting inconsistencies across different libraries; static analysis provides rigorous defect detection and ensures properties like "constant-time" execution; Monte Carlo testing offers statistical input coverage; fuzzing reveals robustness issues with malformed inputs; formal verification delivers strong mathematical assurances of correctness; and KATs (exemplified by tools like Wycheproof) serve as an essential baseline validation by testing against known HFBs and various edge cases. Our accompanying C-port of Wycheproof makes its extensive KAT-collection available for platforms that are not supported by Go, most notably embedded devices.

To advance HFB detection, we proposed a test framework that integrates KATs, Monte Carlo testing, and continuous fuzzing. This approach combines deterministic, statistical, and dynamic testing benefits, empowering developers to bolster the security of their cryptographic software effectively. However, this may still not be sufficient for extremely critical software, which should also be mathematically guaranteed though formal verification.

A key contribution of this survey is the structured collection of real-world HFBs, carefully categorized to illuminate their highly diverse nature and aid in mitigation efforts. We hope this collection will serve as a vital resource for the cryptographic community, offering real-world examples that highlight common pitfalls and reinforce the necessity of specialized testing. By documenting these bugs—ranging from carry propagation flaws to constant-time failures—we aim to improve testing strategies and prevent recurring vulnerabilities.

References

1. Almeida, J.B., Barbosa, M., Barthe, G., et al.: Jasmin: high-assurance and high-speed cryptography. In: 24th ACM Conference on Computer and Communications Security (CCS 2017), pp. 1807–1823. ACM (2017)
2. Almeida, J.B., Barbosa, M., Barthe, G., et al.: The last mile: high-assurance and high-speed cryptographic implementations. In: 41st IEEE Symposium on Security and Privacy (S&P 2020), pp. 965–982. IEEE (2020)
3. Aranha, D.F., Novaes, F.R., Takahashi, A., et al.: LadderLeak: breaking ECDSA with less than one bit of nonce leakage. In: 27th ACM Conference on Computer and Communications Security (CCS 2020), pp. 225–242. ACM (2020)
4. Barthe, G., Grégoire, B., Zanella-Béguelin, S.: Formal certification of code-based cryptographic proofs. In: 36th ACM Symposium on Principles of Programming Languages (POPL 2009), pp. 90–101. ACM (2009)
5. Bhargavan, K., Blanchet, B., Kobeissi, N.: Verified models and reference implementations for the TLS 1.3 standard candidate. In: 38th IEEE Symposium on Security and Privacy (S&P 2017), pp. 483–502. IEEE (2017)
6. Blanchet, B.: Security protocol verification: symbolic and computational models. In: Degano, P., Guttman, J.D. (eds.) POST 2012. LNCS, vol. 7215, pp. 3–29. Springer, Heidelberg (2012). https://doi.org/10.1007/978-3-642-28641-4_2
7. Blessing, J., Specter, M.A., Weitzner, D.J.: Cryptography in the wild: an empirical analysis of vulnerabilities in cryptographic libraries. In: 19th ACM Asia Conference on Computer and Communications Security (ASIACCS 2024), pp. 605–620. ACM (2024)
8. Boston, B., et al.: Verified cryptographic code for everybody. In: Silva, A., Leino, K.R.M. (eds.) CAV 2021. LNCS, vol. 12759, pp. 645–668. Springer, Cham (2021). https://doi.org/10.1007/978-3-030-81685-8_31
9. Bressana, P., Zilberman, N., Soulé, R.: Finding hard-to-find data plane bugs with a PTA. In: 16th International Conference on emerging Networking EXperiments and Technologies (CoNEXT 2020), pp. 218–231. ACM (2020)
10. Brumley, B.B., Barbosa, M., Page, D., Vercauteren, F.: Practical realisation and elimination of an ECC-related software bug attack. In: Dunkelman, O. (ed.) CT-RSA 2012. LNCS, vol. 7178, pp. 171–186. Springer, Heidelberg (2012). https://doi.org/10.1007/978-3-642-27954-6_11
11. Chen, Y., Su, Z.: Guided differential testing of certificate validation in SSL/TLS implementations. In: 10th Joint Meeting on Foundations of Software Engineering (ESEC/FSE 2015), pp. 793–804. ACM (2015)
12. Chudnov, A., et al.: Continuous formal verification of amazon s2n. In: Chockler, H., Weissenbacher, G. (eds.) CAV 2018. LNCS, vol. 10982, pp. 430–446. Springer, Cham (2018). https://doi.org/10.1007/978-3-319-96142-2_26
13. De Ruiter, J., Poll, E.: Protocol state fuzzing of TLS implementations. In: 24th USENIX Security Symposium (USS 2015), pp. 193–206. USENIX Association (2015)
14. Fail0verflow. Console hacking 2010: PS3 epic fail. Presentation at the 27th Chaos Communication Congress (27C3) (2010)
15. Google. OSS-Fuzz: Continuous fuzzing for open source software (2020). https://github.com/google/oss-fuzz
16. Google. Project Wycheproof (2020). https://github.com/google/wycheproof
17. Hax Team. Hax: A Rust verification toolchain for security-critical software (2023). https://github.com/hax-rust/hax

18. Hwang, V.: Formal verification of emulated floating-point arithmetic in Falcon. In: Advances in Information and Computer Security — IWSEC 2024. Springer (2024)

19. Jero, S., Pacheco, M.L., Goldwasser, D., Nita-Rotaru, C.: Leveraging textual specifications for grammar-based fuzzing of network protocols. In: 31st Conference on Innovative Applications of Artificial Intelligence (IAAI 2019), pp. 9478–9483. AAAI Press (2019)

20. Kasak, D.: Rust vs. C: a performance comparison in systems programming. Blog post (2018). https://deniskasak.github.io/rust-vs-c-perf

21. Kocher, P.C.: Timing attacks on implementations of Diffie-Hellman, RSA, DSS, and other systems. In: Advances in Cryptology — CRYPTO 1996, pp. 104–113. Springer (1996)

22. Lazar, D., Chen, H., Wang, X., Zeldovich, N.: Why does cryptographic software fail? A case study and open problems. In: 5th Asia-Pacific Workshop on Systems (APSys 2014), pp. 7:1–7:7. ACM (2014)

23. Libcrux Team. Libcrux: A formally verified cryptographic library for Rust (2023). https://github.com/cryspen/libcrux

24. McConnell, S.: Code Complete, 2nd edn. Microsoft Press (2004)

25. Mouha, N., Raunak, M.S., Kuhn, D.R., Kacker, R.: Finding bugs in cryptographic hash function implementations. IEEE Trans. Reliab. **67**(3), 870–884 (2018)

26. National Security Agency. Software memory safety. Cybersecurity information sheet, NSA (2022). https://media.defense.gov/2022/Nov/10/2003112742/-1/-1/0/ CSI_SOFTWARE_MEMORY_SAFETY.PDF

27. Rukhin, A., Soto, J., Nechvatal, J., et al.: A statistical test suite for random and pseudorandom number generators for cryptographic applications. Special Publication 800-22, National Institute of Standards and Technology (NIST) (2010)

28. Seaborn, T.: Performance analysis of RustCrypto: AES implementations in Rust vs. C (2019). https://rustcrypto.org/performance

29. Smith, B.: Ring: Safe, fast, small crypto using Rust (2023). https://briansmith. org/rustdoc/ring/

30. Steinbach, M.: Wycheproof-C: A C cryptographic test suite (2025). https://github. com/mattc-try/wycheproof-c/

31. Vranken, G.: Differential fuzzing of cryptographic libraries (2019). https://archive. is/https://guidovranken.com/2019/05/14/differential-fuzzing-of-cryptographic- libraries/

32. Weinmann, R.-P.: Assessing and exploiting bignum vulnerabilities. BlackHat 2015 (2015). https://comsecuris.com/slides/slides-bignum-bhus2015.pdf

33. Zalewski, M.: Technical whitepaper for AFL-fuzz (2014). https://lcamtuf. coredump.cx/afl/technical_details.txt

34. Zhivich, M., Cunningham, R.K.: The real cost of software errors. IEEE Secur. Priv. **7**(2), 87–90 (2009)

Secure Secret Sharing Protocol Against Network Data Remanence Side Channel Attacks

Prajwal Thakare, Akash Om Trivedi, and Urbi Chatterjee[✉]

Department of Computer Science and Engineering, Indian Institute of Technology (IIT), Kanpur 208016, India
`urbic@cse.iitk.ac.in`

Abstract. In the setting of lightweight IoT devices and Wireless Sensor Networks (WSNs), a (t, n) Secret Sharing (SS) scheme has been proposed to distribute secrets over n shares where n is the number of disjoint paths between the sender and the receiver and a threshold value t is the number of shares required to reconstruct the original secret. However, studies in NDSS'21 and SPACE'22 have shown that all SS schemes are vulnerable to Network Data Remanence (NDR) attacks under practical scenarios. In this work, we propose a countermeasure to address the vulnerability of SS schemes to NDR attacks. The proposed solution is a Physically Related Function (PReF) based Threshold Changeable SS-Scheme that allows for the threshold value to be modified within a range of integers $[t, u]$ such that $t \leq u$ and $u \leq n$ without requiring the shares to be updated. The PReF can be thought of as a representation or model of Strong Physically Unclonable Functions (PUFs) in a way that abstracts away some of the specific physical details. The modified threshold value is securely transmitted via Physically Related Functions (PReF). Further in the work, we have presented the experimental results of the proposed scheme, where the scheme has been implemented by replicating two Raspberry-pi devices one as a sender and the other as a receiver, and both are connected in a wireless network. The results demonstrate that the probability of having an NDR-planned attack on this new scheme is significantly reduced by a factor of $\frac{1}{n}$ as compared with the basic SS-scheme, where n is the number of disjoint paths available between the sender and the receiver.

1 Introduction

In resource-constrained devices such as Wireless Sensor Networks and the Internet of Things (IoT), data security is of particular concern due to their limited computational resources and memory. These devices often have to operate within strict energy and computational constraints, which makes traditional

Support for this work was provided by the Information Security Education and Awareness (ISEA), an initiative of the Ministry of Electronics and Information Technology (MeitY) and by C3i (cybersecurity and cybersecurity for Cyber-Physical Systems) Innovation Hub, IIT Kanpur.

cryptographic algorithms impractical for such devices. So, there is a need for an alternative security measure that can provide data protection without compromising the performance of the devices. Secret sharing [1,2] is a technique used to distribute sensitive information among multiple parties while ensuring that the information remains secure. In this setup, the sender divides the original secret into multiple shares and transmits it over multiple paths. Out of all the transmitted shares, the receiver collects the required number of shares in order to regenerate the secret. The number of shares required to reconstruct the secret, known as the threshold, can be adjusted to meet the needs of the specific use case. As the computational complexity of Shamir's scheme [3] in its recovery phase is $\mathcal{O}(t \log^2 t)$, a SS-scheme based on the Chinese Remainder Theorem (CRT) is proposed in the literature [4,5]. This method has a complexity of $\mathcal{O}(t)$ for the secret recovery phase which makes it computationally cheaper with respect to Shamir's SS-scheme. This scheme involves the calculation of a set of moduli that are pairwise coprime. The moduli are chosen such that the product of all moduli is greater than the secret value.

While SS schemes discussed above offer an enhanced level of security by distributing secrets among multiple parties, they are susceptible to Network Data Remanence (NDR) attacks [6]. In an ideal scenario, SS schemes assume that all paths between the sender and the receiver are indivisible or atomic, with identical delays. This assumption limits the attacker to a single opportunity to capture the packets. However, real-world networks contradict these assumptions. In practical networks, paths consist of diverse networking devices, such as routers, switches, bridges, and hubs. Each additional component along the path introduces a propagation delay when transmitting a network packet. Consequently, the shares persist in the network for more than one-time quanta, granting the attacker multiple opportunities to intercept the packet by probing the route. Once the attacker retrieves a sufficient number of shares, they can employ polynomial interpolation to reconstruct the original secret. This unauthorized access to sensitive information may enable the attacker to launch further attacks against the system.

To mitigate the risk of NDR attacks in SS schemes, we propose a novel communication protocol for secure parameter sharing. By elevating the issue of exposing threshold (t) in public, this protocol keeps t value secret amongst the concerned parties with minimal security amendments. It also changes the number of shares to reconstruct the secret every time the session is established. The hiding of the t value makes the attacker oblivious to the parameter and forces it to guess the t value. On the other hand, changing the threshold number of shares in every session forces the attacker to perform a Brute-force attack that checks for every possible value of threshold shares in each session till it gets the correct t. We use the concept of Physically Related Functions (PReF) [7] to ensure parameter secrecy in the network. A PReF involves two devices outputting binary strings that are close to each other in terms of their Hamming Distance (HD) for a specific input set known as the related input set. However, for any input not in the related input set, their outputs are not close to each other and it is difficult for an adversary to determine the relationship between the two devices. We are using this construction property of PReF in our proposed scheme to hide t from the attacker.

In a traditional (t, n) Secret Sharing (SS) scheme, t determines the level of security and is fixed during initialization. However, in practice, t may need to be changed due to various reasons such as increasing distrust among participants or stronger adversary attacks. But, to change it, in such traditional (t, n) SS-schemes, requires re-initialization and re-distribution of shares, which can be costly and difficult due to the lack of a trusted communication channel. To address this issue, a threshold changeable SS (TCSS) scheme is proposed in [8]. In this scheme, the dealer prepares primes for share generation for multiple thresholds during initialization and distributes only the shares for the decided t value along all the paths between the sender and the receiver. When the threshold needs to be changed, the dealer only needs to prepare the shares for the changed t value and broadcast a new threshold value along with related public information. The $(t \rightarrow t', n)$ TCSS scheme supports all possible thresholds in the interval $[t, t']$. Compared to traditional schemes, the $(t \rightarrow t', n)$ TCSS scheme offers several advantages such as simplified initialization and no need for new prime computations. This makes it easier to change the threshold value within the range $[t, t']$ which can be used in our proposed scheme for making it more difficult for the attacker to predict the threshold value. Overall, we summarize the contribution of the paper as follows.

- We propose a novel communication protocol for secure parameter sharing by using the notions of Physically Related Functions (PReF) and Threshold Changeable SS-scheme.
- We have implemented the proposed communication protocol over two Raspberry Pi's as the sending and receiving parties of the SS-scheme by connecting them in a wireless network.
- We provide a detailed security analysis for the robustness and correctness of the proposed communication protocol.
- We show that the probability of performing an NDR Planned attack on a (t, n)-SS scheme is depreciated by a factor of $\frac{1}{n}$.

2   Background

In this section, we discuss the preliminary concepts required for our proposed work.

2.1   Physically Related Functions (PReF)

Suppose, there are two parties, P and Q, each with their own hardware devices or circuits (D_P and D_Q), physically implementing related function pairs f_P and f_Q respectively. These functions have input space χ and output space φ. A PReF [9] pair is defined as a pair of functions where there exists a subset of related inputs, denoted as $\chi_{P,Q} \subseteq \chi$, such that for every input x in the subset $\chi_{P,Q}$, $f_P(x) = f_Q(x)$ holds. Whereas for the inputs outside of $\chi_{P,Q}$, the output behaviors of f_P and f_Q are uncorrelated in a computational sense. Specifically, a computationally constrained adversary cannot predict the output of f_Q on the input x' with probability greater than $\frac{1}{|\varphi|}$ (i.e., with probability better than a random guess) given the output of f_P on the same input x' and is not in $\chi_{P,Q}$. Instead of requiring PReFs to have exactly the same output for related inputs, we require their outputs to be close to each other [7] based on a distance function, such as Hamming Distance. It measures the difference between two binary strings. If we consider acceptable Hamming distance as δ, and if x is a related input for the PReFs f_P and f_Q, then the distance between $f_P(x)$ and $f_Q(x)$ must be less than or equal to δ. If another input x' is not a related input, a computationally bounded adversary cannot guess the corresponding output of f_Q on x' with a probability better than $\frac{1}{|\varphi|}$. More formally we can write it as follows.

$$\mathrm{HD}[f_P(x), f_Q(x)] \leq \delta \iff D_p(f_P(x)) = D_Q(f_Q(x))$$

$$\mathrm{HD}[f_P(x'), f_Q(x')] > \delta \iff D_P(f_P(x')) \neq D_Q(f_Q(x')) \tag{1}$$

Now, as we are considering two outputs as the same even if they have a Hamming distance less than or equal to δ, at the prover end we need to correct Hamming distance errors using Error Correcting Codes (ECC) to make these outputs at both the ends as same. Thus, making both the functions give the same output string for the same challenge. Strong PUFs satisfy all of these basic PReF properties, but they additionally require the process of identifying unique related inputs that can be utilized to construct multiple protocols.

2.2 Chinese Remainder Theorem Based SS Scheme

The SS-scheme is a method of sharing a secret S among a finite set P of n participants, in such a way that any t participants can reconstruct the secret S, but no group of $t-1$ participants can do so. Let's denote the SS scheme as a (t, n) scheme. The basic idea behind CRT-based SS-scheme [4] is to split a secret into several shares. Each of these is derived from a different modulus and can be distributed amongst the participants in order to share that secret between the sender and the receiver [8]. Let us assume the sender has a secret value S and wants to send it to the receiver. It chooses n distinct moduli $m_1, m_2, \ldots, m_n$ and distributes the secret value S among the participants as follows.

- The dealer D chooses pairwise co-prime moduli say $m_0, m_1, \ldots, m_n$, where m_0 is a publicly accepted prime number and $m_0 < m_1 < \ldots < m_n$, and these $n+1$ moduli must comply with the following relationship.

$$\prod_{i=1}^{t} m_i > m_0 \prod_{i=1}^{n-t} m_{n-i+1} \tag{2}$$

Table 1. Common Matrix

Threshold value ↓	1	2	3	4	5
2	521	607	677	797	857
3	547	677	719	727	823
4	547	587	599	733	907

- Let $M = \prod_{i=1}^{n} m_i$ and α is a random positive integer satisfying the condition $\prod_{i=1}^{t-1} m_{n-i+1} < S < \prod_{i=1}^{t} m_i$. Then the dealer selects a secret $s \in_R \mathbb{Z}_{m_0}$ and computes $S = s + \alpha \cdot m_0$.
- Now, the share for each of the participant i is $S_i \equiv S \pmod{m_i}$, for $i \in 1, 2, \ldots, n$.

The secret value S can be reconstructed with any of the t or more shares as follows by the combiner.

- Let there is a participant set, say P, that reconstructs the secret by collaborating t or more participants. All the t or more participants in P send their shares to the combiner.
- The combiner computes $S \equiv \sum_{i \in P} S_i \cdot M'_{P \setminus \{i\}} \cdot M_{P \setminus \{i\}} \bmod M_P$ and obtains the secret s by computing $s = S \pmod{m_0}$. Here, $M_P = \prod_{i \in P} m_i$ and $M_{P \setminus \{i\}} = \prod_{j \in P, j \neq i} m_j$. Also, $M'_{P \setminus \{i\}}$ is the multiplicative inverse of $M_{P \setminus \{i\}}$ in Z_{m_i} i.e. $M'_{P \setminus \{i\}} M_{P \setminus \{i\}} \equiv 1 \pmod{m_i}$.

The advantages of using the CRT-based SS-scheme are as follows.

- It allows for efficient sharing and reconstruction of secrets using fast modular arithmetic operations.
- It reduces the complexity of the secret recovery phase from $\mathcal{O}(t \log^2 t)$ to $\mathcal{O}(t)$.
- The use of CRT allows for the distribution of shares across multiple independent communication channels, which can increase security by reducing the likelihood of a single channel being compromised.

Share generation for SS scheme by using CRT [8] requires publicly accepted prime numbers and those prime numbers are used to generate the shares. Generally a permissible range from the user are considered and then prime numbers are generated for each value of the threshold and they are stored in a 2-dimensional matrix. This matrix is then used for dynamic share generation. The algorithm to generate the common matrix can be referred in [8]. For example, if we have $n = 5$, the permissible range for the threshold t is between 2 and 4. After executing the above algorithm a matrix with three rows (i.e. $4 - 2 + 1$) is generated. Each row is having randomly generated primes for each t value mentioned in the first column. The decision to use for share generation is based on t value selected in Sect. 3.1. Here, we have taken 10-bit long primes for the purpose of explaining the working of the algorithm. The generated matrix is given in Table 1.

2.3   Network Data Remanance Side Channel Attack

In this section, we discuss the attacks performed by using the side channel that is created due to the implementation of Multi-path Switching with Secret Sharing (MSSS) [6] in a real network. MSSS is a scheme in which path switching with multi-path routing and SS-scheme are integrated in order to make the scheme more reliable. In an ideal scenario, the sender and the receiver are connected through hops and packets travel instantaneously through these hops. In contrast, the path in a real network is made up of links, hubs, routers, and switches, and packets move through each of them sequentially, using the store and forward design. This indicates that share propagation is not atomic and there may be variations in latency along each path. This implies that when a new message is transmitted, the network still contains the residual portion of earlier messages. This behavior is known as Network Data Remanence (NDR). Depending on their capabilities, an attacker can probe any number of connections and switches on a route in order to eavesdrop on it. We next discuss the most efficient varient of such attackes named *NDR-Planned.*

NDR-Planned: Let n represent the total number of possible paths between the sender and the receiver. Assume that the length of each of the n pathways between the sender and the receiver is the same and is denoted by l. The sender wants to send a message M to the receiver. In order to send the message, the sender divides the message M into t shares, where $t < n$, and chooses t random paths from all the available n paths and delivers the shares at each clock tick.

In NDR planned, the attacker probes the minimum number of paths required to retrieve the secret [10]. Based on their residual shares from previous messages, the attacker employs a specialized algorithm to choose the paths that are most likely to include shares. It is assumed that the attacker has previous knowledge of the remaining network shares and chooses all the nodes that are one tick away from the sender in the first tick. It then gradually advances away from the sender to pick up missed shares in earlier ticks. Let the probability for an NDR Planned attacker to capture exactly m shares in c ticks be $P_{pln}(m,c)$, where P_{pln} refers that the attacker performs a planned attack. We can define $P_{pln}(m,1)$ as follows.

$$
P_{pln}(m,1) = \begin{cases} \dfrac{\binom{t}{m} \cdot \binom{n-t}{t-m}}{\binom{n}{t}}, & (0 < 2t - n \leq m \leq t) \\ & \text{or } (0 \leq m \leq t \leq \dfrac{n}{2}) \\ 0, & \text{otherwise} \end{cases}
\tag{3}
$$

The objective of the NDR Planned attacker is to acquire over t data-carrying paths out of all those that exist between the sender and the receiver (*i.e.,* n). In (3), the first term chooses m data-carrying paths from the t data-carrying paths available, while the second term chooses the $(t - m)$ paths from all the non-data-carrying paths available. So, for $1 < c < l$, $P_{pln}(m,c)$ can be computed as follows.

$$P_{pln}(m, c) = \sum_{i=0}^{f(m)} P_{pln}(m - i, c - 1) \frac{\binom{t-m+i}{i} \cdot \binom{n-t+m-i}{t-i}}{\binom{n}{t}} \tag{4}$$

where,

$$f(m) = \begin{cases} min(m - (2t - n), t), & 2t > n \\ min(m, t), & 2t \leq n \end{cases}$$

Thus, $P_{pln}(t, l - 1)$ represents the probability of message recovery by the NDR Planned attacker.

2.4   Countermeasure Proposed in [6]

Next we discuss the countermeasure in [6] and its estimation of data recovery by an NDR Planned attacker. In MSSS, the sender creates t shares and distributes them across t disjoint paths. In [6], it is proposed the sender produces additional shares and spreads them across both space and time as the sender and the attacker can only use t paths concurrently. Let H be a system parameter that refers to the resilience factor generated by the sender. Instead of employing (t, t)-SS scheme, the countermeasure proposes a (Ht, Ht) SS-scheme that involves dividing the shares into H sets, each containing t shares. These sets of shares are then gradually transmitted, one set at a time, during consecutive clock ticks. At each clock tick c, the sender chooses t paths uniformly at random and sends a share along each of the chosen paths.

The probability is estimated based on the presumption that the attacker tries persistently to obtain all t shares of a certain set. If attacker successfully takes control of every share at time c, it keeps the same distance from the next set of shares to attempt capture at time $c+1$. However, if it fails to capture all t shares at c, it randomly selects t nodes that are one link further away to probe for the next set of shares. For an attacker to retrieve the message, it must obtain all of the shares. Since the final set of shares is transmitted at time $c = H - 1$ and no shares will be available on any intermediate node after time $c = L + H - 2$. Assuming that $n(L - 1) \geq Ht$, the probability of data recovery for the NDR Planned attacker can be calculated using $P_{pln}(m, c)$ defined in (16), to be more specific we denote the probability as $P_{pln}(Ht, L+H-2)$. However, $P_{pln}(m, 1)$ can be computed as in (3), as in that case this countermeasure cannot be applied. If $m < Ht$ and $1 < c < L + H - 1$, the probability can be computed in the following way.

$$P_{pln}(m, c) = \sum_{i=0}^{min(t,m)} P_{pln}(m - i, c - 1) \cdot D_{pln}(m, i) \tag{5}$$

Given that $(m - i)$ shares have already been taken, the chance of an NDR planned attacker capturing i fresh shares before end of c clock ticks is shown in (5) by $D_{pln}(m, i)$.

$$D_{pln}(m,i) = \begin{cases} \dfrac{\binom{n-i}{t-i}}{\binom{n}{t}}, & m\%t = 0 \\[2ex] \dfrac{\binom{t-(m\%t-i)}{i}\binom{n-t+(m\%t-i)}{t-i}}{\binom{n}{t}}, & m\%t > 0 \end{cases} \tag{6}$$

$D_{pln}(m,i)$ can be computed as shown in (6), given that one of the conditions below is true. Otherwise $D_{pln}(m,i)$ is 0.

Condition 1: $2t - n \le i$ and $(m - i)\%t = 0$ and $2t > n$
Condition 2: $i \le (t - m - i)\%t \le n - t$ and $2t > n$
Condition 3: $i \le m\%t$ and $m\%t > 0$ and $2t \le n$

$$P_{pln}(Ht,c) = \begin{cases} \dfrac{P_{pln}((H-1)t,H-1)}{\binom{n}{t}}, & c = H \\[2ex] P_{pln}(Ht,c-1) + \dfrac{P_{pln}((H-1)t,c-1)}{\binom{n}{t}} & c > H, 2t > n \\[1ex] + \sum_{i=1}^{n-t} \dfrac{P_{pln}(Ht-i,c-1)\cdot\binom{n-i}{t-i}}{\binom{n}{t}}, & \\[2ex] \sum_{i=1}^{t} \dfrac{P_{pln}(Ht-i,c-1)\cdot\binom{n-i}{t-i}}{\binom{n}{t}}, & c > H, 2t \le n \end{cases} \tag{7}$$

While the proposed countermeasure reduces the probability of data recovery compared to using MSSS, it has certain limitations: ⓐ The threshold (t) is public information that provides an NDR-planned attacker with a clue to probe for t shares, ⓑ As the sender is sending Ht number of shares instead of t, it increases the congestion in the network, ⓒ The attacker can recover data with higher probabilities as the path length increases. To address these issues and significantly increase the attacker's effort, we propose a secure communication protocol in the below section based on PReF and threshold changeability.

3   Proposed Countermeasure on NDR Planned Attack

In this section, we describe the system model and the adversarial model. Afterward, we propose our communication protocol for secure parameter sharing.

System Setting and Adversarial Model: The proposed system model consists of a Trusted Third Party (TTP) and legitimate participants that can send shares and receive them in order to reconstruct secret messages in the network. The participants have access to the information on n, t, and have a Double Arbiter Physically Unclonable Function (DA-PUF) Hardware. While any Strong PUF can be employed in the protocol, we use a Double Arbiter PUF (DA-PUF) in our description as a representative example. Each Participant also have a set of challenges that can be used while communicating with each other. The TTP has a Physically Related Function based on DA-PUF for each pair of registered participants. It consists of challenge-response pairs of DA-PUF that give related responses for both the involved participants in the SS scheme. Let, T be a TTP, and $P1$, $P2$ are registered legitimate participants in the network. Now, a third participant $P3$ wants to get registered in the network.

- Firstly, $P1$ and $P2$ communicate through a set of related challenges C_{12}, which are selected and provided to $P1$ and $P2$ by T.
- Now, since $P3$ also intends to connect to the network, T requests challenge-response pairs from $P3$ that are generated by its own DA-PUF hardware.
- T initially filters all the related challenges of $P3$ with $P1$ and $P2$, referred to as C'_{13} and C'_{23}, respectively.
- T further filters C'_{13} and C'_{23} to ensure that the resulting challenge sets C_{13}, C_{23}, and C_{12} are mutually exclusive.
- Finally, T transmits C_{13} to both $P1$ and $P3$, and C_{23} to both $P2$ and $P3$.

The protocol is designed in such a way that it successfully hides the changeable threshold across the sessions. In case the number of participants in the network increases, an on-the-fly request can be sent to the TTP. Please note that the challenges need not be private, so the TTP can send it over an insecure network in plain text. In this way, a new participant gets enrolled into the network and gets a unique set of challenges to communicate with each of the existing participants in the network. This enrolment is done in a trusted environment before any participant gets deployed into the network. Moreover, since the protocol shares only the challenges throughout the network in plain text, without revealing their corresponding responses, it significantly enhances resilience against machine learning (ML)-based attacks. Such attacks typically target Strong PUFs by training models on large sets of challenge-response pairs (CRPs).

The adversary has access to the number of disjoint paths (n) that is accessible publicly. However, the measures included in the proposed scheme hide the threshold (t) from all the unconcerned parties making it inaccessible to the adversary. Also, the attacker or any unconcerned authority cannot query the DA-PUF hardware present at a legitimate participant for a particular challenge. The responses for each pair of participants present at the TTP are also inaccessible to the attacker.

3.1 Proposed Communication Protocol for Secure Parameter Sharing

In this section, we first discuss the main properties and the intuitions behind the proposed protocol. Using *Threshold Hiding*, we keep t private and make it accessible only to the concerned parties. It makes an NDR-planned attack harder as it tries to capture t number of shares for secret reconstruction. Secondly, *Threshold Changeability* is another property that makes t dynamic across every session of the SS. In case, the attacker tries to guess it, the above-mentioned property enforces the adversary to perform a brute-force attack. Now, we discuss how we implement these two properties in our proposed protocol.

The *threshold hiding* is achieved by establishing prover-to-prover parameter sharing using PReF. A pair of Physically Related Function (PReF) model (i.e., a related set of challenges) is set on two devices that need to share the secret in the network. Let the embedded PUF hardware at the sender and the receiver

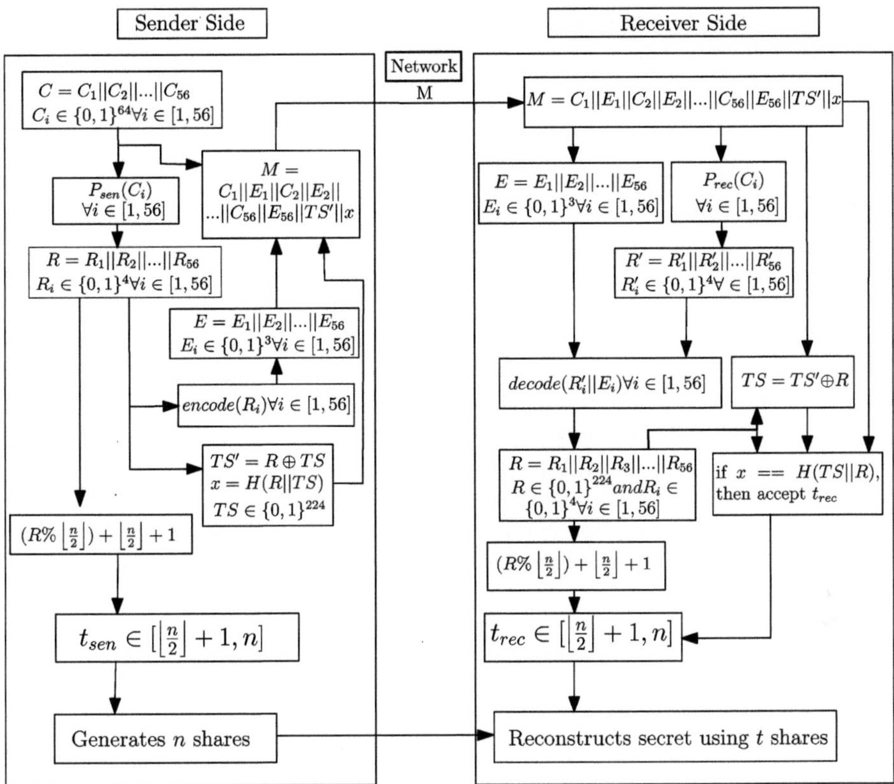

Fig. 1. Overview of the Proposed Protocol.

end be $P_{sen}(C_i)$ and $P_{rec}(C_i)$ respectively, where C_i is a related challenge. The same setup is set between each pair of devices in the network separately for secret communication. While enrolment, the TTP makes sure that it selects a related challenge for which the responses generated from the PUF hardware of the communicating parties are at most one Hamming distance away. Figure 1 clearly explains the overall architecture of the proposed SS-protocol as described below.

- The sender chooses 56 random 64-bit challenges denoted as C_i and takes their 4-bit responses denoted as R_i where $i \in [1,56]$ from the PUF Hardware that collectively makes a 224-bit response R. The challenge and response collectively are as follows.

$$C = C_1||C_2||C_3||...||C_{56} \tag{8}$$

$$R = R_1||R_2||R_3||...||R_{56} \tag{9}$$

where each $C_i \in \{0,1\}^{64}$ and $R_i \in \{0,1\}^4 \ \forall i \in [1,56]$.

- The response R is converted to a threshold value t_{sen} where $t_{sen} \in [\lfloor \frac{n}{2} \rfloor + 1, n]$ at the sender by using below function.

$$t_{sen} = (R \% \lfloor \frac{n}{2} \rfloor) + \lfloor \frac{n}{2} \rfloor + 1 \tag{10}$$

Here, t_{sec} has a range of values in $[1, n]$, but according to 2 in the Chinese Remainder Theorem-based SS-scheme the threshold t can not be strictly less than $\lfloor \frac{n}{2} \rfloor + 1$. The argument is formally substantiated in Sect. 4.
- The sender randomly chooses a 224-bit timestamp TS and calculates $TS' = TS \oplus R$ and $x = H(TS||R)$.
- As PUF is a hardware circuit and it can introduce inherent noise at times, we add an Error Correction Code (ECC) for error detection and correction of the generated responses. The ECC is selected in such a way that for every 4-bit response, it can detect and correct a 1-bit error. So, we are using a Hamming(7,4) code with 3 parity bits overload.
- We have introduced an encoder module at the sender side (i.e. *encode*). It generates helper data for error correction at the receiver end. So, for each response R_i, a 3-bit of helper data is generated by *encode*(). It is established more formally as below.

$$encode(R_i) = E_i$$

$$E = E_1||E_2||E_3||...||E_{56} \tag{11}$$

where each $E_i \in \{0,1\}^3 \; \forall i \in [1,56]$
- Finally, each of these ECCs is then concatenated with corresponding challenges along with TS' and x. The message M transmitted in the network is generated as shown in (12).

$$M = C_1||E_1||C_2||E_2||...||C_{56}||E_{56}||TS'||x \tag{12}$$

- After receiving the message M, the PUF hardware at receiver $P_{rec}(C_i)$ generates a response R'_i for each challenge C_i where $i \in [1,56]$.
- All these R'_i responses constitute to become R' which is the collective 224-bit response of the challenge at the receiver.

$$R' = R'_1||R'_2||R'_3||...||R'_{56} \tag{13}$$

where each $R'_i \in \{0,1\}^4 \; \forall i \in [1,56]$
- Some of these R'_i responses could have error present in them. So, to detect and correct the error we introduced a decoder module (i.e. *decode*) at the receiver side. Each response R'_i along with its corresponding helper data E_i is then passed to the decoder that corrects the error and gives the response R_i. *decode*() gives a response R as an output that collectively looks as below.

$$decode(R'_i|E_i) = R_i$$

$$R = R_1||R_2||R_3||...||R_{56} \tag{14}$$

where each $R'_i \in \{0,1\}^4$ and $E_i \in \{0,1\}^3$ and $R_i \in \{0,1\}^4 \; \forall i \in [1,56]$

- Now, as we have corrected the error at the receiver end, the responses R_i at both sides become identical. Finally, R is converted to the threshold t_{rec} value by using (10).
- The receiver then calculates $TS = TS' \oplus R$ and $x' = H(TS\|R)$. If $x' == x$ (x is received along with M) then it accepts t_{rec}. Else it rejects t_{rec} and identifies the sender as an untrusted party. Thus, the sender and the receiver agree on the same threshold value ($t_{sen} = t_{rec}$) without actually sending the response which derives t at both sides.

<u>Share Generation Phase</u>
1. Create a list *share* with size n and each element as zero.
2. Perform the below step for each element i of the list *share*.
3. $share[i]=(secret + \alpha[t-a]*mat[t-a][0])\% \, mat[t-a][i+1]$.

<u>Share Reconstruction Phase</u>
1. Create two lists namely *mod* and *rem* with size t and initialized with zero.
2. Iterate over each element i of *mod* and set its value to $mat[t - a][i + 1]$.
3. Similarly, each element j of *rem* is set to $share[j]$.
4. The *secret* is revealed by calling Python function named *solve_crt()* that takes two arguments *rem*, *mod* respectively.

Fig. 2. Share Generation and Reconstruction Algorithm.

- **Share Generation:** After completing the matrix generation task shown in Sect. 2.2, we generate shares using the concepts in the threshold changeable SS-scheme. We can generate shares for any value within the range $[a,b]$ multiple times without repeating the matrix generation process. Also, we have the matrices *mat* and *alpha* constructed in Sect. 2.2. The shares can be generated for any threshold value within the given range by using this step. Thus, the *threshold changeability* property is achieved.
- **Share Reconstruction:** As the shares are transmitted to the receiver it only requires to acquire t shares to reconstruct the secret. The overall algorithm for share generation and reconstruction is shown in above Fig. 2.

To gain a better understanding, let us take the same example from Sect. 2.2. The common matrix (mat) and α are already generated in Sect. 2.2. Consider we select $t = 3$, the second row from mat shown in Table 1 and the second element from α are used for share list generation. Now, $\alpha[t - a] = 399151$ and $s = 12$ and $m_0 = 547$. After performing the share generation phase mentioned above the share tuple is $(401, 474, 61, 293, 680)$. Now, the share tuple and the corresponding prime moduli tuple (shown in Table 1) are transmitted to the receiver. The receiver only requires three elements from each tuple, out of the five elements present, to regenerate the secret s.

3.2   Scalability of the Proposed PReF-Based Architecture

An important advantage of using Physically Related Functions (PReFs) in the proposed protocol lies in their ability to scale to a large number of participants without compromising uniqueness or security.

As discussed earlier, each new participant enrolled into the system is assigned unique challenge-response sets that are pairwise disjoint across the network. The Trusted Third Party (TTP) ensures this by filtering the related challenges such that each pair of participants shares a mutually exclusive set. However, this naturally raises the question of how many devices or participants can be supported by the system under these constraints.

Following the theoretical bounds established in [9], the maximum size T of a PReF network is constrained by the correlation probability ε and the uniqueness parameter ε', which together ensure that no two device pairs share the same related input subset. The authors in [9] provide a representative example based on their DA-PUF-based implementation, where the bit mismatch probability q is observed in the range $[0.26, 0.4]$. For an illustrative value of $q = 0.35$, with response size $m = 224$ and a maximum allowable Hamming distance $\delta = 32$, the corresponding correlation probability is calculated as $\varepsilon \approx 1.46 \times 2^{-39}$ [9, Eq. (2)]. Assuming a security-level uniqueness bound of $\varepsilon' = 2^{-128}$, the authors show that the network can theoretically support up to $T = 2^{43}$ unique devices while preserving mutual exclusivity of the input subsets [9, Sec. IV-F].

This upper bound demonstrates that our proposed scheme is not only secure but also practically scalable, supporting hundreds of participants while maintaining the uniqueness of the PUF, error tolerance, and session-based randomness. As the number of participants increases, the TTP can efficiently enlist new devices while preserving the cryptographic integrity of the network.

4   Security Analysis for the Proposed Protocol

The main target here is to share t by keeping the adversary oblivious to the same. As the derivation of t solely depends on the response generated by the PUFs at both the sender and the receiver side, we try to prove that the adversary can generate the response from the challenge with a negligible probability.

Definition IV.1. Conditional Pseudorandomness [7]: Consider a family of functions F, where each function $f_p : X \rightarrow Y$ maps elements from set X to set Y. Let $k \in \mathbb{N}$. For each $p \in [1, k]$, let $X_{0,p}$ be a set such that $f_0(x) = f_p(x)$ for all $x \in X_{0,p}$. We model the devices in the network as functions $f_0, f_1, ..., f_p$, such that for all $t \in [1, k]$, the pair (D_0, D_P) forms a PReF pair. Suppose there exists a polynomial-time adversary A with oracle access to the devices $D_0, D_1, ..., D_p$. We say that D_0 is conditionally pseudorandom if the adversary A cannot distinguish between $D_0(x')$ and a randomly chosen value from the output space Y with more than a negligible advantage, given the following restrictions.

- If $x' \in X \backslash (\bigcup_{p=1}^{k} X_{0,p})$, then the adversary A is prohibited from issuing an oracle query of the form $D_0(x')$.
- If $x' \in X_{0,p}$, then the adversary A is prohibited to make oracle queries of the form $D_0(x')$ or $D_p(x')$.

Definition IV.2. Physically Related Function (PReF) [7]: Let F be a family of functions $f_p : X \to Y$, where X and Y are any arbitrary sets. Two devices in a network, D_P, and D_Q, are functionally modeled as f_p and f_q, respectively. Then, the pair of devices (D_P, D_Q) is considered a PReF pair if there is a unique input set $X_{p,q} \subset X$ such that:

- $f_p(\mathrm{x}) = f_q(\mathrm{x})$ for all $\mathrm{x} \in X_{p,q}$
- D_P and D_Q are conditionally pseudorandom as per the Def.IV.1.

Definition IV.3. Universality [7]: If we have a PReF device instance denoted as D and is functionally modeled as $f_p : X \to Y$, it is considered to fulfill the universality property when the distribution of $f(x)_{x \in X'}$ is statistically similar to the uniform distribution $\bigcup_Y$ over Y for any given input subset $X_0 \subseteq X$. Essentially, this means that for any $X_0 \subseteq X$ and any $y \in Y$, the following holds.

$$\sum_{x \in X'} |Pr[f(x) = y] - Pr[U_Y = y]| \leq negl(n) \tag{15}$$

Next, we prove the security of the proposed scheme.

Theorem IV.1. The PReF-based secure parameter sharing scheme is statistically hiding under a random oracle model with the assumptions that PReF (defined in Def.IV.2) is conditionally pseudorandom (as defined in Def.IV.1) and follows universality (as defined in Def.IV.3).

Proof. Let input to the sender and the receiver side PReF instances be c. Also, U_Y is a uniform distribution over the output set Y. Since PReF follows universality property, for any $c \in X$ and $y \in Y$.

$$Pr[D_P(c) = y] \approx Pr[U_Y = y], Pr[D_Q(c) = y] \approx Pr[U_Y = y]$$

If we model a random oracle function $H : \{0,1\}^{448} \to \{0,1\}^{256}$ for any input $c \in X$, the probability of generating the same hash as that of the sender device for a device D' at the adversary for any randomly chosen t_s where $t_s \in \{0,1\}^{224}$ is shown as below.

$$Pr[H(D_P(c)\|TS) - H(D'(c)\|ts)] = \frac{1}{2^{256}}$$

Now, if the adversary device D' tries to query the oracle function multiple times (say q), the probability of generating the same hash as that of the sender device tends to increase because each query to the oracle provides the adversary with additional information about the output space. So, the probability of generating the same hash as that of the sender device in the qth query to the random oracle is shown as below.

$$Pr[H(D_P(c)||TS) - H(D'(c)||ts)] = 1 - (1 - \frac{1}{2^{256}})^q$$

According to binomial theorem, $(1 + x)^n \approx 1 + nx$. Hence,

$$Pr[H(D_P(c)||TS) - H(D'(c)||ts)] \approx q \cdot \frac{1}{2^{256}}$$

Thus, the probability of breaking the proposed protocol remains negligibly small even with multiple queries.

Range for t Value: As t is generated over a modulus function of (R, n), $t \in [1, n]$, where R is the response of the PUF (refer Eq. 9). As our protocol uses CRT-based SS-Scheme, it relies on $n + 1$ prime numbers $m_0, m_1, ..., m_n$, where $m_i < m_j$ for $i < j$. However, from the requirement stated in Eq. 2, if we order the prime numbers, we can make an observation that t value must be strictly greater than $\lfloor \frac{n}{2} \rfloor$. We will verify this by taking an example where $t = \frac{n}{2}$. Substituting $t = \frac{n}{2}$ in LHS and $t = \frac{n}{2}$ in RHS of Eq. 2, we get: $m_1 \cdot m_2 \cdot ... \cdot m_{\frac{n}{2}} < m_{\frac{n}{2}}^{\frac{n}{2}}$ and $m_0 \cdot m_{\frac{n}{2}+1} \cdot m_{\frac{n}{2}+2} \cdot ... \cdot m_n > m_{\frac{n}{2}+1}^{\frac{n}{2}}$. As we know, $m_{\frac{n}{2}+1}^{\frac{n}{2}} > m_{\frac{n}{2}}^{\frac{n}{2}}$, we get: $m_1 \cdot m_2 \cdot ... \cdot m_{\frac{n}{2}} < m_{\frac{n}{2}+1} \cdot m_{\frac{n}{2}+2} \cdot ... \cdot m_n$. This contradicts the requirement 2 for CRT-based SS-Scheme. Hence, we can say that the range for t value is $[\lfloor \frac{n}{2} \rfloor + 1, n]$.

Improvement over [6]: Given the above-mentioned security analysis, if the adversary now attempts to perform an NDR-planned attack by guessing the t value, the probability (refer to Sect. 2.3) to recover the data is as follows.

$$P_{pln}(m, c) = \sum_{i=0}^{f(m)} P_{pln}(m - i, c - 1) \frac{\binom{t-m+i}{i} \cdot \binom{n-t+m-i}{t-i}}{\binom{n}{t}} \tag{16}$$

where

$$f(m) = \begin{cases} min(m - (2t - n), t), & 2t > n \\ min(m, t), & 2t \leq n \end{cases}$$

Assuming that the adversary guesses threshold t' with uniform probability, the probability of data recovery in this scenario is computed as below.

$$P_{pln}(m, c, t) = \begin{cases} \sum_{t'=0}^{n} \frac{2}{n} \cdot P_{pln}(m, c, t'), & t \text{ is even} \\ \sum_{t'=0}^{n} \frac{2}{n+2} \cdot P_{pln}(m, c, t'), & t \text{ is odd} \end{cases} \tag{17}$$

If the guessed threshold t' is greater than or equal to the actual threshold value t, the data can be correctly recovered. Whereas if the guessed threshold value t' is less than the actual threshold value, the data cannot be retrieved. More formally, we can say it as follows.

$$P_{pln}(m, c, t) = \begin{cases} \frac{2}{n} \cdot \sum_{t'=t}^{n} P_{pln}(m, c, t'), & t' \geq t \text{ \& t is even} \\ \frac{2}{n+2} \cdot \sum_{t'=t}^{n} P_{pln}(m, c, t'), & t' \geq t \text{ \& t is odd} \\ 0, & t' < t \end{cases} \quad (18)$$

The sender needs to select t value close to n, which makes the adversary guess and collude with t' number of hops where $t' >= t$. Now, an NDR-planned attack is based on the assumption that the attacker can tap a small subset of the hops in an intelligent way across the path length between the sender and the receiver to collect shares from a sufficiently large network. But to tap t' number of hops to satisfy the criteria of $t' \geq t$, actually opposes the basic intuition of the NDR-planned attack. This eventually makes the probability of data recovery from an NDR-planned attacker depreciated by a factor of $\frac{1}{n}$ and the message transmissions to resist an NDR-planned attack is reduced by a factor of $\frac{1}{H}$ as compared to [6].

5   Experimental Setup and Results

In this section, we delve into the experimental arrangement for the proposed SS-scheme and explore how it impacts the probability of successfully recovering a secret message when faced with an NDR-planned attack. The scheme is successfully implemented using two Raspberry Pi 3 Model B+ devices, each equipped with a 1.4 GHz CPU and 1GB RAM. One device served as the sender, while the other acted as the receiver, both connected via a wireless network. For the hashing purpose, we have used SHA-256. For the experimental setup, we have considered 10 node disjoint paths between the sender and the receiver with path length l ranging from 2 to 9 and the threshold number of shares ranging between 1 to 9. The scheme is implemented for a n value from 10 to 100 and the average power consumption reported is 8.38mW. The *powertop* command in Linux is used to report the power consumption. The total time required for the complete secret sharing protocol including protocol execution, message transmission, and propagation delays for different values of n at both the sender and receiver ends is reported in Table 2.

In Fig. 3, as we increase the threshold number of nodes, we observe that the probability of data recovery increases more rapidly without employing countermeasures compared to when countermeasures are implemented. Furthermore, despite of decreasing the data recovery by the NDR-planned attacker, the change in threshold value has a minimal impact on the effectiveness of the countermeasure. This makes the threshold value more unpredictable for the attacker. Moreover, comparing the scenarios when the countermeasure is applied and when it is not, we observe that the NDR-planned attacker has minimal impact on the

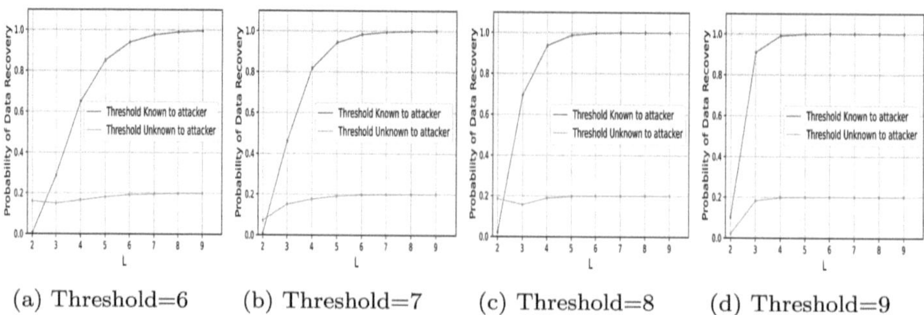

(a) Threshold=6   (b) Threshold=7   (c) Threshold=8   (d) Threshold=9

Fig. 3. Probability of data recovery with and without countermeasure for different threshold values (6–9), path length (2–9), and 10 node disjoint paths.

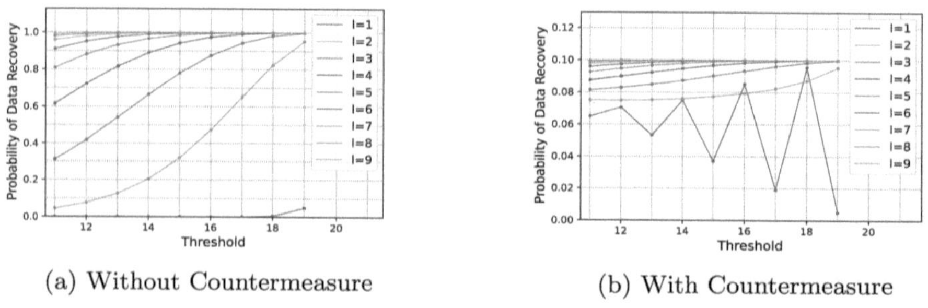

(a) Without Countermeasure   (b) With Countermeasure

Fig. 4. Probability of data recovery with and without countermeasure for different threshold values (11–19) ranging between 11 to 19, constant path length l and 20 node disjoint paths.

probability of data recovery in the former case, even with an increase in the path length. However, in the latter case, an increase in the path length does impact the probability of data recovery.

Table 2. Reported time (in sec.) to execute the protocol.

Threshold value $\rightarrow$	10	15	20	25	30	35	40
Time reported at the sender	7	9	10	10	12	13	13
Time reported at the receiver	4	5	5	8	9	9	11

In Fig. 4(a), when the threshold is increased, regardless of the path lengths, the probability of data recovery by the NDR-planned attacker tends to increase. This does not seem true in the case when the countermeasure is applied as shown in Fig. 4(b). Moreover, Fig. 4(b) shows that the SS-scheme driven by the proposed countermeasure exhibits minimal sensitivity to changes in path lengths. In contrast, when path lengths are increased without applying the countermeasure, it has a detrimental impact on the probability of data recovery by an NDR-planned attacker. In total Fig. 3 and Fig. 4 illustrate that our proposed countermeasure for the SS-scheme exhibits minimal sensitivity to increase in both the threshold value and the path length. This indicates that the countermeasure can effectively mitigate the probability associated with higher thresholds and larger disjoint path lengths, which consequently expands the network's communication infrastructure. As a result, our proposed countermeasure demonstrates scalability, allowing for its application to a greater number of devices within the network.

6   Conclusion

We have developed a communication protocol for secure parameter sharing using the notions of Physically Related Functions (PReF) and Threshold Changeable SS-scheme. We have also validated the proposed communication protocol by providing the security analysis for its robustness and correctness. The scheme significantly reduces the probability of performing an NDR-planned attack on a (t, n) ss scheme. We have simulated the protocol over two Raspberry-pi devices connecting in a wireless network that shows that the protocol can be effectively used for SS in resource-constrained devices.

References

1. Beimel, A.: Secret-sharing schemes: a survey. In: Chee, Y.M., et al. (eds.) IWCC 2011. LNCS, vol. 6639, pp. 11–46. Springer, Heidelberg (2011). https://doi.org/10.1007/978-3-642-20901-7_2
2. Blakley, G.R.: Safeguarding cryptographic keys. In: International Workshop on Managing Requirements Knowledge (MARK), vol. 1979, pp. 313–318 (1979)
3. Shamir, A.: How to share a secret. Commun. ACM **22**(11), 612–613 (1979). https://doi.org/10.1145/359168.359176
4. Asmuth, C., Bloom, J.: A modular approach to key safeguarding. IEEE Trans. Inf. Theory **29**(2), 208–210 (1983)
5. Mignotte, M.: How to share a secret. In: Beth, T. (ed.) Cryptography, pp. 371–375. Springer, Heidelberg (1983)
6. Rashidi, L., et al.: More than a fair share: network data remanence attacks against secret sharing-based schemes. In: Network and Distributed System Security Symposium, NDSS, vol. 28 (2021). https://www.ndss-symposium.org/ndss-paper/more-than-a-fair-share-network-data-remanence-attacks-against-secret-sharing-based-schemes/
7. Boyapally, H., Patranabis, S., Mukhopadhyay, D.: Commitments via physically related functions. IEEE Trans. Inf. Forensics Secur. **18**, 1497–1508 (2023)
8. Jia, X., Wang, D., Nie, D., Luo, X., Sun, J.Z.: A new threshold changeable secret sharing scheme based on the Chinese remainder theorem. Inf. Sci. **473**, 13–30 (2019). https://www.sciencedirect.com/science/article/pii/S0020025518307242

9. Chatterjee, D., Boyapally, H., Patranabis, S., Chatterjee, U., Hazra, A., Mukhopadhyay, D.: Physically related functions: exploiting related inputs of PUFs for authenticated-key exchange. IEEE Trans. Inf. Forensics Secur. **17**, 3847–3862 (2022)
10. Naik, P., Chatterjee, U.: Network data remanence side channel attack on SPREAD, H-SPREAD and reverse AODV. In: Batina, L., Picek, S., Mondal, M. (eds.) Security, Privacy, and Applied Cryptography Engineering, pp. 129–147. Springer, Cham (2022)

Quantum Synthesis of Large S-Boxes: Heuristic and MILP-Based Transpiled-Depth Optimization

Tarun Yadav$^{(\boxtimes)}$, Shweta Singh , and Sudha Yadav

Scientific Analysis Group, DRDO, Metcalfe House Complex, Delhi 110054, India
{`tarunyadav.sag,shweta.singh2416,sudhayadav.sag`}@gov.in

Abstract. Quantum cryptanalysis of block ciphers with Grover's search requires synthesis of round function, where the non-linear S-boxes dominate the circuit cost. Efficient quantum implementations of these S-boxes are a bottleneck for cryptanalysis. In this work, we address this problem and present two new generic strategies for synthesis of quantum circuit for large S-boxes that reduces the NISQ-era transpiled depth after decomposition into the hardware-agnostic universal basis gate set `U+CX`. First, we develop an ANF-based heuristic with global common subexpression elimination and layered scheduling. This approach leverages modest ancilla budgets to eliminate redundant computations and aggressively parallelise low-degree monomials, producing circuits that substantially reduce primitive as well as transpiled depth compared to the classical MMD baseline. Second, we introduce two-phase MILP-based, ancilla-aware synthesis framework for large S-boxes. Phase 1 determines which monomials will be synthesised globally, and how they are reused across outputs. This reduces redundancy and avoids high-degree terms that would lead to deep ladders. Phase 2 arranges the selected monomials into parallel layers. Here the solver explicitly accounts for ancilla usage, balancing the trade-off between fewer layers (smaller depth) and larger ancilla. MILP based synthesis show decisive, multi-fold reductions in transpiled depth in universal basis gate set `U+CX`. For SKINNY and ZUC S0 S-boxes, our synthesis reduces transpiled depth by factors of 18 and 9, respectively, with ancilla usage raised only to 10 and 13 qubits. For higher-degree S-boxes such as AES, SM4, and ZUC S1, we achieve 5 times reduction in transpiled depth by trading additional ancillas, increasing the budget from 5 to 22. To our knowledge, this is the first demonstration of MILP based ancilla-aware, globally optimised synthesis of 8-bit cryptographic S-boxes. By aligning primitive synthesis with transpiled cost, our methods establish a new baseline for depth-optimised resource estimation in the quantum cryptanalysis of symmetric primitives.

Keywords: Quantum circuits · Transpiled depth · S-box · MILP optimization

C. Karfa et al. (Eds.): SPACE 2025, LNCS 16406, pp. 377–406, 2026.
https://doi.org/10.1007/978-3-032-16342-4_21

1   Introduction

Substitution boxes (S-boxes) are fundamental building blocks in symmetric cryptography. They provide the non-linearity required to resist linear and differential attacks, and hence largely determine the cryptanalytic strength of a cipher. In block ciphers such as AES, SM4, and SKINNY, and in stream ciphers such as ZUC, S-boxes serve as the core non-linear transformation. From the perspective of quantum cryptanalysis, the efficient realization of these S-boxes as reversible quantum circuits directly determines the cost of Grover's search or related attacks. Thus, synthesizing low-cost quantum circuits for S-boxes is a decisive step in estimating the quantum security of symmetric primitives.

1.1   Small vs. Large S-Boxes

The cost of quantum synthesis strongly depends on the size of the S-box. Small S-boxes, such as the 4-bit S-box used in PRESENT [1] and GIFT [2], can be realized with only a handful of Toffoli and CNOT gates. For example, optimized circuits for the GIFT S-box required few Toffoli gates and achieve low transpiled depth even after Clifford$+T$ decomposition. As a result, the quantum cost for GIFT often arises from the linear layer where in the idealized model it is free as a wire relabeling, but in hardware-constrained settings it translates into costly SWAP operations that overshadow the S-box cost.

In contrast, large 8-bit S-boxes, as employed in AES [3], SM4 [4], SKINNY [5] and ZUC [6], pose a much greater challenge. Their non-linear structure cannot be captured by shallow reversible networks, and existing methods of synthesis typically yields hundreds of Toffoli gates with depth in the hundreds. When transpiled, these circuits inflate to thousands of Clifford$+T$ or U+CX basis gates with depths in the order of thousands, making the S-box the clear bottleneck in the quantum implementation. This gap between 4-bit and 8-bit implementations highlights the need for specialized optimization methods for large S-boxes.

1.2   Quantum Gates

To execute classical Boolean functions such as S-boxes on a quantum computer, they must be implemented as reversible quantum circuits. The standard model expresses such circuits using a universal gate set, which is later transpiled to Clifford$+T$ or U+CX basis. Below we briefly recall the main gate types relevant to S-box synthesis:

- **NOT (Pauli-X) gate.** A single-qubit gate that flips $|0\rangle$ to $|1\rangle$ and vice versa, corresponding to classical bit negation:

$$X = \begin{bmatrix} 0 & 1 \\ 1 & 0 \end{bmatrix}.$$

– **CNOT (controlled-NOT or CX) gate.** A two-qubit gate that flips the target qubit iff the control qubit is $|1\rangle$. It is the quantum analogue of XOR and is essential for linear layers:

$$\text{CNOT} : |c, t\rangle \mapsto |c, t \oplus c\rangle.$$

– **Toffoli (CCNOT or CCX) gate.** A three-qubit gate that flips the target iff both controls are $|1\rangle$. Generalizations to n controls allow realization of arbitrary AND functions. Toffoli gates form the backbone of reversible S-box synthesis.

$$\text{CCNOT} : |c_1, c_2, t\rangle \mapsto |c_1, c_2, t \oplus (c_1 \cdot c_2)\rangle.$$

• **Realization of Arbitrary AND Functions**
Every Boolean monomial in Algebraic Normal Form (ANF) can be expressed as

$$m(x_1, \ldots, x_n) = \prod_{j \in S} x_j, \quad S \subseteq [n].$$

Such a monomial corresponds to the logical AND of the selected input bits. This is realized directly by an MCX gate with controls $\{x_j : j \in S\}$ and an ancilla target qubit z, yielding

$$|x_1, \ldots, x_n, z\rangle \mapsto |x_1, \ldots, x_n, z \oplus m(x_1, \ldots, x_n)\rangle.$$

Thus, MCX gates provide a reversible implementation of arbitrary AND functions, which form the building blocks of S-box outputs in their ANF representation.

• **Generalized Toffoli (MCX) Gates**
The standard Toffoli gate acts on three qubits, flipping the target bit only when both control qubits are in state $|1\rangle$. This generalizes naturally to a k-controlled Toffoli (multi-controlled X, or MCX) gate with controls $c_1, c_2, \ldots, c_k$ and target t. The action is defined as:

$$|c_1, c_2, \ldots, c_k, t\rangle \mapsto |c_1, c_2, \ldots, c_k, t \oplus (c_1 \cdot c_2 \cdots c_k)\rangle.$$

That is, the target qubit flips if and only if all k control qubits are in the $|1\rangle$ state.

– **Hadamard (H) gate.** The Hadamard gate creates superpositions by mapping the computational basis states as:

$$H = \tfrac{1}{\sqrt{2}} \begin{bmatrix} 1 & 1 \\ 1 & -1 \end{bmatrix},$$

$$H|0\rangle = \tfrac{1}{\sqrt{2}}(|0\rangle + |1\rangle), \quad H|1\rangle = \tfrac{1}{\sqrt{2}}(|0\rangle - |1\rangle).$$

It transforms a definite state into an equal superposition of $|0\rangle$ and $|1\rangle$, which is fundamental for quantum parallelism. Although not directly corresponding to classical logic, H is required for Grover's algorithm and for decomposing multi-controlled operations.

– **Phase (S) and T gates.** Defined as

$$S = \begin{bmatrix} 1 & 0 \\ 0 & i \end{bmatrix}, \quad T = \begin{bmatrix} 1 & 0 \\ 0 & e^{i\pi/4} \end{bmatrix},$$

$$S|0\rangle = |0\rangle, \quad S|1\rangle = i|1\rangle.$$

$$T|0\rangle = |0\rangle, \quad T|1\rangle = e^{i\pi/4}|1\rangle.$$

these introduce controlled phase shifts. Together with H and CNOT, they form the Clifford+T universal gate set. The T gate is considered costly in fault-tolerant implementations, making T-count and T-depth key resource measures.

– **The u gate** The u gate is Qiskit's universal single-qubit operation, parameterised by three Euler angles:

$$u(\theta, \phi, \lambda) = \begin{bmatrix} \cos(\frac{\theta}{2}) & -e^{i\lambda}\sin(\frac{\theta}{2}) \\ e^{i\phi}\sin(\frac{\theta}{2}) & e^{i(\phi+\lambda)}\cos(\frac{\theta}{2}) \end{bmatrix}.$$

This representation covers all possible single-qubit rotations, including X, Y, Z, phase, and Hadamard gates as special cases. In our evaluation, it serves as the basic single-qubit unit in the U+CX basis, reflecting how NISQ(Noisy Intermediate Scale Quantum)-era quantum hardware directly implements arbitrary rotations through physical control pulses.

1.3 Quantum Cost Metrics

The efficiency of a quantum implementation of a classical function can be measured along several dimensions. In the literature on quantum cryptanalysis and quantum circuit synthesis, four metrics are most commonly reported:

– **Qubit count.** The number of logical qubits required. This corresponds to the memory footprint of the circuit. Early works emphasized qubit minimization due to hardware constraints, and qubit count remains important when considering NISQ-era devices. However, for fault-tolerant computation, qubit overhead can often be traded against depth through the use of ancilla qubits, making qubit count alone a misleading performance measure.

– **Gate count.** The total number of quantum gates, usually measured either in a universal gate basis or in primitive reversible gates such as Toffolis and CNOTs. Gate count reflects total operations applied but does not capture parallelism as two circuits with identical gate counts can have very different execution times if one admits more parallel scheduling.

– **Primitive depth.** At the reversible logic level, before decomposition into a hardware or fault-tolerant gate set, circuits are often analyzed in terms of the number of sequential multi-controlled gate layers. This metric has the advantage of being simple to compute and correlates with circuit complexity. However, it is only an indirect proxy for quantum cost and after transpilation, these gates expand into long sequences with nontrivial scheduling constraints, and primitive depth can underestimate the true runtime.

– **Transpiled depth.** In this paper, "transpiled depth" refers to the depth of the circuit after compilation into a universal basis such as Clifford+T or the U+CX set, but before mapping to hardware-native gates. In the Clifford+T model, cost is dominated by the T gate in fault-tolerant implementations. We target the logical U+CX basis, which is the standard device-independent representation adopted in NISQ-era compilers. Although real hardware decomposes U and CX into native operations (e.g., {rz, sx, cz} on IBM devices), the U+CX transpiled depth accurately captures parallelism and qubit-interaction constraints; making it a realistic and hardware-agnostic metric for assessing NISQ costs of practical quantum cryptanalysis.

The coexistence of these metrics reflects different stages in the development of quantum resource estimation. Early studies emphasized qubits and gate count due to hardware scarcity, while later works adopted Toffoli counts and primitive depth as a way to benchmark reversible circuit synthesis algorithms. However, in the context of practical cryptanalysis, where the decisive question is whether a Grover-based search can be completed within a given depth budget, feasibility is determined by the transpiled depth, not the primitive depth measured in gate layers. In particular, two circuits with similar primitive depth can yield vastly different transpiled depths depending on their ancilla structure and synthesis method. This observation motivates our work and we explicitly target transpiled depth minimization as the objective of our synthesis framework, rather than relying on qubit count or primitive depth as proxies.

2   Related Work

2.1   Classical S-Box Design and Optimization

S-boxes are the principal non-linear components in symmetric ciphers and are designed to maximize non-linearity, minimize differential uniformity, and satisfy algebraic criteria while keeping the implementation efficient.

For 8-bit S-boxes like AES, this often involves algebraic constructions (e.g., inversion in $\mathbb{F}_{2^8}$ combined with affine transformations) that balance security and implementation cost [3,7,8]. For lightweight block ciphers such as PRESENT or GIFT, smaller 4-bit S-boxes are adopted to minimize hardware area and energy consumption [1,2], which also makes it possible to apply exhaustive logic optimization or even find the most efficient reversible implementation. Classical optimization techniques therefore trade off between security strength and implementation efficiency, depending on whether the target is high-performance general-purpose cryptography or resource-constrained lightweight designs [9].

2.2   Quantum Circuit Synthesis for S-Boxes

Reversible Synthesis Paradigms. A common approach to build reversible circuits for S-boxes is the Miller–Maslov–Dueck (MMD) method and its extensions [10–12]. These techniques create circuits using a small set of gates: NOT,

CNOT, and Toffoli (sometimes with multiple controls). The cost is usually measured by the number of Toffoli gates or the circuit depth. Other approaches also exist, such as using ESOP forms, XOR–AND graphs, binary decision diagrams (BDDs), spectral techniques, or cycle-based (permutation) synthesis [13]. For linear mixing layers, the classical synthesis method of Patel–Markov–Hayes [14] provides an almost optimal construction of CNOT networks with $O(n^2/\log n)$ cost, establishing the asymptotic bound for general linear transformations. Subsequent work by Xiang et al. [15] optimized such layers specifically for symmetric ciphers, reducing the CNOT gate count through structured decomposition, while Shi and Feng [16] further minimized the overall circuit depth in quantum AES implementations by introducing a low-depth scheduling strategy for the linear layer.

Small vs. Large S-Boxes. For very small S-boxes (3-bit or 4-bit), researchers have already found near-optimal circuits in terms of Toffoli count and depth [9]. However, for larger 8-bit S-boxes (as in AES, ZUC, and SNOW), the problem becomes substantially harder. Straightforward MMD-based synthesis produces hundreds of Toffoli gates and circuit depths in the hundreds even before decomposition into a universal basis [17,18]. Recent efforts have focused on tool-assisted and SAT-based approaches for optimized reversible S-box realization, including LIGHTER-R [19], the SAT-driven constructions of Lin et al. [20], the new SAT-based circuit decision model of Chen et al. [21], and the generalized framework for quantum implementation of both linear and non-linear layers by Baksi et al. [22]. Techniques such as composite-field decomposition can simplify AES's algebraic structure, but unless inversion and affine layers are jointly optimized, the final compiled circuits remain very deep.

Clifford+T Decomposition Details. For fault-tolerant quantum computing, prior work has focused on expressing reversible circuits in the Clifford+T gate set. A Toffoli gate can be broken down into 7 T gates and about 9 Clifford gates. Meet-in-the-middle methods reduce its T-depth to around 3–4 without using ancilla qubits [23]. If 4 ancilla qubits are allowed, Selinger's method can bring the T-depth down to 1, though at the cost of more Clifford gates [24]. Multi-controlled Toffoli gates also have several design trade-offs: ancilla-based ladders with logarithmic overhead, relative-phase Toffoli chains [25,26], or ancilla-free designs with higher depth. The chosen design strongly influences the actual transpiled depth. For arithmetic operations, like addition (important in S-box factorizations and stream ciphers), ripple-carry adders by Cuccaro et al. give efficient depth and gate counts [27]. These form the backbone for both block and stream cipher oracles.

Synthesis Tooling. Open-source frameworks such as REVKIT [28] and the *Munich Quantum Toolkit (MQT)* [29] implement these different synthesis methods and allow optimization passes before converting into universal basis. These frameworks represent circuits as directed acyclic graphs (DAGs), where nodes correspond to gates and edges encode dependencies. Optimizations at the DAG level include gate cancellations, commutations, and local resynthesis, often with T-gate-aware heuristics. General-purpose compilers like *Qiskit* or TKET can further improve the circuits after decomposition, but they often cannot fix inefficiencies caused by poor reversible synthesis choices [30,31]. This highlights the need for synthesis approaches that are already *depth-aware before decomposition*, instead of relying on backend compilers.

2.3 Quantum Resource Estimation in Cryptanalysis

Earlier studies on quantum resources mostly looked at the number of qubits and gates. Later, the focus shifted to Clifford+T measures, especially the number of T gates (T-count) and the number of sequential T layers (T-depth). The most important metric today is the *transpiled circuit depth*, because it shows the actual cost once the circuit is compiled for a quantum computer. NIST's MAXDEPTH rule gives limits on how deep a circuit can be (about 2^{40}–2^{96} cycles depending on the setup) [32]. Since error correction makes non-Clifford gates very expensive, runtime is mainly determined by T-depth. As a result, primitive Toffoli depth is not a reliable cost measure because after transpilation, scheduling constraints and ancilla usage can significantly inflate the realized depth. However, in a NISQ-era model such as Qiskit's U+CX, arbitrary single-qubit rotations are treated as primitive, and transpiled depth reflects realistic execution costs on near-term devices.

For AES, Grassl et al. and later studies estimated the cost of Grover-oracle, including the key schedule, S-box computations, and linear layers [17,33–35]. These optimizations are largely tailored to AES's algebraic structure (e.g., composite-field inversion) and do not extend to generic 8-bit S-boxes. Their results highlighted that S-box depth is the main bottleneck, and they provided design points under different MAXDEPTH assumptions. Luo et al. presented a cipher-specific quantum implementation of SM4 exploiting composite-field arithmetic to reduce Toffoli count and depth [36]. Similar analyses have been carried out for PRESENT, GIFT and other lightweight ciphers, where 4-bit S-boxes reduce non-linear overhead, making linear layers relatively more significant [37] [38].

For stream ciphers, the oracle structure couples state-update arithmetic with non-linear layers. Dutta et al. presented the first comprehensive Grover-based resource estimation for ZUC, introducing arithmetic optimizations (modular doubling/halving modulo $2^n - 1$ as wire permutations, carry-chain scheduling for consecutive additions) and linear-layer synthesis following [14], but used MMD-only reversible synthesis for the 8-bit S-boxes [18].

Beyond heuristic, exact synthesis via optimization has been explored for small functions, often targeting minimal T-count or CNOT count. However, these approaches seldom scale to full 8-bit S-boxes, and typically optimize component-wise counts rather than global transpiled depth with ancilla-awareness and cross-block scheduling.

2.4 Gap and Positioning

Across block and stream cipher studies, prior work predominantly optimizes Toffoli count or primitive depth at the reversible level and relies on backend transpilers for decomposition into a universal gate basis and scheduling. This separation leads to substantial depth difference since two circuits with similar primitive metrics can differ in transpiled depth due to ancilla placement, relative-phase gadgets, and concurrency. To our knowledge, no prior work formulates full 8-bit S-box synthesis as a global, ancilla-aware optimization problem with transpiled depth in a hardware-agnostic basis as the primary objective.

3 Methodology

The synthesis of efficient quantum circuits for 8-bit S-boxes begins with their representation as Boolean functions. Each S-box output can be expressed as a polynomial over $\mathbb{F}_2$, where monomials correspond to logical ANDs of subsets of input variables and addition is realized as XOR. This representation, known as the *algebraic normal form* (ANF), provides a canonical algebraic specification that is particularly suitable for reversible logic synthesis.

From a circuit perspective, the ANF serves as base since each linear term maps to a CNOT, each quadratic term to a Toffoli, and higher-degree terms to multi-controlled Toffolis requiring either ancilla qubits or decompositions into universal gate basis. Thus, the efficiency of a quantum S-box implementation depends on how these monomials are selected, shared across outputs, and scheduled with respect to ancilla usage.

We begin in Sect. 3.1 with a detailed discussion of the ANF representation of Boolean functions, which forms the foundation of our optimization pipeline.

3.1 Algebraic Normal Form (ANF)

Every Boolean function $f : \{0,1\}^n \rightarrow \{0,1\}$ admits a unique representation as a polynomial over $\mathbb{F}_2$ known as its *algebraic normal form (ANF)*:

$$f(x_1, \ldots, x_n) = \bigoplus_{u \in \{0,1\}^n} \lambda_u \cdot \prod_{i=1}^{n} x_i^{u_i}, \tag{1}$$

where $\lambda_u \in \{0,1\}$ are coefficients in $\mathbb{F}_2$, and $\oplus$ denotes XOR. Each monomial $\prod_{i=1}^{n} x_i^{u_i}$ corresponds to an AND of a subset of variables, determined by the support of u. The algebraic degree of f, $\deg(f)$, is the maximum size of such subsets with nonzero coefficient.

For an $n \times m$ S-box (m-bit S-box) $S : \{0,1\}^n \rightarrow \{0,1\}^m$, each output coordinate S_j can be written in ANF:

$$S_j(x_1, \ldots, x_n) = \bigoplus_{u \in \{0,1\}^n} \lambda_{j,u} \cdot \prod_{i=1}^{n} x_i^{u_i}, \qquad j = 1, \ldots, m. \tag{2}$$

Thus, an m-bit S-box is specified by m distinct ANFs, each of which can be interpreted as a set of monomials to be realized by a reversible network.

Example (4-bit S-box). Let the input be $(x_1, x_2, x_3, x_4) \in \{0,1\}^4$, where x_1 is the most significant bit. The PRESENT S-box outputs $S(x) = (S_1, S_2, S_3, S_4)$ are given in algebraic normal form (ANF) as:

$$S_1(x) = 1 \oplus x_1 \oplus x_2 \oplus x_4 \oplus x_2 x_3 \oplus x_1 x_2 x_3 \oplus x_1 x_2 x_4 \oplus x_1 x_3 x_4$$
$$S_2(x) = 1 \oplus x_3 \oplus x_4 \oplus x_1 x_2 \oplus x_1 x_4 \oplus x_2 x_4 \oplus x_1 x_2 x_4 \oplus x_1 x_3 x_4$$
$$S_3(x) = x_2 \oplus x_4 \oplus x_2 x_4 \oplus x_3 x_4 \oplus x_1 x_2 x_3 \oplus x_1 x_2 x_4 \oplus x_1 x_3 x_4$$
$$S_4(x) = x_1 \oplus x_3 \oplus x_4 \oplus x_2 x_3$$

illustrating how linear, quadratic, and cubic monomials coexist.

Implications for Quantum Synthesis. In a quantum circuit, monomials map naturally to multi-controlled Toffoli gates:

- Linear terms x_i are implemented directly as CNOTs from input x_i to the output qubit.
- Quadratic terms $x_i x_j$ correspond to Toffoli gates with two controls.
- Higher-degree terms $x_{i_1} x_{i_2} \cdots x_{i_d}$ correspond to d-controlled Toffolis, realized by decomposition into universal basis gates, with the option of introducing ancillas to reduce depth.

Thus, the ANF serves as the canonical intermediate representation for Boolean synthesis. Once the ANF is known, circuit design reduces to selecting which monomials to implement, how to share them across outputs, and how to schedule them under ancilla constraints.

Key properties of ANFs relevant for optimization include:

1. **Uniqueness:** The ANF is unique for each Boolean function.
2. **Linearity of XOR:** Monomials may be freely added or removed modulo 2, enabling cancellation of repeated subexpressions.
3. **Degree structure:** The distribution of low-degree vs. high-degree monomials strongly impacts the number of Toffoli gates required.
4. **Common subexpressions:** Identical monomials across different outputs can be computed once and fanned out, motivating our layered synthesis strategy.

This ANF representation forms the common foundation for all subsequent synthesis strategies. At the most direct level, each monomial can be realized using multi-controlled Toffoli gates, which leads to the MMD approach described in Sect. 3.2. Our proposed heuristic methods such as ANF+CSE+LS (Sect. 3.3) and MILP-based optimization (Sect. 3.4) build on the same ANF structure, but apply increasingly global reasoning to reduce depth and ancilla usage.

3.2 Maslov–Miller–Dueck (MMD) Synthesis

The Maslov–Miller–Dueck (MMD) algorithm [10] is a classical transformation-based synthesis method that operates directly on the truth table of a Boolean function. Unlike ANF-based approaches, MMD does not require algebraic manipulation. Instead, it applies a sequence of multi-controlled Toffoli (MCX) gates to iteratively transform the given truth table into the identity mapping. This truth-table driven construction guarantees correctness without introducing persistent ancilla qubits, and has been widely adopted in resource estimation for block ciphers [18].

Formally, let $T \in \{0,1\}^{2^n \times m}$ denote the truth table of an $n \times m$ S-box. The algorithm proceeds as follows:

1. *Row-0 normalization.* If $T[0] \neq 0^m$, apply X gates to input/output bits as required so that the all-zero input maps to the all-zero output.
2. *Row iteration.* For $i = 1, \ldots, 2^n - 1$ and for each output bit j, if $T[i][j]$ differs from the identity mapping, apply a gate

$$C^d X(t_j),$$

   where C^d denotes the set of d controls determined by the prefix of row i, and t_j is the target output qubit.
3. *Update.* After each application, update column j of T for all rows where the controls evaluate to 1. The process continues until T is mapped to the identity.

At this abstract level, MMD produces circuits consisting of NOT, CNOT, and d-controlled Toffoli gates (`Toffoli`$_d$; $d = 1, \ldots, 7$), each treated as a primitive MCX. This requires no ancilla. However, for cost estimation each MCX must be decomposed into CCX gates using a ladder construction with one scratch qubit. We account for resources along three dimensions:

Ancilla Count. For `Toffoli`$_d$ the auxiliary ancilla usage are as follows:

$$\#\text{Ancilla}(d) = d - 2, \qquad d \geq 2, \tag{3}$$

while $d = 1$ corresponds to zero ancilla.

Gate Count. Each `Toffoli`$_d$ is expanded into a chain of CCX gates with cost

$$\#\text{CCX}(d) = 2d - 3, \qquad d \geq 2, \tag{4}$$

while $d = 1$ corresponds to a CNOT. For example, `Toffoli`$_7$ contributes 11 CCX gates.

Primitive Depth. For depth we use a bucketed ladder model that reflects empirical decomposition patterns:

$$\text{Depth}_{\text{ladder}}(d) = \delta(d) = \begin{cases} 1, & d \in \{1,2\}, \\ 3, & d \in \{3,4\}, \\ 5, & d \in \{5,6\}, \\ 7, & d = 7. \end{cases} \tag{5}$$

To compute the normalized depth, we begin with the naive unit baseline Base = $\sum_{d\geq 1} n_d$, subtract the counts of higher-degree Toffolis (which were included as 1 in the baseline), and re-add their bucketized costs:

$$Depth_N \;=\; \text{Base} - \sum_{d\geq 3} n_d \;+\; \sum_{d\geq 3} n_d \cdot \delta(d). \qquad (6)$$

The MMD synthesis is appealing because it is constructive, deterministic, and requires no persistent ancilla at the MCX level. It has therefore been the default synthesis strategy in several cipher resource estimates. Maslov and collaborators proposed improved synthesis methods based on Reed–Muller spectra and template simplification [10,11]. These approaches report modest reductions (on the order of 10–16%) in primitive gate count and quantum cost, metrics that scale with the size of k-controlled Toffoli decompositions. Importantly, these improvements are measured only at the primitive circuit level and do not directly address transpiled depth. In contrast, in our proposed approaches, we observe that even with slightly larger primitive depth, the transpiled depth is reduced substantially. For this reason, we adopt the original MMD method as the baseline comparator similar to Dutta et al. [18] and focus our evaluation on transpiled depth.

The drawback of MMD synthesis is the lack of global optimization as high-degree Toffolis are introduced whenever needed to fix truth table rows, without exploiting algebraic structure or cross-output sharing. After decomposition, these high-control Toffolis expand into long CCX chains, which inflates both gate count and depth. As a result, MMD provides a clear and reproducible reference point, but leave the scope to improve synthesis method in terms of transpiled resources.

3.3 ANF Synthesis with Common Sub-Expression Elimination and Layered Scheduling (ANF+CSE+LS)

The algebraic normal form (ANF) representation provides a natural bridge between Boolean functions and reversible synthesis. In the Miller–Maslov–Dueck (MMD) construction, each output polynomial of an S-box $S : \{0,1\}^n \to \{0,1\}^m$ is synthesized independently by mapping its monomials into ladders of multi-controlled Toffoli gates. While this approach is correct and general, it treats outputs in isolation and recomputes common subterms redundantly. The ANF+CSE+LS method builds upon ANF of S-boxes by introducing two key optimizations: common subexpression elimination (CSE) and layered scheduling (LS).

Given a Boolean function $f : \{0,1\}^n \to \{0,1\}$ with truth table values $f(x)$, its ANF coefficients can be obtained by the Möbius transform:

$$f(x_1,\ldots,x_n) = \bigoplus_{u\in\{0,1\}^n} a_u \prod_{i:u_i=1} x_i, \qquad (7)$$

where the coefficients $a_u \in \{0, 1\}$ are computed from the truth table via

$$a_u = \bigoplus_{v \subseteq u} f(v). \tag{8}$$

Equivalently, in vector–matrix form,

$$\mathbf{a} = M \cdot \mathbf{f}, \tag{9}$$

where M is the upper-triangular $2^n \times 2^n$ Möbius matrix over $\mathbb{F}_2$. In practice the Möbius transform can be computed in $O(n2^n)$ time by sweeping over the truth table with XOR updates; this yields the canonical ANF for each S-box output and provides the input representation for synthesis.

Common Sub-expression Elimination (CSE). To mitigate redundancy we apply common subexpression elimination, factoring the ANF both across outputs and within monomials. If two or more outputs require the same product term, or if higher-degree monomials share a common prefix, these intermediate products are computed once and reused. For example,

$$x_{i_1} x_{i_2} x_{i_3} \oplus x_{i_1} x_{i_2} x_{i_4} = (x_{i_1} x_{i_2}) \cdot (x_{i_3} \oplus x_{i_4}), \tag{10}$$

demonstrates that $x_{i_1} x_{i_2}$ can be computed once and shared. Formally, CSE constructs a directed acyclic graph (DAG) $\mathcal{G} = (V, E)$ where each node $v \in V$ corresponds to a partial monomial and sinks represent required output monomials $\mathcal{M}_j$. Circuit size then scales with the number of unique sub-monomials $|V|$ rather than with $\sum_j |\mathcal{M}_j|$.

Each monomial χ_u of degree d is implemented through a ladder decomposition using ancillas:

$$t_1 \leftarrow x_{i_1} \wedge x_{i_2}, \tag{11}$$

$$t_k \leftarrow t_{k-1} \wedge x_{i_{k+1}}, \quad k = 2, \ldots, d-2, \tag{12}$$

$$y_j \oplus = t_{d-2} \wedge x_{i_d}, \tag{13}$$

$$t_k \leftarrow 0 \quad \text{(uncompute)}. \tag{14}$$

This ladder uses $2(d-2)+1 = 2d-3$ Toffoli gates and consumes $d-2$ temporary ancillas. The primitive depth of a ladder depends on the chosen decomposition of multi-controlled Toffoli gates into primitive operations and on sequencing and uncomputation conventions; we capture these empirical depths in a function $\delta(d)$ similar to Eq. 5.

When accounting for primitive depth in ANF+CSE+LS we therefore express per-layer contributions using $\delta(d)$. The unconstrained per-layer contribution is

$$D_{\text{prim}}^{\text{CSE+LS}}(S) = \sum_{\ell=1}^{L} \max_{u \in \mathcal{L}_\ell} \delta\big(\deg(\chi_u)\big), \tag{15}$$

and when an ancilla budget B forces recomputation we include the overhead $\Delta_B(u)$:

$$D_{\text{prim}}^{\text{CSE+LS}}(S; B) = \sum_{\ell=1}^{L} \max_{u \in \mathcal{L}_\ell}\Big(\delta(\deg(\chi_u)) + \Delta_B(u)\Big). \qquad (16)$$

Layered Scheduling (LS). Beyond CSE, we exploit parallelism by partitioning $\mathcal{G}$ into layers $\{\mathcal{L}_\ell\}_{\ell=1}^{L}$ so that independent monomials within the same layer are evaluated concurrently. The per-layer ancilla demand is

$$A_\ell = \sum_{u \in \mathcal{L}_\ell} r(u), \qquad A_{\max} = \max_{\ell} A_\ell, \qquad (17)$$

where $r(u) = \max(0, \deg(\chi_u) - 2)$. When ancillas are scarce, layering interacts with recomputation costs through $\Delta_B(u)$; when ancillas are abundant, many intermediate products can be materialized and retained, reducing recomputation and enabling more parallel execution.

Implementation-level choices that distinguish `pair_temp` (short-lived, local temporaries used for prefix-sharing) from `full_temp` (persistent temporaries preserved across layers for repeated reuse) turn out to be crucial. `pair_temp` reduces immediate recomputation within a layer; `full_temp` unlocks cross-layer reuse, increases locality for mapping, and breaks global dependency chains. Practically, `full_temp` plus a large ancilla budget often produces a DAG that is far easier for the transpiler and mapper to schedule and place.

Two structural mechanisms explain why ANF+CSE+LS with generous ancilla can outperform MMD in transpiled depth. First, enabling ancilla-backed CSE replaces a small number of high-control multi-controlled-X (MCX) gates by a larger number of controlled-controlled-X (CCX/Toffoli) primitives plus temporaries. This MCX-to-CCX trade-off reduces the incidence of deep, high-control bottlenecks as ancilla-assisted CCX decompositions are shallower and more local than ancilla-free MCX decompositions, and CCX networks can be scheduled concurrently on disjoint qubit sets. Second, materializing and retaining temporaries (especially `full_temp`) improves qubit-locality for consumers of those temporaries; better locality reduces SWAP insertion during mapping and enables ancilla-assisted decompositions to be effective in practice. The combined effect is that the synthesized DAG exposes more parallelism and more ancilla-friendly decomposition opportunities, so after `U+CX` decomposition, routing and mapping the final circuit often has lower depth than a compact MMD circuit that exhibits long serialization and mapping overheads.

These effects are not universal: the magnitude of the transpiled-depth improvement depends on the ancilla budget, the temporary strategy (`pair_temp` vs. `full_temp`), the decomposer/transpiler's preference for ancilla-assisted decompositions, and the target coupling map. If ancillas are scarce or if the transpiler forbids ancilla-assisted decompositions, recomputation penalties and mapping-induced SWAPs can negate the advantage. Therefore, when describing methodology and when comparing synthesis approaches we measure both primitive and transpiled quantities. Concretely, the experimental methodology of this study includes primitive depth $D_{\text{prim}}^{\text{ANF+CSE+LS}}$ as Depth$_\text{P}$, counts of MCX by control-degree, CCX (Toffoli) count, CNOT/X counts, maximum simultaneous temporaries (A_{max}), final depth (Depth$_\text{N}$) after U+CX decomposition and mapping, the ancilla budget, and whether `pair_temp` or `full_temp` allocation was used. We also present a converted-cost view where an explicit table mapping MCX of degree k to normalized CCX or depth (derived from the chosen decomposition) correlates primitive structure with observed transpiled depth. Providing these measurements makes it possible to separate the mechanisms of benefit (reduced MCX, increased CCX plus temporaries, improved locality) from superficial primitive-depth comparisons.

For low-degree and low-to-medium-degree S-boxes (algebraic degree 2–3 and up to moderate degree), such as ZUC S0 and SKINNY, most terms are quadratic or cubic and can be synthesized with shallow ladders and modest ancilla demand; in this regime CSE and LS typically yield circuits significantly smaller and shallower than MMD. Importantly, for many low-to-medium degree S-boxes ANF+CSE+LS can reduce primitive depth relative to MMD by eliminating redundant ladders and shortening critical chains via prefix sharing. Moreover, when the ancilla budget is increased (and especially when `full_temp` is enabled) these cases also see further reductions in transpiled depth compared to MMD: additional ancillas allow persistent temporaries and ancilla-assisted CCX decompositions that lower mapping overhead and expose more parallelism, producing shallower final circuits.

For high-degree S-boxes (e.g., AES or ZUC S1 with degree 7), long ladders dominate the critical path and CSE can only partially mitigate depth; here layered scheduling helps but peak ancilla demand grows, and when ancilla are constrained primitive recomputation penalties inflate depth and size. Across this spectrum, the methodological lesson is clear: primitive depth by itself is an incomplete predictor of practical circuit depth once decomposition, mapping and ancilla-aware scheduling are taken into account. Designing synthesis pipelines that explicitly trade high-control MCX sites for ancilla-backed CCX networks and temporaries, and measuring both primitive and transpiled metrics under varying ancilla budgets and temporary strategies, is therefore essential for accurate evaluation. This observation motivates the MILP formulation in Sect. 3.4, which internalizes ancilla allocation and DAG parallelism into a global optimization objective rather than leaving them as post-hoc routing concerns.

3.4   Two-Phase MILP: Global, Ancilla-Aware Synthesis

In Sects. 3.2 and 3.3 we examined two complementary synthesis paradigms: the transformation-based MMD and the ANF+CSE+LS pipeline. A salient, implementation-level observation from Sect. 3.3 is that ANF+CSE+LS can restructure a circuit's DAG so that for a given sufficiently large ancilla budget and persistent temporaries, many high-control MCX bottlenecks are replaced by ancilla-backed CCX networks and short, reusable temporaries. Crucially, this transformation often reduces the transpiled depth even when the synthesized circuit reports larger primitive depth. That empirical gap between primitive metrics and final (U+CX mapping) depth shows that optimizing synthesis solely for primitive-depth or gate-count is insufficient. The MILP formulation developed in this section is motivated directly by this observation: instead of applying factorization and scheduling heuristics as post-hoc choices, we embed ancilla allocation, monomial factoring and layer-parallelism into a single global optimization so the synthesis itself produces DAGs that are inherently ancilla-friendly, locality-aware and compiler-friendly.

Concretely, our MILP workflow is executed in two complementary phases: *Phase-1* performs global factoring and ancilla allocation to produce balanced primitive circuits under a given ancilla budget, and *Phase-2* performs post-decomposition rescheduling and depth-compaction on U+CX basis to directly target the transpiled objective. This two-phase design lets the solver first choose algebraic structure and ancilla placements, then refine timing after decomposition, closing the gap between primitive and transpiled metrics.

Setup and Notation. Let $S : \{0,1\}^n \rightarrow \{0,1\}^m$ be an m-bit S-box. For $u \in \{0,1\}^n$ we write

$$\chi_u(x) = \prod_{i=1}^{n} x_i^{u_i}, \qquad \deg(u) = \|u\|_1.$$

For each output $j \in [m]$, the ANF is

$$S_j(x) = \bigoplus_u \lambda_{j,u}\, \chi_u(x),$$

and $Y_{j,s} = S_j(s)$ denotes its truth-table value at input $s \in \{0,1\}^n$.

Phase 1: Degree-Bounded Monomial Selection with Reuse. Phase 1 determines which monomials will be synthesised globally, and how they are reused across outputs. This reduces redundancy and avoids high-degree terms that would lead to deep ladders.

Decision Variables

$$z_u \in \{0,1\} \qquad \text{Indicator: monomial } u \text{ is synthesised globally,}$$
$$x_{j,u} \in \{0,1\} \qquad \text{Indicator: monomial } u \text{ contributes to output } j.$$

Here z_u ensures a monomial is available globally, while $x_{j,u}$ links it to a specific output function.

Correctness. The selected monomials must reproduce the truth table of each output. For input s, all monomials u with $u \subseteq s$ evaluate to 1. The XOR of these must equal $Y_{j,s}$:

$$\sum_{u:\, u \subseteq s} x_{j,u} \;=\; Y_{j,s} + 2\,k_{j,s}, \qquad \forall j, s, \tag{18}$$

with integer slack $k_{j,s}$. This constraint guarantees exact functional correctness.

Coupling and Degree Bound. Each monomial used in an output must be globally selected:

$$x_{j,u} \leq z_u, \qquad \forall j, u. \tag{19}$$

To avoid long ladders, monomials beyond a maximum degree are disallowed:

$$x_{j,u} = 0 \quad \text{if } \deg(u) > d_{\max}. \tag{20}$$

Objective. The solver minimises a weighted sum:

$$\min \ w_{\text{mono}} \sum_u c_u z_u + w_{\text{use}} \sum_{j,u} x_{j,u} + w_{\text{depth}} D_{\max} + w_{\text{deg5+}} \sum_{\deg(u) \geq 5} z_u, \tag{21}$$

with $c_u = \max(\deg(u) - 1, 0)$. Each term has a clear meaning:

- $\sum_u c_u z_u$: penalises the total "heaviness" of global monomials (encouraging reuse of small-degree terms).
- $\sum_{j,u} x_{j,u}$: penalises widespread usage (encouraging sparse factorizations).
- $D_{\max}$: penalises outputs that rely on many sequential monomials (encouraging shallow ANFs).
- $\sum_{\deg(u) \geq 5} z_u$: applies an extra penalty to degree-5 or higher monomials.

By adjusting weights $(w_{\text{mono}}, w_{\text{use}}, w_{\text{depth}}, w_{\text{deg5+}})$, we bias Phase 1 towards compact, low-degree, highly reusable factorizations.

Outcome. Phase 1 produces a globally consistent set of monomials $\{u : z_u = 1\}$ and their per-output usage $\{x_{j,u} = 1\}$, which are then scheduled in Phase 2.

Phase 2: Ancilla-Aware Layered Scheduling. Phase 2 arranges the selected monomials into parallel layers. Here the solver explicitly accounts for ancilla usage, balancing the trade-off between fewer layers (smaller depth) and larger ancilla.

Derived Data. Each monomial u of degree d requires

$$r_u := \max(0, d - 2)$$

persistent ancilla if it is stored across its ladder. The temporary scratch qubit is reused and not counted.

Decision Variables

$$
\begin{aligned}
y_{u,\ell} \in \{0, 1\} \qquad & \text{Indicator: monomial } u \text{ is assigned to layer } \ell, \\
A_\ell \in \mathbb{Z}_{\geq 0} \qquad & \text{Total ancilla load in layer } \ell, \\
A \in \mathbb{Z}_{\geq 0} \qquad & \text{Peak ancilla across all layers,} \\
D_{\max} \in \mathbb{Z}_{\geq 0} \qquad & \text{Index of last non-empty layer (makespan).}
\end{aligned}
$$

Here $y_{u,\ell}$ is the assignment variable, A_ℓ aggregates ancilla in each layer, A captures the maximum load, and $D_{\max}$ counts sequential layers as a proxy for depth.

Constraints.

1. *Assignment:*

$$\sum_{\ell=1}^{L} y_{u,\ell} = z_u, \qquad \forall u. \tag{22}$$

Every monomial must appear in exactly one layer.

2. *Ancilla accounting:*

$$\sum_{u} r_u\, y_{u,\ell} \leq A_\ell, \qquad \forall \ell, \tag{23}$$

$$A \geq A_\ell, \qquad \forall \ell. \tag{24}$$

These ensure that ancilla usage in each layer is respected and that A correctly represents the peak.

3. *Target contention:*

$$\sum_{u \in \mathcal{M}_j} y_{u,\ell} \leq 1, \qquad \forall j, \ell, \tag{25}$$

preventing two monomials from toggling the same output in the same layer.

4. *Makespan:* $D_{\max}$ is constrained to be at least the index of the last occupied layer. This ensures $D_{\max}$ reflects true sequential depth.

Objective. The Phase 2 objective is:

$$\min\ D_{\max} + w \cdot A. \tag{26}$$

This reflects a simple but powerful trade-off:

- $D_{\max}$ counts the number of sequential layers, i.e. a proxy for depth.
- A penalises excessive ancilla usage.
- The weight w balances the importance of space (ancilla) against time (depth).

In practice, depth dominates the cost function, while $w \cdot A$ prevents the solver from inflating ancilla without consequence.

After solving, the solver reports the layer structure: which monomials are in each layer, the ancilla load A_ℓ, and the peak A. The schedule is then emitted as a Qiskit circuit with an ancilla pool of size A, and transpiled to measure realistic transpiled depth.

Why the MILP Should Outperform ANF+CSE+LS. The empirical behaviors described above explain why the MILP approach should outperform ANF+CSE+LS in our benchmarks. While ANF+CSE+LS applies local heuristics, the MILP simultaneously reasons about monomial factoring, ancilla budgeting and layer scheduling under a single objective that targets real-world cost of transpiled depth. MILP Phase-1 produces globally balanced primitive circuits by choosing factorizations and ancilla placements that minimize long dependency chains; Phase-2 performs post-decomposition rescheduling to compact the transpiled depth further. By making ancilla allocation and DAG parallelism first-class variables, the MILP reduces MCX bottlenecks when beneficial, places temporaries to maximize locality, and produces structures that the transpiler and mapper can exploit directly. The result is a consistent reduction in final (U+CX) depth across S-box families validating the claim that global, ancilla-aware synthesis is necessary to reliably minimize practical quantum resource cost.

4   Results and Discussion

All synthesis methods described in Sect. 3 are implemented in Python, with U+CX decompositions handled through Qiskit's transpiler module and verified against the truth-table specifications of each S-box. We developed both the heuristic and MILP-based approaches to ensure fair comparison under identical cost models. The developed modules automatically extracts ANF representations, applies the chosen synthesis strategy, and compiles the resulting circuits to the same universal gate set U+CX. The complete source code and scripts are available on GitHub[1], ensuring all reported numbers are reproducible.

In this section we present a structured comparison of the three synthesis strategies. We begin with the baseline MMD synthesis (Sect. 4.1), which represents the canonical ANF-to-ladder construction used in prior resource estimates (e.g., Dutta et al. [18]). Next, we introduce results for our heuristic ANF+CSE+Layered Scheduling (Sect. 4.2) and analyze how redundancy elimination and layered parallelism affect both primitive and transpiled costs. Finally, we present the MILP-based synthesis (Sect. 4.3), which incorporates ancilla allocation and global scheduling into a single optimization framework. There are too many metrics to compare and therefore, we have restricted our results to the metrics which are significant in the cost computation. These metrics include ancilla count, primitive-level normalized depth and transpiled-level depth. A comparative discussion in these subsections analyzes the trade-offs and cryptanalytic implications across all methods.

4.1   MMD Based Synthesis

We first evaluate the baseline MMD construction on five representative 8-bit S-boxes: AES, SM4, SKINNY, and the two ZUC S-boxes (S0 and S1). Table 1 and 2 summarize the primitive-level metrics with a full Toffoli breakdown and MCX totals, and the transpiled-level metrics after U+CX decomposition and mapping respectively.

Analysis. The MMD baseline produces circuits with primitive depths in the range 877–945. The per-degree breakdown (Table 1) shows a heavy reliance on high-degree Toffoli gates: across all five S-boxes, MCX totals range from 611

---

[1] https://github.com/tarunyadav/QuantumSynthesis_LargeSBoxes.

Table 1. Primitive-level MMD synthesis results with full Toffoli breakdown (ancilla = 5). MCX = total multi-controlled-X gates (sum of T3–T7). Toffoli$_N$ and Depth$_N$ denote normalized metrics using Dutta's $(2d-3)$ weighting for $C^d X$.

S-box	NOT	CNOT	Toffoli	T3	T4	T5	T6	T7	MCX	Depth$_P$	Toffoli$_N$	Depth$_N$
AES	4	123	206	244	205	123	42	7	621	945	3279	2545
SM4	5	104	198	220	214	136	53	9	632	931	3456	2609
SKINNY	4	95	173	212	205	134	52	8	611	877	3328	2503
ZUC S0 [18]	5	102	199	236	202	136	53	10	637	936	3456	2628
ZUC S1 [18]	4	110	211	221	189	132	62	9	613	930	3400	2580

Table 2. Transpiled-level MMD synthesis results (ancilla $= 5$). Reported are transpiled depth, and dominant decomposed gate counts.

S-box	Ancilla	Depth$_T$	u	cx
AES	5	54,124	46,377	29,907
SM4	5	58,989	51,001	32,900
SKINNY	5	57,081	49,244	31,777
ZUC S0	5	59,021	50,775	32,916
ZUC S1	5	58,916	50,692	33,022

(SKINNY) to 637 (ZUC S0), with many of T_6 and T_7 gates still present. These high-control constructs account for the majority of the normalized Toffoli costs (e.g., 3,456 for SM4 and ZUC S0) and inflate the normalized depth estimates.

After U+CX decomposition and transpilation (Table 2), the final depths explode to 5.4×10^4–5.9×10^4, and total gate count exceeds 8×10^4. Two-qubit operations (cx) alone exceed 3×10^4 in each case. This blow-up confirms that while MMD provides a straightforward and general synthesis, it is pessimistic as a baseline because it directly maps monomials into long Toffoli ladders without factoring or scheduling.

These MMD numbers establish the reference point for subsequent methods. In Sect. 4.2 we show how ANF+CSE+LS changes the Toffoli distribution (trading large MCX gates for more CCX and temporaries) and how this alters both primitive and transpiled depth under different ancilla budgets.

4.2   ANF + CSE + LS Based Synthesis

The ANF+CSE+LS approach extracts algebraic normal forms (ANFs) of the S-box outputs, applies global common-subexpression elimination (CSE) under a given ancilla budget, and then schedules the resulting computations into layers (LS) to maximize parallelism. Each monomial of degree d is mapped to a multi-controlled Toffoli ($C^d X$). The depth of MCX gates is converted into equivalent ladder-depth units using the $(2d-3)$ rule, consistent with the MMD baseline reported in Table 1. The resulting primitive-level normalized depth is denoted Depth_N, and the post-transpile U+CX depth is denoted Depth_T.

Table 3 reports ANF+CSE+LS results for AES, SM4, SKINNY, ZUC S0, and ZUC S1 across ancilla budgets $A \in \{0, 5, 10, \ldots, 240\}$. For each cipher we list the primitive-level normalized depth Depth_N and the post-transpile depth Depth_T. Bold entries indicate the minimum transpiled depth attained for that cipher.

Table 1 reported MMD primitive depths: AES (2545), SM4 (2609), SKINNY (2503), ZUC S0 (2628), and ZUC S1 (2580). Direct comparison shows:

- **AES.** ANF+CSE+LS starts worse (3556 vs. 2545) but overtakes MMD at $A = 70$ (2521). The best value of primitive depth is 2333 at $A = 145$, about 8% lower than MMD. Transpiled depth reduces from 94,280 ($A = 0$) to **47,681** ($A = 205$).
- **SM4.** Starts worse (3586 vs. 2609) but beats MMD by $A = 75$ (2572). The best is 2294 at $A = 235$, 12% lower than MMD. Transpiled depth improves from 97,351 to **48,021** ($A = 190$).
- **SKINNY.** Much lower from the start (349 vs. 2503) and with $A = 15$, $\text{Depth}_N = 262$ achieve minimum depth. This strong advantage stems from SKINNY's low algebraic degree (mostly cubic terms), enabling highly parallel circuits. Minimum transpiled depth is **4775** at $A = 15$.
- **ZUC S0.** Already below MMD (1652 vs. 2628 at $A = 0$), with minimum 1156 at $A = 40$ (a 56% improvement). This reflects the predominance of degree-3 to degree-5 monomials. Transpiled depth drops from 29,578 to **17,991** ($A = 105$).
- **ZUC S1.** Worse at $A = 0$ (3592 vs. 2580) but surpasses MMD by $A = 80$ (2552). Best primitive depth is 2319 at $A = 145$, 10% below MMD. Transpiled depth reduces from 97,863 to **48,270** ($A = 205$).

The first factor that clearly influences the performance of ANF+CSE+LS is the algebraic degree of the S-box. Low-degree S-boxes such as SKINNY and ZUC S0 benefit almost immediately, even when only a handful of ancilla qubits are available. This is because the majority of their algebraic expressions are cubic or quartic, which map to relatively shallow multi-controlled Toffoli gates. These gates not only require fewer control lines but also parallelize well across layers, allowing layered scheduling to compress the circuit depth aggressively. In contrast, high-degree S-boxes such as AES, SM4, and ZUC S1 contain a significant fraction of quintic, sextic, or higher-degree terms. These necessitate deeper multi-controlled gates and create more dependency chains. In such cases, only when a sufficient ancilla budget is available can the CSE routine extract and store common higher-order monomials, which then enables layered scheduling to rebalance the circuit and reduce depth. Thus, the advantage of ANF+CSE+LS is immediate for low-degree designs but deferred until moderate ancilla levels for high-degree ones.

A second important observation arises when contrasting the primitive-level depth with the transpiled U+CX depth. At the primitive level, improvements from CSE+LS appear modest, often only shaving off a few hundred normalized ladder

Table 3. ANF+CSE+LS synthesis results across ancilla budgets. Depth_N is the primitive-level normalized depth under $(2d - 3)$ conversion. Depth_T is the transpiled depth. "−" marks missing values due to maximum ancilla utilization. Ancilla values marked with *, †, ‡ indicate that the actual evaluated ancilla differs from the nominal row index. Bold rows mark the minimum transpiled depth observed for each cipher.

Ancilla	AES		SM4		SKINNY		ZUC S0		ZUC S1	
	Depth_N	Depth_T	Depth_N	Depth_T	Depth_N	Depth_T	Depth_N	Depth_T	Depth_N	Depth_T
0	3556	94280	3586	97351	349	5603	1652	29578	3592	97863
5	3361	92849	3411	95960	288	5104	1484	28270	3405	96466
10	3222	91794	3280	94919	269	4877	1358	27110	3297	95493
15	3136	90908	3205	94164	**262**	**4775**	1282	26369	3210	94658
20	3084	90130	3169	93384	287	4875	1241	25601	3171	93884
25	3017	86396	3081	88668	308	5009	1204	23956	3088	89420
30	2920	81834	3005	85166	326	5106	1191	22860	3005	85013
35	2854	78806	2946	82101	325†	5098†	1170	21559	2940	82138
40	2792	75872	2889	79049	−	−	1156	20607	2885	78828
45	2742	72833	2833	76641	−	−	1177	20619	2836	75436
50	2691	70624	2791	73831	−	−	1168	19723	2785	73479
55	2642	68529	2741	71500	−	−	1158	18730	2735	71548
60	2592	66641	2690	69356	−	−	1182	18814	2691	69840
65	2551	64696	2641	67394	−	−	1214	19117	2648	68180
70	2521	62649	2610	65566	−	−	1230	19059	2618	66351
75	2505	61406	2572	63473	−	−	1234	18815	2589	64494
80	2478	60088	2554	61916	−	−	1242	18540	2552	62187
85	2455	58821	2537	60948	−	−	1253	18327	2522	60931
90	2429	57544	2513	59591	−	−	1271	18287	2488	59615
95	2413	56443	2484	58463	−	−	1287	18238	2477	58557
100	2407	55772	2458	57136	−	−	1299	18028	2451	57236
105	2401	55224	2435	55766	−	−	**1316**	**17991**	2417	55848
110	2424	55258	2398	54442	−	−	1339	18160	2387	54490
115	2407	54463	2408	54132	−	−	1358	18384	2408	54499
120	2391	53521	2413	53651	−	−	1374	18636	2397	53981
125	2373	52693	2406	52966	−	−	1382	18568	2385	53486
130	2362	51814	2398	52050	−	−	1350	18261	2351	52678
135	2353	50889	2385	51016	−	−	1353	18182	2337	51740
140	2343	49995	2376	50085	−	−	1375	18326	2322	50792
145	2333	49593	2373	49394	−	−	1404	18546	2319	49990
150	2355	49627	2396	49418	−	−	1414‡	18559‡	2341	50116
155	2370	49596	2399	49130	−	−	−	−	2330	50070
160	2379	49553	2411	49086	−	−	−	−	2335	49905
165	2379	49345	2425	49044	−	−	−	−	2331	49502
170	2384	49120	2438	48856	−	−	−	−	2329	49181
175	2405	49180	2462	48900	−	−	−	−	2347	49141
180	2431	49285	2480	48862	−	−	−	−	2372	49276
185	2444	49099	2489	48488	−	−	−	−	2371	49034
190	2456	48882	**2489**	**48021**	−	−	−	−	2396	49149
195	2461	48464	2450	48119	−	−	−	−	2375	48586
200	2460	48243	2424	48194	−	−	−	−	2387	48379
205	**2451**	**47681**	2433	48342	−	−	−	−	**2399**	**48270**
210	2456	47856	2402	48456	−	−	−	−	2420	48418
215	2483	48119	2421	48503	−	−	−	−	2425	48543
220	2491	48304	2359	48394	−	−	−	−	2426	48696
225	2504	48262	2333	48215	−	−	−	−	2416	48815
230	2442	47931	2352	48235	−	−	−	−	2331	48398
235	2434	47841	2294	48133	−	−	−	−	2341	48422
240	2436*	47724*	2304	48054	−	−	−	−	2345	48415

Note: *AES results correspond to ancilla = 236 (not 240).
†SKINNY results correspond to ancilla = 32 (not 35).
‡ZUC S0 results correspond to ancilla = 149 (not 150).

units. However, after transpilation, the reductions become much more significant, consistently approaching a factor of two across all families. For instance, AES circuits shrink from 94,280 to 47,681, SM4 from 97,351 to 48,021, and ZUC S1 from 97,863 to 48,270. This divergence highlights the compiler-friendly nature of circuits produced by ANF+CSE+LS while the primitive gate model does not fully capture parallelism and cancellation opportunities, the transpiler is able to exploit the regularity introduced by layered scheduling, leading to much deeper compaction than suggested at first glance.

Finally, the data reveal clear *elbow points* in the trade-off between ancilla allocation and depth reduction (Appendix A Fig. 1). Beyond a certain ancilla threshold, additional workspace yields diminishing returns, and the depth curves begin to flatten. For AES, SM4 and ZUC S1, this elbow appears around $A \approx 140$, indicating that moderate ancilla are sufficient to unlock most of the achievable parallelism. ZUC S0 reaches its minimum much earlier, around $A \approx 40$, while SKINNY achieves near-optimal performance with as few as $A \approx 15$ qubits. These elbow points are useful indicators for cryptanalytic cost models, as they suggest practical ancilla budgets beyond which further qubit investment provides limited advantage.

Taken together, these results establish ANF+CSE+LS as a robust intermediate between the naive MMD baseline and more sophisticated global optimizations. It surpasses MMD immediately for SKINNY and ZUC S0, and with moderate ancilla for AES, SM4, and ZUC S1 (Appendix A Fig. 2). In all cases, the transpiled depth is reduced significantly, demonstrating that ANF+CSE+LS produces circuits that are not only smaller at the primitive level but also significantly more compiler-friendly. However, the approach still relies on local factoring and heuristic layering decisions, which may miss globally optimal trade-offs between ancilla usage, monomial reuse, and depth balancing. This limitation motivates the use of Mixed-Integer Linear Programming (MILP) based synthesis, presented in Sect. 3.4, which aims to capture these trade-offs in a global optimization framework.

4.3 MILP Based Synthesis

The Mixed-Integer Linear Programming (MILP) pipeline is described in Sect. 3.4. The Phase 1 results (Depth_P, Depth_N and Depth_T) in Table 4 closely resemble those of the MMD and ANF+CSE+LS heuristic with a few ancilla usages. Most of metrics of Table 4 are higher than other two methods. However, after applying Phase 2, the transpiled depth drops by a large margin due to ancilla-depth tradeoff optimization (Table 5). This highlights that primitive depths (Depth_P and Depth_N) are not a reliable indicator of the true execution cost as circuits with similar Depth_P may have multifold difference in transpiled depth (Depth_T).

In Phase 2, d_max controls the maximum number of sequential layers and *ancilla* records the peak ancilla load. At small d_max, the solver packs many monomials per layer: ancilla are large but depth is minimal. At large d_max, monomials are spread across more layers and ancilla shrink, while transpiled

Table 4. MILP Phase-1 Results: Reported are primitive depth, normalized depth, transpiled depth, and dominant decomposed gate counts.

S-box	Ancilla	Depth_P	Depth_N	Depth_T	u	cx
AES	5	1,010	3,558	94,542	82,824	53,995
SM4	5	1,028	3,589	97,640	85,589	55,741
SKINNY	4	153	349	5,6571	4,759	2,999
ZUC S0	3	627	1,667	29,668	25,179	15,387
ZUC S1	5	1,032	3,594	98,330	86,207	56,094

depth increases only slightly and quickly saturates. Thus the Phase 2 sweep directly exposes the trade-off between workspace and wall-clock logical time. This is an essential contrast to MMD and ANF+CSE+LS, which either lack ancilla-awareness (MMD) or use only local heuristics (ANF+CSE+LS).

Observations. The Table 5 shows a consistent pattern: the absolute minimum depths are obtained at $d_{\max} = 1$ with very high $ancilla(A)$. But as $d_{\max}$ increases, ancilla quickly drops while Depth_T rises by only a few dozen units. For AES, reducing A from 516 to 22 increases Depth_T by just 115 (11,772 $\rightarrow$ 11,887). For SM4 and ZUC S1, the observation is same as A shrinks to 22 while depth rises by only $\approx$ 120. For SKINNY, Depth_T stays around 3.1 $\times 10^3$ even as A is reduced from 119 (at $d_{\max} = 1$) to 10 (at $d_{\max} = 12$). For ZUC S0, depths around 6.5 $\times 10^3$ are preserved even as ancilla is cut down to 13. Thus the sweep exposes a Pareto frontier where very shallow depths are retained even at drastically reduced ancilla budgets.

Comparison with ANF+CSE+LS. ANF+CSE+LS (Table 3) achieved its best results at moderate ancilla: AES 47,681 ($A = 205$), SM4 48,021 ($A = 190$), SKINNY 4,775 ($A = 15$), ZUC S0 17,991 ($A = 105$), ZUC S1 48,270 ($A = 205$). MILP's Phase-2 sweep shows that even at much lower ancilla, MILP attains depths an order of magnitude smaller. For example:

- AES: at $A = 22$ ($d_{\max} = 24$), MILP has depth 11,887, nearly four times shallower than ANF+CSE+LS, with ten times fewer ancilla.
- SM4: at $A = 22$, MILP has depth 11,902, a four times reduction compared to ANF+CSE+LS, with nine times fewer ancilla.
- SKINNY: at $A = 10$ ($d_{\max} = 12$), MILP's 3,138 beats ANF+CSE+LS (4,775 at $A = 15$) by 34%, with fewer ancilla.
- ZUC S0: at $A = 13$, MILP achieves 6561 depth, about three times shallower than ANF+CSE+LS at $A = 105$.
- ZUC S1: at $A = 22$, MILP's 11,829 is four shallower than ANF+CSE+LS (48,270 at $A = 205$), again with ten times fewer ancilla.

In all cases MILP defines a Pareto-superior frontier as it not only wins at maximum ancilla, but also provides substantially better depths at equal or lower ancilla budgets (Appendix A Fig. 2).

Table 5. MILP Phase-2 results: peak ancilla (A) and transpiled depth ($\mathrm{Depth_T}$) as a function of depth bound $d_{\max}$. Bold entries mark the minimum $\mathrm{Depth_T}$ and minimum *ancilla* per cipher. "–" represents not achieving full bound $d_{\max}$ and therefore, results are same as one of the previous row.

$d_{\max}$	AES		SM4		SKINNY		ZUC S0		ZUC S1	
	A	$\mathrm{Depth_T}$	A	$\mathrm{Depth_T}$	A	$\mathrm{Depth_T}$	A	$\mathrm{Depth_T}$	A	$\mathrm{Depth_T}$
1	**516**	**11772**	**516**	**11779**	119	3082	259	6428	513	11708
2	258	11840	258	11850	60	3128	130	6493	257	11792
3	172	11876	172	11823	40	3119	87	6521	171	11804
4	129	11842	129	11854	30	3117	65	6531	129	11792
5	104	11842	104	11849	24	3104	52	6503	103	11792
6	86	11809	86	11861	20	3132	44	6476	86	11804
7	74	11827	74	11852	17	3125	37	6498	74	11787
8	65	11865	65	11878	15	3129	33	6535	65	11806
9	58	11845	58	11891	–	–	29	6516	57	11811
10	52	11859	52	11882	12	3137	26	6545	52	11832
11	47	11844	47	11855	11	3140	24	6516	47	11799
12	43	11860	43	11876	**10**	**3138**	22	6561	43	11830
13	40	11850	40	11862	–	–	20	6520	40	11807
14	37	11882	37	11886	–	–	19	6550	37	11789
15	35	11858	35	11873	–	–	18	6543	35	11778
16	33	11848	33	11879	–	–	17	6536	33	11809
17	31	11874	31	11880	–	–	16	6528	31	11837
18	29	11863	29	11878	–	–	15	6518	29	11834
19	28	11853	28	11832	–	–	14	6505	27	11837
20	26	11882	26	11885	–	–	**13**	**6561**	26	11818
21	25	11871	–	–	–	–	–	–	25	11770
22	24	11862	24	11899	–	–	–	–	–	–
23	–	–	–	–	–	–	–	–	23	11799
24	**22**	**11887**	**22**	**11902**	–	–	–	–	**22**	**11829**

Comparison with MMD. MMD's transpiled depths (Table 2) are all around 5.4×10^4–5.9×10^4 with $A = 5$. MILP improves dramatically even at very low ancilla:

- AES: 54,124 (MMD) vs. 11,887 (MILP at $A = 22$),
- SM4: 58,989 (MMD) vs. 11,902 (MILP at $A = 22$),
- SKINNY: 57,081 (MMD) vs. 3,138 (MILP at $A = 10$),
- ZUC S0: 59,021 (MMD) vs. 6561 (MILP at $A = 13$),
- ZUC S1: 58,916 (MMD) vs. 11,829 (MILP at $A = 22$),

Thus even in the ancilla regime close to MMD, MILP provides an order of magnitude reduction in transpiled depth (Appendix A Fig. 2).

Why MILP Outperforms. MILP's superiority arises from three interacting mechanisms.

- *Global monomial selection:* Phase 1 balances degree, reuse, and a depth proxy, eliminating long chains and redundant recomputation.
- *Ancilla-aware scheduling:* Phase 2 distributes heavy monomials across layers to reduce peak ancilla without introducing sequential bottlenecks, maintaining compiler-friendly DAG shapes.
- *Compiler synergy:* these globally balanced DAGs decompose into U+CX circuits with shorter ladders, more parallelism, and better cancellation opportunities.

Together, these yield circuits that are not only dramatically shallower than heuristic methods at the same ancilla, but also remain shallow even when ancilla budgets are tightened to realistic device scales.

5   Conclusion

We have presented the first comprehensive quantum-oriented synthesis study of 8-bit cryptographic S-boxes, combining algebraic, heuristic, and optimisation-based approaches. Using MMD as a systematic transformation-based baseline, comparing it against an ANF+CSE+LS heuristic pipeline, and finally applying a two-phase MILP formulation, we mapped out a clear progression of methods and their trade-offs. A key principle throughout our study is that practical comparisons must be made on the transpiled depth. Primitive metrics such as normalized ladder units are useful for explaining structural properties, but they do not reliably predict the actual depth that arises under decomposition and compilation. Since MAXDEPTH dominates the cost of cryptanalytic quantum algorithms, all resource conclusions here are based on transpiled U+CX depth which is prominent than Clifford+T in NISQ-era.

Both of the approaches we developed provide concrete advantages over the MMD baseline. ANF+CSE+LS is a lightweight, scalable pipeline that extracts ANFs, eliminates redundant monomials globally, and layers the remaining computation to maximise concurrency. This heuristic is particularly effective for low-degree S-boxes such as SKINNY and ZUC S0, where modest ancilla budgets are enough to produce circuits that already beat MMD both in transpiled depth and primitive-level metrics. Because it is fast and deterministic, ANF+CSE+LS is valuable for broad ancilla sweeps and for identifying elbow points that guide qubit–depth trade-offs. MILP goes further by embedding factoring, ancilla allocation and layer scheduling into a single global optimisation. Its Phase 2 results demonstrate that MILP consistently produces the shallowest transpiled circuits across all benchmarks, often reducing depth by multiple factors compared to ANF+CSE+LS and by even larger margins relative to MMD. Crucially, MILP produces a Pareto-superior frontier as the lowest depths are reached with abundant ancilla, but nearly the same depths are retained with multifold reduction in ancilla usage. This shows that MILP is not just a low-depth outlier requiring excessive workspace, but the most practical synthesis method across realistic device budgets.

Taken together, these findings establish MILP as the most effective paradigm for minimising transpiled depth across 8-bit S-boxes, while also highlighting the complementary role of ANF+CSE+LS as a fast, algebraic heuristic for low-degree cases. This work is the first application of MILP to full 8-bit cryptographic S-boxes in NISQ-era universal basis (U+CX) setting, where it delivers meaningful reductions in both depth and size, and directly refines quantum resource estimates for symmetric-key cryptanalysis. Future directions include scaling MILP to larger nonlinear components, exploring hybrid flows, and extending optimisation across complete cipher rounds.

A   Appendix

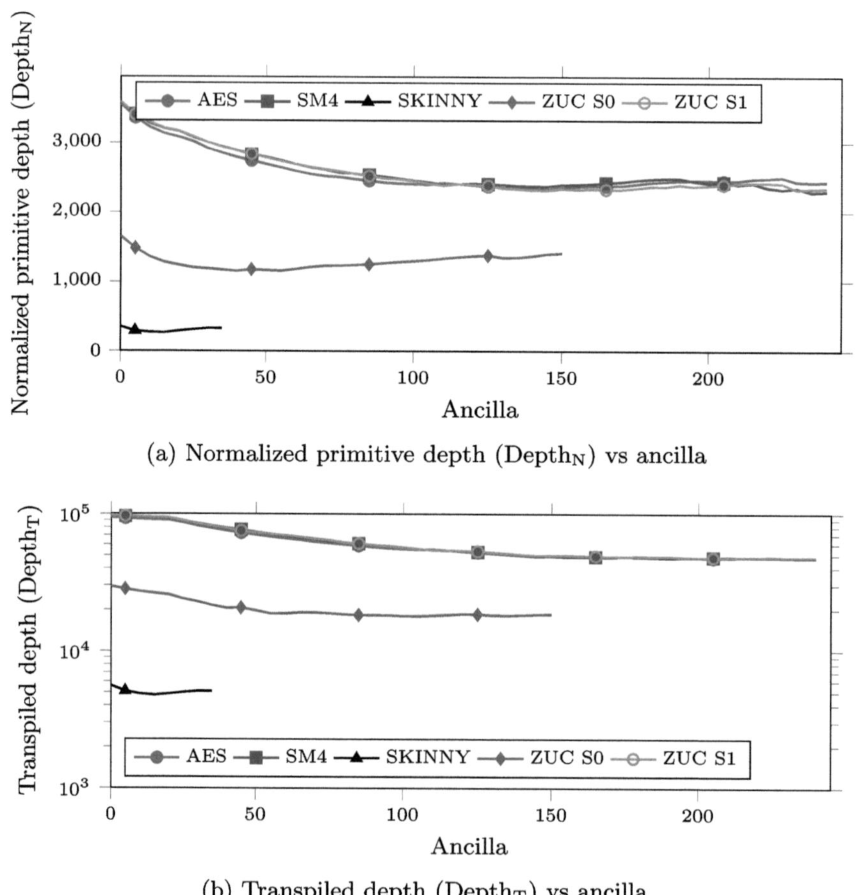

(a) Normalized primitive depth (Depth_N) vs ancilla

(b) Transpiled depth (Depth_T) vs ancilla

Fig. 1. ANF+CSE+LS synthesis depth as a function of ancilla budget for five ciphers. Top: primitive normalized depth (Depth_N). Bottom: transpiled depth (Depth_T) in the hardware-agnostic basis. Elbow points are visible where depth saturates with increasing ancilla.

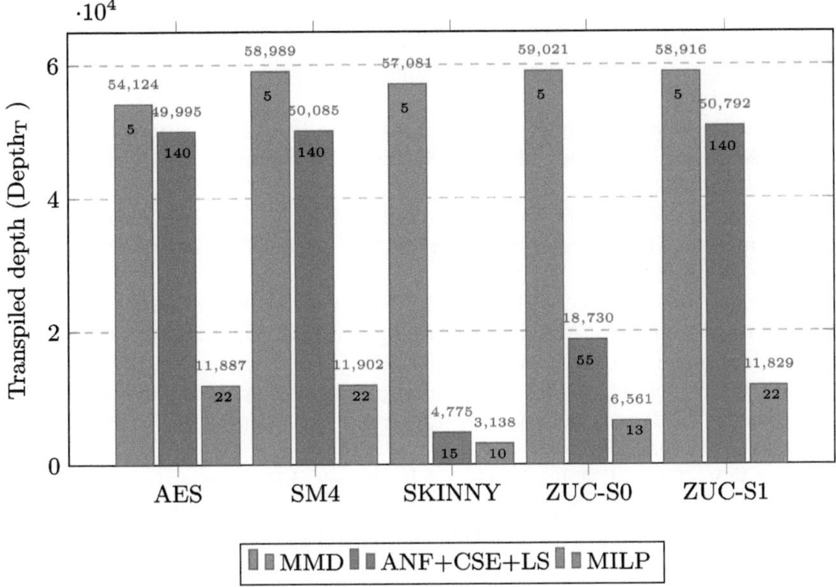

Fig. 2. Transpiled depth (Depth_T) of 8-bit S-boxes across different synthesis approaches. Depth_T values are shown above each bar, and ancilla counts are printed inside the bars. For ANF+CSE+LS, the elbow points are selected; for MILP, the lowest-ancilla configuration is chosen to balance the depth–ancilla tradeoff.

References

1. Bogdanov, A., et al.: PRESENT: an ultra-lightweight block cipher. In: Paillier, P., Verbauwhede, I. (eds.) CHES 2007. LNCS, vol. 4727, pp. 450–466. Springer, Heidelberg (2007). https://doi.org/10.1007/978-3-540-74735-2_31
2. Banik, S., Pandey, S.K., Peyrin, T., Sasaki, Y., Sim, S.M., Todo, Y.: GIFT: a small present. In: Fischer, W., Homma, N. (eds.) Cryptographic Hardware and Embedded Systems – CHES 2017. CHES 2017. LNCS, vol. 10529, pp. 321–345. Springer, Cham (2017). https://doi.org/10.1007/978-3-319-66787-4_16
3. Daemen, J., Rijmen, V.: The Design of Rijndael: AES–The Advanced Encryption Standard. Springer, Berlin, Heidelberg (2002). https://doi.org/10.1007/978-3-662-04722-4
4. State Cryptography Administration of China: GM/T 0002-2012: SM4 Block Cipher Algorithm (2012)
5. Beierle, C., et al.: The SKINNY family of block ciphers and its low-latency variant MANTIS . In: Robshaw, M., Katz, J. (eds.) Advances in Cryptology – CRYPTO 2016. CRYPTO 2016. LNCS, vol. 9815, pp. 123–153. Springer, Berlin, Heidelberg (2016). https://doi.org/10.1007/978-3-662-53008-5_5
6. State Cryptography Administration of China: GM/T 0001-2012: ZUC Stream Cipher Algorithm (2012)

7. Satoh, A., Morioka, S., Takano, K., Munetoh, S.: A compact rijndael hardware architecture with S-Box optimization. In: Boyd, C. (ed.) ASIACRYPT 2001. LNCS, vol. 2248, pp. 239–254. Springer, Heidelberg (2001). https://doi.org/10.1007/3-540-45682-1_15

8. Canright, D.: A very compact S-Box for AES. In: Rao, J.R., Sunar, B. (eds.) CHES 2005. LNCS, vol. 3659, pp. 441–455. Springer, Heidelberg (2005). https://doi.org/10.1007/11545262_32

9. Golubitsky, O., Maslov, D.: A study of optimal 4-bit reversible Toffoli circuits and their synthesis. IEEE Trans. Comput. **61**(9), 1341–1353 (2012). https://doi.org/10.1109/TC.2011.144

10. Maslov, D., DueckG, W., Miller, D.M.: Toffoli network synthesis with templates. IEEE Trans. Comput. Aided Des. Integr. Circuits Syst. **24**(6), 807–817 (2005). https://doi.org/10.1109/TCAD.2005.847911

11. Maslov, D., Dueck, G., Miller, M.: Techniques for the synthesis of reversible Toffoli networks. ACM Trans. Des. Autom. Electron. Syst. **12**(4) (2007). https://doi.org/10.1145/1278349.1278355

12. Shende, V.V., Prasad, A.K., Markov, I.L., Hayes, J.P.: Synthesis of reversible logic circuits. IEEE Trans. Comput. Aided Des. Integr. Circuits Syst. **22**(6), 710–722 (2003). https://doi.org/10.1109/TCAD.2003.811448

13. Wille, R., Drechsler, R.: BDD-based synthesis of reversible logic for large functions. In: 46th ACM/IEEE Design Automation Conference, pp. 270–275, 2009. https://doi.org/10.1145/1629911.1629984

14. Patel, K.N., Markov, I.L., Hayes, J.P.: Optimal synthesis of linear reversible circuits. Quantum Inf. Comput. **8**(3), 282–294 (2008). https://doi.org/10.26421/QIC8.3-4-4

15. Xiang, Z., Zeng, X., Lin, D., Bao, Z., Zhang, S.: Optimizing implementations of linear layers. IACR Trans. Symmetric Cryptol. **2020**(2), 120–145 (2020). https://doi.org/10.13154/tosc.v2020.i2.120-145

16. Shi, H., Feng, X.: Quantum circuits of AES with a low-depth linear layer and a new structure. In: Chung, K.M., Sasaki, Y. (eds.) Advances in Cryptology – ASIACRYPT 2024. ASIACRYPT 2024. LNCS, vol. 15491, pp. 358–395. Springer, Singapore (2025). https://doi.org/10.1007/978-981-96-0944-4_12

17. Grassl, M., Langenberg, B., Roetteler, M., Steinwandt, R.: Applying Grover's algorithm to AES: quantum resource estimates. In: Takagi, T. (eds.) Post-Quantum Cryptography. PQCrypto 2016. LNCS, vol. 9606, pp. 29–43. Springer, Cham (2016). https://doi.org/10.1007/978-3-319-29360-8_3

18. Dutta, S., Ghatak, A., Chattopadhyay, A., Maitra, S.: Quantum cryptanalysis of ZUC and related resource estimation. In: Mukhopadhyay, S., Stănică, P. (eds.) Progress in Cryptology – INDOCRYPT 2024. INDOCRYPT 2024. LNCS, vol. 15495, pp. 329–355. Springer, Cham (2025). https://doi.org/10.1007/978-3-031-80308-6_15

19. Dasu, V.A., Baksi, A., Sarkar, S., Chattopadhyay, A.: LIGHTER-R: optimized reversible circuit implementation for S-boxes. In: 32nd IEEE International System-on-Chip Conference (SOCC), Singapore, pp. 260–265, 2019. https://doi.org/10.1109/SOCC46988.2019.1570548320

20. Lin, D., Yang, C., Xu, S., Tian, S., Sun, B.: On the construction of quantum circuits for S-boxes with different criteria based on the SAT solver. IACR Cryptology ePrint Archive, Report 2024/565, 2024

21. Chen, J., Liu, Q., Fan, Y., Wu, L., Li, B., Wang, M.: New SAT-based model for quantum circuit decision problem: Searching for low-cost quantum implementation. IACR Commun. Cryptol. **1**(1) (2024). https://doi.org/10.62056/anmmp-4c2h

22. Baksi, A., et al.: Quantum implementation of linear and non-linear layers. In: IEEE 37th International System-on-Chip Conference (SOCC), Dresden, Germany, pp. 1–6, 2024. https://doi.org/10.1109/SOCC62300.2024.10737862

23. Amy, M., Maslov, D., Mosca, M., Roetteler, M.: A meet-in-the-middle algorithm for fast synthesis of depth-optimal quantum circuits. IEEE Trans. Comput. Aided Des. Integr. Circuits Syst. **32**(6), 818–830 (2013). https://doi.org/10.1109/TCAD.2013.2244643

24. Selinger, P.: Quantum circuits of T-depth one. Phys. Rev. A **87**(4), 042302 (2013). https://doi.org/10.1103/PhysRevA.87.042302

25. Maslov, D.: Advantages of using relative-phase Toffoli gates with an application to multiple control Toffoli optimization. Phys. Rev. A **93**(2), 022311 (2016). https://doi.org/10.1103/PhysRevA.93.022311

26. Gidney, C.: Halving the cost of quantum addition. Quantum **2**, 74 (2018). https://doi.org/10.48550/arXiv.1709.06648

27. Cuccaro, S., Draper, T., Kutin, S., Moulton, D.: A new quantum ripple-carry addition circuit. arXiv:quant-ph/0410184, 2004. https://doi.org/10.48550/arXiv.quant-ph/0410184

28. Soeken, M., Frehse, S., Wille, R., Drechsler, R.: RevKit: an open source toolkit for the design of reversible circuits. In: De Vos, A., Wille, R. (eds.) RC 2011. LNCS, vol. 7165, pp. 64–76. Springer, Heidelberg (2012). https://doi.org/10.1007/978-3-642-29517-1_6

29. Wille, R., et al.: The MQT handbook: a summary of design automation tools and software for quantum computing. In: IEEE International Conference on Quantum Software (QSW), Shenzhen, China, pp. 1–8, 2024. https://doi.org/10.1109/QSW62656.2024.00013

30. Aleksandrowicz, G., et al.: Qiskit: an open-source framework for quantum computing (0.7.2). Zenodo, 2019. https://doi.org/10.5281/zenodo.2562111

31. Sivarajah, S., Dilkes, S., Cowtan, A., Simmons, W., Edgington, A., Duncan, R.: t—ket⟩: a retargetable compiler for NISQ devices. Quantum Sci. Technol. **6**(1), 014003 (2020). https://doi.org/10.1088/2058-9565/ab8e92

32. Chen, L., et al.: Report on Post-Quantum Cryptography. NISTIR 8105, 2016. https://doi.org/10.6028/NIST.IR.8105

33. Langenberg, B., Pham, H., Steinwandt, R.: Reducing the cost of implementing AES as a quantum circuit. IEEE Trans. Quantum Eng. **1**, 1–12, Art no. 2500112 (2020).https://doi.org/10.1109/TQE.2020.2965697

34. Zhang, M., Shi, T., Wu, W., Sui, H.: Optimized quantum circuit of AES with interlacing-uncompute strategy. IEEE Trans. Comput. **73**(11), 2563–2575 (2024). https://doi.org/10.1109/TC.2024.3449094

35. Jang, K., Baksi, A., Kim, H., Song, G., Seo, H., Chattopadhyay, A.: Quantum analysis of AES. IACR Commun. Cryptol. **2**(1) (2025). https://doi.org/10.62056/ay11zo-3y

36. Luo, Q., Li, Q., Li, X., Yang, G., Shen, J., Zheng, M.: Quantum circuit implementations of SM4 block cipher optimizing the number of qubits. Quantum Inf. Process. **23**, 177 (2024). https://doi.org/10.1007/s11128-024-04394-x

37. Yadav, T., Kumar, M., Kumar, A., Pal, S.K.: A practical-quantum differential attack on block ciphers. Cryptogr. Commun. **17**, 337–357 (2025). https://doi.org/10.1007/s12095-023-00650-6
38. Jang, K., Song, G., Kim, H., Kwon, H., Kim, H., Seo, H.: Efficient implementation of PRESENT and GIFT on quantum computers. Appl. Sci. **11**(11), 4776 (2021). https://doi.org/10.3390/app11114776

A Keystream Generator Inspired by the Experiment of Drawing Balls with Replacement

Ganesh Yellapu[✉]

Center of Excellence-Communication, Bharat Electronics Limited, Bangalore, India
`ganeshyellapu@bel.co.in`

Abstract. Many keystream generator designs rely on mapping internal state bits to the output via a Boolean function. This introduces correlation between the keystream and the generator's state, as well as a functional dependency, rendering the generator vulnerable to various cryptanalytic techniques such as correlation, algebraic, and distinguishing attacks. These attacks can often be leveraged for key recovery.

A core challenge in stream cipher design, therefore, is to develop generators producing keystream with strong statistical properties while ensuring security beyond vulnerability to known cryptanalytic methods—specifically, achieving a security level where key recovery is, in principle, limited only to the exhaustive key search. In this work, we address this challenge with the Random Transposition Cipher (RTC), a generator inspired by the experiment of drawing balls with replacement from an urn. This analogy forms the basis of a hidden Markov model (HMM) of the random transposition shuffling process and constitutes the core of the RTC, superficially resembling the RC4 stream cipher.

We present a detailed security analysis of the RTC, demonstrating its resistance to correlation, algebraic, and distinguishing attacks. Furthermore, we establish that key recovery for the RTC is theoretically infeasible by any method other than the exhaustive search.

Keywords: Algebraic attack · correlation attack · distinguishing attack · entropy · hidden Markov model · keystream generator · nonlinear combiner · nonlinear combiner with memory · nonlinear filter · Pinsker's inequality · random permutations · random transposition shuffling · RC4 · relative entropy · stream cipher · total variation distance · Viterbi decoding algorithm

1 Introduction

A binary additive stream cipher, operating synchronously, generates a keystream sequence $z_1, z_2, \ldots$ of binary digits. Encryption is achieved by combining the

G. Yellapu—This research work is dedicated to the feet of Goddess Kamakshi. I (author) would like to remind myself my parents Y Lakshmi Narayana & Y Alivelu (for their blessings) and my wife Palla Harika for her support to accomplish this work.

C. Karfa et al. (Eds.): SPACE 2025, LNCS 16406, pp. 407–429, 2026.
https://doi.org/10.1007/978-3-032-16342-4_22

plaintext bit sequence $m_1, m_2, \ldots$ with the keystream sequence via the bitwise XOR operation to produce the corresponding ciphertext sequence $c_1, c_2, \ldots$.

From a finite state machine perspective, a keystream generator is defined by an output alphabet of $\{0, 1\}$, a finite state space, a next-state function, an output function, and an initial state [36]. The output function maps the current state to a binary output symbol z_t, while the next-state function determines the subsequent state based on the current state.

A complete stream cipher includes the keystream generator and a resynchronization mechanism, establishing the initial state from a key and an initialization vector (IV). Ideally, a stream cipher should emulate the properties of the one-time pad (Vernam cipher), where plaintext and ciphertext are statistically independent, resulting in zero mutual information [34]. Consequently, desirable characteristics of the keystream sequence include a large period, high linear complexity, and strong statistical properties ensuring indistinguishability from a truly random sequence.

Two common models for keystream generator design are the nonlinear combiner generator and the nonlinear filter generator. Both utilize linear feedback shift registers (LFSRs) and a nonlinear Boolean function as core components [34,36]. A fundamental characteristic of Boolean functions is that their output is invariably correlated with some linear combination of their input variables. Consequently, keystream sequences generated using these models exhibit inherent correlations with the internal state of the generator.

These correlations are exploited by correlation-based attacks, which aim to recover the generator's initial state [7,9,12,24,26,32,33,37,38,40].

To mitigate the correlations introduced by the output Boolean function in combiner and filter generators, the concept of a combiner with memory was proposed. This model employs separate functions for memory update and keystream generation. However, Golic [20] demonstrated the existence of linear correlations between successive outputs and inputs within such combiners. Linear cryptanalysis exploits these correlations to compromise the security of the generator [5,20,21,33]. Consequently, inherent linear correlations exist for any combination of memory update and output functions used within this framework, rendering combiners with memory susceptible to linear attacks.

Algebraic and fast algebraic attacks represent significant threats to security of keystream generators. These techniques aim to construct a system of algebraic equations relating the generator's initial state to observed keystream bits. Solving this system reveals the internal state, and thus compromises the generator [4,11,13].

Efficient algorithms exist for solving such systems of algebraic equations [12]. Furthermore, a design criteria for Boolean functions intended to resist algebraic attacks was proposed in [13].

[5] provides strategies for selecting output and memory update functions to design combiners with memory that are resilient to both correlation and algebraic attacks. Specifically, the work establishes a lower bound on the degree of the

algebraic equations that arise during an algebraic attack providing guidance for function design.

The above classical keystream generator models typically employ regularly clocked shift registers with nonlinearity introduced via the output Boolean function. To resist against cryptanalytic techniques like correlation and algebraic attacks, various cryptographic criteria have been proposed for the output function, including balance, high nonlinearity, high algebraic degree, and high algebraic immunity [8].

Clock-controlled generators represent another classical approach to keystream generator design. Nonlinearity is introduced through irregular clocking of shift registers. However, these generators typically exhibit lower throughput compared to regularly clocked designs and are susceptible to correlation, algebraic, and side-channel attacks [1,25,29].

Distinguishing attacks represent another crucial technique for analyzing keystream generators. The adversary attempts to determine whether a given keystream sequence appears to be random or if it was generated by a specific cipher. In certain scenarios, distinguishing attacks are successful in recovering the key. Overviews of distinguishing attacks against stream ciphers are available in [10,17,23].

The Linear Sequential Circuit Approximation (LSCA) method provides a general framework for mounting distinguishing attacks [18,20,21]. For instance, the keystreams of popular ciphers like RC4 and Grain have been successfully distinguished from random using LSCA [19,28].

Classical keystream generator designs conceptualize the internal state as a single, unified entity. The state is iteratively updated, and keystream bits are derived from it via an output function. This functional dependency between the keystream and the generator's state inevitably reveals information about the state - specifically, in the form of correlations and algebraic relations. Consequently, various cryptanalytic techniques exploit this information to either recover the generator's initial state or distinguish the keystream from a truly random sequence.

This work introduces a new keystream generator, the Random Transposition Cipher (RTC), designed for cryptographic applications. RTC's internal state is composed of three maximum-length linear feedback shift registers (LFSRs) - with lengths of 4, 128, and 128 bits - a 16-element array storing 4-bit words, and a 4-bit counter. The design of RTC is inspired by the experiment of drawing balls with replacement and implements a random transposition shuffle - a card-shuffling method - to uniformly (or near uniformly) permute the array of words. A keystream nibble is then generated by uniformly selecting an element from the permuted array using a vectorial Boolean function. We demonstrate that this process can be formally represented as a hidden Markov model (HMM), providing a rigorous mathematical foundation.

State of the RTC can be intrinsically partitioned into two components: $part_1$, consisting of linear feedback shift registers, and $part_2$, the array of words and the counter. $part_1$ drives both itself and the array, making the array as a time-variant permutation, while $part_2$ exclusively determines the keystream through the output function. By isolating keystream generation to $part_2$, we aim to mitigate the information leakage due to the functional dependency between the keystream and the generator's state and to evade cryptanalytic techniques that attempt to extract any information about the driving state component.

The rest of this article is organized as follows: Sect. 2 revisits the experiment of drawing balls with replacement and its application to random number generation. Section 3 details the hidden Markov model (HMM) for the random transposition shuffling, including its associated decoding problem. Section 4 presents the keystream generator, the Random Transposition Cipher (RTC), based on this HMM along with the security analysis. Finally, Sect. 5 concludes the paper.

2 Revisiting the Experiment of Drawing Balls with Replacement

Let $\mathcal{F}_2$ denote the finite field of two elements, $\{0, 1\}$, and let n be a non-negative integer. Define $S = \{0, 1, \ldots, N - 1\}$ where $N = 2^n$. A bijection $\pi : S \rightarrow S$ is a permutation of S, and the set of all permutations of S is denoted by S_N. S_N forms a symmetric group of order N, where $N! = |S_N|$ represents the cardinality of S_N. A permutation π can be represented as

$$\pi = \begin{pmatrix} 0 & 1 & \cdots & N-1 \\ \pi(0) & \pi(1) & \cdots & \pi(N-1) \end{pmatrix}$$

or equivalently as $(\pi(0), \pi(1), \ldots, \pi(N-1))$.

Let P_N be the set of all $N \times N$ permutation matrices. P_N is a subgroup of the general linear group $GL(N, \mathcal{F}_2)$, the set of all invertible $N \times N$ matrices over $\mathcal{F}_2$, under matrix multiplication. A one-to-one correspondence exists between S_N and P_N. A permutation matrix $P \in P_N$ defined by a transposition (L, R), where $L, R \in S$, is obtained by swapping the L-th and R-th rows of the $N \times N$ identity matrix. For example, when $N = 4$ and $(L, R) = (1, 3)^1$, we have

$$P = \begin{pmatrix} 1 & 0 & 0 & 0 \\ 0 & 0 & 0 & 1 \\ 0 & 0 & 1 & 0 \\ 0 & 1 & 0 & 0 \end{pmatrix}.$$

Consequently, the transformation $P : \mathcal{F}_2^N \rightarrow \mathcal{F}_2^N$ is both linear and bijective.

Let $w > 0$ be an integer. Define $\mathcal{S}_T = \{\{(L_t, R_t)\}_{t=0}^{w-1} | L_t, R_t \in S\}$ as the set of all sequences of transpositions of length w, where $S = \{0, 1, \ldots, N - 1\}$ and $N = 2^n$. Let $\mathcal{S}_{PTM}$ be the set of all products of permutation matrices, where each matrix is defined by a transposition (L_j, R_j) with $L_j, R_j \in S$. That is, $\mathcal{S}_{PTM} = \{\prod_{j=0}^{w-1} P_j | P_j$ is the permutation matrix corresponding to $(L_j, R_j)\}$.

---

^{1} Row index starts from 0.

Given an element $\alpha = \{(L_t, R_t)\}_{t=0}^{w-1} \in \mathcal{S}_T$, there exists a unique $\beta = \prod_{t=0}^{w-1} P_t \in \mathcal{S}_{PTM}$, where P_t is the permutation matrix defined by (L_t, R_t). However, this correspondence is not one-to-one; a single $\beta \in \mathcal{S}_{PTM}$ may correspond to multiple elements of $\mathcal{S}_T$. For instance, consider $N = 4$ and $w = 3$, with $\beta = P_0 P_1 P_2$. Here P_0, P_2 correspond to the transpositions $(L_0, R_0), (L_1, R_1)$ respectively and P_1 represents the identity matrix. Then, four distinct sequences $\alpha_0, \alpha_1, \alpha_2, \alpha_3 \in \mathcal{S}_T$ yield the same β: $\alpha_0 = ((L_0, R_0), (0, 0), (L_2, R_2))$, $\alpha_1 = ((L_0, R_0)(1, 1)(L_2, R_2))$ $\alpha_2 = ((L_0, R_0)(2, 2)(L_3, R_3))$ and $\alpha_3 = ((L_0, R_0)(3, 3)(L_3, R_3))$.

Consider a set of N distinguishable balls, indexed from 0 to $N - 1$. A permutation of these balls can be represented as an element of the symmetric group S_N. Specifically, a permutation $\pi \in S_N$ defines an arrangement of the indexed balls. For example, a permutation $\pi = (6, 7, 4, 5, 1, 0, 2, 3) \in S_8$ is interpreted as follows: place ball 6 into position 0, place ball 7 into position 1, place ball 4 into position 2, place ball 5 into position 3, place ball 1 into position 4, place ball 0 into position 5, place ball 2 into position 6 and place ball 3 into position 7 and the corresponding arrangement is illustrated in Fig. 1.

$$\begin{array}{cccccccc} 0 & 1 & 2 & 3 & 4 & 5 & 6 & 7 \\ \boxed{6} & \boxed{7} & \boxed{4} & \boxed{5} & \boxed{1} & \boxed{0} & \boxed{2} & \boxed{3} \end{array}$$

Fig. 1. An ordered arrangement of 8 indexed balls

Given a container holding N distinguishable balls, a common method for generating independent and identically distributed (i.i.d.) uniform random variables over the set of ball indices is to draw balls with replacement. While this experiment typically does not necessitate reshuffling after each draw, potential predictability arises if a single observer performs all draws, due to memorization or identification of systematic arrangements. To mitigate this bias and ensure statistical independence, we assume shuffling of the balls within the container prior to each draw.

Given an initial ordered arrangement of N distinguishable balls, a sequence of pseudo-random numbers over the set $\{0, 1, \cdots, N - 1\}$ can be generated by simulating the experiment of drawing balls with replacement. This is achieved through the following iterative process:

1. Randomly permute the balls, effectively sampling a permutation from the symmetric group S_N and rearranging the balls accordingly.
2. Randomly select a position (or location) from the set $\{0, 1, ..., N - 1\}$.
3. Output the number of the ball located at index as a pseudo-random number.

Considering the initial arrangement shown in Fig. 1, if $\pi_2 = (3, 6, 5, 4, 2, 0, 1, 7)$ represents a randomly chosen permutation , after applying π_2, the rearrangement depicted in Fig. 2 is obtained. If position 6 is subsequently selected, the output is the number of the ball at position 6, which is 1. This re-arranged configuration (Fig. 2) then serves as the basis for generating the next pseudo-random number.

Fig. 2. Arrangement of balls after permuting

The uniformity of the generated random numbers depends critically on the selection process for both the permutation from S_N and the position from S. Consider a subset S' of S_8 consisting of permutations that map the ball numbered 5 to position 3; i.e., permutations of the form $(*, *, *, 5, *, *, *, *)$ where $*$ denotes any element of S excluding 5. If the permutation selection method systematically excludes elements of S' (selecting only from $S_8 \setminus S'$), while still employing a uniform random number generator to choose the position, the resulting distribution of generated random numbers will be non-uniform. Specifically, the probability of observing the number 5 at position 3 will be zero, while the distribution of any other number in $S \setminus \{5\}$ will remain uniform. This highlights the necessity of a uniformly random selection from the entire permutation group S_N to ensure a uniform distribution of generated random numbers.

If a permutation is selected uniformly at random from S_N, then each ball (or each n-bit number) has an equal probability of occupying any given position. Given an initial ordered arrangement of N balls, the Fisher-Yates shuffle algorithm (Algorithm P, or "Shuffling") provides a method for generating permutations. This algorithm is provably uniform, ensuring that each permutation in S_N is equally likely for the new arrangement [30, 39]. The algorithm consists of $N - 1$ iterations, progressing from index $N - 1$ down to 1. Each iteration i requires a uniformly distributed random number within the range $[0, i]$. Consequently, generating these random numbers often necessitates the use of the modulo operation. However, the modulo operation can introduce bias in the generated random numbers [39].

Several card-shuffling methods have been studied; one example is the random transposition shuffle [16]. In this method, N' cards, labeled 0 through $N' - 1$, are initially arranged face up in a row (card 0 is at the left, card 1 is next, and so on, with card $N' - 1$ at the right of the row) corresponding to the identity permutation of $S_{N'}$. At each step, a pair of random integers (L, R), independently and uniformly chosen from the interval $[0, N' - 1]$, are used to transpose the cards at those locations. If $L = R$, no transposition occurs. A central question is determining how many transpositions, denoted by w, are required to achieve a nearly uniform permutation. For $N' \geq 10$, Diaconis [16] showed that the total variation distance between the resultant permutation's probability distribution and the uniform distribution on $S_{N'}$ approaches 0 when $w = \frac{1}{2}N'log(N') + cN'$, where c is a positive constant. The variation distance exhibits a rapid transition, changing from approximately 1 to approximately 0, over an interval of length $\mathcal{O}(N')$ centered around the cutoff rate of $\frac{1}{2}N'log(N')$. For $c = 4$, the variation distance is bounded between e^{-9} and $e^{-6.3} = 0.0018$; with $c = 5$, these bounds become e^{-11} and $e^{-8.3} = 0.00025$ [31]. The expression $\frac{1}{2}N'log(N')$ is known as the cutoff rate of the random transposition shuffle.

Other card shuffling methods, such as riffle shuffles, top-in-at-random shuffles and overhand shuffles exhibit different cutoff rates $\frac{3}{2}log_2(N')$, $N'log(N')$, $\theta(N'^2 logN')$ respectively [3,6,27]. However, for the purposes of this study, we focus on the random transposition shuffle due to its relatively straightforward implementation compared to these alternatives.

Given a properly chosen value of w, a sequence of w transpositions, denoted as $\{(L_t, R_t)\}_{t=0}^{w-1} = (L_0, R_0), (L_1, R_1), \ldots, (L_{w-1}, R_{w-1})$, can be applied to an initial arrangement of $N(= 2^n)$ balls to generate a new permutation. Each transposition involves swapping the contents of positions L_t and R_t. Through appropriate selection of w and the transposition sequence, the variation distance between the resulting permutation distribution and the uniform distribution over S_N can be minimized.

3   A Hidden Markov Model of the Random Transposition Shuffling

A probability distribution, denoted by μ, over the symmetric group S_N is defined as [2]:

$$\mu(\sigma) = \begin{cases} 1/N & \text{if } \sigma = identity\ permutation, \\ 2/N^2 & \text{if } \sigma = (i,j)\ a\ transposition, \\ 0 & otherwise. \end{cases}$$

This distribution μ models a shuffling process, where a permutation σ is applied to a set of N elements with probability $\mu(\sigma)$. Repeated applications of permutations drawn from μ constitute a random walk, $\{X_t\}$, on S_N with increment distribution μ. This Markov chain is known to be irreducible and aperiodic [2], converging to the uniform distribution on S_N as its stationary distribution, with a cutoff rate of $\frac{1}{2}Nlog(N)$ [16].

Let $\sigma \in S_N$ represent the state of the process $\{X_t\}$ at time t. A random transposition (L, R) is applied, where L and R are independent and uniformly distributed over S. Applying this transposition to σ yields a subsequent state at time $t+1$. The possible successors of σ comprise a set of $\frac{N(N-1)}{2}+1$ permutations, representing all permutations, $\{\sigma, \sigma_{i_1}, \sigma_{i_2}, \cdots, \sigma_{i_{\frac{N^2-N}{2}}}\}$, achievable through a single transposition. The transition probabilities are defined as follows:

$$Prob(\sigma \rightarrow \sigma) = 1/N \qquad\qquad\qquad \text{if } L = R$$
$$Prob(\sigma \rightarrow \sigma_{i_j}) = 2/N^2 \qquad\qquad \text{for some } \sigma_{i_j} \text{ if } L \neq R$$
$$Prob(\sigma \rightarrow \sigma_k) = 0 \qquad\qquad \text{if } \sigma_k \neq \sigma \text{ and } \sigma_k \neq \sigma_{i_j} \text{ for all } j$$

The state transition probabilities of the Markov chain $\{X_t\}$ are represented by the matrix $\mathbf{P} = [p_{ij}]_{N! \times N!}$, where p_{ij} denotes the probability of transitioning from state σ_i to state σ_j. The transition matrix P exhibits symmetry, reflecting the property that the probability of transitioning between two permutations is independent of the order in which they are considered. Furthermore, each row of P contains exactly $\frac{N(N-1)}{2} + 1$ non-zero entries, representing the accessible transitions from a given permutation; all other transition probabilities are zero. Notice that the transition probabilities p_{ij} are independent of time (assumption of stationary transition probabilities of a hidden Markov model [35]).

Let $\mathbf{\Pi} = [\Pi_i]_{1 \times N!}$ denote the initial probability distribution of the Markov chain $\{X_t\}$, where $\Pi_i \geq 0$ for all i and $\sum_{i=0}^{N!-1} \Pi_i = 1$. Given a sequence of transitions $X_0, X_1, \cdots, X_{T-1}$ of the process, we observe that for $t \geq w$, where w is significantly larger than the cutoff rate of the random transposition shuffling, the distribution of $\{X_t\}$ converges to the uniform distribution over the symmetric group S_N. However, for $t < w$, the distribution of $\{X_t\}$ is not necessarily uniform over S_N. To facilitate analysis, we assume a uniform initial distribution, i.e., $\Pi_i = \frac{1}{N!}$ for all i. This assumption is motivated by the convergence to the uniform stationary distribution and enables a clearer understanding of the chain's initial behavior. As the uniform distribution is the stationary distribution of the Markov chain, $\{X_t\}$ is uniformly distributed over S_N for all $t \geq 0$. Consequently, for any state $X_t = \sigma_t$, each n-bit number is equally likely for any of N positions of σ_t. However, although the chain converges to the uniform distribution, the conditional distribution of X_{t+1} given X_t is not uniform because σ_t and σ_{t+1} differ by at most two positions.

Let Y be a uniform random variable over S. At time t, let $\sigma_t \in S_N$ denote the state of the process (i.e., $X_t = \sigma_t$). Given a realization y_t of the random variable Y, the observation $O_t = (O_t^1, O_t^2) = (\sigma_t[y_t], \sigma_t[N-1])$ of the process is generated, where $\sigma_t[y_t]$ represents the element at position y_t of the permutation σ_t. The observation O_t depends solely on the current state σ_t and the random variable y_t; it is independent of both past and future states and observations. This implies that the observations of the process $\{X_t\}$ are conditionally independent, mirroring the observation independence assumption within the framework of a Hidden Markov Model [35]. Formally,

$$Prob(O_0, O_1, \cdots, O_{T-1} | \sigma_0, \sigma_1, \cdots, \sigma_{T-1}, y_0, y_1, \cdots, y_{T-1}) = \prod_{t=0}^{T-1} Pr(O_t | \sigma_t, y_t).$$

Let $\Omega = \{O = (O^1, O^2) | O^1, O^2 \in S\}$ be the set of possible observations of the Markov chain $\{X_t\}$, where $|\Omega| = N^2$. For $0 \leq k \leq N^2 - 1$, define $\phi_i(k)$ as the emission probability of the observation $O_k = (O_k^1, O_k^2)$ when the process is in state σ_i. Given a state $\sigma_i \in S_N$, the observation O^2 is constrained by the permutation σ_i such that $O^2 = \sigma_i[N-1]$. Therefore, only observations of the form $(*, \sigma_i[N-1])$ can be emitted, defining the subset $\Omega_i = \{(O^1, \sigma_i[N-1]) | O^1 \in S\} \subseteq \Omega$. Since the random variable Y is uniformly distributed over S, each observation in Ω_i is equally likely, with probability $\frac{1}{N}$. Hence, the emission probability is given by:

$$\phi_i(k) = \text{Prob}(\text{emitting the observation } O_k = (O_k^1, O_k^2) \text{ given the state } \sigma_i)$$

$$= \text{Prob}(O_k = (O_k^1, O_k^2)|\sigma_i)$$

$$= \frac{1}{N} \quad \text{if } O_k^2 = \sigma_i[N-1]$$

$$= 0 \quad \text{if } O_k^2 \neq \sigma_i[N-1]$$

Consider the hidden Markov model (HMM) defined by the parameters $\lambda = (S_N, \Omega, \mathbf{P}, \mathbf{\Phi}, \mathbf{\Pi})$ for the Markov chain $\{X_t\}$ of random transposition shuffling. Here, S_N represents the state space, Ω the observation space, $\mathbf{P}$ the state transition matrix, and $\mathbf{\Pi}$ the initial state distribution, assumed to be uniform. The emission probability matrix $\mathbf{\Phi}$ (of dimension $N! \times N^2$) exhibits sparsity: each row contains precisely N non-zero probabilities.

1. The decoding problem for the hidden Markov model (HMM) λ seeks to identify the most probable sequence of hidden states, $\widehat{\overline{\sigma}} = (\widehat{\sigma_0}, \widehat{\sigma_1}, \cdots, \widehat{\sigma_{T-1}})$, given an observation sequence $\overline{O} = O_0, O_1, \cdots, O_{T-1}$. Formally, this corresponds to maximizing the posterior probability:

$$\widehat{\overline{\sigma}} = \arg \max_{\overline{\sigma} = (\sigma_0, \sigma_1, \cdots, \sigma_{T-1})} Prob(\overline{\sigma}/\overline{O}).$$

An exhaustive search over all possible state sequences is computationally prohibitive, requiring evaluation of $N!^T$ paths. However, given the constraint that $\sigma_t[N-1] = O_t^2$, the number of candidate paths is reduced to $(N-1)!^T$. For instance, with $N = 16$ and $T = 4$, this narrows the search space to approximately 2^{161} paths.

While the Viterbi algorithm is well-established for the HMM decoding problem, with a general computational complexity of $\mathcal{O}(N!^2 T)$ and space complexity of $\mathcal{O}(N! \times T)$ [15,35], the sparsity of the state transition matrix $\mathbf{P}$ offers further optimization. Each row of $\mathbf{P}$ contains only $\frac{N^2 - N}{2} + 1$ non-zero probabilities, reducing the Viterbi algorithm's computational complexity to $\mathcal{O}((\frac{N^2 - N}{2} + 1) \times N! \times T)$. For $N = 16$, this reduces the complexity of the decoding algorithm to approximately $\mathcal{O}(121 \times 16! \times T)$.

Notably, the state transition matrix $\mathbf{P}$ exhibits a unique structure: all non-zero transition probabilities are uniform except for the self transition. Given the observation $O_t = (O_t^1, O_t^2)$, for $0 \leq t \leq T-1$, there are $(N-1)!$ states and $(N-2)!$ states are possible for σ_t depending on whether $O_t^1 = O_t^2$ and $O_t^1 \neq O_t^2$ respectively . Each of these states emits O_t with a uniform probability of $\frac{1}{N}$. This uniformity may introduce ambiguity during Viterbi decoding, potentially leading to the most probable sequence $\widehat{\overline{\sigma}}$ that differs from the true hidden sequence, denoted as $\widehat{\overline{\sigma}} = (\widehat{\sigma_0}, \widehat{\sigma_1}, \cdots, \widehat{\sigma_{T-1}})$, of states.

2. Given an initial state σ_0, the process evolves through a sequence of random transpositions $\{(L_t, R_t)\}_{t=0}^{T-2}$, resulting in a state sequence $(\sigma_0, \sigma_1, \cdots, \sigma_{T-1})$, where σ_{t+1} is derived from σ_t by applying the transposition (L_t, R_t). Correspondingly, we observe a sequence $\overline{O} = (O_0, O_1, \cdots, O_{T-1})$, where $O_t = (O_t^1, O_t^2) = (\sigma_t[y_t], \sigma_t[N-1])$.

416   G. Yellapu

Conversely, assuming we are given the observation sequence $\overline{O}$ and the values $\{y_t\}_{t=0}^{T-1}$, a key question arises: can we uniquely reconstruct the sequence of random transpositions $\{(L_t, R_t)\}_{t=0}^{T-2}$?.

Recovering the underlying state sequence $\widehat{\overline{\sigma}}$ is a prerequisite to this reconstruction. If $\widehat{\overline{\sigma}}$ is known, the transposition (L_t, R_t) for $0 \leq t \leq T - 2$ can be determined by comparing successive states, $\widehat{\sigma_t}$ and $\widehat{\sigma_{t+1}}$, provided they differ. However, when $\widehat{\sigma_t} = \widehat{\sigma_{t+1}}$, no unique transposition can be identified; in this instance, we have $L_t = R_t$, leading to N possible transpositions.

3. Consider the scenario where only the initial and final observations, $O_0 = (O_0^1, O_0^2)$ and $O_{T-1} = (O_{T-1}^1, O_{T-1}^2)$, are available, with all intermediate observations absent. Given the initial state σ_0, the final state σ_{T-1}, and the sequence $\{y_t\}_{t=0}^{T-1}$, we aim to reconstruct the path connecting these states. While there are $N!^{T-2}$ possible paths between σ_0 to σ_{T-1}, the state transition matrix $\mathbf{P}$ constrains the number of viable paths. Let nP_e^T and nP_o^T denote the number of such paths for even and odd T, respectively. We establish bounds on these quantities:

$$x^{\frac{(T-2)(T-4)}{4}} \leq nP_e^T \leq x^{\frac{T(T-2)}{4}}$$

and

$$x^{\frac{(T-1)(T-3)}{4}} \leq nP_o^T \leq x^{\frac{(T-1)^2}{4}}$$

where $x = \frac{N^2 - N}{2} + 1$ (see Appendix A).

However, given that the hidden process can only be inferred through the sequence of observations, information-theoretic principles suggest that complete recovery of the original sequence (the true sequence) of hidden states is impossible. Any decoding algorithm, including Viterbi, relies on intermediate observations. Without them, the nP_e^T (or nP_o^T) viable paths between σ_0 and σ_{T-1} are indistinguishable. Consequently, reconstructing the sequence of transpositions $\{(L_t, R_t)\}_{t=0}^{T-2}$ that evolved the process from state σ_0 to state σ_{T-1} is infeasible.

4. Now consider a scenario with sparse observations. Given u observations $O_0, O_T, O_{2T}, \cdots, O_{(u-1)T}$ and the sequence $\{y_t\}_{t=0}^{(u-1)T}$, along with the corresponding states $\sigma_0, \sigma_T, \cdots, \sigma_{(u-1)T}$, where $T > 1$, complete reconstruction of the true hidden state sequence is not possible. Specifically, for each interval $[jT, (j+1)T]$, where $0 \leq j \leq u - 2$, the lack of intermediate observations precludes uniquely determining the path between states σ_{jT} and $\sigma_{(j+1)T}$. Without intermediate observations, the number of possible paths is bounded by either nP_e^{T+1} (when $T + 1$ is even) or nP_o^{T+1} (when $T + 1$ is odd), as previously defined. Consequently, the sequence of transpositions $\{(L_t, R_t)\}_{t=jT}^{(j+1)T-1}$ driving the process between σ_{jT} and $\sigma_{(j+1)T}$ remains unrecoverable.

Points 2, 3 and 4 are referred while analyzing the RTC in Sect. 4.2.

4   The Random Transpositions Cipher (RTC)

This section details the Random Transpositions Cipher (RTC), a keystream generator built upon the principle of drawing balls with replacement. As illustrated in Fig. 3 and Fig. 4, the RTC utilizes three maximum-length Linear Feedback Shift Registers (LFSRs) - A, B, and C - with lengths of 4 bits, 128 bits, and 128 bits, respectively. The cipher incorporates a 16-element array F, where each element is a 4-bit word, a 4-bit counter cnt, and a 4-variable vectorial Boolean function G.

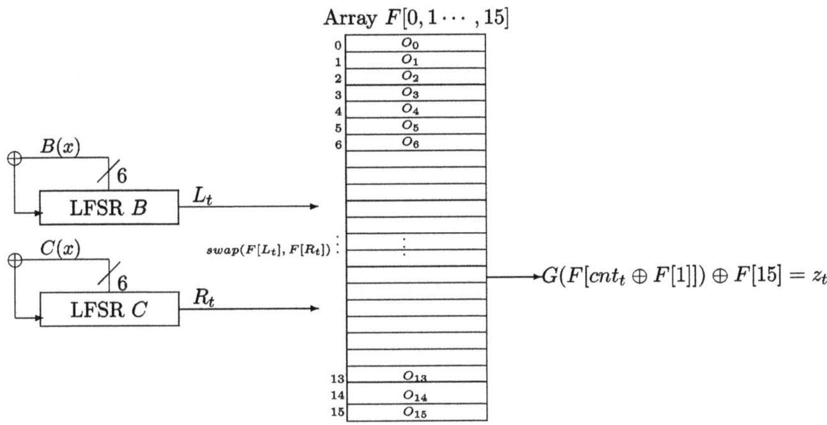

Fig. 3. Overview of the RTC generator

The primitive polynomials and state update function of each shift register, along with the truth table of the function G, are detailed in Table-1. The function G has algebraic degree 3 and nonlinearity 4. The memory elements of all shift registers, memory elements of the 16 element array and memory elements of counter variable represent the state of RTC cipher.

During initialization of the cipher, the array F is initialized with the 16 distinct 4-bit words, representing a permutation of $N = 16$ elements (or balls) numbered 0 through 15. As discussed in Sect. 2, a sequence of w random transpositions, $\{(L_t, R_t)\}_{t=0}^{w-1}$, achieves uniform (or near) permutation[2]. For the RTC cipher, we utilize $w = 23$ random transpositions (with $c = 0$ in the cutoff formula), where $gcd(w, N) = gcd(23, 16) = 1$.

The cipher generates keystream one nibble at a time via a straightforward process. For each nibble, $w = 22$ random transpositions are applied to the array F, utilizing states from shift registers B and C. These transpositions permute the elements of F. Subsequently, two elements, O_{23i+23}^1 and O_{23i+23}^2, are chosen from

---

[2] The cutoff rate for a random transposition shuffle of $N = 16$ elements is approximately $\frac{1}{2}N log(N) \approx 23$ transpositions.

Table 1. Primitive polynomial and state update function of each LFSR A, B and C and, Cryptographic properties of G

LFSR	Primitive polynomial, state and state update function
A	$A(x) = 1 + x + x^4$, $A_t = (a_{t+3}, a_{t+2}, a_{t+1}, a_t)$, $a_{t+4} = a_{t+3} + a_t$
B	$B(x) = 1 + x^{36} + x^{38} + x^{45} + x^{57} + x^{95} + x^{128}$ $B_t = (b_{t+127}, b_{t+126}, \cdots, b_{t+1}, b_t)$ $b_{t+128} = b_{92} + b_{t+90} + b_{t+83} + b_{t+71} + b_{t+33} + b_t$
C	$C(x) = 1 + x^{21} + x^{42} + x^{62} + x^{83} + x^{105} + x^{128}$ $C_t = (c_{t+127}, c_{t+126}, \cdots, c_{t+1}, c_t)$ $c_{t+128} = c_{t+107} + c_{t+86} + c_{t+66} + c_{t+45} + c_{t+23} + c_t$
$G : \mathcal{F}_2^4 \to \mathcal{F}_2^4$	$G[0, 1, \cdots, 15] = \{0, 15, 11, 5, 9, 3, 14, 12, 8, 4, 13, 2, 7, 10, 6, 1\}$ Algebraic degree of G is 3, Nonlinearity of G is 4
Component functions of G	$G(x) = (g_3(x), g_2(x), g_1(x), g_0(x))$ for all $x \in \mathcal{F}_2^4$

the permuted array F at positions determined by $y_{23i+23} = cnt_{23i+23} \oplus F_{23i+23}[1]$ and 15, respectively. The keystream nibble $z_i = (z_{i,3}, z_{i,2}, z_{i,1}, z_{i,0}) \in \{0, 1\}^4$ is then produced as $z_i = G[O^1_{23i+23}] \oplus O^2_{23i+23}$.

4.1 Initialization and Keystream Generation

The cipher requires initialization with a key and an initialization vector (IV) prior to keystream generation. A 128-bit key, represented as $(k_0, k_1, \ldots, k_{127})$, and a 128-bit IV, represented as $(iv_0, iv_1, \ldots, iv_{127})$, are used. The initialization procedure is adopted from the Grain-128 [22]. Initially, the 16-element array F is populated with 4-bit words using shift register A. Subsequently, the cipher is clocked 128 times without keystream output; instead, the component function g_0 of G feeds back into shift registers B and C (see Fig. 4). Given the key and IV, the below procedure initializes the RTC cipher and generates u keystream nibbles for any integer $u > 0$[3].

1: $A_0 = (a_3, a_2, a_1, a_0) \leftarrow (iv_0, iv_1, iv_2, 1)$ $\triangleright$ load shift registers
2: $cnt_0 \leftarrow (iv_3, iv_4, iv_5, iv_6)$
3: $B_0 = (b_{127}, b_{126}, \ldots, b_1, b_0) \leftarrow (k_0, k_1, \ldots, k_{127})$
4: $C_0 = (c_{127}, c_{126}, \ldots, c_1, c_0) \leftarrow (1, 1, 1, 1, 1, 1, 1, iv_7, iv_8, \ldots, iv_{127})$
5: **for** $t \leftarrow 1$ to 15 **do** $\triangleright$ initialize 16 element array F
6:     $loc \leftarrow A_{t-1}$ [4]
7:     $F[loc] \leftarrow t$
8:     update shift register A to get A_t
9: **end for**

---

[3] The keystream generation algorithm is detailed for clarity and reproducibility.
[4] Given $A_t = (a_{t+3}, a_{t+2}, a_{t+1}, a_t) \in \{0, 1\}^4$, we use the same notation, A_t, for the corresponding integer $\sum_{i=0}^{3} a_{t+i} 2^i$.

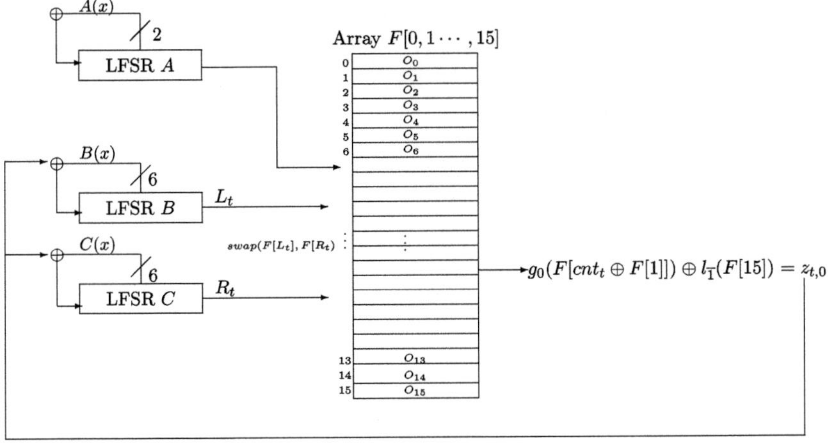

Fig. 4. Initialization of the RTC generator

10: $F[0] \leftarrow 0$
11: **for** $t \leftarrow 0$ to 127 **do**
12:     $y_t \leftarrow cnt_t \oplus F[1]$
13:     $O_t^1 \leftarrow F[y_t]$
14:     $O_t^2 \leftarrow F[15]$
15:     $L_t \leftarrow (b_{t+3}, b_{t+2}, b_{t+1}, b_t)$
16:     $R_t \leftarrow (c_{t+3}, c_{t+2}, c_{t+1}, c_t)$
17:     swap $(F[L_t], F[R_t])$
18:     $cnt_{t+1} \leftarrow cnt_t + 1$
19:     **if** $cnt_{t+1} = 16$ **then**
20:         $cnt_{t+1} \leftarrow 0$
21:     **end if**
22:     update shift register B to get next state B_{t+1}
23:     update shift register C to get next state C_{t+1}
24:     $b_{(t+1)+127} \leftarrow b_{(t+1)+127} \oplus g_0(O_t^1) \oplus l_{\overline{1}}(O_t^2)$
25:     $c_{(t+1)+127} \leftarrow c_{(t+1)+127} \oplus g_0(O_t^1) \oplus l_{\overline{1}}(O_t^2)$
26: **end for**
27: $cnt_0 \leftarrow cnt_{128}$
28: $B_0 \leftarrow B_{128}$
29: $C_0 \leftarrow C_{128}$
30: $F_0 \leftarrow F$
31: $t \leftarrow 0$
32: **for** $i \leftarrow 0$ to $u - 1$ **do**   ▷ generate u keystream nibbles
33:     **for** $j \leftarrow 0$ to 22 **do**   ▷ $w = 23$ transpositions
34:         $y_{23i+j} \leftarrow cnt_{23i+j} \oplus F_{23i+j}[1]$
35:         $O_{23i+j}^1 \leftarrow F_{23i+j}[y_t]$
36:         $O_{23i+j}^2 \leftarrow F_{23i+j}[15]$
37:         $L_j \leftarrow (b_{i+4j+3}, b_{i+4j+2}, b_{i+4j+1}, b_{i+4j})$

38:         $R_j \leftarrow (c_{i+4j+3}, c_{i+4j+2}, c_{i+4j+1}, c_{i+4j})$
39:         swap $(F_{23i+j}[L_j], F_{23i+j}[R_j])$
40:         $cnt_{23i+j+1} \leftarrow cnt_{23i+j} + 1$
41:         **if** $cnt_{23i+j+1} = 16$ **then**
42:             $cnt_{23i+j+1} \leftarrow 0$
43:         **end if**
44:         $j \leftarrow j + 1$
45:     **end for**
46:     $y_{23i+23} \leftarrow cnt_{23i+23} \oplus F_{23i+23}[1]$
47:     $O^1_{23i+23} \leftarrow F_{23i+23}[y_{23i+23}]$
48:     $O^2_{23i+23} \leftarrow F_{23i+23}[15]$
49:     output $z_i = G(O^1_{23i+23}) \oplus O^2_{23i+23}$ ▷ keystream nibble z_i
50:     update shift register B to get next state B_{i+1}
51:     update shift register C to get next state C_{i+1}
52: **end for**

The cipher's initialization begins with loading the key and IV into the shift registers along with initialization of the counter (lines 1 to 4). Specifically, positions 121 through 127 of shift register C (indexed $C[0-6]$) are set to all 1's. The 16-element array F is then initialized using the state of shift register A, with $F[0]$ set to 0 as the maximum-length LFSR A never visits the all-zero state (lines 5 to 10). Lines 11 to 26 establish the cipher's initial state for keystream generation. From lines 27 to 52, the keystream sequence $\{z_i\}_{i=0}^{u-1}$ is generated. For each nibble, the array F is permuted using 23 random transpositions derived from the states of shift registers B and C. Notice that for each transposition (L_j, R_j), the random variables L_j and R_j are independent and, uniform over S as both B and C are maximum-length LFSRs.

The initial state of the cipher, for keystream generation, is defined as $(A_0, B_0, C_0, F_0, cnt_0)$ following line 26. At time t, the contents of registers B, C, array F, and counter are B_t, C_t, F_t, and cnt_t, respectively. Thus, F_t acts as a time-varying permutation, and z_i can be expressed as[5]

$$z_i = G(F_{23(i+1)}[cnt_{23(i+1)} \oplus F_{23(i+1)}[1]]) \oplus F_{23(i+1)}[15], \forall i \geq 0$$
$$= G(O^1_{23(i+1)}) \oplus O^2_{23(i+1)} \tag{1}$$

Following initialization of the array F using the shift register A, the array undergoes permutation with 128 transpositions (c is about 6.6 in the cutoff rate formula). Consequently, the distribution of F_0 is uniform over S_{16}. Because uniform distribution is the stationary distribution of the random transposition shuffling process, the distribution of F_t remains uniform for all t. However, given F_t, the distribution of F_{t+1} is not uniform, as F_t and F_{t+1} differ by at most two positions. To address this, the array is permuted with $w = 23$ transpositions for each keystream nibble, as supported by the ball-drawing experiment.

Beginning with F_0, the sequence $\{F_t\}$ forms a hidden Markov process governed by the random transposition shuffling, with parameters $\lambda = (S_{16}, \Omega,$

---

[5] Here, t denotes time (or clock), and i indexes the keystream.

$\mathbf{P}, \Phi, \Pi$). Here, $|S_{16}| \approx 2^{44.25}$, $|\Omega| = 256$ (and for each state $\sigma_i \in S_{16}$, $|\Omega_i| = 16$), $\mathbf{P} = [p_{ij}]_{16! \times 16!}$, $\Phi = [\phi_i(k)]_{16! \times 256}$, $\Pi = [\pi_i]_{1 \times 16!}$, each $\Pi_i = \frac{1}{16!}$. Each row of $\mathbf{P}$ contains exactly 121 non-zero transition probabilities, with all others equal to 0. Similarly, each row of Φ contains exactly 16 non-zero emission probabilities, and all other probabilities are 0.

For $i \geq 0$, given F_{23i}, distribution of $F_{23(i+1)}$ exhibits near-uniformity over S_{16}, with a minimum entropy of 41.39 bits (see Appendix B). The variation distance between $F_{23(i+1)}$ and the uniform distribution on S_{16} is upper bounded by 0.996 (as $c = 0$ in the cutoff rate formula). More specifically,

- for any $j \in S$, $F_{23(i+1)}[j]$ is approximately equally likely to take on any value in S; that is, $Prob(F_{23(i+1)}[j] = y) \approx \frac{1}{16}$ for all $y \in S$.
- Notably, while $F_{23(i+1)}[1]$ is near-uniform over S, the composite variable $y_{23(i+1)} = cnt_{23(i+1)} \oplus F_{23(i+1)}[1]$ is certainly uniform, due to the uniformity of the counter cnt.

Consequently, both $F_{23(i+1)}[y_{23(i+1)}]$ and $F_{23(i+1)}[15]$ are nearly uniform over S.

If we define $O_{23(i+1)} = (F_{23(i+1)}[y_{23(i+1)}], F_{23(i+1)}[15])$ as the observation of Markov process $\{F_t\}$, for each $z \in \{0,1\}^4$, we have $Prob(z_i = z) \approx \frac{1}{16}$. Clearly, period of $\{z_i\}$ is at least $2^{128} - 1$.[6] Since observations of the Markov process are conditionally independent, given the state sequence $\{F_{23(i+1)}\}_{i=0}^{u-1}$, the keystream nibbles $\{z_i\}_{i=0}^{u-1}$ are conditionally independent and approximately uniform random variables over S.

Consider the array F as an element of $\mathcal{F}_2^{16 \times 4}$. Then we have,

$$F_{t+1} = P_t F_t, \text{ for all } t \geq 0 \tag{2}$$

where P_t is the permutation matrix defined by the transposition (L_t, R_t) and

$$F_{23(i+1)+23} = P_{23(i+1)} F_{23(i+1)}, \text{ for all } i \geq 0 \tag{3}$$

where $P_{23(i+1)} = \prod_{t=23(i+1)}^{23(i+1)+22} P_t \in \mathcal{S}_{\mathcal{PTM}}$. Therefore, for any $i \geq 0$, the transformation from $F_{23(i+1)}$ to $F_{23(i+1)+23}$ is linear and time-variant.

The output function of the generator can be written as $H : \mathcal{F}_2^4 \times \mathcal{F}_2^4 \to \mathcal{F}^4$ where $H(O^1, O^2) = G[O^1] \oplus O^2$, for all $(O^1, O^2) \in \mathcal{F}_2^4 \times \mathcal{F}_2^4$.

4.2 Security Analysis

The internal state of the RTC generator comprises 328 bits, distributed across four components: a 4-bit shift register A, two 128-bit shift registers B and C, a 64-bit array F, and a 4-bit counter variable . However, for keystream generation, only 324 bits are relevant, as shift register A does not contribute to the output.

Given a keystream segment $z_i, z_{i+1}, \ldots, z_{i+u-1}$ for $i = 0$ and $u > 0$, the primary objectives of cryptanalysis are to recover the initial state $(A_0, B_0, C_0, F_0,$

---

[6] The sequence $\{z_i\}$ has a minimum period of $2^{128} - 1$. Although LFSRs B and C return to their initial states, B_0 and C_0 respectively, after one cycle, the array does not necessarily return to its initial state F_0.

cnt_0) of the cipher or to differentiate the keystream from a truly random sequence. To facilitate security analysis, we adopt the assumption that the complete sequence of counter values, $\{cnt_t\}_{t=0}^{\infty}$, is publicly known.

Given the array F and knowing its state at time $t_0 = 23(i_0 + 1)$ corresponding to keystream nibble z_{i_0}, we claim that predicting the state at F_{t_0+23} (corresponding to z_{i_0+1}) solely from F_{t_0} is not possible. This prediction requires knowledge of the sequence of transpositions $\{(L_j, R_j)\}_{j=t_0}^{t_0+22}$, which is equivalent to knowing the contents of the shift registers B and C. Crucially, at any time $t = 23(i + 1)$, the array's contents are not directly dependent on the contents of registers B and C (If F_{t_0} were dependent on B and C, for example through a functional relationship, then observing F_{t_0} would indirectly reveal information about the register contents.). However the array's contents are dependent on the transformation $P_{23(i+1)} = \prod_{t=23(i+1)}^{23(i+1)+22} P_t \in \mathcal{S}_{\mathcal{PTM}}$, governing the evolution from $F_{23(i+1)}$ to $F_{23(i+1)+23}$, which is uniquely determined by the contents of the shift registers and, therefore, by the associated sequence of transpositions $\{(L_t, R_t)\}_{t=23(i+1)}^{23(i+1)+22}$ within $\mathcal{S}_{\mathcal{T}}$. Since contents of the array F are not dependent on bits of B and C, knowing F_{t_0} provides no information regarding the contents of B and C and, consequently, does not facilitate the determination of F_{t_0+23}.

Correlation, Distinguishing and Algebraic Attacks

Let $h : \mathcal{F}_2^4 \to \mathcal{F}_2$ and $h' : \mathcal{F}_2^4 \times \mathcal{F}_2^4 \to \mathcal{F}_2$ be two Boolean functions such that

$$Prob(h'(O^1, O^2) = (h \circ H)(O^1, O^2)) \neq \frac{1}{2}, \text{for all } (O^1, O^2) \in \mathcal{F}_2^4 \times \mathcal{F}_2^4$$

In particular, for $t = 23(i + 1)$, we have,

$$Prob(h'(O^1_{23(i+1)}, O^2_{23(i+1)}) = (h \circ H)(O^1_{23(i+1)}, O^2_{23(i+1)})) \neq \frac{1}{2}$$

$$Prob(h'(O^1_{23(i+1)}, O^2_{23(i+1)}) = \qquad\qquad h(z_i)) \qquad\qquad \neq \frac{1}{2} \qquad (4)$$

Equation (4) is exploitable for correlation and higher order correlation attacks[7].

Consider the array F as an element of $\mathcal{F}_2^{16 \times 4}$. Then correlation attacks require a time-invariant linear transformation $U : \mathcal{F}_2^{16 \times 4} \to \mathcal{F}_2^{16 \times 4}$ such that $F_{t+1} = U \times F_t$ for all $t \geq 0$, F_0 is the initial state of the array. This implies that $F_t = U^t \times F_0$ for all $t \geq 0$, where U^0 represents the identity transformation.

However, the time-varying transformation $P_{23(i+1)}$ mapping $F_{23(i+1)}$ to $F_{23(i+1)+23}$ precludes the exploitation of Eq. (4) by the correlation attacks. Furthermore, as neither shift register B nor C contributes to Eq. (1), it is not possible to recover their respective bits using correlation attacks based on Eq. (4).

We now investigate distinguishing attacks based on the correlation properties of the component Boolean functions of F_t. At time $t = 23(i + 1)$, denote the

---

[7] When the input $(O^1_{23(i+1)}, O^2_{23(i+1)})$ is originated from linear feedback shift registers, Eq. (4) is exploitable for correlation-based attacks.

component Boolean functions of F_t by $(f_{t,3}, f_{t,2}, f_{t,1}, f_{t,0})$ where each $f_{t,j}$ is a balanced Boolean function of 4-variables. Due to the near-uniform distribution of F_t over the space S_{16} (with a minimum entropy of 41.39 bits), these component functions behave statistically as random, balanced Boolean functions. As a result, the Hamming distance $d_H(f_{t,j}, f_{t+23,j})$ between the function $f_{t,j}$ and $f_{t+23,j}$, is a random variable taking values between 0 and 16 inclusive. Thus the correlation between $f_{t,j}$ and $f_{t+23,j}$, denoted by $corr(f_{t,j}, f_{t+23,j})$, is a random variable as

$$corr(f_{t,j}, f_{t+23,j}) = 1 - \frac{d_H(f_{t,j}, f_{t+23,j})}{8}. \tag{5}$$

Therefore attacks exploiting correlation properties of random Boolean functions - such as distinguishing attacks on the RC4 stream cipher [19] - are infeasible. In RC4, the state array S_t evolves slowly over time, as each iteration employs a single transposition operation. This slow state transition enables adversaries to distinguish the keystream from a truly random sequence [19]. For successive states S_t and S_{t+1} of RC4, there exist 254 indices $\{v_i\}_{i=1}^{254}$ where $S_t[v_i] = S_{t+1}[v_i]$, as only one transposition is applied per step which is far below the cutoff rate of the random transposition shuffle for a 256-element array [19]. While the distribution of S_{t+1} asymptotically approaches uniformity over the symmetric group S_{256} relative to the initial state S_0 for large t, the conditional distribution of S_{t+1} given S_t remains non-uniform. In contrast, the RTC generator ensures near-uniform distribution of $F_{23(i+1)}$ over S_{16}, even when conditioned on the prior state $F_{23(i+1)-23}$, thereby mitigating such statistical vulnerabilities.

Algebraic attacks typically require deriving algebraic expressions for z_i in terms of the initial state bits of the generator. However, as shown by equation-(1), the algebraic relationship between z_i and the initial bits F_0 of the array F is insufficient to recover the initial states of shift registers B and C. Specifically, solving equation-(1) can only disclose F_0, which does not provide sufficient information to determine the contents of B and C. To mount an effective algebraic attack on the RTC generator, one must establish algebraic dependencies among the keystream nibbles $\{z_i\}$, the initial states of shift registers B and C, and the initial bits of array F. However, since z_i is not functionally dependent on B and C, deriving such algebraic relationships between z_i and the initial states of these registers is unfeasible. Consequently, the design of the generator inherently resists algebraic attacks by decoupling z_i from the state of B and C.

The RTC's state is intrinsically representable as a combination of two distinct components: $part_1$, comprising the shift registers B and C, and $part_2$, consisting of the array F and the counter cnt. Note that, due to its irrelevance to keystream generation, shift register A is not included in $part_1$[8]. Importantly, $part_1$ functions as a driver, updating the array F, while $part_2$ generates the keystream. A primary security feature of the RTC generator lies in the fact that the keystream is derived solely from $part_2$, without any direct dependency on

---

[8] Only shift registers B and C contribute to keystream generation; therefore, shift register A is excluded from $part_1$.

the state of $part_1$, as demonstrated by Eq. (1). Consequently, keystream z_i is not dependent on the state variables within the driving component, $part_1$, of the generator.

Consider a best case scenario for a cryptanalyst. Given a keystream segment $\{z_i\}_{i=0}^{u-1}$, and assuming full knowledge of the corresponding underlying states $\{F_{23(i+1)}\}_{i=0}^{u-1}$ and the counter sequence $\{cnt_t\}_{t=0}^{u-1}$, including the corresponding observations $\{(F_{23(i+1)}[y_t], F_{23(i+1)}[15])\}_{i=0}^{u-1}$, an attacker cannot reconstruct the original sequence (the true sequence) of hidden states between $F_{23(i+1)}$ and $F_{23(i+1)+23}$. Specifically, within the Hidden Markov Model $\lambda = (S_{16}, \Omega, \mathbf{P}, \mathbf{\Phi}, \mathbf{\Pi})$, it is computationally intractable, for each i, $0 \le i \le u-2$, to determine the original sequence of hidden states (see points 2, 3 and 4 in Sect. 3). Consequently, recovery of the sequence of transpositions $\{(L_t, R_t)\}_{t=23(i+1)}^{23(i+1)+23}$ applied to permute $F_{23(i+1)}$ to obtain $F_{23(i+1)+23}$ remains infeasible[9].

Therefore, for the RTC generator, exhaustive search represents the only feasible method to recover the initial states of shift registers B and C. Any attempt to derive these initial states via a cryptanalytic technique other than the exhaustive search would contradict the fundamental information-theoretic limitation that, given a hidden Markov process $\{X_t\}$, the original sequence of hidden states is unrecoverable when all observations are absent except the first and last.

5   Conclusion

A hidden Markov model (HMM) is proposed to describe the random transposition shuffling process, forming the basis for a new keystream generator, the Random Transposition Cipher (RTC). The RTC comprises shift registers, a 4-bit array, a 4-bit counter, and a vectorial Boolean function for keystream generation. With a 128-bit key and Initialization Vector (IV), the generator achieves a minimum period of $2^{128} - 1$ and produces conditionally independent and aprroximately uniformly distributed 4-bit keystream nibbles, each corresponding to an observation of the underlying HMM.

Cryptanalysis of the RTC demonstrates resistance to conventional correlation, algebraic, and distinguishing attacks. An intrinsic characteristic of the RTC is the functional dependency of the keystream solely on the array's contents and the counter, excluding any direct dependence on the shift register states. This decoupling renders algebraic attacks ineffective and prevents the derivation of correlations between the keystream and the shift register contents.

Furthermore, under a best-case scenario for an attacker, recovering states of the underlying shift registers is framed as a special case of the decoding problem of the hidden Markov model with absent intermediate observations. Given the information-theoretic impossibility of reconstructing the original sequence of hidden states from only the first and last observations of a Markov process, exhaustive search is the sole viable method for a state recovery of the shift registers in the RTC. This fundamental limitation underlines the generator's security properties.

---

[9] For $N = 16$, we have $x = 121$. For $T = 24$ observations, the number of paths nP_e^{24} between $F_{23(i+1)}$ and $F_{23(i+1)+23}$ is bounded by $121^{110} \le nP_e^{24} \le 121^{132}$.

Acknowledgment. The author would like to thank the management of CoE-Communication, Bharat Electronics Limited for their support and encouragement to carry out this work. The author would also like to thank Dr. Venkata Satya Sreedhar Tenneti, Central Research Laboratory, Bharat Electronics Limited and Dr. Sapta Girish Neelam, Central Research Laboratory, Bharat Electronics Limited, for various value-added discussions.

A   Bounds for Number of Paths Between First and Last Observations of the Markov Chain $\{X_t\}$

Let $T \geq 4$ be a positive integer, $x = \frac{N^2 - N}{2} + 1$ and $O_0 = (O_0^1, O_0^2)$, $O_{T-1} = (O_{T-1}^1, O_{T-1}^2)$ be the first and last observations of the Markov process $\{X_t\}$ respectively. We also assume initial state σ_0 and last state σ_{T-1} of the process, correspond to O_0 and O_{T-1}, are also given. Let nP_e^T, nP_o^T denote the number of path vectors between σ_0 and σ_{T-1} for T observations when T is even and odd respectively.

Suppose T is even. Then given σ_0 and σ_{T-1}, using the state transition matrix $\mathbf{P}$, x states are possible for σ_1 and σ_{T-2}, x^2 states are possible for σ_2 and σ_{T-3} and, more generally, x^j states are possible for σ_j and $\sigma_{T-(j+1)}$ for any j, $1 \leq j \leq \frac{T-2}{2}$. Hence, $nP_e^T = x \times x^2 \times \cdots \times x^{\frac{T-2}{2}} \times x^{\frac{T-2}{2}} \times \cdots \times x^2 \times x = x^{\sum_{j=1}^{\frac{T-2}{2}} 2j} = x^{\frac{T(T-2)}{4}}$.

However, moving forward from σ_0 to $\sigma_{\frac{T-2}{2}+1}$, $\sigma_{\frac{T-2}{2}+1}$ has $x^{\frac{T-2}{2}+1}$ possible states, denoted by A. Similarly, moving backward from σ_{T-1} to $\sigma_{\frac{T-2}{2}+1}$, $\sigma_{\frac{T-2}{2}+1}$ has $x^{\frac{T-2}{2}}$ possible states, denoted by B, i.e., the number of possible valid states for $\sigma_{\frac{T-2}{2}+1}$ is $|A \cap B| \leq |B|$. Thus, $nP_e^T \leq x^{\sum_{j=1}^{\frac{T-2}{2}} 2j} = x^{\frac{T(T-2)}{4}}$.

To derive a lower bound of nP_e^T, simply consider the all states σ_j between σ_0 and σ_{T-1} except the two middle states $\sigma_{\frac{T-2}{2}}$ and $\sigma_{\frac{T-2}{2}+1}$. Then we have,

$x^{\sum_{j=1}^{\frac{T-4}{2}} 2j} = x^{\frac{(T-2)(T-4)}{4}} \leq nP_e^T$. Hence $x^{\frac{(T-2)(T-4)}{4}} \leq nP_e^T \leq x^{\frac{T(T-2)}{4}}$.

Suppose T is odd. Then given σ_0 and σ_{T-1}, x states are possible for σ_1 and σ_{T-2}, x^2 states are possible for σ_2 and σ_{T-3}, more generally x^j states are possible for σ_j and $\sigma_{T-(j+1)}$ for any j, $1 \leq j \leq \frac{T-1}{2} - 1$. Starting from either σ_0 or σ_{T-1}, $x^{\frac{T-1}{2}}$ states are possible for the middle node $\sigma_{\frac{T-1}{2}}$. Hence $nP_o^T = x \times x^2 \times \cdots \times x^{\frac{T-1}{2}-1} \times x^{\frac{T-1}{2}} \times x^{\frac{T-1}{2}-1} \times \cdots \times x^2 \times x = x^{\sum_{j=1}^{\frac{T-1}{2}-1} 2j + \frac{T-1}{2}} = x^{\frac{(T-1)^2}{4}}$.

From the same reasoning as above, let A denotes the set of $x^{\frac{T-1}{2}}$ possible states of the middle node $\sigma_{\frac{T-1}{2}}$ when moving forward from σ_0 to $\sigma_{\frac{T-1}{2}}$ and let B denotes the set of $x^{\frac{T-1}{2}}$ possible states of $\sigma_{\frac{T-1}{2}}$ when moving backward from σ_{T-1}. Then, the number of possible valid states for the middle node $\sigma_{\frac{T-1}{2}}$ is

$|A \cap B| \leq |B|^{10}$. Hence, $nP_o^T \leq x^{\sum_{j=1}^{\frac{T-1}{2}-1} 2j + \frac{T-1}{2}} = x^{\frac{(T-1)^2}{4}}$.

---

[10] Although, $|A| = |B| = x^{\frac{T-1}{2}}$, we may have $A \neq B$.

Discarding the middle node $\sigma_{\frac{T-1}{2}}$, a lower bound $x^{\sum_{j=1}^{\frac{T-1}{2}-1} 2j} = x^{\frac{(T-1)(T-3)}{4}}$ for nP_o^T can be obtained. Hence $x^{\frac{(T-1)(T-3)}{4}} \leq nP_o^T \leq x^{\frac{(T-1)^2}{4}}$.

B   Given F_{23i}, Bounds for the Entropy of Distribution of $F_{23(i+1)}$

Let P and Q be two probability distributions on a sample space $\mathcal{X}$.

Definition 1. *The variational distance between P and Q is defined as [2, 16, 31]*

$$V(P,Q) = \frac{\sum_{x\in\mathcal{X}} |P(x) - Q(x)|}{2}.$$

Definition 2. *The informational divergence between P and Q is defined as*

$$D_e(P||Q) = \sum_{x\in\mathcal{X}} P(x)log_e(\frac{P(x)}{Q(x)})\ [11].$$

[11] The informational divergence is also referred to as relative entropy or the Kullback-Leibler distance (KL distance) [41].

It can be written as

$$D_2(P||Q) = \frac{D_e(P||Q)}{log_e(2)}\ [12]. \tag{6}$$

[12] The Pinsker's inequality provides the relation between the variational distance $V(P,Q)$ and the KL distance $D_e(P||Q)$,

$$V(P,Q) \leq \sqrt{\frac{1}{2}D_e(P||Q)} \tag{7}$$

and in terms of $D_2(P||Q)$, we have

$$D_2(P||Q)) \geq \frac{2}{log_e(2)}V(P,Q)^2 \tag{8}$$

Suppose P denotes uniform distribution on the symmetric group S_{16}. Then the entropy of P, denoted as $H(P)$, is $H(P) \approx 44.25$ bits.

Let $w \in \{23, 31, 39, 47, 55\}$ [13]. For $i \geq 0$, given F_{wi} , let Q denotes the distribution of $F_{w(i+1)}$ on S_{16}. Now we use the Pinsker's inequality [41] to measure the entropy of the distribution Q.

---

[11] The subscript e in D_e refers that information is measured in nautural units information (nats).

[12] The subscript 2 in D_2 refers that information is measured in bits.

[13] The values of w represent different lengths of the sequences of transpositions and correspond to $c = 0, 0.5, 1, 1.5, 2$ respectively in the cutoff rate formula.

Suppose $w = 23$ (corresponds to $c = 0$ in the cutoff rate formula for the random transposition shuffling). Then the variation distance between P and Q is bounded in the range $[0.33, 0.996]$ i.e., $0.33 \leq V(P,Q) \leq 0.996$ [31]. Now considering the lower bound, we have

$$D_2(P||Q)) \geq \frac{2}{log_e(2)}0.33^2 \approx 0.314$$

Similarly, considering the upper bound, we have

$$D_2(P||Q)) \geq \frac{2}{log_e(2)}0.996^2 \approx 2.862.$$

Now the entropy of Q, $H(Q)$, is computed as [14,41]

$$\begin{aligned}
H(Q) &= H(P) - D_2(P||Q) \\
&= 44.25 - D_2(P||Q)
\end{aligned} \tag{9}$$

Since $V(P,Q)$ lies in $[0.33, 0.996]$, substituting 0.314 and 2.862 in equation-(9), we have

$$41.39 \leq H(Q) \leq 43.93$$

i.e., when $w = 23$, given F_{wi}, entropy of the distribution Q of $F_{w(i+1)}$ is at least 41.39 bits, indicating a distribution closely resembling the uniform distribution P over the symmetric group S_{16}. For different values of w, bounds for the entropy of Q are given in Table 2.

Table 2. Bounds for the entropy of distribution Q of $F_{w(i+1)}$

constant c	w	Bounds for $V(P,Q)$	$H(Q)$
0	23	$0.33 \leq V(P,Q) \leq 0.996$	$41.39 \leq H(Q) \leq 43.93$
0.5	31	$0.13 \leq V(P,Q) \leq 0.86$	$41.12 \leq H(Q) \leq 44.20$
1	39	$0.050 \leq V(P,Q) \leq 0.52$	$43.47 \leq H(Q) \leq 44.24$
1.5	47	$0.018 \leq V(P,Q) \leq 0.24$	$44.08 \leq H(Q) \leq 44.25$
2.0	55	$0.0067 \leq V(P,Q) \leq 0.095$	$44.22 \leq H(Q) \leq 44.25$

References

1. Al-Hinai, S., Batten, L., Colbert, B., Wong, K.: Algebraic attacks on clock-controlled stream ciphers. In: Batten, L.M., Safavi-Naini, R. (eds.) ACISP 2006. LNCS, vol. 4058, pp. 1–16. Springer, Heidelberg (2006). https://doi.org/10.1007/11780656_1
2. Aldous, D.: Markov chains and mixing times (Second Edition) by David A. Levin and Yuval Peres. Math. Intell. **41**(1), 90–91 (2018). https://doi.org/10.1007/s00283-018-9839-x

3. Aldous, D.J., Diaconis, P.: Shuffling cards and stopping-times. Amer. Math. Mon. **93**, 333–348 (1986)
4. Armknecht, F., Krause, M.: Algebraic attacks on combiners with memory. In: Boneh, D. (ed.) CRYPTO 2003. LNCS, vol. 2729, pp. 162–175. Springer, Heidelberg (2003). https://doi.org/10.1007/978-3-540-45146-4_10
5. Armknecht, F., Krause, M., Stegemann, D.: Design principles for combiners with memory. In: Maitra, S., Veni Madhavan, C.E., Venkatesan, R. (eds.) INDOCRYPT 2005. LNCS, vol. 3797, pp. 104–117. Springer, Heidelberg (2005).https://doi.org/10.1007/11596219_9
6. Bayer, D., Diaconis, P.: Trailing the dovetail shuffle to its lair. Ann. Appl. Probab. **2**, 294–313 (1992)
7. Braeken, A., Lano, J.: On the (im)possibility of practical and secure nonlinear filters and combiners. In: Preneel, B., Tavares, S. (eds.) SAC 2005. LNCS, vol. 3897, pp. 159–174. Springer, Heidelberg (2006).https://doi.org/10.1007/11693383_11
8. Braeken, A.: Cryptographic Properties of Boolean Functions and S-Boxes. Ph.D. thesis, Katholieke Universiteit Leuven (2006)
9. Canteaut, A.: Fast correlation attacks against stream ciphers and related open problems. In: IEEE Information Theory Workshop on Theory and Practice in Information-Theoretic Security, pp. 49–54 (2005)
10. Coppersmith, D., Halevi, S., Jutla, C.: Cryptanalysis of stream ciphers with linear masking. Cryptology ePrint Archive, Report 2002/020 (2002)
11. Courtois, N.T.: Fast algebraic attacks on stream ciphers with linear feedback. In: Boneh, D. (ed.) CRYPTO 2003. LNCS, vol. 2729, pp. 176–194. Springer, Heidelberg (2003).https://doi.org/10.1007/978-3-540-45146-4_11
12. Courtois, N.T.: Higher order correlation attacks, XL algorithm and cryptanalysis of Toyocrypt. In: Lee, P.J., Lim, C.H. (eds.) ICISC 2002. LNCS, vol. 2587, pp. 182–199. Springer, Heidelberg (2003). https://doi.org/10.1007/3-540-36552-4_13
13. Courtois, N.T., Meier, W.: Algebraic Attacks on stream ciphers with linear feedback. In: Biham, E. (ed.) EUROCRYPT 2003. LNCS, vol. 2656, pp. 345–359. Springer, Heidelberg (2003). https://doi.org/10.1007/3-540-39200-9_21
14. Cover, T.M., Thomas, J.A.: Elements of Information Theory, 2nd edn. Wiley-Interscience, Hoboken (2006)
15. Dholakia, A.: Introduction to Convolutional Codes with Applications. Kluwer Academic Publishers, Dordrecht (1994)
16. Diaconis, P., Shahshahani, M.: Generating a random permutation with random transpositions. Zeitschrift für Wahrscheinlichkeitstheorie und Verwandte Gebiete **57**(2), 159–179 (1981). https://doi.org/10.1007/BF00535487
17. Englund, H.: Some Results on Distinguishing Attacks on Stream Ciphers. Ph.D. thesis, Lund University (2007)
18. Golic, J.: Linear models for keystream generators. IEEE Trans. Comput. **45**(1), 41–49 (1996)
19. Golic, J.: Linear models for a time-variant permutation generator. IEEE Trans. Inf. Theory **45**(7), 2374–2382 (1999)
20. Golic, J.D.: Correlation via linear sequential circuit approximation of combiners with memory. In: Proceedings of the 11th Annual International Conference on Theory and Application of Cryptographic Techniques, pp. 113–123. EUROCRYPT'92 (1993)
21. Golić, J.D.: Linear cryptanalysis of stream ciphers. In: Preneel, B. (ed.) FSE 1994. LNCS, vol. 1008, pp. 154–169. Springer, Heidelberg (1995). https://doi.org/10.1007/3-540-60590-8_13

22. Hell, M., Johansson, T., Maximov, A., Meier, W.: A stream cipher proposal: grain-128. In: Information Theory, 2006 IEEE International Symposium on, pp. 1614–1618 (2006)
23. Hell, M., Johansson, T., Brynielsson, L.: An overview of distinguishing attacks on stream ciphers. Cryptogr. Commun. 1(1), 71–94 (2009). https://doi.org/10.1007/s12095-008-0006-7
24. Johansson, T., Jönsson, F.: Improved fast correlation attacks on stream ciphers via convolutional codes. In: Stern, J. (ed.) EUROCRYPT 1999. LNCS, vol. 1592, pp. 347–362. Springer, Heidelberg (1999). https://doi.org/10.1007/3-540-48910-X_24
25. Johansson, T.: Reduced complexity correlation attacks on two clock-controlled generators. In: Ohta, K., Pei, D. (eds.) ASIACRYPT 1998. LNCS, vol. 1514, pp. 342–356. Springer, Heidelberg (1998). https://doi.org/10.1007/3-540-49649-1_27
26. Johansson, T., Jönsson, F.: Theoretical analysis of a correlation attack based on convolutional codes. IEEE Trans. Inf. Theory 48, 2173–2181 (2002)
27. Jonasson, J.: The overhand shuffle mixes in T(n2logn) steps. Ann. Appl. Probab. 16(1), 231–243 (2006). https://doi.org/10.1214/105051605000000692
28. Khazaei, S., Hasanzadeh, M.M., Kiaei, M.S.: Linear sequential circuit approximation of grain and trivium stream ciphers. IACR Cryptol. ePrint Arch., p. 141 (2006)
29. Klein, A.: Stream Ciphers. Springer, Bücher, London (2013). SpringerLink
30. Knuth, D.E.: The Art of Computer Programming: Seminumerical Algorithms, vol. 2. 2 edn
31. Matthews, P.: A strong uniform time for random transpositions. J. Theor. Probab. 1, 411–423 (1988)
32. Meier, W., Staffelbach, O.: Fast correlation attacks on stream ciphers. In: Barstow, D., et al. (eds.) EUROCRYPT 1988. LNCS, vol. 330, pp. 301–314. Springer, Heidelberg (1988). https://doi.org/10.1007/3-540-45961-8_28
33. Meier, W.: Fast correlation attacks: methods and countermeasures. In: Joux, A. (ed.) FSE 2011. LNCS, vol. 6733, pp. 55–67. Springer, Heidelberg (2011). https://doi.org/10.1007/978-3-642-21702-9_4
34. Menezes, A.J., Vanstone, S.A., Oorschot, P.C.V.: Handbook of Applied Cryptography. CRC Press, Boca Raton (1996)
35. Oliver, I.: Markov Processes for Stochastic Modeling. Elsevier, Amsterdam (2009)
36. Rueppel, R.A.: Analysis and Design of Stream Ciphers, 1st edn. Springer-Verlag, Berlin, Heidelberg (1986). https://doi.org/10.1007/978-3-642-82865-2
37. Siegenthaler, T.: Correlation-immunity of nonlinear combining functions for cryptographic applications (corresp.). IEEE Trans. Inf. Theory 30(5), 776–780 (1984)
38. Siegenthaler, T.: Decrypting a class of stream ciphers using ciphertext only. IEEE Trans. Comput. C-34(1), 81–85 (1985)
39. Wikipedia contributors: Fisher–Yates shuffle — Wikipedia, The Free Encyclopedia (2026). https://en.wikipedia.org/w/index.php?title=Fisher%E2%80%93Yates_shuffle&oldid=1332159908. Accessed 22 Jan 2026
40. Yellapu, G.: Correlation (fast) attack against nonlinear combination generator. J. Discret. Math. Sci. Cryptogr. 18(6), 705–715 (2015). https://doi.org/10.1080/09720529.2014.943391
41. Yeung, R.W.: Information Theory and Network Coding, 1st edn. Springer, Cham (2008). https://doi.org/10.1007/978-0-387-79234-7

Author Index

MIX
Papier aus verantwortungsvollen Quellen
Paper from responsible sources
FSC® C105338

If you have any concerns about our products,
you can contact us on
ProductSafety@springernature.com

In case Publisher is established outside the EU,
the EU authorized representative is:
Springer Nature Customer Service Center GmbH
Europaplatz 3, 69115 Heidelberg, Germany

Printed by Libri Plureos GmbH
in Hamburg, Germany